MMPI
Instruments

Assessing Personality and Psychopathology

SIXTH EDITION

JOHN R. GRAHAM
CARLO O. C. VELTRI
TAYLA T. C. LEE

OXFORD
UNIVERSITY PRESS

OXFORD
UNIVERSITY PRESS

Oxford University Press is a department of the University of Oxford.
It furthers the University's objective of excellence in research, scholarship,
and education by publishing worldwide. Oxford is a registered trade mark
of Oxford University Press in the UK and in certain other countries.

Published in the United States of America by Oxford University Press
198 Madison Avenue, New York, NY 10016, United States of America.

© 2023, 2012, 2006, 2000, 1994, 1991 by Oxford University Press

CIP data is on file at the Library of Congress.
ISBN 9780190065560

9 8 7 6 5 4 3 2 1
Printed by Marquis, Canada

To my best friend, Mary Ann.
—JRG

To Christa, and my adorable critters, Micah and Ephram.
—COCV

To Dan and Coop. Thanks for always catching me—cradle and all.
—TTCL

To our mentor and friend, Jack.
—COCV & TTCL

CONTENTS

PREFACE

The Minnesota Multiphasic Personality Inventory (MMPI) family of instruments are the most widely used tests of personality and psychopathology in the United States and are commonly used in countries around the world. They are used in inpatient and outpatient mental health settings, medical centers, and correctional settings. MMPI instruments are also used in the screening of applicants for jobs that involve public trust and safety. They are frequently admitted as evidence in civil and criminal legal proceedings. However, the MMPI family of instruments are in a period of transition, which began with the publication of the MMPI–2–Restructured Form (MMPI-2-RF) in 2008 and continued with the publication of the Minnesota Multiphasic Personality Inventory–Adolescent–Restructured Form (MMPI-A-RF) in 2016 and the Minnesota Multiphasic Personality Inventory–3 (MMPI-3) in 2020. Since the last edition of this book, hundreds of articles examining the use of MMPI instruments with adults and adolescents have been published. We intend this book to act as a bridge for graduate students and clinicians alike in the coming years as they navigate this period of MMPI transition.

NEW TO THIS EDITION
MMPI Instruments: Assessing Personality and Psychopathology has two primary audiences. We have worked to write the book in such a manner that it will be an appropriate text for graduate assessment courses in psychology and related disciplines. In addition, we have endeavored to make it useful as a comprehensive guide for clinicians interpreting MMPI instruments. In revising this text, the primary changes from the previous edition we made include the following:

- Added a chapter on the MMPI-3
- Added a chapter on the MMPI-A-RF
- Updated research on the MMPI-2, MMPI-2-RF, and MMPI-A

The last edition of this book covered the Minnesota Multiphasic Personality Inventory–2 (MMPI-2) and Minnesota Multiphasic Personality Inventory–Adolescent (MMPI-A), as well as the (then) recently published MMPI-2-RF. Since that time, there have been important changes to the MMPI family. First, two new MMPI instruments have been released. The MMPI-A-RF was published in 2016. This instrument is a shortened, alternative form of the MMPI-A similar in goals and design to the MMPI-2-RF. The MMPI-3, released in 2020, provides contemporary normative samples as well as updates to the item and scale content coverage found on the MMPI-2-RF. The release of the MMPI-3 means that a MMPI instrument with new norms is now available to clinicians for the first time in 30 years. Given the importance of making an informed choice when selecting which version of the MMPI to use with test takers, we have included chapters on each of these instruments in this edition of the book.

Second, in addition to these new instruments, hundreds of articles, chapters, and books have been published about the MMPI instruments since the last edition of this book was completed. Empirical research continues to inform our use of these tests. Much of the research supports long-standing practices, but some findings require changes in how we interpret the tests or suggest new applications for them. Thus, this edition reviews and incorporates these new data into our interpretations of scales on the MMPI instruments.

All of these changes indicate to us that the MMPI instruments have entered a period of transition. We view this transition as an exciting opportunity to improve clinical assessment using the MMPI instruments, but we also recognize it can be difficult, confusing, or frustrating to achieve clinical competence with new test instruments. Our hope for this book is that it can serve as a bridge to help clinicians, graduate students, and teachers who use the MMPI instruments to cross the turbulent waters of transition and remain grounded in empirically based assessment practices.

Given our goals of providing comprehensive, empirically based information about the MMPI instruments and guiding MMPI users through this period of transition, we have made several changes to the structure of the book. Our first 11 chapters of the book continue to focus specifically on the MMPI-2, while the remaining four chapters are each focused on one of the other MMPI instruments. In all of these chapters, we have attempted to place the MMPI scales being discussed in their historical context, as this can both inform their current use as well as identify areas in need of future research.

A reader seeking to develop the deepest knowledge of the tests, as well as basic competency using all five of the instruments, would be best served reading the entire book. However, we recognize that some readers will be interested in using only one or two of the MMPI instruments. For readers interested in the MMPI-2, the first 11 chapters are the best path to acquiring the competencies needed to use it. For readers interested in learning about the MMPI-2-RF, MMPI-3, MMPI-A, or MMPI-A-RF, we have worked to make the final four chapters of the book readable as stand-alone resources. It is our suggestion that you begin with the chapter detailing the version of the test about which you wish to learn. However, you will find that there are some matters we could not cover comprehensively in a single chapter. In those instances, we refer you back to an earlier chapter to help you develop a deeper understanding of the matter. Liberal use of the table of contents, headings within each chapter, and the subject index will help identify the passages in the referenced chapter that will be most useful to you.

The MMPI instruments have long been the most widely used personality tests in the United States and around the world. When these tests are used appropriately by informed professionals, they contribute to accurate and useful evaluations in a variety of contexts. It is our hope that this book will contribute to more effective and appropriate use of the MMPI instruments in assessing personality and psychopathology.

JRG Kent, OH
COCV Northfield, MN
TTCL Muncie, IN
November 2021

ACKNOWLEDGMENTS

We appreciate the assistance provided by others in the preparation of this revision. We are grateful to the authors and publishers who granted permission to reproduce their works. Katie Nickerson, Tami Brown, and Alicia Gomez at the University of Minnesota Press were especially helpful in granting permissions, providing information about the MMPI instruments, and offering general support for this project. Deb Ringwelski at Pearson Assessments answered numerous questions about the MMPI instruments and the associated products and support offered by Pearson. We are also grateful to Beverly Kaemmer for encouraging us to undertake this revision. Megan Keen and Colette Delawalla, graduate students at Ball State University, assisted in numerous ways including conducting multiple literature reviews, obtaining articles, compiling reference lists, proofreading, and providing feedback on draft chapters. We are thankful to Darla Frandrup for her assistance in preparing all the sample cases used in this edition. Oxford University Press provided resources and clerical support for the project. Finally, we extend our gratitude and love to our partners—Mary Ann Stephens, Christa Veltri, and Daniel Lee—who understand how important this book is to each of us and provided support and encouragement throughout the preparation of this revision.

CHAPTER 1

DEVELOPMENT OF THE MMPI AND MMPI-2

DEVELOPMENT OF THE ORIGINAL MMPI

Original Purpose

The Minnesota Multiphasic Personality Inventory (MMPI) was first published in 1943. The test authors, Starke Hathaway, PhD, and J. Charnley McKinley, MD, worked at the University of Minnesota Hospitals and expected the MMPI to be useful for routine diagnostic assessments. During the 1930s and 1940s, a primary function of psychologists and psychiatrists was to assign appropriate psychodiagnostic labels. An individual interview or mental status examination and individual psychological testing usually were used with each patient. Hathaway and McKinley believed a group-administered, paper-and-pencil personality inventory would provide a more efficient and reliable way of arriving at appropriate psychodiagnostic labels.

Rationale

Hathaway and McKinley used the empirical keying approach in the construction of the various MMPI scales. This approach, which requires empirical determination of items that differentiate between groups of persons, represented a significant innovation at the time of the MMPI's construction. Most prior personality inventories were constructed according to a logical keying approach, where test items are selected and keyed according to the subjective judgment of the test author concerning what kinds of responses are likely to be indicative of the attributes being measured. Both clinical experience and research data seriously questioned the adequacy of this logical keying approach. It became increasingly apparent that test takers could falsify or distort their responses to items in order to present themselves in any way they chose. Further, empirical studies indicated that the subjectively keyed responses often were not consistent with differences actually observed between groups of persons. In the newly introduced empirical keying procedure, responses to individual test items were treated as unknowns, and empirical item analysis was utilized to identify test items that differentiated between criterion groups (e.g., patients who were depressed versus nonclinical individuals). Such an approach to item responses overcame many of the difficulties associated with the earlier, subjective approaches.

Clinical Scale Development

The first step in the construction of the basic MMPI scales was to collect a large pool of potential inventory items.[1] Hathaway and McKinley selected a wide variety of personality-type statements from sources such as psychological and psychiatric case histories and reports, textbooks, and earlier published scales of personal and social attitudes. From an initial pool of approximately 1,000 statements, the test authors selected 504 that they judged to be reasonably independent of each other.

The next step was to select appropriate criterion groups. One criterion group, referred to as the "normal cases" (and later the "Minnesota normals"), consisted primarily of 724 relatives and visitors of medical patients in the University of Minnesota Hospitals. This group also included 265 recent high school graduates who were attending precollege conferences at the University of Minnesota, 265 Works Progress Administration workers, and 254 medical patients at the University of Minnesota Hospitals. The second major group, referred to as "clinical participants," was made up of psychiatric patients at the University of Minnesota Hospitals. This second group included 221 patients representing all of the major psychiatric categories used clinically at the time of the construction of the test. Clinical participants were divided into subgroups of discrete diagnostic samples according to their clinically determined diagnostic labels. The different subgroups of clinical participants formed were hypochondriasis, depression, hysteria, psychopathic deviate, paranoia, psychasthenia, schizophrenia, and hypomania.

The next step in scale construction was to administer the original 504 test items to the non-patients comprising the Minnesota normals and to the patients in each of the clinical groups. An item analysis was conducted separately for each of the clinical groups to identify the items in the pool of 504 that differentiated significantly between the specific clinical group and non-patients. Individual MMPI items identified by this procedure were included in the resulting MMPI scale intended for use in classifying individuals into that specific clinical group. Eight scales, collectively known as the Clinical scales, were created using these procedures. To cross-validate the Clinical scales, they were administered to new groups of individuals with no known mental difficulties, patients with relevant clinical diagnoses, and sometimes

---

[1] Information concerning Clinical and Validity scale development is abstracted from a series of articles by Hathaway (1956, 1965); Hathaway and McKinley (1940, 1942); McKinley and Hathaway (1940, 1944); McKinley, Hathaway, and Meehl (1948); and Meehl and Hathaway (1946).

also to patients with other clinical diagnoses. If significant differences were found among scores for these groups, the Clinical scales were considered to have been adequately cross-validated and thus were ready for use in the differential diagnosis of new patients whose diagnostic features were unknown.

At a somewhat later time, two additional Clinical scales were constructed. First, the Masculinity–Femininity (Mf) scale originally was intended to assess homosexuality, which was considered a mental disorder at the time the scale was constructed. Because of difficulties in identifying adequate numbers of items that differentiated between gay and heterosexual men, Hathaway and McKinley subsequently broadened their approach in the construction of the Mf scale. In addition to the few items that discriminated between gay and heterosexual men, other items were identified that were differentially endorsed by men and women in the non-patient samples. Also, some items from Terman and Miles' (1936) Attitude–Interest Analysis Test were added to the original item pool and included in the Mf scale. As a result of these changes, the final scale assessed stereotypically masculine and feminine interests, rather than sexual identity. Second, the Social Introversion (Si) scale was developed by Drake (1946) and came to be included as one of the basic MMPI scales. Drake selected items for the Si scale by contrasting item response frequencies for groups of college women who scored higher or lower on the Social Introversion–Extroversion scale of the Minnesota T-S-E Inventory (Evans & McConnell, 1941). The Si scale was cross-validated by comparing scores of women in college who participated in many extracurricular activities with those who participated in few or no extracurricular activities. Subsequently, the scale's use was extended to men as well as women.

Validity Scale Development

Because Hathaway and McKinley were aware that test takers could falsify or distort their responses to the items in self-report inventories, they also developed four scales—hereafter referred to as the Validity scales—to detect deviant test-taking attitudes. The Cannot Say (?) score was simply the total number of items in the MMPI that the individual taking the test either omitted or responded to as both true and false. Obviously, the omission of large numbers of items, which tends to lower the scores on the Clinical scales, calls into question the interpretability of the whole resulting profile of scores.

The L scale, originally called the Lie scale of the MMPI, was designed to detect rather unsophisticated and naive attempts on the part of test takers to present themselves in an overly favorable way. The L scale items were rationally derived and cover everyday situations in order to assess the strength of a person's unwillingness to admit even very minor weaknesses in character or personality. For example, one item involves a claim of reading every editorial in daily newspapers. Most people would be quite willing to admit that they do not read every editorial every day, but persons determined to present themselves in a favorable way might not be willing to admit to such a perceived shortcoming.

The Infrequency (F) scale of the MMPI was designed to detect individuals whose approach to the test-taking task is different from that intended by the test authors. F scale items were selected by examining the endorsement frequency of the non-patient group and identifying the items endorsed in a particular direction by fewer than 10% of that group. Because few non-patients endorse these items in a given direction, a person who does endorse an item in that direction is exhibiting an unusual response. A large number of such unusual responses call into question the extent to which a person taking the test complied with the instructions. Hathaway and McKinley believed the most common reason for elevated scores on the F scale was responding to test items without reading and considering their content.

The Correction (K) scale of the MMPI was constructed by Meehl and Hathaway (1946) to identify clinical defensiveness in test takers. It was noted that some persons with clearly observable psychological difficulties who took the MMPI obtained scores on the Clinical scales that were not as elevated as would be expected given their clinical status. Items in the K scale were selected empirically by comparing the responses of a group of patients who were known to have clinically significant difficulties but who produced normal scores on the Clinical scales of the MMPI to responses from a group of people producing normal Clinical scale scores and for whom there was no extratest indication of psychopathology. A high K scale score was intended to indicate defensiveness and call into question the person's responses to all of the other items.

The K scale was also used later to develop a correction factor for some of the Clinical scales. Meehl and Hathaway reasoned that if the effect of a defensive test-taking attitude—as reflected by a high K score—is to lower scores on the Clinical scales, then it might be possible to determine the extent to which the scores on the Clinical scales should be raised in order to reflect more accurately a person's behavior. By comparing the diagnostic efficiency of each Clinical scale with various portions of K scale scores added as a correction factor, Meehl and Hathaway determined the appropriate weight of the K scale score for each Clinical scale to correct for the defensiveness indicated by the K scale score. Certain Clinical scales were not K corrected because the simple raw score on those Clinical scales seemed to result in the most accurate prediction about a person's clinical condition. Other scales have proportions of K, ranging from .2 to 1.0, added to adjust the Clinical scales appropriately.

Modified Approach to MMPI Utilization

After a decade of clinical use and additional validity studies, it became apparent that the MMPI was not adequate to successfully carry out its original purpose, namely, the valid psychodiagnosis of new patients. Although patients in any particular clinical category (e.g., depression) were likely to obtain high scores on the corresponding Clinical scale, they also often obtained high scores on other Clinical scales. Also, many individuals with no observable clinical difficulties obtained high scores on one or more of the Clinical scales. Clearly, the Clinical scales were not pure measures of the symptom syndromes suggested by the scale names.

Several reasons have been suggested for the failure of the MMPI to fulfill its original purpose. Further research revealed that many of the Clinical scales of the MMPI are highly intercorrelated, making it unlikely that only a single scale would be elevated for an individual. These intercorrelations were due, to a large extent, to item overlap between scales. Also, the unreliability of the specific psychiatric diagnoses of patients used in the development of the MMPI scales contributes to their failure to differentiate among clinical groups.

Although the limited success of the MMPI scales in differentiating among clinical groups might have been bothersome in the 1940s, this limitation is not particularly critical today. This is because over time, the MMPI came to be used in a way quite different from what was originally intended. It was assumed the Clinical scales were indicating something other than error variance because reliable differences in scores were found among individuals known to differ in other important ways. The modified approach to the MMPI treated each of its scales as an unknown; and, through clinical experience and empirical research, the correlates of each scale were identified (indeed, more than 10,000 studies have been published about the MMPI). According to this approach, when a person obtained a score on a particular scale, the clinician attributed to that person the characteristics and behaviors previous research and experience had identified for other individuals with similar scores on that scale. To lessen the likelihood that excess meaning would be attributed because of the Clinical scale names, numbers were assigned to the original scales, and today they replace the clinical labels. These can be seen in Table 1.1.

In addition to identifying empirical correlates of high scores on each of the numbered scales, attempts were made to identify empirical correlates for low scores and for various combinations of scores on the scales (e.g., two highest scales in the profile). Some investigators developed very complex rules for classifying individual profiles and identified behavioral correlates of profiles that met the criteria (Gilberstadt & Duker, 1965; Marks et al., 1974). Thus, even though the MMPI was not particularly successful in terms of its original purpose, the test was used to

TABLE 1.1 *MMPI and MMPI-2 Clinical Scale Numbers and Names*

Present Scale Number	Original Scale Name
1	Hypochondriasis (Hs)
2	Depression (D)
3	Hysteria (Hy)
4	Psychopathic Deviate (Pd)
5	Masculinity–Femininity (Mf)
6	Paranoia (Pa)
7	Psychasthenia (Pt)
8	Schizophrenia (Sc)
9	Hypomania (Ma)
0	Social Introversion (Si)

generate descriptions of and inferences about individuals on the basis of their scores. It is this behavioral description approach to the utilization of the test in everyday practice that led to the great popularity of the MMPI family of instruments among practicing clinicians.

DEVELOPMENT OF THE MMPI-2

The original MMPI was a widely used instrument. Several national surveys revealed that it was the most frequently used personality test in the United States (Harrison et al., 1988; Lubin et al., 1984). Nonetheless, critics expressed concern about certain aspects of the test. Specifically, there were serious concerns about the adequacy of the original standardization sample, which consisted primarily of persons who were visiting friends or relatives at the University of Minnesota Hospitals. The sample was one of convenience, and little to no effort was made to ensure it was representative of the U.S. population. Second, there were concerns about the item content of the original MMPI. Some of the language and references in the items had become archaic or obsolete. Other items had content that was not in keeping with contemporary standards for psychological tests (e.g., culturally insensitive item wording) or was objectionable to test takers (e.g., items regarding bowel movements). Because the original MMPI items had never been subjected to careful editorial review, some included poor grammar, inappropriate punctuation, and complicated sentence structures confusing to many test takers. Finally, there was concern that the original MMPI item pool was not broad enough to permit assessment of certain characteristics judged important by many test users, such as suicide attempts or the use of drugs other than alcohol.

The Restandardization Project

In response to concerns about the MMPI, in 1982, the University of Minnesota Press appointed a restandardization committee, consisting of James N. Butcher, W. Grant Dahlstrom, and John R. Graham, to consider the need for and feasibility of a revision of the MMPI.[2] Based on the recommendations of the committee, a decision was made to revise the MMPI. However, though the committee believed changes were needed, they also determined it was necessary to make every effort to maintain continuity between the original MMPI and its revision. This would ensure that the considerable research base accumulated since the test's publication would still be relevant to the new version.

The restandardization project had several goals. A primary goal of the project was to collect a contemporary normative sample more representative of the general population than had been true of the MMPI's original sample. Additionally, efforts were made to improve the MMPI item pool by rewriting some items, deleting items judged to be objectionable, and generating new items to expand the content dimensions of

---

[2] Although not involved in the early stages of the restandardization project, Auke Tellegen later was appointed to the restandardization committee.

the item pool. Only minor revisions of the existing Validity and Clinical scales were part of the restandardization project, although it was hoped the project would produce data that later could lead to more comprehensive efforts to make improvements in these basic scales. Also, it was anticipated that the new test items would be useful in generating new scales.

MMPI-2 Items and Scales

The MMPI-2 has several sets of scales. Some of these scales were carried over from the MMPI (e.g., the Clinical scales), while others were entirely new to the instrument (e.g., the Content scales). These scales were derived from a preliminary item pool of 704 items used for the restandardization project. This pool of potential items contained all 550 items from the MMPI and additional items designed to assess other important constructs. Some of the original MMPI items were reworded, but the changes were slight and did not change the meanings of the items or endorsement patterns (Ben-Porath & Butcher, 1989).

Several criteria were employed in deciding which items were to be included in the final booklet. All items entering into the standard Validity and Clinical scales were provisionally included, as were items needed to score supplementary scales judged to be important. Additional items were maintained because they would be included in new scales developed from the item pool. The final MMPI-2 includes 567 items.

MMPI-2 Norms

During the restandardization project, procedures intended to facilitate obtaining a large normative group broadly representative of the U.S. population were used (Butcher et al., 1989).[3] Census data from 1980 were used to guide participant solicitation. Potential participants were selected in various regions of the United States using community or telephone directories. Letters were sent to prospective participants explaining the nature of the project and asking them to participate. To enhance the representativeness of the overall sample, persons from specific samples were recruited (e.g., military personnel and Native American individuals). All participants completed a biographical-information form, a life-events form, and an experimental test form containing all 704 items considered for inclusion on the MMPI-2 (referred to as Form AX). Participants were tested in groups in convenient locations in their communities and paid $15 for completing the procedures.

Using these procedures, approximately 2,900 participants were tested. After eliminating people because of test invalidity or incompleteness of other forms, a final sample of 2,600 community participants (1,138 men and 1,462 women) was

---

[3] Throughout this book, we will use terms for sociocultural group memberships consistent with current guidelines from the American Psychological Association (2020). However, when referring to previously published work, such as the original and revised MMPI-2 Manuals (Butcher et al., 1989; 2001) or empirical studies, we maintain use of original terms for sociocultural group memberships to retain how individuals would have self-identified.

constituted. Of this number, 841 couples were included in the sample. Couples independently completed the test items and two additional forms describing the length of their relationships and rating each other on 110 characteristics using a modified version of the Katz Adjustment Scales (Katz & Lyerly, 1963). To collect test–retest data, a subgroup of participants, including 111 women and 82 men, were retested approximately one week after the initial testing.

The racial and ethnic composition of the sample was recorded as follows: Caucasian, 81%; African American, 12%; Hispanic, 3%; Native American, 3%; and Asian American, 1%. Participants ranged in age from 18 to 85 years (M = 41.04; SD = 15.29) and in formal education from 3 to 20 years (M = 14.72; SD = 2.60). Most men (61.6%) and women (61.2%) in the sample were married. Approximately 32% of the men and 21% of the women had professional or managerial positions, and approximately 12% of the men and 5% of the women were laborers. The median family income was $30,000–$35,000 for men and $25,000–$30,000 for women. Approximately 3% of men and 6% of women included in the normative sample indicated that they were involved in treatment for mental health problems at the time of their participation in the study.

At the time of its publication, the normative sample for the MMPI-2 was clearly more representative of the general population than the original MMPI normative sample. Some concerns were initially raised that individuals with higher educational levels seemed overrepresented in the normative sample; however, it was argued these levels better reflected the experiences of persons most likely to take the test. Butcher (1990a), Dahlstrom and Tellegen (1993), and Long et al. (1994) found only a negligible relationship between educational level of the MMPI-2 normative sample and scores on the MMPI-2 Validity and Clinical scales. Schinka and LaLone (1997) constituted a subsample of the MMPI-2 standardization sample that was matched to 1995 projected census data for gender, ethnic identification, age, and education. They concluded that the MMPI-2 normative sample was a very close approximation of the then current U.S. population and that small demographic differences (including education) between the normative sample and the U.S. population were not clinically meaningful.

Current Status of MMPI-2

Reviews of the MMPI-2 after it was published were positive, with Nichols (1992) concluding that "the psychodiagnostician selecting a structured inventory for the first time will find that no competing assessment device for abnormal psychology has stronger credentials for clinical description and prediction" (p. 565). Survey data indicate that the MMPI-2 is widely used by psychologists. Camara et al. (2000) found 86% of psychologists reported using the MMPI/MMPI-2, second in use only to the revised version of the Wechsler Adult Intelligence Scale (Wechsler, 1981; 94%). Similar results were presented in a more recent survey conducted by C. V. Wright and colleagues (2017). This survey suggested the MMPI-2 and the Restructured Form of the MMPI-2 (MMPI-2-RF; Ben-Porath & Tellegen, 2008/2011; Tellegen &

Ben-Porath, 2008/2011) were the most used broadband measures of personality and psychopathology in outpatient (83.8%) and inpatient (94.9%) settings. The MMPI-2 is the personality assessment instrument most emphasized in PhD and PsyD programs (Belter & Piotrowski, 2001; Mihura et al., 2017). It is also the psychological test considered by internship directors to be most essential for practicing psychologists (Piotrowski & Belter, 1999). Use of the MMPI-2 is supported by an extensive research base. Indeed, since 1989, approximately 3,000 articles, books, and dissertations have reported studies that included the MMPI-2. Although some of these studies used the MMPI-2 scales to evaluate other tests and constructs, most provided important information about the psychometric properties of the MMPI-2 and its use in various settings and for a wide array of purposes.

Although the MMPI-2 has not been revised since its publication in 1989, several developments should be noted. A revised test manual (Butcher et al., 2001) presents scoring information and interpretive guidelines for some scales that were added to the MMPI-2 after its publication in 1989. This updated manual contains information about new Validity scales, Infrequency Psychopathology (F_p; Arbisi & Ben-Porath, 1995) and Superlative Self-Presentation (S; Butcher & Han, 1995), as well as the Hostility (Ho; Cook & Medley, 1954) Supplementary scale. Content Component scales, developed by Ben-Porath and Sherwood (1993) to aid in interpretation of Content scale scores, are also included. Finally, the updated manual included the Personality Psychopathology Five (PSY-5) scales, which connect the MMPI-2 to dimensional models of personality disorders. These scales were described in greater detail in a monograph by Harkness et al. (2002). Scales that were developed subsequent to the updated MMPI-2 manual that have been added to most standard scoring packages for the instrument are also described in published monographs. This includes the Restructured Clinical scales (RC; Tellegen et al., 2003) and the Symptom Validity Scale (FBS; Ben-Porath et al., 2009). All of these scales will be discussed in detail in subsequent chapters of this book.

After the publication of the MMPI-2, several additional MMPI tests were developed. The first of these tests is the Minnesota Multiphasic Personality Inventory-Adolescent (MMPI-A), which was published in 1992 (Butcher et al., 1992). This test was developed concurrently with the MMPI-2 and was intended to provide a version of the MMPI appropriate for use with adolescents ages 14–18. The next two versions of the MMPI developed were the Minnesota Multiphasic Personality Inventory-2-Restructured Form (MMPI-2-RF; Ben-Porath & Tellegen, 2008/2011) and the Minnesota Multiphasic Personality Inventory-Adolescent-Restructured Form (MMPI-A-RF; Archer et al., 2016). The MMPI-2-RF and MMPI-A-RF were developed as alternatives to the MMPI-2 and MMPI-A, respectively. In both cases, the motivation for restructuring the instrument was to address the need for shorter tests, while also attempting to represent the substantive content of the MMPI item pool in psychometrically sound scales. The MMPI-2-RF uses the same normative sample as the MMPI-2 and draws on a subset of 338 MMPI-2 items to create 51 mostly original scales. Archer and colleagues (2016) engaged in a test development process similar to that used to create the MMPI-2-RF to develop the MMPI-A-RF. These efforts resulted in a 241-item, 48-scale, alternative test for use with 14- to 18-year-olds. The last of the tests added to the MMPI family is the Minnesota Multiphasic Personality Inventory-3 (MMPI-3; Ben-Porath & Tellegen, 2020). Two new normative samples intended to reflect the projected 2020 census were collected in the United States (one Spanish speaking and one English speaking), and a number of new items were added to the MMPI-2-RF item pool for use in developing the MMPI-3. This new instrument contains 335 items that are used to score 52 different scales. It is normed for use with adults ages 18 and over. Each of these four MMPI instruments are discussed in detail in subsequent chapters.

CHAPTER 2

ADMINISTRATION AND SCORING

QUALIFICATIONS OF TEST USERS

The MMPI-2 is easily administered and scored by hand or by computer. Although these procedures can be carried out by a properly trained and supervised clerk, administrative assistant, or technician, the MMPI-2 is a sophisticated psychological test. Its use is restricted to qualified professionals who have adequate training in test theory, personality structure and dynamics, and psychopathology and psychodiagnosis. Before purchasing MMPI-2 materials for the first time, users must provide to the test distributor (Pearson Assessments) credentials indicating they (1) are licensed to practice psychology independently, (2) have a graduate degree in psychology or a closely related field and have completed graduate courses in tests and measurement or a workshop or other course approved by the test distributor, or (3) have been granted the right to administer tests at this level in their jurisdiction. These criteria are consistent with standards established by the American Psychological Association and other professional organizations. Users of the MMPI-2 also should have detailed knowledge of the inventory itself. Familiarity with all material included in the MMPI-2 manual (Butcher et al., 2001) is essential. Additionally, users should be familiar with MMPI-2 interpretive procedures presented in books such as this one.

WHO CAN TAKE THE MMPI-2?

To produce meaningful MMPI-2 results, the test taker must read well enough to understand the items and respond to them appropriately. The MMPI-2 manual (Butcher et al., 2001) reports that, based on contemporary reading proficiency levels, a sixth grade reading level is required to comprehend the content of all the MMPI-2 items and to respond to them appropriately. If the examiner has doubt about the reading competence of a test taker, a standardized test of reading comprehension should be administered. Sometimes persons with less than a sixth grade reading level can meaningfully complete the MMPI-2 if it is administered using a standard audio version available from the test distributor.

The MMPI-2 is intended for use with persons who are 18 years of age or older. The MMPI-A (Butcher et al., 1992) or MMPI-A-RF (Archer et al., 2016) should be used with persons who are younger than 18. Because all versions of the MMPI were normed on 18-year-olds, any version can be used with persons of this age. The clinician should decide for each individual case whether to use the adolescent or adult instrument with 18-year-olds. Ordinarily, the MMPI-A or MMPI-A-RF would be selected for 18-year-olds who are still in high school and the MMPI-2 for 18-year-olds who are in college, working, or otherwise living a more independent lifestyle. Adolescent versions of the MMPI are discussed in Chapters 14 and 15. There is no upper age limit to who can take the MMPI-2.

The clinical condition of potential examinees is an important consideration in deciding who can take the MMPI-2. Completion of the test is a challenging and tedious task for many individuals. Persons who are very depressed, anxious, or agitated often find the task quite difficult, as do many who have experienced cognitive injuries or decline. Frequently it is possible to break the testing session into several shorter periods for such individuals. Sometimes persons who are in great distress find it easier to complete the test if the items are presented by means of the standardized audio version.

ADMINISTERING THE MMPI-2

The MMPI-2 is a well standardized instrument, assuring that differences in test results are due to differences in test takers and not to the manner in which the test is administered. Approved administration methods for the MMPI-2 include a pencil/paper version where the test taker reads items from a paper booklet and marks their responses on an answer sheet or a computerized version that uses software available from Pearson Assessments. For most people, the test can be administered either individually or in groups using the approved administration method most convenient for the examiner. For individuals of average or above-average intelligence—without complicating factors, such as limited reading ability or significant emotional distress—the testing time typically is between an hour and an hour and a half. Pencil/paper administrations typically take longer than computerized administrations. For individuals with reading difficulties or other complicating factors, the testing time may exceed 2 hours.

Although it might at times seem more convenient to send the MMPI-2 home to be completed, this procedure is unacceptable. The test should always be completed in a professional setting with adequate supervision. This increases the likelihood that the test will be taken seriously and that the results will be valid and useful. In forensic evaluations, examiners may be asked to verify that the responses that were scored and interpreted are indeed those of the individual under consideration. Such verification is difficult if the test was not completed under direct supervision.

Before the MMPI-2 is administered, the examiner should establish a positive rapport with the person to be tested. The best way to ensure cooperation is to explain why the MMPI-2 is being administered, who will have access to the results, and why it is in the best interest of the test taker to cooperate with the testing. The test should be administered in a quiet, comfortable place. The examiner or a proctor should be readily available to monitor the test taking and to answer questions that may arise. Care should be taken to make sure that the test taker reads the instructions and understands them. Questions that arise during the course of testing should be handled promptly and confidentially. Most questions can be handled by referring the test taker back to the standardized test instructions.

TESTING MATERIALS

There is one English version of the MMPI-2. Regardless of which approved administration method is used, items are presented in the same order and arranged so that those required for scoring the original Validity (L, F, K) and Clinical scales appear first. It is possible to score these standard scales by administering only the first 370 items. However, if less than the entire test is completed, some Validity scales (VRIN, TRIN, F_B, F_P, FBS), the Content and Content Component scales, the Restructured Clinical (RC) scales, the Personality Psychopathology Five (PSY-5) scales, and many of the Supplementary scales cannot be scored. As such, we recommend administration of the entire test in all but the most unusual circumstances.

The MMPI-2 has been translated into many other languages. This includes both translations intended for people living in the United States that do not speak English as their first language (e.g., Spanish for individuals living in the United States) and for individuals living in places where they use a different primary language (e.g., Italian). A full listing of approved translations of the MMPI-2 and contact information for obtaining access to translated versions of the instrument are available at the University of Minnesota Press, Test Division's website (https://www.upress.umn.edu/test-division/translations-permissions/available-translations).

The approved pencil/paper administration of the MMPI-2 requires the test taker read the test's items from a booklet and record their answers on an answer sheet. The test booklet is typically in softcover form, though an optional hardcover version of the test booklet is available for use when a table or desk surface is not available. Printed booklets are available in English, Spanish for the United States, French for Canada, and Hmong from Pearson Assessments (pearsonassessments.com). Users interested in other translations will need to contact the distributors identified on the University of Minnesota Press, Test Division's website (https://www.upress.umn.edu/test-division/translations-permissions/available-translations).

Several different answer sheets are available for the MMPI-2. The one to be used depends on how the examiner plans to score the test. If the test is to be hand scored, one kind of answer sheet should be used. If it is to be computer scored, a different kind of answer sheet is needed. Before administering the test, examiners should determine how scoring will be accomplished. Reference the Pearson Assessments' website (pearsonassessmsents.com) for specific information about which answer sheets to use.

Pearson Assessments also offers software that permits computerized administration of the MMPI-2. Specifically, Pearson Assessments' Q-Local and Q-Global software can be used to administer the test. In both programs, the test taker reads the MMPI-2 items displayed on the computer screen and records their answers using the keyboard or mouse. A meta-analysis of the results of five MMPI-2 studies (Finger & Ones, 1999) concluded that differences between computerized and conventional administrations are attributable to sampling error and that computer and booklet forms are psychometrically equivalent.

For persons who may have difficulty completing a written form of the MMPI-2 (either pencil/paper or computerized administrations), a standardized audio version of the items is available from Pearson Assessments. Items are read and repeated in a neutral voice, and test takers mark their answers on a paper answer sheet or using the computer. This version is useful for people with reading difficulties or for those with disabilities that make completion of the standard form difficult or impossible. The audio version is available in English, French for Canada, Spanish for the United States, and Hmong. Several early MMPI studies have demonstrated that the standard booklet form and a tape-recorded form yielded very similar results (Henning et al., 1972; Reese et al., 1968; Urmer et al., 1960). Differences between the two versions were no greater than for two administrations of the standard form. Although all of these studies employed the original MMPI, there is no reason to believe that results would be different for the MMPI-2.

Sometimes it may seem more convenient to read MMPI-2 items to test takers and have them record their responses or respond out loud. This is a procedure that should be avoided because having individual clinicians read items represents a significant deviation from standardized procedures. At least one study suggests this practice with the MMPI-2 may lead to more defensive responding on the part of the test taker (E. L. Edwards et al., 1998). This may be because the examiner's tone of voice, facial expressions, and other nonverbal behaviors affect responses, and therefore scores, in unknown ways. This is especially problematic when either the test taker or the person administering the test may be motivated to produce a particular test result.

SCORING THE MMPI-2

Once the test taker has responded to the MMPI-2 items, scoring can be accomplished by computer or by hand. For computerized scoring, Pearson Assessment's Q-Local and Q-Global software can be used. This software also allows the user to choose from among several computer-generated score or interpretive reports. If the test was computer administered using one of these software systems, test responses are stored in the program's memory, and scoring programs can be applied directly to them. It is also possible to hand-enter a test taker's responses into these systems to score the instrument if a pencil/paper version of the test was administered. Another automated scoring option is to mail the responses to Pearson Assessments in Minneapolis, where they are scored and returned to users (usually within a week). All of the automated scoring options offered by Pearson Assessments are paid for on a per use basis. Individuals interested in available computer services should contact Pearson Assessments for details.

Some test users, particularly those who are not high-volume users, may prefer to hand score the MMPI-2, using templates available from Pearson Assessments. Scoring keys are available for all 121 of the standardly scored scales of the MMPI-2. Additional information about how to hand-score the MMPI-2 can be found in the instrument's manual (Butcher et al., 2001). Importantly, although hand scoring is a relatively straightforward clerical task, it should be completed with great care, as counting and recording errors are rather common. In fact, Allard and Faust (2000) demonstrated that scoring errors are quite common for several objective personality tests and that the errors occur with both hand scoring and computer scoring that is dependent on keyboard entry of responses.

T–SCORE TRANSFORMATIONS

To put a test-taker's scores in the same metric as the normative sample, raw scores on the various MMPI-2 scales are converted to T scores to facilitate interpretation. T scores are standardized scores with a mean of 50 and a standard deviation of 10. Because raw scores for MMPI-2 scales are not normally distributed, linear T scores— which maintain the same distributions as the raw scores on which they are based—do not have exactly the same meaning for every scale. For example, if linear T scores are used, a score of 65T on any one of the Clinical scales would not necessarily have the same percentile value as a score of 65T on one of the other Clinical scales.

To address this problem, for the eight basic Clinical scales (excluding Scales 5 and 0), the MMPI-2 utilizes a different kind of T score, called a Uniform T score. The use of Uniform T Scores ensures that a T score of a given level (e.g., 65) has the same percentile value for all Clinical scales (Butcher et al., 2001). A composite (or average) distribution of raw scores of the MMPI-2 normative sample on the eight basic Clinical scales was derived. The distribution of each of the eight Clinical scales was adjusted so that it would match this composite distribution. This procedure re-sulted in Uniform T scores that are percentile equivalent and whose distributions are closely matched in terms of skewness and kurtosis (Tellegen & Ben-Porath, 1992). The change in the distribution of any particular scale is not great, so the profile re-tains most of its familiar characteristics. Percentile equivalents for various Uniform T scores are reported in Table 2.1.

Uniform T scores also are used for the Content, PSY-5, and RC scales. However, Uniform T scores were not derived for Clinical scales 5 and 0 or for the Validity scales because the distributions of scores for these scales differ from those of the other eight Clinical scales. For these scales, linear T-score transformations were derived. Linear T scores are also used for other MMPI-2 Supplementary scales.

Whether the MMPI-2 is scored by hand or computer, the examiner will need to choose which normative sample to apply when determining the test taker's standard scale scores. The MMPI-2 has gender-based norms for men and women. There were important differences in raw scores between men and women, so separate norms were

TABLE 2.1 *Percentile Equivalents for Uniform T Scores*

Uniform T Score	Percentile Equivalent
30	≤1
35	4
40	15
45	34
50	55
55	73
60	85
65	92
70	96
75	98
80	≥99

Note. Excerpted (Table 4) from the *MMPI®-2 (Minnesota Multiphasic Personality Inventory®-2) Manual for Administration, Scoring, and Interpretation, Revised Edition* by James N. Butcher, John R. Graham, Yossef S. Ben-Porath, Auke Tellegen, W. Grant Dahlstrom, and Beverly Kaemmer. Copyright © 2001 by the Regents of the University of Minnesota. Used by permission of the University of Minnesota Press. All rights reserved. "MMPI®" and "Minnesota Multiphasic Personality Inventory®" are registered trademarks of the Regents the Regents of the University of Minnesota.

developed for these two groups. Use of gendered norms assumes that the differences in raw scores between men and women reflect differing degrees of willingness to admit to symptoms and problems rather than actual differences in the base rates of those characteristics. However, the use of separate norms for men and women is problematic when the MMPI-2 is used in employment screening. The Civil Rights Act of 1991 explicitly prohibits consideration of race, color, religion, national origin, or sex in employment practices, thus prohibiting the use of gendered norms. Non-gendered norms were subsequently developed. The use of non-gendered norms is appropriate in employment screening applications of the MMPI-2 or whenever the use of gendered norms is prohibited. Non-gendered T scores are based on 1,138 men and 1,138 women in the MMPI-2 normative sample (Ben-Porath & Forbey, 2003). Ben-Porath and Forbey (2003) compared gendered and non-gendered scale scores. Although they found significant differences for some scales, they concluded that different interpretations would not be reached about individuals based on gendered versus non-gendered scores.

MMPI-2 PROFILES
Once scoring is complete, test taker's scores on the MMPI-2 are summarized in profile sheets. When the MMPI-2 is scored by computer, profiles for the various sets of scales are provided in the output. When hand scoring is utilized, profile sheets are available from Pearson Assessments for the Validity, Clinical, Content, PSY-5, RC, and

Supplementary scales. Both methods of scoring provide two versions of the Clinical scale profile: K-corrected and non-K-corrected. Historically, test users relied upon the K-corrected Clinical scale profiles; however, this practice has been questioned over the past several decades. The test manual (Butcher et al., 2001) discusses circumstances in which the non-corrected scores may be preferable. Generally speaking, K-corrected scores may lead to overestimates of clinical symptoms for persons who are not clients or patients, particularly when the test taker approaches the MMPI-2 in a defensive manner. In such cases, the non-corrected scores may more accurately reflect adjustment level compared with the normative sample. Non-K-corrected and K-corrected scores tend to be very similar when the MMPI-2 is used in clinical settings. Thus, these authors recommend that non-K-corrected scores be used routinely (see Chapter 3 for additional details).

CHAPTER 3

THE VALIDITY SCALES

FOR THE MMPI-2 TO YIELD ACCURATE AND USEFUL information, the person taking the test must do so in the manner indicated by the standard instructions. Test takers are expected to read each item, consider its content, and give a direct and honest response to the item, using the true–false response format provided. Whenever extreme deviations from these procedures occur, the resulting protocol should be considered invalid and should not be interpreted further. Less extreme deviations in test taking do not necessarily invalidate test results but should be carefully inspected to see if cautious interpretation of other scales is needed.

Validity indicators were developed for the MMPI-2 specifically to assess test-taking approaches that might distort the results of other scales. These indicators are the Cannot Say (?) missing item count, and the Variable Response Inconsistency (VRIN), True Response Inconsistency (TRIN), Infrequency (F), Back F (F$_B$), Infrequency Psychopathology (F$_p$), Symptom Validity (FBS), Lie (L), Correction (K), and Superlative Self-Presentation (S) scales.

Research has demonstrated the Validity scales are correlated with other extra-test behaviors (e.g., symptoms, personality characteristics) in addition to providing important information about test-taking approaches. However, we recommend the Validity scales be used exclusively to assess test-taking attitudes and that inferences about personality and psychopathology be derived from other MMPI-2 scales. The items included in each of the Validity scales, the keyed response for each item, and linear T-score transformations for raw scores are presented in appendixes of the MMPI-2 manual (Butcher et al., 2001).[1] This information for the FBS scale can be

---

[1] Although scale composition information and T-score transformations were presented in appendixes of prior editions of this book, concerns about test security led the University of Minnesota Press to adopt a policy that precludes the presentation of such information in books such as this one.

found in the FBS Test Monograph (Ben-Porath et al., 2009). Score transformations based on the non-gendered normative data are available in the Appendix of Ben-Porath and Forbey's (2003) non-gendered norms monograph.

Nichols et al. (1989) stressed the importance of differentiating between non-content-based invalid responding and content-based invalid responding. In the former, test takers complete the MMPI-2 in a way that is not related to the content of items (e.g., random responding). In the latter, test takers read and consider each item and then respond consistently in a manner that distorts their true underlying personality or psychopathology (i.e., overreporting, underreporting). MMPI-2 Validity scales assessing both categories of response sets will be reviewed in the subsequent sections of this chapter.

SCALES ASSESSING NON-CONTENT-BASED INVALID RESPONDING

The first step in interpreting the MMPI-2 is determining if the test taker has responded without considering item content. Their responses may be random or may follow some systematic approach (e.g., all true, all false) unrelated to item content. Test responses might be unrelated to item content for any number of reasons such as poor reading comprehension, a desire to complete the task as quickly as possible, passive-aggressive resistance to psychological testing, or any number of other motivations and factors that might result in the test taker failing to attend to and respond deliberately to each item on the test. Regardless of the reason, it is important to identify when the test has been completed without regard to item content. The Cannot Say (?), VRIN, and TRIN scales are examined for this purpose. If scores on any of these scales indicate invalid responding, then none of the other scales on the test should be interpreted.

Cannot Say Score

The Cannot Say (?) score simply counts the number of items that the test taker did not answer or to which they provided an unscorable response (e.g., marking both true and false for the same item). There are many reasons people omit items on the MMPI-2. Occasionally, items are omitted because of carelessness or confusion. Omitted items may reflect an attempt to avoid admitting undesirable things about oneself without directly lying. Indecisive people, who cannot decide between the two response alternatives, may leave many items unanswered or answer both true and false to some items. Sometimes items are omitted because of a lack of information or experience necessary for a meaningful response or because the test taker does not understand the item.

Regardless, a large number of omissions can lower scores on other scales. Therefore, the validity of a protocol with many omitted items should be questioned. The MMPI-2 manual (Butcher et al., 2001) suggests protocols with 30 or more omitted items must be considered highly suspect, if not completely invalid. This criterion is very liberal. Our practice is to interpret with great caution protocols with more than 10 omitted items and not to interpret at all those with more than 30 omitted items. When more than a few items are omitted, it can be very helpful to determine on which scales the omitted items are scored. Obviously, even fewer than 10 omitted items can be a problem if all of the items are on a single scale. If item omissions are limited to a few scales, then other scales may still be interpreted. Computer scored MMPI-2s report the percentage of items on each scale that were answered. Dragon and colleagues (2012) found the criterion validity of MMPI-2 substantive scales was not affected significantly when up to 10% of items were randomly omitted. Therefore, we recommend only interpreting scales with an item response rate of at least 90%. When a scale is elevated despite having a response rate below 90%, it can be interpreted with caution as it may be an underestimate of the test taker's standing on that scale.

As indicated in Chapter 2, it is best to try to ensure that few or no items are omitted. If encouraged before beginning the MMPI-2 to answer all items, most people will omit very few. Also, if the examiner visually scans the answer sheet when the test is completed and encourages the test taker to try to answer previously skipped items, then most people will do so. Computer administration of the MMPI-2 tracks omitted items and asks the test taker to reconsider and answer as many of those items as possible.

Variable Response Inconsistency Scale

The Variable Response Inconsistency (VRIN) scale provides an indication of a tendency to respond inconsistently to MMPI-2 items (Butcher et al., 2001). The scale consists of 67 item response pairs with either similar or opposite content. Each time a person answers items in a pair inconsistently, one raw-score point is added to the score on the VRIN scale. For some item pairs, two true responses result in a point being scored on the scale; for other item pairs, two false responses result in a point being scored; and for still other item pairs, a true response and a false response result in a point being scored. Hand scoring VRIN is very complicated, and it is recommended it be scored by computer (Iverson & Barton, 1999). If hand scoring is done, considerable care should be exercised.

A completely random response set produces a T score on the VRIN scale of 96 for men and 98 for women. All-true and all-false response sets result in VRIN T scores near 50. Persons who deliberately overreport on the MMPI-2—as well as those who honestly admit to serious psychopathology—typically have about average T scores on the VRIN scale (Wetter et al., 1992).

The MMPI-2 manual (Butcher et al., 2001) suggests VRIN raw scores equal to or greater than 13 (T ≥ 80) indicate inconsistent responding that invalidates the protocol. Several empirical studies have confirmed that scores at or above this cutoff are indicative of random responding (Berry et al., 1991; Gallen & Berry, 1996; Paolo & Ryan, 1992; Pinsoneault, 2007), although slightly lower cutoff scores may yield more accurate results in settings with unusually high base rates of random responding (Gallen & Berry, 1996).

There also are data suggesting partial random responding (i.e., random responding during some but not all of the test) produces elevated VRIN scale scores, but the optimal cutoff scores for identifying various degrees of randomness have not been determined (Berry et al., 1991; Gallen & Berry, 1996; Pinsoneault, 2007). Partial random responding is most likely to occur later in the test (Berry et al., 1992; Gallen & Berry, 1996).

In summary, the VRIN scale was developed to identify persons who respond to the MMPI-2 items inconsistently, typically because they did not read the content of the items and responded instead in a random or near-random way. The VRIN scale can be especially helpful in understanding elevated F scale scores. A high F scale score and a high VRIN scale score would support the notion of random responding. However, a high F scale score and a low or moderate VRIN scale score would suggest the protocol did not result from random responding.

True Response Inconsistency Scale

The True Response Inconsistency (TRIN) scale was developed for the MMPI-2 to identify persons who tend to repeatedly respond either "true" (acquiescence) or "false" (nonacquiescence) regardless of the content of items (Butcher et al., 2001). In either case, the resulting protocol is likely to be invalid and uninterpretable.

The TRIN scale consists of pairs of items for which answering either "true" or "false" to both items in the pair means the test taker is providing contradictory (i.e., inconsistent) information. The TRIN raw score is obtained by subtracting the number of pairs of items to which test takers responded inconsistently with two false responses from the number of pairs of items to which they responded inconsistently with two true responses, and then adding a constant value of 9 to the difference. TRIN scale raw scores can range from 0 to 23. Higher TRIN scale raw scores indicate a tendency to give true responses indiscriminately, and lower TRIN scale raw scores indicate a tendency to give false responses indiscriminately. When TRIN scale raw scores are converted to T scores, raw scores above 9 and below 9 are converted to T scores greater than 50, with the likelihood of a true or false response set indicated by the letters "T" or "F" following the T scores. As with the VRIN scale, the TRIN scale involves complex scoring that is best done by computer (Iverson & Barton, 1999). If hand scoring is done, considerable care should be exercised.

The MMPI-2 manual (Butcher et al., 2001) suggests TRIN scale raw scores of 13 or greater (T ≥ 80 in the true direction) or of 5 or less (T ≥ 80 in the false direction) indicate inconsistent responding that might invalidate the protocol. An analogue study by Wetter and Tharpe (1995) found TRIN scale scores are sensitive to randomly inserted true or false responses, and the TRIN scale uniquely contributes to the detection of this response set.

SCALES ASSESSING CONTENT–BASED INVALID RESPONDING

Scales for Detecting Overreporting

Sometimes people respond to the MMPI-2 in a manner that portrays them as having more problems and symptoms than they really do. The motivations for overreporting are varied. Some test takers may do so to convince mental health professionals they are desperately in need of their help. Other test takers may be motivated to try to avoid responsibility for

s by appearing to be very psychologically disturbed (e.g., not guilty by reason
pleas) or for the purpose of enhancing monetary gains (e.g., personal injury or
disability claims). Regardless of motivation, it is important to detect individuals who are
overreporting so test takers will not be described as more maladjusted than they really are.

Infrequency Scale

The Infrequency (F) scale of the original MMPI was developed to detect atypical
ways of responding to test items, such as when test takers respond randomly (Meehl
& Hathaway, 1946). Items in the MMPI's F scale were answered in the scored direction by fewer than 10% of the MMPI normative sample. During development of the
MMPI-2, several of the original F scale items were deleted because of objectionable
content, but the scale was otherwise unchanged, leaving the MMPI-2's F scale with
60 items (Butcher et al., 2001).

The item content of the F scale includes such diverse characteristics as paranoid
thinking, antisocial attitudes or behavior, hostility, and poor physical health. In
general—because the scales of the MMPI-2 are intercorrelated—high scores on the
F scale usually are associated with elevated scores on the Clinical scales, especially
Scales 6 and 8. In the MMPI-2 normative sample, scores on the F scale are related to
race and ethnicity, with individuals who identified as African American, American
Indian, and Hispanic American scoring on average three to five T-score points higher
on the F scale than those who identified as Caucasian (Butcher et al., 2001).

Although scores on the F scale were originally intended to identify random responding, it soon became apparent there were other explanations for high scores.
People who are experiencing severe psychopathology typically endorse a large number
of F scale items in the scored direction, as do individuals with less severe psychopathology who are overreporting. Repeatedly answering items indiscriminately true
or false will also lead to high F scale scores. Fortunately, MMPI-2 scales directly
assessing random responding (VRIN), fixed true or false responding (TRIN), and
overreporting (F_p) aid in understanding the reasons for high F scale scores.

HIGH SCORES ON THE F SCALE

It is possible to establish some ranges of T scores on the F scale and to discuss possible
interpretations associated with scores in each range. The MMPI-2 manual (Butcher
et al., 2001) indicates that—because of the relationship between F scale scores and
genuine psychopathology—scores on this scale may have different meanings in clinical and nonclinical settings. The manual also suggests different scores for identifying
invalid responding in inpatient, outpatient, and nonclinical settings.

T ≥ 100 (Inpatients); T ≥ 90 (Outpatients); T ≥ 80 (Nonclinical Settings)

When T scores on the F scale are this high, the possibility of a non-content-based
invalid response style should first be ruled out. This is because F scores this high may
be the result of random responding or acquiescent responding (i.e., a fixed "true"
response bias). The influence of these non-content-based invalid response styles on F
scores can be examined using scores on the VRIN and TRIN scales, both of which
were described earlier in this section. If the VRIN scale T score is equal to or greater
than 80, then random responding is likely the cause of the elevated F scale. If the T

score on the TRIN scale is equal to or greater than 80 (in the "true" direction), then the elevation on F is likely due to acquiescent responding. It is also possible F scale scores in this range have resulted from attempts to present an unrealistically negative picture when completing the MMPI-2. The F_P scale—discussed later in this chapter—is especially helpful in identifying individuals who overreported. Finally, among hospitalized psychiatric patients, F scale T scores greater than 100 often are suggestive of very serious psychopathology.

T = 80–99 (Inpatients); T = 70–89 (Outpatients); T = 65–79 (Nonclinical Settings)

Answering false to all or most of the MMPI-2 items can produce an F scale score at this level. If this is the case, the TRIN scale T score is likely to be equal to or greater than 80 (in the "false" direction). Alternatively, persons with scores at this level may have exaggerated symptoms, perhaps as a "cry for help." However, scores at this level may also be indicative of serious psychological problems.

T = 55–79 (Inpatients); T = 55–69 (Outpatients); T = 40–64 (Nonclinical)

Persons with T scores at this level on the F scale likely approached the test in a valid manner. Persons with scores at the upper end of this range may be accurately reporting psychological problems.

LOW SCORES ON THE F SCALE

T ≤ 54 (Inpatient and Outpatient); T ≤ 39 (Nonclinical)

Persons with F scale T scores in this below-average range may be denying or minimizing psychological problems. An underreporting response set should be considered. More information about underreporting is presented later in this chapter.

Back Infrequency Scale

Items on the F scale appear in the first part of the MMPI-2 test booklet. Thus, there were concerns an invalid response style in the latter parts of the test would not be detected. The Back Infrequency (F_B) scale was developed to address this need. The procedures used to develop the F_B scale were similar to those used for the F scale (Butcher et al., 2001). Items were selected for the F_B scale if (a) they were endorsed in the scored direction by fewer than 10% of the normative sample, and (b) they appeared later in the test booklet. The F_B scale consists of 40 items occurring between Item No. 281 and Item No. 555 in the test booklet.

When the F scale score indicates a valid approach (discussed earlier in this chapter), an elevated F_B scale score could indicate the test taker responded to items in the second half of the test booklet in an invalid manner. In this situation, those scales whose items exclusively appear early in the booklet (i.e., L, F, K, the Clinical scales and their subscales, the Health Concerns Content scale [HEA] and its content component scales, and the Posttraumatic Stress Disorder scale [PK]) can still be interpreted, but all other scales should not be interpreted.

Only limited data are available concerning optimal F_B scale cutoff scores for identifying invalid protocols. The MMPI-2 manual (Butcher et al., 2001) suggests that when the F_B scale is significantly elevated (T ≥ 110 in clinical settings; T ≥ 90 in nonclinical settings) and is at least 30 T-score points higher than the F scale's T score, the test taker is likely to have changed their approach in the latter part of the test, and scales with items in the latter part of the test should not be interpreted. This applies to any scale not listed in the previous paragraph.

The VRIN and TRIN scales should be interpreted prior to interpreting the F_B scale, as either random responding or acquiescent responding will produce very high F_B scale scores. Persons who are overreporting psychopathology also will produce very high scores on the F_B scale. Persons overreporting psychopathology are likely also to have elevated scores on the F_P scale.

Infrequency Psychopathology Scale

Recognizing that in some clinical settings, high F scale scores are often due—at least in part—to severe psychopathology, Arbisi and Ben-Porath (1995) developed the Infrequency Psychopathology (F_P) scale to supplement the F and F_B scales. The 27 items in the F_P scale were answered infrequently by both psychiatric inpatients and persons in the MMPI-2 normative sample. The resulting items are far less likely to reflect genuine psychopathology than the items on the F and F_B scales.

Several studies have confirmed that the F_P scale is less sensitive to genuine psychopathology than the F and F_B scales (Arbisi & Ben-Porath, 1998; Ladd, 1998; Tolin et al., 2004). Using data collected by Graham, Watts, and Timbrook (1991), Arbisi and Ben-Porath (1995) demonstrated that the F_P scale added incrementally to the F scale in discriminating between persons overreporting and psychiatric inpatients.

Gass and Luis (2001) noted that four F_P scale items also appear on the L scale and seem to indicate defensiveness rather than overreporting. They suggested deleting these items from the F_P scale could increase its effectiveness. However, Arbisi et al. (2003b) demonstrated the original F_P scale was more effective in identifying overreporting than the revised scale suggested by Gass and Luis.

Although Arbisi and Ben-Porath (1995) did not establish optimal F_P cutoff scores, they suggested T scores over 100 on the F_P scale likely indicate overreporting. The MMPI-2 manual (Butcher et al., 2001) suggests that an F_P scale score equal to or greater than 100 may indicate overreporting or random responding, although the latter would also result in a significant elevation on the VRIN scale. Thus, it is important to first consider the possibility of non-content-based random responding when interpreting F_P scores.

Rogers et al. (1995) examined MMPI-2 scores of individuals receiving psychiatric outpatient services who took the test with standard instructions and also with instructions to make their problems seem much worse than they really were. Scale scores on F_P accurately identified the exaggerated protocols, although the F scale was about equally effective in making this distinction. Several subsequent studies indicated that the F_P scale may be more accurate than the F scale in identifying individuals receiving psychiatric inpatient and outpatient care who were instructed to exaggerate their symptoms and problems (Arbisi & Ben-Porath, 1998; Berry et al., 1996). Additional research also demonstrated that the F_P scale added incrementally to the F scale in the detection of prisoners instructed to fake bad (Gallagher, 1997) and college students instructed to feign schizophrenia (Bagby, Rogers, Buis, et al., 1997).

Rogers et al. (2003) conducted a meta-analysis of 65 MMPI-2 feigning studies. They concluded that both F and F_p are effective in identifying individuals who are overreporting psychopathology. They expressed a preference for the F_p scale because optimal cutting scores were consistent across settings, and it demonstrated low false-positive rates.

HIGH SCORES ON THE F_p SCALE

Protocols with F_p scale T scores equal to or greater than 100 are likely to be invalid and should not be interpreted (Butcher et al., 2001). As with the other overreporting scales, non-content-based invalid responding will cause elevated F_p scores and should always be ruled out (see the discussion of the VRIN and TRIN scales earlier in this chapter). F_p scale scores at this level also occur when test takers overreport psychopathology. F_p scale scores between 70 and 99 suggest some exaggeration of symptoms and problems—perhaps as a "cry for help"—but the protocol may still be valid and interpretable. F_p scale scores equal to or less than 69 suggest the test taker accurately described their mental health status.

Symptom Validity Scale

The Symptom Validity Scale (FBS)—originally called the Fake Bad Scale—was developed by Lees-Haley et al. (1991). The FBS was not originally part of the MMPI-2 and thus not included in the test manual. When it was added to the test, a test monograph was published to inform users about scale development and interpretation (Ben-Porath et al., 2009).

Lees-Haley et al. (1991) developed FBS in an attempt to detect the noncredible reporting of emotional distress among personal injury claimants. Items for the FBS were selected rationally based on unpublished frequency counts of suspected malingerers' MMPI item responses and "observations of personal injury malingerers." Subsequent research demonstrated the FBS scale does not work for its intended purpose. In a study utilizing a sample of workplace accident victims, Bury and Bagby (2002) found the FBS was ineffective in detecting feigned psychopathology and concluded its use for this purpose is inadvisable. Butcher et al. (2008) analyzed data from a variety of settings and concluded the FBS is likely to classify an unacceptably large number of individuals who are experiencing genuine psychological distress as overreporters. A meta-analysis of MMPI-2 overreporting studies (Rogers et al., 2003) revealed the FBS was quite ineffective in identifying persons who are overreporting emotional distress.

Some authors have suggested FBS scores may be effective in identifying the noncredible reporting of cognitive deficits during neuropsychological examinations (e.g., Greiffenstein et al., 2002; Larrabee, 2003). However, a well-conducted analogue study by Dearth et al. (2005) found the FBS was not as effective as the F, F_B, or F_p scales in identifying persons who gave noncredible responses during a neuropsychological examination.

N. W. Nelson et al. (2006) conducted a meta-analysis of 19 studies investigating the FBS's utility. Results indicated FBS was superior to the F_B and F_p scales in differentiating between persons who gave noncredible reports of cognitive deficits compared with persons known to have such deficits. However, the FBS scale underperformed the F, F$_B$, and F$_p$ scales in detecting noncredible reporting of emotional problems. N. W. Nelson and colleagues (2010) replicated these results in an expanded meta-analysis that included 32 studies examining the utility of FBS scores. Results suggested FBS scores were able to differentiate between overreporting and comparison groups with a large effect. Moderation analyses suggested FBS scores demonstrated especially large effect size differences when identifying overreporting among those who were also known to have provided insufficient effort on performance validity tests as well as among individuals being evaluated for traumatic brain injuries. Additional research has suggested the FBS scale is effective in identifying noncredible reports of pain symptoms (Bianchini et al., 2008). More research is needed to determine the extent to which the FBS and other MMPI-2 Validity scales can detect the overreporting of cognitive deficits during neuropsychological examination as well as the extent to which any of the scales adds incrementally to established neuropsychological effort tests such as the Digit Memory Test (Hiscock & Hiscock, 1989), the Test of Memory Malingering (Tombaugh, 1997), or the Letter Memory Test (Inman et al., 1998).

There have been concerns the FBS incorrectly identifies persons with bona fide medical problems as overreporting somatic difficulties (Butcher et al., 2003). However, in the FBS test monograph, Ben-Porath et al. (2009) rebutted these claims with both a literature review and original data analyses. They concluded the use of appropriate cutoff scores resulted in few persons with genuine medical/neurological problems being incorrectly identified as noncredible responders. There also have been claims the FBS is biased against women (Nichols et al., 2009). However, Lee et al. (2012) presented data suggesting that when appropriate cutoff scores are used, the FBS is equally valid for men and women in differentiating between persons simulating cognitive problems and persons with bona fide cognitive problems. Dean et al. (2008) found no differences in FBS scale scores between individuals who identified as Caucasian, Hispanic, and African American who were referred to a neuropsychological clinic or were patients in a vocational rehabilitation program. In summary, having reviewed existing research literature very carefully, we conclude that—when appropriate cutoff scores are used—the FBS scale has utility in identifying persons who give noncredible reports of cognitive or somatic problems.

HIGH SCORES ON THE FBS SCALE
Based on their review of the literature, Ben-Porath et al. (2009) established ranges of T scores on the FBS and the possible interpretations associated with scores in each range.

T ≥ 100
When T scores on the FBS are this high, the possibility of a non-content-based invalid response style must first be considered. Either random responding or acquiescent responding will result in very high FBS scores. Thus, the VRIN and TRIN scales should always be interpreted prior to interpretation of FBS scores (see earlier in this chapter for their interpretive guidelines). If non-content-based invalid responding is ruled out, then scores in this range indicate the test taker likely overreported somatic or cognitive symptoms, as they endorsed an unusual combination of somatic and cognitive problems that is unlikely even in individuals with genuine and severe medical problems.

Substantive scales should be interpreted cautiously, if at all, as they are unlikely to present an accurate picture of the test taker's functioning. This is especially true for substantive scales assessing constructs reflecting somatic and cognitive difficulties.

T = 80–99

Scores on FBS within this range may be a product of random responding or acquiescent responding (see the interpretive guidelines for the VRIN and TRIN scales earlier in this chapter). However, if there are no indications of non-content-based invalid responding, then scores in this range can indicate the test taker overreported somatic or cognitive issues, as they endorsed an unusual combination of somatic and cognitive problems when compared to individuals with genuine and severe medical problems. Scores in this range may also reflect the exaggeration of somatic or cognitive difficulties experienced by the test taker. Regardless, scores on the substantive scales, especially those reflecting somatic or cognitive symptoms, are likely to overestimate the problems and difficulties experienced by the test taker and should be interpreted cautiously.

T = ≤ 79

Persons with T scores at this level on the FBS scale are likely to be accurately reporting somatic and cognitive problems.

Scales for Detecting Underreporting

People taking the MMPI-2 sometimes engage in underreporting, a response style characterized by minimizing one's problems or exaggerating one's virtues. The causes of underreporting are varied and may include self-deception, personal blind spots, and responding to item content in a socially desirable manner. Some test takers may underreport to convince mental health professionals they have few or very mild psychiatric symptoms. Other test takers may be motivated to try to present themselves as being especially psychologically fit (e.g., parents undergoing child custody evaluation, persons seeking employment as law enforcement officers). Regardless, it is important to assess underreporting so test takers will not be described as being better adjusted than they really are.

Lie Scale

The Lie (L) scale for the original MMPI was constructed to detect deliberate and unsophisticated attempts to present oneself in an unrealistically favorable way (Meehl & Hathaway, 1946). All 15 rationally derived items in the original L scale were maintained in the MMPI-2. These items deal with minor personality flaws and weaknesses to which most people are willing to admit (e.g., getting along with everyone they meet). However, individuals who deliberately try to present themselves in a very favorable way are unwilling to admit even such minor shortcomings, resulting in high L scale scores.

Many test takers will endorse several L scale items in the scored direction. The average number of L items endorsed by persons in the MMPI-2 normative sample was approximately three. However, Duris et al. (2007) found persons with strong Christian beliefs answered L scale items in the scored direction more often. A meta-analysis of 12 studies examining the MMPI-2 in religious samples—primarily seminary students and clergy of the Christian faith—indicated the tendency to endorse some L items in the scored direction was likely to elevate scores by approximately five T-score points (Rosen et al., 2016). This suggests religiousness is unlikely to lead to clinically significant elevations on L.

Persons completing the MMPI-2 in certain nonclinical settings (e.g., personnel screening, child custody evaluations) understandably want to present themselves in a positive way. For example, Bathurst et al. (1997) reported average L scale T scores of approximately 55 for parents involved in child custody determinations; while Bagby et al. (1999) reported average L scale T scores of approximately 60 for parents in a similar situation. Moderately elevated scores on the L scale under these kinds of situations do not necessarily indicate underreporting of significant psychological symptoms and problems.

HIGH SCORES ON THE L SCALE

T ≥ 80 (Clinical and Nonclinical Settings)
When the L scale T score is equal to or greater than 80, the TRIN scale must first be consulted, as these scores may result from a pervasive nonacquiescent response style (see TRIN scale score interpretation described earlier in this chapter). Once nonacquiescence is ruled out, L scale scores at this level indicate the test taker was not honest and frank in answering items on the inventory and may have claimed virtues and denied negative characteristics to a greater extent than most people do. The result of such a test-taking attitude is the person's scores on other scales may be lowered artificially in the direction of appearing better adjusted psychologically. The resulting protocol should not be interpreted. This level of L scale scores is typically found when test takers are instructed to appear very well adjusted and free of emotional problems and symptoms.

T = 65–79 (Clinical Settings); T = 70–79 (Nonclinical Settings)
L scale T scores at this level may result from a pervasive nonacquiescent response set, and the TRIN scale should be consulted to rule out this possibility (presented earlier in this chapter). Otherwise, L scale scores in this range suggest the test taker has not responded to items honestly, trying to instead appear as a very virtuous and well-adjusted person. Other MMPI-2 scores may not represent accurately the psychological status of the test taker (i.e., those scales may indicate better psychological adjustment than is accurate), and the protocol should be interpreted very cautiously or not at all.

T = 65–69 (Nonclinical Settings)
L scale T scores at this level are suggestive of an overly positive self-presentation. The test taker may have minimized psychological and behavioral difficulties, but the resulting protocol can be interpreted if the defensiveness is considered.

T = 60–64 (Clinical and Nonclinical Settings)
Scores at this level may reflect an unsophisticated defensiveness in which respondents are denying negative characteristics and claiming positive ones because they judge it to be in their best interest to do so. However, the MMPI-2 protocol is likely valid and interpretable if this test-taking attitude and the circumstances of the

evaluation are considered. Persons completing the MMPI-2 in nonclinical settings (e.g., personnel screening, child custody evaluations) often have L scale scores at this level. These scores do not necessarily indicate significant psychological problems, or symptoms are present but being hidden. Persons with strong Christian or other religious beliefs may obtain scores at this level.

AVERAGE SCORES ON THE L SCALE

T = 50–59
L scale scores at this level suggest a valid protocol.

LOW SCORES ON THE L SCALE

T < 50
T scores below 50 on the L scale are considered low scores and have no additional interpretive significance.

CorrectionScale
The Correction (K) scale was developed for the MMPI as a more subtle index of attempts by examinees to deny psychopathology and to present themselves in a favorable light (McKinley et al., 1948; Meehl & Hathaway, 1946). Items on the K scale were empirically identified by contrasting responses of clearly disturbed psychiatric patients who produced normal scores on the MMPI with responses from a nonclinical sample. The 30 items on the K scale were unchanged in the transition to the MMPI-2 (Butcher et al., 2001). The items in the K scale cover several different content areas in which a person can deny problems (e.g., hostility, suspiciousness, family dissension, lack of self-confidence, excessive worry).

Although very high scores on the K scale typically indicate underreporting, moderate elevations sometimes reflect greater ego strength and psychological resources (McGrath et al., 1998). There is no definite way to determine when moderately elevated K scale scores indicate clinical defensiveness and when they indicate positive adjustment. However, if moderately high K scale scores are found for persons who do not seem to be disturbed psychologically and who appear to be functioning reasonably well, then the possibility the score reflects psychological well-being should be considered.

In addition to identifying deviations in test-taking attitudes, the K scale was also used to develop an algorithm for adjusting scores on some of the Clinical scales (see Chapter 1 for additional information on the development of the K correction). Because most of the data concerning the interpretation of the MMPI's Clinical scales scores were based on K-corrected scores, the K correction was maintained with the MMPI-2. The test distributor, Pearson Assessments, offers profile sheets for plotting both K-corrected and non-K-corrected scores, and many computer-generated reports include both K-corrected and non-K-corrected scores for the Clinical scales.

However, research results tend not to support the use of K-corrected scores. Barthlow et al. (2002) correlated therapist ratings of clients with K-corrected and non-K-corrected MMPI-2 Clinical scale scores and found no meaningful differences between the two sets of correlations. Archer et al. (1998) reported similar results using a sample of psychiatric inpatients. Of course, these studies utilized psychiatric samples for which little defensiveness was present.

Several studies have also examined the utility of the K correction in nonclinical samples and have again failed to find convincing empirical support for its use. Weed and Han (1992) concluded that the standard K correction failed to produce higher correlations between Clinical scale scores and ratings of symptoms and personality characteristics for couples in the MMPI-2 normative sample or for couples involved in marriage counseling. Instead, they found non-K-corrected Clinical scales had higher correlations with spousal ratings for four of the five scales. Sellbom et al. (2007) conducted a predictive validity study using police officer applicants, a group for whom considerable defensiveness would be expected. They found non-K-corrected scores were more closely related than K-corrected scores to behavioral measures of police officer misconduct. Similarly, Detrick et al. (2001) examined a sample of police officer candidates and found K-corrected Clinical scores typically demonstrated lower correlations with conceptually relevant scales on the Inwald Personality Inventory (a well-respected instrument in the area of safety officer screening) than non-K-corrected scales.

Ben-Porath and Forbey (2004) presented data for a variety of clinical and nonclinical samples, including several reviewed here. They found that correlations between non-K-corrected Clinical scale scores and conceptually relevant criterion measures (self-report and therapist ratings) were consistently stronger than correlations between K-corrected scores and the criterion measures. Given these results, it is these authors' practice and strong recommendation to use non-K-corrected scores when interpreting a MMPI-2 profile.

HIGH SCORES ON THE K SCALE

T ≥ 65 (Clinical Settings); T ≥ 75 (Nonclinical Settings)

K scale scores at this level indicate test takers probably approached the MMPI-2 in a very defensive manner. The higher the score, the more likely it is the person was underreporting, and the protocol might best be considered invalid. The absence of significant elevations on substantive scales is not interpretable. High scores on the K scale may also result from a fixed, false response style, and the TRIN scale should be examined prior to interpretation of the K scale to rule out this possibility (see interpretive guidelines for the TRIN scale earlier in this chapter).

In nonclinical settings (e.g., personnel screening, child custody evaluations), T scores in the 65–74 range are fairly common and should not necessarily be interpreted as invalidating the test results. However, scores in this range in nonclinical settings suggest moderate defensiveness that should be considered as other MMPI-2 scales are interpreted.

AVERAGE SCORES ON THE K SCALE

T = 40–64

Average scores on the K scale indicate the test taker is likely to have presented a balanced self-view. Both positive and negative behaviors and personality characteristics are likely to have been acknowledged.

LOW SCORES ON THE K SCALE

T < 40

Low scores on the K scale may result from an acquiescent response style. The TRIN scale should always be interpreted prior to reviewing K scale scores to rule out this possibility (see discussion of the TRIN scale interpretation earlier in this chapter). Historically, low scores on the K scale have sometimes been interpreted as an exaggeration of problems indicative of a "cry for help." The data supporting this interpretation is limited, and we recommend relying upon the overreporting validity scales (i.e., F, F_B, F_p, and FBS) when considering the possibility of symptom exaggeration (see the guidelines for each of these scales found earlier in this chapter).

Superlative Self-Presentation Scale

Butcher and Han (1995) developed the Superlative Self-Presentation scale (S) to assess the tendency of some persons to present themselves on the MMPI-2 as highly virtuous, responsible individuals who are free of psychological problems, have few or no moral flaws, and get along extremely well with others. This manner of self-presentation is very common in situations such as personnel screening or child custody evaluations.

The 50 items in the S scale were identified by contrasting the responses of men applying to work as airline pilots and men in the MMPI-2 normative sample. Butcher and Han (1995) suggested there are five major content dimensions in the S scale items: (1) belief in human goodness, (2) serenity, (3) contentment with life, (4) patience and denial of irritability and anger, and (5) denial of moral flaws. They also reported that S scale scores are highly correlated with K scale scores in the MMPI-2 normative sample: .81 for men and .92 for women. S scale scores were less highly correlated with L scale scores: .46 for men and .34 for women.

Higher S scale scorers in the MMPI-2 normative study were characterized by their spouses as less dysphoric, hostile, and impulsive and as more self-confident, sociable, relaxed, cheerful, and cooperative than lower scorers on the scale. Butcher and Han (1995) concluded that higher scores on the S scale are suggestive of persons who are unrealistically reporting positive attributes and good adjustment. These investigators did not report data concerning how well this scale can detect defensiveness or underreporting response sets or the extent to which higher scores reflect these response sets rather than genuinely superior adjustment.

In a subsequent study, Baer, Wetter, Nichols, et al. (1995) found higher S scale scores in a nonclinical sample when participants were instructed to complete the MMPI-2 while pretending to be well adjusted and psychologically and emotionally healthy in order to get a very desirable job. In addition, the S scale added to the L and K scales in discriminating between persons who took the test with standard instructions and those who pretended to be perfectly well adjusted. Baer, Wetter, and Berry (1995) also found the S scale was effective in identifying students who tried to appear very well adjusted when taking the MMPI-2. Bagby, Rogers, Nicholson, et al. (1997) reported the S scale was effective in distinguishing students who completed the MMPI-2 with standard instructions from students who completed the test with instructions to try to appear very well adjusted, but it was not as effective in distinguishing psychiatric patients who responded honestly from those who were instructed to underreport symptoms and problems. The L scale was more effective than the S scale for this latter discrimination.

Lim and Butcher (1996) found that students who were instructed to either deny psychological problems or to claim excessive virtue had higher S scale scores than when they completed the MMPI-2 with standard instructions. The classification rates for the S scale were not much different from those obtained with the L scale. Unfortunately, these investigators did not determine if the S scale added incrementally to the accuracy of classification rates based on the L scale alone. Interestingly, students in the two faking conditions (denying psychological problems versus claiming excessive virtue) did not differ significantly from each other on the S scale or on the other Validity scales and indexes used in the study.

Baer and Miller (2002) conducted a meta-analysis of MMPI-2 studies examining underreporting of psychopathology. They concluded the S scale is effective in detecting underreporting, but they found no consistent support to suggest the scale does so any better than L and K. They recommended using L and K for identifying underreporting because of their more extensive research base. However, the meta-analysis did indicate the S scale is a bit more effective than the L or K scales in detecting underreporting when test takers have been coached to avoid detection of underreporting.

HIGH SCORES ON THE S SCALE

T ≥ 70 (Clinical Settings); T ≥ 75 (Nonclinical Settings)

S scale T scores at this level suggest the test has been completed in such a defensive manner that the results may be invalid. In clinical settings, protocols with scores at or about 70 probably should not be interpreted at all. In nonclinical settings—where some defensiveness is often typical—protocols with S scale T scores at or above 75 should not be interpreted at all. However, in nonclinical settings, protocols with S scale T scores between 70 and 74 may be interpreted, keeping in mind the scores on other scales may underestimate problems to a moderate degree. Because high scores on the S scale may result from a pervasive nonacquiescent response style, the TRIN scale should always be interpreted prior to interpretation of S scale scores (see guidelines for interpreting TRIN found earlier in this chapter).

AVERAGE SCORES ON THE S SCALE

T = 40–69

Average scores on the S scale indicate the person was not very defensive in responding to the MMPI-2 items, and scores on the other scales are interpretable.

LOW SCORES ON THE S SCALE

T < 40

Although persons who are overreporting symptoms and problems may score well below average on the S scale, there is not sufficient research evaluating the use of the S scale as an indicator of overreporting. Thus, we recommend relying exclusively on the overreporting scales—discussed earlier in this chapter—to evaluate the possibility of an overreporting response set.

OTHER VALIDITY INDICATORS

F Minus K Index

Gough (1950) found that people trying to create the impression of severe psychopathology scored considerably higher on the F scale than on the K scale. He suggested the difference between the F scale raw score and the K scale raw score could serve as an index for detecting overreporting. This is referred to as the F Minus K Index (F-K Index). We recommend the possibility of overreporting be considered whenever the F scale raw score is much greater than the K scale raw score. As the difference becomes greater, the likelihood of overreporting becomes greater. However, most MMPI-2 research on the F-K Index has indicated it is not as effective as the F scale in identifying overreporting (Graham, Watts, & Timbrook, 1991; Rogers et al., 1995, 2003).

A metanalysis of underreporting studies with the MMPI-2 revealed that while the F-K Index was somewhat effective in differentiating between underreporting and standard instruction groups, the index was less effective than the L scale and about as effective as the K scale (Baer & Miller, 2002). Thus, there is little to recommend the use of the F-K Index over these other measures.

PROFILE INVALIDITY

In order to produce a valid MMPI-2 protocol, a person must first read and consider each item. Then they must respond openly and honestly to the item indicating whether it is "true" or "false" for them. Some persons answer MMPI-2 items in a manner so different from the standard instructions that the resulting protocols are simply not interpretable. For example, a person who approaches the test in a deliberate and extreme attempt to feign psychopathology will produce a protocol that should not be interpreted. Other persons may not follow the test instructions exactly, but their deviation from the instructions is less extreme. For example, a client seeking psychological or psychiatric treatment for the first time may somewhat exaggerate their symptoms and problems to ensure their request for help is taken seriously. Or consider a parent completing the MMPI-2 as part of child custody proceedings who responds in a moderately defensive manner as part of their efforts to share the best possible version of themselves with the examiner. These more moderate tendencies must be considered when the resulting protocol is interpreted, but they do not necessarily render the protocol uninterpretable.

In ideal circumstances, the test examiner should be aware of contextual factors that increase the chances of a test taker deviating from the standard instructions. The examiner should use their rapport with the test taker to increase the test taker's investment in the psychological testing. Whenever possible, examiners are encouraged to provide test takers with basic information about the testing such as what the testing will include, how long testing will take, the purpose of the testing, and how participation in the testing may benefit the client. The examiner should work to provide the test taker with a distraction-free environment for completing the testing, familiarize the test taker with the test administration method and instructions, and ensure the test taker knows they are welcome to ask the examiner questions during testing. We also recommend examiners consider implementing therapeutic assessment practices as a means of improving assessment utility in general, including increasing rates of valid MMPI-2 protocols (e.g., Finn, 1996, 2007).

Efforts should be made to ensure test takers follow the standard instructions for completing the MMPI-2. If cooperation cannot be elicited, the test should not be administered. However—particularly in situations in which large numbers of people are tested at once—some persons complete the MMPI-2 without following these instructions. It is important for the MMPI-2 user to know how to detect the resulting invalid protocols. If profile invalidity is suspected, it may be helpful to consider what is known about the test taker's behavior from observation. Lack of congruence between the MMPI-2 results and observed behaviors could be accounted for by the adoption of a response set or style.

If a particular MMPI-2 protocol is deemed invalid, then the examiner may be able to discuss the situation with the test taker and readminister the test. The examiner should indicate the test results will not be helpful because the instructions may not have been followed and ask the individual to complete it again. Attention should be given to the standard instructions, and the test taker should be urged to follow them. Often, a second administration yields a valid and interpretable protocol (Butcher et al., 1997; Cigrang & Staal, 2001; Gucker & McNulty, 2004). If retesting is not possible, or if it does not yield a valid protocol, then no interpretation of the protocol should be made. The only thing an invalid protocol tells us about a person is that, because the test items were not responded to in a valid manner, the test results are not likely to present an accurate picture of what the person really is like. For example, it may be tempting to conclude that a person who presents a very defensive protocol—one in which even average numbers of symptoms and problems are denied—is really a maladjusted person who is trying to conceal that maladjustment. Such a conclusion, without substantial extra-test data, is not justified. The person could just as well be a well-adjusted person who, because of circumstances, felt the need to present themselves as even better adjusted than they really are. For example, such motivation often is present when parents complete the MMPI-2 as part of a child custody evaluation.

Please note, the invalid profiles described in the subsequent sections are modal profiles resulting from all MMPI-2 items being answered in the identified invalid manner. In practice, persons may begin the MMPI-2 in a valid manner and then change to an invalid approach later in the test. Thus, many invalid profiles will approximate the modal ones presented here, but they will not match them exactly. For a broader discussion of response styles and how to assess them, we refer the reader to Burchett and Bagby (2014).

Non–Content-Based Invalid Responding

Random Responding

One form of deviation from following standard test instructions involves responding randomly or near randomly to the test items. A person may respond in a clearly random manner or may use an idiosyncratic response pattern—such as marking every block of eight items as "true," "true," "false," "false," "true," "true," "false," "false"—and repeat this pattern with each such subsequent block. There are various reasons why persons respond randomly to the test items. Sometimes they cannot read well enough to understand the items but are reluctant to inform the examiner that this is the case. Other times test takers are confused or uncooperative because they do not want to take the test but feel they cannot directly refuse to do so. Regardless of motivation, the responses are made without regard to item content, and the resulting protocol must be considered invalid.

The VRIN scale (discussed earlier in this chapter) was developed specifically to identify random responding. According to the MMPI-2 manual (Butcher et al., 2001), VRIN scale T scores equal to or greater than 80 indicate random responding that invalidates the protocol. Subsequent research studies have confirmed this is the optimal VRIN scale cutoff score for identifying random responding (Berry et al., 1991; Gallen & Berry, 1996; Paolo & Ryan, 1992). In addition to having a very high VRIN scale score, a profile generated entirely by random responding exhibits very elevated T scores on the F, F_B, and F_p scales (usually greater than 100); the FBS T score is moderately elevated (low to mid 70s); the K and S scale T scores are at or near 50; and the L scale is moderately elevated (T = 60–70). The Clinical scales are characterized by generally elevated scores, usually with the highest score on Scale 8 and the second-highest score on Scale 6. T scores on Scales 5 and 0 are likely to be below 70.

Patterns of scores on the standard Validity and Clinical scales like those described for random responding also are obtained when individuals approach the test with either an overreporting or a true–false fixed response set. The VRIN scale is very helpful in determining when the profile likely results from a random response set. If random responding seems unlikely, then the TRIN scale should be examined next to determine if an acquiescent or nonacquiescent response set is likely. Obviously, a protocol resulting from random responding should not be interpreted.

True–False Fixed Responding

The TRIN scale score is very helpful in detecting an all true or all false fixed response set. Responding "true" to all items in the MMPI-2 will result in TRIN scale T scores of 120 using the norms for both men and women; however, any T score equal to or greater than 80 on the TRIN scale (in the true direction) indicates indiscriminate true responding to enough items that the resulting protocol should be considered invalid. If all of the MMPI-2 items are answered in the true direction, the resulting profile includes an extremely elevated F scale score (well above a T score of 100); L, K, and S scale T scores well below 50; and extreme elevations on the right side of the Clinical scale profile, usually with the highest scores on Scales 6 and 8. The F_B and F_p scales will also be quite elevated, usually at about the same level as the F scale, and the FBS will be moderately elevated (T = 67 for men and T = 70 for women). Obviously, a profile resulting from all-true responding should never be interpreted.

Responding "false" to all MMPI-2 items will yield a TRIN scale T score of 114 for men and 120 for women; however, any T score equal to or greater than 80 on the TRIN scale (in the false direction) indicates indiscriminate false responding to enough items that the resulting protocol should be considered invalid. Persons who respond false to all of the MMPI-2 items will produce profiles displaying simultaneous elevations on the F, F_p, FBS, L, K, and S scales, while the T scores on the F_B and VRIN scales will be near 50. The Clinical scales on the left side of the profile (i.e., 1, 2, 3, and 4) will be noticeably more elevated than those Clinical scales on the right side, perhaps with the lone exception of Scale 8. Obviously, a protocol resulting from all-false responding should not be interpreted.

Content-Based Invalid Responding

OVERREPORTING

Some persons may inaccurately present themselves as being more symptomatic or dysfunctional than they truly are when completing the MMPI-2. An extreme example would be when a person deliberately responds to test items in a manner intended to communicate that they are experiencing severe mental illness when in fact they are not. This response set often is referred to as "faking bad" or "malingering." However, because these terms presume an external motivation for presenting oneself as having more psychological symptoms than is really the case, we prefer to use the broader term "overreporting" to characterize this response style. Furthermore, the MMPI-2's validity scales, while capable of detecting overreporting, are unable to assess any motivation or intentionality on the part of the test taker. Any attempt to identify causes for an overreporting response set requires information from sources other than the MMPI-2.

The Validity scales of the MMPI-2 are quite effective in identifying persons who overreport when completing the test. Graham, Watts, and Timbrook (1991) reported that when college students are instructed to simulate serious psychopathology on the MMPI-2, they tend to over endorse uncommon items, thus producing scores on the F scale and Clinical scales much higher than those of patients experiencing severe mental illness. Subsequent research replicated the general findings from that initial study (e.g., Storm & Graham, 2000; Wetter et al., 1992).

An overreporting protocol on the MMPI-2 is characterized by a very elevated F scale T score (usually well above 100). Likewise, the F_p and F_B scales are elevated, usually at about the same level as the F scale. The FBS scale is likely to be moderately elevated (T = 80–90). Because persons overreporting typically respond consistently—albeit not honestly—to the content of the items, both the TRIN scale and VRIN scale scores are not significantly elevated. Scores on the Clinical scales are very elevated, with Scales 6 and 8 typically being the most elevated, while Scales 5 and 0 usually are the least elevated.

At first glance, the overreporting profile looks similar to the profile one might expect to obtain from a person who is actually experiencing severe mental illness. However, there are several critical differences. Scores on the F, F_B, F_p, and FBS scales are usually higher for the overreporting protocol. The usual range of F scale T scores for a person with severe psychopathology is 70–90, whereas in the overreporting profile, the F scale T score is well above 100. Likewise, the F_B and F_p scale T scores above 100 are characteristic of an overreporting profile. In addition, in an overreporting protocol the Clinical scales tend to be more extremely elevated than in a valid protocol from an individual experiencing severe mental illness.

In addition to Graham, Watts, and Timbrook (1991), a number of other studies have confirmed the ability of MMPI-2 Validity scales to identify overreporting on the test. Rogers et al. (2003) reported the results of a meta-analysis of 62 MMPI-2 overreporting studies. They calculated very strong effect size differences for the F, F_B, and F_p

scales as well as the F-K Index when comparing mean scales scores for overreporters to mean scale scores for genuine psychiatric patients. However, they concluded the F_p scale was the most effective indicator of overreporting because it also demonstrated very consistent optimal cut scores when distinguishing between overreporters and genuine patients across a variety of settings and diagnoses.

Many MMPI-2 overreporting studies have compared genuine clinical samples with nonclinical individuals—typically college students—who took the test under instructions to overreport, raising some questions about the generalizability of the Validity scales utility when people overreporting in clinical settings may be better able or better motivated to feign psychopathology. Several studies have demonstrated the F scale is effective in identifying prison inmates who took the MMPI-2 with instructions to overreport symptoms and problems (Gallagher, 1997; Iverson et al., 1995). In the Gallagher study, the F_p scale added significantly to the F scale in identifying the over-reporters. Berry et al. (1996) examined scores of mental health outpatients who completed the MMPI-2 with standard instructions or with instructions to exaggerate their symptoms and problems. They found the F, F_B, and F_p scales and the F minus K index were all effective in discriminating between the groups. Arbisi and Ben-Porath (1998) reported both the F and F_p scales discriminated between psychiatric inpatients who completed the MMPI-2 with standard instructions or with instructions to exaggerate their symptoms and problems, but the F_p scale was a more accurate indicator than the F scale in this setting where there is a high base rate of serious psychopathology.

Although it is clear that persons who overreport when responding to the MMPI-2 produce very high F scale scores, the optimal cutoff score for identifying overreporting is less clear. Various studies have identified optimal F scale T-score cutoffs ranging from 75 to 120. Most studies have found that F scale T scores greater than 100 are indicative of overreporting. However, as Graham, Watts, and Timbrook (1991) cautioned, F scale raw scores that are beyond the T-score ceiling for the scale (120) are optimal when trying to identify overreporting among psychiatric inpatients. As mentioned earlier in this chapter, the F_p scale, which was designed specifically to identify overreporting in settings in which there is a high base rate of severe psychopathology, is a valuable addition to the F scale in inpatient settings. Although optimal cutoff scores should be determined in each setting when the MMPI-2 is used, it is clear that more confidence concerning overreporting can be had when F or F_p scale scores are more extreme.

Many MMPI-2 overreporting studies have instructed participants to feign serious or severe psychopathology, but can the MMPI-2 detect less extreme forms of over-reporting? Wetter et al. (1992) instructed students to feign either severe or moderate psychopathology. They found the F scale was significantly elevated in both feigning conditions and only slightly lower for the moderate condition (T = 108) than for the severe condition (T = 119). This study suggests the F scale can identify less extreme forms of overreporting, but different optimal cutoff scores may be needed.

Feigning Specific Disorders

Some studies have examined the extent to which persons can feign specific forms of psychopathology when responding to the MMPI-2 and the extent to which the MMPI-2 Validity scales can identify this test-taking approach. When nonclinical persons have been asked to feign schizophrenia, paranoid psychosis, posttraumatic stress disorder, or borderline personality disorder, they have produced scores quite similar to those of persons who are given general instructions to feign psychopathology (Bagby, Rogers, Buis, et al., 1997; Gold & Frueh, 1999; Rogers et al., 1993; Sivec et al., 1994, 1995; Wetter et al., 1993; Wetter & Deitsch, 1996). Their profiles were characterized by high-ranging scores on the F and F_p scales and on Scales 6 and 8. Scores on F and F_p were quite effective in discriminating persons who overreported symptoms of these particular disorders from persons taking the MMPI-2 with standard instructions and from patients with the actual disorders. Similar conclusions were reached in a meta-analysis examining the detection of feigned PTSD with MMPI-2 validity scales (Nijdam-Jones et al., 2020). Results of this meta-analysis suggested large effect size differences in scores on F and F_p, but also the F-K Index and F_B, when individuals instructed to feign PTSD were compared to individuals who took the test under standard instructions.

When nonclinical persons have been asked to feign symptoms of depression, somatoform disorder, or closed head injury, they have produced moderately high scores on the F scale and on most of the Clinical scales (Bagby, Rogers, Buis, et al., 1997; Berry et al., 1995; Sivec et al., 1994, 1995). Scores on F and F_p were most effective in differentiating these feigned protocols from those completed under standard conditions, but classification accuracies were lower than those reported for identifying the feigning of more severe forms of psychopathology. One study suggested a similar pattern of findings for feigned attention-deficit hyperactivity disorder in adults (Young & Gross, 2011).

In general, it would appear persons who try to feign general psychopathology or specific psychopathology involving extreme and unusual symptoms produce a clearly recognizable pattern of scores on the Validity and Clinical scales. Cardinal features of the pattern are extreme elevations on the F and F_p scales and general elevation on the Clinical scales, with Scales 6 and 8 being the most elevated. When persons try to feign other specific forms of psychopathology, they produce more elevated scores than patients who actually have the disorders, and they are accurately identified by scores on the F and F_p scales. However, different optimal cutoff scores may be appropriate for identifying the feigning of some specific kinds of psychopathology, and the Validity scales may be less accurate for some specific kinds of feigning than others.

Effects of Coaching

In forensic settings, concerns have been raised about the possibility that persons who want to feign psychological disturbance when they complete the MMPI-2 could do so more effectively if they were coached, which can mean they have information about the symptoms of the disorder they want to simulate or about how the MMPI-2 identifies overreporting. Wetter and Corrigan (1995) reported the results of a survey indicating almost half of a sample of practicing attorneys and approximately one-third of a sample of law students believed that clients referred for psychological testing always or usually should be given information about the validity scales of psychological tests they will be taking. A more recent survey of a sample of attorneys from the United States—most of whom were practicing in family/juvenile law, personal injury law, and criminal law—demonstrated similar findings (Spengler et al., 2020). In this survey, 73% of attorneys reported they strongly agreed or agreed they should advise clients about what is involved in psychological testing. Approximately 53% endorsed strongly agreeing or agreeing that they should disclose information to their clients about MMPI-2 Validity scales and their use in detecting invalid responding.

Many studies have demonstrated that giving test takers information about the symptoms of disorders they are asked to simulate does not permit them to avoid detection by the MMPI-2 Validity scales (Bagby, Rogers, Nicholson, et al., 1997; Elhai et al., 2000; Rogers et al., 1993; Wetter et al., 1993, 1994). For example, Bagby, Rogers, Nicholson, et al. (1997) found that clinical psychology graduate students and psychiatric residents, who can be assumed to have considerable information about psychological testing and psychopathology, were readily detected when they attempted to feign schizophrenia on the MMPI-2. However, work by Veltri and Williams (2013) suggests identification of individuals who are overreporting psychiatric symptoms after receiving coaching on both symptoms and the presence of validity scales may be more difficult when the feigned disorder is not schizophrenia and is instead generalized anxiety disorder or posttraumatic-stress disorder.

Some research has been conducted to determine the extent to which overreporting on the MMPI-2 can be detected when test takers have been given information (coached) about how the Validity scales function and/or how to avoid detection of overreporting when completing the test. Several studies reported it was more difficult to detect overreporting when such coaching had taken place (Rogers et al., 1993; Storm & Graham, 2000). However, even when test takers have been coached about the Validity scales, a large portion of the coached overreporters were correctly identified. Not all research in this area has yielded consistent results. Bagby et al. (2002) found the MMPI-2 Validity scales were equally effective in identifying coached and uncoached simulators of general psychopathology. In most studies, both the F and F_p scales have been effective in identifying coached overreporters, with the F_p scale doing better in some studies.

In contrast, Rogers et al. (1993) found that persons who were given information about how the Validity indicators of the MMPI-2 function and how to avoid detection were more effective in simulating schizophrenia without being detected by the standard Validity indicators. Viglione et al. (2001) examined the effect of giving very limited coaching and then asking test takers to overreport. They found giving a simple caution to avoid exaggeration of responses made detection of overreporting somewhat more difficult.

Although only limited research data are available at this time, there is reason to be concerned that some persons who are informed about how the Validity scales of the MMPI-2 function may be able to avoid detection. More research is needed to determine just how much of a problem this is and if there are more effective ways to identify the informed overreporting.

Exaggeration

Sometimes individuals with genuine psychological symptoms exaggerate them when responding to the MMPI-2. This is a rather common occurrence among persons who are trying to communicate to others that they desperately need professional help. In these circumstances, the resulting scores will depend on what actual symptoms and problems are being exaggerated. Thus, it is not possible to identify a prototype for this response set. The major clue such a response set might be operating is that scores on the F and F_p scales and the Clinical scales seem to be much higher than would be expected given the person's history and observations made during the interview and testing.

There has been some research investigating symptom exaggeration on the MMPI-2. Rogers et al. (1995) asked psychiatric outpatients to take the MMPI-2 first using standard instructions and then again while attempting to convince the examiner their problems were worse than they really were and that they needed immediate hospitalization. Patients produced very similar configurations of scores in both conditions; but when they exaggerated their problems, their scores were considerably higher than when they followed standard instructions. Both the F and F_p scales were quite effective in identifying the protocols produced by patients who exaggerated their symptoms and problems. Arbisi and Ben-Porath (1998) examined scores of psychiatric inpatients who completed the MMPI-2 with standard instructions or with instructions to exaggerate their symptoms and problems. Those who exaggerated produced significantly higher scores on most scales. The F and F_p scales were both effective in identifying exaggeration, but the F_p scale was somewhat more accurate than the F scale. Exaggeration does not necessarily invalidate a protocol, but interpretations must be modified to take into account that the scores obtained represent an overreporting of symptoms and problems.

UNDERREPORTING

Sometimes test takers are motivated to deny problems or to appear better adjusted psychologically than is the case. This response set is relatively common when persons complete the MMPI-2 as part of a job application process or child custody evaluation.

In an initial MMPI-2 underreporting study, Graham, Watts, and Timbrook (1991) compared scores of men and women in college who completed the test with standard instructions and with instructions to present a very positive impression of themselves, as if they were being evaluated for a job they really wanted. The mean profiles of persons in the underreporting condition had somewhat lower scores on most of the Clinical scales. The T scores were well above 50 on the L and K scales. Graham, Watts, and Timbrook (1991) also found it was more difficult to detect underreporting than overreporting protocols.

Baer and Miller (2002) conducted a meta-analysis of 14 studies of underreporting on the MMPI-2. They found the MMPI-2 Validity scales were effective in discriminating between underreporters and those who completed the test with standard instructions. Although the identification of underreporters was not as accurate as for overreporting (e.g., Rogers et al., 2003), the overall effect size ($d = 1.25$) across studies was quite impressive. Persons who completed the MMPI-2 with instructions to try to appear to be very well adjusted psychologically tended to obtain high scores on the L, K, and S scales and average or below-average scores on the F, F_B, and F_p scales. Baer and Miller (2002) concluded, "relying on L and K, for which much larger bodies of supporting data are available, may be the most defensible approach" (p. 24).

Regarding cutoff scores for underreporting Validity scales, Baer and Miller (2002) reminded readers that optimal cutoff scores are likely to vary as a function of the base rates of underreporting in particular settings, as well as on the kinds of errors (false positive versus false negative) judged to be the most important to avoid. Obviously, setting relatively high cutoff scores will increase the likelihood persons identified as underreporting are truly doing so, but at the cost of missing many underreporters. Conversely, establishing relatively low cutoff scores will improve the identification of underreported protocols, but it will also result in many valid protocols being mistaken as underreported.

In summary, when persons complete the MMPI-2 with the intention of denying problems and appearing much better adjusted than they really are, they tend to produce elevated scores on the L, K, and S scales, and below-average scores on the F, F_B, and F_p scales. The L and K scales are quite effective in identifying underreporting. Although it is not possible to specify a single, empirically derived, optimal cutoff score for these scales, those score ranges offered in the interpretive guidelines described earlier in this chapter for each validity scale will serve to alert examiners to the possibility test takers may have approached the MMPI-2 in an invalid manner.

As was discussed in relation to overreporting on the MMPI-2, it is important to acknowledge what underreporting indicators do and do not tell us. When we have evidence a person has underreported in responding to the MMPI-2 items, we can only conclude that the resulting scores do not give an accurate picture of the person's psychological adjustment and personality characteristics. In such a case, we do not know what the person is really like. A person who underreports could be quite well adjusted psychologically or could be quite disturbed psychologically. We cannot tell from the MMPI-2 scores which may be more likely. Furthermore, the test does not provide us any information about the motivation for engaging in underreporting. Other data, including interview- and history-based information, may help in making these determinations.

Defensiveness

Sometimes persons are motivated to present unrealistically favorable impressions but do not do so to such an extent that their protocols should be considered invalid. For example, persons taking the MMPI-2 as part of employment screening or child custody evaluations may want to emphasize positive characteristics and minimize negative ones. The resulting scores may underestimate problems and symptoms but are not necessarily uninterpretable.

In a defensive profile, the L, K, and S scale scores typically are more elevated than the F, F_B, and F_p scale score. T scores equal to or greater than 70 on L, K, or S should alert the clinician that the test taker may have underreported symptoms and problems to such an extent the protocol probably is invalid. T scores in the 60–69 range on these scales also suggest underreporting but probably indicate a defensive test-taking attitude that does not necessarily invalidate the protocol.

If the Validity scales indicate defensiveness, and no Clinical scale T scores are above 60, then the Clinical scores may not reflect accurately the psychological status of the test taker. However, based on these scores alone we cannot infer the person is covering up significant problems, as the protocol could also reflect a well-adjusted person who wanted to create an unrealistically favorable impression.

If the Validity scales indicate defensiveness and there are Clinical scale scores greater than 60, then another variable needs to be considered. Defensive protocols involve significant elevations on the K scale, which impacts the size of the K corrections performed on some of the Clinical scales. Consequently, the person could have significantly elevated T scores on Clinical Scales 1, 4, 7, 8, and 9 without endorsing many—or even any—items on those scales. The K correction itself may be large enough to cause a significantly elevated score. In such cases, it would be inappropriate to infer significant problems and symptoms from the elevated scores. When defensiveness is suspected, test users should always refer to the non-K-corrected Clinical scales. Any elevations on the non-K-corrected scales may be interpreted in the usual manner with the caveat that the elevated scores may actually underestimate the severity of problems and symptoms because of the test taker's defensive response style.

Sometimes in a defensive profile either the L or K scale score is elevated but not both. This is because the two scales seem to be measuring somewhat different aspects of defensiveness. Persons who have elevated scores on the K scale are generally denying symptoms and problems. Persons who have elevated scores on the L scale are presenting themselves as honest, moral, and conforming. Although these two aspects of defensiveness often occur simultaneously, in some circumstances they do not.

Effects of Coaching

Several studies have examined the effects on underreporting of providing test takers with information about the Validity scales. Using a sample of college students, Baer, Wetter, and Berry (1995) found the standard Validity scales were effective in detecting the students who were instructed to underreport symptoms and problems. However, detection of underreporting became more difficult when students were given information about the underreporting Validity scales.

Baer and Sekirnjak (1997) replicated the procedures used by Baer, Wetter, and Berry (1995) with a sample of outpatient mental health clients. Clients in the underreporting group were either given no information about the underreporting scales or were told the MMPI-2 contains scales for identifying underreporting, so they should try to appear both psychologically healthy and honest in responding to the items. Results were similar to those reported by Baer, Wetter, and Berry (1995). Clients who were instructed to underreport but were not given any information about the Validity scales were readily detected by the standard Validity scales. However, clients who were informed of underreporting Validity scales were less readily detected. The S scale seemed to be especially effective.

Relatively few studies have examined the effects of coaching on the ability of the MMPI-2 to detect underreporting. The Baer and Miller (2002) meta-analysis included five studies where participants were coached in avoiding detection of underreporting. They concluded the Validity scales were somewhat less effective in identifying test takers who had received such coaching.

In summary, it appears persons who are informed there are underreporting scales on the MMPI-2 and who are told to try to appear both psychologically healthy and honest produce scores that resemble nonclinical persons and are difficult to detect with the traditional Validity scales. There is some preliminary indication the S scale may be more effective than the L and K scales in detecting coached underreporting. However, more research is needed before we can conclude just how effectively coached underreporters can avoid detection, and if there are ways—other than the use of the standard Validity scales—to identify the coached underreporting effectively.

What is especially needed are studies with larger samples that report classification data (i.e., positive predictive power and negative predictive power) for the different test-taking conditions and the various Validity scales and indexes. Clinicians using the MMPI-2 in settings where there is strong motivation to underreport and where test takers may have been coached about the Validity scales should be alert to the possibility that underreporting on the MMPI-2 may not be readily detected. In such instances, information outside the MMPI-2 scores (e.g., history, mental status, information from significant others) may be helpful in assessing the validity of self-report.

CHAPTER 4

THE CLINICAL SCALES

IN THIS CHAPTER, EACH MMPI-2 Clinical scale is discussed in an attempt to elucidate the dimensions of personality and psychopathology it assesses. In addition, descriptors are presented for scores at various levels on each scale.

The Clinical scales of the MMPI-2 are basically the same as those found in the original MMPI. A few items were deleted from some scales because they had become dated or were judged to have objectionable content, usually having to do with religious beliefs or bowel or bladder functions. Some items were modified slightly to modernize them, eliminate sexist references, or improve readability. The items included in each Clinical scale and the keyed response for each item are presented in appendixes of the MMPI-2 manual (Butcher et al., 2001), as are tables for converting raw scores to T scores. Score transformations based on the non-gendered normative data are available in the Appendix of Ben-Porath and Forbey's (2003) non-gendered norms monograph.

RELIABILITY OF CLINICAL SCALES

Table 4.1 reports coefficients of internal consistency (alphas) for the Clinical scales. Because of the empirical keying approach and the absence of efforts to make the Clinical scales internally consistent, most of the scales have relatively low internal consistency coefficients, especially in nonclinical samples. This reflects the varied and heterogeneous content of items in the Clinical scales. High scores on a specific scale can represent quite different patterns of item endorsement. For example, someone with a high score on Scale 4 may have endorsed primarily (a) items having to do with

TABLE 4.1 *Internal Consistency Coefficients (Alphas) for MMPI-2 Clinical Scales for Men and Women in Normative Sample*

	Men		Women	
Scale	α	n	α	n
1—Hs	.77	1,116	.81	1,432
2—D	.59	1,095	.64	1,374
3—Hy	.58	1,095	.56	1,378
4—Pd	.60	1,063	.62	1,345
5—Mf	.58	1,056	.37	1,342
6—Pa	.34	1,097	.39	1,407
7—Pt	.85	1,099	.87	1,421
8—Sc	.85	1,076	.86	1,370
9—Ma	.58	1,062	.61	1,347
0—Si	.82	1,070	.84	1,345

Note. Excerpted (Table E-4) from the *MMPI®-2 (Minnesota Multiphasic Personality Inventory®-2) Manual for Administration, Scoring, and Interpretation, Revised Edition* by James N. Butcher, John R. Graham, Yossef S. Ben-Porath, Auke Tellegen, W. Grant Dahlstrom, and Beverly Kaemmer. Copyright © 2001 by the Regents of the University of Minnesota. Used by permission of the University of Minnesota Press. All rights reserved. "MMPI®" and "Minnesota Multiphasic Personality Inventory®" are registered trademarks of the Regents of the University of Minnesota.

antisocial attitudes and behaviors; or (b) items suggesting negative opinions and feelings about family members; or (c) some of each kind of item.

Table 4.2 reports test–retest coefficients for subgroups of men and women in the MMPI-2 normative sample who completed the test twice with an interval of approximately one week between administrations. These data indicate Clinical scale scores are quite stable over a relatively short period of time, with Scale 6 having the least stability and Scale 0 the most stability. Table 4.2 also reports test–retest coefficients for a group of older men who completed the MMPI-2 twice with a 5-year interval between the two tests. As one might expect, the scores were less stable over the longer period; however, the coefficients are comparable to those of other self-report inventories for similar time intervals. It is noteworthy that the 5-year coefficient for Scale 0 (Si) is almost as high as for the 1-week interval, suggesting characteristics associated with Scale 0 scores are likely to be quite stable.

VALIDITY OF CLINICAL SCALES

Since the MMPI's publication, hundreds of studies have examined relationships between the Clinical scales and relevant extratest characteristics such as symptoms, personality traits, diagnosis, and response to treatment. These studies were conducted in a variety of nonclinical, medical, mental health, forensic, and correctional settings. Because of the continuity between the Clinical scales of the original MMPI and the MMPI-2, this research is relevant to determining the validity of the Clinical scales. Similar studies have also been reported using the MMPI-2. The accumulated

TABLE 4.2 *Test–Retest Coefficients for MMPI-2 Clinical Scales*

Scale	1-Week Interval MMPI-2 Normative Sample[a]		5-Year Interval Normative Aging Sample[b]
	Men (n = 82)	Women (n = 111)	Men (n = 1,072)
1—Hs	.76	.75	.75
2—D	.79	.80	.71
3—Hy	.70	.74	.65
4—Pd	.79	.69	.67
5—Mf	.83	.74	.67
6—Pa	.67	.56	.55
7—Pt	.72	.68	.83
8—Sc	.72	.54	.71
9—Ma	.80	.65	.64
0—Si	.93	.92	.85

Note. [a]Excerpted (Table E-1) from the *MMPI®-2 (Minnesota Multiphasic Personality Inventory®-2) Manual for Administration, Scoring, and Interpretation, Revised Edition* by James N. Butcher, John R. Graham, Yossef S. Ben-Porath, Auke Tellegen, W. Grant Dahlstrom, and Beverly Kaemmer. Copyright © 2001 by the Regents of the University of Minnesota. Used by permission of the University of Minnesota Press. All rights reserved. "MMPI®" and "Minnesota Multiphasic Personality Inventory®" are registered trademarks of the Regents of the University of Minnesota.
[b]Excerpted (Table 37.3) from Change and Stability in Personality: A Five-Year Study of the MMPI-2 in Older Men by Avron Spiro, M. Richard Levenson, Carolyn M. Aldwin, and Raymond Bose. In *Basic Sources on the MMPI-2* by James N. Butcher (Ed.). Copyright © 2000 by the Regents of the University of Minnesota. Reproduced by permission of the University of Minnesota Press. All rights reserved. "MMPI®" and "Minnesota Multiphasic Personality Inventory®" are registered trademarks of the Regents of the University of Minnesota.

database suggests the MMPI-2 Clinical scales are meaningfully related to conceptually relevant extratest characteristics. For example, higher scorers on Scale 1 have reported more somatic complaints than lower scorers; higher scorers on Scale 4 have been characterized as more antisocial than lower scorers; and higher scorers on Scale 8 have been more likely to show symptoms of psychotic disorders. Research findings concerning correlates of the Clinical scales in these varied settings are the primary source of the inferences suggested later in this chapter.

DEFINING HIGH AND LOW SCORES ON CLINICAL SCALES

The definition of high scores on the Clinical scales has varied considerably in the MMPI-2 literature. Some researchers considered T scores above 65 on the MMPI-2 as high scores, others defined high scores in terms of the upper quartile in a distribution, and still others presented descriptors for several T-score levels on some scales. In this chapter, the T-score cutoffs used to indicate high scores on the Clinical scales are clearly stated, and they are not the same for all scales. For most Clinical scales, interpretive guidelines are presented for several different T-score levels.

Low scores also have been defined in different ways in the literature, sometimes as T scores at or below 40 (or 39) and other times as scores in the lowest quartile of a distribution. However, this latter approach led to T scores well above 50 sometimes being considered low scores. Compared with high scores, very limited information is available in the literature concerning the meaning of low scores. Several MMPI-2 studies have sought to clarify the meaning of low scores on the Clinical scales. Keiller and Graham (1993) examined extratest characteristics of high-, medium-, and low-scoring persons in the MMPI-2 normative sample on eight Clinical scales. They concluded low scores were associated with fewer than an average number of symptoms and problems as well as above-average overall adjustment. Timbrook and Graham (1992) examined the relationship between low scores and ratings of symptoms for psychiatric inpatients. They found for some scales, the lower scorers were rated as having less severe symptoms than high and average scorers. For other scales, the low scorers were rated as having more severe symptoms than average and high scorers. For example, low-scoring men on Scale 2 were rated as more uncooperative; however, some of these findings probably emerged because of the intercorrelations of the Clinical scales. For example, the men who had low scores on Scale 2 could have had high scores on Scale 4 that might better account for the uncooperativeness associated with low scores on Scale 2. Graham et al. (1997) studied the meaning of low scores in an outpatient mental health setting but were only able to study Clinical Scales 9 and 0 because of the infrequent occurrence of low scores. Low scorers on Scale 9 did not differ significantly from average scorers in terms of symptoms and problems. However, the characteristic attributes of low scorers on Scale 0 were very much the opposite of high scorers.

Because of the inconsistent data concerning the meaning of low scores on the MMPI-2, our recommendation is to adopt a conservative approach to the interpretation of low scores on the Clinical scales. In nonclinical settings (e.g., personnel selection), low scores in a valid protocol should be interpreted as indicating more positive overall adjustment than average or high scores. However, if the Validity scales indicate the test was completed in a defensive manner, low scores should not be interpreted. In clinical settings, we recommend low scores on the Clinical scales not be interpreted—except for Scales 5 and 0, for which we provide limited suggested inferences.

INTERPRETATION OF SCORES ON CLINICAL SCALES

The approach used in this chapter will be to suggest interpretive inferences about persons who have high scores on each of the Clinical scales. In general, T scores greater than or equal to 65 are considered to be high scores, although inferences about persons with scores at several different T-score levels are presented for some scales. For Scales 5 and 0, inferences also will be suggested for below-average scores. It should be understood the T-score levels specified have been established somewhat arbitrarily, and clinical judgment will be necessary in deciding which inferences should be applied to scores at or near the cutoff scores.

Not every inference presented in this chapter will apply to every person who has a T score at the specified level. Greater confidence may be placed in inferences based on more extreme scores; however, all inferences should be treated as hypotheses to be considered in the context of other information available about the test taker. It is reasonable to infer higher scores might also be associated with more severe symptoms and problems (e.g., depression for Scale 2). A study by Graham et al. (2003) supported this notion, as they found patients with very high scores on the Clinical scales had more severe symptoms and problems than those with moderately high scores.

The descriptors suggested for each Clinical scale are quite heterogeneous in nature. For example, descriptors for high scorers on Scale 8 include confused and disorganized thinking, depression, anxiety, drug abuse, and physical complaints. This heterogeneity is accounted for in part by the varied content of items in Scale 8 and in part by the general maladjustment or demoralization component present in each Clinical scale (Tellegen et al., 2003). In clarifying the meaning of high scores on a particular Clinical scale, it will be helpful to examine several other sources of MMPI-2 information. The Harris–Lingoes subscales and the Content and Content Component scales—discussed in Chapter 6 of this book—provide information about the kinds of items endorsed by a person who obtains a high score on a Clinical scale. Examination of the Restructured Clinical (RC) scales (Chapter 7 of this book) can provide helpful information about the extent to which a high score on a Clinical scale resulted from endorsement of items having to do with the core construct for that scale (e.g., aberrant experiences for Scale 8) versus endorsement of items suggestive of general maladjustment or demoralization. Finally, consideration of other Supplementary scales (see Chapter 8) can help clarify the likelihood of some particular descriptors suggested for high scorers (e.g., the Addiction Admission Scale [AAS] in relation to an inference of drug abuse problems for a high scorer on Scale 8).

In summary, the descriptors listed for each Clinical scale should be considered a starting point in the interpretation. Consideration of other information will help to focus the interpretation in terms of determining which of the many descriptors are most likely for a particular person with an elevated score on a Clinical scale. The process of refining interpretations based on multiple sources of information will be discussed further and illustrated with a case in Chapter 11 of this book.

SCALE 1 (HYPOCHONDRIASIS)

Scale 1 originally was developed to identify patients who manifested a pattern of symptoms associated with a diagnosis of hypochondriasis. This syndrome was characterized in clinical terms by preoccupation with the body and concomitant fears of illness and disease, similar to the current DSM diagnostic category of illness anxiety disorder (American Psychiatric Association, 2013). Although such fears usually are not delusional in nature, they tend to be persistent despite contradictory information. One item was deleted from the original MMPI Scale 1 due to objectionable content, leaving 32 items in the MMPI-2.

Of all the Clinical scales, Scale 1 seems to be the most homogeneous and, thus, unidimensional. All items deal with somatic concerns or general physical competence. Factor analysis (Comrey, 1957b) indicated much of the variance in Scale 1 is accounted for by a single factor, characterized by the denial of good health and the admission of a variety of somatic symptoms. Patients with genuine physical problems typically have somewhat elevated T scores on Scale 1 (approximately 60). Older persons tend to also have slightly elevated Scale 1 scores, probably reflecting the declining health often—but not always—associated with aging.

Interpretation of High Scores on Scale 1

Persons with extremely high scores on Scale 1 (T ≥ 80) may present with dramatic and sometimes bizarre somatic concerns. If Scale 3 also is very elevated, the possibility of a conversion disorder should be considered. Individuals with chronic pain often have high scores (T = 70–80) on both Scales 1 and 3. Somatic delusions may be present when both Scales 1 and 8 are very high.

Persons with more moderate elevations on Scale 1 (T = 60–80) tend to have generally vague, nonspecific somatic concerns. When specific symptoms are elicited, they may include chronic pain, headaches, and gastrointestinal discomfort. Persons experiencing problems associated with eating often have moderately elevated scores. High scores are often associated with reports of chronic weakness, lack of energy, fatigue, and sleep disturbance. High Scale 1 scorers often are preoccupied with health problems, and they tend to develop physical symptoms in response to stress.

Medical patients with real physical problems generally obtain T scores around 60 on Scale 1. When medical patients produce T scores much above 60, a strong psychological component to the illness should be considered. Moderately high scores tend to be associated with psychiatric diagnoses such as somatic symptom, pain, anxiety, and depressive disorders. High scorers on Scale 1 often are prescribed antidepressant or anxiolytic medications. Acting-out behavior is rare among high scorers.

High Scale 1 scorers (T ≥ 60) in both psychiatric and non-psychiatric samples tend to be characterized by a rather distinctive set of personality attributes. They are likely to be selfish, self-centered, and narcissistic. Their outlook toward life tends to be pessimistic, defeatist, and cynical. They are generally dissatisfied and unhappy and are likely to make those around them miserable. They complain a great deal and communicate in a whiny manner. They are demanding of others and very critical of what others do—although they are likely to express hostility in rather indirect ways. High scorers on Scale 1 often are described as dull, unenthusiastic, unambitious, and lacking ease in oral expression. High scorers may not show signs of major incapacity. Rather, they appear to be functioning at a reduced level of efficiency. Problems are much more likely to be long-standing than situational or transient.

Extremely high and moderately high scorers typically see themselves as physically ill and seek medical explanations and treatment for their symptoms. They tend to lack insight concerning the causes of their somatic symptoms, and they resist psychological interpretations. These tendencies—coupled with their generally cynical outlook—suggest they are not good candidates for traditional psychotherapy or counseling. They tend to be very critical of their therapists and may terminate therapy if they perceive the therapist as suggesting psychological reasons for their symptoms or as not giving them enough support and attention.

Summary of Descriptors for Scale 1

High scores on Scale 1 indicate persons who

1. have excessive bodily concern
2. may have conversion disorders (if T ≥ 80 and Scale 3 also is very high)
3. may have somatic delusions (if T ≥ 80 and Scale 8 also is very high)
4. describe generally vague somatic complaints that if specific may include chronic pain, headaches, and gastrointestinal discomfort
5. may have problems associated with eating
6. describe experiences of chronic weakness, lack of energy, fatigue, and sleep disturbance
7. are preoccupied with health problems and tend to develop physical symptoms in response to stress
8. if medical patients, may have a strong psychological component to their illnesses
9. frequently receive diagnoses of somatic symptom, pain, depressive, or anxiety disorders
10. often are prescribed antidepressant or anxiolytic medications
11. are not likely to act out in antisocial ways
12. seem selfish, self-centered, and narcissistic
13. have a pessimistic, defeatist, cynical outlook toward life
14. are unhappy and dissatisfied
15. make others miserable
16. complain a great deal
17. communicate in a whiny manner
18. are demanding and critical of others
19. express hostility indirectly
20. are described as dull, unenthusiastic, and unambitious
21. lack ease in oral expression
22. may not show signs of major incapacity
23. seem to have functioned at a reduced level of efficiency for long periods of time
24. see themselves as physically ill and seek medical treatment
25. lack insight and resist psychological interpretations
26. are not very good candidates for traditional psychotherapy or counseling
27. tend to become critical of therapists
28. may terminate therapy prematurely when therapists suggest psychological reasons for symptoms or are perceived as not giving enough attention and support

SCALE 2 (DEPRESSION)

Scale 2 was developed originally to assess symptomatic depression. The primary characteristics of symptomatic depression are poor morale, lack of hope for the future, and a general dissatisfaction with one's life situation. Of the 60 items originally composing Scale 2 on the MMPI, 57 were retained in the MMPI-2. Many items in the scale deal with various aspects of depression, such as denial of happiness and personal worth, psychomotor retardation, withdrawal, and lack of interest in one's surroundings. Other items in the scale cover a variety of other symptoms and behaviors, including somatic complaints, worry or tension, denial of hostile impulses, and difficulty in controlling one's own thought processes.

Scale 2 is an excellent index of examinees' discomfort and dissatisfaction with their life situations. Whereas very elevated scores on this scale suggest clinical depression, more moderate scores indicate a general attitude or lifestyle characterized by poor morale and lack of involvement. The average score for older persons is approximately 5–10 T-score points above the mean for the total MMPI-2 normative sample. Persons recently hospitalized or incarcerated tend to show moderate elevations on Scale 2. These elevations may reflect dissatisfaction with current circumstances rather than clinical depression.

Interpretation of High Scores on Scale 2

High scorers on Scale 2 (particularly if the T scores exceed 70) often display depressive symptoms. They may report feeling depressed, sad, blue, unhappy, or dysphoric. They tend to feel hopeless and to be pessimistic about the future both in general and more specifically in regard to overcoming their problems. They may talk about attempting suicide; and in clinical settings, high scorers on Scale 2 are more likely than other patients to have made suicide attempts. Self-depreciation, guilt, and anhedonia are common. Behavioral manifestations may include a lack of energy, refusal to speak, crying, and psychomotor retardation. Patients with such high scores often are diagnosed with a depressive disorder. Other symptoms of high scorers include physical complaints, sleep disturbances, bad dreams, weakness, fatigue or loss of energy, agitation, tension, poor concentration, and fearfulness. They also are described as irritable, high-strung, and prone to worry and fretting. They often have unhealthy patterns of eating. They may have a sense of dread that something bad is about to happen to them.

High scorers also tend to feel insecure and show a marked lack of self-confidence. They report feeling useless and unable to function in a variety of situations. They do not have strong achievement motivation. They act helpless and give up easily when faced with adversity. They see themselves as having failed to achieve adequately in school and at work.

A lifestyle characterized by social withdrawal and lack of intimate involvement with other people is common. High scorers tend to be described as introverted, shy, retiring, timid, reclusive, and secretive. Also, they tend to act aloof and maintain psychological distance from other people. They may feel others do not care about them, and their feelings are easily hurt. They often have a severely restricted range of interests and may withdraw from activities in which they previously participated. They are extremely cautious and conventional in their activities, and they are not very creative in problem solving.

High scorers may have great difficulty in making even simple decisions. They may feel overwhelmed when faced with major life decisions such as vocation or marriage. They tend to be very overcontrolled and to deny their own impulses. They are likely to avoid unpleasantness and will make concessions to avoid confrontations.

Because high Scale 2 scores suggest great personal distress, they indicate the examinee is likely to be motivated for treatment. Extremely high scores may indicate insufficient energy to engage actively in therapy. Patients with high scores on Scale 2 often are given antidepressant medications.

Summary of Descriptors for Scale 2

High scores on Scale 2 indicate persons who

1. display depressive symptoms (particularly if T ≥ 70)
2. feel depressed, sad, blue, unhappy, and dysphoric
3. feel hopeless and pessimistic about the future
4. talk about committing suicide and in clinical settings, may be more likely than other patients to have made suicide attempts
5. have feelings of self-depreciation and guilt
6. experience anhedonia
7. lack energy, may refuse to speak, and show psychomotor retardation
8. often are diagnosed with depressive disorders
9. report physical complaints, sleep disturbances, bad dreams, weakness, fatigue, and loss of energy
10. are agitated, tense, and fearful
11. have poor concentration
12. are described as irritable, high-strung, and prone to worry and fretting
13. have unhealthy patterns of eating
14. may have a sense of dread that something bad is about to happen to them
15. feel insecure and lack self-confidence
16. feel useless and unable to function
17. do not have strong achievement motivation
18. act helpless and give up easily
19. feel like failures at work or in school
20. have lifestyles characterized by withdrawal and lack of involvement with other people
21. are introverted, shy, retiring, timid, reclusive, and secretive
22. are aloof and maintain psychological distance from other people
23. may feel others do not care about them
24. have their feelings easily hurt
25. have restricted ranges of interests
26. may withdraw from activities in which they previously participated
27. are very cautious and conventional and are not creative in problem solving
28. have difficulty making decisions
29. feel overwhelmed when faced with major life decisions
30. are overcontrolled and deny their own impulses
31. avoid unpleasantness and make concessions to avoid confrontations
32. because of personal distress, are likely to be motivated for psychotherapy or counseling
33. if scores are very high, may have insufficient energy to engage actively in therapy
34. often are prescribed antidepressant medications

SCALE 3 (HYSTERIA)

Scale 3 was developed to identify patients who were having hysterical reactions to stress situations. The hysterical syndrome was characterized by involuntary psychogenic loss or disorder of function. All 60 items in the original MMPI Scale 3 were retained in the MMPI-2 scale. Some items deal with a general denial of physical health and a variety of rather specific somatic complaints—including heart or chest pain, nausea and vomiting, fitful sleep, and headaches. Another group of items involves a general denial of psychological or emotional problems and of discomfort in social situations. Still other items have to do with holding naively optimistic views of other people. High raw scores are more common among women than among men in both clinical and nonclinical settings.

It is important to consider the level of scores on Scale 3. Marked elevations (T ≥ 80) suggest the possibility of a conversion disorder. It also has been noted chronic pain patients often have Scale 3 T scores in the 70–80 range. Moderately elevated scores are associated with characteristics consistent with conversion disorders, such as vague somatic complaints and self-centeredness. However, scores in this range do not typically suggest a classic conversion reaction. As with Scale 1, patients with genuine medical problems for whom there is no indication of psychological components to the conditions tend to obtain T scores of about 60 on this scale.

Interpretation of High Scores on Scale 3

Marked elevations on Scale 3 (T ≥ 80) are suggestive of persons who often feel overwhelmed and who react to stress, as well as avoid responsibility, by developing physical symptoms. Their symptoms usually do not fit the pattern of any known organic disorder. They may include—in some combination—headaches, stomach discomfort, chest pains, weakness, or tachycardia. Under stress, the symptoms may appear suddenly, and they are likely to disappear just as suddenly when the stress subsides.

High scorers on Scale 3 typically do not seem to be experiencing acute emotional turmoil, but they may report feeling sad, depressed, and anxious at times. They also may report lack of energy and feeling worn out. Sleep disturbances are rather common. The most frequent diagnoses for high Scale 3 scorers in clinical settings are conversion disorder, somatic symptom disorder, and pain disorder. High scorers often are prescribed antidepressant and anxiolytic medications.

A salient feature of the day-to-day functioning of high scorers is a marked lack of insight concerning the possible underlying causes of their symptoms. In addition, they show little insight concerning their own motives and feelings. High scorers often express rather naïve and Pollyannaish views of the world.

High scorers are often described as immature psychologically and at times even childish or infantile. They are quite self-centered, narcissistic, and egocentric; and they expect a great deal of attention and affection from others. They often use indirect and devious means to get the attention and affection they crave. When others do not give the desired attention and affection, high scorers may feel angry and resentful; but these feelings are likely to be denied and not expressed openly or directly.

High scorers on Scale 3 in clinical settings tend to be more interpersonally involved than many other patients. Although their needs for affection and attention drive them into social interactions, their interpersonal relationships tend to be rather superficial and immature. They seem to be interested in people primarily because of what they can get from them rather than because of a sincere interest in them.

Because of their needs for acceptance and affection, high scorers may initially be quite enthusiastic about treatment. However, they view themselves as having medical problems and want to be treated medically. They are slow to gain insight into the underlying causes of their behavior and are quite resistant to psychological interpretations. If therapists insist on examining the psychological causes of symptoms, premature termination of treatment is likely. High scorers may be willing to talk about problems in their lives so long as they are not perceived as causing their symptoms, and they often respond quite well to direct advice and suggestion. In therapy, they often discuss worry about failure in school or work, marital unhappiness, lack of acceptance socially, and problems with authority figures.

Summary of Descriptors for Scale 3
High scores on Scale 3 indicate persons who

1. often feel overwhelmed
2. react to stress and avoid responsibility by developing physical symptoms (especially if $T \geq 80$)
3. may report headaches, stomach discomfort, chest pains, weakness, or tachycardia
4. have physical symptoms that may appear and disappear suddenly
5. do not typically seem to be experiencing acute emotional turmoil
6. may report feeling sad, depressed, and anxious at times
7. report lack of energy, feeling worn out, and sleep disturbances
8. frequently receive diagnoses of conversion, somatic symptom, or pain disorder
9. often are prescribed antidepressant and anxiolytic medications
10. lack insight concerning possible underlying causes of symptoms
11. show little insight concerning their own motives and feelings
12. often are described as psychologically immature, childish, and infantile
13. are self-centered, narcissistic, and egocentric
14. expect a great deal of attention and affection from others
15. use indirect means to get attention and affection
16. feel angry when they do not get enough attention and affection
17. do not express negative feelings openly or directly
18. may express naïve and Pollyannaish beliefs about the world
19. in clinical settings, tend to be more interpersonally involved than many patients
20. tend to have superficial and immature interpersonal relationships
21. are interested in others primarily because of what they can get from them
22. because of strong needs for acceptance and affection, may initially be quite enthusiastic about treatment
23. believe they have medical problems and want medical treatment
24. are slow to gain insight into underlying causes of their behavior during therapy

25. are quite resistant to psychological interpretations
26. may terminate treatment prematurely if therapists focus on psychological causes of symptoms
27. may be willing to talk about problems so long as they are not connected to their physical symptoms
28. often respond quite well to direct advice and suggestion
29. in treatment, may discuss failure at work or school, marital unhappiness, lack of social acceptance, or problems with authority figures

SCALE 4 (PSYCHOPATHIC DEVIATE)

Scale 4 was developed to identify patients diagnosed with psychopathic personality, asocial or amoral type. Whereas persons in the original criterion group characteristically engaged in less severe delinquent acts like lying, stealing, sexual promiscuity, and excessive drinking, individuals who engaged in more extreme criminal behavior were included. All 50 items in the original MMPI scale were maintained in the MMPI-2. The items cover a wide array of topics including absence of satisfaction in life, family problems, juvenile delinquency, sexual problems, and difficulties with authorities. Interestingly, the keyed responses include both admissions of social maladjustment and assertions of social poise and confidence.

Scores on Scale 4 tend to be related to age, with younger persons scoring slightly higher than older persons. In the MMPI-2 normative samples, people who identified as Caucasian or Asian American scored somewhat lower on Scale 4 (5–10 T-score points) than those who identified as African American, Native American, or as being Hispanic.

One way of conceptualizing what Scale 4 assesses is to think of it as a measure of rebelliousness. The highest scorers on the scale may rebel by acting out in antisocial and criminal ways, and moderately high scorers are likely to express their rebelliousness in more socially acceptable ways.

Interpretation of High Scores on Scale 4

Extremely high scores (T ≥ 75) on Scale 4 tend to be associated with difficulty in incorporating the values and standards of society. Such high scorers are likely to engage in a variety of antisocial, and even criminal, behaviors. These behaviors may include lying, cheating, stealing, and sexual acting out. They can also include excessive use of alcohol or other drugs, including use of substances that leads to problems with the law (e.g., convictions for driving under the influence).

High scorers on Scale 4 tend to rebel against authority figures and often are in conflict with authorities of one kind or another. They frequently have stormy family relationships and regularly blame family members for their difficulties. Underachievement in school, poor work history, and marital problems are also characteristic of high scorers.

High scorers are very impulsive persons who seek immediate gratification. They often do not adequately plan their behavior and may act without considering the consequences of their actions. They are very impatient and have a limited frustration tolerance. Their behavior may involve poor judgment and considerable risk taking. They tend not to learn from experience and may find themselves in the same difficulties time and time again.

High scorers are described by others as immature and childish. They are narcissistic, self-centered, selfish, and egocentric. Their behavior often is ostentatious and exhibitionistic. They are insensitive to the needs and feelings of others, and their interest in others is usually related to how they can be used to further their own goals. Although they tend to be seen as likable and generally create good first impressions, their relationships tend to be shallow and superficial. This may be in part due to rejection by the people they mistreat, but it also seems to reflect their own inability to form warm attachments with others.

In addition, high scorers typically are extroverted and outgoing. They are talkative, active, adventurous, energetic, and spontaneous. Others view them as intelligent and self-confident. Although they have a wide range of interests and may become involved in many activities, they lack definite goals, and their behavior lacks clear direction.

High scorers tend to be hostile and aggressive. They are resentful, rebellious, antagonistic, and stubborn. They tend to be sarcastic, and their attitudes are characterized by cynicism and lack of trust. They often feel they are mistreated by others. Men and women with high Scale 4 scores may act in aggressive ways, but women are likely to express aggression in more passive, indirect ways. Often there does not appear to be any guilt associated with the aggressive behavior. Whereas high scorers may feign guilt and remorse when their behaviors get them into trouble, such responses typically are short-lived, disappearing when the immediate crisis passes.

High scorers typically are not seen as being overwhelmed by emotional turmoil, but at times they may admit feeling sad, fearful, and worried about the future. They may experience absence of deep emotional response, which may produce feelings of emptiness, boredom, and depression. Among psychiatric patients, high scorers tend to receive personality disorder diagnoses with antisocial personality disorder occurring most frequently.

Because of their verbal facility, outgoing manner, and apparent intellectual resources, high scorers often are perceived as good candidates for psychotherapy or counseling. Unfortunately, the prognosis for change is poor. Although they may agree to treatment to avoid something more unpleasant (e.g., jail or divorce), they generally are unwilling to accept responsibility for their own problems, and they terminate treatment as soon as possible. In therapy, they tend to intellectualize excessively and blame others for their difficulties.

Summary of Descriptors for Scale 4

High scores on Scale 4 indicate persons who

1. have difficulty incorporating the values and standards of society
2. may engage in antisocial acts—such as lying, cheating, stealing, sexual acting out, and excessive use of alcohol or other drugs
3. are rebellious toward authority figures

4. have stormy relationships with families
5. blame family members for difficulties
6. have histories of underachievement
7. tend to have marital problems
8. are impulsive and seek instant gratification
9. do not plan their behavior well
10. tend to act without considering the consequences of their actions
11. are impatient and have limited frustration tolerance
12. show poor judgment and take risks
13. tend not to learn from experience
14. are seen by others as immature and childish
15. are narcissistic, self-centered, selfish, and egocentric
16. are ostentatious and exhibitionistic
17. are insensitive to the needs and feelings of others
18. are interested in others in terms of how they can be used
19. are likable and create good first impressions
20. have shallow, superficial relationships
21. seem unable to form warm attachments with others
22. are extroverted and outgoing
23. are talkative, active, adventurous, energetic, and spontaneous
24. are judged by others to be intelligent and self-confident
25. have wide ranging interests, but their behavior lacks clear direction
26. tend to be hostile, resentful, rebellious, antagonistic, and stubborn
27. have sarcastic, cynical, and suspicious attitudes
28. may act in aggressive ways, although women may do so in less direct ways
29. may feign guilt and remorse when in trouble
30. are not seen as overwhelmed by emotional turmoil
31. may admit feeling sad, fearful, and worried about the future
32. experience absence of deep emotional response
33. may feel empty, bored, and depressed
34. in clinical settings, are likely to receive diagnoses of antisocial personality disorder
35. may agree to treatment to avoid something more unpleasant
36. have poor prognosis for psychotherapy or counseling
37. tend to terminate treatment prematurely
38. in treatment tend to intellectualize excessively and blame others for difficulties

SCALE 5 (MASCULINITY–FEMININITY)

At the time the MMPI was developed, being romantically or sexually attracted to individuals who were similarly gendered (referred to as "homosexuality" during this period) was considered a mental disorder. Thus, in their efforts to create a comprehensive differential diagnostic instrument, Hathaway and McKinley included a scale to identify homosexuality in men, which later became Clinical Scale 5. The test authors identified only a very small number of items that differentiated gay and heterosexual patients. As such, items also were added to the scale if they differentiated between men and women in the MMPI standardization sample. Items from Terman and Miles' (1936) Attitude-Interest Analysis Test were also added to the scale. The test authors attempted unsuccessfully to develop a corresponding scale for identifying homosexuality in women. Although Hathaway and McKinley considered Scale 5 to be in need of revision, it has come to be used routinely in its original form. However, it is not used for its original purpose. Rather, it is used to assess whether an individual has traditionally masculine or feminine interests.

Scale 5 has been used routinely for both men and women and was constructed around conventional ideas about biological sex, gender, and sexual orientation. Fifty-two of the items are keyed in the same direction for men and women, whereas four items—all dealing with explicit sexual material—are keyed in opposite directions for men and women. After obtaining raw scores, T-score conversions are reversed on the basis of gender so that a high raw score for men is transformed to a high T score, whereas a high raw score for women is transformed to a low T score. The result is that high T scores for both men and women are indicative of deviation from traditional gender responses.

In the MMPI-2, 56 of the 60 items in the original MMPI Scale 5 were maintained. Although a few of the items in Scale 5 have explicit sexual content, most items are not sexual in nature and cover a diversity of topics, including work and recreational interests, worries and fears, excessive sensitivity, and family relationships.

Butcher (1990a) reported a correlation of .35 between Scale 5 scores and years of education for men in the MMPI-2 normative sample. For women, the correlation was –.15. Long et al. (1994) found that men in the MMPI-2 standardization sample with the highest educational levels (college degrees or beyond) had an average score more than 5 T-score points higher on Scale 5 than the lowest educational group (less than high school diploma). The most educated women scored more than 5 T-score points lower than the least educated women. These differences probably reflect the broader interest patterns of more educated men and women and are not large enough to necessitate different Scale 5 interpretations for persons with differing levels of education.

Scores on Scale 5 do not seem to be related to symptoms or problems for non-clinical persons (Long & Graham, 1991), psychiatric inpatients (Graham, 1988), or mental health center outpatients (Graham et al., 1999). In fact, several studies have indicated that moderate Scale 5 elevations may actually be associated with more positive functioning (Reed et al., 1996; Tanner, 1990). Although several older studies have reported Scale 5 elevations for some individuals who committed specific kinds of sexual offenses (G. C. N. Hall et al., 1991; Walters, 1987), relationships between Scale 5 scores and sexual aggression or other kinds of sexual problems are not established well enough to permit prediction of these problem behaviors in individual cases.

Interpretation of Scores on Scale 5

High scores for men on Scale 5 are indicative of a lack of traditionally masculine interests. High scorers tend to have aesthetic and artistic interests, and they are likely to participate in housekeeping and childrearing activities to a greater extent than other men.

High scores on Scale 5 are very uncommon among women. When they are encountered, they generally indicate rejection of a highly traditional feminine role.

Women having high Scale 5 scores are interested in sports, hobbies, and other activities that tend to be stereotypically more masculine than feminine. They often are seen as assertive and competitive.

Men who score low on Scale 5 are presenting themselves as very traditionally masculine. They are likely to have stereotypically masculine preferences in work, hobbies, and other activities. Women who score low on Scale 5 are indicating they have many stereotypically feminine interests. They are likely to derive satisfaction from roles as a spouse or as a mother. However, women with low Scale 5 scores may be highly traditionally feminine or may have adopted a more androgynous lifestyle. This androgynous lifestyle is more likely for women with low Scale 5 scores who also are well educated.

Summary of Descriptors for Scale 5

High Scale 5 scores for men indicate persons who

1. lack traditionally masculine interests
2. have aesthetic and artistic interests
3. are likely to participate in housekeeping and childrearing to a greater extent than many men

High Scale 5 scores for women indicate persons who

1. may be rejecting a highly traditional feminine role
2. are likely to be interested in sports, hobbies, and other activities that are stereotypically more masculine than feminine
3. are seen as assertive and competitive

Low Scale 5 scores for men indicate persons who

1. are presenting themselves as extremely masculine
2. tend to have stereotypically masculine preferences in work, hobbies, and other activities

Low Scale 5 scores for women indicate persons who

1. have many stereotypically feminine interests
2. are likely to derive satisfaction from having a role as a spouse or mother
3. may be traditionally feminine or more androgynous

SCALE 6 (PARANOIA)

Scale 6 originally was developed to identify patients who were judged to have paranoid symptoms such as ideas of reference, feelings of persecution, grandiose self-concepts, suspiciousness, excessive sensitivity, and rigid opinions and attitudes. Although the scale was considered preliminary because of problems in cross-validation, a major reason for its retention was that it produced relatively few false positives. Persons who score high on the scale usually have paranoid symptoms. However, some patients with clearly paranoid symptoms can achieve average scores on Scale 6.

All 40 of the items in the original MMPI scale were maintained in the MMPI-2. Although some of the items in the scale clearly refer to psychotic behaviors (e.g., suspiciousness, ideas of reference, delusions of persecution, and grandiosity), other items cover such diverse topics as sensitivity, cynicism, asocial behavior, excessive moral virtue, and complaints about other people. It is possible to obtain a T score greater than 65 on this scale without endorsing any of the items referencing psychotic symptoms.

Interpretation of High Scores on Scale 6

When T scores on Scale 6 are greater than 70, and especially when Scale 6 also is the highest scale in the profile, persons may clearly exhibit psychotic behavior. Their thinking may be disturbed, and they may have delusions of persecution or grandeur. Ideas of reference also are common. They may feel mistreated and picked on, they may be angry and resentful, and they may harbor grudges. Projection is a common defense mechanism. Among psychiatric patients, diagnoses of schizophrenia, paranoid delusional disorder, or paranoid personality disorder are most frequent; and past hospitalizations are common.

When Scale 6 scores are within a T-score range of 60–70, psychotic symptoms are not as common as for higher scores. However, persons with scores within this range are characterized by a variety of traits and behaviors that suggest a paranoid orientation. They tend to be excessively sensitive and overly responsive to the opinions of others. They feel they are getting a raw deal out of life and tend to rationalize and to blame others for their own difficulties. Also, they are seen as suspicious and guarded and commonly exhibit hostility, resentment, and an argumentative manner. They tend to be very moralistic and rigid in their opinions and attitudes. Rationality is likely to be greatly overemphasized. Persons who score in this range may also describe depression, sadness, withdrawal, and anxiety; and they are seen by others as emotionally labile and moody. Prognosis for psychotherapy is poor because these persons do not like to talk about emotional problems and are likely to rationalize much of the time. They have great difficulty in establishing rapport with therapists. In therapy, they are likely to reveal hostility and resentment toward family members.

Summary of Descriptors for Scale 6

Extreme elevations (T ≥ 70) on Scale 6 indicate persons who

1. may exhibit psychotic behavior
2. may have disturbed thinking, delusions of persecution or grandeur, and ideas of reference
3. feel mistreated and picked on
4. feel angry and resentful
5. harbor grudges
6. utilize projection as a defense mechanism
7. in clinical settings, often receive diagnoses of schizophrenia, paranoid delusional disorder, or paranoid personality disorder
8. if psychiatric patients, previous hospitalizations are common

Moderate elevations (T = 60–70) on Scale 6 indicate persons who

1. have a paranoid orientation
2. tend to be excessively sensitive and overly responsive to the opinions of others
3. feel they are getting a raw deal out of life
4. tend to rationalize and blame others for difficulties
5. are suspicious and guarded
6. have hostility, resentment, and an argumentative manner
7. are moralistic and rigid in their opinions and attitudes
8. overemphasize rationality
9. may describe depression, sadness, withdrawal, and anxiety
10. are seen by others as emotionally labile and moody
11. have poor prognosis for psychotherapy
12. do not like to talk about emotional problems
13. rationalize excessively in therapy
14. have difficulty establishing rapport with a therapist
15. in therapy, reveal hostility and resentment toward family members

SCALE 7 (PSYCHASTHENIA)

Scale 7 originally was developed to measure the general symptomatic pattern labeled psychasthenia. Although this diagnostic label is not used commonly today, it was popular when the scale was developed. Among currently diagnostic categories, obsessive–compulsive disorder probably is closest to describing the symptoms captured in the psychasthenia construct. Persons given diagnoses of psychasthenia had thinking characterized by excessive doubts, compulsions, obsessions, and unreasonable fears. This symptom pattern was much more common among outpatients than among hospitalized patients, so the number of cases available for scale construction was small.

All 48 items in the original MMPI scale were maintained in the MMPI-2 version of the scale. They cover a variety of symptoms and behaviors. Many of the items deal with uncontrollable or obsessive thoughts, feelings of fear or anxiety, and doubts about one's own ability. Unhappiness, physical complaints, and difficulties in concentration also are represented in the scale.

Interpretation of High Scores on Scale 7

Scale 7 is a reliable index of psychological turmoil and discomfort. High scorers tend to be extremely anxious, tense, and agitated. They worry a great deal, even over small problems, and they are fearful and apprehensive. They are high-strung and jumpy and report difficulties in concentrating. High scorers often also report feeling sad and unhappy, and they tend to be pessimistic about the future. Some high scorers express physical complaints that may center on the heart, the gastrointestinal system, or the genitourinary system. Complaints of fatigue, exhaustion, insomnia, and bad dreams are common. High scorers on Scale 7 often are given anxiety-, obsessive–compulsive-, or trauma-related diagnoses.

High scorers on Scale 7 tend to be very introspective, and they sometimes report fears that they are losing their minds. Obsessive thinking, compulsive and ritualistic behavior, and ruminations—often centering on feelings of insecurity and inferiority—are common among highest scorers. They lack self-confidence; are self-critical, self-conscious, and self-degrading; and are plagued by self-doubts. High scorers tend to be very rigid and moralistic and to have high standards of behavior and performance for themselves and others. They are likely to be perfectionistic and highly conscientious; they may feel guilty about not living up to their own standards and depressed about falling short of goals.

In general, high scorers are neat, orderly, organized, and meticulous. They are persistent and reliable, but they lack ingenuity and originality in their approach to problems. They are seen by others as dull and formal. They have great difficulties in decision making. They do not cope well with stress, often distorting the importance of problems and overreacting to stressful situations.

High scorers tend to be shy and do not interact well socially. They are described as hard to get to know, and they worry a great deal about popularity and social acceptance. Other people often see them as sentimental, peaceable, soft-hearted, trustful, sensitive, and kind. Other adjectives used to describe them include dependent, unassertive, and immature.

Although high scorers may be motivated for treatment because they feel so uncomfortable and miserable, they are not very responsive to brief psychotherapy or counseling. Despite some insight into their problems, they tend to rationalize and intellectualize a great deal. They often are resistant to interpretations and may express hostility toward the therapist. However, they tend to remain in treatment longer than most patients, and they may show very slow but steady progress. Problems presented in treatment may include difficulties with authority figures and poor work or study habits.

Summary of Descriptors for Scale 7
High scores on Scale 7 indicate persons who

1. are experiencing psychological turmoil and discomfort
2. feel anxious, tense, and agitated
3. are worried, fearful, apprehensive, high-strung, and jumpy
4. report difficulties in concentrating
5. often report feeling sad and unhappy
6. feel pessimistic about the future
7. report physical complaints centering on the heart, genitourinary system, or gastrointestinal system
8. complain of fatigue, exhaustion, and insomnia
9. in clinical settings, often are given anxiety-, obsessive–compulsive- or trauma-related diagnoses
10. are introspective
11. may fear they are losing their minds
12. have obsessive thinking, compulsive and ritualistic behavior, and ruminations

13. feel insecure and inferior
14. lack self-confidence
15. are self-critical, self-conscious, and self-degrading
16. are plagued by self-doubts
17. tend to be very rigid and moralistic
18. have high standards of performance for self and others
19. are perfectionistic and highly conscientious
20. may feel depressed and guilty about falling short of goals
21. are neat, organized, and meticulous
22. are persistent and reliable
23. lack ingenuity in their approach to problems
24. are seen by others as dull and formal
25. have difficulties in making decisions
26. do not cope well with stress
27. often distort the importance of problems and overreact to stress
28. tend to be shy and do not interact well socially
29. are described as hard to get to know
30. worry about popularity and social acceptance
31. are seen by others as sentimental, peaceable, soft-hearted, sensitive, and kind
32. may be motivated for treatment because of inner turmoil
33. are not very responsive to brief therapy or counseling
34. show some insight into their problems
35. rationalize and intellectualize excessively
36. are resistant to psychological interpretations in therapy
37. may express hostility toward therapists
38. remain in treatment longer than most patients
39. make slow but steady progress in treatment
40. in treatment, discuss problems that may include difficulty with authority figures and poor work or study habits.

SCALE 8 (SCHIZOPHRENIA)

Scale 8 was developed to identify patients with diagnoses of schizophrenia. This category included a heterogeneous group of disorders characterized by disturbances of thinking, mood, and behavior, reflected today in the dysfunctions included in the DSM-5's schizophrenia spectrum disorders category (American Psychiatric Association, 2013). Misinterpretations of reality, delusions, and hallucinations may be present. Ambivalent or constricted emotional responsiveness is common. Behavior may be withdrawn, aggressive, or bizarre.

All 78 of the items in the MMPI original scale were maintained in the MMPI-2 version of Scale 8. Some of the items clearly refer to psychotic symptoms, such as bizarre mentation, peculiarities of perception, delusions of persecution, and hallucinations. Other topics covered include social alienation; poor family relationships; sexual concerns; difficulties in impulse control and concentration; and fears, worries, and dissatisfactions.

Experiences unrelated to psychosis may also elevate Scale 8 scores. For example, scores on Scale 8 are related to race and ethnicity. Individuals who identified as African American, Native American, and Hispanic in the MMPI-2 normative sample scored approximately 5 T-score points higher than those who identified as Caucasian (Butcher et al., 2001). These mildly elevated scores do not necessarily suggest greater overt psychopathology but rather may be indicative of the alienation and social estrangement experienced by some underrepresented groups. Further, elevations of Scale 8 are found in persons who are reporting unusual experiences, feelings, and perceptions related to the use of prescription and nonprescription drugs, especially amphetamines. Also, some persons with medical disorders such as epilepsy, stroke, or closed head injury endorse sensory and cognitive items that lead to above-average scores on Scale 8 (e.g., Dikmen et al., 1983; Dodrill, 1986; Gass, 1991, 1992; Gass & Lawhorn, 1991).

Interpretation of High Scores on Scale 8

Although one should not assign a diagnosis solely on the basis of the score on Scale 8, T scores greater than 75 suggest the possibility of a psychotic disorder. Scale 8 scores add incrementally to information from semi-structured diagnostic interviews in predicting psychotic disorders. When T scores are greater than 75, confusion, disorganization, and disorientation may be present. Unusual thoughts or attitudes (perhaps delusional in nature), hallucinations, and extremely poor judgment may be evident. High scorers often have long histories of inpatient or outpatient psychiatric treatment.

High scores on Scale 8, however, do not necessarily indicate psychotic disorders. They can be produced by an individual who is in acute psychological turmoil or by a person experiencing less severe difficulties who is endorsing many items describing unusual experiences as a cry for help. In interpreting high scores on Scale 8, it is important to consider the possibility they reflect the reporting of unusual symptoms associated with substance misuse or with medical disorders such as epilepsy, stroke, or closed head injury.

High scores on Scale 8 may suggest social alienation. High scorers tend to feel as if they are not a part of their social environments. They feel isolated, alienated, misunderstood, and unaccepted by their peers. They believe they are getting a raw deal from life. They are withdrawn, seclusive, secretive, and inaccessible and may avoid dealing with people and with new situations. They are described by others as shy, aloof, and uninvolved; and they often report having few or no friends.

High scorers may be experiencing a great deal of apprehension and generalized anxiety, and they often report having bad dreams and problems with concentration. They may feel sad, blue, and depressed. They may feel helpless and pessimistic about the future, and they may report suicidal ideation. They may feel very resentful, hostile, and aggressive, but they are unable to express such feelings directly. A typical response to stress is withdrawal into daydreams and fantasies, and some high scorers may have a difficult time in separating reality and fantasy.

High scorers may be plagued by self-doubts. They feel insecure, inferior, incompetent, and dissatisfied. They give up easily when confronted with problem situations and often feel like failures. Sexual preoccupation and sex-role confusion are common.

Their behavior often is characterized by others as nonconforming, unusual, unconventional, and eccentric. Physical complaints may be present, and they usually are vague and long-standing in nature.

High scorers may at times be very stubborn, moody, and opinionated. At other times, they are seen as generous, peaceable, and sentimental. Other adjectives used to describe high scorers include immature, impulsive, adventurous, sharp-witted, conscientious, and high-strung. Although they may have a wide range of interests and may be creative and imaginative in approaching problems, their goals generally are abstract and vague; and they seem to lack the basic information required for problem solving.

The prognosis for psychotherapy for high scorers is not good because of the long-standing nature of their problems and their difficulties relating in a meaningful way to therapists. However, high scorers tend to stay in treatment longer than most patients, and eventually they may come to trust their therapists. Medical consultation to evaluate the appropriateness of psychotropic medications may be indicated. In some cases, high scorers may require the structured environment of an inpatient treatment program. Focusing on specific and practical problems in therapy may be more beneficial than a more insight-oriented approach.

Summary of Descriptors for Scale 8

High scores on Scale 8 indicate persons who

1. may have a psychotic disorder (especially if $T \geq 75$)
2. may be confused, disorganized, and disoriented
3. may report unusual thoughts or attitudes and hallucinations
4. may show extremely poor judgment
5. often have histories of inpatient or outpatient psychiatric treatment
6. may be in acute psychological turmoil
7. may be reporting unusual symptoms associated with drug use or medical problems such as epilepsy, stroke, or closed head injury
8. tend to be isolated from others
9. do not feel part of their social environments
10. feel alienated, misunderstood, and unaccepted by peers
11. may feel they are getting a raw deal from life
12. are withdrawn, seclusive, secretive, and inaccessible
13. avoid dealing with people and new situations
14. are described by others as shy, aloof, and uninvolved
15. often report having few or no friends
16. experience apprehension and generalized anxiety
17. report bad dreams and problems with concentration
18. may feel sad, blue, and depressed
19. may feel helpless and pessimistic about the future
20. may report suicidal ideation
21. feel resentful, hostile, and aggressive
22. are unable to express negative feelings directly
23. typically respond to stress by withdrawing into daydreams and fantasies

24. may have difficulty separating reality and fantasy
25. are plagued by self-doubts
26. feel insecure, inferior, incompetent, and dissatisfied
27. give up easily when confronted with problem situations
28. often feel like failures
29. may have sexual preoccupation and sex-role confusion
30. are nonconforming, unusual, unconventional, and eccentric
31. have vague and long-standing physical complaints
32. may at times be stubborn, moody, and opinionated
33. may at times be seen as generous, peaceable, and sentimental
34. are described as immature, impulsive, adventurous, sharp-witted, conscientious, and high-strung
35. have a wide range of interests
36. may be creative and imaginative in approaching problems
37. have abstract and vague goals
38. seem to lack the basic information required for problem solving
39. have a poor prognosis for psychotherapy because of the long-standing nature of their problems and inability to relate in a meaningful way to a therapist
40. tend to stay in treatment longer than most patients
41. may eventually come to trust therapists
42. may require medical referral to evaluate the appropriateness of psychotropic medications
43. in some cases, may require the structured environment of an inpatient treatment program
44. may benefit most from focusing on specific and practical problems in therapy

SCALE 9 (HYPOMANIA)

Scale 9 originally was developed to identify psychiatric patients manifesting hypomanic symptoms. Hypomania is characterized by elevated mood, accelerated speech and motor activity, irritability, flight of ideas, and brief periods of depression. All 46 items in the original MMPI scale were maintained in the MMPI-2 version of the scale. Some of the items deal specifically with features of hypomanic disturbance (e.g., activity level, excitability, irritability, and grandiosity). Other items cover topics such as family relationships, moral values and attitudes, and physical or bodily concerns. No single content dimension accounts for much of the variance in scores, and most of the sources of variance represented in the scale are not duplicated in other clinical scales.

Scores on Scale 9 are related to age and ethnicity (Butcher et al., 2001). For older persons, T scores below 50 are common. Individuals in the MMPI-2 normative sample who identified as African American, Native American, or Hispanic scored somewhat higher (5–10 T-score points) than those who identified as Caucasian.

Scale 9 can be viewed as a measure of psychological and physical energy, with high scorers having excessive energy. When Scale 9 scores are high, characteristics suggested by other aspects of the MMPI-2 are more likely to be observed. For example, high scores on Scale 4 suggest antisocial tendencies. If Scale 9 is elevated along with Scale 4, these tendencies are more likely to be expressed overtly in behavior.

Interpretation of High Scores on Scale 9

Extreme elevations (T ≥ 80) on Scale 9 may be suggestive of a manic episode. Patients with such scores are likely to show excessive, purposeless activity and accelerated speech; they may experience hallucinations or delusions of grandeur; and they are emotionally labile. Some confusion may be present, and flight of ideas is common.

Persons with more moderate elevations are not likely to exhibit severe symptoms, but there is a definite tendency toward overactivity and unrealistic self-appraisal. High scorers are energetic and talkative, and they prefer action to thought. They have a wide range of interests and are likely to have many projects going at once. However, they do not utilize energy wisely and often do not see projects through to completion. They may be creative, enterprising, and ingenious, but they have little interest in routine or details. High scorers tend to become bored and restless very easily, and their frustration tolerance is quite low. They have great difficulty in inhibiting expression of impulses; and periodic episodes of irritability, hostility, and aggressive outbursts are common. An unrealistic and unqualified optimism is also characteristic of high scorers. They seem to think nothing is impossible, and they have grandiose aspirations. Also, they have an exaggerated appraisal of their own self-worth and self-importance and are not able to see their own limitations. High scorers have a greater-than-average likelihood of misusing alcohol and other drugs and getting into trouble with the law.

High scorers are very outgoing, sociable, and gregarious. They like to be around other people and generally create good first impressions. They impress others as being friendly, pleasant, enthusiastic, poised, and self-confident. They tend to try to dominate other people. Their relationships are usually quite superficial; and as others get to know them better, they become aware of their manipulations, deceptions, and unreliability.

Despite the outward picture of confidence and poise, high scorers are likely to harbor feelings of dissatisfaction concerning what they are getting out of life. They may feel upset, tense, nervous, anxious, and agitated, and they describe themselves as prone to worry. Periodic episodes of depression may occur.

In psychotherapy, high scorers may reveal negative feelings toward domineering parents, may report difficulties in school or at work, and may admit to a variety of delinquent behaviors. High scorers are resistant to interpretations, are irregular in their attendance, and are likely to terminate therapy prematurely. They engage in a great deal of intellectualization and may repeat problems in a stereotyped manner. They do not become dependent on the therapist, who may be a target for hostility and aggression.

Summary of Descriptors for Scale 9

High scores on Scale 9 indicate persons who

1. if T ≥ 80, may exhibit behavioral manifestations of manic episodes, including
   a. excessive, purposeless activity
   b. accelerated speech
   c. hallucinations
   d. delusions of grandeur

      e. emotional lability

      f. confusion

      g. flight of ideas

2. are overactive
3. have unrealistic self-appraisal
4. are energetic and talkative
5. prefer action to thought
6. have a wide range of interests
7. may have many projects going at once
8. do not utilize energy wisely
9. often do not see projects through to completion
10. may be creative, enterprising, and ingenious
11. have little interest in routine or detail
12. tend to become bored and restless very easily
13. have low frustration tolerance
14. have difficulty inhibiting expression of impulses
15. have periodic episodes of irritability, hostility, and aggressive outbursts
16. are characterized by unrealistic and unqualified optimism
17. have grandiose aspirations
18. have an exaggerated appraisal of self-worth
19. are unable to see their own limitations
20. have a greater-than-average likelihood of misusing alcohol and other drugs
21. may get into trouble with the law
22. are outgoing and gregarious
23. are sociable and like being around other people
24. create good first impressions
25. impress others as friendly, pleasant, enthusiastic, poised, and self-confident
26. try to dominate other people
27. have quite superficial relationships with other people
28. eventually are seen by others as manipulative, deceptive, and unreliable
29. beneath an outward picture of confidence and poise, harbor feelings of dissatisfaction
30. may feel upset, tense, nervous, anxious, and agitated
31. may describe themselves as prone to worry
32. may experience periodic episodes of depression
33. in psychotherapy may reveal negative feelings toward domineering parents, difficulties in school or at work, and a variety of delinquent behaviors
34. have a poor prognosis for psychotherapy
35. are resistant to interpretations
36. are irregular in therapy attendance
37. are likely to terminate therapy prematurely
38. engage in a great deal of intellectualization
39. repeat problems in a stereotyped manner
40. do not become dependent on therapists
41. may make therapists targets of hostility and aggression

SCALE 0 (SOCIAL INTROVERSION)

Scale 0 was developed later than the other Clinical scales and was designed to assess a person's tendency to withdraw from social contacts and responsibilities. Items were selected by contrasting high and low scorers on the Social Introversion–Extroversion scale of the Minnesota T-S-E Inventory (Evans & McConnell, 1941). Only data from women were used to develop the scale, but its use has been extended to men as well.

All but one of the 70 items in the original scale were maintained in the MMPI-2 version. The items are of two general types. One group of items deals with social participation, whereas the other group deals with general neurotic maladjustment and self-depreciation. High scores can be obtained by endorsing either kind of item, or both. Scores on Scale 0 are quite stable over extended periods of time.

Interpretation of Scores on Scale 0

The most salient characteristic of high scorers on Scale 0 is social introversion. High scorers are very insecure and uncomfortable in social situations. They tend to be shy, reserved, timid, and retiring. They feel more comfortable when alone or with a few close friends, and they do not participate in many social activities. They may be especially uncomfortable around individuals to whom they are romantically or sexually attracted.

High scorers lack self-confidence, and they tend to be self-effacing. They are hard to get to know and are described by others as cold and distant. They are sensitive to what others think of them and are likely to be troubled by their lack of involvement with other people. They are overcontrolled and are not likely to display their feelings directly. They are passive, submissive, and compliant in interpersonal relationships; and they are overly accepting of authority.

High scorers also are described as serious and as having a slow personal tempo. Although they are reliable and dependable, their approach to problems tends to be cautious, conventional, and unoriginal; and they give up easily. They are somewhat rigid and inflexible in their attitudes and opinions. They also have great difficulty in making even minor decisions. They typically do not have strong needs to achieve.

High scorers tend to worry, to be irritable, and to feel anxious. They often are preoccupied with health problems. They are described by others as moody. Guilty feelings and episodes of depression may occur. High scorers seem to lack energy and do not have many interests. In treatment settings, they may have difficulty forming therapeutic alliances; and they often report feeling quite uncomfortable and tense during sessions.

Low scorers on Scale 0 tend to be sociable and extroverted. They are outgoing, gregarious, friendly, and talkative. They have a strong need to be around other people, and they mix well with other people. They are seen by others as verbally fluent and expressive. They are active, energetic, and vigorous. They are interested in power, status, and recognition; and they tend to seek out competitive situations.

Summary of Descriptors for Scale 0

High scores on Scale 0 indicate persons who

1. are socially introverted
2. are very insecure and uncomfortable in social situations
3. tend to be shy, reserved, timid, and retiring
4. feel more comfortable alone or with a few close friends
5. do not participate in many social activities
6. may be especially uncomfortable around individuals to whom they are romantically or sexually attracted
7. lack self-confidence and tend to be self-effacing
8. are hard to get to know
9. are described by others as cold and distant
10. are sensitive to what others think of them
11. are likely to be troubled by their lack of involvement with other people
12. are quite overcontrolled and not likely to display feelings openly
13. are passive, submissive, and compliant in interpersonal relationships
14. are overly accepting of authority
15. are described as serious and as having a slow personal tempo
16. are reliable and dependable
17. tend to have a cautious, conventional, and unoriginal approach to problems
18. tend to give up easily
19. are somewhat rigid and inflexible in attitudes and opinions
20. have great difficulty making even minor decisions
21. do not have a strong need to achieve
22. tend to worry, to be irritable, and to feel anxious
23. often are preoccupied with health problems
24. are described by others as moody
25. may experience episodes of depression
26. do not have many interests
27. in treatment settings, have difficulty forming therapeutic alliances
28. report feeling uncomfortable and tense during treatment sessions

Low scores on Scale 0 indicate persons who

1. are sociable and extroverted
2. are outgoing, gregarious, friendly, and talkative
3. have a strong need to be around other people
4. mix well socially
5. are seen as expressive and verbally fluent

CHAPTER 5

CODE TYPES

FROM THE MMPI'S INCEPTION, Hathaway and McKinley emphasized that configural interpretation of scores was diagnostically richer and thus more useful than interpretation that examined single scales without regard for relationships among the scales. They reasoned that people grouped together on the basis of scores on more than one Clinical scale would be more similar to each other than those grouped together on the basis of having high scores on a single Clinical scale. Thus, it would be expected that there would be more reliable and specific behavioral correlates for configurations of scales than for single scales. This configural interpretation strategy became commonly referred to as the "code type approach." Meehl (1951), Meehl and Dahlstrom (1960), Taulbee and Sisson (1957), and others also stressed configural approaches to MMPI interpretation. Subsequent research with both the MMPI and MMPI-2 identified reliable extratest correlates for some frequently occurring code types (e.g., Arbisi et al., 2003a; Archer et al., 1995; Dahlstrom et al., 1972; Graham et al., 1999; Lewandowski & Graham, 1972; Sellbom, Graham, & Schenk, 2005).

DETERMINING CODE TYPES

Described very simply, code types indicate which Clinical scales are the highest ones in the profile. Though it is possible that many Clinical scales could be elevated, historically, code types have been constrained to describing the two or three highest Clinical scale scores. These are referred to as two- and three-point code types, respectively.

Two-point code types tell us which two Clinical scales are the highest ones in the profile. Thus, a 2–7 two-point code type tells us that the Scale 2 score is the highest and Scale 7 score is the second highest in the Clinical scale profile. For most two-point code types, the order of the scales is interchangeable. For example, we often talk about code types such as 27/72, and we make basically the same interpretations for the 2–7 code type as we do for the 7–2 code type. In this chapter, whenever scale order makes a difference in interpretation, then specific mention is made in the interpretive description for those particular code types. Two-point code types tell us nothing about the absolute level of scores for the two scales in the code type or the level of scores of other clinical scales.

Three-point code types tell us which three Clinical scales are the highest in the profile. For example, a 2–7–8 code type is one where in the profile the Scale 2 score is the highest, Scale 7 score is the second highest, and Scale 8 score is the third highest. For most three-point code types, the order of scales is interchangeable. Again, specific mention is made in the descriptive information when the order of scale elevation has implications for code type interpretation.

Early approaches to code type interpretation did not consider the extent to which the code types were defined. Definition refers to the difference in scores between the scales included in the code type and those excluded from the code type. Research has demonstrated well-defined code types have stronger evidence supporting their reliability and validity than code types that are not well-defined. For example, in a simulation study, Munley et al. (2004) found that as the degree of code type definition increases, code type stability also increases. McNulty et al. (1998) found the strength and number of conceptually relevant correlates were greater for defined code types than for those that were not defined.

Given these findings, our recommendation is to interpret only defined code types—ones in which the lowest Clinical scale included in the code type is at least 5 T score points higher than the next highest Clinical scale in the profile. We can be more confident the descriptors associated with a defined code type accurately characterize the person whose profile we are interpreting. Obviously, not every MMPI-2 protocol will have a defined code type; and when this occurs, the code type approach to interpretation should not be used. Rather, inferences about the examinee should be based on the interpretation of individual scales.

When determining definition, the T score difference between the lowest scale included in the code type and the next highest Clinical scale in the profile should be considered. For example, for a two-point code type, we would examine the T score difference between the second- and third-highest Clinical scales in the profile. For a three-point code type, we would examine the T score difference between the third- and fourth-highest scales. Once this difference is identified, the code type can be categorized as well-defined if the difference is 5 or more T score points. T score differences of less than 5 points should not be considered meaningful given the standard errors of measurement for the Clinical scales (Graham, Timbrook, et al., 1991).

Defined code types can be interpreted whenever the included Clinical scales have T scores greater than 60. Typically, the list of descriptors for a particular code type includes both symptoms and personality characteristics. We recommend inferences concerning both symptoms and personality characteristics be considered when the scores on the scales in the code type are very high. When the scores are not as high, inferences about symptoms should not be made (or should be made with considerable caution), but inferences about personality characteristics would apply. As a general rule, the inferences concerning symptoms probably should not be included unless T scores on the scales in the code type are greater than 65. Obviously, when T scores are considerably higher than 65, there is an even greater likelihood inferences concerning symptoms will be appropriate.

Historically, code types have identified using scores from all Clinical scales, except Scales 5 and 0. This is because Scales 5 and 0 were added after the original publication of the MMPI and do not seem to measure clinical symptoms and problems directly. The other eight Clinical scales can be combined to form 28 different two-point code types and 56 different three-point code types—if we ignore the order based on scale elevations. In this chapter, we present interpretive information only for those code types that we believe (a) occur relatively frequently in a variety of settings, and (b) which have been adequately reported upon in the literature.[1] Generally, descriptors for the various code types in this chapter are based on studies comparing persons with a particular code type to other persons in the same setting without that code type. It should be emphasized that the descriptors for two- and three-point code types were not rationally generated by combining descriptors for the individual scales included in the code types. Code type descriptions are modal patterns and obviously do not describe unfailingly each individual presenting with a specific code type. Rather, these descriptors are more likely to apply to persons with that code type than to persons without that code type. The descriptive information is not presented separately by gender because earlier research did not analyze data by gender, and most MMPI-2 studies have found far more similarities than differences in correlates for men and women (e.g., Graham et al., 1999).

RELIABILITY OF CODE TYPES

Only limited data are available concerning the stability of scale configurations for the MMPI-2. However, because of the continuity between the original and revised instruments, it can be assumed that the stability of MMPI-2 configurations is very similar to the stability of configurations on the original MMPI. Research on the temporal stability of MMPI code types suggested about one-fourth to one-third of people had the same two-point code type on two successive test administrations, and about one-fourth had the same three-point code type (e.g., Chojnacki & Walsh, 1992; Graham, 1977; Faschingbauer, 1974). It should be noted the stability indicated by these MMPI studies is likely somewhat lower than would be expected using the MMPI-2 code

---

[1] The following sources were consulted in preparing the descriptors of code types: W. Anderson and Bauer (1985); Arbisi et al. (2003a); Archer et al. (1995); Carson (1969); Dahlstrom et al., (1972); Davis and Sines (1971); Drake and Oetting (1959); Duckworth and Anderson (1986); Gilberstadt and Duker (1965); Good and Brantner (1961); Graham et al. (1999); Gynther et al. (1973); Hovey and Lewis (1967); Kelley and King (1979a, 1979b); Lachar (1974); Lewandowski and Graham (1972); Marks et al. (1974); Merritt et al., (1998); L. D. Nelson and Marks (1985); Persons and Marks (1971); and Sellbom, Graham, and Schenk (2005).

types because of the past practice of using code types that were not well-defined. In fact, Graham et al. (1986) reported that MMPI configurations tended to be more stable when the scales in the code types were more elevated initially and when there was a greater difference between these scales and other scales in the profile (i.e., the code types were well-defined).

Graham, Timbrook, et al. (1991) reported temporal stability of two- and three-point code types for the MMPI-2 normative sample. The percentages of two- and three-point code types that remained the same for retesting a week later were 26% and 15%, respectively. Because the subgroup of the normative sample who took the test twice was relatively small, the analysis of Graham, Timbrook, et al. could not be restricted to well-defined code types. Thus, the obtained percentages are somewhat lower than would be expected if only well-defined code types had been used in the analyses.

Ryan et al. (1995) reported code type stability for two groups of individuals abusing substances with test–retest intervals of 5 and 13 months. For the shorter interval, 20% of the participants had the same two-point code type, and 14% had the same three-point code type. For the longer interval, 12% had the same two-point code type, and 6% had the same three-point code type. As with the study of Graham, Timbrook, et al. (1991), these values probably would have been higher if only defined code types had been used. In addition, some of the changes in code types for these abusers could have reflected actual changes that occurred during treatment.

Munley et al. (2004) used a simulation design to estimate the effects on stability of varying degrees of code type definition. As expected, they found the stability of two-point code types increased as the differences between the scores on the scales comprising a two-point code type and the next highest Clinical scale in the profile became larger (e.g., increased from 3 points difference to over 15 points difference). In other words, stability of the code type increased as the code type became more well-defined. Consistent with these findings, Livingston et al. (2006) found that code types of injured workers were more stable over a 21-month period when the initial code types were well-defined.

In summary, research generally supports that code types are relatively stable over time. Well-defined code types are likely to be more stable than those that are not well-defined. When code types change from one test administration to another, those changes typically are not dramatic; and inferences based on the two code types are likely to be very similar.

VALIDITY OF CODE TYPES

The validity of code types can be demonstrated to the extent there are relevant extratest correlates for specific code types that differentiate them from protocols without those same code types. Because of the similarities between the MMPI and MMPI-2 Clinical scales, we are able to draw on research using both instruments in examining extratest correlates. Gynther et al. (1973) and Lewandowski and Graham (1972) demonstrated that reliable extratest correlates could be identified for profiles classified according to their two highest Clinical scales. Graham et al. (1999) investigated correlates of two- and three-point MMPI-2 code types for mental health center outpatients.

Code type correlates for private practice clients were identified by Sellbom, Graham, and Schenk (2005). Arbisi et al. (2003a) and Archer et al. (1995) reported correlates for commonly occurring two-point code types for psychiatric inpatients. In combination, these studies have demonstrated MMPI-2 code type correlates were consistent across settings and with those previously reported for the original MMPI.

INTERPRETIVE GUIDELINES FOR TWO-POINT CODE TYPES

12/21

The most prominent feature of the 12/21 code type is somatic discomfort. Individuals with this code type present as physically ill, although there may be no clinical evidence of an organic basis for their symptoms. They are preoccupied with health and bodily functions, and they are likely to overreact to minor physical dysfunction. They may report a wide variety of somatic complaints, or the symptoms may be restricted to a particular system. Although headaches and cardiac complaints may occur, the digestive system is more commonly involved. Ulcers—particularly of the upper gastrointestinal tract—are common; and anorexia, nausea, and vomiting may be present. Individuals with the 12/21 code type also may complain of dizziness, insomnia, weakness, fatigue, and tiredness. They tend to react to stress with increased focus on physical symptoms, and they resist attempts to explain their symptoms in terms of emotional or psychological factors.

Persons with the 12/21 code type may report feelings of depression, unhappiness, or dysphoria; brooding; and loss of initiative. They also may feel anxious, tense, and nervous. They are high-strung and prone to worry about many things, and they tend to be restless and irritable.

Persons with the 12/21 code type report feeling very self-conscious. They are introverted and shy in social situations, and they tend to be somewhat withdrawn and reclusive. They may be particularly uncomfortable when interacting with potential romantic or sexual partners. They harbor many doubts about their own abilities, and they are indecisive about even minor, everyday matters. They are hypersensitive to how others perceive them, and they may be somewhat suspicious and untrusting in interpersonal relations. They also tend to be passive–dependent in their relationships, and they may harbor anger and hostility toward people they believe do not offer them enough attention and support.

Excessive use of alcohol may be a problem for individuals with the 12/21 code type, especially among psychiatric patients. Their histories may include blackouts, job loss, arrests, and family problems associated with alcohol misuse. Persons with the 12/21 code type most often are given diagnoses of anxiety, obsessive compulsive, or trauma-related disorders; depressive disorders; or somatic symptom and related disorders; although a small proportion of individuals with this code type have diagnoses of a schizophrenia spectrum disorder. In this latter group (schizophrenia spectrum), Scale 8 usually is elevated, along with Scales 1 and 2.

Individuals with the 12/21 code type are not seen as good candidates for traditional psychotherapy. They can tolerate high levels of discomfort before becoming motivated to change. They utilize repression and somatization excessively, and they lack insight and self-understanding. In addition, their passive–dependent lifestyles make it difficult for them to accept responsibility for their own behavior. Although long-term change after psychotherapy is not likely, short-lived symptomatic changes may occur.

13/31

The 13/31 code type is more common among women and older persons than among men and younger persons. Psychiatric patients with the 13/31 code often have somatic symptom and related disorders diagnoses. Classical conversion symptoms (i.e., manifestation of a medical problem with no organic cause) may be present, particularly if Scales 1 and 3 are very elevated and Scale 2 is considerably lower than Scales 1 and 3 (i.e., the so-called conversion-V pattern). Whereas some anxiety and depression may be reported by 13/31 persons, they typically are not experiencing disabling emotional turmoil. Rather than being grossly incapacitated in functioning, the 13/31 individual is likely to continue functioning but at a reduced level of efficiency.

The somatic difficulties presented by 13/31 persons include headaches, chest pain, back pain, and numbness or tremors of the extremities. Eating problems—anorexia, nausea, vomiting, and obesity—are common. Other physical complaints include weakness, fatigue, dizziness, and sleep disturbance. These physical symptoms increase in times of stress, and often there is a clear secondary gain associated with the symptoms.

Individuals with the 13/31 code type may present themselves as psychologically healthy, responsible, and without fault. They make excessive use of denial, projection, and rationalization; and they blame others for their difficulties. They prefer medical explanations for their symptoms and lack insight into the psychological factors related to their symptoms. They manifest an overly optimistic and Pollyannaish view of their situations and of the world in general, and they do not show appropriate concern about their symptoms and problems.

Persons with the 13/31 code type tend to be rather immature, egocentric, selfish, and histrionic. They are insecure and have a strong need for attention, affection, and sympathy. They are highly dependent, but they are uncomfortable with the dependency and experience conflict because of it. Although they tend to be outgoing and socially extroverted, their social relationships tend to be shallow and superficial; and they may lack genuine emotional involvement with other people. They tend to exploit social relationships in an attempt to fulfill their own needs. They lack skills in dealing with sexual or romantic partners and are likely to have little interest in sexual activities.

Individuals with the 13/31 code type harbor resentment and hostility toward other people, particularly those who are perceived as not fulfilling their needs for attention. Most of the time they are overcontrolled and likely to express their negative feelings in indirect, passive ways; but they occasionally lose their tempers and express themselves in angry, but not violent, ways. Behaving in a socially acceptable manner is important to persons with this code type. They need to convince other people that they are logical and reasonable. As a result, they tend to be conventional and conforming in their attitudes and values.

Because of their unwillingness to acknowledge psychological factors related to their symptoms, persons with the 13/31 code type are difficult to motivate in traditional psychotherapy. They are reluctant to discuss psychological factors that might be related to somatic symptoms; and if therapists insist on doing so, people with this code type are likely to terminate therapy prematurely. Sometimes it is possible to get these persons to discuss psychological problems so long as no direct link to somatic symptoms is suggested. In therapy, they expect therapists to provide definite answers and solutions to their problems, and they may terminate therapy when therapists fail to respond to their demands. Because 13/31 persons tend to be suggestible, they often will try activities suggested by their therapists.

14/41

The 14/41 code type is not encountered frequently in clinical practice and is much more likely to be found for men than for women. Persons with the 14/41 code type frequently report severe somatic symptoms, particularly nonspecific headaches. They also may appear to be indecisive and anxious. Although they are socially extroverted, they lack skills with potential romantic or sexual partners. They may feel rebellious toward home and parents, but direct expression of these feelings is not likely. Excessive use of alcohol may be a problem. Persons with the 14/41 code type may have a history of binge drinking alcohol for periods of several days, as well as job loss and family problems associated with their drinking behavior. In school or on the job, they lack drive and do not have well-defined goals. They are dissatisfied and pessimistic in their outlook toward life; and they are demanding, grouchy, and often referred to as "bitchy" in interpersonal relationships. Because they are likely to deny psychological problems, they tend to be resistant to traditional psychotherapy.

18/81

Persons with the 18/81 code type often harbor feelings of hostility and aggression; and they are not able to express these feelings in a modulated, adaptive manner. Either they inhibit expression almost completely, which results in feelings of being "bottled up," or they are overly belligerent and abrasive.

Individuals with the 18/81 code type feel socially inadequate, especially around potential romantic or sexual partners. They lack trust in other people, keep them at a distance, and feel generally isolated and alienated. A nomadic lifestyle and a poor work history are common.

Psychiatric patients with the 18/81 code type often have diagnoses of schizophrenia, although diagnoses of anxiety disorders and schizoid personality disorder are sometimes given. These persons tend to be unhappy and depressed, and they may display flat affect. They present somatic concerns (including headaches and insomnia), which at times are so intense they border on being delusional. Persons with this code type also may be confused in their thinking, and they are very distractible.

19/91

Persons with the 19/91 code type are likely experiencing a great deal of distress and turmoil. They tend to be very anxious, tense, and restless. Somatic complaints—including gastrointestinal problems, headaches, and exhaustion—are common; and they are reluctant to accept psychological explanations of their symptoms. Although on the surface, persons with the 19/91 code type appear to be verbal, socially extroverted, aggressive, and belligerent, they are basically passive–dependent persons who are trying to deny this aspect of their personalities.

Individuals with the 19/91 code type often appear to have a great deal of ambition. They expect a high level of achievement from themselves, but they lack clear and definite goals. They are frustrated by their inability to achieve at a high level. The 19/91 code type is sometimes found for individuals with brain damage/injury who are experiencing difficulties in coping with their limitations and deficits. It should be emphasized, however, that this code type or other MMPI-2 data should not be used to diagnose brain damage.

23/32

Although persons with the 23/32 code type typically do not experience disabling anxiety, they report feeling nervous, agitated, tense, and worried. They also report feeling sad, unhappy, and depressed; and suicidal ideations may be present. Fatigue, exhaustion, weakness, and sleep disturbances are common. They lack interest and involvement in their life situations and have difficulty getting started on projects. Decreased physical activity is likely; and somatic complaints, usually gastrointestinal in nature, may occur.

Individuals with the 23/32 code type are rather passive, docile, and dependent. They are plagued by self-doubts; and they harbor feelings of inadequacy, insecurity, and helplessness. They tend to elicit helping behaviors from other people. However, persons with the 23/32 code type are very interested in achievement, status, and power. They may appear to be competitive, industrious, and driven; but they do not really place themselves in directly competitive situations where they might experience failure. They seek increased responsibility, but they dread the stress and pressure associated with it. They often feel that they do not get adequate recognition for their accomplishments, and they are easily hurt by even mild criticism.

Persons with the 23/32 code type tend to be emotionally overcontrolled. They have difficulty expressing their feelings, and they may feel bottled up much of the time. They tend to deny unacceptable impulses; and when denial fails, they feel anxious and guilty. Persons with the 23/32 code type feel socially inadequate, and they tend to avoid social involvement. They are especially uncomfortable with potential romantic or sexual partners, and sexual dysfunctions may be reported.

The 23/32 code type is more common for women than for men. Rather than indicating incapacitating symptoms, it suggests prolonged periods of suboptimal functioning. Problems are long-standing, and individuals with this code type have learned to tolerate a great deal of unhappiness. Among psychiatric patients, diagnoses of depressive disorders often are assigned to persons with the 23/32 code type. Antisocial personality disorder diagnoses are rare among persons with this code type.

Response to traditional psychotherapy is likely to be poor for persons with the 23/32 code type. They are not introspective, lack insight into their own behavior, resist psychological formulations of their problems, and tolerate a great deal of unhappiness before becoming motivated to change.

24/42

Persons with the 24/42 code type often come to the attention of professionals after they have been in trouble with their families or with the law. They are likely to appear angry, hostile, resentful, critical, argumentative, and untrusting. They are impulsive and struggle to delay gratification. They have little respect for social standards and often find themselves in direct conflict with societal values. Their acting-out behavior may involve excessive use of alcohol and other drugs, which is likely to have resulted in arrests, job loss, and family discord. Some patients with this code type have histories of eating disorders.

Individuals with the 24/42 code type feel frustrated by their own lack of accomplishment and are resentful of demands placed on them by other people. After periods of acting out, they may express a great deal of remorse and guilt about their misdeeds. They may report feeling depressed, anxious, and worthless; but others often question the sincerity of these expressions. Despite the frequent resolutions to change made by 24/42 persons, they are likely to act out again in the future. It has been noted in the literature that when Scales 2 and 4 are grossly elevated, suicidal ideation and attempts are quite possible. Often the suicide attempts seem to be directed at making other people feel guilty.

When they are not in trouble, 24/42 persons may seem to be energetic, sociable, and outgoing. They often create favorable first impressions, but their tendency to manipulate others commonly elicits feelings of resentment in long-term relationships. Beneath the outer facade of being competent, comfortable persons, 24/42 individuals tend to be introverted, self-conscious, and passive–dependent. They harbor feelings of inadequacy and self-dissatisfaction, and they are uncomfortable in social interactions—particularly those involving potential romantic or sexual partners. At times, they appear to be rigid and overly intellectualized.

Personality disorder diagnoses often are given to persons with the 24/42 code type, although among persons seeking treatment, diagnoses of depressive disorders are common. Although persons with this code type may express the need for help and the desire to change, the prognosis for traditional psychotherapy is not good. They are likely to terminate therapy prematurely when the situational stress subsides or when they have extracted themselves from their current difficulties. Even when they stay in therapy, not much improvement is likely.

26/62

There is only limited research concerning the correlates of this code type. Patients with the 26/62 code type have been described as having prominent personality problems, including suspiciousness and mistrust, resentfulness, hostility, and aggressiveness. They also may be described as depressed and fatigued, and they may be preoccupied with health problems. These individuals generally do not cope well with stress, experience sleep disturbances, lack energy, and feel hopeless. They may have past suicide attempts.

27/72

Persons with the 27/72 code type tend to be anxious, tense, and high-strung. They worry excessively, and they are very sensitive to real and imagined threat. They tend to anticipate problems that often do not occur and overreact to minor stress. Obsessive thoughts and compulsive behaviors often are reported. Somatic symptoms also are common among persons with this code type and involve rather vague complaints of fatigue, tiredness, and exhaustion. Insomnia, anorexia, and bulimia may be reported. Persons with this code type often show symptoms of clinical depression, including feelings of sadness, weight loss, lack of energy, slowed thought processes, and suicidal ideation. They may speak slowly and hesitantly. They feel pessimistic and hopeless about the world in general and more specifically about the likelihood of overcoming their problems, and they ruminate about their problems much of the time.

Individuals with the 27/72 code type are immature and have a strong need for achievement and for recognition of their accomplishments. They have high expectations for themselves, and they feel guilty when they fall short of their goals. They tend to be indecisive, and they harbor feelings of inadequacy, insecurity, and inferiority. They are intropunitive, blaming themselves for the problems in their life situations. Individuals with the 27/72 code type are rigid in their thinking and problem solving, and they are meticulous and perfectionist in their daily activities. They also may be very religious and extremely moralistic.

Persons with the 27/72 code type tend to be docile and passive–dependent in their relationships with other people. In fact, they often find it difficult to be even appropriately assertive. They have the capacity for forming deep, emotional ties; and in times of stress, they become overly clingy and dependent. They tend to elicit nurturance and helping behavior from other people.

Psychiatric patients with the 27/72 code type often have diagnoses of anxiety disorders, depressive disorders, or obsessive–compulsive disorder. Diagnoses of antisocial personality disorder are rare among persons with this code type. Because of the intense discomfort they experience, individuals with a 27/72 code type are motivated for psychotherapy. They tend to remain in psychotherapy longer than many patients, and slow but steady progress can be expected.

28/82

Persons with the 28/82 code type often report feeling anxious, agitated, tense, and jumpy. Sleep disturbance, inability to concentrate, confused thinking, and forgetfulness also characterize them. Such persons are inefficient in carrying out their responsibilities, and they tend to be unoriginal in their thinking and problem solving. They are likely to present themselves as physically ill; and somatic complaints may include dizziness, blackout spells, overeating, nausea, or vomiting. They resist psychological interpretations of their problems, and they are resistant to change. They underestimate the seriousness of their problems, and they tend to be unrealistic about their own capabilities.

Individuals with the 28/82 code type are basically dependent and ineffective, and they have problems in being assertive. They are irritable and resentful much of the time, fear loss of control, and do not express themselves directly. They attempt to deny undesirable impulses, and they may experience periods of cognitive dissociation during which they experience negative emotions that are not later remembered. When informed of these episodes, they may feel guilty and depressed. Persons with the 28/82 code type are sensitive to the reactions of others, and they are suspicious of the motivations of others. They may have histories of being hurt emotionally, and they fear being hurt again. They avoid close interpersonal relationships, and they keep people at a distance emotionally. This lack of meaningful involvement with other people increases their feelings of despair and worthlessness.

If both Scales 2 and 8 are very elevated, the 28/82 code type is suggestive of serious and chronic psychopathology. The most common diagnoses given to psychiatric patients with this code type are bipolar disorder and schizoaffective disorder. This is a common code type among patients who have been assigned posttraumatic stress disorder diagnoses. Individuals with this code type may be guilt-ridden and appear to be clinically depressed. Withdrawal, flat affect, soft and reduced speech, cognitive slowing, and tearfulness also are common. Psychiatric patients with the 28/82 code type may be preoccupied with suicidal thoughts, and they may have a specific plan for killing themselves.

29/92

Persons with the 29/92 code type tend to be self-centered and narcissistic. They ruminate excessively about self-worth. Although they may express concern about achieving at a high level, it often appears that they set themselves up for failure. In younger persons, the 29/92 code type may be suggestive of an identity crisis characterized by a lack of personal and vocational direction.

Persons with this code type report feeling tense and anxious; and somatic complaints, often centering on the upper gastrointestinal tract, are common. Although they may not appear to be clinically depressed at the time they are examined, their histories typically suggest periods of serious depression. Excessive use of alcohol may be employed as an escape from stress and pressure.

The 29/92 code type suggests individuals who are denying underlying feelings of inadequacy and worthlessness and defending against depression through excessive activity. Alternating periods of increased activity and fatigue may occur. Psychiatric patients with the 29/92 code type often are diagnosed with a bipolar disorder. This code type sometimes is found for patients with brain damage who have lost emotional control or who are trying to cope with deficits through excessive activity. It should be emphasized, however, that this code type or other MMPI-2 information should not be used to diagnose brain damage.

34/43

The most salient characteristic of 34/43 persons is chronic, intense anger. They harbor hostile and aggressive impulses, but they are unable to express their negative feelings appropriately. If Scale 3 is significantly higher than Scale 4, passive, indirect expression of anger is likely. Persons with Scale 4 significantly higher than Scale 3 appear to be overcontrolled most of the time, but brief episodes of aggressive acting out may occur. Prisoners with the 4–3 code type often have histories of violent crimes.

In some rare instances, individuals with the 34/43 code type successfully dissociate themselves from their aggressive acting-out behavior. Individuals with this code type lack insight into the origins and consequences of their behavior. They tend to be extrapunitive, blaming other people for their difficulties. Although others are likely to define the behavior of persons with this code type as problematic, they are not likely to view it in the same way.

Persons with the 34/43 code type are reasonably free of disabling anxiety and depression, but complaints of headaches, upper gastrointestinal discomfort, and other somatic distress may occur. Although these persons may experience psychological distress, the experience does not seem to be related directly to external stressors. Histories of excessive use of alcohol and other substances are frequently associated with this code type.

Many of the difficulties of persons with the 34/43 code type may stem from deep, chronic feelings of hostility toward family members. They demand attention and approval from others. They tend to be cynical and suspicious of others. They are sensitive to rejection, and they become hostile when criticized. Although outwardly they appear to be socially conforming, inwardly they are quite rebellious. They may be sexually maladjusted. Marital instability and sexual promiscuity are common. Suicidal thoughts and attempts are characteristic of individuals with the 34/43 code type and are most likely to follow episodes of excessive drinking and acting-out behavior. Personality disorder diagnoses, especially those characterized by passive–aggressive behaviors, often are associated with the 34/43 code type, and diagnoses of substance-related disorders may also be assigned.

36/63

Individuals with the 36/63 code type may report moderate tension and anxiety and may have physical complaints—including headaches and gastrointestinal discomfort—but their problems do not seem to be acute or incapacitating. Most of their difficulties may stem from deep, chronic feelings of hostility toward family members. They do not express these feelings directly, and much of the time they may not even recognize the hostile feelings. When they become aware of their anger, they try to justify it in terms of the behavior of others. In general, individuals with the 36/63 code type are defiant, uncooperative, and hard to get along with. They may express mild suspiciousness of and resentment about others. They are very self-centered and narcissistic. They deny serious psychological problems and express a very naive, Pollyannaish attitude toward the world.

38/83

Persons with the 38/83 code type appear to be in a great deal of psychological turmoil. They report feeling anxious, tense, and nervous. Also, they are fearful and worried, and phobias may be present. Depression and feelings of hopelessness are common among 38/83 individuals, and they struggle making even minor decisions. A wide variety of physical complaints (e.g., gastrointestinal and musculoskeletal discomfort, dizziness, blurred vision, chest pain, genital pain, headaches, insomnia) may be presented. They tend to be vague and evasive when talking about their complaints and difficulties.

Persons with the 38/83 code type are rather immature and dependent and have strong needs for attention and affection. They are not involved actively in their life situations, and they are apathetic and pessimistic. They approach problems in an unoriginal, stereotypical manner.

The 38/83 code type suggests the possibility of disturbed thinking, especially when both scales are quite elevated. Individuals with this code type may complain of not being able to think clearly, problems in concentration, and lapses of memory. They often express unusual, unconventional ideas, and their ideational associations may be rather loose. Obsessive ruminations, blatant delusions or hallucinations, and irrelevant, incoherent speech may be present. The most common diagnosis for psychiatric patients with the 38/83 code type is schizophrenia, but sometimes somatic symptom and related disorder diagnoses are assigned. Although response to insight-oriented psychotherapy is not likely to be good for persons with this code type, they often benefit from a supportive psychotherapeutic relationship.

46/64

Persons with the 46/64 code type seem to be immature, narcissistic, and self-indulgent. They are passive–dependent individuals who make excessive demands on others for attention and sympathy, but they are resentful of even the mildest demands made on them by others. Women with the 46/64 code type seem overly identified with a stereotypical feminine role and may be very dependent. Individuals with this code type do not get along well with others in social situations, and they are especially uncomfortable around potential romantic or sexual partners. They are suspicious of the motivations of others, feel they are getting a raw deal from life, and avoid deep emotional involvement. They often have poor work histories, and marital problems are quite common. Repressed hostility and anger are characteristic of persons with the 46/64 code type. They may appear sarcastic, irritable, sullen, argumentative, and generally obnoxious. They seem to be especially resentful of authority and may derogate authority figures.

Individuals with the 46/64 code type tend to deny serious psychological problems. They rationalize and transfer blame to others, especially family members, accepting little or no responsibility for their own behavior. They are somewhat unrealistic and grandiose in their self-appraisals. Because they deny serious emotional problems, they generally are not receptive to traditional counseling or psychotherapy.

Among psychiatric patients, frequent diagnoses associated with the 46/64 code are schizophrenia and personality disorders, especially those characterized by passive–aggressive behavior. Concerns about psychotic disorder are greater when Scales 4 and 6 are very elevated and when Scale 6 is higher than Scale 4. Psychiatric patients with this code type often have histories of substance abuse and difficulties with the law. Individuals with the 46/64 code type present vague emotional and physical complaints. They report feeling nervous and depressed, and they are indecisive and insecure. Physical symptoms may include asthma, hay fever, hypertension, headaches, blackout spells, and cardiac complaints.

47/74

Persons with the 47/74 code type may alternate between periods of gross insensitivity to the consequences of their actions and excessive concern about the effects of their behavior on others. Episodes of acting out, which may include excessive drinking and sexual promiscuity, may be followed by temporary expressions of guilt and self-condemnation. However, the remorse typically does not inhibit further episodes of acting out. Individuals with the 47/74 code type may present vague somatic complaints, including headaches and stomach pain. They also may report feeling tense, fatigued, and exhausted. They are rather dependent, insecure individuals who require almost constant reassurance of their self-worth. Personality disorder diagnoses, especially those characterized by passive–aggressive behavior, often are assigned to persons with the 47/74 code type. In psychotherapy, persons with this code type tend to experience reductions in symptoms when provided support and reassurance, but long-term changes in personality are unlikely.

48/84

Individuals with the 48/84 code type do not seem to fit into their environments. They are seen by others as odd, peculiar, and eccentric. They are nonconforming and resentful of authority, and they may espouse radical religious or political views. Their behavior is erratic and unpredictable, and they have marked problems with impulse control. They do not seem to learn from their mistakes. They tend to be angry, irritable, and resentful; and they may act out in asocial or antisocial ways. When crimes are committed by persons with this code type, the behaviors tend to be vicious and assaultive, often appearing senseless, poorly planned, and poorly executed. Prostitution, promiscuity, and sexual deviation are fairly common among individuals with the 48/84 code type. Excessive alcohol and drug use—particularly use of hallucinogens—may also occur. Histories of individuals with this code type usually indicate underachievement, uneven performance, marginal adjustment, and irresponsibility.

Persons with the 48/84 code type harbor deep feelings of insecurity, and they have exaggerated needs for attention and affection. They have poor self-concepts, and seemingly set themselves up for rejection and failure. They may have periods during which they experience frequent suicidal ideation and feel agitated and depressed. They are quite distrustful of other people, and they avoid close relationships. When they are involved interpersonally, they have impaired empathy and try to manipulate others into satisfying their needs. They lack basic social skills and tend to be socially withdrawn and isolated. The world is seen as a threatening and rejecting place. Their response to it is to withdraw or to strike out in anger as a defense against being hurt. They accept little responsibility for their own behavior, and they rationalize excessively, blaming their difficulties on other people. Persons with this code type tend to harbor serious concerns about their masculinity or femininity. Psychiatric patients with this code type are more likely than many other patients to have histories of being sexually abused. They may be preoccupied with sexual thoughts, but they are afraid they cannot perform adequately in sexual situations. They may indulge in excessive fantasy in an attempt to cope with these feelings of inadequacy. They may also engage in antisocial sexual acts.

Psychiatric patients with the 48/84 code type tend to have diagnoses of schizophrenia or personality disorders. If both Scales 4 and 8 are very elevated, and particularly if Scale 8 is much higher than Scale 4, the likelihood of psychosis and bizarre symptomatology—including hallucinations, unusual thinking, and paranoid suspiciousness—increases.

49/94

When both scales in the 49/94 code type are very elevated, a marked disregard for social standards and values is likely. Such persons frequently get in trouble with the authorities because of antisocial behavior. They seem to have a poorly developed conscience and fluctuating ethical values. Excessive alcohol use, fighting, marital problems, sexual acting out, and a wide array of delinquent acts are characteristic behaviors. This is a common code type among persons who misuse alcohol and other substances.

Individuals with the 49/94 code type are narcissistic, selfish, and self-indulgent. They are quite impulsive and are unable to delay gratification of their impulses. They show poor judgment—often acting without considering the consequences of their behavior—and they fail to learn from experience. They are not willing to accept responsibility for their actions, instead rationalizing shortcomings and failures as well as blaming difficulties on other people. They have low frustration tolerance; and they often appear moody, irritable, and caustic. They harbor intense feelings of anger and hostility, which are expressed in occasional emotional outbursts.

Persons with the 49/94 code type tend to be ambitious, energetic, restless, and overactive. They often seek out emotional stimulation and excitement. In social situations, they tend to be uninhibited, extroverted, and talkative; and they create a good first impression. However, due to self-centeredness and distrust of people, their relationships are likely to be superficial and not particularly rewarding. They seem incapable of forming deep emotional ties, and they keep others at an emotional distance. Beneath the facade of self-confidence and security, individuals with the 49/94 code type are immature, insecure, and dependent persons who are trying to deny these aspects of themselves. A diagnosis of antisocial personality disorder is often associated with the 49/94 code type, although psychiatric patients with this code type sometimes have symptoms of bipolar disorder or disorders characterized by paranoid thinking.

68/86

Persons with the 68/86 code type harbor intense feelings of inferiority and insecurity. They lack self-confidence and self-esteem, and they feel guilty about perceived failures. Anxiety, depression, withdrawal from everyday activities, and emotional apathy are common. Feelings of hopelessness and pessimism as well as suicidal ideation may be present.

Persons with the 68/86 code type are not likely to be emotionally involved with other people, and they tend to have histories of having few or no friends. They are suspicious and distrustful of others, and they avoid deep emotional ties. They are seriously deficient in social skills and are most comfortable when alone. They are quite resentful of demands placed on them; and other people see them as moody, irritable, unfriendly, and negativistic. They do not make good first impressions and are seen by others as odd or strange. They are not very work oriented and do not have strong achievement orientations. In general, their lifestyles can be characterized as solitary.

Diagnoses of paranoid or schizoid personality disorders are common among persons with this code type. Psychiatric patients with this code type often are assigned a diagnosis of schizophrenia particularly if Scales 6 and 8 are both quite elevated and are considerably higher than Scale 7. Such individuals are likely to manifest clearly psychotic behavior. These individuals tend to be preoccupied with their inner world; and their thinking can be described as fragmented, tangential, and circumstantial. Thought content is likely to be bizarre. Difficulties in concentrating and attending, deficits in memory, and poor judgment are common. Delusions of persecution or grandeur as well as hallucinations may be present. Feelings of unreality may also be reported.

Persons with the 68/86 code type often are preoccupied with abstract or theoretical matters to the exclusion of specific, concrete aspects of their life situations. Their affect may be blunted, and their speech may be rapid and at times incoherent. They seem to lack effective defenses and respond to stress and pressure by withdrawing into fantasy and daydreaming. Often it is difficult for persons with this code type to differentiate between fantasy and reality. Medical consultation to determine appropriateness of antipsychotic medication should be considered.

69/96

Persons with the 69/96 code type are rather dependent and have strong needs for affection. They are sensitive to real or imagined threat, and they feel anxious and tense much of the time. In addition, they may appear tearful and trembling. A marked overreaction to minor stress also is characteristic of persons with the 69/96 code type. A typical response to severe stress is withdrawal into fantasy. These individuals are unable to express emotions in an adaptive, modulated way. They may alternate between over and undercontrolled emotional outbursts.

Psychiatric patients with the 69/96 code type frequently have diagnoses of schizophrenia, and they are likely to show signs of thought disorder, especially if both scales are quite elevated. They complain of difficulties in thinking and concentrating, and their stream of thought may be slowed. They are ruminative, overideational, and obsessional. They may have delusions and hallucinations, and their speech seems to be irrelevant and incoherent. They may appear disoriented and perplexed, and they may show poor judgment.

78/87

Individuals with the 78/87 code type typically are in a great deal of emotional turmoil. They readily admit to psychological problems, and they seem to lack adequate defenses to keep themselves reasonably comfortable. They report feeling depressed and pessimistic, and they may experience suicidal ideation. They also tend to be worried, tense, and anxious; and they are preoccupied with health problems. When first seen professionally, they may appear to be confused and in a state of panic. They show poor judgment and do not learn from experience. They are introspective, ruminative, and overideational.

Persons with the 78/87 code type harbor chronic feelings of insecurity, inadequacy, and inferiority; and they tend to be indecisive. They lack even an average number of socialization experiences, are not socially poised or confident, and withdraw from social interactions. They are passive–dependent individuals who are unable to take a dominant role in interpersonal relationships. Sexual relationships are especially difficult for them. They often feel quite inadequate, and sexual performance may be poor. In an apparent attempt to compensate for these deficits, they may engage in rich sexual fantasies.

Diagnoses of schizophrenia, depressive disorders, obsessive–compulsive disorder, posttraumatic stress disorder, and personality disorders are all represented among individuals with the 78/87 code type. Schizoid is the most common personality disorder diagnosis assigned to persons with this code type. The relative elevations of Scales 7 and 8 are important in differentiating psychotic from nonpsychotic disorders. When Scale 8 is much higher than Scale 7, the likelihood of a psychotic disorder is greater. Even when a psychotic label is applied to persons with the 78/87 code type, blatant psychotic symptoms may not be present.

89/98

Persons with the 89/98 code type tend to be rather self-centered and infantile in their expectations of other people. They demand a great deal of attention and may become resentful and hostile when their demands are not met. Because they fear emotional involvement, they avoid close relationships and tend to be socially withdrawn and isolated. They seem especially uncomfortable in sexual relationships, and poor sexual adjustment is common.

Individuals with this code type are characterized as hyperactive and emotionally labile. They appear agitated and excited, often talking excessively in a loud voice. They are unrealistic in their self-appraisal; and others find them grandiose, boastful, and fickle. They are vague, evasive, and deny talking about their difficulties; and they may state they do not need professional help.

Although persons with the 89/98 code type have a high need to achieve and may feel pressured to do so, their actual performance tends to be mediocre at best. Their feelings of inferiority and inadequacy as well as their low self-esteem limit the extent to which they involve themselves in competitive or achievement-oriented situations. They engage in excessive fantasy and daydreaming.

The 89/98 code type is suggestive of serious psychological disturbance, particularly when Scales 8 and 9 are quite elevated. The most common diagnosis for persons with this code type is schizophrenia, and severe thought disorder may be evident. Such individuals are likely to be confused, perplexed, and disoriented; and they may report feelings of unreality. They have difficulty concentrating. They may seem preoccupied with their inner experiences; and thinking may appear odd, unusual, and circumstantial. Their speech may be disorganized—including clang associations, neologisms, and echolalia. Delusions and hallucinations may be present.

INTERPRETIVE GUIDELINES FOR THREE-POINT CODE TYPES

As stated earlier in this chapter, three-point code types tell us which three Clinical scale scores are the highest in the profile. Far less research has been conducted concerning three-point code types than two-point code types. The three-point code types included in this section are those that occur reasonably frequently in a variety of clinical settings and for which some empirical data are available. Because profiles classified according to three-point code types result in rather homogeneous groupings, the descriptors presented for any particular code type are likely to fit many individuals with that code type rather well. However, it must again be emphasized that the descriptions provided represent modal patterns. Not every descriptor will apply to every person with a particular three-point code type.

Unlike two-point code types, the scales in three-point code types are not interchangeable. For example, though the 123/213/231 code type is made up of the same scales that comprise the 132/321 code type, individuals who have these two code types are likely to have some different characteristics and difficulties. In this case, the 123/213/231 is more characteristic of generalized somatic complaints, while the 132/321 suggests conversion-type difficulties. Thus, when a three-point code type is identified, it is important to not only consider which three Clinical scales have the highest scores and whether the identified code type is well-defined, but also the order of the scales that comprise the three-point code type.

123/213/231

Persons with this code type usually are diagnosed as having somatic symptom and related disorders, anxiety disorders, or depressive disorders. Somatic complaints—particularly those associated with the gastrointestinal system—are common, and often there appears to be clear secondary gain associated with the symptoms. Persons with this code type often show signs of depression. Sleep disturbance, perplexity, despondency, and feelings of hopelessness and pessimism occur often. Persons with this code type may feel life is a strain and may abuse alcohol and other substances as a way of coping. They vacillate between dependency and self-assertion, and they often keep other people at an emotional distance. They tend to feel fatigued as well as have low energy and sex drive. Such persons may show relatively good work and marital adjustment, but they are not very achievement oriented and rarely take risks in their lives.

132/312

This configuration, in which Scales 1 and 3 often are significantly higher than Scale 2, has been referred to as the "conversion valley." Persons with this code type may show classic conversion symptoms, and diagnoses of conversion disorder or somatic symptom disorder (with or without the predominant pain specifier) are common. Physical symptoms often develop during times of increased stress. Persons with this code type use denial and repression excessively, lack insight into the causes of their symptoms, and resist psychological explanations of their problems. Although these individuals are rather sociable, they tend to be passive–dependent in relationships. It is important for them to be liked and approved of by others, and their behavior typically is conforming and conventional. They tend to seek medical treatment for their symptoms and are likely to terminate treatment prematurely if they are pressed to deal with psychological matters.

138

Persons with this code type frequently have diagnoses of schizophrenia or paranoid personality disorder. They are likely to have rather bizarre somatic symptoms that may be delusional in nature. Depressive episodes, suicidal ideation, and sexual or religious preoccupation may occur. Clear evidence of thought disorder may be observed. These individuals are often agitated, excitable, loud, and short-tempered. They typically have histories of excessive use of alcohol and feel restless and bored much of the time. They are ambivalent about forming close relationships, and they often feel suspicious and jealous.

139

Persons with this code type often are diagnosed as having a somatic symptom or related somatic disorder or an organic brain disorder. If they are given the latter diagnosis, they may show spells of irritation, physical aggression, and outbursts of temper. It should be emphasized that this code type or other MMPI-2 data should not be used to arrive at organic diagnoses.

237/273/372

Persons with this code type are likely to report physical complaints and symptoms of depression and anxiety. In addition, they may find it difficult to trust other people.

247/274/472

Persons with this code type frequently have diagnoses of a personality disorder, especially those that include passive–aggressive behaviors. This is a very common code type among patients who abuse alcohol or other substances. Family and marital problems are common among these individuals. They may feel depressed and pessimistic, and they may experience suicidal ideation and obsessive–compulsive thoughts and behaviors. They also may feel anxious, fearful, worried, and highstrung. They overreact to stress and exhibit poor impulse control. They tend to be angry, hostile, and immature, with strong unfilled needs for attention and support. They may feel they are getting a raw deal from life. They may be in conflict about dependency and sexuality, or express being uncomfortable around potential romantic or sexual partners. They tend to be phobic, ruminative, and overideational; and they experience guilt associated with their anger. Although they often have strong achievement needs, they are afraid to compete for fear of failing. They have difficulty enduring anxiety during treatment and may respond best to directive, goal-oriented treatment.

278/728

Persons with this code type experience a great deal of emotional turmoil, and they tend to have rather solitary lifestyles. They tend to feel tense, nervous, and fearful; and they have problems in concentrating and attending. They may also feel sad, depressed, despondent, pessimistic, and hopeless; and they often ruminate about suicide. However, their affect appears to be blunted or otherwise inappropriate. Multiple somatic complaints may be presented, and eating problems often are reported by women with this code type. Psychiatric patients with this code type are more likely than other patients to have histories of having been sexually abused. These persons lack basic social skills and are shy, withdrawn, introverted, and socially isolated. They tend to be passive in relationships. They feel inadequate and inferior. They tend to set high standards for themselves and feel guilty when these standards are not met. They tend to show interest in obscure, esoteric subjects. They may use alcohol or other drugs as a way of coping with stress.

The diagnostic picture for the 278/728 code type is mixed. Diagnoses of depressive disorders and anxiety disorders are common. Schizophrenia spectrum and other psychotic disorders, as well as Cluster A personality disorders (i.e., paranoid, schizoid, and schizotypal), are also frequent diagnoses assigned to individuals with this code type. In making a differential diagnosis, it often is helpful to try to understand why Scale 8 is elevated along with Scales 2 and 7. If examination of the Harris–Lingoes subscales indicates that the Scale 8 elevation is accounted for primarily by items in the Sc3 (Lack of Ego Mastery, Cognitive) or Sc6 (Bizarre Sensory Experiences) subscales, a psychotic disorder is more likely than if items in the Sc4 (Lack of Ego Mastery, Conative) seem to account for much of the Scale 8 elevation. High scores on the Bizarre Mentation (BIZ) Content scale or the RC8 (Aberrant Experiences) scale also support psychotic diagnoses.

468/648/684/846/864

There is not much research concerning the correlates of this code type. However, mental health center clients with this code type have been described as being in acute psychological turmoil. They were anxious, depressed, and agitated. They were more likely than other clients to have diagnoses of major depressive disorder, persistent depressive disorder (dysthymia), and antisocial personality disorder. They also were more likely to have histories of previous psychiatric hospitalizations, suicide attempts, and having been physically abused. Some of these clients had psychotic symptoms, including paranoid ideation. They tended to be antisocial and to have low tolerance for frustration. They were seen as critical, hostile, angry, aggressive, argumentative, and resentful. They often had family and work problems.

478/748

Although there are limited data concerning correlates of this code type, mental health center clients with the 478/748 code type were described as having psychotic symptoms, including delusions, hallucinations, loose cognitive associations, and poor reality testing. They were characterized as eccentric and suspicious, and they tended to have past psychiatric hospitalizations. Depression, suicidal ideation, anxiety, and agitation also were characteristic of these clients. They were seen as histrionic, insecure, and introverted persons who tended to make self-degrading comments and to engage in self-punishing behaviors.

687/867

This code type, in which Scales 6 and 8 typically are much more elevated than Scale 7, has been referred to as the "psychotic valley." It suggests very serious psychopathology, and the most common diagnosis for persons with the code type is schizophrenia. Hallucinations, delusions, and extreme suspiciousness are common. Their affect tends to be blunted. Persons with this code type tend to be shy, introverted, and socially withdrawn, but they may become quite aggressive when consuming alcohol. They tend to have problems with memory and concentration. Although persons with this code type may not be experiencing disabling emotional turmoil, they often are unable to handle the responsibilities of everyday life and may require inpatient treatment. Psychotropic medications often are prescribed.

OTHER CONFIGURAL ASPECTS

Regardless of their absolute elevations and whether or not they are the highest scales in the profile, the relative elevations of Scales 1, 2, and 3 provide important interpretive information. When Scales 1 and 3 are 10 or more T-score points higher than Scale 2, individuals probably are using denial and repression excessively. They tend to have little or no insight into their own needs, conflicts, or symptoms. They are reasonably free of depression, anxiety, and other emotional turmoil; but somatic symptoms are likely. These persons seek medical explanations for their problems and are resistant to psychological explanations. When Scale 2 is equal to or higher than Scales 1 and 3, the individuals are not likely to be so well defended. They may report emotional turmoil and a wide variety of symptoms.

The relationship between Scales 3 and 4 gives important information about anger control. Even when these two scales are not the most elevated ones in the profile, their relative positions are meaningful. When Scale 4 is 10 or more T-score points higher than Scale 3, problems with poor control of anger are common. Such persons tend to express anger openly without adequately considering the consequences of their actions. When Scale 3 is 10 or more T-score points higher than Scale 4, we expect the individual to have adequate control of their emotions, and they are not likely to express anger openly. When scores on Scales 3 and 4 are about equally elevated—especially when they are both above T scores of 65—persons may be overcontrolled and not express anger openly most of the time, but periodic angry outbursts may occur.

CHAPTER 6

CONTENT INTERPRETATION

HATHAWAY AND MCKINLEY UTILIZED empirical keying procedures to construct the original MMPI Clinical scales. Items were included in a scale if they empirically differentiated between diagnostic criterion groups. Little emphasis was placed on the content of the items identified in this manner, and only for Scale 7 were attempts made to ensure internal consistency. This approach was purposeful, reflecting efforts to shift away from interpretations that assumed test takers interpreted and responded to item content in the same way and move toward interpretations based in empirical findings (Meehl, 1945). In fact, early in the history of the MMPI, some clinicians seemed to believe that examination of the content of the items endorsed by test takers would spoil the empirical approach to assessment.

As use of the MMPI progressed, however, others argued that item content likely reflected important information about how the test taker viewed themselves and their difficulties (e.g., Wiggins, 1966). Thus, interpretation of the instrument shifted toward interpretative strategies that combined both the test taker's responses to content and empirical findings about what scale scores were likely to mean about a test taker's social, emotional, and behavioral functioning. The purpose of this chapter is to discuss some approaches to the interpretation of content dimensions of the MMPI-2. These approaches are viewed as supplementary to empirical interpretation of the standard MMPI-2 Clinical scales and should not be used instead of them.

THE HARRIS–LINGOES SUBSCALES

Development of the Harris–Lingoes Subscales

Because little attention was given by Hathaway and McKinley to scale homogeneity, most of the standard Clinical scales are quite heterogeneous in terms of item content. The same total raw score on a Clinical scale can be obtained by individuals endorsing very different combinations of items. Some investigators suggested that systematic analysis of subgroups of items within the standard MMPI Clinical scales could add significantly to the interpretation of protocols (e.g., Comrey, 1957a, 1957b, 1957c, 1958a, 1958b, 1958c, 1958d; Comrey & Marggraff, 1958; Graham et al., 1971; Harris & Lingoes, 1955, 1968; Pepper & Strong, 1958).

The subscales developed by Harris and Lingoes (1955, 1968) represent the most comprehensive effort of this kind. Their scales have come to be widely used clinically and are routinely scored and reported by automated scoring and interpretation services. Harris and Lingoes constructed subscales for 6 of the 10 standard Clinical scales (Scales 2, 3, 4, 6, 8, and 9). They did not develop subscales for Scales 1 or 7 because they considered them to have homogeneous content. Harris and Lingoes also did not develop subscales for Scales 5 and 0 because these scales were not considered to be standard Clinical scales.

Each of the Harris–Lingoes subscales was constructed rationally by examining the content of items within a standard Clinical scale and grouping together items that seemed similar or were judged to reflect a single attitude or trait. A label was assigned to each subscale on the basis of the investigators' clinical judgments of the content of items in the subscale. Harris and Lingoes did not avoid placing an item in more than one subscale. Thus, item overlap among the subscales is considerable and may account, at least in part, for the high correlations between certain subscales. In total, Harris and Lingoes developed 31 subscales; however, three subscales that involve combining items from several other subscales generally are not scored or used in clinical interpretation.

Although the Harris–Lingoes subscales were constructed using the MMPI item pool, they can be scored for the MMPI-2. However, several items scored on some of the subscales were deleted during the MMPI revision process, so the MMPI-2 has fewer items for those subscales. Although only a few items were deleted, some of the subscales were already so short that the deletions are of serious concern. The MMPI-2 booklet numbers of the items in each Harris–Lingoes subscale and the scored response for each item are presented in Appendix B of the MMPI-2 manual (Butcher et al., 2001). Linear T-score transformations for the Harris–Lingoes subscale raw scores based on data from the MMPI-2 normative sample are presented by gender in Appendix A of the MMPI-2 manual (Butcher et al., 2001). Score transformations based on the non-gendered normative data are available in the Appendix of Ben-Porath and Forbey's (2003) non-gendered norms monograph.

Reliability of the Harris–Lingoes Subscales

Harris and Lingoes (1955) reasoned intuitively that the subscales should be more homogeneous than the parent scales from which they were drawn, but they did not offer any evidence in this regard. Unpublished analyses of the MMPI-2 normative data provide mixed evidence in support of this assumption, as internal consistency (α) of the subscales ranged from .17 (Hy5) to .73 (Hy1) for men (n = 1,138; median = .57) and from .11 (Hy5) to .74 (D1 & Hy1) for women (n = 1,462; median = .57).[1]

The test–retest data from the MMPI-2 normative sample were used to calculate the test–retest correlation in the subset of men and women who took the test two times (9 days apart on average). Results suggest that the temporal stability of the subscales is less than the parent scales, but stability is adequate for most scales. Test–retest coefficients ranged from .58 (Pa3) to .86 (Hy1 & Hy3) for men (n = 82; median = .76) and from .58 (Ma4) to .88 (Hy3) for women (n = 111; median = .75).

Validity of the Harris–Lingoes Subscales

Although the Harris–Lingoes subscales have been in existence for more than 65 years and have gained fairly wide usage among clinicians (largely because they are scored routinely by some automated scoring and interpretation services), only limited empirical research concerning the validity of these subscales has been published. This dearth of published research is especially true if the review is limited to only those studies using the MMPI-2.

Graham et al. (1999) reported correlations between MMPI-2 versions of the Harris–Lingoes subscale scores and extratest characteristics for a large sample of mental health center outpatients. Their results indicated that most of the subscales have reliable extratest correlates and that the correlates are consistent with the symptoms, behaviors, and characteristics suggested by the item content of each scale. However, results suggested the subscale scores generally have poor discriminant validity, as indicated by meaningful associations between specific subscales and extratest characteristics that would not be expected based on scale content.

Yamout and colleagues (2017) examined the ability of scores on Clinical Scales 1 and 3, Harris–Lingoes Hy4 (Somatic Complaints), and Restructured Clinical Scale 1 to detect nonepileptic events (i.e., a non-epileptic or pseudo-seizure where an individual has behavioral symptoms of a seizure that are not accompanied by electrographic changes). Results indicated when using a traditional cut score of T > 65, scores on Hy4 were better at discriminating accurately between individuals experiencing epileptic and nonepileptic seizures than scores on the other examined Clinical and Restructured Clinical scales.

Two MMPI-2 studies have examined relationships between Scale 4 and the Harris–Lingoes Pd subscales and measures of psychopathy and antisocial behavior. Meloy and Gacono (1995) found the Pd2 (Authority Problems) subscale was a better predictor than Scale 4 of scores on the Hare Psychopathy Checklist-Revised (Hare, 1991). Lilienfeld (1999) reported similar results using his Psychopathic Personality Inventory (Lilienfeld & Andrews, 1996) as a criterion measure.

---

[1] The source of the internal consistency (α) estimates and the test–retest correlations is unpublished analyses of data collected during the MMPI restandardization project. These data are available from the first author (JRG).

Evidence supporting the construct validity of the Harris–Lingoes subscales is mixed. For example, work by Comrey (1957a, 1957b, 1957c, 1958a, 1958b, 1958c, 1958d; Comrey & Marggraff, 1958) has suggested there were some significant differences between the logically derived Harris–Lingoes subscales and factors derived from analysis of the MMPI item pool. However, in general, the Comrey studies revealed factors within each Clinical scale that are similar to the Harris–Lingoes subscales. However, Almagor and Koren (2001) factor analyzed items in MMPI-2 versions of the Harris–Lingoes subscales using large samples of Israeli and American psychiatric patients. Their results generally did not support the Harris–Lingoes breakdown of most Clinical scales into specific content areas.

Interpretive Guidelines for the Harris–Lingoes Subscales

Scores on the Harris–Lingoes subscales provide information concerning the kinds of items endorsed in the scored direction on a particular Clinical scale. As with many of the other scales discussed in this book, it is not possible to establish absolutely firm cutoff scores to define high scorers on the Harris–Lingoes subscales. Generally, high scores have been defined as T scores greater than 65. However, because some of the subscales have very few items and are relatively unreliable, and because there is only limited research concerning extratest correlates of the subscales, they should not be interpreted independently of their parent Clinical scale. Thus, the subscales generally should not be interpreted unless their parent Clinical scale is significantly elevated (T ≥ 65).

Use of the Harris–Lingoes subscales should be limited to trying to understand why high scores have been obtained on the Clinical scales. For example, an individual with self-reported and observed difficulties with depression who has a substantial history of treatment for these types of symptoms could produce a profile with elevations on Scales 2, 7, and 8. The Scale 2 and Scale 7 elevations are consistent with the person's history and with clinical observation. However, the Scale 8 elevation is somewhat troublesome. Why does this individual, for whom there is no history or clinical indication of thought disorder, score relatively high on Scale 8? Reference to the Harris–Lingoes subscale scores might reveal that most of the Scale 8 elevation is coming from items in the Lack of Ego Mastery, Conative (Sc4) subscale. This subscale assesses depression and despair and whether the patient feels that life is a strain much of the time. These characteristics would be highly consistent with those based on the rest of the profile and with the individual's history.

The Harris–Lingoes subscales can also be considered in relation to the empirical correlates for the Clinical scales. For any of the Clinical scales, a variety of behaviors and characteristics has been associated with higher scores. For example, elevated scores on Scale 4 have been associated with family problems, antisocial behavior, and absence of social anxiety. Usually, not all of the descriptors associated with elevated scores on a scale will be characteristic of any specific individual with an elevated score on that scale. Examination of the Harris–Lingoes subscales can be helpful in determining which of the many different descriptors should be emphasized. For example, if an individual had a high score on Clinical Scale 4 and achieved a high score on Pd1

(Familial Discord) but not on other Scale 4 subscales, in our interpretation, we would emphasize the correlates associated with family problems. On the other hand, if the Pd2 (Authority Problems) subscale was the only elevated Scale 4 subscale, we would emphasize the correlates having to do with acting-out behaviors.

Given limited reliability and validity evidence supporting their use, we recommend interpretation of the Harris–Lingoes subscales include only content interpretation. As such, the descriptions that follow for the subscales are based primarily on examination of the content of the items in each subscale. The descriptions can be used to generate hypotheses concerning why persons have obtained high scores on the parent Clinical scales. Because not every descriptor will be characteristic of every person who has a high score on a subscale, the hypotheses need to be evaluated in relation to other information available about the person being assessed. Descriptions are not provided for low scorers on the subscales because it is difficult to know what low scores mean. Therefore, it is recommended that low scores on the Harris–Lingoes subscales not be interpreted.

SUBJECTIVE DEPRESSION (D1)

High scorers on the D1 subscale report that they

1. feel unhappy, blue, or depressed much of the time
2. lack energy for coping with the problems of their everyday lives
3. are not interested in what goes on around them
4. feel nervous or tense much of the time
5. have difficulties in concentrating and attending
6. have poor appetite and trouble sleeping
7. brood and cry frequently
8. lack self-confidence
9. feel inferior and useless
10. are easily hurt by criticism
11. feel uneasy, shy, and embarrassed in social situations
12. tend to avoid interactions with other people, except for relatives and close friends

PSYCHOMOTOR RETARDATION (D2)
High scorers on the D2 subscale report that they

1. feel immobilized and withdrawn
2. lack energy to cope with everyday activities
3. avoid other people
4. do not have hostile or aggressive impulses

PHYSICAL MALFUNCTIONING (D3)
High scorers on the D3 subscale report that they

1. are preoccupied with their own physical functioning
2. do not have good health

3. experience a wide variety of specific somatic symptoms that may include weakness, hay fever or asthma, poor appetite, nausea or vomiting, and convulsions

MENTAL DULLNESS (D4)
High scorers on the D4 subscale report that they

1. lack energy to cope with the problems of everyday life
2. feel tense
3. experience difficulties in concentrating
4. have poor memory and/or show poor judgment
5. lack self-confidence
6. feel inferior to others
7. get little enjoyment out of life
8. may have concluded that life is no longer worthwhile

BROODING (D5)
High scorers on the D5 subscale report that they

1. brood, ruminate, and cry much of the time
2. lack energy to cope with problems
3. may have concluded that life is no longer worthwhile
4. feel inferior, unhappy, and useless
5. are easily hurt by criticism
6. may feel that they are losing control of their thought processes

DENIAL OF SOCIAL ANXIETY (Hy1)
Because it is not possible to obtain a T score greater than 65 on this subscale (Krishnamurthy et al., 1995), it is not helpful in understanding why a high score was obtained on Scale 3.

NEED FOR AFFECTION (Hy2)
High scorers on the Hy2 subscale report that they

1. have strong needs for attention and affection from others and fear that those needs will not be met if they are more honest about their feelings and attitudes
2. have optimistic and trusting attitudes toward other people
3. see others as honest, sensitive, and reasonable
4. do not have negative feelings about other people
5. try to avoid unpleasant confrontations whenever possible

LASSITUDE–MALAISE (Hy3)
High scorers on the Hy3 subscale report that they

1. feel uncomfortable and are not in good health
2. feel weak, fatigued, or tired
3. do not have specific somatic complaints
4. have difficulties in concentrating, poor appetite, and sleep disturbance
5. feel unhappy and blue
6. see their home environments as unpleasant and uninteresting

SOMATIC COMPLAINTS (Hy4)

High scorers on the Hy4 subscale report that they

1. have many somatic complaints
2. experience pain in the heart and/or chest
3. have fainting spells, dizziness, or balance problems
4. experience nausea and vomiting, poor vision, shakiness, or feeling too hot or too cold
5. express little or no hostility toward other people

INHIBITION OF AGGRESSION (Hy5)

High scorers on the Hy5 subscale report that they

1. do not experience hostile and aggressive impulses
2. are not interested in reading about crime and violence
3. are sensitive about how others respond to them
4. are decisive

While items on Hy5 reflect the content described above, the internal consistency of this subscale is so low that it is not likely to be very useful in understanding why a high score was obtained on Scale 3 (e.g., α = .17 and .11 in men and women, respectively, who provided data during the MMPI restandardization project).

FAMILIAL DISCORD (Pd1)

High scorers on the Pd1 subscale report that they

1. see their home and family situations as quite unpleasant
2. have felt like leaving their home situations
3. see their homes as lacking in love, understanding, and support
4. feel that their families are critical, quarrelsome, and refuse to permit adequate freedom and independence

AUTHORITY PROBLEMS (Pd2)

High scorers on the Pd2 subscale report that they

1. resent societal and parental standards and customs
2. have been in trouble in school or with the law
3. have definite opinions about what is right and wrong
4. stand up for what they believe
5. are not greatly influenced by the values and standards of others

SOCIAL IMPERTURBABILITY (Pd3)

Because it is not possible to obtain a T score greater than 65 on this subscale (Krishnamurthy et al., 1995), it is not helpful in understanding why a high score was obtained on Scale 4.

SOCIAL ALIENATION (Pd4)

High scorers on the Pd4 subscale report that they

1. feel alienated, isolated, and estranged

2. feel that other people do not understand them
3. feel lonely, unhappy, and unloved
4. feel that they get a raw deal from life
5. see other people as responsible for their problems and shortcomings
6. are concerned about how other people react to them
7. experience regret, guilt, and remorse for their actions

SELF-ALIENATION (Pd5)
High scorers on the Pd5 subscale report that they

1. are uncomfortable and unhappy
2. have problems in concentrating
3. do not find daily life interesting or rewarding
4. experience regret, guilt, and remorse for past deeds but are vague about the nature of this misbehavior
5. find it hard to settle down
6. may use alcohol excessively

PERSECUTORY IDEAS (Pa1)
High scorers on the Pa1 subscale report that they

1. view the world as a threatening place
2. feel that they are getting a raw deal from life
3. feel misunderstood
4. feel that others have unfairly blamed or punished them
5. are suspicious and untrusting of other people
6. blame others for their own problems and shortcomings
7. feel that others are trying to influence or control them
8. believe that others are trying to poison or otherwise harm them

POIGNANCY (Pa2)
High scorers on the Pa2 subscale report that they
1. are more high-strung and more sensitive than other people
2. feel more intensely than others
3. feel lonely and misunderstood
4. look for risky or exciting activities to make them feel better

NAIVETE (Pa3)
High scorers on the Pa3 subscale report that they

1. have very optimistic attitudes about other people
2. see others as honest, unselfish, generous, and altruistic
3. are trusting
4. have high moral standards
5. do not experience hostility and negative impulses

SOCIAL ALIENATION (Sc1)

High scorers on the Sc1 subscale report that they

1. are getting a raw deal from life
2. believe that other people do not understand them
3. believe that other people have it in for them
4. believe that other people are trying to harm them
5. feel that their family situations are lacking in love and support
6. feel that their families treat them more as children than as adults
7. feel lonely and empty
8. have never had love relationships with anyone
9. harbor hostility and hatred toward family members

EMOTIONAL ALIENATION (Sc2)

High scorers on the Sc2 subscale report that they

1. experience feelings of depression and despair
2. may wish that they were dead
3. are apathetic and frightened
4. have sadistic or masochistic needs

LACK OF EGO MASTERY, COGNITIVE (Sc3)

High scorers on the Sc3 subscale report that they

1. feel that they might be losing their minds
2. have strange thought processes and feelings of unreality
3. have problems with concentration and memory

LACK OF EGO MASTERY, CONATIVE (Sc4)

High scorers on the Sc4 subscale report that they

1. feel that life is a strain and that they experience depression and despair
2. have difficulty in coping with everyday problems and worry excessively
3. respond to stress by withdrawing into fantasy and daydreaming
4. do not find their daily activities interesting and rewarding
5. have given up hope of things getting better
6. may wish that they were dead

LACK OF EGO MASTERY, DEFECTIVE INHIBITION (Sc5)

High scorers on the Sc5 subscale report that they

1. feel that they are not in control of their emotions and impulses and are frightened by this perceived loss of control
2. tend to be restless, hyperactive, and irritable
3. may have periods of laughing and crying that they cannot control
4. may have experienced episodes during which they did not know what they were doing and later could not remember what they had done

BIZARRE SENSORY EXPERIENCES (Sc6)

High scorers on the Sc6 subscale report that they

1. experience feelings that their bodies are changing in strange and unusual ways
2. experience skin sensitivity, feeling hot or cold, voice changes, muscle twitching, clumsiness, problems in balance, ringing or buzzing in the ears, paralysis, and weakness
3. experience hallucinations, unusual thought content, and ideas of external influence

AMORALITY (Ma1)

High scorers on the Ma1 subscale report that they

1. perceive other people as selfish, dishonest, and opportunistic and because of these perceptions feel justified in behaving in similar ways
2. derive vicarious satisfaction from the manipulative exploits of others

PSYCHOMOTOR ACCELERATION (Ma2)

High scorers on the Ma2 subscale report that they

1. experience acceleration of speech, thought processes, and motor activity
2. feel tense and restless
3. feel excited or elated without cause
4. become bored easily and seek out risk, excitement, or danger as a way of overcoming the boredom
5. have impulses to do something harmful or shocking

IMPERTURBABILITY (Ma3)

High scorers on the Ma3 subscale report that they

1. do not experience social anxiety
2. feel comfortable around other people
3. have no problem in talking with others
4. are not concerned about the opinions, values, and attitudes of other people
5. feel impatient and irritable toward others

EGO INFLATION (Ma4)

High scorers on the Ma4 subscale report that they

1. are important persons
2. are resentful when others make demands on them, particularly if the persons making the demands are perceived as less capable
3. have been treated unfairly

SUBSCALES FOR SCALE 0

Development of the Scale 0 Subscales of the MMPI-2

As stated previously, Harris and Lingoes (1955, 1968) did not develop subscales for Scales 5 and 0 because these were not considered standard Clinical scales. Research suggested, however, that Scale 0 content was quite heterogeneous. As such, Ben-Porath and colleagues (1989) developed Scale 0 subscales for the MMPI-2. Factor analyses of Scale 0 item responses provided by college students who identified as men or women were used to construct provisional subscales. Internal consistency procedures were then used to refine the subscales. The three subscales resulting from these procedures are mutually exclusive, internally consistent, moderately independent, and representative of the major content dimensions of Scale 0. Item numbers and scored directions for each of the subscales are reported in Appendix B in the MMPI-2 manual (Butcher et al., 2001). Linear T-score values for raw scores on the subscales by gender can be found in Appendix A in the MMPI-2 manual. Non-gendered T score transformation for these scales can be found in the Appendix of Ben-Porath and Forbey (2003).

Reliability of the Scale 0 Subscales

Internal consistency (alpha) coefficients were computed for the subscales for men and women in the normative sample (Ben-Porath et al., 1989). These coefficients ranged from .75 (Si3) to .81 (Si1) for men (n = 1,138; median = .77) and from .75 (Si2) to .84 (Si1) for women (n = 1,462; median = .78). They reported similar coefficients for a college sample, as did Sieber and Meyers (1992). Test–retest reliability coefficients were computed for the subscales using a subsample of 82 men and 111 women from the MMPI-2 normative sample who took the test twice with approximately a 1-week interval between testing sessions (Ben-Porath et al., 1989). The test–retest coefficients ranged from .77 (Si3) to .91 (Si1) for men (n = 82; median = .88) and from .87 (Si2) to .90 (Si1) for women (n = 111; median = .88).

Validity of the Scale 0 Subscales

Ben-Porath et al. (1989) provided some preliminary validity data for the Scale 0 subscales. Scores on the subscales were correlated with behavioral ratings for a sample of 822 couples from the normative sample who participated in the study together and independently rated each other. The patterns of correlations were judged to offer support for the convergent and discriminant validity of the subscales.

Sieber and Meyers (1992) examined the validity of the Scale 0 subscales by correlating them with other self-report measures of constructs believed to be differentially related to the three subscales. The results were very similar for men and women. These authors found that persons with elevated Si1 subscale scores were more socially anxious, were less social, and had lower self-esteem; those with elevated Si2 subscale scores were shyer and less social; and persons with elevated Si3 subscale scores possessed lower self-esteem and had a more external locus of control.

Ward and Perry (1998) confirmed the comprehensiveness, reliability, and distinctness of the Scale 0 subscales when applied to several clinical samples. Graham et al. (1999) correlated scores on the Scale 0 subscales with extratest characteristics for a large sample of mental health center outpatients. Their results were consistent with previously reported characteristics and suggested that there also are reliable behavioral correlates for the subscales among mental health outpatients.

Interpretation of the Scale 0 Subscales

Given the relatively positive support for the reliability and validity in normative and clinical samples, both content and empirical interpretations of Scale 0 subscales is possible. Examination of the Scale 0 subscales can help in clarifying the meaning of high scores on Scale 0. For example, some high scorers on Scale 0 will have high scores on both Si1 (Shyness/Self-Consciousness) and Si2 (Social Avoidance), suggesting that they are uncomfortable in social interactions and cope by avoiding most social situations. Other high scorers on Scale 0 will have high scores on Si1 but not on Si2, suggesting that, despite social discomfort, they are not likely to avoid social interactions. Because each of the Scale 0 subscales seems to be homogeneous and bipolar, both high and low scores are interpretable. Ben-Porath et al. (1989) recommended that T scores of 65 or greater be considered high scores on the subscales. Although the subscale developers did not recommend any cutoff for low scores, it seems reasonable to consider T scores below 39 as low scores.

SHYNESS/SELF-CONSCIOUSNESS (Si1)

High scores on the Si1 subscale indicate persons who

1. feel shy, anxious, and uncomfortable in social situations
2. feel easily embarrassed
3. feel ill at ease in new situations
4. are not talkative or friendly
5. lack self-confidence and give up easily
6. in clinical settings, have symptoms of depression
7. in clinical settings, lack energy

Low scores on the Si1 subscale indicate persons who

1. are extroverted
2. initiate social contact with other people
3. are talkative and friendly
4. are self-confident and do not give up easily

SOCIAL AVOIDANCE (Si2)

High scores on the Si2 subscale indicate persons who

1. do not enjoy being involved with groups or crowds of people
2. actively avoid getting involved with other people
3. are shy
4. do not have high aspirations or strong achievement needs
5. in clinical settings, report depression, anxiety, somatic symptoms, and obsessive–compulsive thoughts and behaviors

Low scores on the Si2 subscale indicate persons who

1. enjoy being involved with groups or crowds of people
2. initiate social contact with other people

SELF/OTHER ALIENATION (Si3)
High scores on the Si3 subscale indicate persons who

1. have low self-esteem
2. lack interest in activities
3. feel unable to effect changes in their life situations
4. have a more external locus of control
5. are interpersonally very sensitive
6. feel insecure
7. do not have strong achievement needs
8. in clinical settings, feel depressed, sad, and hopeless
9. in clinical settings, report obsessive–compulsive thoughts and behaviors

Low scores on the Si3 subscale indicate persons who

1. have high self-esteem
2. appear to be interested in activities
3. feel able to effect changes in their life situations

THE MMPI-2 CONTENT SCALES
Wiggins (1969) used the entire MMPI item pool to form 13 content-based scales. Due to the deletion of some MMPI items and the addition of new items, when the MMPI-2 was published in 1989, Wiggins's scales were no longer adequate. Thus, instead of using Wiggins's scales on the MMPI-2, Content scales based on the MMPI-2 item pool were developed by Butcher et al. (1990) to assess the content dimensions of the revised instrument.

Development of the Content Scales
The MMPI-2 Content scales were developed using a combination of rational and statistical procedures. The first step in the development was to define clinically relevant content areas represented by the items in the MMPI-2. Numerous categories were rationally identified, and a definition was written for each. Three clinical psychologists served as judges and assigned items to the content categories. Judges were free to add categories, and items could be assigned to more than one category. Items assigned to a category by two or three of the judges were placed into provisional scales. Raters then met and reviewed all the item placements. Any disagreements were discussed until there was full agreement by all three raters concerning item placement. For one of the original categories, sufficient items could not be identified, so it was dropped from further consideration.

In the next step of scale development, item responses for two samples of psychiatric patients and two samples of college students were used to identify items in the provisional scales that did not correlate highly with total scores for the scales and detracted from internal consistency. Such items were dropped from the scales. At this stage, some preliminary scales were eliminated from further consideration because of unacceptably low internal consistencies. Additionally, the data indicated that another content category, cynicism, which had been previously identified by item factor analysis, was not represented in the Content scales. Thus, a 20-item cynicism scale was added. Another way of ensuring appropriate item placement was to examine correlations between each item in the inventory and total scores on the provisional Content scales. Items that correlated higher with a score from a scale other than the one on which it was placed were deleted or moved to the other scale.

A final step involved examination of the content of the items in each Content scale to determine rationally whether the items fit conceptually with the definition of the content domain. Some items that were statistically related to the total score for a scale but whose content did not seem appropriate for that scale were eliminated. These multistage procedures yielded a set of 15 scales that were judged to be internally consistent, relatively independent, and representative of clinically relevant content dimensions in the MMPI-2 item pool. Although item overlap between scales was kept to a minimum, some overlap was permitted when the constructs assessed by the scales were conceptually related. Table 6.1 presents a listing of the 15 Content scales.

Item numbers and scored directions for each of the Content scales are presented in Appendix B of the MMPI-2 manual (Butcher et al., 2001). Content scales are scored using Uniform T scores, which permits scores for the Content scales to be expressed on the same metric as the Clinical scales, thus ensuring comparability within the set of Content scales and between the Content scales and the Clinical scales. Uniform T-score transformations for the Content scales are reported separately for men and women in Appendix A in the MMPI-2 manual. Score transformations based on the non-gendered normative data are available in the Appendix of Ben-Porath and Forbey's (2003) non-gendered norms monograph.

Reliability of the Content Scales

Table 6.1 reports internal consistency (α) coefficients for the Content scales based on responses of men and women in the normative sample. As would be expected, the internal consistency of the Content scales is quite high, ranging from .72 (TPA & FRS) to .86 (CYN) for men (median = .78) and from .68 (TPA) to .86 (DEP) for women (median = .80). In general, the Content scales are more internally consistent than the Clinical scales and similar in internal consistency to the Wiggins scales, which they were developed to replace.

Table 6.1 also reports test–retest reliability coefficients for the Content scales for 82 men and 111 women in the normative sample. The average retest interval was approximately nine days. These coefficients indicate that the Content scales are quite stable over this short time interval, with test–retest coefficients ranging from .78 (BIZ) to .91 (SOD) for men (median = .83) and from .79 (TPA) to .91 (WRK) for women (median = .86). In fact, the Content scales appear to be more stable than the basic Clinical scales.

Validity of the Content Scales

Butcher and colleagues (1990) reported several kinds of preliminary validity data for the Content scales. Correlations between the Content scales and other MMPI-2 scales are reported in Table 6.2 These correlational data contribute significantly to our

TABLE 6.1 *Reliability of the MMPI-2 Content Scales*

Scale		Number of Items	Internal Consistency[a]		Test-Retest Reliability[b]	
			Men ($n = 1,138$)	Women ($n = 1,462$)	Men ($n = 82$)	Women ($n = 111$)
ANX	Anxiety	23	.82	.83	.90	.87
FRS	Fears	23	.72	.75	.81	.86
OBS	Obsessiveness	16	.74	.77	.83	.85
DEP	Depression	33	.85	.86	.87	.88
HEA	Health Concerns	36	.76	.80	.81	.85
BIZ	Bizarre Mentation	23	.73	.74	.78	.81
ANG	Anger	16	.76	.73	.85	.82
CYN	Cynicism	23	.86	.85	.80	.89
ASP	Antisocial Practices	22	.78	.75	.81	.87
TPA	Type A Behavior	19	.72	.68	.82	.79
LSE	Low Self-Esteem	24	.79	.83	.84	.86
SOD	Social Discomfort	24	.83	.84	.91	.90
FAM	Family Problems	25	.73	.77	.84	.83
WRK	Work Interference	33	.82	.84	.90	.91
TRT	Negative Treatment Indicators	26	.78	.80	.79	.88

Note.
[a] Cronbach's coefficient alpha.
[b] Average retest interval was 9 days. Excerpted (Table E-12) from *Development and Use of the MMPI-2 Content Scales* by James N. Butcher, John R. Graham, Carolyn L. Williams, and Yossef S. Ben-Porath. Copyright © 1990 by the Regents of the University of Minnesota. Reproduced by permission of the University of Minnesota Press. All rights reserved. "MMPI®" and "Minnesota Multiphasic Personality Inventory®" are registered trademarks of the Regents of the University of Minnesota.

understanding of the construct validity of the Content scales. Some of the Content scales correlate highly with the Clinical scales, suggesting that they can be interpreted in similar ways. For example, the HEA (Health Concerns) scale and Scale 1 (Hypochondriasis) correlate .89 for men and .91 for women in the normative sample, suggesting that both are measures of health concern. Likewise, the SOD (Social Discomfort) scale and Scale 0 (Social Introversion) correlate .85 for men and .84 for women. However, other Content scales are not so highly correlated with Clinical scales with similar labels, suggesting that these scales are assessing unique characteristics as well as common ones. For example, the correlation between the DEP

TABLE 6.2 *Correlations of the MMPI-2 Content Scales with the Clinical Scales for Men and Women in the MMPI-2 Normative Samples*

	1 (Hs)	2 (D)	3 (Hy)	4 (Pd)	5 (Mf)	6 (Pa)	7 (Pt)	8 (Sc)	9 (Ma)	0 (Si)
					Men (*n* = 1,138)					
ANX	.50	.45	.04	.50	.20	.33	.80	.69	.31	.43
FRS	.34	.22	.02	.16	.01	.09	.37	.35	.06	.28
OBS	.40	.26	−.16	.29	.12	.18	.77	.64	.31	.44
DEP	.48	.52	.02	.58	.16	.38	.80	.75	.27	.48
HEA	.89	.45	.39	.35	.10	.25	.50	.55	.18	.29
BIZ	.38	.03	−.09	.36	.08	.33	.51	.62	.48	.11
ANG	.33	.01	−.21	.36	−.02	.15	.55	.53	.42	.19
CYN	.33	.07	−.43	.26	−.17	−.16	.51	.53	.42	.32
ASP	.26	.01	−.36	.37	−.15	−.12	.45	.50	.51	.18
TPA	.29	.05	−.30	.22	−.05	.04	.53	.48	.38	.25
LSE	.42	.42	−.11	.27	.07	.18	.72	.61	.11	.59
SOD	.24	.39	−.19	.04	.11	.09	.40	.36	−.20	.85
FAM	.32	.21	−.11	.57	.18	.21	.59	.66	.43	.31
WRK	.49	.44	−.09	.41	.14	.21	.81	.73	.23	.59
TRT	.46	.40	−.12	.40	.02	.19	.72	.68	.20	.56
					Women (*n* = 1,462)					
ANX	.58	.60	.17	.51	.10	.39	.83	.71	.34	.48
FRS	.34	.20	−.01	.13	.00	.06	.39	.33	.11	.32
OBS	.45	.40	−.06	.36	.08	.25	.79	.65	.36	.47
DEP	.54	.63	.12	.61	.01	.44	.83	.77	.31	.55
HEA	.91	.45	.48	.33	.00	.25	.55	.59	.29	.31
BIZ	.36	.11	−.03	.39	−.14	.31	.51	.65	.50	.15
ANG	.39	.20	−.06	.44	.00	.25	.62	.60	.44	.27
CYN	.41	.17	−.24	.32	−.24	−.06	.51	.54	.46	.35
ASP	.30	.09	−.25	.37	−.28	−.09	.44	.51	.51	.23
TPA	.32	.15	−.16	.23	−.05	.13	.53	.49	.36	.28
LSE	.44	.53	−.04	.31	.01	.23	.74	.61	.14	.65
SOD	.24	.43	−.17	.06	.07	.19	.43	.35	−.17	.84
FAM	.40	.32	.04	.61	.04	.33	.60	.72	.45	.33
WRK	.52	.58	.02	.44	.04	.29	.82	.72	.27	.63
TRT	.45	.50	−.05	.42	−.04	.26	.72	.69	.24	.61

Note. Excerpted (Tables 25 & 26) from *Development and Use of the MMPI-2 Content Scales* by James N. Butcher, John R. Graham, Carolyn L. Williams, and Yossef S. Ben-Porath. Copyright © 1990 by the Regents of the University of Minnesota. Reproduced by permission of the University of Minnesota Press. All rights reserved. "MMPI®" and "Minnesota Multiphasic Personality Inventory®" are registered trademarks of the Regents of the University of Minnesota.

(Depression) scale and Scale 2 (Depression) was .52 for men and .63 for women, suggesting that these two measures of depression are not interchangeable.

Studies reporting correlates of the Content scales have been conducted in a variety of settings. Butcher et al. (1990) presented data concerning extratest correlates for the Content scales for 800 couples who participated in the MMPI-2 standardization project (Butcher et al., 2001). Subsequently, reliable and conceptually relevant correlates of the Content scales have been reported for psychiatric inpatients (Archer et al., 1996; Dwyer et al., 1992); mental health outpatients (Graham et al., 1999); college students (Ben-Porath et al., 1993); older Australian residents (Strassberg et al., 1991); chronic-pain patients (Strassberg & Russell, 2000); and traumatic brain injury patients (Palav et al., 2001).

Some studies have examined the validity of specific Content scales. Schill and Wang (1990) reported that the Anger (ANG) Content scale correlated positively with a measure of anger expression and negatively with an anger control measure. For men, ANG was correlated significantly with verbal expression of aggression; and, for women, with physical expression of aggression. O'Laughlin and Schill (1994) found that self-monitored aggression correlated positively and significantly with ANG. Carr and Graham (1996) found that college students who identified as men and scored higher on ANG reported experiencing anger more frequently, regardless of provocation; and that ANG scores were not helpful in trying to predict if the anger would be expressed inwardly or outwardly. College students who identified as women and who scored higher on the ANG scale also reported experiencing anger more frequently, lacking anger control, and expressing their anger outwardly. Clark (1994) reported that in a pain management program, higher ANG scores were associated with anger externalization, while higher Cynicism (CYN) Content scale scores were associated with anger internalization.

Butcher et al. (1990) reported data concerning scores of chronic-pain patients, psychiatric patients, and nonclinical persons on the Health Concerns (HEA) Content scale. As expected, chronic-pain patients scored significantly higher than the other groups on the HEA scale. A T-score cutoff of 65 on the HEA scale correctly classified most of the chronic-pain patients and incorrectly classified very few other persons. Boone (1994) reported that scores on the Depression (DEP) Content scale were highly correlated with other self-report measures of depression, hopelessness, and suicidality in a psychiatric inpatient sample.

Butcher et al. (1990) examined Work Interference (WRK) Content scale scores for several groups of men who would be expected to differ on this scale. The scores of pilot applicants, military personnel, psychiatric inpatients, and individuals in alcohol-related treatment were compared. The pilot applicants, who would be expected to have the most positive work attitudes, scored lowest on the WRK scale, whereas the psychiatric and alcohol-treatment patient groups obtained the highest scores.

Lilienfeld (1996) reported that the Antisocial Practices (ASP) Content scale measures some of the core personality features of psychopathy as well as generalized social deviance. S. R. Smith et al. (1999) demonstrated the utility of the ASP scale in differentiating clients with diagnoses of antisocial personality disorder from clients with other personality disorder diagnoses. Lee and Forbey (2010) demonstrated scores on

ASP and ANG were moderately and positively related to sexual preoccupation in a large sample of college students who identified as men.

Using college student participants, several studies have found that scores on the Low Self-Esteem (LSE) Content scale were related to other self-report measures of negative self-value, ineptitude, and negative comparisons with others (Brems & Lloyd, 1995; Englert et al., 2000; McCurdy & Kelly, 1997). Rice and Stuart (2010) demonstrated scores on LSE and DEP were positively related to larger discrepancies between expectations and self-evaluations of one's performance—a characteristic related to maladaptive perfectionism—in a large sample of college students.

Clark (1996) examined the utility of the Negative Treatment Indicators (TRT) scale for men in a chronic-pain treatment program. Higher scorers on the TRT scale tended to show greater decreases in symptoms of depression during treatment and smaller improvements in physical capacities. Higher scorers also were more likely to terminate treatment prematurely. Gilmore et al. (2001) found that persons with higher TRT scale scores were less likely to return for treatment after a screening interview. Among persons who returned for treatment, higher TRT scale scorers were involved in treatment for fewer days and were rated as having lower motivation, poorer participation, and poorer comprehension of treatment materials. Michael et al. (2009) found that TRT scale scores were significantly related to distress and functioning at the time of intake interviews but were unrelated to changes in distress or functioning when patients received cognitive behavioral or interpersonal therapy. Craig and Olson (2004) reported that for a small sample of African American men, the TRT scale was not predictive of treatment success.

Several studies have examined the extent to which Content scale scores are related to specific clinical problems. Egeland et al. (1991) found that mothers at high risk for child abuse obtained above-average scores on all the Content scales except LSE. Their highest scores were on the ASP, CYN, ANG, and Bizarre Mentation (BIZ) scales. Bosquet and Egeland (2000) reported that higher ASP scores of women who completed the MMPI-2 during pregnancy were predictive of insensitivity, hostility, and harshness toward their children when they were 13–24 months old. McAnulty and colleagues (2014) demonstrated that lower scores on Fears (FRS), in combination with higher scores on the Repression (R) Supplementary scale, were related to non-attendance at a residential treatment program in a small sample of women who committed nonviolent offenses. They also demonstrated scores on DEP—in combination with higher scores on Clinical Scale 4, Supplementary Scale Responsibility (Re), and the Addiction Admissions Scale (AAS)—were useful in predicting which of these women did not complete the residential treatment program.

Hjemboe and Butcher (1991) found that the Family Problems (FAM) Content scale strongly differentiated couples in marital counseling from couples in the MMPI-2 normative sample and that FAM scale scores were negatively and significantly related to measures of marital adjustment. Kopper et al. (2001) reported significant relationships between several Content scales and self-reported suicidal ideation among college students. For women, ANG, along with several Validity and Clinical scales, contributed to the prediction of suicidal ideation; whereas for men, the Type A

(TPA) Content scale, along with several Validity and Clinical scales, contributed to the prediction of suicidal ideation.

In a study that has implications for the use of the MMPI-2 in the area of health psychology, Kawachi et al. (1998) found that among older men, scores on the TPA Content scale were significantly related to cardiovascular disease. Gass (1991) reported that some brain-injured patients obtain artificially elevated scores on some of the MMPI-2 Clinical scales because of the neurologic complaint items that those scales contain. By contrast, he concluded that the Content scales are especially useful in understanding the emotional status of patients with brain injuries because these scales include relatively few neurologic complaint items.

Butcher et al. (1995) stressed the importance of demonstrating that new scales developed for the MMPI-2 add significantly to the prediction of relevant extratest characteristics beyond what is possible using already existing scales. Several studies have demonstrated such incremental validity for the MMPI-2 Content scales for samples of psychiatric patients. Ben-Porath et al. (1991) investigated the contribution of the MMPI-2 Content scales to the differential diagnosis of schizophrenia and major depression in an inpatient psychiatric setting. They found both the Clinical scales and the Content scales were related to the differential diagnosis of these two conditions and that the Content scales contained information relevant to this diagnostic question beyond that available from the Clinical scales alone. For patients who identified as men, the DEP and BIZ Content scales added to the diagnostic discrimination. For patients who identified as women, the BIZ Content scale added to the diagnostic discrimination. Similarly, Wetzler et al. (1998) found the DEP Content scale added significantly to the Clinical scales in identifying patients with depressive diagnoses; and the BIZ and DEP Content scales added significantly to the Clinical scales in identifying patients with psychotic diagnoses. Bagby et al. (2005) found the DEP and ANX Content scales were predictive of bipolar and unipolar depression, and the BIZ and LSE Content scales were predictive of schizophrenia.

Using a large sample of college students, Ben-Porath et al. (1993) found the MMPI-2 Content scales added to the Clinical scales in the prediction of relevant characteristics assessed by other self-report measures. Archer et al. (1996) reported that for a sample of adult psychiatric inpatients, most Content scales added to the prediction of relevant self-reported and clinician-rated characteristics. Strassberg et al. (1991) reported incremental validity for four Content scales (DEP, ANX, LSE, HEA) in predicting scores on self-report measures of depression, anxiety, and physical health in a sample of older Australian residents.

Barthlow et al. (1999) examined the extent to which Content scales add incrementally to the Clinical scales in predicting therapist-rated characteristics of mental health outpatients. Although the incremental validity tended to be modest, most Content scales added significantly to the variance in ratings accounted for by corresponding Clinical scales. These investigators concluded that because each set of scales (i.e., Clinical and Content) added to the other, the two sets should be used together in MMPI-2 interpretation.

Carter and colleagues (2019) examined whether select Clinical and Content scales added to the prediction of diagnoses of nonaffective psychosis beyond that offered by a semi-structured diagnostic interview in a sample of individuals presenting for inpatient treatment. Results suggested higher scores on Clinical Scale 8 and Content Scale BIZ, as well as lower scores on Content Scale ANX, discriminated nonaffective psychosis from other mental health conditions. Scores on these scales also added to the prediction of psychotic symptoms beyond that offered by the diagnostic interview data.

In summary, there is considerable evidence to support the validity of the MMPI-2 Content scales. The scales appear to be related significantly to relevant extratest characteristics; and in most cases, relationships between Content scales and extratest characteristics are stronger than between Clinical scales and those characteristics. Additionally, there have been several demonstrations that the Content scales add significantly to the Clinical scales in the prediction of relevant extratest characteristics. Taken together, these data indicate the Content scales can be quite helpful in understanding persons who complete the MMPI-2 and that they add significantly to the standard Validity and Clinical scales.

However, not everyone has shared this positive view. Jackson et al. (1997) suggested that "convergent and discriminant validity of MMPI-2 Content scales are seriously compromised by the presence of substantial, confounding, general variance" (p. 111), which they believed reflected social desirability and acquiescence response sets. Their arguments are similar to those previously made about scales of the original MMPI (e.g., Edwards, 1957; Jackson & Messick, 1961). J. Block (1965) presented data that clearly rebutted the response-set arguments. The accumulated evidence that the MMPI-2 Content scales have stable and conceptually relevant extratest correlates suggests that the scales are assessing important aspects of personality and psychopathology, which may, in part, overlap with tendencies to endorse items in stylistic ways.

Content Component Scales

Although an important goal in developing the MMPI-2 Content scales was to maximize the internal consistency of the individual scales, Ben-Porath and Sherwood (1993) suggested that for 12 of the 15 Content scales, it is possible to subdivide the items to form Component scales. For example, they indicated that the items in the ASP Content scale could be subdivided into two parcels of items: one dealing with antisocial attitudes and the other dealing with antisocial behaviors. Ben-Porath and Sherwood reasoned that in some cases, interpretation of the Content scales scores could be augmented by additional information about which kinds of items were endorsed in obtaining a particular T score on a scale.

Development of the Content Component Scales

To create the Content Component scales, Ben-Porath and Sherwood (1993) first factor analyzed items within each of the 15 Content scales using data from the MMPI-2 normative sample, a college sample, and a psychiatric inpatient sample. Results were utilized to develop preliminary versions of the Component scales. Next, several statistical procedures were utilized to enhance the internal consistency of the Component scales. Finally, rational analyses were employed to ensure the conceptual independence of the item clusters and to determine appropriate labels for the resulting Component scales. The resulting Content Component scales for 12 of the 15 Content scales are listed in Table 6.3. Component scales were not developed for

TABLE 6.3 *MMPI-2 Content Component Scales*

Fears (FRS)
  FRS1: Generalized Fearfulness
  FRS2: Multiple Fears

Depression (DEP)
  DEP1: Lack of Drive
  DEP2: Dysphoria
  DEP3: Self-Depreciation
  DEP4: Suicidal Ideation

Health Concerns (HEA)
  HEA1: Gastrointestinal Symptoms
  HEA2: Neurological Symptoms
  HEA3: General Health Concerns

Bizarre Mentation (BIZ)
  BIZ1: Psychotic Symptomatology
  BIZ2: Schizotypal Characteristics

Anger (ANG)
  ANG1: Explosive Behavior
  ANG2: Irritability

Cynicism (CYN)
  CYN1: Misanthropic Beliefs
  CYN2: Interpersonal Suspiciousness

Antisocial Practices (ASP)
  ASP1: Antisocial Attitudes
  ASP2: Antisocial Behavior

Type A Behavior (TPA)
  TPA1: Impatience
  TPA2: Competitive Drive

Low Self-Esteem (LSE)
  LSE1: Self-Doubt
  LSE2: Submissiveness

Social Discomfort (SOD)
  SOD1: Introversion
  SOD2: Shyness

Family Problems (FAM)
  FAM1: Family Discord
  FAM2: Familial Alienation

Negative Treatment Indicators (TRT)
  TRT1: Low Motivation
  TRT2: Inability to Disclose

Note. Excerpted (Table 2) from *The MMPI-2 Content Component Scales: Development, Psychometric Characteristics, and Clinical Application* by Yossef S. Ben-Porath and Nancy E. Sherwood. Copyright © 1993 by the Regents of the University of Minnesota. Reproduced by permission of the University of Minnesota Press. All rights reserved. "MMPI®" and "Minnesota Multiphasic Personality Inventory®" are registered trademarks of the Regents of the University of Minnesota.

the Anxiety (ANX), Obsessiveness (OBS), and Work Interference (WRK) scales. Appendix B in the MMPI-2 manual (Butcher et al., 2001) lists the items included in each Component scale (and their scored direction). Uniform T-score transformations for raw scores for the Component scales, based on data from the MMPI-2 normative sample, are also presented in Appendix A in the MMPI-2 manual. Score transformations based on the non-gendered normative data are available in the Appendix of Ben-Porath and Forbey's (2003) non-gendered norms monograph.

Reliability of the Content Component Scales

Ben-Porath and Sherwood (1993) reported internal consistency coefficients for the Component scales for the normative, college, and psychiatric samples. The internal consistencies of the Component scales were quite variable and generally lower than those of their parent Content scales. The lower internal consistency probably can be attributed, at least in large part, to the fact that these scales contain many fewer items than their parent scales. As might be expected, for many of the Component scales, internal consistency was lower for the normative and college samples than for the psychiatric sample, perhaps reflecting the restriction of range of some of the Component scale scores in the normative sample. Ben-Porath and Sherwood (1993) pointed out that the internal consistencies of the Component scales are similar to those of the more widely used Harris–Lingoes subscales. Ben-Porath and Sherwood also reported test–retest reliability coefficients for a subsample of persons from the MMPI-2 normative sample. These coefficients also were quite variable, ranging from .47 (FRS1) to .90 (SOD1) (median = .77) for men and .67 (BIZ1) to .88 (SOD1) (median = .79) for women. Although these coefficients are somewhat lower than those previously reported for the parent Content scales, they are comparable to those previously reported for the Harris–Lingoes subscales.

Validity of the Content Component Scales

Ben-Porath and Sherwood (1993) reported correlations between Component scale scores and extratest ratings of persons in the MMPI-2 normative sample. Although the ratings available did not cover the full range of characteristics assessed by the Component scales, and the magnitude of the resulting correlations probably was attenuated because of the restricted range of scores in the normative sample, the patterns of correlations were interpreted as offering some preliminary support for the external validity of the Component scales.

Graham et al. (1999) determined extratest characteristics of the Content Component scales for a large sample of mental health outpatients. Although for many scales, the correlations with extratest measures were similar for the parent Content scales and their corresponding Content Component scales, there were some instances where there were differential patterns of correlations. For example, having a history of being physically abusive or of committing domestic violence was more strongly related to the Explosive Behavior (ANG1) Component scale than to the Irritability (ANG2) Component scale.

Clark (1996) found the Negative Treatment Indicators (TRT) Content scale and the Low Motivation (TRT1) Content Component scale were equally effective in predicting changes in depression and physical capacity for men in a chronic-pain treatment program. The Inability to Disclose (TRT2) Component scale was not very effective in predicting these changes.

Ben-Porath and Sherwood (1993) recommended the Component scales be used to enhance the interpretation of the parent Content scales and not be used independently of the parent scales to generate inferences. They indicated the Component scales should be interpreted only when T scores on a parent Content scale are equal to or greater than 60. Differential elevations on Content Component scales within a parent Content scale may be especially useful in specifying the symptoms and problems associated with elevations on the Content scales. This differential elevation is most likely when parent Content scale scores are moderately high (T = 60–75).

McNulty, Ben-Porath, et al. (1997) suggested that scores on the Content Component scales are likely to be most helpful when the parent Content scale is elevated (T > 60) and the score on one of the Component scales is at least 10 T-score points greater than the other Component scale(s) within the parent Content scale. Their analyses of data for a sample of mental health center clients supported the notion that for some Content scales, differential elevations of the Component scales added important information about which correlates of the Content scales should be emphasized or deemphasized in the interpretation.

Interpretation of the Content and Content Component Scales

The data summarized here and examination of the content of items in each Content scale can be used to generate interpretive inferences about persons who have high scores (T > 65) on the scales. Given only one previous study has examined low score meanings on the Content scales (Graham, Ben-Porath, et al., 1997), it is not recommended that low scores on the Content scales be used to generate interpretive statements.

Special attention should be given to interpretation of the WRK and TRT scales. Because of the manner in which these scales were constructed, each scale seems to be saturated with general maladjustment and demoralization. Thus, persons who are in a great deal of psychological turmoil and feeling demoralized are likely to obtain higher scores on these scales regardless of their specific attitudes about work or treatment. Elevated scores on these scales are most informative when there are indications that the test taker is not generally maladjusted or demoralized.

The Content Component scales should be interpreted only when the parent Content scale T score is greater than or equal to 60. In such cases, the relative T scores for Component scales for a particular Content scale should be examined. If there is a differential pattern among Component scales (i.e., one scale at least 10 T-score points higher than another scale), the item content of the Component scales may offer some additional information about which Content scale correlates should be emphasized or deemphasized in the interpretation.

It is especially important to consider test-taking attitude when interpreting the Content scales. Because the scales contain primarily items with face-valid content, scores on these scales are very susceptible to distortion related to test-taking attitude. Persons who underreport when completing the MMPI-2 are likely to obtain low scores on most of the scales, and persons who overreport problems in taking the MMPI-2 are likely to obtain high scores on most of the scales. Clearly, the Content scales are most useful when test takers have approached the MMPI-2 in a cooperative, open manner.

Clinicians should view scores on the Content scales as direct communication between test takers and examiners. Characteristics reflected by high scores on the Content scales are those that the test takers want examiners to know about. Rapport with clients often is increased when the Content scale results are used to give feedback to clients, indicating an awareness of the things they were trying to communicate when they completed the MMPI-2.

ANXIETY (ANX)

High scores on the ANX scale are indicative of persons who

1. feel anxious, nervous, worried, and apprehensive
2. have problems with concentration
3. complain of sleep disturbance
4. are uncomfortable making decisions
5. may have somatic symptoms
6. may report feeling sad, blue, or depressed
7. may have suicidal ideation
8. feel that life is a strain and are pessimistic about things getting better
9. feel hopeless
10. feel insecure and lack self-confidence
11. feel overwhelmed by the responsibilities of daily life
12. in clinical settings, frequently have anxiety- or trauma-related disorder diagnoses

ANX Content Component Scales

There are no Component scales for the ANX Content scale.

FEARS (FRS)

High scores on the FRS scale are indicative of persons who

1. feel fearful and uneasy much of the time
2. report multiple specific fears or phobias
3. are not very competitive

FRS Content Component Scales

Both the Generalized Fearfulness (FRS1) and Multiple Fears (FRS2) Component scales contain items having to do with fearfulness and anxiety. However, the FRS1 scale seems to assess a more global state of anxiety and fearfulness, whereas the FRS2 scale includes items dealing with fear associated with specific objects (e.g., lightning, animals, fire, blood).

OBSESSIVENESS (OBS)

High scores on the OBS scale are indicative of persons who

1. have great difficulty making decisions
2. are rigid and dislike change
3. fret, worry, and ruminate about trivial things
4. may feel depressed, sad, and despondent
5. lack self-confidence
6. tend to feel hopeless
7. often report sleep disturbances
8. report obsessive–compulsive symptoms
9. lack interest in things

OBS Content Component Scales
There are no Content Component scales for the OBS Content scale.

DEPRESSION (DEP)
High scores on the DEP scale are indicative of persons who

1. feel depressed, sad, blue, or despondent
2. feel fatigued and lack interest in things
3. are pessimistic and feel hopeless
4. may recently have been preoccupied with thoughts of death and suicide and may have made suicide attempts
5. cry easily
6. are indecisive and lack self-confidence
7. feel that life is a strain
8. feel guilty; feel like a failure
9. are not very achievement oriented and think their performance of tasks does not live up to their expectations
10. have health concerns
11. often report sleep disturbances
12. feel lonely and empty much of the time
13. are emotionally withdrawn
14. have few or no friends
15. are overly sensitive interpersonally
16. have difficult interpersonal relationships
17. in clinical settings, frequently have depressive disorder diagnoses

DEP Content Component Scales
High scores on all four of the DEP Content Component scales are indicative of sadness and depression. The Lack of Drive (DEP1) Component scale has items that focus on life being empty and meaningless and on giving up hope about a better future. The Dysphoria (DEP2) Component scale focuses on mood, with high scorers indicating that they feel

sad, blue, and unhappy most of the time. The Self-Depreciation (DEP3) Component scale has to do primarily with feeling inadequate and guilty about past behaviors.

As the scale name indicates, the last DEP Component scale, the Suicidal Ideation (DEP4) scale, has to do with the admission of recent or current thoughts of death and suicide. Four of its five items deal directly with suicidal ideation or behavior. The fifth asks about the experience of hopelessness. Given the items signal potential suicide risk, these authors recommend inspecting responses to DEP4 when the test taker completes the instrument and discussing any items endorsed in the keyed direction with them.

HEALTH CONCERNS (HEA)

High scores on the HEA scale are indicative of persons who

1. deny good physical health
2. are preoccupied with bodily functioning
3. may develop somatic symptoms in times of stress
4. feel worn out and lack energy
5. report a variety of specific somatic symptoms, including some that could be suggestive of a neurological disorder
6. do not cope well with their difficulties
7. feel anxious and overwhelmed much of the time
8. may report feeling sad, depressed, and pessimistic
9. often report sleep disturbances
10. in clinical settings, frequently have depressive disorder diagnoses

HEA Content Component Scales

The items in the Gastrointestinal Symptoms (HEA1) Component scale suggest symptoms of nausea, constipation, and stomach discomfort. The Neurological Symptoms (HEA2) Component scale has to do with sensory and motor experiences sometimes associated with neurological disorders (e.g., numbness in skin, convulsions, dizzy spells, balance problems). The General Health Concerns (HEA3) Component scale indicates an exaggerated general concern about illness and disease.

BIZARRE MENTATION (BIZ)

High scores on the BIZ scale are indicative of persons who

1. may have psychotic thought processes
2. may report unusual thought content
3. may report auditory, visual, or olfactory hallucinations
4. report feelings of unreality
5. may seem to be disoriented
6. feel that other people say bad things about them
7. tend to be suspicious
8. may believe that other people are trying to harm them
9. may believe that other people can read their minds or control their thinking or behavior

10. have blunted affect
11. often report having few or no friends
12. may have histories of suicide attempts
13. may have histories of substance misuse
14. may have histories of having been sexually abused
15. do not have strong achievement orientation
16. in clinical settings, frequently have schizophrenia spectrum and other psychotic disorder diagnoses

BIZ Content Component Scales

High scores on either the Psychotic Symptomatology (BIZ1) or Schizotypal Characteristics (BIZ2) Component scales suggest the presence of psychotic symptoms. However, high BIZ1 scale scores are more likely to indicate feelings that one's thoughts and behaviors are being controlled by others.

ANGER (ANG)

High scores on the ANG scale are indicative of persons who

1. feel angry and hostile much of the time
2. are seen by others as irritable, grouchy, impatient, and stubborn
3. are aggressive, critical, and argumentative
4. may feel like swearing or smashing things
5. have temper tantrums
6. may lose control and be physically abusive
7. are impulsive and have low frustration tolerance
8. feel that they are unfairly treated
9. are very sensitive to criticism
10. often have interpersonal problems
11. may have histories of having been physically abused
12. may report feeling sad, depressed, and hopeless

ANG Content Component Scales

Persons who score significantly higher on the Explosive Behavior (ANG1) Component scale than on the Irritability (ANG2) Component scale are describing themselves as angry and resentful and sometimes losing control and striking out physically at people and things. When the reverse pattern is present (i.e., ANG2 significantly higher than ANG1), it is likely that such persons are chronically angry and resentful, but they are less likely to exhibit problems in controlling expression of these feelings.

CYNICISM (CYN)

High scores on the CYN scale are indicative of persons who

1. see other people as dishonest, selfish, and uncaring
2. are suspicious of the motives of others
3. are guarded and untrusting in relationships

4. may be hostile and overbearing
5. may be demanding themselves but resent even mild demands placed on them by others
6. are not friendly or helpful
7. have low achievement orientation
8. may have paranoid ideation
9. may have histories of having been physically abused

CYN Content Component Scales

Items in the Misanthropic Beliefs (CYN1) Component scale suggest a contemptuous and distrustful view of other people who are seen as lying to stay out of trouble, demanding more respect than they give to others, and using unfair means to gain profit or advantage. The Interpersonal Suspiciousness (CYN2) Component scale focuses on mistrust of the motives of other people and a perception that others often behave in a manner intended to get undue credit for the accomplishments of the test taker.

ANTISOCIAL PRACTICES (ASP)

High scores on the ASP scale are indicative of persons who

1. are likely to have been in trouble in school or with the law
2. believe that there is nothing wrong with getting around laws as long as they are not broken
3. may enjoy hearing about the antics of criminals
4. have generally cynical attitudes about other people, seeing them as selfish and dishonest
5. resent authority
6. blame others for their own difficulties
7. are manipulative
8. are cold-hearted
9. are self-centered
10. are viewed as dishonest, not trustworthy, and not believable
11. may have substance use problems
12. are aggressive, angry, and resentful
13. are impulsive
14. in clinical settings, frequently have antisocial personality disorder diagnoses

ASP Content Component Scales

Higher scorers on the Antisocial Attitudes (ASP1) Component scale are expressing nonconforming attitudes (e.g., getting around a law is acceptable if you do not break it; lying to stay out of trouble is understandable), but they are not necessarily acknowledging past antisocial behaviors. The Antisocial Behaviors (ASP2) Component scale focuses on history of problems in school and with the law.

TYPE A BEHAVIOR (TPA)

High scores on the TPA scale are indicative of persons who

1. are hard-driving, fast-moving, and work-oriented
2. feel there is never enough time to get things done
3. do not like to wait or be interrupted
4. frequently are hostile, irritable, and easily annoyed
5. tend to be overbearing and critical in relationships
6. tend to hold grudges and want to get even
7. have increased risk for cardiovascular problems
8. in clinical settings, may have paranoid ideation

TPA Content Component Scales

The Impatience (TPA1) Component scale focuses on irritability toward other people and a strong dislike of having to wait or stand in line. The items in the Competitive Drive (TPA2) Component scale primarily reflect experiences of jealousy and competitiveness in interpersonal relationships.

LOW SELF-ESTEEM (LSE)

High scores on the LSE scale are indicative of persons who

1. have very poor self-concepts
2. anticipate failure and give up easily
3. have feelings of ineptitude and think their performance of tasks does not live up to their expectations
4. compare themselves unfavorably with others
5. are overly sensitive to criticism and rejection
6. find it difficult to accept compliments
7. are passive in relationships
8. have difficulty making decisions
9. may have many worries and fears

LSE Content Component Scales

Persons with high scores on the Self-Doubt (LSE1) Component scale are expressing many negative attitudes about themselves. They doubt their own abilities, compare themselves unfavorably with other people, and may feel that they can never change. Persons with high scores on the Submissiveness (LSE2) Component scale are easily influenced by other people and tend to be passive and submissive in interpersonal relationships.

SOCIAL DISCOMFORT (SOD)

High scores on the SOD scale are indicative of persons who

1. are shy and socially introverted
2. are socially awkward
3. would rather be alone than around other people

4. dislike parties and other group activities
5. do not initiate conversations
6. have limited interests
7. often feel nervous
8. frequently report sleep disturbances
9. may be preoccupied with health and illness
10. may report feeling depressed and hopeless
11. are overly sensitive interpersonally
12. have low energy levels
13. may be emotionally withdrawn
14. in clinical settings, frequently have depressive or social anxiety disorder diagnoses

SOD Content Component Scales

While high scores on both the Introversion (SOD1) and Shyness (SOD2) Component scales suggest introversion, each scale focuses on a somewhat different aspect. The items in the SOD1 Component scale deal with a person's preference for being alone rather than around other people, particularly in groups or at parties; whereas SOD2 items focus on the uncomfortable feelings experienced when meeting new people or being the focus of attention.

FAMILY PROBLEMS (FAM)

High scores on the FAM scale are indicative of persons who

1. describe considerable discord in their current families or families of origin
2. describe their families as lacking in love, understanding, and support
3. resent the demands and advice of their families
4. feel angry and hostile toward their families
5. see marital relationships as involving unhappiness and lack of affection
6. often feel they are getting a raw deal from life
7. may have histories of having been physically abused
8. may report feeling depressed and hopeless
9. in clinical settings, frequently have depressive disorder diagnoses

FAM Content Component Scales

The items in the Familial Discord (FAM1) Component scale express anger, hate, and resentment toward family members and a desire to get away from family. The Familial Alienation (FAM2) Component scale focuses on feelings that family members are not very understanding or supportive.

WORK INTERFERENCE (WRK)

As previously noted, the WRK scale can be elevated by extreme psychological distress, regardless of the specific attitudes about work the individual may have. As such, elevated scores on WRK are most informative when there are indications that the test taker is not generally maladjusted or demoralized. In cases where high levels of maladjustment are indicated, high scores on WRK should be interpreted cautiously.

High scores on the WRK scale are indicative of persons who

1. are reporting a wide variety of attitudes and behaviors likely to contribute to poor work performance
2. may be questioning their own career choices
3. say their families have not approved of their career choices
4. are not ambitious and are lacking in energy
5. express negative attitudes toward coworkers
6. often feel overwhelmed and unable to cope with stress
7. feel insecure
8. often feel like failures
9. have poor self-concepts
10. are obsessive and have problems concentrating
11. have difficulty making decisions and may show poor judgment
12. feel anxious, tense, worried, and fearful
13. feel depressed, sad, and hopeless
14. may have suicidal ideation
15. have low energy level
16. do not have strong achievement orientation
17. often report somatic symptoms
18. may report sleep disturbances
19. in clinical settings, frequently have depressive disorder diagnoses

WRK Content Component Scales

There are no Component scales for the WRK Content scale.

NEGATIVE TREATMENT INDICATORS (TRT)

As previously noted, the TRT scale can be elevated by extreme psychological distress, regardless of the specific attitudes about treatment the individual may have. As such, elevated scores on TRT are most informative when there are indications that the test taker is not generally maladjusted or demoralized. In cases where high levels of maladjustment are indicated, high scores on TRT should be interpreted cautiously.

High scores on the TRT scale are indicative of persons who

1. have negative attitudes toward doctors and mental health treatment
2. may terminate treatment prematurely
3. feel no one can understand them
4. believe they have problems that they cannot share with anyone
5. give up easily when problems are encountered
6. feel unable to make significant changes in their lives
7. are experiencing intense emotional distress
8. often report sleep disturbances
9. frequently report somatic symptoms

10. feel depressed, sad, and hopeless
11. may have suicidal ideation
12. have low energy levels
13. often feel anxious and insecure
14. are poor problem solvers
15. often show poor judgment

TRT Content Component Scales

Items in the Low Motivation (TRT1) Component scale have to do with feelings of helplessness and pessimism about working out one's problems. The items in the Inability to Disclose Component scale (TRT2) indicate a person's unwillingness and/or inability to reveal personal information to others.

CRITICAL ITEMS

Critical items are those whose content has been judged to be indicative of serious psychopathology. Koss, Butcher, and Hoffman (1976) and Lachar and Wrobel (1979) each developed lists of critical items for the MMPI that were carried over to the MMPI-2. The MMPI-2 Extended Score Report—available from Pearson Assessments—provides the individual item numbers and content for critical items from either list whenever they are endorsed by the test taker.

Recommendations Concerning Use of the Critical Items

Koss (1979) summarized the usefulness of critical items. She pointed out that critical-item sets overlap considerably with Scales F and 8, and most critical items are keyed in the true direction. Thus, critical-item endorsements can be misleading for persons who are displaying an acquiescent response set or are overreporting their symptoms and problems.

MMPI-2 users who interpret critical items should understand that individual items are not as reliable as scales because of the vulnerability to error of single-item responses. A test taker can misinterpret or mismark a single item, leading the test interpreter to an erroneous conclusion, whereas that same mistake in the context of a longer scale would not have much impact on the individual's total score on that scale. As such, critical-item responses should not be overinterpreted. In a valid MMPI-2 protocol, endorsement of critical items should lead the clinician to inquire further into the areas assessed by the items. Special attention should be given to endorsements of critical items dealing with suicidal ideation and bizarre thoughts and behaviors.

CHAPTER 7

RESTRUCTURED CLINICAL (RC) AND PERSONALITY PSYCHOPATHOLOGY FIVE (PSY-5) SCALES

SUBSEQUENT TO THE PUBLICATION of the MMPI-2 in 1989, several important new scales were developed using the MMPI-2 item pool and included in standard scoring of the instrument. Among these additions are two sets of scales, the Personality Psychopathology Five (PSY-5) scales (Harkness et al., 2002) and the Restructured Clinical (RC) scales (Tellegen et al., 2003), both of which are discussed in this chapter. Scores on these scales have strong evidence supporting their reliability and validity in a variety of contexts in which the MMPI-2 is frequently used. These scales have especially strong evidence supporting their construct validity (Sellbom, 2019), which allows the MMPI-2 to be linked to modern models of psychopathology such as the Hierarchical Taxonomy of Psychopathology (HiTOP; Kotov et al., 2021) and the Alternative Model of Personality Disorders (AMPD) described in the Diagnostic and Statistical Manual of Mental Disorders (DSM-5; American Psychiatric Association, 2013).

Given their strong psychometric properties, identical or slightly modified versions of the RC and PSY-5 scales are also scored on other versions of the MMPI, including the MMPI-2-Restructured Form (MMPI-2-RF; Ben-Porath & Tellegen, 2008/2011; Tellegen & Ben-Porath, 2008/2011) and the recently released third edition of the MMPI (MMPI-3; Ben-Porath & Tellegen, 2020a; 2020b).[1] Information on these

---

[1] Abbreviations for RC scales do not differ across the MMPI-2 and MMPI-2-RF. To reflect differences in the MMPI-2 and MMPI-2-RF PSY-5 scales, MMPI-2-RF versions include "-r" at the end of their abbreviations. Both RC and PSY-5 scales scored on the MMPI-3 differ from their predecessors. However, Ben-Porath and Tellegen (2020a; 2020b) did not adopt a method of denoting these revisions in scale abbreviations. Instead, MMPI-2 abbreviations are used for these scales on the MMPI-3. To prevent confusion, in cases where we are not referring to MMPI-2 versions of these scales, we will clearly indicate which version of the scales we are describing.

instruments is available in Chapter 12 (MMPI-2-RF) and Chapter 13 (MMPI-3) of this book. However, the RC scales scored on the MMPI-2-RF are identical in composition to those scored on the MMPI-2. There is also initial evidence the revised versions of the RC scales scored on the MMPI-3 and modified versions of the PSY-5 scales scored on the MMPI-2-RF and MMPI-3 are equivalent to MMPI-2 versions of the scales (Ben-Porath & Tellegen, 2020b; Harkness, McNulty, et al., 2014). Thus, information regarding validity presented in this chapter will include that obtained from studies of the MMPI-2, MMPI-2-RF, and MMPI-3 versions of these scales. We also think the information in this chapter can be applied to understanding and interpreting these scales, regardless of which version of the MMPI is used in an assessment.

RESTRUCTURED CLINICAL (RC) SCALES

The empirical keying methodology used in constructing the original Clinical scales of the MMPI resulted in scales that were quite heterogeneous in content and not very independent of one another. Many authors (e.g., Dahlstrom & Welsh, 1960) reported high intercorrelations among the MMPI Clinical scales. To some extent, these relationships were due to items appearing on more than one scale. However, Welsh (1956) demonstrated that even with overlapping items removed, some of the Clinical scales were strongly intercorrelated. Early factor-analytic studies (e.g., Eichman, 1961; Welsh, 1956) revealed a major source of shared variance among the Clinical scales was a factor variously labeled as anxiety, general maladjustment, or emotional distress. Factor analyses of the MMPI-2 Clinical scales produced similar results (Butcher et al., 1989). This ubiquitous "first factor" variance may have been a product of the empirical keying approach used in developing the MMPI Clinical scales. This process involved contrasting distinct diagnostic groups of hospitalized psychiatric patients (e.g., depression, schizophrenia) with a group of nonclinical individuals. As such, it is likely some of the items that were differentially endorsed by these two groups and, thus, identified for inclusion in each Clinical scale were associated with the common emotional distress and unhappiness that led to the patients seeking treatment.

While it is important to know to what extent a test taker is experiencing emotional distress, having that distress reflected in every single Clinical scale makes it difficult to know to what extent high scores on individual scales should be interpreted as indicating characteristics associated with the core constructs of the scales (e.g., depression or aberrant thinking) and to what extent they are the product of a test taker's high level of emotional distress. Thus, clinicians often have used code types, subscales, and Content scales to help clarify the meaning of high scores on the Clinical scales. Nonetheless, many of these approaches to refining interpretation have had difficulties with heterogeneity and excessive intercorrelation, as well.

Tellegen et al. (2003) developed the Restructured Clinical (RC) scales to overcome some of the limitations of the original Clinical scales and to help refine interpretations of them. They stated, "the RC Scales were designed to preserve the important descriptive properties of the existing MMPI-2 Clinical Scales while enhancing their distinctiveness" (p. 1). Table 7.1 provides a list of the RC scales Tellegen et al. (2003) developed for the MMPI-2 and later included in full on the MMPI-2-RF.

TABLE 7.1 *The MMPI-2 and MMPI-2-RF Restructured Clinical Scales*

RCd	Demoralization (dem)	24 items
RC1	Somatic Complaints (som)	27 items
RC2	Low Positive Emotions (lpe)	17 items
RC3	Cynicism (cyn)	15 items
RC4	Antisocial Behavior (asb)	22 items
RC6	Ideas of Persecution (per)	17 items
RC7	Dysfunctional Negative Emotions (dne)	24 items
RC8	Aberrant Experiences (abx)	18 items
RC9	Hypomanic Activation (hpm)	28 items

Note. Excerpted from the *MMPI®-2 (Minnesota Multiphasic Personality Inventory®-2) Restructured Clinical (RC) Scales: Development, Validation, and Interpretation* by Auke Tellegen, Yossef S. Ben-Porath, John L. McNulty, Paul A. Arbisi, John R. Graham, and Beverly Kaemmer. Copyright © 2003 by the Regents of the University of Minnesota. All rights reserved. Reproduced by permission of the University of Minnesota Press. "MMPI®" and "Minnesota Multiphasic Personality Inventory®" are registered trademarks of the Regents of the University of Minnesota.

Development of the RC Scales

Our description of RC scale development presents the overall approach to scale construction. Some methodological details have been omitted for the sake of brevity, but they can be found in the monograph by Tellegen et al. (2003).

The first step in constructing the RC scales was to develop a scale measuring the general emotional distress factor observed in the Clinical scales, which Tellegen et al. (2003) labeled Demoralization (RCd). It was anticipated removal of demoralization from the Clinical scales would result in a set of restructured scales that would be less intercorrelated and have greater discriminant validity than their original Clinical scale counterparts. Based on the two-factor model of affect described by Watson and Tellegen (1985), demoralization was conceptualized as equivalent to the pleasant–unpleasant dimension of self-reported affect. Because Scale 2 and Scale 7 are known to be related to anxiety, depression, and other emotional distress, these scales were thought to contain items assessing the demoralization dimension. Using four clinical samples, factor analyses of items in Scale 2 and Scale 7 yielded a set of items marking the demoralization factor. These items were scored in a provisional scale, which was then used to identify additional demoralization markers by correlating the provisional scale with all other MMPI-2 items.

The next step was to identify the core component of each original Clinical scale after the demoralization factor was removed. Separate factor analyses were conducted for each Clinical scale including the scale's items and the items from the provisional RCd scale. Factors were extracted and rotated to yield a clear demoralization factor—which included all the provisional RCd items as well as any items on the target Clinical scale that were primarily demoralization markers—and a second factor identified as the substantive core for the Clinical scale being analyzed (e.g., health concerns for Scale 1).

The third step in constructing the RC scales involved identifying items with high loadings on the factor representing the core of each scale to serve as a "seed" scale for each RC scale. This was accomplished by assigning to a given seed scale those items that had the highest loadings on the scale's core factor that also did not have salient loadings on the demoralization factor. An additional requirement was items correlated only minimally with the core factor seed scales created to reflect other Clinical scales. Overlapping items were then removed, as were items that detracted from the internal consistency of a seed scale. This step was designed to make the seed scales maximally distinct in order to enhance the discriminant validity of the final RC scales.

The 12 seed scales (Demoralization plus one for each Clinical scale) were then correlated with all other MMPI-2 items in four clinical samples. Items were selected for the RC scales if they had high correlations with a particular seed scale (i.e., convergence) and low correlations with other seed scales (i.e., discrimination). Items were then deleted from a scale if they did not contribute to the scale's internal consistency or, for six scales, if they were not appropriately correlated with conceptually relevant external criterion measures. Ultimately, RC scales were not developed for Scales 5 and 0 because they were not judged to assess core components of psychopathology. However, Tellegen et al. (2003) indicated restructured versions of Scale 5 and Scale 0 would be developed later.

These complex psychometric and statistical procedures resulted in restructured versions of Clinical Scales 1, 2, 3, 4, 6, 7, 8, and 9 and a Demoralization scale. The names, abbreviations, and number of items for each RC scale are reported in Table 7.1.

Intercorrelations of RC Scales and Clinical Scales

As seen in Table 7.2, congruent with the goals of the RC Scale development process, RC scales' intercorrelations are weaker than those demonstrated by the Clinical scales. This greater independence of the RC scales provides the opportunity for the scales to have greater discriminant validity than the Clinical scales, an issue discussed later in this chapter. Table 7.2 also reports correlations between the RC scales and the original Clinical scales for the MMPI-2 normative sample. In most comparisons, RC scales and the corresponding Clinical scales have strong positive correlations—suggesting the scales are assessing similar but not identical constructs. The very high correlations (.89 for men and .92 for women) between RC1 and Scale 1 indicate these two scales are essentially measuring the same construct (somatic concerns). The exception to these patterns of correlations is for the RC3 scale and Scale 3 (–.42 for men and –.24 for women). This pattern of correlations was expected given that the RC3 scale does not include the somatic items found in Scale 3; these were assigned to the RC1 scale. Instead, items in Scale 3 indicating naive positive perceptions of other people are scored in the reverse direction on RC3, and the resulting scale is labeled Cynicism.

The data in Table 7.2 also address the extent to which the emotional distress factor, which Tellegen et al. (2003) referred to as Demoralization, was successfully removed (or at least reduced) from the RC scales compared with the original Clinical scales. Based on the intercorrelations observed between scales, as well as the relations between the Clinical and RC scales with scores on RCd, Tellegen et al. (2003) concluded the RC scales are substantially less saturated with Demoralization than the

TABLE 7.2 *Intercorrelations of MMPI-2 RC and Clinical Scales for Men (n = 1,138) and Women (n = 1,462) in MMPI-2 Normative Sample*

Scale	RCd	RC1	RC2	RC3	RC4	RC6	RC7	RC8	RC9	1	2	3	4	6	7	8	9
RCd	—	.40	.44	.37	.34	.36	.68	.35	.32	.45	.53	.03	.53	.36	.83	.75	.23
RC1	.47	—	.27	.25	.22	.32	.39	.40	.22	.89	.44	.37	.30	.24	.48	.56	.20
RC2	.53	.27	—	.05	.03	.08	.18	.07	.25	.37	.64	.25	.27	.20	.35	.32	.29
RC3	.42	.34	.09	—	.27	.42	.50	.37	.47	.29	.11	-.42	.22	-.19	.46	.47	.34
RC4	.36	.25	.13	.27	—	.26	.33	.38	.47	.21	.02	-.04	.63	.24	.39	.49	.43
RC6	.42	.35	.09	.45	.27	—	.40	.49	.32	.33	.16	-.06	.38	.38	.39	.49	.35
RC7	.73	.46	.31	.49	.34	.43	—	.49	.53	.43	.28	-.24	.33	.21	.82	.72	.33
RC8	.38	.39	-.01	.40	.34	.52	.46	—	.49	.37	.03	-.07	.31	.29	.50	.62	.50
RC9	.34	.28	-.16	.46	.48	.38	.49	.52	—	.21	-.21	-.25	.25	.11	.48	.51	.72
1	.52	.92	.36	.38	.24	.34	.48	.38	.27	—	.53	.41	.33	.23	.53	.56	.15
2	.66	.48	.66	.19	.09	.20	.42	.10	-.10	.56	—	.35	.34	.26	.47	.39	-.21
3	.12	.47	.21	-.24	.01	-.03	-.12	.01	-.14	.53	.35	—	.25	.32	-.05	.01	-.09
4	.57	.32	.30	.29	.64	.42	.37	.36	.31	.36	.37	.26	—	.41	.46	.55	.36
6	.42	.24	.25	-.10	.24	.41	.30	.28	.17	.24	.31	.22	.41	—	.34	.39	.15
7	.86	.55	.45	.46	.39	.45	.83	.48	.47	.59	.61	.09	.51	.43	—	.84	.33
8	.77	.59	.38	.49	.53	.58	.72	.64	.53	.60	.48	.15	.64	.47	.84	—	.46
9	.27	.27	-.22	.39	.44	.39	.34	.54	.74	.25	-.07	.01	.42	.21	.37	.51	—

Clinical scales. However, they also noted several scales (especially RC2 and RC7) are not free of Demoralization because of the conceptual relationships between the constructs underlying RCd, RC2, and RC7. They also speculated the somewhat higher correlations between RCd and RC9 scale compared to RCd and Scale 9 may reflect the narrower focus of the RC9 scale on hypomanic activation—which includes affective states associated with the experience of unpleasant emotions reflected in the Demoralization construct. The strong correlations between some RC scales and their Clinical scale counterparts raise the question of the extent to which the RC scales add significantly to the Clinical scales in predicting external criterion measures. This issue will be addressed later in this chapter.

Forbey et al. (2004) compared RC scales and Content scales for 1,020 mental health center clients. Comparing these two sets of scales is especially interesting because the methodology used in constructing the Content scales was intended to produce more homogeneous scales than the Clinical scales, and item overlap between Content scales was minimized. Thus, one might expect the RC scales and corresponding Content scales to be more similar than the pairs of RC scales and Clinical scales. As expected, there were strong correlations between most RC scales and their corresponding Content scales (e.g., RC1 and Health Concerns [HEA]; RC8 and Bizarre Mentation [BIZ]).

Reliability of the RC Scales

Table 7.3 reports internal consistency and test–retest reliability coefficients for the RC scales for the MMPI-2 normative sample and for the three clinical samples. Because internal consistency was a consideration in the development of the RC scales, it is not surprising the RC scales have higher internal consistency values than the Clinical scales. In all samples, the RC scales had acceptable internal consistency, with the coefficients being somewhat higher for the clinical than for the normative samples.

There were 82 men and 111 women from the MMPI-2 normative sample who completed the test twice with a retest interval of approximately 1 week. As the data in Table 7.3 indicate, the stability of the RC scales over this short time period is acceptable and in most cases greater than for the corresponding Clinical scales.

Validity of the RC Scales

The correlations between RC scales and the Clinical and Content scales—discussed earlier—provide some information concerning the validity of the RC scales. These data indicate most RC scales are measuring characteristics similar, but not identical, to their Clinical and Content scale counterparts. For several scales (e.g., RC1), the correlations are so high it seems the RC scales may be redundant with corresponding Clinical and Content scales (e.g., Scale 1 and HEA). The RC3 scale, which was altered from its Clinical Scale counterpart more than any other scale, seems to be assessing only a part of what Scale 3 measures (naiveté/cynicism). Both the RC3 scale and the Cynicism (CYN) Content scale are measuring similar characteristics. Whereas the RC3 scale seems to be a rather pure measure of misanthropic beliefs, the Cynicism scale seems to measure these beliefs along with suspiciousness.

TABLE 7.3 *Internal Consistency (Alpha) Coefficients and Test–Retest Coefficients for RC Scales*

| | Alpha Coefficients | | | | | | | | Test–Retest Correlations | |
| | MMPI–2 Normative Sample | | Outpatient Sample | | Inpatient Sample I | | Inpatient Sample II | | MMPI–2 Normative Sample (Subset) | |
Scale	Men (n = 1,138)	Women (n = 1,462)	Men (n = 410)	Women (n = 610)	Men (n = 722)	Women (n = 501)	Men (n = 1229)		Men (n = 82)	Women (n = 111)
RCd	.87	.89	.93	.93	.95	.95	.93		.89	.90
RC1	.73	.78	.88	.89	.86	.88	.88		.81	.79
RC2	.68	.62	.83	.82	.85	.87	.84		.76	.77
RC3	.80	.79	.81	.80	.86	.84	.84		.76	.87
RC4	.76	.74	.81	.77	.83	.82	.83		.90	.87
RC6	.63	.65	.80	.78	.86	.85	.85		.77	.54
RC7	.81	.83	.87	.87	.90	.90	.89		.91	.87
RC8	.70	.71	.81	.81	.87	.85	.84		.80	.75
RC9	.79	.76	.80	.78	.84	.83	.83		.88	.86

Note. Excerpted (Tables 4.4 and 4.5) from the *MMPI®-2 (Minnesota Multiphasic Personality Inventory®-2) Restructured Clinical (RC) Scales: Development, Validation, and Interpretation* by Auke Tellegen, Yossef S. Ben-Porath, John L. McNulty, Paul A. Arbisi, John R. Graham, and Beverly Kaemmer. Copyright © 2003 by the Regents of the University of Minnesota. All rights reserved. Reproduced by permission of the University of Minnesota Press. "MMPI®" and "Minnesota Multiphasic Personality Inventory®" are registered trademarks of the Regents of the University of Minnesota.

While scale intercorrelations are of interest, more telling indicators of scale validity are relationships between scales and external criterion measures. Convergent validity is indicated when a scale correlates significantly with external criterion measures with which it is conceptually related. Discriminant validity is indicated when a scale is not related (or less related) to external criterion measures with which one would not expect strong relationships. Several studies have reported data relevant to these issues.

Tellegen et al. (2003) reported correlations between RC scales and several different kinds of external criterion measures for an outpatient mental health center sample and for two psychiatric inpatient samples. These correlations generally supported the convergent validity of the RC scales. For example, for outpatients, scores on RC1 had their highest correlation with therapist ratings of somatic symptoms (.58 for men and .35 for women); scores on RC2 had their highest correlation with therapist ratings of depression (.57 for men and .34 for women); and scores on RC4 had their highest correlation with therapist ratings of antisocial behaviors (.36 for men and .35 for women).

In terms of discriminant validity, data presented by Tellegen et al. (2003) suggested that although scores on the RC scales also were significantly related to some criterion measures with which they are not closely related conceptually, these correlations tended to be of lesser magnitude than the correlations observed between RC scale scores and conceptually relevant criterion measures. By comparison, some Clinical scales had correlations with conceptually relevant therapist ratings similar in strength to those of corresponding RC scales. The clear exception was Scale 4, for which correlations with therapist ratings of antisocial and acting-out behaviors were noticeably lower than similar correlations for the RC4 scale. In addition, Clinical scales were more likely than RC scales to be significantly correlated with therapist ratings of characteristics not conceptually related to the scales. This difference in discriminant validity was most marked for the RC4 scale versus Clinical Scale 4.

Sellbom et al. (2004) examined correlations between RC scales and Clinical scales and external criterion measures for 813 clients at a university clinic who identified as men and women. Similar to data reported by Tellegen et al. (2003), results of Sellbom and colleagues' (2004) study indicated most RC scales and their Clinical scale counterparts had convergent correlations of similar strength with conceptually relevant external criterion measures. For example, the correlation between the RC1 scale and therapist ratings of somatic symptoms was .25; the corresponding correlation for Clinical Scale 1 was also .25. Correlations with therapist ratings of antisocial behavior were .35 for the RC4 scale and .25 for Clinical Scale 4. However, once again, there was evidence of greater discriminant validity for the RC scales than for the Clinical scales. Additionally, scores on RCd were related moderately with markers of general maladjustment and depression; and more Clinical scales than RC scales were significantly correlated with these same outcomes. This provides some evidence to suggest efforts to isolate the assessment of general maladjustment to a single scale in the restructuring process (i.e., RCd) were successful.

Forbey et al. (2004) compared the external validity of the RC scales and the Content scales using both outpatient and inpatient samples. Both the RC scales and their Content scale counterparts were strongly correlated with conceptually related criterion measures. For example, the RC1 scale correlated .44 with therapist ratings of somatic symptoms; and the HEA Content scale correlated .45 with this variable. The RC4 scale and Antisocial Practices (ASP) Content scale correlations with therapist ratings of antisocial behaviors were .37 and .30, respectively. Once again, results suggested the discriminant validity of the RC scales was generally greater than for the Content scales. The authors pointed out some Content scales (Fears [FRS], Family Problems [FAM], and Anger [ANG]) assess areas not well represented by RC scales. Unfortunately, adequate criterion measures were not available in their study to examine the validity of these Content scales compared with the RC scales. They also acknowledged the construct of social introversion is not adequately assessed by the RC scales.

Overall, these early studies examining RC scale validity suggest Tellegen and colleagues (2003) were able to create scales with equal or better convergent and stronger discriminant validity than existing MMPI-2 scales. Other studies have reached similar conclusions about the convergent and discriminant validity of the RC scales in a variety of settings, including: (a) outpatient mental health settings (Sellbom, Ben-Porath & Graham, 2006; Sellbom, Graham, & Schenk, 2006; Shkalim, 2015; Simms et al., 2005; van der Heijden et al., 2013; Wallace & Liljequist, 2005), (b) inpatient psychiatric hospitals (Arbisi et al., 2008; Handel & Archer, 2008), (c) university clinics (Forbey & Ben-Porath, 2008; Osberg et al., 2008; Sellbom & Ben-Porath, 2005), (d) clinics evaluating candidates for bariatric surgery (Wygant et al., 2007), and (e) among patients with chronic low back pain (Tarescavage, 2015). Nonetheless, there have been exceptions. For example, in their study of clients at a university clinic, Binford and Liljequist (2008) found the RC4 scale had better convergent and discriminant validity than Scale 4 or the ASP Content scale. However, they did not find significant differences in convergent or discriminant validity between the RCd and RC2 scales and Scale 2 or the Depression (DEP) Content scale.

The strong evidence supporting discriminant validity for the RC scales suggests scores on these scales may have utility for the task of differential diagnosis. The ability of RC scales to aid in this task has been examined in several studies. Kamphuis and colleagues (2008) found the RC scales were superior to the Clinical scales in discriminating between patients with Axis I disorders (substance use or major depression) who did or did not also have Axis II disorders. E. J. Wolf et al. (2008) found the Clinical and RC scales were equally effective in predicting PTSD diagnoses based on structured interviews, but the RC scales were superior to the Clinical scales in predicting comorbid diagnoses with PTSD. Lee and colleagues (2018) demonstrated select RC scales were useful for differentiating depressive disorders from schizophrenia. These results also suggested RC scale scores were equally as able to detect these conditions when compared to their Clinical scale counterparts, but that the RC scales were generally better at discriminating between these conditions. McCord and Drerup (2011) demonstrated the Clinical and RC scales were both able to differentiate between individuals with and without depression in a sample of individuals presenting to a neuropsychology clinic with chronic pain and additional mental health difficulties. However, results also suggested this differentiation was made with fewer RC scales when compared to Clinical scales, which led the authors to conclude the differential diagnosis task might be more efficiently completed using RC scale scores.

Additional studies have examined the ability of RC scales to assess symptoms of mental disorders, but without comparing these scales to their Clinical scale counterparts. Some of this work has focused on assessing PTSD. For example, scores on RCd were demonstrated to be the best predictor of global PTSD symptoms in a study conducted by Sellbom and colleagues (2012) using data from 347 individuals undergoing disability evaluations. Arbisi et al. (2011) demonstrated scores on RCd and RC7 differentiated between subsamples of post-deployment National Guard soldiers who did and did not screen positive for PTSD symptoms. Other studies have focused on personality pathology. Specifically, J. L. Anderson and colleagues (2015) examined the ability of MMPI-2-RF scales, including scores on the RC scales, to assess DSM-defined personality disorder symptom counts derived from a structured interview in samples of Dutch clinical and forensic inpatients. Results suggested scores on conceptually relevant RC scales were associated with personality disorder symptomology. For example, scores on RC4 and RC9 were related to examined Cluster B personality disorder symptoms; avoidant and obsessive–compulsive personality symptoms were both related to scores on RC7; and paranoid and schizotypal personality disorders symptoms were associated with scores on RC7 and RC6, respectively.

Other work has continued to examine the question of differential diagnosis. For example, using data drawn from a large mental health and addiction center, Sellbom and colleagues (2012) examined the ability of MMPI-2-RF scale scores, including scores on the RC scales, to differentiate between and uniquely predict diagnoses of major depression, bipolar disorder, and schizophrenia derived via structured interview. They examined this question in several different ways statistically, but results across the various analyses suggested scores on RCd and RC2 were likely to be useful for identifying major depression; and scores on RC6 and RC8 were likely to be useful for identifying schizophrenia. A less definitive pattern of predictors was demonstrated for distinguishing bipolar disorder from the other included conditions, but results did suggest some utility of scores on RC8 and RC9 for this purpose. Haber and Baum (2014) also studied differential diagnosis in a sample of individuals receiving treatment at a university-based psychology clinic and replicated the finding that scores on RCd and RC2 are useful in identifying depressive symptoms.

In their introduction to the RC scales, Tellegen et al. (2003) proposed low scores (i.e., T < 39) on RC3 were likely to return meaningful information about a test taker. When the MMPI-2-RF was released, low score interpretations were expanded to include all RC scales except RC6 and RC8 (Ben-Porath & Tellegen, 2008/2011). The suggested interpretations were primarily based on item content. However, correlations presented by Tellegen and Ben-Porath (2008/2011) in the instrument's *Technical Manual* demonstrated low scores on RC2 were associated with extraversion and social engagement and that low scores on RC9 were related to problems with low energy levels and being withdrawn from one's environment.

Subsequent work has sought to further establish an empirical basis for low score interpretations of the RC scales. Kremyar and colleagues (2020) demonstrated low scores on RC1 were related to test takers reporting fewer medical and physical difficulties, confirming content-based interpretations provided in the MMPI-2-RF manual. Low scores on RC2 were demonstrated to be associated with higher levels of positive affect, self-esteem, and life satisfaction in a large sample of college students (J. T. Hall et al., 2021). Corey et al. (2018) investigated the ability of MMPI-2-RF scales to assess problem behavior in law enforcement officers. They demonstrated low scores on externalizing scales, including RC4, and were indicators of overcontrolled behavior associated with poor performance outcomes, such as those due to low assertiveness and stress reactivity.

Since their release in 2003, there have also been studies examining the validity of specific RC scales or the ability of RC scales to assess specific constructs. Results from some of these empirical investigations have implications for the interpretation of RC scales and will be briefly summarized following.

J. T. Hall and colleagues (2018) conducted a comprehensive study of the construct validity of RCd in a large sample of college students. Results replicated past work suggesting high scores on RCd reflect psychological distress and emotional discomfort. However, they extended the construct network of this scale by demonstrating high scores are also associated with depressive attribution styles (i.e., attributions about negative events that tend to be internal, global, and stable); having an external locus of control; maladaptive responses to stress; and engaging in excessive reassurance seeking. Scores on RCd have also been associated with tendencies toward catastrophizing in samples of spine surgery and spinal cord stimulator patients (A. R. Block et al., 2013; Marek et al., 2020). In a psychiatric inpatient sample, Stanley and colleagues (2018) demonstrated high scores on RCd were associated with past suicide attempts and that this association was stronger when scores on RC9 were also elevated.

Scores on RCd and other internalizing and somatic RC scales, which includes RC1, RC2, and RC7, have also been demonstrated to be related to treatment engagement and outcomes in mental health samples. For example, Tarescavage and colleagues (2015) examined the association between premature termination from therapy and RC scale scores in a mental health clinic and demonstrated scores on RC2 and RC7 were related to a higher likelihood of premature termination from therapy. Tylicki et al. (2019) extended this work by examining associations between MMPI-2-RF scales and treatment outcomes in a large sample of individuals receiving outpatient treatment. Results suggested scores on RCd and RC1 were both related to negative treatment outcomes, which was defined using a composite variable comprised of tendencies toward non-engagement or noncompliance with treatment recommendations, not reaching therapy goals, and having lower functioning at the time treatment was terminated.

Scores on RC3 are intended to assess cynicism (Tellegen et al., 2003). Work by Ingram and colleagues (2011) suggested scores on this scale may reflect not only a cynical worldview, but a larger pattern of manipulative and hostile interactions that impact relationships. Specifically, in a small sample of undergraduate students, those authors demonstrated scores on RC3 were strongly related to measures of Machiavellian personality traits and alienation. Scores on RC3 were also investigated by Arbisi et al. (2013) in a large sample of U.S. National Guard soldiers. Results suggested scores on RC3 from a pre-deployment assessment were associated with lower odds of using mental health services at approximately 8 months post-deployment. Remarkably, scores on RC3 remained a significant predictor of non-engagement in treatment even after accounting for self-stigma and attitudes toward mental health. Tylicki et al. (2019) demonstrated scores of 60T or higher on RC3 were associated with heightened risk for poor treatment outcomes in a large community outpatient sample. Overall, these results support the interpretation of scores on RC3 as reflecting a hostile and cynical worldview and suggest these traits may prevent or impede individuals with high scores from seeking out and engaging meaningfully in services that could assist them.

Scores on RC4 are intended to reflect antisocial attitudes and behaviors (Tellegen et al., 2003), and recent research suggests these attitudes may impact treatment completion. Specifically, the association of scores on RC4 and participation in court-ordered drug treatment was examined by Mattson and colleagues (2012) in a sample of 133 men and women evaluated as part of their involvement with the court. Results of correlational and relative risk analyses suggested scores on RC4 above 65T were significantly related to an increased risk of treatment non-completion.

Scores on RC8 have been demonstrated to be related to psychotic symptoms (Tellegen et al, 2009). However, scores on this scale may also reflect less pronounced manifestations of psychosis. Specifically, in two small samples of college students, Hunter et al. (2014) examined the ability of MMPI-2-RF scales to differentiate individuals identified as likely "schizotypes"—individuals displaying personality and cognitive characteristics suggesting they are at an increased risk for developing schizophrenia—from a matched control group. Results suggested scores on RC8, in combination with several other MMPI-2-RF scales, were effective in differentiating these two groups. These results were replicated using data from a large sample of college students by Schuder and colleagues (2016).

Several investigators have examined the construct validity of the RC scales using factor analyses. Tellegen et al. (2006) identified eight factors that corresponded with the eight RC scales (excluding the Demoralization scale). However, Hoelzle and Meyer (2008) concluded a five-factor solution was optimal. An externalizing, antisocial factor was associated with elevations on RC4 and RC9. A depressive/withdrawal factor was associated with elevations on RC2 and RCd. RC1 defined a somatic factor, and RC6 and RC8 defined a psychotic factor. Finally, a cynicism factor was associated with RC3 scale elevations. Three factors similar to the externalizing, depressive/withdrawal, and psychotic factors demonstrated by Hoelzle and Meyer (2008) emerged in a factor analysis of the RC scales conducted using data from a psychiatric inpatient sample (Sellbom et al., 2008b). Specifically, an externalizing factor was comprised of items from RC4 and RC9. A thought dysfunction factor was comprised of items from RC6 and RC8. Sellbom et al. (2008b) called their last factor "internalizing" rather than "depressive/withdrawal," as it reflected a broader set of loadings from items that are scored on RCd, RC1, RC2, and RC7. Subsequently, this three-factor structure was replicated in a combined clinical and forensic sample by van der Heijden and colleagues (2012). It should be noted this three-factor structure is also similar to that reported for the RC scales in the MMPI-2-RF manual (see Chapter 12 of this book).

The consistent emergence of three factors reflecting externalizing, internalizing, and thought dysfunction from analyses of the RC scales is important, as it provides a link between the instrument and modern models of psychopathology such as the HiTOP model (Kotov et al., 2021). Development of the HiTOP model has been spurred by known problems with comorbidity between and heterogeneity within categorical diagnoses, such as those described in the DSM-5 (American Psychiatric Association, 2013). Proponents of HiTOP seek to develop a new method of organizing psychopathological symptoms, namely, by developing an empirically derived, dimensional framework. The current HiTOP model proposes there are six broad spectra of psychopathology: somatoform, internalizing, disinhibited externalizing, antagonistic externalizing, detachment, and thought dysfunction—most of which are further divided into subspectra. The factor analyses described in the previous paragraph suggest the structure of RC scales assesses three, possibly four, of these dimensions, and thus aligns well with the HiTOP model. Sellbom (2019) provides a comprehensive review of the connections between the HiTOP model and the RC and other MMPI-2-RF scales. Generally, these data support the construct validity of RC scales as broad measures of psychological dysfunction as defined by the HiTOP model.

Some construct validity studies have focused on specific RC scales. For example, Thomas and Locke (2010) examined the construct validity of the RC1 scale in a large sample of individuals experiencing epileptic or psychogenic nonepileptic seizures. Results of factor analyses indicated the scale was comprised of several facets, including malaise and gastrointestinal, head-pain, and neurological difficulties. However, while these results suggested a multidimensional model best described the scale's structure, the authors also examined a unidimensional model. Results suggested this simpler model also had adequate fit. Overall, these results support the construct validity of RC1 and suggest it reflects broadly defined somatization.

Other construct validity studies have focused on connections between RC scale scores and theoretical models of mood, psychopathology, and personality. For example, the theoretical underpinning of the RC scale development process was based on Tellegen et al.'s (1999a, 1999b) model of mood. This model posits a pleasantness–unpleasantness dimension (sometimes referred to as happiness–unhappiness) reflecting variations in hedonic capacity that is related to, but distinct from, positive and negative affect. The unpleasantness pole of this dimension is associated with the emotional discomfort experienced by individuals high on negative affect or low on positive affect. Broadly, research has supported that scores on RCd assess the pleasantness–unpleasantness dimension, while scores on RC2 and RC7 reflect distinctive aspects of positive and negative affect, respectively (Sellbom & Ben-Porath, 2005, Shkalim et al., 2016; Simms et al., 2005). Scores on these scales have also been associated with internalizing psychopathology in a manner congruent with this theory (Sellbom et al., 2008a; Shkalim et al., 2017). Taken together, this work suggests strong connections between RCd, RC2, and RC7 and Tellegen et al.'s (1999a; 1999b) theoretical model of mood.

Several general conclusions about the RC scales seem appropriate. The RC scales demonstrate convergent validity similar to, and in some cases greater than, corresponding Clinical and Content scales. Although Demoralization is still represented to some degree in the RC scales, they are less saturated with this general factor than either the Clinical or Content scales. This reduction of the Demoralization factor in the RC scales has resulted generally in improved discriminant validity for these scales. Some RC scales are more focused measures of important core constructs than their Clinical and Content scale counterparts. Finally, empirical work supports the construct validity of these scales and their alignment with contemporary models of psychopathology and affect.

The RC scales have not been without critics. For example, an entire issue of the *Journal of Personality Assessment* (*JPA*; October 2006) was devoted to concerns about the RC scales and responses by the authors of the scales to those concerns. It is not possible to discuss all of the concerns and responses raised in the special issue here. However, a brief summary of the major issues may be useful to readers.

In the *JPA* special issue, one concern expressed was the possibility that the RC scales were redundant measures of constructs already assessed by existing MMPI-2 scales with strong evidence supporting their validity (e.g., RCd, the Content scales; Nichols, 2006). A second concern raised was that the RC scales were less valid measures of the constructs reflected in the Clinical scales (e.g., RC3 and RC9; Butcher et al., 2006; Nichols, 2006). A third concern raised was that the RC scales were less able to detect complex psychopathological syndromes than the Clinical scales (Caldwell, 2006; Nichols, 2006; Rogers et al., 2006). Further, Rogers et al. (2006) challenged the construct validity of the RC scales, reporting a failed attempt to replicate the factor structure used by Tellegen et al. (2003) to construct the scales. Rogers et al. (2006) also expressed concern that the RC scales were developed without taking socially desirable responding into account, suggesting they were likely to be more susceptible to noncredible responding.

Tellegen et al. (2006) responded to these criticisms, pointing out errors of logic and presenting new data to address some of the concerns. Specifically, they reviewed existing studies or provided new evidence demonstrating the RC scale scores had similar or better convergent validity and improved discriminant validity for assessing both narrow and multifaceted constructs when compared to existing Clinical, Content, and Supplementary scales. They acknowledged psychological distress as being a key component of many psychopathological syndromes, but they argued it was unnecessary to assess this construct in every scale as it may limit their discriminant validity. Tellegen and colleagues (2006) also identified ways in which Rogers et al. (2006) used different criteria in their factor analyses than those used in development of the RC scales, and they were able to replicate the RC factor structure using the Rogers et al. criteria. Finally, they reviewed evidence from a study by Sellbom, Ben-Porath, Graham, and colleagues (2005) that demonstrated RC scales were no more susceptible to invalidating response styles than the Clinical or Content scales.

Interpretation of RC Scales

Item numbers and scoring directions for the RC scales are provided in the MMPI-2 RC scales monograph (Tellegen et al., 2003). The monograph also includes uniform T-score equivalents for RC scale raw scores for the MMPI-2 normative samples.

Score transformations based on the non-gendered normative data are available in the Appendix of Ben-Porath and Forbey's (2003) non-gendered norms monograph.

The RC scale monograph (Tellegen et al., 2003) and the research studies described here indicate some of the RC scales can add significantly to the interpretation of MMPI-2 protocols. Not only can the scales clarify the meaning of elevated scores on the Clinical scales, they can also be used to generate inferences about test takers independently of the Clinical scales. However, as with any other MMPI-2 scale, clinicians need to first assess the validity of the test protocol before interpreting RC scale scores. Sellbom, Ben-Porath, Graham, et al. (2005) demonstrated the RC scales are susceptible to the effects of overreporting and underreporting.

Tellegen et al. (2003) suggested tentative interpretive guidelines for the RC scales. They recommended—as with most MMPI-2 scales—a T score equal to or greater than 65 (approximately the 92nd percentile for the MMPI-2 normative sample) be considered a high score for most RC scales. However, for some RC scales, they also discussed the meaning of even more elevated T scores—typically at T > 70 or T > 80—representing the upper extremes of the distribution. For several RC scales, interpretations of low scores (T < 39) are suggested.

We recommend the following strategy for integrating Clinical and RC scale information. First, consider that for any particular Clinical scale/RC scale pair (e.g., Scale 1 and RC1), there are four possibilities: (a) neither the Clinical nor RC scale score is high; (b) both the Clinical and RC scale scores are high; (c) the Clinical scale score is high, but the corresponding RC scale score is not high; or, finally, (d) the Clinical scale score is not high but the corresponding RC scale score is high. Sellbom et al. (2004) found in mental health center and university clinic settings, most often, either both a Clinical scale and its RC scale counterpart would be elevated, or neither scale would be elevated. Having only one elevated scale in the Clinical/RC pair was less common but occurred frequently enough that attending to this pattern of scores is likely to be important in MMPI-2 interpretation. For most Clinical/RC scale pairs, Sellbom et al. (2004) found it was more common for the Clinical scale to be elevated and the corresponding RC scale not to be elevated than vice versa. Similar results were demonstrated by Bowden and colleagues (2014) in a sample of individuals with seizure disorders.

After a pattern of scale elevations for a particular test taker on a particular set of Clinical/RC scales is identified, interpretation of these scales should proceed by taking the observed pattern into account. If neither the Clinical nor RC scale T score is high, no interpretations should be made of either scale. If both the Clinical and RC scale T scores are high, inferences about the core construct for the Clinical scale (e.g., health concerns for Scale 1) can be made with considerable confidence. Inferences about characteristics of the test taker in addition to those associated with the core construct may also be appropriate based on the high score on the Clinical scale. For example, a high Scale 7 score and a high RC7 scale score suggest inferences about characteristics associated with the core construct of dysfunctional negative emotions (e.g., anxiety, irritability, and fearfulness). Additional inferences, based on the high Scale 7 score, would also be in order (e.g., organized, persistent, tendency to stay in treatment longer than most patients).

When the Clinical scale score is high, but the RC scale score is not, one should be quite cautious about making inferences the test taker has characteristics consistent with the core construct associated with the Clinical scale. The high Clinical scale score may very well be a product of demoralization and not indicative of characteristics associated with the core construct. In such cases, the RCd scale score also is likely to be high.

Finally, if the Clinical scale score is not high, but the RC scale score is high, inferences about characteristics related to the core construct (e.g., health concerns for RC1) are appropriate. The lower Clinical scale score is likely to result from the absence of demoralization in the protocol. The person may have endorsed items consistent with the core construct for the scale but not many items having to do with demoralization, leading to a Clinical scale score that is not high. Obviously, in such cases, one would not expect a high RCd scale score.

Demoralization (RCd)

The RCd scale reflects the pleasantness–unpleasantness (also known as the happiness–unhappiness) dimension from Tellegen and colleagues' (1999a; 1999b) model of mood and affect and is associated with the "distress" dimension of internalizing psychopathology posited in recent quantitative models of psychopathology. Scores on RCd provide an indication of the overall emotional discomfort and turmoil a person is experiencing. High scorers (T ≥ 65) on this scale are likely also to have high scores on other RC, Clinical, and Content scales, especially those that have strong affective components.

Very high scores (T ≥ 80) on the RCd scale indicate persons who

1. are experiencing significant emotional turmoil
2. report feeling depressed
3. report being anxious and unable to concentrate
4. report somatic complaints that may increase in times of stress
5. feel overwhelmed by the demands of their life situations
6. feel incapable of coping with their current life circumstances
7. may be experiencing suicidal thinking or engaging in suicide-related behavior
8. should be evaluated for suicide risk (particularly if RC9 is > 65)
9. should be evaluated for disorders characterized by high levels of dysphoric affect, such as depressive, generalized anxiety, and trauma-related disorders
10. may be motivated for treatment because of emotional distress
11. need intervention to relieve emotional distress
12. are at risk for poor treatment outcomes

High scores (T = 65–79) indicate persons who

1. feel sad and unhappy
2. feel anxious much of the time
3. are dissatisfied with their life situations
4. have poor self-concepts and feel like failures

5. have low self-efficacy and view themselves as unworthy and incapable
6. react poorly to stress
7. tend to imagine the worst possible outcomes for actions or events
8. respond to negative events with internal, global, and stable attributions
9. are pessimistic about their lives getting better
10. may engage in excessive reassurance seeking

Low scores (T < 39) indicate persons who report a greater than average level of morale and life satisfaction.

Somatic Complaints (RC1)

Items on RC1 inquire about an individual's general sense of physical well-being and specific somatic difficulties and reflect a broad somatoform construct similar to that posited in dimensional models of psychopathology. The RC1 scale is very similar to Scale 1 and the HEA Content scale. Indeed, like these latter two scales, the cardinal feature of high scorers (T ≥ 65) on the RC1 scale is somatic preoccupation.

High scores on the RC1 scale indicate persons who

1. report multiple somatic complaints, including gastrointestinal problems, head pain, and neurological symptoms
2. have increased somatic symptoms in times of stress
3. are quite resistant to considering psychological factors that may be related to somatic symptoms
4. are at risk for terminating therapy before goals are met
5. if physical explanations for their somatic symptoms can be ruled out, should be further evaluated for somatoform disorders

Low scores (T < 39) indicate persons who report a sense of physical well-being and are likely to describe having fewer medical and physical difficulties than is typical.

Low Positive Emotions (RC2)

Items on RC2 ask about the test taker's experience of positive emotions, social engagement, and interest and ability to engage in activities. The RC2 scale reflects the positive affect dimension of Tellegen and colleagues' (1999a; 1999b) model of mood and affect. It also has conceptual connections with aspects of the internalizing and detachment spectra described in dimensional models of psychopathology. Scores on this scale are intended to reflect the test taker's low capacity for positive emotional experiences, a core component of depressive syndromes (i.e., anhedonia).

High scores (T ≥ 65) on the RC2 scale indicate persons who

1. lack positive emotional experiences in life
2. have deficits in their ability to experience joy and happiness (anhedonia)
3. are unhappy and demoralized
4. lack energy to handle the demands of their life situations
5. find it difficult to take charge, make decisions, and get things done

6. tend to be introverted, passive, and withdrawn in social situations
7. often feel bored and isolated
8. are pessimistic
9. have low expectations of success and are not likely to place themselves in competitive situations
10. may meet criteria for major depression or other depressive disorders
11. should be evaluated for disorders characterized by social withdrawal or avoidance, such as social anxiety disorder
12. should be evaluated for antidepressant medications
13. may have difficulty engaging in treatment because of low positive emotionality
14. are at risk for terminating therapy before goals are met
15. if $T \geq 75$, may need inpatient treatment for depression

Low scores ($T < 39$) on the RC2 scale indicate persons who

1. report a high level of psychological well-being
2. are likely to be satisfied with their life
3. report a wide range of emotionally positive experiences
4. report feeling confident and energetic
5. have high levels of positive affect
6. have positive self-esteem
7. are extraverted and socially engaged
8. are optimistic about the future

Cynicism (RC3)

Clinical Scale 3 has two major components—somatic complaints and avowal of excessive trust of others. As mentioned earlier, the somatic complaints component was assigned to the RC1 scale. The RC3 scale assesses the second component but is scored in the opposite direction from Scale 3. Thus, RC3 reflects cynical (as opposed to naïve) beliefs about others.

High scores ($T \geq 65$) indicate persons who

1. have cynical beliefs
2. see other people as untrustworthy, uncaring, and concerned only about themselves
3. may be hostile or manipulative when interacting with other people
4. feel alienated from others
5. need help in developing interpersonal trust
6. may have difficulty engaging in therapy or forming therapeutic relationships
7. are at risk for negative treatment outcomes

Low scores ($T < 39$) on the RC3 scale indicate persons who

1. disavow cynical beliefs
2. see others as well-intentioned and trustworthy
3. may be naive, gullible, and overly trusting of others

Antisocial Behavior (RC4)

Clinical Scale 4 is often elevated in persons with histories of antisocial attitudes and behaviors. However, because Scale 4 is quite saturated with a general demoralization factor, high scores do not necessarily indicate antisocial proclivities. The RC4 scale is a purer measure than Scale 4 of antisocial characteristics and reflects both the antagonistic and disinhibited aspects of externalizing tendencies reflected in dimensional models of psychopathology.

High scores (T ≥ 65) on the RC4 scale indicate persons who

1. report histories of antisocial behaviors
2. find it difficult to conform to societal norms and expectations
3. are likely to have been in trouble with the law
4. are at increased risk for substance abuse
5. behave aggressively toward other people
6. are critical, argumentative, and antagonistic
7. have conflictual relationships with other people
8. may have significant family problems
9. should be evaluated for Cluster B personality disorders
10. are not likely to be motivated for treatment
11. may not be very compliant in treatment
12. may be at risk for not completing recommended treatments
13. need help in developing better self-control

Low scores (T < 39) on the RC4 scale indicate persons who report higher than average levels of behavioral constraint. Individuals achieving low scores on RC4 are likely to be overcontrolled.

Ideas of Persecution (RC6)

Items on RC6 inquire about an individual's beliefs about others wanting to harm them and, like Clinical Scale 6, reflect persecutory ideation. However, because the RC6 scale is less saturated with Demoralization than Scale 6, it is a purer measure of persecutory thinking. Scores on RC6 reflect aspects of a liability toward thought dysfunction described in dimensional models of psychopathology. However, it is important to note that elevations on this scale do not necessarily indicate the presence of thinking that is delusional in nature. Elevations can occur in individuals who are suspicious and cautious around people for other reasons (e.g., as a result of traumatic experiences).

High scores (T ≥ 65) indicate persons who

1. feel targeted, controlled, or victimized by others
2. are suspicious of the motivations of others
3. have difficulty in forming relationships
4. may have difficulty forming therapeutic relationships
5. if T ≥ 80, may experience paranoid delusions or hallucinations
6. if T ≥ 80, should be evaluated further for schizophrenia and other psychotic spectrum disorders, including Cluster A personality disorders

Low scores on this scale are not interpreted.

Dysfunctional Negative Emotions (RC7)

The RC7 scale reflects the negative affect dimension of Tellegen and colleagues' (1999a; 1999b) model of mood and affect and is associated with the "fear" dimension of internalizing psychopathology described in dimensional models of psychopathology. Items on RC7 assess the test taker's experience of negative emotions, such as anxiety, anger, and fear. Given the negative emotions reflected in RC7, test takers with high scores on this scale will also frequently report experiencing demoralization. However, while these experiences are correlated, negative emotionality is distinct from demoralization, which tends to pervade many different kinds of psychopathology.

High scores (T ≥ 65) on the RC7 scale indicate persons who

1. report negative emotional experiences, including anxiety, fear, and irritability
2. worry excessively
3. experience intrusive ideation
4. report feeling sad and unhappy
5. are insecure and excessively sensitive to perceived criticism
6. are self-critical and guilt-prone
7. ruminate and brood about perceived failures
8. should be evaluated for disorders related to fearfulness (i.e., phobias, social anxiety, and obsessive–compulsive disorders), trauma-related disorders, and Cluster C personality disorders
9. may be motivated for treatment because of emotional distress
10. are at risk for terminating therapy before goals are met
11. should be evaluated for anxiolytic medications

Low scores (T < 39) on the RC7 scale indicate persons who report below average levels of negative emotional experiences.

Aberrant Experiences (RC8)

Like Clinical Scale 8, items on RC8 inquire about the test taker's experience of unusual thinking and perceptual experiences. However, because the RC8 scale is less saturated with Demoralization than Clinical Scale 8, it has the potential to be a more focused measure of sensory, perceptual, cognitive, and motor disturbances suggestive of psychotic disorders. Scores on RC8 reflect aspects of a liability toward thought dysfunction described in dimensional models of psychopathology.

High scores (T ≥ 65) on the RC8 scale indicate persons who

1. report unusual sensory, perceptual, cognitive, or motor experiences
2. may experience hallucinations or delusions
3. may experience bizarre sensory experiences
4. have impaired reality testing
5. may report feeling anxious or depressed
6. have impaired occupational and interpersonal functioning
7. may be experiencing subclinical levels of thought disturbance that reflect a vulnerability to psychotic disorders
8. in mental health settings, should be evaluated further for psychosis spectrum disorders, including schizophrenia

9. may require treatment in structured settings
10. should be evaluated for antipsychotic medications
11. may find it difficult to participate appropriately in treatment because of disordered thinking

Low scores on the RC8 scale are not interpreted.

Hypomanic Activation (RC9)

Although the RC9 scale and Clinical Scale 9 do not share many items, they seem to be very similar scales. Neither scale is heavily saturated with the demoralization factor, and both seem to be assessing similar constructs. In most samples, items on RC9 appear to reflect disinhibited aspects of externalizing tendencies reflected in dimensional models of psychopathology, likely due to its assessment of impulsive behavior and sensation-seeking tendencies.

High scores (T ≥ 65) on the RC9 scale indicate persons who

1. experience racing thoughts
2. experience high energy levels
3. have heightened mood
4. are irritable and aggressive
5. show poor impulse control
6. may engage in antisocial behaviors
7. may abuse substances
8. are sensation seekers and risk takers
9. should be evaluated further for bipolar disorders
10. may find appropriate participation in treatment difficult because of excessive behavioral activation
11. should be evaluated for mood-stabilizing medications
12. if T ≥ 75, may experience manic episodes

Low scores (T < 39) on the RC9 scale indicate persons who have below average levels of activation and engagement with their environments. Individuals with low scores on RC9 are likely to experience low energy levels and be withdrawn from their environment. They should be evaluated for depressive disorders, especially if scores on RC2 are also elevated.

PERSONALITY PSYCHOPATHOLOGY FIVE (PSY-5) SCALES

Widiger (1997) and others have articulated concerns about a categorical classification system of mental disorders and have suggested dimensional approaches that conceptualize personality disorders as extensions of normal range personality functioning. Harkness, McNulty, and Ben-Porath (1995) subscribed to the notion that understanding broad bandwidth personality constructs was likely to be useful in clinical practice, especially when thinking about personality pathology; but they felt existing scales for assessing such constructs (e.g., the NEO Personality Inventory-Revised; NEO-PI-R; Costa & McCrae, 1992) were not adequate for assessing both adaptive and maladaptive personality functioning. Thus, they developed the PSY-5 scales to assess personality traits relevant to both adaptive and maladaptive personality (Harkness, McNulty, & Ben-Porath, 1995). The conceptualization underlying the scales is similar, but not identical, to the five-factor model of personality. The PSY-5 model has been independently replicated (Harkness et al., 2012) and aligns with personality dimensions outlined in dimensional models of psychiatric dysfunction (Sellbom, 2019). This alignment includes models recently proposed to describe personality dysfunction (e.g., the AMPD; American Psychiatric Association, 2013) and psychopathology more broadly (e.g., HiTOP; Kotov et al., 2021).

The PSY-5 Constructs

The constructs the PSY-5 scales were designed to measure were identified by having lay persons (hospital volunteers and college students) rate personality descriptors using the method of psychological distances. This methodology has been described in several places, but the most concise description is in a monograph published by the University of Minnesota Press (Harkness et al., 2002).

Harkness first assembled a large pool of descriptors of personality and personality disorders. A total of 120 descriptors of maladaptive personality were selected from descriptions of personality disorders in the *Diagnostic and Statistical Manual III-R* (American Psychiatric Association, 1987) and were reworded so they could be understood by lay persons. In addition, 16 descriptors of psychopathy (Cleckley, 1982) were similarly reworded. Finally, 94 descriptors of adaptive personality traits relevant to everyday life were generated based on personality dimensions described by Tellegen (1982). The lay raters were asked to group similar descriptors together, and these ratings were subjected to mathematical analyses to identify clusters of personality features.

The 60 clusters of personality features resulting from these procedures were then examined by other lay persons who were asked to group similar features together; and these ratings were subjected to latent root methods, ultimately yielding five broad constructs representing the full range of adaptive and maladaptive personality. It is these five constructs (Aggressiveness, Psychoticism, Constraint, Negative Emotionality/Neuroticism, and Positive Emotionality/Extraversion) that were the basis for the construction of the PSY-5 scales of the MMPI-2, as well as subsequent versions of the PSY-5 scales scored on the MMPI-2-RF and MMPI-3 (which are described in Chapters 12 and 13 of this book). It should be noted that to keep the poles of all five dimensions oriented such that high scores were associated with more maladaptive manifestations of personality, the Constraint construct later was reversed and relabeled as Disconstraint and Positive Emotionality/Extraversion later was reversed and relabeled as Introversion/Low Positive Emotionality.

Harkness et al. (2002) provided brief descriptions of the PSY-5 constructs, which were expanded upon by Harkness, Reynolds, and Lilienfeld (2014). Aggressiveness (AGGR) is hypothesized to reflect individual differences in agenda protection—characteristics that allow a person to overcome social and environmental obstacles that could prevent them from reaching their goals. The core personality difference captured by AGGR is the readiness to assert oneself and dominate others to protect and advance yourself. As such, AGGR is largely focused on offensive and instrumental aggression and may include enjoyment of intimidating others to accomplish one's goals. This dimension aligns with the antagonism dimension proposed in the AMPD and the antagonistic externalizing spectrum in the HiTOP model.

Psychoticism (PSYC) has to do with disconnection from reality—including unshared beliefs as well as unusual sensory and perceptual experiences—and feeling alienated and having unrealistic expectations of harm. Harkness, Reynolds, and Lilienfeld (2014) described PSYC as drawing from multiple brain systems that work together to create internal representations of external reality. They hypothesized PSYC specifically captures individual differences in the degree to which new and existing information about the external world is integrated into internal models of reality. PSYC aligns with the AMPD dimension of the same name and the thought disorder spectrum in the HiTOP model.

Disconstraint (DISC) involves risk-taking, impulsivity, and ignoring traditional moral beliefs and behaviors. It most closely aligns with the HiTOP model's disinhibited externalizing spectrum and the AMPD's disinhibition domain trait. Harkness, Reynolds, and Lilienfeld (2014) describe DISC as capturing individual differences in the ability to weigh long-term benefits and risks versus those present in the immediate environment. They explain that individuals who are low on DISC will be likely to change their immediate behaviors to better conform with their predictions of future consequences, while individuals who are high in DISC will act to maximize benefits and minimize risks in the present with less regard for any possible future outcomes.

Harkness, Reynolds, and Lilienfeld (2014) place Negative Emotionality/Neuroticism (NEGE) within a brain system devoted to the detection of danger in our environment. As such, NEGE captures a predisposition to experience negative emotions (e.g., fear, anxiety), to focus on problematic features of incoming information, to worry, to be self-critical, to feel guilty, and to concoct worst-case scenarios. The internalizing spectrum from the HiTOP model (especially the "fear" sub-spectrum) and the AMPD's negative affectivity domain trait demonstrate considerable conceptual overlap with NEGE.

Harkness, Reynolds, and Lilienfeld (2014) theorize that Introversion/Low Positive Emotionality (INTR) is part of a broader resource acquisition brain system. They describe this system—responsive to both internal need states and external opportunities—as being responsible for the recognition, planning, activation, coordination, and reinforcement of goal-driven actions. INTR detects individual differences in capacity to experience positive emotions (e.g., joy) and positive engagement as well as social introversion. INTR is keyed such that high scores are indicative of limited capacity. Conceptually, it is congruent with the construct named detachment in both the AMPD and HiTOP models.

Construction of the PSY–5 Scales

Using the constructs derived from the procedures described earlier, Harkness, McNulty, and Ben-Porath (1995) identified MMPI-2 items judged to be assessing each construct. First, 114 college students were trained to understand each of the PSY-5 constructs. These students then examined each MMPI-2 item and identified those they believed assessed a PSY-5 construct. Items identified in this manner by a majority of raters were selected for preliminary PSY-5 scales.

TABLE 7.4 *Personality Psychopathology-Five (PSY-5) Scales*

Aggressiveness	AGGR	18 items
Psychoticism	PSYC	25 items
Disconstraint	DISC	29 items
Negative Emotionality/Neuroticism	NEGE	33 items
Introversion/Low Positive Emotionality	INTR	34 items

Note. Excerpted from *MMPI®-2 Personality Psychopathology Five (PSY-5) Scales: Gaining an Overview for Case Conceptualization and Treatment Planning* by Allan R. Harkness, John L. McNulty, Yossef S. Ben-Porath, and John R. Graham. Copyright © 2002 by the Regents of the University of Minnesota. All rights reserved. Reproduced by permission of the University of Minnesota Press. "MMPI®" and "Minnesota Multiphasic Personality Inventory®" are registered trademarks of the Regents of the University of Minnesota.

Experts then reviewed the preliminary scales to make sure items in a scale could be clearly keyed to indicate the construct, were direct measures of that construct, and were relevant to only one construct. The preliminary scales were revised and then subjected to psychometric analyses based on data from four large samples. Any item that correlated more strongly with a scale other than the one on which it was initially placed was deleted. An item is not scored on more than one PSY-5 scale. Uniform T scores were generated for each raw score based on data from the MMPI-2 normative sample. Table 7.4 lists the MMPI-2's PSY-5 scales and the number of items in each scale. Item numbers and scored directions for each of the PSY-5 scales can be found in Appendix B of the MMPI-2 manual (Butcher et al., 2001). Tables for converting raw scores on the PSY-5 scales to Uniform T scores are in Appendix A of the MMPI-2 manual. Score transformations based on the non-gendered normative data are available in the Appendix of Ben-Porath and Forbey's (2003) non-gendered norms monograph.

Reliability of the PSY-5 Scales

Table 7.5 presents data from several sources on the reliability of the PSY-5 scales. Harkness et al. (2002) reported internal consistency coefficients for the MMPI-2 normative sample and for three clinical samples; and Trull et al. (1995) published similar data for two samples of psychiatric patients. Subsequently, internal consistency data were reported for college students (Sharpe & Desai, 2001) and Dutch psychiatric patients (Egger et al., 2003). In all of these nonclinical and clinical samples, the PSY-5 scales had acceptable internal consistency (>.60). In general, the scales were a bit more internally consistent for clinical than for nonclinical samples.

Because the PSY-5 scales are thought to measure rather enduring personality characteristics, scores on these scales should be relatively stable over time. Harkness, et al. (2002) reported test–retest reliability coefficients for the MMPI-2 normative sample (1-week interval) and for the Boston VA Normative Aging sample (5-year interval). Trull et al. (1995) reported test–retest coefficients for the PSY-5 scales for psychiatric patients for whom repeat MMPI-2s were available after 3 and 6 months. Langwerden et al. (2021) reported test–retest coefficients for the PSY-5 scales over a 20-year interval using a subsample derived from the Dutch language normative samples for the MMPI-2 and MMPI-2-RF. The reliability coefficients for these various samples are reported in Table 7.6. These coefficients suggest that the PSY-5 scales are

TABLE 7.5 *Internal Consistency (Alpha) Coefficients for PSY-5 Scales*

| Scale | Alpha Coefficients | | | | |
	Normative (*n* = 2,567)	College (*n* = 2,928)	Psych. A[a] (*n* = 328)	Psych. B[b] (*n* = 156)	CDC[c] (*n* = 1,196)
AGGR	.68	.71	.70	.73	.72
PSYC	.70	.74	.84	.78	.74
DISC	.71	.69	.73	.68	.75
NEGE	.84	.84	.88	.88	.86
INTR	.71	.74	.86	.85	.81

Note. AGGR = Aggressiveness, PSYC = Psychoticism, DISC = Disconstraint, NEGE = Negative Emotionality/ Neuroticism, INTR = Introversion/Low. Positive Emotionality. Excerpted (Tables 1 and 2) from *MMPI®-2 Personality Psychopathology Five (PSY-5) Scales: Gaining an Overview for Case Conceptualization and Treatment Planning* by Allan R. Harkness, John L. McNulty, Yossef S. Ben-Porath, and John R. Graham. Copyright © 2002 by the Regents of the University of Minnesota. All rights reserved. Reproduced by permission of the University of Minnesota Press. "MMPI®" and "Minnesota Multiphasic Personality Inventory®" are registered trademarks of the Regents of the University of Minnesota.
[a]State hospital psychiatric patients.
[b]Private hospital psychiatric patients.
[c]Chemical dependency.

TABLE 7.6 *Test–Retest Reliability Coefficients for PSY-5 Scales*

Scale	1–Week[a]	3–Month[b]	6–Month[b]	5–Year[c]	20–Year[d]
AGGR	.82	.65	.62	.74	.73
PSYC	.78	.83	.67	.69	.30
DISC	.88	.84	.86	.74	.56
NEGE	.88	.78	.84	.82	.65
INTR	.84	.76	.70	.79	.63

Note. AGGR = Aggressiveness, PSYC = Psychoticism, DISC = Disconstraint, NEGE = Negative Emotionality/ Neuroticism, INTR = Introversion/Low Positive Emotionality.
[a]*N* = 111 men and women in MMPI-2 normative sample. Excerpted (Table 3) from *MMPI®-2 Personality Psychopathology Five (PSY-5) Scales: Gaining an Overview for Case Conceptualization and Treatment Planning* by Allan R. Harkness, John L. McNulty, Yossef S. Ben-Porath, and John R. Graham. Copyright © 2002 by the Regents of the University of Minnesota. All rights reserved. Reproduced by permission of the University of Minnesota Press. "MMPI®" and "Minnesota Multiphasic Personality Inventory®" are registered trademarks of the Regents of the University of Minnesota.
[b]*N* = 44 psychiatric outpatients. From Trull, T. J., Useda, J. D., Costa, P. T., & McCrae, R. R. (1995). Comparison of the MMPI-2 Personality Psychopathology Five (PSY-5), the NEO-PI, and the NEO-PI-R. *Psychological Assessment, 7,* 508–516.
[c]*N* = approximately 959–998 men in Boston VA Normative Aging Sample. From Harkness, A. R., Spiro, A., Butcher, J. N., & Ben-Porath, Y. S. (1995, August). *Personality Psychopathology Five (PSY-5) in the Boston VA Normative Aging Study.* Paper presented at the 103rd Annual Convention of the American Psychological Association, New York. Reproduced by permission from the authors.
[d]*N* = 65 adults from the 1992 and 2012 Dutch language standardization samples. Test-retest coefficients in this sample were calculated using the revised versions of the PSY-5 scored on the MMPI-2-RF. From Langwerden, R. J., van der Heijden, P. T., Egger, J. I. M., & Derksen, J. J. L. (2021). Robustness of the maladaptive personality plaster: An investigation of stability of the PSY-5-r in adults over 20 years. *Journal of Personality Assessment, 103*(1), 27–32. https://doi.org/10.1080/00223891.2020.1729772

temporally stable even for patients who are undergoing psychiatric treatment and for nonpatients over relatively long periods of time.

Validity of the PSY-5 Scales

Bagby and colleagues (2002) reported data that support the construct validity of the PSY-5 scales. These investigators conducted confirmatory factor analyses of items in the PSY-5 scales for college student and psychiatric patient samples. They reported a good fit between the hypothesized model underlying the PSY-5 scales and their factor-analytic results.

Some validity studies have examined relationships between PSY-5 scales and scales from other self-report inventories. Harkness, McNulty, and Ben-Porath (1995) correlated PSY-5 scales with scales from Tellegen's Multidimensional Personality Questionnaire (MPQ; Tellegen, 1982). Given MPQ constructs were the basis, at least in part, for the determination of the PSY-5 constructs, it is not surprising that expected relationships between the two sets of scales were obtained. For example, the PSY-5 AGGR scale's highest correlation was with the MPQ Aggression scale; and the PSY-5 DISC scale correlated most highly (and negatively) with the MPQ Constraint super factor scale. Harkness, Spiro, et al. (1995) correlated PSY-5 scales with scales from the 16 Personality Factor Questionnaire (16PF; Cattell, Eber, & Tatsuoka, 1970). Again, correlations between the sets of scales were consistent with definitions of the PSY-5 constructs. For example, the PSY-5 DISC scale had its highest positive correlation with the 16PF Happy-Go-Lucky versus Sober scale, and its highest negative correlations with the Conscientious versus Expedient and Assertive versus Humble scales of the 16PF.

PSY-5 scales have also been correlated with scores on the NEO and NEO-PI-R for older, nonclinical men (Trull et al., 1995) and psychiatric patients (Bagby et al., 2008; Egger et al., 2003). Data from these studies demonstrated expected patterns of relationships that generally supported the construct validity of the PSY-5 scales.

J. L. Anderson et al. (2013) compared the PSY-5 as measured using the MMPI-2-RF to the Personality Inventory for DSM-5 (PID-5; Krueger et al., 2012). The PID-5 is a self-report inventory designed to measure domain and facet level personality traits derived from the DSM-5's AMPD (American Psychiatric Association, 2013). In a sample of college students, J. L. Anderson and colleagues (2013) demonstrated that the PSY-5 and the AMPD traits were empirically associated in a manner consistent with the theoretical conceptualization of how these two models of personality overlap. AGGR-r was generally most strongly correlated with PID-5 Antagonism and its facet traits, PSYC-r with PID-5 Psychoticism, DISC-r with PID-5 Disinhibition, NEGE-r with PID-5 Negative Affectivity, and INTR-R with PID-5 Detachment. Finn and colleagues (2014) examined the relationship between the PSY-5 and the AMPD using two non-treatment-seeking samples (college student and military service members). Finn et al. used the SCID-II Personality Questionnaire (SCID-II-PQ; First et al., 1997) to construct AMPD domain trait proxy scales from self-report questions designed to identify markers of DSM-IV personality disorders. Their general findings replicated J. L. Anderson et al.'s (2013) earlier results.

Harkness, McNulty, et al. (2014) utilized a college student sample to examine correlations between the PSY-5 scales and the Oxford-Liverpool Inventory of Feelings and Experiences (O-LIFE; Mason et al., 1995). The O-LIFE is a self-report inventory designed to measure four aspects of schizotypy: unusual experiences, cognitive distortions, introvertive anhedonia, and impulsive nonconformity. The correlations between the O-LIFE factors and the PSY-5 were generally consistent with conceptual expectations (e.g., unusual experiences was most strongly correlated with PSYC-r, introvertive anhedonia was most strongly correlated with INTR-r). However, NEGE-r was moderately to highly correlated with all four O-LIFE factors.

Sharpe and Desai (2001) examined relationships between PSY-5 scale scores and scales from the Buss and Perry Aggression Questionnaire (AQ; Buss & Perry, 1992). AGGR scale scores were significantly correlated with the total score and all subscale scores of the AQ. However, the AGGR scale was especially important in predicting scores on the Verbal Aggression subscale of the AQ, a measure assessing an assertiveness or instrumental component of aggression.

Harkness, McNulty, et al. (2014) correlated the PSY-5 scales with the Externalizing Spectrum Inventory (ESI; Krueger et al., 2007). The ESI consists of 415 self-report items combined to score 23 subscales reflecting different manifestations of externalizing behaviors. DISC-r was meaningfully correlated with a majority of the subscales; and it was especially strongly correlated with rebelliousness, excitement seeking, and ESI subscales measuring substance use. AGGR-r was moderately correlated with both physical aggression and relational aggression. Somewhat surprisingly, NEGE-r demonstrated moderate magnitude associations with both impatient urgency and problematic impulsivity.

McDermut et al. (2019) investigated the relationships between the PSY-5, dysfunctional beliefs, and emotions. Overall, they found NEGE-r was the PSY-5 scale most closely associated with self-reported depression, anxiety, and anger. However, they found the relationship between NEGE-r and those emotional states was partially mediated by self-reported dysfunctional beliefs as measured by the short-form of the Dysfunctional Attitude Scale (DAS-SF1; Beevers et al., 2007). In other words, McDermut and colleagues identified dysfunctional beliefs as one of the mechanisms through which NEGE-r was connected to affective states.

The PSY-5 scales also have been correlated with history variables for male and female mental health center clients (Harkness et al., 2002) and for men and women referred to a court clinic for forensic evaluations (Petroskey et al., 2003). In both samples, PSY-5 scales were correlated with expected history variables (e.g., AGGR with history of being physically abusive; INTR with history of previous suicide attempts). Harkness et al. (2002) also reported relationships between PSY-5 scales and therapist ratings of their clients. Again, expected relationships were observed. The highest correlation for the AGGR scale was with therapist ratings of aggressive behavior, and the highest correlation for the DISC scale was with therapist ratings of antisocial behavior. Although the NEGE and INTR scales were correlated significantly with many therapist ratings, it is interesting to note the ratings having to do with anger and antisocial behaviors were noticeably lacking among the correlates for these two scales.

In a Veteran's Affairs psychiatric inpatient sample, Harkness, McNulty, et al. (2014) reviewed patient records and found PSYC-r to be strongly related to increased psychotic symptom counts at hospital intake. Bryant and McNulty (2017) used the same sample but examined variables in patients' records related to a history of substance use, which were again recorded during hospital intake. They found DISC-r to be the strongest PSY-5 correlate for each of these variables. Bryant and McNulty also examined history of substance use upon intake at an outpatient community mental health center and again identified DISC-r as the PSY-5 scale most strongly correlated with each variable.

Using a sample of private practice clients, Wygant et al. (2006) found the PSY-5 scales added incrementally to the Clinical and Content scales in predicting personality disorder criteria. The AGGR scale was most related to criteria for narcissistic, antisocial, and paranoid disorders; PSYC was most related to borderline, paranoid, and schizotypal disorders; DISC was most strongly related to antisocial disorders; and INTR was most strongly related to avoidant disorders. NEGE was significantly related to all of the personality disorders, but it was most strongly related to borderline and schizotypal disorders.

Wygant and Sellbom (2012) investigated the relationship between psychopathy and the PSY-5 in a sample undergoing court-ordered psychological assessment. They compared forensic evaluators' ratings using the Psychopathy Checklist: Screening Version (PCL:SV; S. D. Hart et al., 1995) to PSY-5 scale scores. The PCL:SV provides a total score as well as scores for four facets of psychopathy: Interpersonal, Affective, Lifestyle, and Antisocial. Wygant and Sellbom found that AGGR, DISC, and NEGE each accounted for unique and meaningful variance in the overall PCL:SV score. The AGGR scale was strongly associated with all four facets of psychopathy. In contrast, DISC was only positively correlated with the Antisocial facet, while NEGE was inversely correlated with both the Interpersonal and Affective facets.

A study by M. W. Miller et al. (2004) demonstrated the PSY-5 scales can be helpful in understanding the diversity of symptoms reported by patients with diagnoses of PTSD. Three groups of PTSD patients were identified on the basis of cluster analysis of PSY-5 scale scores: (a) low pathology, (b) externalizing, and (c) internalizing. The low pathology group had PSY-5 scale scores within a normal range, the externalizing group was characterized by high NEGE and DISC, and the internalizing group was characterized by high NEGE and INTR. The groups differed in terms of comorbid disorders, with the externalizers showing higher rates of alcohol-related and antisocial personality disorders and the internalizers showing higher rates of panic and major depressive disorder. The findings suggested premorbid personality characteristics may influence the expression of posttraumatic symptomatology.

J. L. Anderson et al. (2018) used the PSY-5-r scales to predict future incidents of aggression in a forensic psychiatric inpatient population. For this study, they examined documented incidents of verbal and physical aggression that occurred after 533 patients had completed the MMPI-2 or MMPI-2-RF but while they remained institutionalized. While all five scales contributed uniquely to these predictions, NEGE-r and AGGR-r were the two strongest predictors of future documented incidents of both verbal and physical aggression.

Caillouet et al. (2010) examined relationships between PSY-5 scale scores and several measures of negative job performance of law enforcement officers. The PSY-5 scales were only mildly related to supervisor ratings of job misconduct. However, stronger relationships were found between PSY-5 scale scores and involuntary employment termination. The relationships were stronger among officers who did not have elevated L and K scale scores, with elevated scores on the AGGR and DISC scales having the strongest relationships.

Taken together, these various studies suggest strong support for the construct validity of the PSY-5 scales. The PSY-5 scales seem to be related to important personality characteristics and behaviors consistent with the constructs underlying the scales. Although some extratest characteristics are related to more than one PSY-5 scale, there are some data suggesting the scales have discriminant validity. For example, Petroskey et al. (2003) found the AGGR scale was positively correlated with antisocial personality disorder diagnoses and histories of violence among criminal offenders but negatively correlated with or unrelated to diagnoses of depression and anxiety disorders. The PSYC scale was positively related to diagnoses of schizophrenia but unrelated to antisocial personality disorder diagnoses. A. R. Harkness (personal communication, December 8, 2004) found correlations between PSY-5 scales and Demoralization (RCd) were modest compared with other MMPI-2 scales.

In summary, research involving the PSY-5 scales indicates they are a useful source of information about the underlying personality characteristics of clinical and nonclinical test takers. Harkness and Lilienfeld (1997) and Harkness and McNulty (2006) have made some interesting suggestions concerning the use of information about personality traits, such as that provided by the PSY-5 scales, in treatment planning. Vendrig et al. (2000) found pain patients with higher scores on the Introversion/ Low Positive Emotionality (INTR) scale showed greater improvements in treatment satisfaction and self-rated emotional change. However, the PSY-5 scales were not related to measures of physical change (e.g., pain intensity, fear of movement).

Interpretation of the PSY-5 Scales

Harkness et al. (2002) provided some preliminary guidelines for interpreting scores on the PSY-5 scales. Based on item response theory, it was determined high scores (T ≥ 65) on all five scales are interpretable. However, research supports only interpreting low scores (T < 39) for the DISC, INTR, and AGGR (Rouse et al., 1999; Weisenburger et al., 2008) scales. Harkness et al. (2002) acknowledged their interpretive guidelines are likely to be modified, refined, and expanded as more research is conducted with the PSY-5 scales. The interpretive inferences that follow are based on the Harkness et al. (2002) recommendations and these authors' examination of research concerning the PSY-5 scales.

Aggressiveness (AGGR)

The AGGR scale largely captures individual differences in offensive and instrumental aggression and may include enjoyment of intimidating others to accomplish one's goals. This trait aligns with the antagonism domain trait proposed in the AMPD and the antagonistic externalizing spectrum in the HiTOP model. Both high and low scores on this scale are interpreted.

High scores (T ≥ 65) on the AGGR scale indicate persons who

1. are both verbally and physically aggressive
2. may use aggression to dominate and control others
3. may enjoy intimidating other people
4. may react aggressively when provoked
5. have histories of behavioral problems in school
6. have histories of arrests
7. if male, often have histories of committing domestic violence
8. in clinical or forensic settings, tend to have diagnoses of antisocial personality disorder
9. in forensic settings, may exhibit traits consistent with psychopathy
10. in treatment, may attempt to control and dominate therapists
11. in treatment, may benefit from discussion of the costs and benefits of their aggressiveness

Low scores (T < 39) indicate persons who are passive, submissive, and not very aggressive in interactions with other people.

Psychoticism (PSYC)

The PSYC scale identifies disconnection from reality, feelings of alienation, and unrealistic expectations of harm. PSYC aligns with the AMPD domain trait of the same name as well as the thought disorder spectrum in the HiTOP model. Low scores are not interpreted for this scale.

High scores (T ≥ 65) on the PSYC scale indicate persons who

1. are experiencing a disconnection from reality
2. may experience unshared beliefs or unusual sensory or perceptual experiences
3. may report delusions of reference
4. may have bizarre, disoriented, or circumstantial thinking
5. have an unrealistic expectation of harm
6. feel alienated
7. have few or no friends
8. have poor work histories
9. are not very achievement oriented
10. in therapy, may benefit from frequent opportunities to engage in reality checking

Disconstraint (DISC)

The DISC scale measures differences in self-control, risk-taking behaviors, and tendencies to follow rules and expectations. It most closely aligns with the HiTOP model's disinhibited externalizing spectra and the AMPD's disinhibition domain trait. Both high and low scores are interpreted for this scale.

High scores (T ≥ 65) on the DISC scale indicate persons who

1. are impulsive and lack self-control
2. take physical risks
3. are easily bored by routine and seek out excitement
4. are rebellious
5. are less bound by traditional moral constraints
6. often have histories of substance abuse
7. often have histories of school problems and arrests
8. in forensic settings, tend to have histories of violence and antisocial personality disorder diagnoses
9. in treatment, may benefit from exploring more constructive ways to satisfy needs for novelty, excitement, and risk-taking

Low scores (T < 39) on the DISC scale indicate persons who

1. are self-controlled and not impulsive
2. do not take many physical risks
3. have high tolerance for boredom
4. tend to follow rules and laws
5. may respond better to structured treatment approaches

Negative Emotionality/Neuroticism (NEGE)

The NEGE scale captures a predisposition to experience negative emotions (e.g., fear, anxiety) and fixate on problematic features of incoming information. The internalizing spectrum from the HiTOP model and the AMPD's negative affectivity domain trait demonstrate considerable conceptual overlap with NEGE. Low scores on this scale are not interpreted.

High scores (T ≥ 65) on the NEGE scale indicate persons who

1. have a predisposition to experience negative affect
2. focus on problematic features of incoming information
3. concoct worst-case scenarios
4. may have few or no friends
5. are self-critical
6. worry excessively
7. feel guilty
8. may report feeling sad or blue
9. are pessimistic
10. hold dysfunctional beliefs about themselves and their relationships
11. are not very achievement oriented
12. in clinical settings, may have histories of suicide attempts
13. in clinical settings, often receive diagnoses of depression or dysthymia

14. are very anxious
15. may report somatic symptoms
16. may benefit from therapy designed to identify and deal with their tendencies to process information in anxiety-producing ways

Introversion/Low Positive Emotionality (INTR)

The INTR scale detects individual differences in capacity to experience positive emotions (e.g., joy) and positive engagement as well as social introversion. Conceptually, it is congruent with the construct named detachment in both the AMPD and HiTOP model. Both high and low scores on this scale are interpreted.

High scores (T ≥ 65) on the INTR scale indicate persons who

1. seem to have little capacity to experience joy and pleasure
2. are socially introverted
3. have low need to achieve
4. report feeling sad, blue, or depressed
5. report somatic symptoms
6. often feel anxious
7. are pessimistic about the future
8. in clinical settings, tend to have diagnoses of depression
9. in clinical settings, may have histories of suicide attempts
10. tend to show little emotional response in therapy

Low scores on the INTR scale (T < 39) indicate persons who

1. have the capacity to experience joy and pleasure
2. are quite sociable
3. have lots of energy
4. if scores are very low, may exhibit symptoms of hypomania
5. are likely to be quite emotionally responsive in therapy

CHAPTER 8

SUPPLEMENTARY SCALES

IN ADDITION TO ITS UTILIZATION in the construction of the Validity and Clinical scales, the original MMPI item pool was used to develop numerous other scales by variously recombining the 567 items using item-analytic, factor-analytic, and intuitive procedures. Dahlstrom and colleagues (1972, 1975) identified more than 450 Supplementary scales that were developed for the MMPI. The scales had quite diverse labels, ranging from more traditional ones, such as "Dominance" and "Suspiciousness," to more unusual ones, such as "Success in Baseball." The scales varied considerably in terms of what they were supposed to measure, the manner in which they were constructed, their reliabilities, the extent to which they were cross-validated, the availability of normative data, and the amount of additional validity data that were generated. The scales also varied in terms of how frequently they were used in clinical and research settings. Some scales were used only by their constructors, whereas others were employed extensively in research studies or used routinely in clinical interpretation of the MMPI.

Only a select few MMPI Supplementary scales were maintained in the MMPI-2 (Butcher et al., 1989, 2001). For the most part, the extent to which existing research data supported a scale's reliability and validity determined which scales were retained. However, some scales were maintained despite limited scientific support. For example, the Harris–Lingoes subscales (see Chapter 6) were retained because the MMPI-2 authors judged them to be a helpful supplementary source of information in interpreting the Clinical scales. In addition to maintaining some of the existing MMPI Supplementary scales, new scales were developed for the MMPI-2. Several new Validity scales (described in Chapter 3 of this book) and Content scales (described in Chapter 6 of this book) were developed. Other scales also were created as part of the

MMPI-2 development process and will be described in this chapter. Subsequent to the publication of the MMPI-2, several additional scales for assessing substance use and marital distress were published. They too will be described in this chapter.

The same format will be used for discussing each Supplementary scale. Scale development information will be presented, and reliability and validity data will be reported. Interpretive suggestions for each scale also will be given. As with the Clinical and Validity scales, no absolute cutoff scores can be specified for the Supplementary scales. In general, T scores greater than or equal to 65 should be considered as high scores. Whenever information about specific cutoff scores for a scale is available, that information will be presented. The higher the scores are, the more likely it is that the interpretive information presented will apply. For scales that have data concerning the meaning of low scores available, the interpretation of low scores is discussed in this chapter. However, as with other scales discussed earlier in this book, low scores should not be interpreted for most of the Supplementary scales because there is not enough research information available to have confidence in interpretive statements based on low scores.

Although an attempt was made to rely on research studies for interpretive information, in some cases, examining item content was necessary in generating descriptors. For Supplementary scales that were developed from the original MMPI and maintained in the MMPI-2, research data from the original MMPI also were used to generate interpretive suggestions. Because these scales are essentially the same in the two versions of the test, this approach seems appropriate. Archer et al. (1997) concluded that the Supplementary scales did not add much to the Clinical scales in predicting self-reported and psychologist-rated symptoms of psychiatric inpatients. However, it should be noted that their study did not include conceptually relevant extratest measures for most of the Supplementary scales. Graham et al. (1999) were able to identify meaningful correlates for many Supplementary scales in their study of community mental health center clients. Nonetheless, it should be emphasized that the Supplementary scales are not intended to replace the standard Validity and Clinical scales. Rather, they are to be used in addition to them.

Scores and profile plots for the Supplementary scales can be generated by hand or obtained via computerized score reports available from Pearson Assessments. It should be noted that most of the Supplementary scales can be scored only if the entire 567-item MMPI-2 is administered. The composition and scoring of each Supplementary scale are presented in Appendix B of the MMPI-2 manual (Butcher et al., 2001). Appendix A in the MMPI-2 manual presents Linear T-score conversions for the Supplementary scales. Score transformations based on the non-gendered normative data are available in the Appendix of Ben-Porath and Forbey's (2003) non-gendered norms monograph.

ANXIETY (A) AND REPRESSION (R) SCALES

Scale Development

Whenever the basic Validity and Clinical scales of the MMPI or MMPI-2 have been factor analyzed to reduce them to their most common denominators, two basic dimensions have emerged consistently (e.g., Block, 1965; Butcher et al., 1989;

Eichman, 1961, 1962; Welsh, 1956). Welsh (1956) developed the Anxiety (A) scale to assess the first of these basic dimensions. Specifically, by factor analyzing MMPI scores for Veterans Administration patients who identified as men, Welsh identified a factor that he originally labeled "general maladjustment" and later called "anxiety." This factor was defined by high positive loadings from Scales 7 and 8 and a high negative loading from the Correction (K) Scale. The A scale was developed to assess this factor by identifying the items most highly associated with it. After being administered to new groups of psychiatric patients, the scale was refined by using internal consistency procedures. The original A scale included 39 items, all of which are included in the MMPI-2 version of the scale. The items are keyed in such a way that high scores on the A scale are associated with greater psychopathology.

The Repression (R) scale was constructed by Welsh (1956) to measure the second major dimension emerging from factor analyses of the basic Validity and Clinical scales of the MMPI. This factor was defined by positive loadings from Scales 1, 2, and 3 and a negative loading from Scale 9. A procedure similar to that used in developing the A scale also was employed with the R scale. It resulted in a final scale containing 40 items, 37 of which are included in the MMPI-2 version of the scale.

Reliability and Validity

In the MMPI-2 normative sample, internal consistency coefficients for the A scale were .89 for men and .90 for women. Corresponding internal consistency coefficients for the R scale were .67 and .57 (for men and women, respectively; Butcher et al., 2001). Thus, it appears that the A scale is quite internally consistent, whereas the R scale is less so. In this same sample, test–retest reliabilities (with an average interval of 1 week) for the A scale were .91 for men and .91 for women. Corresponding values for the R scale were .79 for men and .77 for women (Butcher et al., 2001). Thus, the stability of scores on the A and R scales over these relatively short periods of time seems to be quite acceptable.

It has been suggested by some researchers that the major sources of variance in MMPI responses are associated with response sets. A response set exists when persons taking a test answer the items from a particular perspective or attitude about how they would like the items to show themselves to be. A. L. Edwards (1964) argued that the first factor of the MMPI, the one assessed by the A scale, simply assesses examinees' willingness, while describing themselves on the test, to endorse socially undesirable items. Messick and Jackson (1961) suggested that R scale scores simply indicate the extent to which examinees are unwilling to admit (acquiesce) on the test to many kinds of emotional difficulties. This interpretation appears to be supported by the fact that all of the items in the R scale are keyed in the false direction. J. Block (1965) refuted the response set or bias arguments by demonstrating that the same two major factor dimensions emerge even when the MMPI scales were altered to control for social desirability and acquiescence effects with the use of techniques developed by A. L. Edwards (1964) and others. J. Block also was able to identify through his research reliable, meaningful extratest correlates for his two factor dimensions. Thus, overall, there is little evidence to support the idea that A, R, and other MMPI scale scores measure only response styles.

Empirical studies on the MMPI suggested scores on A were positively related to emotional discomfort, pessimism, and experiencing self-doubt as well motivation to change in psychotherapy (e.g., J. C. Duckworth & Duckworth, 1975; Sherriffs and Boomer, 1954; Welsh, 1965). In their study of MMPI-2 scale correlates, Graham et al. (1999) reported that mental health center clients with higher scores on the A scale had a wide variety of symptoms, including anxiety, depression, and somatic complaints. They were also more likely than lower scorers to have histories of inpatient mental health treatment and suicidal ideation.

Empirical studies using the MMPI version of the R scale suggested scores on this scale were related to somatization and depression and that individuals with high R scores were described as denying, rationalizing, and lacking self-insight (e.g., J. C. Duckworth & Duckworth, 1975; Welsh, 1956). Using the MMPI-2 version of the scale, Archer et al. (1997) found R scores were positively related to ratings of psycho-motor retardation for women in an inpatient psychiatric setting. Graham et al. (1999) identified relatively few correlates of the R scale among mental health center clients. However, higher scoring clients were described by their therapists as being preoccupied with health and presenting somatic complaints. Clients who identified as men and produced higher R scores were seen as nervous and depressed, lacking energy, and having restricted affect. They also were more concrete in their thinking and felt pessimistic. Higher scoring clients who identified as women also were seen as anxious, introverted, and shy. These women often felt overwhelmed and that life is a strain. They expressed many fears and were lacking in energy.

Interpretation of High A Scale Scores

High scores on the A scale indicate persons who

1. are generally maladjusted
2. are anxious and uncomfortable
3. are depressed
4. have somatic complaints
5. have a slow personal tempo
6. may admit to having suicidal ideation
7. are pessimistic
8. are apathetic, unemotional, and unexcitable
9. are shy and retiring
10. lack confidence in their own abilities
11. are hesitant and vacillating
12. are inhibited and overcontrolled
13. are influenced by diffuse personal feelings
14. are defensive
15. rationalize and blame others for difficulties
16. lack poise in social situations
17. are conforming and overly accepting of authority
18. are submissive, compliant, and suggestible
19. are cautious

20. are fussy
21. are seen as cool, distant, and uninvolved
22. become confused, disorganized, and maladaptive under stress
23. are likely to have histories of inpatient mental health treatment
24. are uncomfortable enough to be motivated to change in psychotherapy

Interpretation of High R Scale Scores
High scores on the R scale indicate persons who

1. are passive/submissive
2. are unexcitable
3. are conventional and formal
4. are slow and painstaking
5. may show psychomotor retardation
6. are introverted
7. have somatic complaints

EGO STRENGTH (ES) SCALE

Scale Development
The Ego Strength (Es) scale was developed by Barron (1953) specifically to predict the response of neurotic patients to individual psychotherapy. To identify items for the Es scale, item responses provided after 6 months of psychotherapy were contrasted for 17 patients who were judged as having clearly improved and 16 patients who were judged as unimproved. The 52 items of the MMPI-2 Es scale are scored in the direction most often chosen by the improved patients (see Appendix B of the MMPI-2 manual for item composition and scoring; Butcher et al., 2001). The Es scale items deal with physical functioning, reclusiveness, moral beliefs, personal adequacy, ability to cope, phobias, and anxieties.

Reliability and Validity
For men and women in the MMPI-2 normative sample, internal-consistency values for the Es scale were .60 and .65, respectively. Test–retest coefficients (average of 1-week interval) for subsamples of men and women in the MMPI-2 normative sample were .78 and .83, respectively (Butcher et al., 2001).

Though Es was developed to predict response to treatment, there is mixed evidence supporting its use for this purpose. A review by Dahlstrom et al. (1975) identified inconsistent findings concerning the relationship between Es scale scores on the original MMPI and treatment outcome. Indeed, MMPI-based research on Es suggests the relationship between Es scale scores and treatment outcome is not a simple one; and that factors such as kind of patients, type of treatment, and nature of the outcome measure must be considered. In general, however, high Es scale scores appear to predict positive change in traditional, individual psychotherapy for patients experiencing symptoms that would be described as "neurotic."

Several studies suggest the Es scale can be viewed as an indication of overall psychological adjustment. Schuldberg (1992) found MMPI-2 Es scale scores of college students were positively related to other self-report measures of psychological health. Graham et al. (1999) reported that mental health center clients with higher Es scale scores were rated as having fewer symptoms and being less likely to report life was a strain, as well as better coping with stress, than clients with lower Es scale scores. In addition, clients with higher Es scale scores were rated by their therapist as having more energy and interests and being more competitive. Windle (1994) found that men with alcohol-related problems who also had made suicide attempts had lower Es scale scores than other men with only alcohol-related problems. Rosch et al. (1991) compared Es scores of college students who identified as women who were in treatment for bulimia, in treatment for other problems, or were not in treatment. They reported those being treated for bulimia had lower Es scale scores than those being treated for other problems and those who were not in treatment. Archer et al. (1997) reported that Es scale scores were negatively related to ratings of psychomotor slowing and unusual thought content in an inpatient psychiatric setting.

Consistent gender differences in Es scale scores have been reported, with men obtaining higher raw scores than women (Butcher et al., 1989; Distler et al., 1964; Getter & Sundland, 1962; Taft, 1957). This gender difference originally was interpreted as reflecting the greater willingness of women to admit to problems and complaints (Getter & Sundland, 1962). However, a reasonable alternative explanation of the gender difference on the Es scale is that men score higher than women because the scale contains a number of items dealing with stereotypical masculine role identification (Holmes, 1967). Regardless, we recommend test users exercise caution when interpreting Es scale scores using the non-gendered norms.

Interpretation of High Es scale Scores

It is necessary to be very cautious in interpreting Es scale scores in protocols that are suggestive of defensiveness. In such circumstances, Es scale scores tend to be artificially high and are not predictive of positive response to therapy. Likewise, caution should be exercised in interpreting Es scale scores in protocols suggestive of exaggeration of symptoms. In such circumstances, Es scale scores tend to be artificially low and are not predictive of a negative response to therapy.

High scores on the Es scale indicate persons who

1. have fewer and less severe symptoms
2. lack chronic psychopathology
3. are stable, reliable, and responsible
4. are tolerant and lack prejudice
5. are alert, energetic, and adventuresome
6. may be sensation seekers
7. are determined and persistent
8. are self-confident, outspoken, and sociable
9. are intelligent, resourceful, and independent
10. have a secure sense of reality

11. deal effectively with others
12. create favorable first impressions
13. gain acceptance of others
14. are energetic and have many interests
15. seek help because of situational problems
16. can tolerate confrontations in psychotherapy

Interpretation of Low Es scale Scores

In many ways, persons with low scores on the Es scale are the opposite of those with high scores. Lower scorers are likely to have more severe problems that are less likely to be situational in nature. They do not seem to have many psychological resources for coping with stress, and the prognosis for change in treatment for these persons is not very positive.

DOMINANCE (DO) SCALE

Scale Development

The Dominance (Do) scale was developed by Gough et al. (1951) as part of a larger project concerned with political participation. High school and college students were given a definition of dominance (strength in face-to-face personal situations; ability to influence others; not readily intimidated or defeated; feeling safe, secure, and confident in face-to-face situations) and were asked to nominate peers who were the most and least dominant. High- and low-dominance criterion groups were defined on the basis of these peer nominations; and both groups were given a 150-item questionnaire, which included some MMPI items. Analyses of the responses identified items that differentiated between high- and low-dominance criterion groups. The items are keyed in such a way that a high score on the Do scale is suggestive of high dominance—see Appendix B of the MMPI-2 manual for the 25 items that comprise the scale along with their scored direction (Butcher et al., 2001).

Reliability and Validity

Internal-consistency (alpha) coefficients for men and women in the MMPI-2 normative sample were .74 and .79, respectively (Butcher et al., 2001). Test–retest coefficients (1-week interval) for subsamples of men and women in the MMPI-2 normative sample were .84 and .86, respectively (Butcher et al., 2001).

Empirical evidence using the MMPI version of Do supported that scores were related to social dominance (Gough et al., 1951). Similar findings have been demonstrated when the MMPI-2 version of the scale was investigated. Hedayat and Kelly (1991) reported a correlation of .86 between Do scale scores of female psychiatric day-treatment clients and ratings of dominance completed by staff members. Archer et al. (1997) found Do scale scores of psychiatric inpatients were positively related to a measure of grandiosity provided by staff members. Graham et al. (1999) reported correlates of the Do scale for clients at a community mental health center. Clients with higher Do scale scores tended to have fewer symptoms, including anxiety, depression, and somatic complaints; they were less passive and socially awkward; and they were more achievement oriented.

Interpretation of High Do scale Scores
High Do scale scores may indicate persons who

1. appear poised and self-assured
2. are secure
3. are optimistic
4. are resourceful and efficient
5. are realistic and achievement oriented
6. feel adequate to handle problems
7. are persevering
8. have a dutiful sense of morality
9. are comfortable in social situations
10. are not easily intimidated by others
11. if psychiatric patients, are likely to have fewer symptoms—including anxiety, depression, and somatic complaints—and may be rather grandiose

SOCIAL RESPONSIBILITY (RE) SCALE

Scale Development
The Social Responsibility (Re) scale was developed by Gough et al. (1952) as part of a larger project concerning political participation. The samples used in constructing the Re scale consisted of 50 men in a college fraternity, 50 women in a college sorority, 123 social science students from a high school, and 221 ninth-grade students. In each sample, the most and least responsible individuals were identified. Responsibility was defined as willingness to accept the consequences of one's own behavior, dependability, trustworthiness, integrity, and sense of obligation to the group. For the high school and college samples, peer nominations were used to identify persons high and low in responsibility. Teachers provided ratings of responsibility for the ninth-grade sample. MMPI item responses of the most and least responsible persons in each sample were examined. Items that demonstrated the best discrimination between most and least responsible persons in all samples were included in the Re scale. The 30 items of the MMPI-2 Re scale are reported in Appendix B of the manual along with their scored direction (Butcher et al., 2001).

Reliability and Validity
Internal-consistency (alpha) coefficients for men and women in the MMPI-2 normative sample were .67 and .61, respectively (Butcher et al., 2001). Test–retest coefficients (with 1-week interval) for subsamples of men and women in the MMPI-2 normative sample were .85 and .73, respectively (Butcher et al., 2001).

Research using the MMPI version of the Re scale suggested scores were related to having a sense of responsibility and being seen by others as willing to accept the consequences of their own behavior, as dependable and trustworthy, and as having integrity and a sense of responsibility to the group (e.g., Gough et al., 1952). High scorers were also more likely than low Re scale scorers to be in positions of leadership and responsibility (e.g., Knapp, 1960), and be rigid in their acceptance of existing values and unwilling to explore others' values (J. C. Duckworth & Duckworth, 1975). Little work has been done using the MMPI-2 version of the scale. However, Graham et al. (1999) determined correlates of Re scores for mental health center clients. Clients with higher Re scale scores had fewer symptoms, including anxiety, depression, and somatic complaints. They were seen by their therapists as more secure and less socially awkward than other clients.

Interpretation of High Re scale Scores
High scores may indicate persons who

1. are seen by themselves and others as dependable and trustworthy
2. have deep concern over ethical and moral problems
3. have a strong sense of justice and integrity
4. set high standards for themselves
5. reject privilege and favor and demonstrate a willingness to accept the consequences of their behaviors
6. have a sense of responsibility toward others and may be in positions of leadership
7. place excessive emphasis on carrying their own share of burdens and duties
8. are secure and self-confident
9. are comfortable in social situations
10. have trust and confidence in the world in general
11. are rigid in acceptance of existing values and unwilling to explore others' values
12. if psychiatric patients, tend to have fewer symptoms—including anxiety, depression, and somatic complaints—compared to other clients

COLLEGE MALADJUSTMENT (MT) SCALE

Scale Development
The College Maladjustment (Mt) scale was constructed to discriminate between emotionally adjusted and maladjusted college students (Kleinmuntz, 1961). Items in Mt were selected from the MMPI item pool by comparing responses of students who identified as men and women, 40 of whom were believed to be adjusted and 40 demonstrating general maladjustment. Namely, the students in the adjusted group had contacted a university clinic to arrange for a routine mental health screening examination as part of teacher certification procedures, and none of them admitted to a history of psychiatric treatment. The students in the maladjusted group had contacted the same clinic for help with emotional problems and had remained in psychotherapy for three or more sessions. Item-analytic procedures identified 43 items that discriminated between the adjusted and maladjusted groups, 41 of which were retained on the MMPI-2. Items in Mt are scored such that higher scores on the scale are more indicative of greater maladjustment (see Appendix B of the MMPI-2 Manual for item composition and scoring; Butcher et al., 2001).

Barthlow et al. (2004) factor analyzed items in the MMPI-2 Mt scale and identified three interpretable factors. A factor labeled "Low Self-Esteem" was represented by items having to do with lack of self-confidence and negative comparisons of self with others. A second factor, labeled "Lack of Energy," was represented by items having to do with feeling tired and having difficulty in starting to do things. A third factor, labeled "Cynicism/Restlessness," had somewhat more heterogeneous content than the other factors and was represented by items having to do with negative impressions of other people, restlessness, and having ideas that are too bad to talk about.

Reliability and Validity

Internal-consistency (alpha) coefficients for Mt in the MMPI-2 normative sample were .84 and .86 for men and women, respectively (Butcher et al., 2001). The test–retest coefficients (1-week interval) for both men and women in the MMPI-2 normative sample were .90 (Butcher et al., 2001).

Research on the original MMPI Mt scale suggested scores assess maladjustment but are more accurate when used to identify existing emotional problems than for predicting future emotional problems (Kleinmuntz, 1961, 1963; Parker, 1961). Studies using the MMPI-2 version of Mt have found that higher scores are associated with the presence of symptoms of emotional/internalizing forms of psychopathology, including depression, anxiety, and trauma-related disorders (Lauterbach et al., 2002; Svanum & Ehrmann, 1993). However, scores on the Mt scale were not related to symptoms of substance use disorders. Students who identified as women tended to obtain higher Mt scale raw scores than students who identified as men, and students with poorer academic performance scored higher than those with better academic performance (Lauterbach et al., 2002).

Similar findings to those just described were demonstrated by Barthlow et al. (2004), who found higher Mt scores were related to increased emotional turmoil and distress (e.g., depression, anxiety, insecurity)—but not acting-out behaviors—in a sample of individuals receiving services at a mental health clinic. Results of this study also suggested correlations between Mt scale scores and emotional distress were similar to those of other MMPI-2 scales and indexes associated with general maladjustment. Indeed, results suggested that Mt scores demonstrated little to no incremental validity when predicting maladjustment beyond other MMPI-2 measures of the construct (e.g., Welsh's A scale, low scores on the Es scale, or the mean score on the eight Clinical scales).

Interpretation of High Mt-Scale Scores

Because the Mt scale has not been studied systematically in settings other than colleges and universities, its use is only recommended with college students.

In addition to suggesting general maladjustment, high Mt-scale scores for college students may indicate persons who

1. are ineffectual
2. are pessimistic
3. procrastinate

4. are anxious and worried
5. develop somatic symptoms during times of increased stress
6. feel that life is a strain much of the time

POSTTRAUMATIC STRESS DISORDER (PK) SCALE

Scale Development

The Posttraumatic Stress Disorder (PK) scale was developed by Keane et al. (1984) by contrasting the MMPI item responses of 60 men who were Vietnam combat veterans with diagnoses of PTSD based on structured interviews and a psychophysiological assessment procedure and 60 men who were veterans with diagnoses other than PTSD. They identified 49 items that these two groups answered significantly differently. A raw cutoff score of 30 correctly classified 82% of cross-validation groups of veterans with and without PTSD diagnoses.

The content of the PK scale items is suggestive of emotional turmoil. Some items deal with anxiety, worry, and sleep disturbance. Others are suggestive of guilt and depression. In their responses to certain items, test takers are reporting the presence of unwanted and disturbing thoughts; and in others, they are describing lack of emotional control. Feeling misunderstood and mistreated is also represented in item content. The 46 items comprising the MMPI-2 PK scale as well as their scored direction are found in Appendix B of the MMPI-2 Manual (Butcher et al., 2001).

Although PK scale scores typically are determined from the administration of the entire MMPI-2, Lyons and Scotti (1994) demonstrated that scores based on a separate administration of the PK scale were quite congruent with scores based on administration of the entire MMPI-2. However, a major disadvantage of the stand-alone administration is that important information concerning test-taking attitudes is lost when the Validity scales cannot be scored. Thus, we recommend PK only be interpreted if the entire MMPI-2 was administered and response distortion ruled out.

Reliability and Validity

Internal-consistency coefficients for the PK scale for men and women in the MMPI-2 normative sample were .85 and .87, respectively (Butcher et al., 2001). A test–retest reliability coefficient (average of a 1-week interval) of .87 was reported for subsamples of men and women in the MMPI-2 normative sample (Butcher et al., 2001).

A substantial number of MMPI studies have reported support for the general utility of the PK scale for identifying individuals diagnosed with PTSD, although the specific classification rates and optimal cutoff scores have varied—sometimes widely—from study to study (e.g., Butler et al., 1988; Hyer et al., 1990; Vanderploeg et al., 1987). Generally, the MMPI PK scale was more effective in discriminating between individuals with PTSD and nonpatients than between individuals with PTSD and those with other diagnoses. Lyons and Wheeler-Cox (1999) reviewed MMPI-2 PK scale research studies and concluded that a raw score cutoff of > 28 was optimal for discriminating veterans with PTSD from those with other disorders. There have also been studies examining PTSD from a dimensional, rather than categorical, perspective (Adkins et al., 2008; L. A. Neal et al., 1994, 1995; Sloan et al., 1996; C. G. Watson et al., 1994). Results from this research have suggested positive correlations between MMPI-2 PK scale scores and symptoms of PTSD as determined by structured interviews or other methods.

Most of the PK scale research has focused on combat-related PTSD. However, several studies have suggested that scores on the MMPI-2 PK scale may also be related to civilian trauma, such as abuse. Sinnett et al. (1995) reported that clients in two private practice settings who identified as women and were victims of abuse scored higher on the PK scale than other women clients in these settings who were not victims of abuse. Noblitt (1995) similarly reported that a small group of psychiatric patients who mostly identified as women and reported having experienced ritual abuse scored higher on the PK scale than patients who did not report such abuse.

Studies of civilian trauma have also included index traumas other than abuse. For example, Bowler et al. (1998) found that approximately half of a sample of persons who had been assigned PTSD diagnoses following a chemical spill had T scores greater than 65 on the PK scale. Haisch and Meyers (2004) found that PK scale scores of police officers were significantly related to job stress, job pressure, and perceived lack of support on the job. M. P. Duckworth and Iezzi (2005) studied individuals reporting chronic pain following motor vehicle accidents. Those with higher PK scores had more physical impairment and greater psychological distress and used more maladaptive pain-coping strategies. Overall, research in civilian populations suggests the utility of PK scores in detecting PTSD symptoms is not tied to specific index traumas.

There is accumulating evidence that scores on the PK scale are related to general distress. For example, Lyons and Wheeler-Cox (1999) demonstrated depressed patients without PTSD had higher PK scale scores than nonpatients; and more than 20% of women with somatization disorder diagnoses had PK scale raw scores of 28 or higher. Thus, it may be that very high PK scale scores are indicative of PTSD, but more moderate elevations on the scale reflect general distress and not specifically posttraumatic stress.

In summary, there appears to be considerable evidence that scores on the PK scale are related to PTSD diagnoses among veterans. Studies, such as that by Keane et al. (1984), which have used well-defined criteria to establish the diagnosis of PTSD, report higher classification rates than other studies that have used less reliable diagnostic procedures. Using the PK scale to classify veterans as experiencing PTSD or not will produce more false-positive than false-negative errors. It is not clear to what extent scores on the PK scale are susceptible to faking by persons who are motivated to appear to have PTSD but who really do not have the disorder. Because higher PK scale scores of mental health clients tend to be associated with more symptoms of psychological maladjustment (Graham et al., 1999), the use of the scale to arrive at differential diagnoses between PTSD versus other disorders may be limited. The utility of the PK scale in identifying PTSD associated with noncombat stress is also unclear. As with other MMPI-2 scales, it is not responsible clinical practice to use a single scale to assign diagnostic labels.

Interpretation of High PK scale Scores

In addition to being associated with symptoms and behaviors typically associated with PTSD and an increased possibility a PTSD diagnosis, high scores on the PK scale indicate persons who

1. are reporting intense emotional distress
2. report symptoms of anxiety and sleep disturbance
3. feel guilty and depressed
4. may be having unwanted and disturbing thoughts
5. fear loss of emotional and cognitive control
6. feel misunderstood and mistreated

MARITAL DISTRESS SCALE (MDS)

Scale Development

The Marital Distress Scale (MDS) of the MMPI-2 was developed by Hjemboe et al. (1992) to assess distress in marital relationships. Tentative items were selected by correlating MMPI-2 item responses with scores on the Dyadic Adjustment Scale (DAS; Spanier, 1976) for 150 couples involved in marital counseling and 392 couples from the MMPI-2 normative sample. The DAS is a 31-item inventory assessing relationship consensus, cohesion, affection, and satisfaction. Additional items were added to the tentative MDS on the basis of correlations between other MMPI-2 items and scores on the tentative scale. Items were later eliminated if their content was judged not to be specifically related to marital distress or if their removal led to improved discriminant validity. The final scale consists of 14 items. The content of certain items seems to be related obviously to marital distress (e.g., having quarrels with family members; believing one's home life is unpleasant). Several items in the scale have less obvious relationships to marital distress (e.g., not being able to make up one's mind; feeling that one's life goals are not within reach). The items are scored in the direction most often chosen by persons experiencing less positive marital adjustment—see Appendix B in the MMPI-2 Manual (Butcher et al., 2001). Although Hjemboe et al. (1992) reported uniform T-score equivalents for raw scores on the MDS, the T scores presented in Appendix A of the MMPI-2 manual are linear T scores (Butcher et al., 2001). Score transformations based on the non-gendered normative data are available in the Appendix of Ben-Porath and Forbey's (2003) non-gendered norms monograph.

Reliability and Validity

Hjemboe et al. (1992) reported an internal-consistency (alpha) coefficient of .65 for the developmental sample. Alpha coefficients for men and women in the MMPI-2 normative sample were .61 and .68, respectively (Butcher et al., 2001). Test–retest reliability coefficients (approximately 1-week interval) for men and women in the MMPI-2 normative sample were .78 and .81, respectively (Butcher et al., 2001).

Hjemboe et al. (1992) provided initial evidence supporting the use of MDS as a measure of marital adjustment. However, results of their study are difficult to evaluate because most of the persons used in the validity analyses were also used for scale development purposes.

Subsequent studies offer mixed support for the validity of MDS scores. Graham et al. (1999) identified correlates of MDS scores for mental health center clients. For clients who identified as men, higher MDS scores were associated with higher therapist ratings of family problems; but this relationship was not observed for clients who identified as women. Scores on MDS for clients who identified as men were also related to a wide variety of symptoms and negative characteristics including depression, anger, and suicidal ideation. O'Reilly et al. (2003) found that MDS scores were related to the number of marital problems reported by couples involved in marital counseling and added significantly to other MMPI-2 scales in predicting number of marital problems. However, the MDS also seemed to be assessing general maladjustment in a manner similar to other MMPI-2 measures such as Welsh's A scale, the Es scale (reversed), and the mean T score for the eight Clinical scales. Overall, these results provide support for the validity of MDS scores but call to question their discriminant validity.

Interpretation of MDS Scores

Because limited data are available concerning the validity of the MDS, the scale should be interpreted cautiously. High scores (T > 60) may be indicative of significant marital distress, and additional assessment in this area is recommended. Obviously, the scale may not be of much help when assessing persons who are admitting to marital problems and seeking help for them. However, when the MMPI-2 is used as part of a more general assessment, high MDS scores should alert clinicians that marital problems may be contributing to other symptoms such as anxiety or depression.

In addition to suggesting distress in marriages or other intimate relationships, high scores on the MDS indicate persons who

1. are generally maladjusted
2. may be experiencing depression
3. may feel like failures much of the time
4. feel that life is a strain
5. are angry
6. have few or no friends and may feel rejected by other people

HOSTILITY (HO) SCALE

Scale Development

The Hostility (Ho) scale was one of several developed by Cook and Medley (1954) to predict the rapport of teachers with pupils in a classroom. Teachers who scored very high or very low on the Minnesota Teacher Attitude Inventory (MTAI), an instrument known to predict teacher–pupil interactions, were identified and their MMPI responses compared. Of the 250 items that these groups endorsed significantly differently, 77 whose content most clearly reflected hostility were included in a preliminary version of the Ho scale. The preliminary scale was refined by having five clinical psychologists independently select the items most clearly related to hostility. Han et al. (1995) factor analyzed Ho scale item responses for a mixed sample of persons in the MMPI-2 normative sample, couples in marital counseling, individuals with substance use problems, and general psychiatric patients. They identified four clusters of items: cynicism, hypersensitivity, aggressive responding, and social avoidance. The 50 items comprising the MMPI-2 Ho scale and the direction in which they are scored are reported in Appendix B of the MMPI-2 Manual (Butcher et al., 2001).

Reliability and Validity

Internal consistency coefficients for the Ho scale for men and women in the MMPI-2 normative sample are .87 and .85, respectively (Butcher et al., 2001). The test–retest coefficients (1-week interval) for subsamples of men and women in the MMPI-2 normative sample were .85 and .88, respectively (Butcher et al., 2001).

Studies of college students (A. Brown & Zeichner, 1989; Hardy & Smith, 1988; K. E. Hart, 1966; Houston & Vavak, 1991; M. K. Pope et al., 1990; T. W. Smith & Frohm, 1985; Swan et al., 1991), employed women (Houston & Kelly, 1989), married couples (T. W. Smith et al., 1990), adults in the MMPI-2 normative sample (Han et al., 1995), healthy men (Carmody et al., 1989), and medical patients (Blumenthal et al., 1987) have generally supported the validity of the Ho scale. In these studies, high scorers tended to experience more anger and were more likely to display overtly hostile behavior than lower Ho scale scorers. They were more irritable, antagonistic, and resentful. High scorers on the Ho scale also were more cynical, suspicious, and untrusting. They were not very friendly, attributed hostility to others, and blamed others for their problems. These high scorers perceived and sought less social support. Previous research has indicated that there is a strong emotional distress component to the Ho scale, with higher scorers having higher levels of anxiety, depression, and somatic complaints and lower self-esteem (Blumenthal et al., 1987).

Graham et al. (1999) determined correlates of the Ho scale in an outpatient mental health center. Although high scores can suggest a cynical mistrust of others, emotional distress, or general maladjustment, they found that the primary characteristic being measured by the Ho scale was cynicism. Based on this finding, they concluded that clinicians who use the Ho scale in outpatient clinical settings should be cautious not to infer that high scorers will be more hostile or aggressive than those with lower scores.

Interest in the Ho scale increased dramatically following research indicating that the anger component of the Type A personality construct was related significantly to health problems, especially coronary heart disease (e.g., R. B. Williams et al., 1980). Following evidence that patients undergoing coronary angiography were more likely to have severe coronary artery disease if they had high Ho scale scores, three prospective studies offered support for the link between hostility, as measured by the Ho scale, and significant health problems. Barefoot et al. (1983) conducted a 25-year follow-up of physicians who had completed the MMPI during medical school and found that Ho scale scores were positively related to subsequent coronary heart disease incidence and to mortality from all causes. Shekelle et al. (1983) reported that Ho scale scores predicted myocardial infarction and cardiac deaths at 10-year follow-up and coronary heart disease deaths and death from all causes at 20-year follow-up. Barefoot et al. (1989) found that Ho scale scores were related to early mortality for lawyers who had taken the MMPI in law school approximately 25 years earlier.

Not all studies have supported the relationship between Ho scale scores and serious health problems. Colligan and Offord (1988) found that unusually large proportions of people from a community sample and general medical patients obtained Ho scale scores higher than cutoffs proposed by previous researchers, suggesting a more conservative interpretation of Ho scores as predictors of coronary heart disease. Maruta et al. (1993) reported that in a 20-year follow-up study of 620 general medical patients, the Ho score was a significant predictor of the development of coronary heart disease. However, when age and gender were accounted for, the Ho score was no longer a significant predictor.

Interpretation of Ho scale Scores

Higher Ho scale scores indicate persons who

1. are very cynical, suspicious, and mistrusting
2. experience higher levels of anger, especially in interpersonal situations
3. are seen as unfriendly
4. attribute hostility to others
5. blame others for their problems
6. perceive and seek less social support
7. have higher levels of anxiety, depression, and somatic complaints
8. have poor self-concepts
9. are at increased risk for serious health problems, such as coronary heart disease
10. are not well adjusted psychologically

OVERCONTROLLED–HOSTILITY (O–H) SCALE

Scale Development

Megargee and colleagues (1967) suggested there are two major types of persons who commit acts of extreme physical aggression. Habitually aggressive (undercontrolled) persons, the first type, have not developed appropriate controls against the expression of aggression, so when provoked they respond with aggression of an intensity proportional to the degree of provocation. The second type, chronically overcontrolled persons, have very rigid inhibitions against the expression of any form of aggression. Most of the time the overcontrolled individuals do not respond even with aggression appropriate to provocation; but occasionally, when the provocation is great enough, they may act out in an extremely aggressive manner. Megargee and his associates (1967) believed that the most aggressive acts typically are committed by overcontrolled rather than undercontrolled persons.

The Overcontrolled–Hostility (O–H) scale was developed to assess the overcontrolled personality just described. The original O-H scale was constructed by identifying items answered differently by extremely assaultive prisoners, moderately assaultive prisoners, prisoners convicted of nonviolent crimes, and men who had not been convicted of any crime. Items were scored so that higher scores on the O–H scale were indicative of more assaultive (overcontrolled) persons. Appendix B of the MMPI-2 manual identifies the 28 items comprising the O-H scale along with their scored direction (Butcher et al., 2001).

Reliability and Validity
Internal-consistency (alpha) coefficients for men and women in the MMPI-2 normative sample were .34 and .24, respectively (Butcher et al., 2001). Test–retest coefficients for men and women from the MMPI-2 normative sample were .68 and .69, respectively (Butcher et al., 2001).

Results of research comparing scores on the original MMPI's O–H-scale between violent and nonviolent offenders were mixed, with some studies finding increased O-H-scale scores among more violent criminals and other studies reporting no difference (e.g., Fisher, 1970; Megargee et al., 1967). Using the MMPI-2, Verona and Carbonell (2000) reported that one-time violent female offenders had higher O–H-scale scores than nonviolent offenders.

Archer et al. (1997) reported that O–H-scale scores of psychiatric inpatients were positively related to extratest measures of grandiosity and negatively related to measures of uncooperativeness. Graham et al. (1999) found that, for men, therapists rated mental health center clients with high O–H-scale scores as less depressed than other clients; and these high-scoring men were less likely to have been arrested. Women clients with high O–H-scale scores were rated as more optimistic than other women clients. Both clients identifying as men and women who scored high on the O–H scale presented themselves as less depressed, hostile, and obsessive–compulsive. In summary, there is little evidence to suggest that high scores on the O–H scale in groups other than prisoners are associated with violent acts.

Caldwell (2005) suggested that the O–H scale can provide information about parenting characteristics in child custody evaluations, stating that high-scoring parents may bottle up anger and express it in undercontrolled ways. However, Bow, Flens, et al. (2006) cited survey data indicating that clinicians who used the MMPI-2 in child custody evaluations did not find the O–H scale to be very useful. These authors could find no data published in peer-review journals concerning behaviors associated with O–H scale scores in settings where custody evaluations are conducted.

Interpretation of High Scores on the O–H Scale
In correctional settings, high scores on the O–H scale tend to be associated with aggressive and violent acts. However, the validity of the O–H scale is such that individual predictions of violence from scores are not likely to be very accurate. The O–H scale has potential use in other settings because it tells clinicians something about how persons typically respond to provocation. Higher scorers on the O–H scale tend to respond to provocation appropriately most of the time, but occasional exaggerated aggressive responses may occur.

High scores also may be indicative of persons who

1. typically do not express angry feelings
2. are more socialized and responsible
3. have strong needs to excel
4. are dependent on others
5. are trustful
6. describe nurturing and supportive family backgrounds
7. if psychiatric inpatients, tend to be rather grandiose but cooperative
8. if mental health center clients, present themselves as having fewer symptoms and negative characteristics than other clients

MACANDREW ALCOHOLISM SCALE-REVISED (MAC-R)

Scale Development
The MacAndrew Alcoholism (MAC) scale (MacAndrew, 1965) was developed to differentiate psychiatric patients with and without alcohol-related disorders. The scale was constructed by contrasting the MMPI responses of 200 men with alcohol-related difficulties seeking treatment at an outpatient clinic with responses of 200 men identified as psychiatric outpatients without alcohol-related disorders from the same facility. These analyses identified 51 items that differentiated the two groups. Because MacAndrew was interested in developing a subtle scale, two items that deal directly with excessive drinking behavior were eliminated from the scale. The items were keyed in the direction selected most often by the individuals with alcohol-related problems.

Four of the original MAC scale items were among those eliminated from the MMPI-2 because of objectionable content. Because the original MAC scale was typically interpreted in terms of raw scores, a decision was made to maintain a scale of 49 items in the MMPI-2. Thus, the four objectionable items were replaced with four new items selected because they differentiated men with and without alcohol-related difficulties and the new scale was referred to as the MacAndrew Alcoholism Scale-Revised (MAC-R; Butcher et al., 1989). The items comprising the MAC-R scale and the direction in which they are keyed are reported in Appendix B of the MMPI-2 Manual (Butcher et al., 2001). Weed et al. (1995) factor analyzed the MAC-R items for a mixed sample of patients with alcohol-related disorders and other psychiatric difficulties. They found six factors that they labeled cognitive impairment, school maladjustment, interpersonal competence, risk taking, harmful habits, and stereotypically masculine interests.

Reliability and Validity
The MAC-R scale does not seem to have particularly good internal consistency due, at least in part, to the heterogenous nature of the item content it includes. Internal-consistency (alpha) coefficients for the MMPI-2 normative sample were .56 for men and .45 for women (Butcher et al., 2001). Butcher et al. (1995) reported alpha coefficients of .51 and .61, respectively, for a composite sample of males and females

with substance-related difficulties, other psychiatric problems, and nonpatients. C. S. Miller et al. (2007) reviewed 210 studies in which MAC/MAC-R data were reported and found that reliability data were reported for only 9% of the studies. The median internal consistency value for these studies was .48.

For subsamples of men and women in the MMPI-2 normative sample, test–retest reliability coefficients (1-week interval) for the MAC-R scale were .62 and .78, respectively. These relatively modest test–retest reliability coefficients can be explained, at least in part, by limited variability of scores in these groups.

Research concerning the MAC-R scale has indicated that individuals engaging in problematic substance use score higher than those who are not misusing substances (e.g., T. G. Brown & Fayek, 1993; Cavaiola et al., 2002; Clements & Heintz, 2002; Rouse et al., 1999; Stein et al., 1999; Wasyliw et al., 1993; Weed et al., 1995). Although the name of the scale implies scores are specific to alcohol-related problems, past studies have demonstrated the MAC and MAC-R scales can detect problems with other drugs, such as cocaine, as well as problematic gambling (e.g., T. G. Brown & Fayek, 1993; Graham, 1978). Cooper-Hakim and Viswesvaran (2002) reported results of a meta-analysis of 161 studies involving the MAC and MAC-R scales. They concluded that with a raw score cutoff of 27, a 72% correct classification of individuals with and without substance-related problems was achieved. The more traditional cutoff score of 24 also yielded a 72% correct classification. Craig (2005) reviewed 71 MAC-R studies published between 1988 and 2001 and concluded that the scale "significantly correlates with measures of alcohol and substance abuse in both male and female adolescents and adults across a diverse spectrum of the use-abuse continuum" (p. 444).

Despite a large body of research suggesting MAC-R scores are effective for detecting substance-related difficulties, other work suggests scale scores are not likely to be useful for monitoring symptoms over time. Specifically, research on the MMPI MAC scale has suggested scores for individuals with substance-related difficulties are not likely to change as a result of treatment (e.g., Gallucci et al., 1989; Huber & Danahy, 1975; Rohan, 1972). This may be, in part, because the scale is comprised of items assessing characteristics that contribute to substance use, such as risk taking, rather than recent behaviors related to substance use (Weed et al., 1995). Nonetheless, though it has been suggested MAC/MAC-R scores may be useful for identifying a personality style prone to developing problems with substances, no previous research has examined this predictive relationship.

Several studies have suggested caution is needed when using MAC-R scores in assessments of members of underrepresented racial and ethnic groups, as well as women. Studies examining the utility of MAC scores in samples of Black Americans with and without substance-related problems noted concerns about poor classification rates (Graham & Mayo, 1985; Walters et al., 1983, 1984). Greene et al. (2003) reported that MAC-R scores were not related to several different measures of substance misuse among members of two Native American nations. Several studies using the MMPI also suggest the MAC scale does not work as well with women as with men (Gottesman & Prescott, 1989; Schwartz & Graham, 1979).

Ward and Jackson (1990) suggested MAC scale scores may be a function of both psychiatric diagnosis and substance use/misuse, a notion supported by subsequent research. Patients who misuse substances who have other psychiatric diagnoses (i.e., MacAndrew's secondary alcoholics) tend to obtain relatively low scores on the MAC scale (e.g., Ward & Jackson, 1990) and are not easily discriminated from psychiatric patients who do not misuse substances. Patients with diagnoses of antisocial personality disorder often obtain relatively higher scores on the MAC scale whether or not they misuse substances (e.g., A. W. Wolf et al., 1990). Thus, patients with diagnoses of antisocial personality disorder who do not have substance-related disorders are often misidentified as having substance use problems.

Interpretation of Scores on the MAC-R Scale

High scores on the MAC-R scale suggest the possibility of alcohol- or other substance-related problems. Of course, no decisions about substance misuse should be made on the basis of MAC-r scale scores alone. High scores on the scale should alert clinicians to seek additional information concerning the possibility of substance-related difficulties. Obviously, it would be irresponsible and negligent clinical practice to reach conclusions about substance-related problems based on a test score alone.

The following guidelines are based on our review of empirical research literature on the MAC and MAC-R. In general, raw scores of 28 and above on the MAC-R scale are suggestive of potential substance-related problems. In such cases, additional information about alcohol and drug use should be obtained. Scores between 24 and 27 may also be suggestive of substance-related difficulties; but at this level, there will be many false positives (i.e., individuals without substance-related disorders who are misidentified as having difficulties with alcohol or drugs by their scores). Scores below 24 suggest that substance-related problems are not very likely. Incorrect classification of individuals without substance-related disorders as having such problems is especially likely to occur for individuals who have many of the characteristics often associated with the diagnosis of antisocial personality disorder. Individuals with substance-related disorders who also have other psychiatric diagnoses, such as schizophrenia or major affective disorders, are likely to have relatively low scores on the MAC-R scale and may not be identified as having substance-related problems on the basis of this scale. Black Americans who have a problematic pattern of substance use are likely to obtain elevated MAC-r scale scores, but the false-positive rate will be higher among Black Americans than White Americans.

Historically, the MAC scale was sometimes described as assessing an addiction-prone personality. This led to the suggestion that persons with higher scores are at greater risk for developing substance use problems even if they are not currently misusing substances. The existing literature simply does not support such interpretations. We strongly recommend limiting interpretations of MAC-r scale scores to focus on the possibility of current substance misuse. MAC-r scale scores do not provide scientifically supported predictions of future vulnerability to develop substance use problems.

Although most items on the MAC-R scale are not obviously related to substance use/misuse, some data suggest that individuals with alcohol-related disorders who take the MMPI-2 with intentions of hiding problems or shortcomings may produce lower scores on the MAC-R scale than when they take the test more honestly (Wasyliw et al., 1993). Thus, we recommend extreme caution in interpreting low MAC-r scale scores when the Validity scales of the MMPI-2 indicate the test taker has approached the MMPI-2 in a defensive manner.

In addition to the possibility of substance-related problems, high scores on the MAC-R scale may indicate persons who

1. are socially extroverted
2. are exhibitionistic
3. are self-confident and assertive
4. may experience blackouts
5. enjoy competition and risk taking
6. have difficulties in concentrating
7. have histories of behavior problems in school or with the law
8. are aggressive

ADDICTION ADMISSION SCALE (AAS)

Scale Development

Weed and colleagues (1992) developed the Addiction Admission Scale (AAS), emphasizing items in the MMPI-2 that have obvious content related to substance misuse (e.g., having a drug or alcohol problem, expressing true feelings only when drinking). A tentative scale composed of 14 items was refined using internal-consistency procedures, resulting in the elimination of three items that did not contribute to scale homogeneity. Scores on the 11-item version of the scale were correlated with each of the other MMPI-2 items. Two additional items were identified for inclusion in the scale. Thus, the final AAS has 13 items (see Appendix B of the MMPI-2 Manual; Butcher et al., 2001). Raw scores on the AAS are transformed to linear T scores using the MMPI-2 normative data (see Appendix A of the MMPI-2 Manual). Score transformations based on the non-gendered normative data are available in the Appendix of Ben-Porath and Forbey's (2003) non-gendered norms monograph.

Reliability and Validity

Weed et al. (1992) reported an internal-consistency coefficient (alpha) of .74 for a combined sample of individuals with substance-related disorders, psychiatric patients, and persons in the MMPI-2 normative sample. In a comprehensive literature review, C. S. Miller et al. (2007) found only two studies that reported internal consistency data for the AAS. The median value was .58. Weed et al. (1992) reported test–retest reliability coefficients of .89 and .84, respectively, for men and women in the MMPI-2 normative sample (1-week interval between testing). Factor analysis of the AAS items yielded one very strong factor associated with admission of problem drinking, and two weaker factors, one reflecting the use of drugs other than alcohol and the other having to do with social problems associated with alcohol or drug use (Weed et al., 1995).

The utility of the AAS was examined by Weed et al. (1992) using samples of individuals with substance-related disorders (832 men, 380 women), psychiatric inpatients (232 men, 191 women), and the MMPI-2 normative sample (1,138 men and 1,462 women). For both men and women, the individuals who had substance-related disorders had the highest mean AAS scores, and persons in the normative sample had the lowest mean scores. The mean scores of the psychiatric patients were between the means of the other two groups. Other research has supported the relationship between AAS scores and various indicators of substance-related difficulties. In the MMPI-2 normative sample (Butcher et al., 1989), higher AAS scorers were more likely to be described by their partners as drinking alcohol excessively and misusing nonprescription drugs. In several studies, mental health patients with higher AAS scores were more likely to have indicators of substance misuse (Stein et al., 1999; Wong & Besett, 1999), and similar relationships were observed in a forensic setting (Ben-Porath & Stafford, 1993) and for college student samples (Clements & Heintz, 2002; Svanum et al., 1994). Rouse et al. (1999) reported that psychotherapy patients with substance-related problems scored significantly higher on the AAS than those without such difficulties.

Although Weed et al. (1992) did not recommend cutoff scores for the AAS, examination of their data suggests that a T score of 60 yielded optimal classification. When men with T scores greater than 60 on the AAS were considered to be misusing substances, and those with T scores equal to or below 60 were not, 72% of the individuals with substance-related disorders, 51% of the psychiatric patients, and 87% of persons in the normative sample were correctly classified. A T-score cutoff of 60 for women yielded correct classification of 58% of the individuals with substance-related disorders, 66% of psychiatric patients, and 95% of persons in the normative sample. Greene et al. (1992) reported similar classification rates for the AAS with substance misuse and general psychiatric samples. Although classification rates in other studies have varied (e.g., Clements & Heintz, 2002; Stein et al., 1999), in general, the data have suggested that T scores greater than 60 on the AAS are suggestive of substance-related problems that should be evaluated carefully with other corroborating data.

Overall, these data suggest AAS has promise in discriminating between individuals with and without substance-related difficulties but that it may be less useful in discriminating between individuals with substance use and other psychiatric difficulties. Namely, using the AAS for this purpose may lead to many psychiatric patients being misclassified as having substance-related difficulties. However, this may reflect the nature of the psychiatric samples used in previous studies. The study of Weed et al. (1992) did not eliminate from the psychiatric samples patients who also had alcohol or drug problems. In fact, Greene et al. (1992) reported that between 10% and 20% of psychiatric patients in the study's setting typically also received a diagnosis of alcohol or drug dependence.

Interpretation of AAS Scores

In summary, persons who obtain high scores (T > 60) on the AAS are openly acknowledging substance-related problems, and additional assessment in this area is indicated. Because the content of the items in the AAS is highly face valid, persons not wanting to reveal substance use problems can easily obtain lower scores. Therefore, it is difficult to determine if low scores indicate the absence of substance use problems or the denial of such problems in persons who actually experience difficulties due to substance use. Examination of the Validity scales of the MMPI-2 could be helpful in this regard. Validity patterns suggesting exaggeration are of less concern because persons are not often motivated to appear to have alcohol or drug problems when they really do not have them. However, in certain forensic cases, this motive should be considered (e.g., a case in which a defendant could receive a more favorable outcome if judged to have a substance-related disorder).

In addition to the possibility of problems related to substance use, high scores on the AAS may indicate persons who

1. have histories of acting-out behavior
2. are impulsive
3. are risk takers
4. have poor judgment
5. are angry and aggressive
6. are critical and argumentative
7. have family problems
8. are agitated and moody

ADDICTION POTENTIAL SCALE (APS)

Scale Development

The Addiction Potential Scale (APS) was developed by Weed et al. (1992) using the MMPI-2 item pool. The 39 items in the scale are those that 434 men and 164 women in an inpatient chemical-dependency program answered differently from 120 men and 90 women in an inpatient psychiatric unit and from 584 men and 706 women in the MMPI-2 normative sample. The patients in the chemical-dependency program included persons who had difficulties due to alcohol only, other drugs only, or both alcohol and other drugs. Several tentative items were eliminated from the scale because their content obviously related to substance misuse. The items are keyed in the direction most often chosen by individuals with substance-related disorders (see Appendix B of the MMPI-2 Manual; Butcher et al., 2001). Raw scores on the APS are transformed to linear T scores using the MMPI-2 normative data (see Appendix A of the MMPI-2 Manual). Score transformations based on the non-gendered normative data are available in the Appendix of Ben-Porath and Forbey's (2003) non-gendered norms monograph.

The content of the items in the APS is quite heterogeneous, and many of the items do not seem to have obvious relevance to substance use. Some items seem to be related to extroversion, excitement seeking, and risk taking. Other seem to assess self-doubts, self-alienation, and cynical attitudes about other people. Sawrie et al. (1996) factor analyzed the items in the APS and identified five major clusters of items: (a) satisfaction/dissatisfaction with self, (b) powerlessness/lack of self-efficacy, (c) antisocial acting out, (d) surgency, and (e) risk taking/recklessness. A somewhat different factor structure for the APS was reported by Weed et al. (1995), who considered a six-factor solution to be most interpretable: (a) harmful habits, (b) positive treatment attitudes, (c) forthcoming, (d) hypomania, (e) risk taking, and (f) passivity.

Reliability and Validity

Although items included in the APS were based, in part, on their contribution to internal consistency, no internal-consistency coefficients were reported by the scale's developers. Weed et al. (1995) later reported alpha coefficients of .70 and .73, respectively, for men and women in a combined sample of individuals with substance-related problems, psychiatric patients, and nonpatients. Alpha coefficients for men and women in the MMPI-2 normative sample were .48 and .43, respectively. In a comprehensive literature review, C. S. Miller et al. (2007) found only two studies that reported internal consistency data for the APS. The median value was .58. The test–retest reliability coefficients for men and women in the MMPI-2 normative sample (1-week interval) were .89 and .84, respectively (Butcher et al., 2001).

In cross-validating the APS, Weed et al. (1992) drew different participants from the same settings used in scale development. They reported data suggesting APS scores discriminated quite well between individuals with substance use problems and persons in the normative sample and between individuals with substance use problems and patients with other psychiatric difficulties. Although the scale developers did not recommend cutoff scores for the APS, examination of their data reveals that the optimal T-score cutoff for both men and women who participated seemed to be 60. When men with T scores greater than 60 were considered to have substance-related problems, and those with T scores equal to or less than 60 as not having these types of difficulties, 71% of the individuals with substance-related difficulties, 86% of persons in the normative sample, and 82% of the psychiatric patients were correctly classified. A T-score cutoff of 60 for women correctly classified 70% of individuals with substance-related difficulties, 87% of the normative sample, and 81% of the psychiatric patients. By lowering the cutoff score, greater proportions of the individuals with substance-related difficulties could be correctly classified, but more persons in the normative sample and more psychiatric patients were incorrectly classified as having substance-related difficulties. Classification rates in subsequent studies have generally been lower than those reported by Weed et al. (1992), and the APS generally did a poorer job of identifying people with substance-related disorders than either the MAC-R scale or the AAS (e.g., Greene et al., 1992; Rouse et al., 1999; Stein et al., 1999). Although the APS has been related to various indicators of substance misuse, it also seems to indicate a general need to admit serious personal problems and to profess a desire for change (Weed et al., 1995).

Interpretation of APS Scores

The limited data available concerning the APS suggest it has some promise for discriminating between persons with and without substance-related difficulties. However, the APS does not seem to be as effective as either the MAC-R scale or the AAS in identifying substance use problems in a variety of settings. The label of "Addiction Potential" suggests the scale assesses a potential for or vulnerability to substance-related problems, whether or not misuse is currently taking place. However, there are no data concerning this very important issue. Available data address the ability of the scale to identify persons who currently are misusing substances or have done so in the past. The extent to which the scale can predict future use-related problems and can identify current substance misuse by persons who are denying substance-related problems has not been investigated.

Despite the limited data available concerning the APS, it should be considered as one indicator of possible substance-related problems. Of course, it is not appropriate to reach conclusions about substance-related problems on the basis of MMPI-2 scores alone. High APS scores (T > 60) should alert clinicians that additional information concerning possible substance misuse and disorders should be obtained. However, when MAC-R scale or AAS scores are suggestive of substance-related difficulties and the APS score is not, greater weight should be given to the MAC-R and AAS scores.

MASCULINE GENDER ROLE (GM) AND FEMININE GENDER ROLE (GF) SCALES

Scale Development

Peterson and Dahlstrom (1992) developed the Masculine Gender Role (GM) and Feminine Gender Role (GF) scales for the MMPI-2 as separate measures of the masculine and feminine components in the bipolar Masculinity–Femininity (Mf or Scale 5) scale of the MMPI. Items in the GM scale were those endorsed in the scored direction by a majority of men in the MMPI-2 normative sample and endorsed in that same direction by at least 10% fewer women in the MMPI-2 normative sample. Correspondingly, items in the GF scale were those endorsed in the scored direction by a majority of women in the MMPI-2 normative sample and endorsed in that same direction by at least 10% fewer men in the MMPI-2 normative sample. Only 9 of 47 items in the GM scale and 16 of the 46 items in the GF scale also appear on Clinical Scale 5 (Mf; see Appendix B of the MMPI-2 Manual for item compositions and keyed directions; Butcher et al., 2001).

Examination of the content of the items in the GM scale suggests they deal primarily with the denial of fears, anxieties, and somatic symptoms. Some GM scale items have to do with interest in stereotypically masculine activities, such as reading adventure stories, and with denial of interests in stereotypically feminine occupations, such as nursing and library work. Other groups of GM scale items have to do with denial of excessive emotionality and presentation of self as independent, decisive, and self-confident.

The largest group of items in the GF scale has to do with the denial of asocial or antisocial acts, such as getting into trouble with the law or at school and excessive use of alcohol or other drugs. Many GF scale items also have to do with liking stereotypically feminine activities, such as cooking and growing houseplants, and with disliking stereotypically masculine activities, such as reading mechanics magazines and auto racing. Some GF scale items involve admissions of emotional sensitivity. There are also several items expressing early identification with a female figure and satisfaction with being female.

Reliability and Validity

Internal-consistency (alpha) coefficients for the GM scale for men and women in the MMPI-2 normative sample were .67 and .75, respectively (Butcher et al., 2001). Test–retest reliability coefficients (1-week interval) for the GM scale for subsamples of men and women in the MMPI-2 normative sample were .82 and .89, respectively (Butcher et al., 2001).

The internal-consistency (alpha) coefficient for the GF scale was .57 for both men and women in the MMPI-2 normative sample (Butcher et al., 2001). Test–retest reliability coefficients (1-week interval) for the GF scale were .85 and .78, respectively, for men and women in the MMPI-2 normative sample (Butcher et al., 2001).

Peterson and Dahlstrom (1992) suggested that the conjoint interpretation of the GM and GF scales can yield a gender-role typology. Used in this manner, a high score on the GM scale and a low score on the GF scale would indicate stereotypic masculinity; a high score on the GF scale and a low score on the GM scale would indicate stereotypic femininity; high scores on both the GM and GF scales would indicate androgyny; and low scores on both the GM and GF scales would indicate an undifferentiated orientation. However, subsequent research by Johnson et al. (1996) did not support this use of the GM and GF scales. These researchers found that the GM and GF scales had only modest correlations with other sex-role measures (e.g., Bem Sex-Role Inventory, Sex-Role Behavior Scale) and that classifying students into gender-role types using the GM and GF scales was not very accurate.

Peterson and Dahlstrom (1992) reported some preliminary data concerning behavioral correlates of the GM and GF scales for men and women in the MMPI-2 normative sample. GM scale scores for both men and women were positively related to high self-confidence, persistence, and lack of feelings of self-reference and other positive characteristics. GF scale scores were related to negative characteristics, including hypercritical behavior and poor temper control for men and misuse of alcohol and nonprescription drugs for men and women. Research by Castlebury and Durham (1997), which involved college student participants, supported the notion that for both men and women, higher GM scale scores are associated with greater self-confidence and general well-being. Similar results were reported by Woo and Oei (2006, 2008) for mental health patients.

Interpretation of GM- and GF-scale Scores

The limited research published about the GM and GF scales does not support their use as measures of gender roles. High scorers (both men and women) on the GM scale are likely to be better adjusted than those who score lower on this scale. However, better MMPI-2 measures of psychological adjustment are available, so the routine use of the GM and GF scales is not recommended.

CHAPTER 9

CULTURAL AND CONTEXTUAL CONSIDERATIONS

THE ORIGINAL MMPI WAS developed for use with adult psychiatric patients. The demographic characteristics of the MMPI-2 normative sample were based on the 1980 U.S. census. Understandably, questions are raised concerning the use of the instrument with persons whose demographic characteristics are different from those of the normative sample. Additional questions are posed when the test is used in contexts other than traditional psychiatric settings. This chapter reviews information addressing these concerns. Throughout this text, we strived to use bias-free language when discussing various cultural groups. Thus, we adopted recommended language from the American Psychological Association (2020) in our summarizations. We did not think, however, that it was appropriate to assume we knew which groups were reflected in past studies that used different terminology. As such, when reporting directly about a published study, we have maintained use of the terminology adopted by the original authors.

ADOLESCENTS

Although the original MMPI was intended for use with adults, it quickly became popular as an instrument for assessing adolescents (e.g., Hathaway & Monachesi, 1963). However, many concerns were expressed about its use with adolescents (e.g., Archer, 1987; C. L. Williams, 1986). As such, in 1992 a version of the MMPI developed specifically for use with adolescents, the Minnesota Multiphasic Personality Inventory-Adolescent (MMPI-A), was published (Butcher et al., 1992). More recently, a restructured version of this instrument, the Minnesota Multiphasic Personality Inventory-Adolescent-Restructured Form (MMPI-A-RF; Archer et al., 2016) was published. Both the MMPI-A and MMPI-A-RF are appropriate for persons between the ages of 14 and 18. Because both the MMPI-2 and adolescent versions of the MMPI can be used with 18-year-olds, clinicians must decide which version is most appropriate for each 18-year-old. Generally, it is advisable to use the MMPI-2 for mature 18-year-olds who are in college or otherwise living independently from caregivers, and the MMPI-A or MMPI-A-RF for less mature 18-year-olds who have not adopted independent lifestyles. The MMPI-A is discussed in detail in Chapter 14 of this book. The MMPI-A-RF is described in Chapter 15.

OLDER ADULTS

The MMPI-2 normative sample included persons ranging in age from 18 to 84 years (mean = 41.71; Butcher et al., 2001). However, older adults (70 years of age or older) were somewhat underrepresented (4.6% of men; 5.3% of women). Although the MMPI-2 manual does not report scores separately by age groups, the committee that developed the MMPI-2 conducted appropriate analyses and concluded age-specific norms were not needed (Butcher et al., 1989).

Butcher et al. (1991) compared scores of men in the MMPI-2 normative sample with those of a group of healthy older men from the Normative Aging Study (NAS). Ages of men in the NAS ranged from 40 to 90 years ($M = 61.27$). Scores of the two groups of men were very similar. Of the 567 MMPI-2 items, only 14 differed by more than 20% in endorsement percentages between the two groups. Interestingly, the item with the greatest difference in endorsement had to do with enjoying the use of marijuana, supporting speculation that differences between older and younger persons may reflect cohort effects. The content of the remaining items endorsed differently by the groups suggests the older men were indicating less stress and turmoil in their lives and greater satisfaction and contentment.

Within each of their samples, Butcher et al. (1991) compared scores of men of different ages. The differences between age groups were small and probably not clinically important. Butcher et al. (1991) concluded the differences may represent the single or combined effects of cohort factors and age-related changes in physical health status rather than age-related changes in psychopathology per se. They also concluded that special, age-related norms for the MMPI-2 are not needed for older men. Spiro et al. (2000) compared MMPI-2 scores of men in the Boston NAS who took the test twice with a 5-year interval. They found statistically significant but small changes on several scales, including Scales 1, 2, and 3.

Priest and Meunier (1993) studied a small group of women who were 60 years of age or older attending an elder hostel program and found their scores were quite similar to those of women in the MMPI-2 normative sample. Strassberg et al. (1991) reported that older adult men and women in Australia who were not in clinical settings had MMPI-2 scores very similar to those of older adults in the United States. They had modest elevations on Clinical Scales 1 and 2 and the Low Self-Esteem (LSE) Content scale and somewhat below-average scores on Scales 4, 6, and 9. Strassberg et al. also reported the Clinical and Content scale scores of the Australian older adults were related significantly to conceptually relevant extratest characteristics.

Aaronson et al. (1996) reported that older men who were VA domiciliary residents endorsed fewer MMPI-2 critical items than younger residents. These results are difficult to interpret because the older residents also were more defensive, suggesting they could have underreported actual symptoms and problems.

In sum, it seems appropriate to conclude there may be some differences between scores of older adults and younger adults. However, the differences tend to be small (less than 5 T-score points) and, thus, not clinically important. They may reflect changes in concerns, attitudes, and behaviors often, but not always, associated with aging. The use of age-specific norms for older adults does not seem appropriate. Because differences associated with normal aging are small, clinically elevated scores (T ≥ 65) on MMPI-2 scales of older adults are likely to indicate the same kinds of symptoms and problems associated with such elevated scores for younger adults.

UNDERREPRESENTED RACIAL AND ETHNIC GROUPS

Almost all of the data used in the development of the original MMPI was provided by White Americans, and the MMPI-2 normative sample underrepresented some racial and ethnic groups (e.g., people who identified as Asian or Hispanic; see Butcher et al., 1989). Therefore, there have been understandable concerns the MMPI-2 might not be appropriate for assessing members of underrepresented racial and ethnic groups.

Timbrook and Graham (1994) identified two general approaches to studying possible test bias on the MMPI-2. They found many studies simply compare mean score differences between racial and ethnic groups and interpret higher group mean scores for the underrepresented group as indicating test bias. This approach is problematic, however, as the presence or absence of mean scale differences between cultural groups does not address directly the issue of test bias (Pritchard & Rosenblatt, 1980). The second, more methodologically sound, approach they identified is to examine whether or not MMPI-2 scores are equally valid for members of the groups being studied, also known as tests of predictive bias. These studies typically use statistical regression-based moderation techniques to examine potential test bias, as they can investigate two different ways a score could be differentially valid. This includes (a) whether there is any evidence of scores having differential abilities for predicting an extratest outcome across the included groups (i.e., slope bias, which answers the question, "are the scale equally associated with conceptually relevant extratest measures?"), and (b) whether scores consistently over- or underpredict an extratest outcome for one group compared to others (i.e., intercept bias, which answers the question, "do members of one group consistently score higher or lower on scale compared to members of other groups?"). Evidence supporting the presence of either of these types of test bias suggests interpretations of a test score are likely to be less accurate for one cultural group when compared to other groups.

More recently, a third way of examining potential test bias has emerged in the literature—that of measurement invariance (Marsh et al., 2012). Examinations of measurement invariance are concerned with the extent to which test scores (and the items that comprise that score) are equally valid indicators of the latent attribute being assessed across groups. Tests of measurement invariance often use Confirmatory Factor

Analysis (CFA) or Item Response Theory (IRT) to examine a test's measurement model across groups. This typically includes examinations of at least four types of equivalence. These include equivalence of: (a) factor structure (i.e., whether the same items comprise similar factors across groups or configural invariance), (b) item loadings (i.e., whether items that comprise a factor are equally related to the factor across groups or metric invariance), and (c) item error variances (i.e., whether the items are equally precise in measuring the attribute across groups or residual invariance). The fourth examination of equivalence (d) is that of scalar invariance, which is an inspection of similarity across groups in intercepts if CFA is used and thresholds if IRT is used. Practically, results of measurement invariance analyses suggesting invariance between groups could indicate a test's items are more or less valid indicators of the attribute being assessed for a particular cultural group. For this reason, Han and colleagues (2019) argued that the measurement invariance of a scale should be examined prior to tests of predictive bias. We have no knowledge of published, peer-reviewed studies examining the measurement invariance of MMPI-2 scales.

In the sections that follow, we make an attempt to summarize what is known about the appropriateness of using the MMPI-2 with members of underrepresented racial and ethnic groups. However, research on this issue has been limited. Additionally, what research has been conducted should be viewed in light of several research-related issues. Specifically, past research has often failed to acknowledge the heterogeneity of cultural backgrounds represented within groups such as Hispanic people or Native Americans and have either not identified cultural identities or have combined persons from varied cultural backgrounds under a single racial or ethnic group. For example, Allen (1998) pointed out there are 510 federally recognized Native entities in the United States; but researchers have typically collapsed these distinctions into a single grouping as if Native Americans share a single, common identity. Second, researchers have often asked participants to select a single racial or ethnic identity from a set list of options. This might force an artificial choice for many individuals, such as people with multiracial identities, people who come from parts of the world with different racial or ethnic identity constructs, and people who do not see their identity listed on the form. These participants must often decide between a predetermined option that does not accurately describe their sense of identity or select "other." Third, the importance of acculturation as a moderating variable—a crucial consideration in communities of immigrants—has rarely been considered in any systematic way. Fourth, tests of predictive bias assume the criterion being predicted by scale scores are themselves unbiased indicators and capture a universal (etic) construct (Hill et al., 2012). To the extent either of these assumptions is not true, tests of predictive bias may misrepresent the cultural fairness of a scale's scores. Finally, none of the data following can speak to ways in which a clinician's biases may enter into the interpretation of the instrument. Interested readers should see Knaster and Micucci (2013) for commentary and empirical study on this issue.

Black Americans

Including individuals who identified as African American in the MMPI-2 normative sample in approximately the same proportion as the 1980 US census was an important improvement over the original MMPI, whose normative sample was comprised almost exclusively of White American people. However, this increase in representation did not necessarily mean the test was unbiased. As such, some subsequent work has examined whether there is any evidence of test bias for MMPI-2 scales when used with individuals who identify as Black.

Appendix H of the original MMPI-2 manual (Butcher et al., 1989) reported MMPI-2 summary data separately for the various racial and ethnic groups included in the normative sample. These data indicated African Americans scored slightly higher than Caucasians on most scales. However, T-score differences of more than 5 points—the traditional demarcation for indicating a clinically meaningful difference—occurred only for Scale 4 for women (6 T-score points). There are two limitations to these findings that warrant mention. First, these summary data did not match African Americans and Caucasians on age, socioeconomic status, or other demographic variables. This is important because differences between Black and White Americans on the original MMPI were much smaller when such variables were taken into account. Second, the manual did not present data concerning whether these small differences between scores achieved by African Americans and Caucasians in the normative sample were associated with differences in associations with external measures.

Shondrick et al. (1992) reported MMPI-2 data for 106 Caucasian and 37 African American men who were undergoing forensic evaluations. The groups differed significantly only on Clinical Scale 9 and the Cynicism (CYN) and Antisocial Practices (ASP) Content scales, with African Americans scoring higher than Caucasians in each case. Frueh et al. (1996) reported patients that identified as Black men and who had diagnoses of PTSD scored higher on Scales 6 and 8 and the F-K Index than patients with this diagnosis who identified as White. Neither of these studies included comparisons of the association of these scales for the various groups with extratest data.

A meta-analysis by G. C. N. Hall et al. (1999) examined the results of 25 MMPI/MMPI-2 studies of African American and European American men and 12 MMPI/MMPI-2 studies of African American and European American women. These authors concluded that, although African American men scored higher than European American men on seven MMPI/MMPI-2 scales and African American women scored higher than European American women on eight scales, the effect sizes associated with these differences were small and not clinically meaningful. For no scale did the meta-analytic mean difference between African American and European American groups exceed 5 T-score points.

Finding significant mean score differences between groups does not necessarily mean a test is biased. As Pritchard and Rosenblatt (1980) pointed out, for a test to be biased, the accuracy of inferences or predictions based on test scores must be different for different groups. Several MMPI-2 studies have examined these issues.

Timbrook and Graham (1994) compared the scores of African Americans and individuals who identified as White in the MMPI-2 normative sample matched for age, education, and family income. They found the African American men scored statistically significantly higher than the men who were White only on Scale 8, while the same was true for women on Scales 4, 5, and 9. In all instances, the group mean differences were less than 5 T-score points. Timbrook and Graham also determined the accuracy with which MMPI-2 scores predicted partner ratings of conceptually relevant characteristics. Accuracy of predictions did not differ between African American men and men who identified as White for any scale. For women, the only significant difference in predictive accuracy was that Scale 7 slightly underpredicted anxiety ratings for African Americans compared to those who identified as White. The authors concluded there was no evidence of test bias against African Americans in this sample.

McNulty, Graham, et al. (1997) compared MMPI-2 scores of African American and Caucasian clients at a community mental health center. Among clients, African American men scored significantly higher than Caucasian men on only the L scale and the Fears (FRS) Content scale. Clients who identified as African American women scored significantly higher than clients who identified as Caucasian women on only Scale 9 and the LSE Content scale. No significant group differences between African Americans and Caucasians were found in the strength of relationships between MMPI-2 scores and therapist ratings of conceptually relevant client characteristics. The authors concluded the MMPI-2 was not biased against African Americans in this outpatient mental health setting. Castro et al. (2008) conducted a similar study in a different outpatient mental health center setting. They found clients who identified as Black scored significantly higher than those who identified as White on Scales 1, RC1, RC3, RC6, and RC8. However, using information from client records as outcomes, they found no evidence of differential prediction between the two groups of clients. Using a sample of veterans receiving services in a VA outpatient hospital, Frueh et al. (1997) found patients with diagnoses of PTSD who identified as Black or White did not differ on any MMPI-2 scales or on external ratings of psychopathology or diagnoses. Overall, work in outpatient settings provides no evidence of MMPI-2 scales being biased against individuals who identify as Black at a clinically meaningful level.

Similar conclusions were reached by Arbisi et al. (2002) who investigated potential cultural biases in an inpatient setting. They found African American inpatients scored meaningfully higher than Caucasian inpatients on Scales 4, 6, and 9; on the Bizarre Mentation (BIZ) and Family Problems (FAM) Content scales; and on the revised MacAndrew's Alcoholism Scale (MAC-R) scale. However, using information from record reviews as outcomes, results of regression analyses indicated differences in predictive accuracy between African American and Caucasian patients were small and not clinically significant.

Discrepant findings from those just described were found by Monnot et al. (2009) who provided evidence for test bias for several MMPI-2 scales in their study of African American and Caucasian individuals receiving inpatient treatment for substance-related difficulties. Because of the large sample size, many statistically significant differences in MMPI-2 scores were found between the two groups of patients. However, for only one Clinical scale (Scale 9) and two RC scales (RC2 and RC6) were differences large enough to be considered clinically meaningful. For those scales with clinically meaningful differences in scores, African American patients scored higher than Caucasian patients. Regression analyses examining whether MMPI-2 scores differentially predicted diagnoses derived from a structured interview revealed there were slope and prediction biases for many of the scales examined. In general,

MMPI-2 scales modestly overpredicted the presence of conceptually relevant diagnoses for African American patients. However, the results of this study are difficult to interpret given there was a differential prevalence of many of the diagnoses in the two groups, which could suggest other meaningful differences between the groups or bias in the outcome variable (i.e., structured interview derived diagnoses). As such, replication is needed prior to drawing strong conclusions from this study. Nonetheless, this work does underscore the importance of examining test bias in a variety of populations and contexts, as conclusions may differ greatly.

Several studies of the original MMPI suggested caution in using the MacAndrew Alcoholism (MAC) scale with individuals who identified as Black (Graham & Mayo, 1985; Walters et al., 1983, 1984). Those studies indicated individuals with alcohol-related problems who identified as Black tended to obtain relatively high scores on the MAC, but classification rates were poor because Black psychiatric patients without alcohol-related problems also tended to obtain rather high MAC scores. This suggests there may be predictive bias in MAC scores, though no published studies have examined this possibility explicitly. Furthermore, all of these studies used military personnel or veterans, so the extent to which the findings can be generalized to other Black Americans is unclear. Nonetheless, we recommend caution if using the MAC-R with individuals who identify as Black.

Although more research is needed concerning potential test bias in MMPI-2 scale scores, some tentative conclusions may be reached. Score differences between people who identify as Black and White tend to be small, especially when groups are matched on other demographic variables such as age and socioeconomic status. Scores on MMPI-2 scales do not typically demonstrate a pattern of differential association with relevant extratest characteristics for Black and White individuals. Thus, there does not seem to be any generalizable and meaningful pattern of test bias in MMPI-2 scale scores against individuals who are Black. However, given findings in substance-related treatment settings, one exception to this general conclusion is that we do recommend caution when using the MMPI-2 with individuals who are Black in these contexts because scale scores may modestly overpredict diagnoses.

Hispanic and Latinx People

Approximately 3% of the MMPI-2 normative sample identified as Hispanic. Although this level of representation in the normative sample is inadequate based on the modern demographic characteristics of the United States, it does roughly approximate the number of respondents identifying as Hispanic on the 1980 US census. Appendix H of the original MMPI-2 manual (Butcher et al., 1989) reported scores separately for people who identified as Caucasian and Hispanic in the normative sample. Although ethnic backgrounds of the Hispanic individuals were not described, the geographical areas in which the normative data were collected suggest that most were Mexican American. Careful examination of these data reveals Hispanic men (n = 35) in the normative sample scored slightly higher than Caucasian men on most scales. However, none of the differences between Hispanic and Caucasian men were greater than 5 T-score points. Hispanic women (n = 38) in the normative sample scored higher than Caucasian women on all scales except L, K, 5, and 0. On the L and

K scales, the Hispanic women scored lower than those who were Caucasian; and on Scales 5 and 0, there were no differences between the two groups. For Scales F, 1, 4, 7, 8, and 9, the differences were greater than 5 T-score points. However, the Hispanic and Caucasian groups in the normative sample were not matched for variables such as age or education. In addition, the manual did not present data concerning whether the differences in group means were also associated with differences in predicting extratest criteria.

Subsequent empirical studies have also demonstrated score differences between individuals who identify as White and those who identify as Hispanic or Latinx. Velasquez et al. (1998) summarized more than 170 studies involving Latino participants. Unfortunately, most of the studies are unpublished, so their results and conclusions are difficult to evaluate. Most of the studies involved comparisons between Latino and other ethnic groups. Many found higher scores for Latino groups on some MMPI/MMPI-2 scales. A meta-analysis by Hall et al. (1999) examined the results of 13 studies that compared MMPI/MMPI-2 scores of European-American and Latino-American men and found the Latino-American men scored higher than European-American men on the L, F, and K scales and lower on all of the Clinical scales. They concluded the differences between the groups in mean scores derived from combining data from across all the studies included in the meta-analysis were small and probably not clinically meaningful, as even the largest differences were less than 5 T-score points. Despite their breadth, results from Valasquez et al. (1998) and Hall et al. (1999) do not permit conclusions concerning whether mean score differences observed between the examined cultural groups are the result of test bias. We need extratest data to know if observed differences are also associated with differences in the accurate prediction of relevant extratest variables.

Several authors (Butcher et al., 2007; Velasquez, 1995; Velasquez et al., 1997, 1998) have made recommendations for using the MMPI-2 with Hispanic and Latinx individuals. Some of these recommendations apply to the general use of the test (e.g., administer the entire test; explain to test takers how completing the MMPI-2 will be helpful to them). Other recommendations are more specific to culturally sensitive use of the MMPI-2. One such recommendation is test users should always consider the impact of acculturation on MMPI-2 performance. However, data concerning the relationships between measures of acculturation and MMPI-2 scores for individuals who are Hispanic have been mixed. For example, whereas Canul and Cross (1994) found L scores were negatively related to acculturation in a sample of Mexican Americans, Lessenger (1997) found no significant relationships between scores on a measure of acculturation and MMPI-2 scores in a sample of 100 Mexican American males with substance-related difficulties.

We offer several recommendations concerning the use of the MMPI-2 with individuals who are Hispanic or Latinx. First, administer the test using the language with which the test taker is most facile. There are several different Spanish-language versions of the MMPI-2 available (https://www.upress.umn.edu/test-division/translations-permissions/available-translations). Second, an individual's level of acculturation should be considered when interpreting MMPI-2 results. Modestly elevated scores (T = 50–60) may be the product of low acculturation. Finally, elevated scores (T ≥ 65) on the Clinical and Content scales are likely to reflect the same symptoms and problems that have been reported for individuals identifying as White on these scales.

Native Americans

There are data from 38 Native American men and 39 Native American women in the MMPI-2 normative sample. Appendix H of the original MMPI-2 manual (Butcher et al., 1989) summarized scores for these two groups. Individuals who identified as Native American scored higher than those who identified as Caucasian on most scales. The Native American men scored more than 5 T-score points higher than the Caucasian men on Scales F and 4. The Native American women scored more than 5 T-score points higher than the Caucasian women on Scales F, 1, 4, 5, 7, and 8. Although the Native American groups were small and not necessarily similar to the Caucasian groups in terms of age, socioeconomic status, or other demographic characteristics, the score differences between the Native American and Caucasian groups are potentially important. However, the test manual does not report any extratest data that would allow this determination to be made.

Robin et al. (2003) compared MMPI-2 Validity, Clinical, Content, and Supplementary scale scores of 535 Southwestern and 297 Plains Native American nation members with scores of persons from the MMPI-2 normative sample. Although differences between the two Native American samples were expected, no meaningful differences were found for any MMPI-2 scales. However, there were differences in scores between the combined Native American groups and the normative sample. The Native American group had meaningfully higher scores for Validity scales L and F; for Clinical scales 4, 8, and 9; for the Health Concerns (HEA), BIZ, CYN, ASP, and Negative Treatment Indicators (TRT) Content scales; and for the Addiction Admission Scale (AAS) and MAC-R scale. Although differences between groups for these scales were smaller when they were matched for age, gender, and education, they were still large enough to be clinically meaningful (i.e., > 5 T-score points).

In a companion study to Robin et al. (2003), Greene et al. (2003) used the same two Native American samples and calculated correlations between MMPI-2 scores and measures of clinical symptoms and behaviors generated from a modified version of the Schedule for Affective Disorders and Schizophrenia (SADS; Endicott & Spitzer, 1978). Meaningful correlations (≥ .30) were obtained between most MMPI-2 scales and conceptually relevant measures from the SADS. For example, breaking rules was correlated with Scale 4 and the ASP Content scale; suicide attempts with the Depression (DEP) Content scale; and alcohol and drug use with the AAS. The MAC-R scale was not correlated meaningfully with any of the measures of alcohol or drug problems. This finding is especially troubling because Robin et al. (2003) reported the Native Americans groups scored meaningfully higher on the MAC-R scale than those in the MMPI-2 normative sample. The SADS provided conceptually relevant measures for only some MMPI-2 scales, leaving relevant extratest correlates for other scales unexamined in the literature.

Pace et al. (2006) examined MMPI-2 scores of two Native American samples—namely, groups from the Eastern Woodland Oklahoma and Southwest Plains

Oklahoma nations—and compared their scores with data from the MMPI-2 normative sample. Both Native American groups scored significantly and meaningfully higher than the normative sample on most of the MMPI-2 Validity and Clinical scales. Level of acculturation was not a significant factor influencing MMPI-2 scale differences. The authors concluded the MMPI-2 should be used with great caution with Native Americans, and scores should be interpreted in the context of clients' unique beliefs and environmental circumstances. This caution is consistent with these authors' position that MMPI-2 results should always be interpreted while considering such factors for all people who complete the test. Absent from the Pace et al. study was the extratest criterion information needed to inform interpretation of elevated scores for members of these Native American tribes.

What conclusions can be reached about using the MMPI-2 with Native Americans? First, one should expect Native Americans to obtain modestly elevated scores on many MMPI-2 scales. These scores may likely be reflecting cultural factors rather than psychopathology. When T scores on Clinical and Content scales are above 65, the scores probably reflect the same symptoms and problems for Native Americans as they do for individuals who are White. However, we recommend special caution in inferring substance abuse problems from the MAC-R for Native Americans. Instead, we recommend using high scores on the AAS as indications of potential substance abuse problems, as its items reflect explicit substance use content. Additional research is needed to more clearly establish relationships between MMPI-2 scores and conceptually relevant extratest characteristics for Native Americans. Future research should also more carefully consider the heterogeneity of Native American nations and the extent to which findings for one tribe will generalize to others.

Asian Americans

Data in Appendix H of the original MMPI-2 manual (Butcher et al., 1989) suggest there were few differences between the individuals who were Asian American and those who were Caucasian in the normative sample. However, because so few Asian Americans were included in the MMPI-2 normative sample (6 men, 13 women), it is not appropriate to reach conclusions about these score differences.

Stevens et al. (1993) compared a small sample of individuals from China studying at a U.S. university with a matched sample of Caucasian American students from the same university. The Chinese men scored significantly higher than the Caucasian American men on Scale 0, suggesting the Chinese men were more introverted. The Chinese women scored higher than the Caucasian American women on the L scale, suggesting the Chinese women presented themselves as somewhat more virtuous. Similar results were reported by Robers (1992) in a sample of Chinese American students.

Tran (1996) and Dong and Church (2003) reported Vietnamese Americans had MMPI-2 scores within the nonclinical range but that their scores were slightly higher than those observed in the MMPI-2 normative sample, especially for Scales F and 8. Dong and Church's sample was comprised of Vietnamese refugees, and they also assessed participants' experience of trauma and level of acculturation. Results demonstrated there was a significant, positive correlation between severity of trauma and mean elevation of MMPI-2 Clinical scales. Results also indicated refugees who reported being less acculturated had higher MMPI-2 scores. Thus, these results suggest the somewhat elevated scores observed in this particular sample may not have been a result of cultural group membership; rather, they may have been a product of psychological symptoms related to past trauma or low acculturation.

Tsai and Pike (2000) compared Asian American college students (who were mostly of Chinese, Vietnamese, and Korean descent) with varying degrees of acculturation to a group of college students who identified as White. They found Asian American students with lower levels of acculturation had higher scores than the White students on most MMPI-2 scales, with the greatest differences on the F scale and Scale 8. Asian American students who were highly acculturated did not differ meaningfully from the White students. However, as Kwon (2002) pointed out, the design did not control for socioeconomic differences between groups, making it difficult to have confidence that differences were due only to levels of acculturation.

Additional research is needed concerning use of the MMPI-2 with individuals who are Asian American. It will be especially important to determine if MMPI-2 scores are differentially associated with important extratest characteristics for Asian Americans when compared to other ethnic and racial groups. Nonetheless, existing research supports recommendations from Okazaki and Sue (1995), who stressed the importance of considering the acculturation levels of Asian Americans when conducting psychological assessments. They recommended assessors "be more conservative and cautious in interpreting the results of less acculturated individuals whose scores deviated from the American norms" (p. 117).

Several conclusions can be reached about the use of the MMPI-2 with Asian Americans. First, scores achieved by Asian Americans in nonclinical settings are likely to be within normal limits, although some moderately high scores (T scores between 50 and 60) may be expected. Test users should consider whether these moderately elevated scores are likely to be the product of experienced stress or level of acculturation. However, very high MMPI-2 T scores (T ≥ 65) are likely to reflect symptoms and problems consistent with the findings reported for test takers who identify as White.

MEDICAL PATIENTS

The MMPI-2 is widely used in medical settings. One survey revealed almost 90% of health psychologists use the MMPI-2 (Piotrowski & Lubin, 1990). Other surveys suggest the instrument is frequently used in neuropsychological evaluations (Camara et al., 2000; S. R. Smith et al., 2010) and chronic pain evaluations (Piotrowski, 1998). It will not be possible in this chapter to review even briefly the voluminous research literature concerning the relationship between MMPI-2 data and characteristics of medical patients. Rather, suggestions will be made about ways in which the MMPI-2 can be helpful in working with patients with medical problems. Additional information on this issue is covered by Arbisi and Seime (2006), who summarized uses of the MMPI-2 in such settings.

Screening for Psychopathology

One important use of the MMPI instruments with medical patients is to screen for serious psychopathology not reported or minimized by patients. The indicators of serious psychopathology discussed elsewhere in this book (e.g., overall scale elevation) should be considered when examining the profiles of medical patients. Though some providers assume medical problems are highly emotionally distressing to patients and will cause highly elevated scores on the MMPI-2, research does not support this idea. For example, Colligan et al. (2008) reported MMPI-2 scores for family medicine outpatients, 590 of whom were women and 653 of whom were men. Scores on the L, K, and S scales were slightly above average. All Clinical scale scores were within normal limits, with scores on Scales 1, 2, and 3 being approximately 5 T-score points above the mean for the MMPI-2 normative sample.

Screening for Substance-Related Difficulties

Substance-related difficulties are quite common among persons being treated primarily for medical conditions. The MMPI-2 can be useful in alerting clinicians to the possibility of substance misuse. Some patients develop physical symptoms because of chronic use of substances, some develop substance use problems because of their medical problems, and some have substance use problems not directly related to their physical symptoms. Regardless, early awareness of these problems facilitates treatment planning.

Many of the same MMPI-2 indices useful for detecting substance-related difficulties in clinical settings are useful for detecting these kinds of problems in medical patients. For example, the 24/42, two-point code type often is found among men in treatment for alcohol use disorders, and this same code type and the 46/64 code type often are found for women in treatment for alcohol use disorders. Neither of these code types is common among medical patients who do not misuse alcohol. Thus, when these code types are encountered in medical patients, the possibility of alcohol related difficulties should be explored carefully.

The MAC-R was described in Chapter 8 of this book. If significant elevation is found on the MAC-R scale scores for patients in a medical setting, careful consideration should be given to the possibility these persons have a problematic pattern of substance use. It should be stressed research concerning the MAC-R scale has emphasized misuse of alcohol and other nonprescribed drugs. Little is known about the extent to which the MAC-R is sensitive to the misuse of prescribed drugs, such as those used by patients with chronic pain.

Medical patients with T scores greater than 60 on the AAS (Weed et al., 1992) are openly reporting substance-related problems, and additional assessment is indicated. Because most of the items in the AAS have content obviously related to substance misuse, the absence of elevated scores on this scale should not be interpreted as indicating the absence of substance-related difficulties. Such scores could indicate either actual absence or conscious denial of significant substance use problems.

T scores greater than 60 on the Addiction Potential Scale (APS; Weed et al., 1992) also indicates additional information concerning possible substance misuse should be obtained. However, as discussed in Chapter 8 of this book, research findings concerning the validity of the APS have been mixed, suggesting scores on this scale should be given less consideration than scores on MAC-R and AAS.

Establishing Homogeneous Subtypes

Some investigators have used the MMPI-2 to establish more homogeneous subtypes within a particular medical disorder. Most of this research has been in relation to chronic pain. The goals underlying the subtyping approach have been to identify etiological factors unique to particular subtypes and to determine specific treatment interventions appropriate for the subtypes.

Sometimes the subtyping has been based on MMPI-2 code types or other configural aspects of test performance. For example, Slesinger et al. (2002) reported MMPI-2 code types involving Scales 1, 2, and 3 were very common among patients in an inpatient, chronic-pain program. There were some suggestions in the MMPI literature that there are differential treatment outcomes associated with these various code types. However, Keller and Butcher (1991) concluded that using this approach to predict treatment outcome was not very effective.

Other efforts have focused on cluster analyses of patients' MMPI-2 profiles. Keller and Butcher (1991) studied 590 chronic-pain patients using cluster analysis and identified three MMPI-2 clusters. The clusters differed from each other primarily in terms of scale elevation rather than scale configuration. Few differences between clusters were identified in patient characteristics as determined from clinical records. They concluded the MMPI-2 is useful with chronic-pain patients primarily as a way to assess their general level of distress and disability and that Scale 2 was especially useful in this regard. Using hierarchical cluster analysis, Riley and Robinson (1998) identified four MMPI-2 cluster types among pain patients. Riley and Robinson demonstrated that relationships between extratest psychological variables (e.g., cognitive coping and activity level) were different for the cluster types, suggesting differential approaches to treating chronic pain might be indicated for patients with differing MMPI-2 profiles. Gatchel et al. (2006) found chronic pain patients with more than four elevated Clinical scale scores were more likely to have Axis I diagnoses than patients with profiles with no clinical elevations. They also found patients with profiles with no clinical elevations were more likely than those with other types of profiles to be employed 1 year after pain treatment. Haggard et al. (2008) reported chronic pain patients with more than four elevated Clinical scale scores had more physical diagnoses and reported poorer physical and mental health than patients with profiles with no clinical elevations.

We think the subtyping approach is limited, as there have been few efforts to establish empirically that persons in the various subtypes differ in important ways (e.g., in their responsiveness to treatment interventions of various kinds). Indeed, existing data seem to indicate MMPI-2 scores can categorize medical patients according to the severity of psychopathology. Patients in the most severe groups tend to be more distressed and in some ways, may respond less well to medical treatment than patients whose MMPI-2 profiles suggest less severe psychopathology.

Psychological Effects of Medical Conditions

The MMPI-2 can be used to understand how persons with medical problems are affected psychologically by them. Past research suggests patients with such varied disorders as chronic pain (Keller & Butcher, 1991; Slesinger et al., 2002), eating disorders (Cumella et al., 2000), and fibromyalgia (Gerson & Fox, 2003) may have MMPI-2 scores suggestive of significant psychological distress and maladjustment. Similar results were demonstrated for the original MMPI for individuals with head injuries (Diamond et al., 1988; Nockleby & Deaton, 1987), stroke (Gass & Lawhorn, 1991), and cancer (Chang et al., 1988). Sometimes the distress is in the form of exaggerated somatic concerns, which will be reflected in high scores on Scales 1 and 3, RC1, and the HEA Content scale. However, often the psychological distress manifests as symptoms of depression—reflected in high scores on Scale 2, the DEP Content scale, RCd, and RC2—or anxiety, reflected in high scores on Scale 7, the Anxiety (ANX) Content scale, Welsh's Anxiety (A) scale, and RC7. Thus, it seems clinicians should especially consider indicators of emotional disturbance discussed previously in this book.

Interpreting high MMPI-2 scores for medical patients can be challenging because some items in the MMPI-2 scales may reflect symptoms and behaviors that are the products of particular medical disorders. For example, patients could endorse items suggesting problems with concentration and attention related to anxiety, but the items could also reflect deficits directly related to traumatic brain injury.

Some work has been done to identify ways of correcting MMPI-2 scores to account for item endorsements that were likely a product of the medical, not psychological, condition of the test taker. Gass (1991) and Alfano et al. (1993) identified MMPI-2 items associated with traumatic brain injury and developed procedures for correcting scores on some scales to remove the effects of these items. Gass (1992) developed a similar correction factor for use with stroke patients. When the correction factors were applied to scores of individuals who had experience brain injury or stroke, corrected scores tended to be significantly lower than uncorrected scores. Those authors opined the corrected scores portrayed the emotional status of patients more accurately. Similarly, L. D. Nelson et al. (2004) identified MMPI-2 items that persons with epilepsy could answer in the scored direction because of symptoms related to their epilepsy. When MMPI-2 scales were corrected to remove these items, lower scores were obtained for most scales. However, no extratest data were presented to address whether the corrected scores more accurately reflected the psychological status of patients than the uncorrected scores.

Arbisi and Ben-Porath (1999) reviewed the use of correction factors with individuals who experienced brain injury and expressed concerns about their routine use. A danger in using the correction factors that is important to highlight is the items, although related to the medical disorders (e.g., traumatic brain injury), could also be indicative of important psychological disorders (e.g., depression). Thus, the corrected scores could underestimate the severity of the psychological disorders. According to Arbisi and Ben-Porath (1999), there is inadequate evidence to support the notion that corrected scores more accurately portray the psychological status of patients than do uncorrected scores. These authors also expressed some methodological concerns about the manner in which the correction factors have been applied to scores. Their article should be consulted for details of those concerns.

Response to Medical Treatment

The MMPI-2 also can provide important information concerning how medical patients are likely to respond psychologically to medical interventions. Several examples can be given to illustrate this potential use.

Tsushima et al. (2004) conducted a MMPI-2 study of patients undergoing gastric bypass surgery with a 1-year follow-up. Less successful patients had higher presurgery scores on Scales F, 3, 5, 6, and 7 and the HEA Content scale. Higher scores on Scale 5 and HEA were the best predictors of poor postsurgery weight loss.

Vendrig et al. (1999) used selected MMPI-2 scales to predict improvement in Dutch pain patients following a 4-week outpatient intervention program. Scales indicative of emotional distress were negatively related to improvement in self-reported pain intensity and disability, but no MMPI-2 scales were predictive of changes in physical abilities following the intervention. Also studying Dutch patient responses to an intervention program, Vendrig (1999) found only the Harris–Lingoes Lassitude–Malaise (Hy3) subscale was predictive of return to work following the intervention, with higher scores associated with failure to return to work.

In summary, a general finding in the literature has been that persons who are well adjusted emotionally before they develop serious medical problems or before they are treated for such problems seem to handle the illness-related stress better than persons who are emotionally less well adjusted. Additionally, better-adjusted persons seem to have better posttreatment courses than do less well-adjusted persons.

Predisposing Factors

Numerous research projects have sought to identify factors that place persons at risk for serious medical problems such as coronary heart disease or cancer. The MMPI has been utilized in some of these projects.

Both the Type A (TPA) Content scale and Hostility (Ho) Supplementary scale have been linked to coronary heart disease (CHD). For example, among a group of older (mean age = 61 years) men currently free of CHD, higher scorers on the TPA scale were significantly more likely to experience CHD, death, or nonfatal myocardial infarction during a follow-up period of approximately 7 years (Kawachi et al., 1998). Based on research conducted using the original MMPI, there are data suggesting the Ho scale of the MMPI-2 may be helpful in identifying psychological risk factors in CHD (Barefoot et al., 1983; Colligan & Offord, 1988; Hearn et al., 1989; Leon et al., 1988; McCranie et al., 1986; Persky et al., 1987; Shekelle et al., 1983; R. B. Williams et al., 1980). However, research results were not completely consistent. Studies differed in terms of participant age, geographic location, follow-up period, and methods used to assess CHD.

Other studies have examined whether the MMPI Clinical scales can predict future pain symptoms. Fordyce et al. (1992) conducted a prospective study of more than 1,600 industrial employees who completed the MMPI and were followed for an average of 3 years. The Harris–Lingoes Hy3 subscale was significantly related to whether or not the workers filed a back-injury report during the follow-up period. Applegate et al. (2005) conducted a study involving more than 2,300 individuals who completed the MMPI at the time of entry into college between 1964 and 1966. They were surveyed in 1997 to determine the presence of various chronic pain symptoms. Although scores on Scales 1, 3, and 5 for men and Scales 1, 3, and 6 for women were significantly related to number of pain symptoms in later life, the relationships were very modest and probably not clinically meaningful.

PERSONNEL SCREENING

The MMPI was developed in a psychiatric hospital setting; however, the MMPI and MMPI-2 have been used frequently in selecting employees for sensitive occupations (e.g., safety officers, airline pilots) and students for training programs (Butcher, 1979, 1985).

Using the MMPI-2 to screen for psychopathology among applicants is most justified when individuals are considered for employment in public safety occupations involving susceptibility to occupational stress, personal risk, and personal responsibility (Butcher, 1991). Such sensitive occupations include those of air traffic controller, airline pilot, police officer, firefighter, and nuclear power plant operator. Routine use of the MMPI-2 for personnel selection is not recommended. For many jobs, the primary requirements are appropriate ability and training, and personality factors may be relatively unimportant or irrelevant. Consistent with the Americans with Disabilities Act, the psychological screening process, which typically includes administration of the MMPI-2, is undertaken only after conditional offers of employment have been extended to applicants. Results of psychological evaluations can subsequently lead to withdrawal of conditional offers.

Research data suggest the MMPI-2 can be used in pre-employment settings to identify individuals who are likely to have poor job performance. This work was summarized by Detrick et al. (2001). Generally, higher scores on MMPI-2 scales were associated with poorer job performance (e.g., Hargrave & Hiatt, 1987; Hiatt & Hargrave, 1988; Pallone, 1992). Higher scores on Scales 4 and 9 were especially predictive of poor job performance (e.g., Bartol, 1991; Costello et al., 1996). Interestingly, B. Neal (1986) found that moderately high scores on the K scale were associated with more positive supervisory ratings.

The MMPI-2 also contains a scale, the Negative Work Attitudes (WRK) Content scale, specifically developed to measure personality characteristics that might be associated with poor job performance. Butcher et al. (1990) reported some preliminary data concerning WRK scale scores of men who could be assumed to have differing levels of work performance. Airline pilots, who were assumed to have highly successful work skills, scored well below the mean for the MMPI-2 normative sample; and active-duty military personnel, who volunteered to participate and were as a group not experiencing occupational problems, scored at about the mean for the MMPI-2 normative sample. Individuals hospitalized due to severe psychiatric difficulties and individuals with alcohol-related disorders, who were assumed to have a poorer work history, scored well above the mean for the normative sample. Although these group data are encouraging, research is needed in which scores on the WRK scale are compared with measures of actual job performance. Importantly, as suggested by the latter finding in individuals with mental health and substance-related difficulties, the

WRK scale appears to be saturated with general maladjustment (or demoralization). Thus, test takers who are demoralized or depressed are likely to have elevated WRK scale scores that may have little to do with negative work attitudes.

One of the most widely studied uses of the MMPI-2 in pre-employment contexts is its use in evaluations of police officer candidates. Kornfeld (1995) reported descriptive MMPI-2 data for applicants for police officer position in small- and medium-sized towns who identified as White and for those who identified as a member of an underrepresented ethnic or racial group. As had been reported previously for the MMPI, most applicants were quite defensive. Interestingly, the mean scores of individuals who identified as White and those from underrepresented racial and ethnic applicants were quite similar. However, it should be noted that the underrepresented sample included only five individuals who were Hispanic, four individuals who were African American, and two individuals who were Asian American. Similarly, defensive MMPI-2 results were also reported by Detrick et al. (2001) for police officer applicants in small to mid-sized suburban cities. Scores on the L and K scales were in the 60–65 T-score range. Differences between gendered and ungendered scores were trivial.

Detrick et al. (2001) compared MMPI-2 scores of their police officer applicants with scores on the Inwald Personality Inventory (IPI), a well-established instrument for predicting law enforcement job performance. Modest but significant correlations were obtained between MMPI-2 and IPI scores. Interestingly, relationships between the two instruments were stronger when non-K-corrected MMPI-2 scores were used. The issue of K-corrected versus non-K-corrected scores was discussed in detail in Chapters 2 and 3 of this book.

Sellbom et al. (2007) examined relationships between police officer integrity and misconduct and MMPI-2 scores. The MMPI-2s were administered to police officer candidates after a conditional offer of employment was rendered. For those who were eventually hired, various measures of employment problems were noted (e.g., breaking rules and regulations, citizen complaints, supervisor ratings, and involuntary dismissal). Although high scores on Scales 8 and 9 and low scores on Scale 3 were related to problem behaviors, the RC3, RC4, RC6, and RC8 scale scores were even more predictive of problems. Consistent with other research reviewed in this book, non-K-corrected scores on the Clinical scales were more strongly related to problem behaviors than K-corrected scores.

Caillouet and colleagues (2010) examined questions similar to that of Sellbom et al. (2007) in a large sample of police officer candidates from the Southern United States, but used the Personality Psychopathology- Five (PSY-5) scales as potential predictors of problematic performance on the job instead of Clinical and RC scales. Results of their study demonstrated small, but significant, associations between scores on Psychoticism (PSYC), Disconstraint (DISC), Negative Emotionality/Neuroticism (NEGE), and Aggressiveness (AGGR) and being forced to leave employment as an officer. No meaningful associations between the PSY-5 scales and on the job misconduct were observed.

Research examining the use of the MMPI-2 in other pre-employment contexts has also been conducted. For example, Butcher (1994) reported data for 437 pilot applicants for a major airline. Consistent with earlier studies with the original MMPI, the applicants were generally quite defensive. Butcher speculated that because the L and K scales were developed in clinical settings, their utility in personnel selection may be limited and that new measures of defensiveness may be needed. The Superlative (S; Lim & Butcher, 1996) scale, which was described in Chapter 3 of this book, may prove to be useful in this regard. Because elevated scores on the MMPI-2 Clinical scales were quite rare in the pilot applicant sample, Butcher (1994) recommended that T scores greater than 60 should be considered extreme in these kinds of settings.

Because most test takers in personnel selection situations have scores suggestive of defensive responding, this issue deserves careful consideration. Some clinicians re-administer the MMPI-2 when an initial testing results in scores indicating a degree of defensiveness that invalidates the results. Other clinicians deal with anticipated defensiveness by instructing test takers to avoid trying to present themselves in an unrealistically favorable way when responding to MMPI-2 items. Several research studies have addressed the effects of these practices on test scores.

Butcher et al. (1997) examined MMPI-2 scores of airline pilot applicants. They found 73% of the applicants produced valid results on an initial testing. The applicants who produced invalid results were asked to complete the MMPI-2 again. They received altered instructions that explained how the MMPI-2 scales were constructed and were told that because of defensiveness, their results would not help the psychologists understand them. On retest, 79% of the applicants who initially produced invalid results produced valid results. Their Validity scale scores were less defensive and resembled scores of applicants who had produced valid results on the first administration of the MMPI-2. Similar results were obtained by Cigrang and Staal (2001) in their study of applicants for military training instructor positions and by Walfish (2010) in a sample of individuals undergoing fitness for duty evaluations.

Butcher and colleagues (2000) reasoned that because giving altered instructions designed to reduce defensiveness deviates from standardized test administration procedures, it is important to know to what extent such altered instructions affect scores of people more generally. Do persons who complete the MMPI-2 initially with such altered instructions obtain different scores from persons who complete the test with standard instructions? A sample of 218 college students completed the MMPI-2 with altered instructions very similar to those used in the Butcher et al. (1997) study, and their scores were compared with 150 college students who completed the test with standard instructions. The scores of students who identified as men in the two conditions did not differ significantly for any scales. For women, students who received the altered instructions had lower scores on the L, K, and S scales. However, the differences were judged to be trivial.

In summary, persons completing the MMPI-2 in personnel selection situations often produce moderately defensive scores, and some applicants respond so defensively that their results are considered invalid. When asked to retake the MMPI-2 with instructions to be more open and honest in responding to items, most applicants produce valid results. Because the use of altered instructions intended to avoid anticipated defensiveness during initial assessment does not seem to affect scores significantly, the standard MMPI-2 norms can be utilized in such circumstances. Given research concerning this issue is rather limited, it is our recommendation that standard instructions for completing the MMPI-2 be used in initial administration with applicants. However, for those applicants who produce invalid results, re-administration of the MMPI-2 with emphasis on following the standard instructions may produce valid protocols. Pearson Assessments markets a computerized MMPI-2 report—*The MMPI-2 Minnesota Report: Revised Personnel System (Third Edition)*—intended for use in personnel selection situations. This report provides profiles of scores on the standard Validity and substantive scales. In keeping with Americans with Disabilities Act guidelines, both gendered and nongendered T scores are provided for the Clinical and Content scales. A narrative interpretation of scores and an Adjustment Rating Report also are available. Based on a set of MMPI-2 decision rules, examinees are rated on several adjustment dimensions: Openness to Evaluation, Social Facility, Addiction Potential, Stress Tolerance, and Overall Adjustment. There are no studies published evaluating the use of the MMPI-2's version of this interpretive report; however, the validity of evaluations based on the MMPI version of the interpretive report were encouraging (e.g., Butcher, 1988; Muller & Bruno, 1988).

CHAPTER 10

FORENSIC APPLICATIONS OF THE MMPI-2

PSYCHOLOGISTS ARE FREQUENTLY ASKED to offer expert opinions about a variety of legal issues. Their opinions often are based in part on psychological assessment data (Archer, 2006), and the MMPI-2 frequently is a source of these data. T. A. Wright et al. (2017) surveyed a random sample of members of the American Psychological Association Practice Organization and found that among psychologists who primarily practice in a forensic setting, 97% use one or more of the MMPI instruments. Archer et al. (2006) surveyed forensic psychologists and found they used the MMPI-2 more frequently than any other assessment instrument. Lally (2003) surveyed 64 diplomates in forensic psychology and found the MMPI-2 was recommended or judged as acceptable for use in addressing a variety of forensic questions including malingering, mental state at time of offense, risk of physical or sexual violence, competency to stand trial, and competency to waive Miranda rights.

A survey of 77 board-certified neuropsychologists revealed the MMPI-2 and MMPI-2-RF were the most frequently used tests measuring "mood or personality" in forensic evaluations (LaDuke et al., 2018). A survey of psychologists who conducted child custody evaluations found the MMPI-2 was used by 97% of the respondents (Ackerman & Pritzl, 2011). An international survey of forensic psychologists and psychiatrists practicing in the United States, Canada, Australia, New Zealand, and Europe found that the MMPI family of instruments was in the top five most frequently used psychological tests for each of 10 different types of forensic evaluations including insanity, aid in sentencing, disability, child custody, and child protection evaluations—where it was the most frequently used instrument (T. M. S. Neal & Grisso, 2014). Thus, it seems clear that the MMPI-2 is a very popular instrument among psychologists who conduct forensic evaluations.

Several factors make the MMPI-2 an attractive instrument among forensic psychologists (K. S. Pope et al., 2006). The MMPI-2 uses a standard set of items and is administered and scored in a standardized manner. Its scales are reliable, and interpretation is based on a vast body of empirical research. Of special appeal to forensic psychologists is that the MMPI-2 includes validity scales designed to detect test-taking approaches that can invalidate the protocol (e.g., response styles like underreporting or overreporting). These scales are particularly useful in forensic settings because the situational demands increase the likelihood the individual being evaluated may present themselves in unrealistically positive or negative ways. In addition, psychologists offering expert testimony based on MMPI-2 results find it is easy to communicate the basis of their opinions to non-psychologists.

ADMISSIBILITY OF MMPI-2 EVIDENCE

Ogloff (1995) pointed out that it is the responsibility of a judge to determine whether expert testimony meets the legal criteria for admissibility. If expert testimony is based on test results, the judge must also make a determination of the admissibility of the test results. In most jurisdictions, the criteria for admissibility of expert testimony currently are based on the Federal Rules of Evidence (FRE) and a United States Supreme Court decision concerning the admissibility of scientific evidence (*Daubert v. Merrell Dow Pharmaceuticals, Inc.*, 1993).

Prior to the adoption of the FRE in 1976, most jurisdictions used an earlier court decision (*Frye v. United States*, 1923), which stated that to be admissible, scientific evidence must be generally accepted by the field in which it is offered, that it is used in the relevant areas of the field, and that the techniques used in producing the evidence comport with the state of the art in the field (Ogloff, 1995). The FRE adopted a more liberal view of expert testimony, maintaining that general acceptance is not a requirement for admissibility of evidence and that all evidence relevant to the issue at hand is admissible.

In its *Daubert* decision, the U.S. Supreme Court ruled that the FRE displaced the earlier *Frye* test of general acceptance as a standard for determining admissibility of scientific evidence and expert testimony based on that evidence (*Daubert v. Merrell Dow Pharmaceuticals, Inc.*, 1993). The *Daubert* decision also stated some specific issues to be considered in determining admissibility of evidence. Trial judges are to determine whether expert witnesses are proposing to testify to scientific knowledge that will assist the trier of fact to understand and determine a fact in issue. A technique is considered to be scientific to the extent that (a) it leads to hypotheses or statements that can be (or have been) tested empirically, (b) information is available concerning error rates associated with the technique, and (c) it has been subjected to peer review and publication. Although general acceptance of a technique within a scientific community is not a requirement for admissibility of evidence based on that technique, such acceptance can be offered in support of its admissibility. Although most jurisdictions follow a standard based on *Daubert*, some states still use the *Frye*-based standard of general acceptance within a field.

The MMPI-2 fares quite well on all of these criteria (Kane & Dvoskin, 2011). Its development and validation are firmly based in empirical research. Error rates (e.g., positive predictive power, negative predictive power) have been established for many uses of the test. There is a very large body of MMPI-2 research published in peer-reviewed scientific journals. That the MMPI-2 is widely used by psychologists and that it has received very positive evaluations by reviewers (see Archer, 1992; Nichols, 1992) indicate acceptance by the scientific community of psychologists.

Bow, Gould, et al. (2006) surveyed forensic psychologists and found that 95% of respondents indicated that the MMPI-2 meets *Daubert* criteria. Otto (2002) reviewed a legal database and identified 19 cases where the admissibility of testimony based on MMPI/MMPI-2 results was challenged. Otto advised, "those using the MMPI-2 in appropriate ways in forensic contexts should do so with little reservation about evidentiary issues revolving around Frye or Daubert issues" (p. 80). However, Ogloff and Douglas (2003) cautioned psychologists to limit expert testimony based on MMPI-2 results to issues in which there is clear scientific evidence that its scores are related to the behaviors in question.

SOME IMPORTANT ISSUES IN USING THE MMPI-2 IN FORENSIC SETTINGS

Norms

Several issues are especially important in deciding to what extent the MMPI-2 will be useful in forensic settings. Should the standard MMPI-2 norms be used, or are special forensic norms needed? This issue becomes especially important in relation to forensic questions in which those being assessed typically differ in a systematic way from the standard norms. For example, parents completing the MMPI-2 in relation to child custody issues typically produce a defensive pattern on the MMPI-2 Validity scales (Bathurst et al., 1997). However, it is appropriate to use the standard MMPI-2 norms for all applications of the test. These are the norms that have been utilized in determining the meaning of scores on all the MMPI-2 scales, and to use other norms would render this important research base useless. Perhaps forensic comparison samples can help alleviate this tension by providing mean scores for each MMPI-2 scale in a particular setting (e.g., parents undergoing child custody evaluations) while still utilizing the standard norms and the existing research as the basis for score interpretation.

Correlates of Scales and Code Types

Most of the research concerning the correlates of MMPI-2 scores and code types has been based on participants in various mental health settings (e.g., hospitals, clinics). An important question is the extent to which the scales and configurations of scales have similar correlates in forensic settings. For example, does significant elevation on Scale 2 indicate greater likelihood of depressed mood in both clinical and forensic settings? If not, then the MMPI-2 cannot be interpreted similarly in the two settings.

In relation to psychopathology and personality characteristics, we would expect the MMPI-2 scales to have similar correlates in both clinical and forensic settings. Decades of research have established that the scales have very similar symptom and personality correlates across settings that have included psychiatric inpatients, mental health outpatients, college counselees, medical patients, and nonclinical student and community groups. Several studies have confirmed that the MMPI-2 scales have similar correlates in forensic settings. In a study conducted at a criminal court forensic diagnostic center, Ben-Porath and Stafford (1993) identified correlates for MMPI-2 scales that were quite congruent with previously reported correlates in other settings. For example, Scale 2 scores were related positively to sad mood; Scale 4 scores were related positively to problematic alcohol use; and Scale 8 scores were related positively to the number of previous psychiatric hospitalizations. Also, scores on the Anger (ANG) Content scale were related positively to histories of violent behavior; scores on the Antisocial Practices (ASP) Content scale were related positively to a variety of criminal activities; scores on the Family Problems (FAM) Content scale were related positively to marital problems; and scores on three substance use scales (MacAndrew Alcoholism Scale-Revised [MAC-R], Addiction Admission Scale [AAS], and Addiction Potential Scale [APS]) were related positively to misuse of alcohol and other substances. Unfortunately, this sample did not include a large proportion of individuals with severe mental illness, and thus many previously reported correlates could not be studied.

Ricketts (2003) reported that the MMPI-2 Content scales and Content Component scales were related to symptoms and problems of forensic cases evaluated at a court-sponsored clinic in ways that were very similar to those reported previously for psychiatric patients. For example, the Depression (DEP) Content scale was significantly related to diagnoses of depression; and FAM Content scale to histories of poor family relationships. Sellbom et al. (2009) found that in a forensic sample, four MMPI-2 scales (Scale 4, RC4, ASP, and Disconstraint [DISC]) were significantly related to extratest measures of psychopathy and antisocial behaviors, with RC4 having the strongest relationship with the extratest variables. Petroskey et al. (2003) found that correlates of the MMPI-2 Personality Psychopathology – Five (PSY-5) scales were very similar for forensic and mental health samples. In summary, the existing data demonstrates directly that the MMPI-2 scales are related to psychopathology and personality characteristics in similar ways in forensic and clinical settings.

When the MMPI-2 scales are used to infer behaviors or characteristics different from those that have been previously studied, it is important to demonstrate that the scales are actually related to these behaviors and characteristics. For example, Osberg and Poland (2001) examined relationships between MMPI-2 scales and number of previous criminal offenses. They found that higher scorers on Scale 9 and on several Harris–Lingoes subscales reported more offenses. However, we should not assume that MMPI-2 scales will be related to variables such as criminal history, adjustment to incarceration, or offenses against persons versus property offenses. These relationships must be established through empirical research.

Use with Underrepresented Racial and Ethnic Groups

Psychologists have long questioned whether the MMPI-2 is appropriate for use with individuals belonging to racial and ethnic groups that have been historically underrepresented in psychological research (see Chapter 9 of this book for a general discussion). This issue is an especially important consideration in forensic settings given the high stakes of these contexts.

Ben-Porath and colleagues (1995) examined the association between race and MMPI-2 scores in men undergoing court-ordered forensic psychological evaluations that identified as Caucasian and African American. They concluded that overall, the Caucasians and African Americans produced highly comparable MMPI-2 scores. The two groups did not differ significantly on any of the Validity or Clinical scales. However, the African American men scored higher than the Caucasian men on the Cynicism (CYN) and ASP Content scales. In a follow-up study, Gironda (1999) found that the MMPI-2 scales predicted extratest characteristics equally well for Caucasian and African American men undergoing these court-ordered evaluations.

Although only limited data are available concerning the accuracy of predicting extratest characteristics for members of historically underrepresented racial and ethnic groups in forensic settings, data from other settings would suggest that the MMPI-2 scales are likely equally accurate for White and Black Americans (see Chapter 9). Nonetheless, it will be important for additional studies to determine the accuracy of prediction for other racial and ethnic groups (e.g., individuals who are Latinx, Hispanic, Native American, Asian American) in forensic settings.

Profiling

Psychologists who are involved in forensic evaluations often are asked to determine if the MMPI-2 scores of a particular person indicate that the person did or did not commit a specific crime (e.g., murder, sexual aggression), will or will not behave in particular ways in the future (e.g., function as a good or bad parent, become violent), or has or has not experienced some particular damages (e.g., emotional distress associated with a traumatic incident). This process has been referred to as "profiling" and involves specifying the typical MMPI-2 scores of a particular group (e.g., murderers, sexual aggressors, good or bad parents) and then determining the probability that a person does or does not match the prototype.

There has been very little empirical support for the notion that there are prototypical MMPI-2 profiles associated with particular crimes or other forensic-related behaviors or that important decisions about persons in forensic settings can be made by comparing their test results to these prototypical profiles. For example, Butcher (1995) indicated that no single pattern of MMPI-2 scores exists among persons who are claiming psychological damages in personal injury litigation. Otto and Collins (1995) reached a similar conclusion concerning the use of the MMPI-2 in child custody evaluations. Their review of the literature failed to identify studies of the relationship between MMPI-2 patterns and good or bad parenting. In cases where support has been demonstrated for the utility of a prototypical profile, there were methodological concerns that call into question the use of these prototypes in real-world forensic evaluations. For example, although Ridenour et al. (1997) reported that the MMPI-2 could accurately identify individuals who had engaged in child molestation, the generalizability of their findings is questionable because they used a non-offending comparison group rather than a group of offenders who had crimes other than child molestation—and they did not cross-validate their findings.

In summary, it seems clear that there is not sufficient empirical research to support the profiling approach to the use of the MMPI-2 in forensic settings. Persons known to have committed particular offenses (e.g., sexual offending) or to have particular characteristics (e.g., good parenting skills) are not likely to produce a specific set of MMPI-2 scores. Thus, the MMPI-2 is of limited utility in assisting courts in determining if an accused person has or has not committed particular crimes or if persons involved in civil litigation do or do not have particular characteristics (e.g., good or bad parenting skills, psychological damages). This does not mean that the MMPI-2 cannot be of any help in these determinations. Some of the inferences that can be made accurately from MMPI-2 scores can be highly relevant to issues that courts are addressing. For example, MMPI-2 results strongly suggesting that a parent in a child custody evaluation is likely to have severe substance use problems would be very helpful to the court in deciding what arrangements are in the best interests of the children in this family.

Administration and Scoring

Chapter 2 of this book presents details concerning how the MMPI-2 should be administered. Those details should also be followed when administering the test in forensic settings. Adherence to standardized administration is especially important in forensic evaluations because it will ensure that the clinician will later be able to testify that they are sure that the person in question completed the test under standard conditions, without help from others, and without consulting books or other sources that could influence the results.

Once administration of the MMPI-2 is complete, several scoring options are available (see Chapter 2 of this book). Regardless of which option is chosen, care should be taken to avoid scoring errors, especially in high-stakes situations like those reflected in forensic evaluations. Importantly, during expert testimony, clinicians may be asked questions about scores and indexes that they did not use in their interpretation and about which they are not well informed. Thus, clinicians who use the MMPI-2 should familiarize themselves with all of the scores and indexes that are contained in the scoring report that they utilize.

Interpreting the MMPI-2

As stated earlier in this chapter, one of the advantages of using the MMPI-2 in forensic evaluations is that interpretation typically is done in a rather standardized manner by relying on the extensive empirical research literature concerning the meaning of scores. We recommend clinicians limit their interpretations to issues for which the MMPI-2 has been adequately validated and to avoid making interpretations that cannot be supported by reference to empirical research. When questioned about the validity of MMPI-2 inferences made in forensic evaluations, it usually will be sufficient to cite secondary sources such as this book. However, clinicians using the MMPI-2 in forensic settings should be prepared to identify and cite specific research studies to support their inferences. It is our practice to only make statements in forensic reports and during expert testimony that are supported by references to specific empirical research literature. Although this often means making many fewer statements than might be made in clinical settings, it certainly makes defending those interpretations much easier.

SOME FORENSIC USES OF THE MMPI-2

Detecting Invalid Responding

Non-Content-Based Invalid Responding

Persons taking the MMPI-2 in forensic settings may not see the benefit of engaging cooperatively in the test-taking process, or they may be experiencing significant difficulties that could prevent them from appropriately responding to MMPI-2 items. As such, it is important to screen for non-content-based invalid responding. The MMPI-2 includes several scales to help identify persons who engaged in these response styles, including scores that are indicative of nonresponding (Cannot Scale [CNS]), randomly endorsing test items (Variable Response Inconsistency [VRIN]), or indiscriminately responding either "true" or "false" to test items (True Response Inconsistency [TRIN]). Readers should refer to Chapter 3 of this book for detailed information concerning interpretation of these indicators.

Overreporting

Persons taking the MMPI-2 in forensic settings sometimes are strongly motivated to present themselves as much more psychologically disturbed and maladjusted than they really are. They may also be motivated to present themselves as more impaired by cognitive or medical problems than they actually are. Examples of situations in which this tendency might be present include evaluations of persons in relation to pleas of not guilty by reason of insanity (NGRI) or incompetency to stand trial; or evaluations of persons who are claiming psychological damages because of some traumatic event such as an automobile accident or medical malpractice. Gallagher and colleagues (1997) reported that 16% of male inmates admitted to deliberately distorting their responses on the MMPI-2.

The MMPI-2 has several scales intended to assess overreporting of general maladjustment, as well as overreported psychological, cognitive, and somatic difficulties. These include the Infrequency (F), Back Infrequency (F_B), Infrequency Psychopathology (F_p), and Symptom Validity (FBS) scales. Readers should refer to Chapter 3 for detailed information concerning interpretation of these indicators. Broadly, however, high scores on F and F_B reflect attempts by the test taker to appear more maladjusted than they really are. Extreme scores on F_p are indicative of overreporting of symptoms infrequently endorsed by psychiatric inpatients; thus, this scale is likely to be especially useful in settings where the base rate of psychopathology is high. The FBS is useful in identifying persons who are overreporting cognitive and somatic symptoms.

Most research concerning the detection of overreporting using MMPI-2 Validity scale scores has not been conducted in forensic settings. However, there is no reason to believe that the indicators of overreporting that have worked well in other settings would not also work well in forensic settings. Furthermore, several studies conducted in forensic settings have supported the utility of the MMPI-2 Validity scales in identifying overreporting. Past work has demonstrated the F scale was quite effective in differentiating between students who were instructed to malinger on the MMPI-2 and both general psychiatric patients and forensic inpatients (Bagby et al., 1994, Bagby et al., 1995). Iverson et al. (1995) found the F scale was quite effective in identifying minimum security inmates who were given instructions to malinger psychopathology in completing the MMPI-2. Using a sample of from a correctional reception center Gallagher (1997) also found the F scale effectively identified men who were malingering. In this study, the F_p scale added significantly to the discrimination between prisoners who were instructed to malinger and correctional psychiatric patients who were assumed to have taken the MMPI-2 honestly.

Overreporting of trauma-related symptoms is likely in some forensic contexts, such as personal injury evaluations. Several studies have addressed the utility of the MMPI-2 Validity scales in identifying feigned symptoms of PTSD. Bury and Bagby (2002) found that, while the F and F_B scales were effective in this regard, the F_p scale had the highest predictive powers. Elhai et al. (2004) found that persons asked to feign symptoms of PTSD resulting from child sexual abuse obtained much higher scores on the F and F_p scales than actual victims of child sexual abuse. However, this study did not report predictive powers for the scales.

It may also be important to assess overreporting of somatic and cognitive symptoms in some forensic contexts, such as competency to stand trial or personal injury evaluations. As discussed in Chapter 3 of this book, Lees-Haley and colleagues (1991) developed the FBS to detect overreporting of emotional distress among personal injury claimants. However, subsequent research has not supported the validity of the FBS for that purpose (Ben-Porath et al., 2009; Bury & Bagby, 2002; Butcher et al., 2003; Rogers et al., 2003). Instead, a review by Ben-Porath et al. (2009) and meta-analyses by N. W. Nelson and colleagues (2006, 2010) suggest scores on this scale are best used to detect overreported somatic and cognitive difficulties. Other MMPI-2 Validity scales may also be useful in this regard. For example, Berry et al. (1995) found that persons instructed to feign symptoms of closed-head injury obtained higher scores than patients with closed-head injuries on the F, F_B, and F_p scales. However, this study did not report predictive powers for these scales in relation to discriminating between the malingering and patient groups.

Underreporting

There are some circumstances in forensic settings in which examinees have strong motivation to underreport symptoms and try to appear better adjusted psychologically than they really are. Obvious examples include parents evaluated in relation to child custody issues or persons who are seeking release from psychiatric or correctional facilities.

As discussed in Chapter 3 of this book, it is much more difficult to identify underreporting than overreporting on the MMPI-2. However, data from non-forensic settings indicate that persons who try to appear better adjusted than they really are when completing the MMPI-2 are likely to produce above-average scores on the Lie (L) and Correction (K) scales. Scores on L may also be used to detect individuals who attempt to present themselves as having good morals and virtues, something that may be particularly relevant to assess in forensic settings. Research in forensic contexts suggests this general interpretation also holds in these types of evaluations. For example, Bagby et al. (1995) concluded the L scale was effective in identifying persons instructed to fake good when completing the MMPI-2 in comparison with forensic patients who completed the test under standard instructions. Please see Chapter 3 for more detailed information about the identification of underreporting on the MMPI-2.

Coaching

Psychologists who use the MMPI-2 in forensic settings are understandably concerned about the possibility examinees can prepare themselves to underreport or overreport without being detected by the Validity scales. A survey by Wetter and Corrigan (1995) revealed almost half of a sample of practicing attorneys and approximately one-third of a sample of law students reported that they felt obligated to give their clients information about the validity scales of psychological tests they would be taking. Similar results were demonstrated in a more recent survey of a sample of attorneys from the United States, most of whom were practicing in family/juvenile law, personal injury law, and criminal law (Spengler et al., 2020). In this survey, about half of the sample agreed that they should disclose information to their clients about MMPI-2 Validity scales.

Data concerning effects of coaching on MMPI-2 Validity scales and indexes were presented in detail in Chapter 3 of this book. In summary, giving examinees specific information concerning the symptoms of disorders that they are trying to simulate when completing the MMPI-2 did not affect the accuracy with which the Validity scales and indexes could identify people who were overreporting. However, giving examinees specific information about the nature of the Validity scales and how they work decreased the likelihood that overreporting would be correctly identified by the Validity scales and indexes. Thus, clinicians using the MMPI-2 in forensic settings should be aware that persons who have been given specific information about the MMPI-2 Validity scales may be able to underreport or overreport without being detected.

Assessing Clinical Condition

The primary purpose for which the MMPI-2 scales have been most comprehensively validated is the assessment of the clinical condition of test takers. Therefore, we recommend using the standard guidelines for evaluating the clinical condition or status of persons assessed in forensic settings. Detailed guidelines for interpreting code types and individual scale scores are provided in prior chapters of this book. Please see Chapter 11 for a general interpretive framework for organizing and integrating MMPI-2 scale interpretations.

Screening for Substance Use Problems

Often it is important to determine if persons undergoing forensic evaluations have significant substance use problems. For example, this possibility may be raised as a mitigating circumstance in relation to criminal charges; it can be important in making decisions about child custody; or it can be related to disposition of criminal cases. Although it is not possible or appropriate to conclude that a person is or is not experiencing substance-related difficulties solely on the basis of test data, the MMPI-2 has three scales that were designed specifically to identify substance use problems. These include MAC-R, AAS, and APS, each of which were described in detail in Chapter 8 of this book. Broadly, elevated scores on these scales serve as indicators of the possibility of substance use problems that should be investigated further using other sources of information such as reports of significant others or physical test results.

Most studies examining MAC-R, AAS, and APS support using these scales to detect substance-related difficulties (e.g., Craig, 2005; Stein et al., 1999; Weed et al., 1995). However, research concerning the validity of the APS suggests scores on this scale do not seem to add much to the MAC-R or the AAS in identifying substance use problems (Greene et al., 1992; Rouse et al., 1999; Stein et al., 1999). As such, we suggest emphasizing scores on MAC-R and AAS during interpretation.

While a majority of research on the validity of the MMPI-2 indicators of substance use problems has taken place in clinical settings, there is no reason to believe these empirical findings would differ in a forensic setting. A study by Ben-Porath and Stafford (1993) indicated that scores on the MAC-R, AAS, and APS scales are related to a wide variety of problems with alcohol and drugs in a sample of persons evaluated at a forensic diagnostic center.

Concerns Regarding Assessment of Substance Use Problems

Although the MMPI-2 substance use scales can provide important information about the possibility of problematic substance use, there are several issues that should be kept in mind when using them in forensic settings. First, current research does not address how persons score on these scales when they previously misused substances but no longer do. Clinical and anecdotal evidence suggests that scores on the MAC-R scale are likely to remain high even after persons have stopped misusing substances. Second, research to date has addressed only problems related to nonprescription drug misuse, so little is known about the substance use scales in relation to problematic use of of prescription drugs. Third, several investigators have cautioned against using the MAC-R scale with Black Americans and members of other underrepresented racial and ethnic groups because several studies using the original MMPI suggested that individuals identifying as Black who did not misuse substances also tended to obtain high scores on the original MAC scale (e.g., Walters et al., 1983, 1984). However, studies using the MMPI-2 have not demonstrated significant MAC-R scale differences between African Americans and Caucasians (Ben-Porath et al., 1995; McClinton et al., 1995). The study by Ben-Porath et al. is especially important because it was conducted at a criminal court diagnostic clinic. The McClinton et al. study also concluded that the MAC-R, AAS, and APS worked equally well in identifying substance use problems for African American and Caucasian mental health center clients. Finally, it is important to keep in mind that no conclusions should be reached about substance use problems based only on the MMPI-2 scales. High scores on these scales should be seen as one indicator that substance use problems may exist and that corroborating information should be collected.

Predicting Dangerousness

Predicting future violent or dangerous behavior is relevant to many of the purposes for which forensic assessments are conducted (e.g., civil commitment, release from prison or hospital, child custody). K. Heilbrun and Heilbrun (1995) discussed the importance of these predictions and the role the MMPI-2 can and cannot play in them. Their conclusion—with which we agree—was that there is no direct and accurate way to predict from MMPI-2 scores which individuals will or will not act dangerously or violently in the future.

Nonetheless, as K. Heilbrun and Heilbrun (1995) pointed out, predicting dangerousness involves the consideration of many different kinds of information, some of which may be indicated by MMPI-2 scale scores. This could include aspects of an individual's current mental status (e.g., having psychotic symptoms) or dynamic risk factors (e.g., substance use, marital problems), both of which are related in complex ways to dangerousness.

Once such relevant factor to assessing dangerousness that could be assessed with MMPI-2 scale scores is psychopathic personality traits. K. Heilbrun and Heilbrun (1995) suggested that psychopathy (as measured by Scale 4 of the MMPI-2) is related to acting dangerously, particularly when coupled with below-average intelligence (A. B. Heilbrun, 1979). However, Sellbom and Ben-Porath (2006) cautioned that Scale 4 is too heterogeneous in content to be used in this manner and suggested the RC4 scale would be a more appropriate scale for such predictions.

Another relevant factor is the association several MMPI-2 scales have with acting in physically aggressive or violent ways. Persons in correctional settings who score higher on the Overcontrolled–Hostility (O–H) scale are more likely to display extreme physical aggression than those who score lower on this scale (see Chapter 8 of this book). Scores on the ANG Content scale suggest problems with the control of anger (see Chapter 6 of this book). Sellbom, Ben-Porath, Lilienfeld, et al. (2005) studied the prediction of violent recidivism among offenders undergoing treatment in a batterers' intervention program. Their results indicated RC4 and RC9 scores were predictive of recidivism—even when historical and demographic variables were taken into account.

Megargee and colleagues (1979) developed a configural system for classifying the MMPI scores of inmates since modified for use with the MMPI-2 (Megargee, 1994). Their evidence suggests membership in certain categories in their system was strongly related to aggressive behavior while in prison. Hutton, Miner, and Langfeldt (1993) demonstrated that the Megargee typology also can reliably and usefully describe different categories of patients in a forensic psychiatric setting. However, at least one study has questioned the utility of the Megargee typology with African American forensic patients (Hutton & Miner, 1995).

Research suggests some caution in applying MMPI-2 scale scores or typologies to detecting characteristics related to aggressive or violent behaviors is needed, however.

For example, the 4–3 code type also been associated with problems with anger control (see Chapter 5 of this book), but Fraboni et al. (1990) found that neither the 4–3 nor the 48/84 code types successfully discriminated between violent and nonviolent offenders. No differences in Clinical or Content scale scores were found between groups of female offenders who had murdered their child, a partner, or a nonfamily adult (McKee et al., 2001). This may be, in part, because the relationships between MMPI-2 scores and the likelihood of acting dangerously are so modest that using them to make individual predictions about dangerousness is not appropriate (e.g., Nussbaum et al., 1996). Nonetheless, these measures serve as sources of information, to be considered along with other data, relevant to dangerousness.

In summary, there is not adequate research evidence to support using MMPI-2 scales or profiles to directly predict dangerous or violent behavior. However, there are MMPI-2 scales and configurations of scales that provide relevant information for the prediction of dangerousness by aiding in the identification of risk factors and protective factors that influence the likelihood of future violence. Thus, we recommend psychologists use MMPI-2 data in combination with other types and sources of data to inform—but not directly make—inferences about future dangerousness.

Assessing Sanity

Rogers and McKee (1995) defined insanity as "a legal term used to describe the acquittal . . . of a criminal defendant because of a severe mental disorder on the basis of specified legal criteria" (p. 104). Although the specific criteria differ from one jurisdiction to another, all sets of criteria require the presence of some mental disorder or intellectual disability. Criteria usually also include cognitive incapacity (i.e., lack of awareness of the wrongfulness of the act), affective incapacity (i.e., inability to appreciate the wrongfulness of the act), or volitional incapacity (i.e., inability to refrain from the criminal behavior in question) resulting from the mental disorder or intellectual disability. Many jurisdictions exclude mental disorders that result from repetitive antisocial behavior or voluntary intoxication.

Because determinations of legal insanity involve reaching conclusions about a person's mental status at the time of the offense—typically a time distant from that of the evaluation—and because insanity is defined in very narrow legal terms, psychological tests, including the MMPI-2, tend not to be very useful in determining legal sanity. Existing research does not support the notion that there are specific aspects of MMPI-2 results that are related directly to legal insanity. Rogers and McKee (1995) presented MMPI-2 data on individuals deemed legally sane and insane and concluded there were few meaningful differences between these two classes of defendants, although they found defendants judged to be insane were likely to have lower scores on Scale 4 and on the ASP Content scale than defendants judged to be sane.

Given the legal definition of insanity, it is not surprising there is no typical profile or set of scores on the MMPI-2 that indicates insanity. However, Rogers and McKee (1995) suggested several ways in which the MMPI-2 can contribute relevant information to an insanity evaluation. First, because defendants who make NGRI pleas may be strongly motivated to exaggerate their emotional problems, it is important to assess their test-taking attitudes. As discussed in a previous section of this chapter and in

Chapter 3, the MMPI-2 Validity scales and indexes are quite effective in identifying persons who are overreporting when they complete the test. Second, the vast research literature concerning the correlates of scales and code types permits accurate inferences about symptoms and personality characteristics that can add to the data upon which determinations of sanity versus insanity are based. Third, several MMPI-2 scales, especially Scale 4, RC4, and ASP, offer information about antisociality that can address, at least in part, the criterion that excludes conditions related only to repetitive antisocial behavior.

In summary, existing research does not support the notion there are specific MMPI-2 scales, code types, or patterns of scores that directly indicate someone was legally sane or insane at the time an act was committed. This determination should result from consideration of a comprehensive database including information from a variety of sources. However, the MMPI-2 can add useful information concerning the possibility of overreporting, current symptoms and behaviors indicative of severe mental disorder, and the likelihood of repetitive antisocial behavior.

Assessing Competency to Stand Trial

Psychologists often are asked to offer opinions about a defendant's competency to stand trial on criminal charges. Competency in this context has to do with whether the defendant has the ability to consult meaningfully with their attorney with a reasonable degree of understanding and has a rational as well as factual understanding of the proceedings against them (*Dusky v. United States*, 1960). Ogloff (1995) concluded the MMPI-2 has limited utility for such evaluations because the competency criteria are functional and do not focus on the defendant's mental state or character. Offering a different perspective, Lawrence (1985) concluded that "psychological test results in competency evaluations are not only useful as an adjunct to other collected data but are often indispensable" (p. 66).

Clearly, a determination concerning competency to stand trial requires information that cannot be obtained from tests like the MMPI-2. Using interviews, record reviews, or standardized competency instruments, assessors should collect relevant information from defendants, attorneys, and others who might be aware of such information. However, the MMPI-2 can add to the available data in several important ways.

Defendants who are claiming to be incompetent to stand trial sometimes overreport severe psychopathology as a reason for their claimed incompetency. As discussed in an earlier section of this chapter, the Validity scales of the MMPI-2 can be very useful in detecting such overreporting (see also Chapter 3). H. A. Miller (2004) studied criminal defendants found incompetent to stand trial because of mental illness. MMPI-2 scores were correlated with scores from the Structured Interview of Reported Symptoms (SIRS; Rogers, 1992), an established instrument for identifying overreporting of psychopathology. The F, F_B, and F_p scales of the MMPI-2 were highly correlated with most SIRS scores, suggesting they are good indicators of symptom overreporting.

Previous research has documented that having a psychotic diagnosis is associated with being judged incompetent to stand trial (e.g., Daniel et al., 1985; Rogers et al., 1988). Thus, the presence of indicators of severe psychopathology on a valid MMPI-2 protocol suggests the presence of psychiatric problems that may interfere with a defendant's ability to communicate effectively with their attorney or to have a rational understanding of the proceedings against them.

In summary, little empirical research exists directly examining the use of the MMPI-2 in the assessment of competency to stand trial. However, the MMPI-2 can provide relevant data about psychiatric symptoms the defendant is experiencing as well as whether the defendant is engaging with the assessment process in an open and honest manner. Obviously, information from the MMPI-2 should only be considered in conjunction with many other kinds of information when making determinations about competency.

Domestic Relations Evaluations

With approximately half of all new marriages in the Unites States ending in divorce (Raley & Bumpass, 2003) and many divorcing or separating couples having minor children, domestic relations courts are quite busy making decisions about child custody and visitation arrangements. Although 40 years ago, mental health professionals offered expert opinions in a relatively small proportion of child custody cases, clinician involvement has become much more commonplace today (Melton et al., 2018).

Domestic relations courts have great latitude in making decisions about child custody and visitation arrangements. Most criteria are modeled after the Uniform Marriage and Divorce Act (UMDA, 1979), although specific standards may differ between jurisdictions (Emery et al., 2005; Melton et al., 2018). The UMDA directs courts to make decisions that are "in the best interests of the child." Several specific guidelines deal with matters about which psychologists are trained to offer expert opinions. Among other criteria, the UMDA indicates that courts should consider "the interaction and interrelationship of the child with his parent or parents, his siblings, and any other person who may significantly affect the child's best interest; the child's adjustment to his home, school, and community; and the mental and physical health of all individuals involved." Clearly, the training and experience of psychologists qualify them to offer opinions about such matters. Otto et al. (2003) have provided a comprehensive discussion of psychological assessment in child custody cases (see also Fuhrman & Zibbell, 2012; Gould & Martindale, 2009).

It is important to consider the sources of information that psychologists utilize in developing opinions about what is best for a particular child. Ackerman and Pritzl (2011) surveyed psychologists who regularly conduct child custody evaluations and asked them how many hours they typically spend gathering information from various sources. Ackerman and Pritzl reported that the largest amount of time was spent interviewing parents (7.1 hours), children (3.6 hours), significant others (2.3 hours), and collateral contacts (3.2 hours). However, conducting psychological testing (6.1 hours), reviewing records (5.6 hours), and observing parent–child interactions (3.7 hours) were also heavily utilized sources of information. Ackerman and Pritzl also reported that the MMPI-2 was the most widely used psychological test with adults, as 97% of survey respondents reported using it. The MMPI-A was the most widely used psychological test with children (66%).

Experts should base their child custody and visitation arrangement opinions on data drawn from a variety of sources (American Psychological Association, 2010). Review of school, legal, and treatment records; interviews with children and significant adults; and observations of children interacting with significant adults provide much of the needed information. However, additional relevant information can be obtained from MMPI-2 results. Domestic relations courts typically have been quite receptive to expert opinion informed by MMPI-2 data (Otto & Collins, 1995).

In virtually every jurisdiction, the mental health of parents and other significant adults (e.g., stepparents, grandparents, other caregivers) is an important consideration in deciding what is in the best interests of children. Because the MMPI-2 has demonstrated strong validity in the assessment of clinically relevant symptoms and functioning, MMPI-2 data may directly inform these considerations.

However, most parents assessed as part of child custody proceedings approach psychological testing in a defensive manner. They understandably want to present a very favorable impression of themselves. In trying to do so, they tend to minimize symptoms and problems and to endorse items that will emphasize how honest, conscientious, virtuous, and well-adjusted they are. Several studies have reported MMPI-2 scores of parents who completed the test as part of child custody evaluations. Mean scores suggest moderate levels of defensive responding and absence of significant elevations on the Clinical scales (Bagby et al., 1999; Bathurst et al., 1997; Siegel, 1996; Strong et al., 1999). The typical pattern on the Validity scales is one with above-average scores on the L and K scales and below-average scores on the F scale.

Thus, we have come to expect some moderate defensiveness in the MMPI-2 results of parents evaluated as part of child custody or visitation proceedings. It is important to consider what such results do and do not indicate about these individuals. When the T scores on the L or K scales are between 50 and 65, the results are very typical for the circumstances and probably do not indicate an attempt to deny or hide significant psychological problems. However, if the T scores on the L or K scales are greater than 65, then the results should be considered invalid and uninterruptible. In this circumstance, it is not possible to know if the extreme defensiveness does or does not indicate the test taker is trying to deny or hide serious emotional problems. All that is clear is that the absence of elevations on other scales—which is likely to accompany the very defensive pattern on the Validity scales—does not necessarily indicate good adjustment. In this circumstance, extratest sources of information are necessary to try to make a determination about psychological adjustment.

Occasionally, adults assessed as part of child custody or visitation proceedings will produce a pattern on the Validity scales suggesting the open admission, and perhaps even exaggeration, of problems and symptoms. Typically, F-scale scores will be well above average, and L- and K-scale scores are typically at average or below-average levels. Consider several possible interpretations of this pattern of scores. First, the person may have such serious psychological problems that revealing them cannot be avoided even in a situation in which the demand characteristics are clearly to try to do so. Second, the pattern may reflect a person who is overreporting problems and symptoms because they really do not want custody. For example, this may occur when a grandparent or some other person has pressured the parent to seek custody the parent really does not want. Again, information from other sources will be helpful in trying to decide how to interpret these results most appropriately.

Assuming the Validity scale scores are not suggestive of extreme defensiveness or exaggeration, MMPI-2 scores and code types can be interpreted very much as they are in other settings. These scales are most likely to be helpful in describing the mental health of the individual being evaluated, though identified difficulties may or may not be directly related to the capacity of the individual to be an effective caregiver. Indeed, there is no single scale or pattern of scales directly related to effective or ineffective parenting (Otto & Collins, 1995).

One area of MMPI-2 research relevant to child custody evaluations is that of parental abuse of children. Key et al. (2020) reported the mean scores of parents undergoing a parental capacity examination following substantiated claims of abuse or neglect. In their sample, the mean score on L was 71T, and 52% of the sample produced L scores ≥ 70T. No other Validity scale or substantive scale mean score was substantially elevated. Ezzo et al. (2007) compared MMPI-2 scores of parents involved in custody litigation whose parental rights had been suspended because of suspected child maltreatment with scores of parents involved in custody litigation where child maltreatment was not suspected. The former group scored significantly higher than the latter on 7 of 10 Clinical scales. However, for no Clinical scale was the mean T score for the suspected maltreatment group greater than 65. The authors concluded that MMPI-2 scores could not be used to determine if child maltreatment had or had not occurred. Gambetti et al. (2019) replicated Ezzo and colleagues' study using samples of Italian parents undergoing psychological assessment as part of either custody litigation or parental fitness evaluation. The results and conclusions reported by Gambetti et al. were nearly identical to Ezzo et al.'s earlier work.

Although MMPI-2 scores do not permit direct inferences concerning how effective persons are likely to be as parents, many of the inferences made during a comprehensive MMPI-2 interpretation can provide potentially relevant information. For example, if a person has been described—based on their MMPI-2 scores—as impulsive, unstable, unpredictable, and aggressive and as having very poor judgment, then this would certainly be relevant to how this person might be expected to function as a parent. However, it is important to make clear that inferences about parenting are typically not directly related to MMPI-2 scores. Rather, they are higher order inferences based on demonstrated relationships between MMPI-2 scores and those behaviors and characteristics that might reasonably be expected to influence parenting. It should also be kept in mind that parental characteristics that might be in the best interests of one child may not necessarily be in the best interests of another child who has different needs.

Professional guidelines for child custody evaluations (American Psychological Association, 2010) caution psychologists to utilize multiple sources of data and consider the context of the assessment when drawing conclusions and offering recommendations and opinions. The MMPI-2 can play an important role in such evaluations, but users should keep in mind that there are limitations to its contributions and should use the test as one of several sources of assessment information.

Personal Injury Evaluations

Psychologists often are called on to evaluate the mental status of individuals who allege that they have suffered psychological damages as a result of some traumatic event in which they were involuntary participants or witnesses. Example events include vehicle accidents, violent assaults, medical malpractice, sexual harassment, workplace injuries, and many other negative experiences. Kane and Dvoskin (2011) identified the MMPI-2 as the most frequently and widely used psychological test in personal injury evaluations.

Psychologists typically are asked to address several issues in personal injury evaluations (Kane & Dvoskin, 2011; K. S. Pope et al., 2000). First, does the person claiming to have been psychologically damaged really have significant psychological or emotional problems? Because there often is strong motivation in these kinds of cases for the claimants to exaggerate problems and symptoms, it becomes very important to assess the credibility of the reported symptoms and problems. Second, are the current psychological or emotional problems directly attributable, at least in part, to the traumatic event claimed as the cause of the problems? In this regard, it becomes very important to determine if there was a preexisting condition that could account, at least in part, for the damages blamed on a particular traumatic incident. Likewise, it is important to determine if there have been other events subsequent to the identified event that could account, at least in part, for current psychological problems. Finally, psychologists often are asked to make some statements about the likely course of recovery.

The MMPI-2 is well suited to address some of these issues and not as well suited to address others. The Validity scales of the MMPI-2 can be very useful in assessing the extent to which claimants are presenting accurate reports of their symptoms and problems as well as the extent to which they are exaggerating such problems. Because its Clinical scales were developed to assess mental status (i.e., clinical condition) and demonstrate strong validity in this regard, the MMPI-2 can directly address problems and symptoms currently experienced by claimants. Although not totally useless in regard to preexisting conditions, other traumatic events that could account for current problems and symptoms, or likely course of recovery from current problems, the MMPI-2 is of limited utility in relation to these issues.

In personal injury evaluations, where the motivation to present an unrealistically negative picture of one's psychological status often is strong, it is especially important to be able to address the issue of credibility. Psychologists have long noted in the general literature the possible influence personal injury litigation may have on symptom presentation (e.g., Binder & Rohling, 1996). Youngjohn et al. (1997) found that persons with diagnoses of head injury who were involved in litigation concerning their injuries tended to have more extreme MMPI-2 scores than nonlitigants, even when severity of injury was equated. In a similar study, Dush et al. (1994) found that chronic-pain patients who were involved in litigation concerning their injuries had more extreme MMPI-2 scores than nonlitigant pain patients. While these findings may suggest individuals with more severe symptoms are more likely to litigate than those with less severe symptoms, they could also suggest exaggeration or fabrication of difficulties. MMPI-2 Validity scales have demonstrated strong utility in detecting overreported cognitive and somatic symptoms in personal injury contexts (e.g., Berry et al., 1995; Dearth et al., 2005; Larrabee, 2003; N. W. Nelson et al., 2010). However, it is not at all clear that any of the MMPI-2 Validity scales adds incrementally to established cognitive effort tests (e.g., Test of Memory Malingering; Tombaugh, 1997) in detecting the overreporting of cognitive deficits.

Greiffenstein and colleagues (2010) reviewed concerns raised in the literature about "examiner effects" on an examinee's response style. This concern, as applied to the MMPI-2, is that Validity scale scores and the interpretation of those scores in personal injury litigation may be influenced by whether the evaluator has been hired by the defendant or the plaintiff. Greiffenstein et al. (2010) point out that often these kinds of concerns are raised during expert testimony and can be used to raise doubts about the accuracy of Validity scale performance regardless of whether the individual was assessed by the plaintiff's expert (i.e., calling into question "passing" results on Validity scales) or the defendant's expert (i.e., calling into question results on Validity scales indicative of noncredible responding). Greiffenstein et al. (2010) reviewed forensic case files and identified 80 cases where the same litigant was administered the MMPI-2 twice, once by an expert selected by the plaintiff and again by an expert selected by the defense. They then compared the mean Validity scale scores from the plaintiff's administration and the defense's administration. The mean scale score differences were not statistically significant for any of the eight Validity scales. Furthermore, the mean T-score differences were less than 2 points on every scale.

Because the MMPI-2 scales were designed to assess clinical condition, once the likelihood of overreporting has been ruled out, scores on the Clinical, RC, PSY-5, Content, and Supplementary scales can directly address the presence or absence of current psychopathology. The indicators of psychopathology found across these scales were discussed thoroughly in earlier chapters of this book.

PRESENTING EXPERT OPINIONS BASED ON THE MMPI-2

A detailed discussion of how to write forensic reports and how to prepare and present expert testimony in court is beyond the scope of this chapter. Others have presented very helpful suggestions about these issues (e.g., Brodsky, 2013; Brodsky & Gutheil, 2016; K. S. Pope et al., 2000; Weiner, 1987, 1995). Only in extraordinarily rare cases will the MMPI-2 be the only source of support for expert opinions. Typically, historical information, clinical interviews, and other assessment data will also be available and will be integrated with MMPI-2 data in support of expert opinions. This section will offer some guidelines concerning the presentation of expert testimony based on MMPI-2 results. However, many of the guidelines also will apply to testimony based on other assessment data.

1. Be familiar with the MMPI-2. Although psychologists have an ethical and professional responsibility to be familiar with all techniques they employ, it is especially important for them to be well informed about instruments used in conducting forensic evaluations where every statement is likely to be scrutinized, questioned, or challenged. Clinicians should understand how the

original MMPI scales were developed and how the MMPI-2 scales are related to those of the original instrument. It is especially important to have a full understanding of the Validity scales and how they can be used to identify test-taking approaches that deviate from the instructions. Knowledge about the normative sample with which test takers are being compared is essential. An understanding of the research literature relevant to the MMPI-2 interpretations being made is critical. This literature may never have to be discussed in testimony, but one should always be prepared to do so.

2. Be sure the MMPI-2 is appropriate for the specific forensic issues that are in question. One of the most common mistakes made by psychologists who use the MMPI-2 in forensic evaluations is trying to use the instrument for purposes for which it is not suited and for which it has not been adequately validated. In previous sections of this chapter, information was provided about issues that can be addressed appropriately with MMPI-2 data. The MMPI-2 is very well suited for identifying response styles and for assessing current clinical conditions. As Weiner (1995) pointed out, test data—including MMPI-2 results—are not well suited for concluding what someone is likely to have done in the past or is likely to do in the future. Such postdictions and predictions should be made cautiously.

3. Be sure the MMPI-2 was administered appropriately and scored correctly. As discussed in Chapter 2 of this book, the MMPI-2 should be administered in a standardized way, in a professional setting, and with appropriate supervision. Psychologists must be able to verify that these procedures were followed and that the test results are, in fact, those of the person who is the focus of the evaluation. Extra care should be taken to ensure the accuracy of hand scoring of item response. Computer scoring of test responses is quite reliable, but if keyboard entry of item responses is utilized, then extra care is required to ensure that the data were entered correctly.

4. Be familiar with all aspects of any computerized scoring and interpretation services utilized. Butcher (1995) discussed the advantages of utilizing computerized interpretations in forensic evaluations. They tend to be more thorough and better documented than more traditional interpretations. They reduce the likelihood that information will be selectively emphasized or ignored by clinicians. They are rapid, efficient, and reliable; and there are data suggesting a high level of external validity. However, interpretations typically contain many scores and indexes, some of which are not very familiar to most clinicians. Even if some of these scores and indexes are not emphasized in a particular interpretation, it can be very embarrassing for clinicians not to be able to respond meaningfully to questions about them. It also is important that users of computerized interpretations understand how the interpretive statements are generated, and that they have made determinations about which of the statements in the interpretive report apply to the person they are evaluating. The descriptions included in interpretive reports are based on a particular MMPI-2 prototype, and not every descriptor will apply to every person for whom a computerized interpretation is generated.

5. Limit inferences based on MMPI-2 data to those supported by empirical research. It is our practice to only make statements in forensic reports or in expert testimony for which supporting empirical research can be cited. This means far fewer statements are made than in other kinds of assessment situations, but it makes it much easier to defend what is said if the statements and inferences are challenged. Typically, experts can respond to challenges using secondary sources such as this book, but they should be prepared to cite original research reports if pressed to do so.

6. Present information about the MMPI-2 in a manner understandable to the recipients of the information. This is an obligation psychologists have in all assessment situations, but it is especially critical in forensic evaluations where the recipients of the interpretations are lay persons (e.g., attorneys, judges, juries). Chapter 11 of this book includes guidelines for presenting feedback about MMPI-2 results to persons who have taken the test. These same guidelines are largely applicable to the presentation of MMPI-2 results and interpretations to lay persons in forensic settings.

Psychologists should not assume the persons to whom information is being communicated have any background concerning the MMPI-2. Prior to presenting information about any MMPI-2 results, psychologists should educate their audiences by describing the development of the MMPI-2 scales, the norms utilized in interpreting scores, the ways in which the Validity scales can detect patterns of responding that deviate from the instructions, and the empirical nature of interpretations. Visual aids, such as sample profile sheets, often are useful in this regard.

Present information using language readily understood by the audience and avoid technical jargon. It is preferable to make statements about the likelihood of certain characteristics and behaviors among persons who produce MMPI-2 results similar to those of the person being evaluated as opposed to making definitive statements that the person whose score was evaluated does or does not have such characteristics and behaviors. For example, it would be better to state that persons with a 48/84, 2-point code type often show very poor judgment than to state that a particular person who produced a 48/84 code type shows very poor judgment.

It is important to keep in mind that inferences based on MMPI-2 data really are probability statements. A person with a particular code type is more likely to have certain characteristics than someone without that code type, or a person with a very high score on a scale is more likely to have certain characteristics than a person with a lower score on that scale. Because no psychological test—including the MMPI-2—is perfectly valid for any purpose, we can never be absolutely confident that every characteristic associated with a particular score or configuration of scores will fit every person who has that score or configuration. Attorneys often will try to get psychologists to assign probability values to particular inferences—for example, what proportion of persons with the 48/84 code type actually show poor judgment. Although there is a strong research base underlying inferences such as these from MMPI-2 data, it generally does not permit these kinds of specific probability statements to be made.

In summary, the MMPI-2 can be very useful in addressing some issues relevant in forensic settings. It is especially useful in assessing deviations from standard test-taking approaches (e.g., overreporting, underreporting) and determining a current clinical condition. However, psychologists are cautioned to limit their MMPI-2 interpretations to areas for which the test was developed and for which adequate validity data are available.

CORRECTIONAL SETTINGS

The earliest studies of the MMPI in relation to criminal activities were conducted by Capwell (1945) and Hathaway and Monachesi (1953, 1957). Since then, numerous studies have examined the utility of the MMPI-2 in correctional settings. Although it is often assumed that inmates will be uncooperative and likely to produce invalid protocols if required to complete the MMPI-2, this does not seem to be the case. McNulty et al. (2003) reported that approximately 79% of inmates who were administered the MMPI-2 at their time of entry into the correctional system produced valid protocols. This rate of profile validity is very similar to that encountered in many clinical settings.

Over the years, various methods of using the MMPI-2 to classify prisoners and to predict their behavior while incarcerated as well as upon release have been developed and examined empirically. According to Megargee and Carbonell (1995), research has typically identified significant relationships between standard MMPI scales (especially Scale 4) and criminal behavior. Scale 4 (and sometimes Scales 8 and 9) have been related to disciplinary infractions in prison and to repeat offenses after release. Unfortunately, the magnitude of these relationships has been so modest that accurate prediction in individual cases is not likely. Experimental scales were developed specifically to predict institutional and post-release behaviors using the original MMPI (e.g., Panton, 1958). However, Megargee and Carbonell concluded these experimental scales tended to be related only modestly to criterion behaviors and typically added little to prediction using the standard scales such as Scale 4.

There are several resources available to the reader interested in a detailed understanding of the use of the MMPI-2 in correctional settings. Megargee and Carbonell (1995) presented an excellent review of the research literature. Megargee's 2006 book, *Using the MMPI-2 in Criminal Justice and Correctional Settings*, includes comprehensive guidelines for interpreting MMPI-2 data in correctional settings. These resources describe the vital role that classification procedures play in correctional settings. Efficient and valid systems for classifying offenders contribute significantly to effective utilization of the limited resources available in virtually all correctional settings.

CHAPTER 11

AN INTERPRETIVE STRATEGY

IN 1956, PAUL MEEHL made a strong plea for a "good cookbook" for psychological test interpretation. Meehl's proposed cookbook was to include detailed rules for categorizing test responses and empirically determined extratest correlates for each category of test responses. The rules could be applied automatically by a nonprofessional worker (or by a computer) with the interpretive statements selected for a particular type of protocol from a larger library of empirically determined statements. Although efforts have been made to construct such cookbooks (e.g., Gilberstadt & Duker, 1965; Marks & Seeman, 1963; Marks et al., 1974), the current status of psychological test interpretation is far from the automatic process Meehl envisioned. All tests, including the MMPI-2, provide opportunities for standardized observation of the current behavior of examinees. On the basis of these test behaviors, inferences are made about other extratest behaviors. The clinician serves as both information processor and clinical judge in the assessment process. The major purpose of this chapter is to suggest one approach (but by no means the only one) to using MMPI-2 data to make meaningful inferences about examinees.

The MMPI-2 should be used to generate hypotheses or inferences about an examinee because the interpretive data presented earlier will not apply completely and unfailingly to each person with specified MMPI-2 scores. In interpreting MMPI-2 scores, one is dealing with probabilities. A particular extratest characteristic is more likely to apply to a person with a higher score on a scale than a person with a lower score on that scale, but there can never be complete certainty that it will. The inferences generated from an individual's MMPI-2 scores should thus be validated against other information about that individual, such as that available from interviews, behavioral observations, and other tests included in the assessment process.

The MMPI-2 is most valuable as an assessment tool when it is used in conjunction with other psychological tests, interview and observational data, and appropriate background information. Although blind interpretation of the MMPI-2 certainly is possible, and in fact is the procedure involved in computerized interpretation, such interpretations should be used only to generate preliminary hypotheses. Much more accurate person-specific inferences are likely to occur when the MMPI-2 is viewed in the context of all information available about an individual. This position is consistent with research findings by investigators such as Kostlan (1954) and Sines (1959).

Two kinds of interpretive inferences can be made on the basis of MMPI-2 data. First, some characteristics of an examinee with particular MMPI-2 scores are those that differentiate that examinee from other persons in a particular setting (e.g., hospital or clinic). For example, it is possible to infer from a hospitalized patient's MMPI-2 scores that they are likely to misuse alcohol or other substances. Because most patients do not misuse substances, this inference clearly differentiates this particular patient from most other patients. A second kind of inference is one that involves a characteristic common to many individuals in a particular setting. For example, the inference that a hospitalized psychiatric patient does not know how to handle stress in an effective manner is one that probably is true for most patients in that setting. Although the differential, patient-specific inferences tend to be more useful than the general ones, the latter are important in understanding an individual case, particularly for clinicians and others involved in the treatment process who might not have a clear understanding of what behaviors are shared by most persons in a particular setting.

Whereas Meehl (1956) envisioned the assessment process as dealing exclusively with non-test behaviors that are directly and empirically tied to specific aspects of test performance (i.e., first-order inferences), the current status of the assessment field is such that only limited relationships of this kind have been identified. Often it is possible and necessary to make higher-order inferences about examinees based on a conceptualization of their personalities. For example, currently no clear data indicate that a particular kind of MMPI-2 profile is predictive of a future suicide attempt. However, if the first-order inferences we make from an individual's MMPI-2 scores are that they are extremely depressed, agitated, and emotionally uncomfortable; are socially alienated; and show poor judgment much of the time, then the higher-order inference that such a person has a higher risk of suicide than patients in general is a logical one. Although it is legitimate to rely on such higher-order inferences in interpreting the MMPI-2, one should have greater confidence in the first-order inferences that are derived from research about the meaning of MMPI-2 scores and configurations.

A GENERAL STRATEGY

In our clinical work, we utilize an approach to MMPI-2 interpretation that involves trying to answer the following questions about each MMPI-2 protocol:

1. What was the test-taking attitude of the examinee, and how should this attitude be taken into account in interpreting the protocol?
2. What is the general level of adjustment (or maladjustment) of the examinee?

3. What other characteristics (e.g., symptoms, attitudes, defenses) can be inferred about or expected from the examinee?

4. What diagnoses, if any, are consistent with the MMPI-2 scores produced by the examinee?

5. What are the implications for treatment with the examinee, if treatment is planned or anticipated?

Test–Taking Attitude

The ideal examinee is one who approaches the task of completing the MMPI-2 in a serious and cooperative manner. This individual reads each MMPI-2 item and responds to the item in an honest, direct manner. When such an ideal situation is realized, the examiner can be confident the test responses are a representative sample of the examinee's behavior and can proceed with the interpretation of the protocol. However, examinees may approach the MMPI-2 with an attitude that deviates from this ideal situation for many different reasons. Identification of test-taking attitude for each individual examinee is important because these influences must be considered prior to generating inferences from the MMPI-2 scores. In addition, such attitudes may be predictive of the way an examinee approaches other parts of the assessment process. Forbey and Lee (2011) found that over- and underreporting approaches detected by MMPI-2 Validity scales generalized to other self-report measures completed as part of the same evaluation. Response styles may even say something about how the test taker approaches other aspects of their life. For example, a test taker whose MMPI-2 Validity scales suggests attempts to present themselves in an excessively positive light may approach other interpersonal interactions in a similarly defensive manner.

Qualitative aspects of an examinee's test behavior often serve to augment inferences based on the more quantitative scores and indexes. One such factor is the amount of time required to complete the MMPI-2. Excessively long testing times may be indicative of indecisiveness, psychomotor retardation, confusion, or passive resistance to the testing procedures. Extremely short times suggest that examinees were quite impulsive in responding to the test items or did not read and consider their content.

Examinees occasionally become very tense, agitated, or otherwise upset while taking the MMPI-2. Such behavior may be predictive of similar responses to other stressful situations. Some examinees, such as those who are obsessive or indecisive, share qualifications to their true–false responses by writing these in the margins of the answer sheet or verbalizing them to the test administrator.

Although the qualitative features of test performance just discussed can offer important information, the Validity scales are the primary objective sources of inferences about test-taking attitude. As discussed in Chapter 3, engagement in non-content-based invalid responding can distort scores on Validity scales assessing over- and underreporting (i.e., make them higher or lower than they would be if the individual had not engaged in non-content-based invalid responding). As such, it is important to follow a prescribed order when interpreting the Validity scales.

The process of interpreting the Validity scales begins by considering the possibility of nonresponding, as well as non-content-based random and fixed responding.

This is done by inspecting scores on Cannot Say (? or CNS), Variable Response Inconsistency (VRIN), and True Response Inconsistency (TRIN). Scores on CNS indicate the number of items omitted by the examinee. A large number of omitted items may indicate indecisiveness, ambivalence, or an attempt to avoid admitting negative things about oneself without deliberately lying. Examinees who answer all or most of the items are not availing themselves of this simplistic way of attempting to present a positive picture of themselves.

High scores on the VRIN scale indicate that the examinee probably responded to the items without reading and considering their content. When the TRIN T score is high (in either the true or false direction), the possibility of a yea-saying or naysaying response set must be considered. If CNS is greater than 30 or there are extreme elevations on VRIN or TRIN, then the protocol should be considered invalid and not be interpreted.

If there are no indications of non-content-based invalid responding, the interpretation of the Validity scales proceeds with a consideration of whether the test taker may have engaged in over- or underreporting. The possibility of overreporting is examined by inspecting scores on the infrequency scales— Infrequency (F), Back Infrequency (F_B), Infrequency Psychopathology (F_p), and Symptom Validity (FBS). Empirical work suggests this process should begin with interpretation of F, followed by the other overreporting scales that assess more specific types of overreported symptoms (e.g., Arbisi & Ben-Porath, 1995; Steffan et al., 2010).

Scores on the F scale reflect the extent to which an examinee's responses to a finite pool of items compare to those of the normative sample. Scores on F that are considerably higher than average suggest that examinees are admitting to many behaviors and attitudes that were not typically endorsed in the normative sample. Examinees could have responded to the test items randomly (refer to VRIN to evaluate this possibility) or with a deliberate intention of appearing very emotionally disturbed. Another possibility is that the examinees are experiencing severe emotional difficulties and are using the MMPI-2 as a vehicle to express a cry for help. Scores on F that are considerably below average indicate that the examinees are admitting fewer than an average number of attitudes and behaviors that were not typically endorsed in the normative sample. They may be overly defensive and trying to create unrealistically positive pictures of themselves (refer to the underreporting Validity scales to rule out these possibilities). Scores on F in the average range indicate that examinees have been neither hypercritical of themselves nor overly denying in responding to the test items.

Whereas F scores provide information about examinees' attitudes in responding to the first 361 items of the test, the F_B scale provides similar information for items that occur later in the test booklet. F_B scores should be interpreted very similarly to those of F. The F_p scale was developed to detect overreporting in settings where there is a high base rate of serious psychopathology. Compared with the F scale, high scores ($T \geq 100$) on the F_p scale are less likely to indicate genuine psychopathology and more likely to indicate overreporting. Very high scores on FBS suggest the examinee reported a large number of responses that are unusual even for someone with serious medical problems.

Once the overreporting scales have been interpreted, the possibility of underreporting should be considered. Test takers can exaggerate or present themselves as having problems and difficulties they do not actually experience while simultaneously presenting other aspects of themselves in an overly positive light. As such, regardless of whether a protocol is suggestive of overreporting or not, the possibility of underreporting should be examined. This is done via inspection of scores on the Lie (L), Correction (K), and Superlative Self-Presentation (S) scales. Above-average scores on the L scale indicate that examinees may have presented themselves as more virtuous than they really are. When L scores are moderately high, the protocol can be interpreted, but adjustments should be made to take into account the examinee's defensiveness. Extremely high scores on the L scale indicate that the protocol is invalid and should not be interpreted.

The K scale can serve as another index of defensiveness. Above-average K scores indicate that examinees have been overly defensive, whereas below-average scores indicate lack of defensiveness and a highly self-critical attitude. Average-range scores on the K scale suggest that examinees have been neither overly defensive nor overly self-critical in endorsing the MMPI-2 items. High scores on the S scale also indicate an attempt to present oneself as highly virtuous, responsible, free of psychological problems, having few or no flaws, and getting along well with others.

The configuration of the Validity scales also is important for understanding examinees' test-taking attitudes. In general, persons who are approaching the test with the intention of presenting themselves in an overly favorable way have L, K, and S scores greater than scores on the F, F_B, F_p, and FBS scales. On the other hand, persons who are using the test to be overly self-critical, to exaggerate their problems, or both, produce L, K, and S scores that are significantly lower than the F, F_B, F_p, and FBS scores.

In summary, a first step in interpreting the MMPI-2 is to make some judgments concerning the test-taking attitude of the examinee. If the decision is made that the test was approached in a manner that invalidates the protocol (e.g., inconsistent responding, underreporting, overreporting), no additional interpretation of the scores is in order. Scores on scales other than those on the Validity scales should not be viewed as providing an accurate assessment of the test taker. Invalid protocols only tell us how the test taker likely approached (a) the MMPI-2 and (b) other instruments administered as part of the assessment battery (Forbey & Lee, 2011). Invalid protocols can also be a source of information for generating higher-order inferences about how the test taker relates to the world more generally. If there are less extreme response sets operating (e.g., defensiveness or exaggeration), it may be possible to make some tentative interpretations of the profile; but adjustments in interpretations must be made.

Adjustment Level

There are several important components to psychological adjustment level. First, how emotionally comfortable or uncomfortable are examinees? Second, how well do they carry out the responsibilities of their life situations regardless of how conflicted and uncomfortable they might be? For most people, these two components are very much related. Persons who are psychologically comfortable tend to function well and vice versa. However, for certain individuals (e.g., those with anxiety disorder diagnoses) a great deal of discomfort and turmoil can be present, but adequate functioning continues. For other persons (e.g., some individuals with diagnoses of schizophrenia or antisocial personality disorder), serious impairment in coping with responsibilities can be found without great emotional discomfort. The MMPI-2 permits inferences about both aspects of adjustment level.

Several MMPI-2 scales are excellent indicators of experienced distress. Elevated scores on Clinical Scale 2, the Depression (DEP) Content scale, and the RCd (Demoralization) and RC2 (Low Positive Emotions) Restructured Clinical (RC) scales suggest that the examinee is feeling depressed and demoralized. Elevated scores on Clinical Scale 7, the Anxiety (ANX) Content scale, and the RC7 (Dysfunctional Negative Emotions) scale indicate that the examinee is likely to be experiencing considerable anxiety.

Overall elevation on the Clinical scales is a simple but meaningful index of the extent to which an examinee is not coping well with the demands of their life situation. In general, as more of the Clinical scales are elevated (and as the degree of elevation increases), the greater the probability that serious psychopathology and impaired functioning are present. An index of scale elevation can be obtained by calculating the average T scores for eight Clinical scales (excluding Scales 5 and 0), with higher scores indicating poorer coping. Graham et al. (2002) demonstrated that this simple index was strongly related to maladjustment in mental health center clients as assessed by intake workers and therapists.

Scores on several other MMPI-2 scales also are related to coping. High scorers on the Welsh's Anxiety (A) and RCd scales and low scorers on the Ego Strength (Es) scale are not likely to be coping very well. The RC2 scale indicates someone who lacks positive emotional engagement with the world. Scale 7 and the RC7 scale are good measures of anxiety, irritability, and other forms of emotional reactivity.

Whenever there is evidence of emotional distress and reduced ability to effectively cope, it is especially important to review the MMPI-2 for signs of acute suicidal ideation. The Suicidal Ideation (DEP4) Content Component scale is one indicator that should be reviewed. We also recommend reviewing the responses to those few items explicitly dealing with suicidal ideation and behavior (i.e., items 303, 506, 520, 524, & 546). We generally recommend avoiding interpretation of Content Component scales unless their associated parent scales are also elevated, and we generally suggest very cautious interpretation of responses to individual items. However, we believe these instances are the lone exceptions to our general practices because these indicators raise explicit concerns about suicidality. Although the MMPI-2 cannot be used to assess suicide risk, we recommend conducting a suicide risk assessment whenever any of these indicators are present.

Characteristic Traits and Behaviors

A next step in the interpretive process is to describe the test taker's symptoms, personality traits, attitudes, defenses, and so forth in enough detail to allow an overall understanding of the person. Although not every protocol permits inferences about all the following points, in general, we try to make statements or inferences about each of these:

1. symptoms
2. major needs (e.g., dependency, achievement, autonomy)

3. perceptions of the environment, particularly of significant other people in the examinee's life situation
4. reactions to stress (e.g., coping strategies, defenses)
5. self-concept
6. emotional control
7. interpersonal relationships
8. psychological resources.

Inferences about these various aspects of behavior and personality are based on analysis of defined code types and scores on individual Clinical, RC, Content, PSY-5, and Supplementary scales. Because inferences based on well-defined code types are more likely to apply to a particular examinee with that code type than inferences based on a single MMPI-2 scale, begin by determining if a protocol has a defined code type and review inferences related to it. If there is a defined code type, inferences appropriate to the code type should be generated. If both scales in the defined code type are elevated (T ≥ 65), include inferences having to do with symptoms as well as those having to do with personality characteristics. However, if the scales in the defined code type have T scores between 60 and 65, you should emphasize inferences about personality characteristics and not those associated with psychiatric symptoms.

Next, you should examine each Clinical scale score and determine if any inferences are appropriate for a score at its level. If a defined code type was identified, you should not consider individually the Clinical scales that make up the code type. However, other Clinical scales should be examined to determine if inferences are appropriate for scores at their levels.

High scores on the Clinical scales typically suggest many inferences with varying content. Obviously, not all of the inferences for a scale will apply to everyone with a high score on that scale. For example, high scores on Scale 4 lead to inferences that include family problems, antisocial behaviors, and negative emotionality (e.g., depression and worry). Examination of some other MMPI-2 scales can sometimes clarify the meaning of a high score on a Clinical scale for a particular person. The Harris–Lingoes subscales may indicate greater focus on some inferences over others. For example, if a high Scale 4 score is accompanied by a high score on the Pd2 subscale (Authority Problems), you should focus on the antisocial aspects. However, if the high Scale 4 score is accompanied by a high score on the Pd1 subscale (Family Problems) but not on the Pd2 subscale, you should focus on the inferences having to do with family problems. Obviously, if scores on the Harris–Lingoes subscales are very similar to each other, these scales will not be helpful in clarifying the meaning of a high Clinical scale score. The Harris–Lingoes subscales should only be used to clarify interpretation of the Clinical scale from which they are derived. If a Harris–Lingoes subscale is high, but its associated Clinical scale is not elevated, then the Harris–Lingoes subscale should not be interpreted.

Examination of the Restructured Clinical (RC) scales can also help focus interpretations of the Clinical scales (Sellbom, Ben-Porath, McNulty, et al., 2006). If there is a high score for a Clinical scale (e.g., Scale 4) and the corresponding RC scale (e.g., RC4) is also high, the focus should be on the core construct of the Clinical scale (e.g., antisocial behavior). However, if a Clinical scale score is high but the corresponding

RC scale score is not high, it is likely that the Clinical scale is high because the test taker endorsed many items having to do with demoralization and not because of characteristics associated with the core construct. In this case, you would expect RCd to also be high. Occasionally, an RC scale score will be high and its corresponding Clinical scale score will not be high. In such cases, the high RC scale score suggests a focus on the core constructs that the scale assesses. The absence of a high score on the corresponding Clinical scale is likely due to the absence of great personal distress, and you would not expect RCd to be high.

The Content scales can also be used to clarify the interpretation of high scores on Clinical scales. Again, let us consider the example of a high score on Scale 4, suggesting possible antisocial behaviors, family problems, and negative affect. If you find that the Antisocial Practices (ASP) Content scale also is high, you should focus on the antisocial inferences for Scale 4. However, if the ASP scale is not very high but the Family Problems (FAM) Content scale is high, you should focus on the inferences having to do with family problems and not on those having to do with antisocial behaviors.

The Content Component scales can potentially be of assistance in determining the focus of inferences associated with a high Content scale score. Much like the Harris–Lingoes subscales for the Clinical scales, the Content Component scales can clarify the kinds of symptoms and behaviors the examinee acknowledged. For example, if there is a high score on the Anger (ANG) Content scale that is accompanied by a higher score on the Explosive Behavior (ANG1) scale than on the Irritability (ANG2) Content Component scale, you should emphasize the inferences based on the ANG scale that have to do with problems with anger control. However, if there is a high ANG Content scale score with the ANG2 scale score higher than the ANG1 scale score, inferences about problems with anger control are less critical. Ben-Porath and Sherwood (1993) emphasized that the Content Component scales for a particular Content scale should be interpreted only when the T score on the Content scale is greater than 60 and when there is a difference of at least 10 T-score points between Content Component scale scores. As we suggested earlier about the Harris–Lingoes subscales, the Content Component scales should not be used by themselves to generate inferences.

This part of the interpretive process typically will yield a large number of inferences. Because some of the MMPI-2 scales are not independent of each other, there may be considerable overlap in the inferences that have been generated. Importantly, because these redundancies arise from the intercorrelation of MMPI-2 scales, the number of times a particular inference occurs should not be used to make statements about the severity of a test-taker's difficulties in a specific area. Rather, information about severity of symptoms will be reflected in the degree to which the scale scores leading to the inferences were elevated (i.e., how much higher than T = 65 the scores were).

Initially there may appear to be inconsistencies among the various inferences that have been generated. You should first consider the possibility that the apparent inconsistencies are accurately reflecting different facets of the examinee's personality and behavior. Consider, for example, a profile with high scores (T ≥ 65) on both Clinical scales 2 and 4 . The Scale 2 score suggests sensitivity to the needs and feelings of others, whereas the Scale 4 score suggests insensitivity to the needs and feelings of others. It is possible that the same individual may show both characteristics at different times. In fact, research with the 24/42 code type indicates that persons with this code type tend to alternate between periods of great sensitivity and insensitivity to others.

Sometimes inconsistencies in inferences cannot be reconciled as easily as in this example. In these instances, you must decide in which inferences to have the most confidence. In general, inferences based on defined code types will be more accurate than those based on a single scale. Greater confidence should be placed in inferences that occur for several scales than in those that occur for only a single scale. However, you should consider that item overlap may account for similar inferences based on two or more scales. Inferences based on scales with very high scores should receive greater emphasis than those based on moderately high scores. Finally, greater emphasis should be placed on inferences based on scales that have stronger evidence supporting their validity for assessing the particular characteristic in question. While novice MMPI-2 users may have limited information about relative validity of scale scores; as users become more informed about the test, more information will be available to inform this issue.

Some inferences about an examinee do not result directly from scores on a scale or from configurations of scales. Rather, they are higher-order inferences generated from a basic understanding of the examinee. For example, there are no data indicating that scores on particular MMPI-2 scales are predictive of suicide attempts. However, it would be reasonable to be concerned about such attempts in a person whose MMPI-2 scores led to inferences of serious depression, agitation, social alienation, and poor problem solving.

Diagnostic Impressions

Although the usefulness of psychiatric diagnoses has been questioned by many clinicians, referral sources often request information about diagnosis. In addition, it often is necessary to assign diagnostic labels for purposes such as insurance claims, disability status, or competency status. Many of the interpretive sections earlier in this book presented diagnostic inferences for two- and three-point code types and for individual scales. Inferences relevant to diagnoses would have been recorded earlier as you considered code types and scores on the individual scales. You should keep in mind that one cannot assign diagnoses based solely on MMPI-2 data. The criteria for most diagnoses include information not available from test data (e.g., age at onset of symptoms; previous occurrences of the problem behavior). You should determine the diagnoses that are most consistent with the MMPI-2 data and then consider these possible diagnoses in the context of everything else that is known about a particular person.

In using the MMPI-2 for diagnostic purposes, you should consider that many research studies concerning diagnostic inferences were based on the original MMPI. However, because of the continuity between the original MMPI and the MMPI-2, data based on the original instrument are applicable to the MMPI-2. It also is important to know that many of the studies of the relationship between MMPI data and diagnoses were conducted prior to the publication of the DSM-5 (American Psychiatric Association, 2013). In presenting diagnostic inferences for particular scores and configurations of scores in this book, the earlier diagnostic labels were translated into more contemporary ones.

Treatment Implications

A primary goal of many assessments is to make meaningful recommendations about treatment. Sometimes, when demand for treatment exceeds the resources available, the decision is whether or not to accept a particular person for treatment. Such a decision may involve clinical judgment about how much the person needs treatment as well as how likely the person is to continue in treatment and respond favorably. When differential treatment procedures are available, the assessment may be useful in deciding which procedures are likely to be most effective. When the decision has been made before the assessment that a person will receive a particular treatment procedure, the assessment still can be helpful in providing information about problem areas to be considered in treatment and alerting the therapist (or others involved in treatment) to assets and liabilities that could facilitate or hinder progress in therapy. The MMPI-2 can provide information relevant to many of these aspects of treatment. Butcher (1990b) and Finn (1996, 2007) have provided interesting descriptions of how the MMPI-2 can be useful in relation to treatment. Results of a meta-analysis reported by Poston and Hanson (2010) indicated that psychological assessment as a treatment intervention produces positive outcomes and enhances the treatment process.

Many of the inferences generated from well-defined code types and scores on individual scales have direct relevance to treatment considerations. Of special importance is the pattern of scores on the Validity scales. A defensive pattern (L, K, and S scores considerably higher than scores on the F-family of scales) suggests that the examinee is not willing to talk about problems or symptoms and is not likely to be very receptive to therapeutic intervention. By contrast, an examinee whose scores on the F-family of scales are considerably higher than those on L, K, and S is admitting to problems, symptoms, and emotional distress. This person is likely to be motivated to begin treatment and talk about problems.

MMPI-2 indicators of personal distress and emotional turmoil are relevant to treatment planning. Generally, persons in more distress are more receptive to therapeutic intervention and may be willing to tolerate the effort and discomfort of therapy in order to feel better. Primary indicators of distress include Clinical Scales 2 and 7; RC scales RCd, RC2, and RC7; Content Scales DEP, ANX, and Fears (FRS), and Welsh's A.

Well-defined code types and high scores on individual scales can provide additional information relevant to treatment, and those inferences would have been recorded earlier in the interpretive process as each of these sources was considered. For example, high Scale 4 scorers typically are not accepting responsibility for any of their difficulties, may agree to treatment only to avoid more unpleasant circumstances, and tend to terminate treatment prematurely. On the other hand, persons with the 27/72 code type are agreeable to treatment because of their emotional distress, tend to remain in treatment longer than most patients, and can be expected to show slow but steady progress in treatment. These are just a few of the treatment-related inferences stemming from examination of code types and individual scales.

Several of the MMPI-2 scales were developed specifically to provide information about treatment. The Es Supplementary scale was designed to predict response to psychotherapy. In dealing with individuals who are admitting problems and voluntarily seeking treatment, higher Es scores indicate a more favorable response to individual psychotherapy. With other kinds of persons or treatment procedures, the relationship between Es scores and treatment outcome is less clear; but in general, higher Es scores can be interpreted as suggestive of greater psychological resources that can be used in treatment. However, it should be noted that persons who approach the MMPI-2 in a defensive manner tend to have relatively high Es scores that are not indicative of a positive prognosis for treatment. Also, persons who are exaggerating problems and symptoms tend to have very low Es scores, which do not necessarily indicate a negative prognosis.

The Negative Treatment Indicators (TRT) Content scale was designed to assess attitudes that would indicate a negative response to treatment. Higher scorers on the TRT scale may be unwilling or unable to change their life situations, pessimistic about the possibility of positive change, uncomfortable discussing problems with others, and rigid and noncompliant in therapy. A limitation of the TRT scale is that its scores are strongly related to maladjustment in general and depression and demoralization in particular. Therefore, persons who are depressed, demoralized, or generally maladjusted may have elevated TRT scores that do not necessarily reflect negative attitudes about treatment.

Many of the inferences about treatment will not come directly from scores on specific MMPI-2 scales or configurations of scales. Rather, they are higher-order inferences based on other inferences that already have been made about the examinee. For example, if it has been inferred from the MMPI-2 that an examinee is in a great deal of emotional turmoil, it can further be inferred that this person is likely to be motivated enough to change in psychotherapy. On the other hand, if it has been inferred that a person is very reluctant to accept responsibility for their own behavior and blames others for problems and shortcomings, the prognosis for traditional psychotherapy is very poor. A person who has been described on the basis of MMPI-2 scores as very suggestible is apt to respond more favorably to direct advice than to insight-oriented therapy. A person described as antisocial who enters therapy rather than going to jail may terminate therapy prematurely. Obviously, there are many other examples of higher-order inferences related to treatment.

Specific Referral Questions

The interpretive strategy just described is intended to help the clinician generate as many meaningful inferences as possible about test takers' MMPI-2s. It should be recognized that the MMPI-2 sometimes is administered as part of an evaluation intended to address specific questions or issues. For example, a court-ordered evaluation may ask about competency to stand trial, a police department may want recommendations about which applicants to hire, or another psychologist may want an opinion about the suicide risk of a client. Unless these specific questions or issues are dealt with directly, it is unlikely that the MMPI-2 interpretation will be regarded as useful. Sometimes the MMPI-2 data are directly relevant to the issue of concern. For example, scores on the substance misuse scales (e.g., MacAndrew Alcoholism Scale - Revised [MAC-R] and Addiction Admission Scale [AAS]) permit inferences about alcohol or other drug problems. At other times, conclusions about issues of concern are dependent on clinical integration of many different kinds of MMPI-2 data and higher-order inferences.

Integrating MMPI-2 Results into the Assessment

Once interpretation of the MMPI-2 is complete, inferences about the test taker based on the MMPI-2 should be integrated into the other information obtained during the assessment. This process begins by comparing inferences made about the test taker based on the MMPI-2 to those derived from other sources of information, including interview data. Ideally, the clinician will see MMPI-2 results converge with data from other sources. However, this is not always the case. Inferences derived solely from MMPI-2 results should be given less weight than those that are consistently derived from multiple sources of information. Additionally, discrepancies in inferences derived from the MMPI-2 and other sources of information should be recorded. The clinician should consider possible explanations for inconsistent or diverging results and include a summary of their reasoning about these issues in their report. Additional details about the process of integrating assessment information using an empirically guided procedure are available in Suhr (2015).

Computerized Interpretation

In addition to electronic administration and scoring services, the test distributor, Pearson Assessments, offers computerized interpretive reports for use in a variety of settings (e.g., mental health, medical, forensic, personnel). Each report includes scores and profiles for a large number of MMPI-2 scales as well as narrative statements believed to characterize persons producing those scores. It is important to understand that the statements in the reports represent the inferences of skilled and knowledgeable clinicians and vary in the extent to which they are based on empirical research. The reports may be useful as part of a more comprehensive assessment.

Automated interpretation of the MMPI-2 is not as simple and straightforward as electronic administration and scoring. Interpretive statements are written for various MMPI-2 scores and patterns of scores by the expert(s) who developed the interpretation program. Once a scored protocol is entered into the interpretive program, the software finds all the interpretive statements previously identified as appropriate for the specific scores and patterns of scores present in the scored protocol. These statements are then presented to the user.

There are guidelines for the use of computer-based tests and computer-generated test interpretations, such as those reflected in the Ethical Guidelines (American Psychological Association, 2017) and Guidelines for Psychological Assessment and Evaluation (American Psychological Association & APA Task Force on Psychological Assessment and Evaluation Guidelines, 2020) produced by the American

Psychological Association and in the Standards for Educational and Psychological Testing developed jointly by the American Educational Research Association, the American Psychological Association, and the National Council on Measurement in Education (American Educational Research Association, American Psychological Association, & National Council on Measurement in Education, 2014). Generally, these guidelines state that it is the responsibility of test developers of computerized reports to demonstrate the equivalence of computerized and conventional versions of a test. Developers offering interpretations of test scores should describe how the interpretive statements are derived from the original scores and should make clear the extent to which interpretive statements are based on quantitative research versus clinical opinion. When statements in an interpretive report are based on expert clinical opinion, users should be given information that will allow them to weigh the credibility of the opinion. Developers are expected to provide whatever information is needed to qualified professionals engaged in scholarly review of their interpretive services.

These guidelines also make it very clear that professionals are responsible for any use they make of computer-administered tests or computer-generated interpretations (American Educational Research Association, American Psychological Association, & National Council on Measurement in Education, 2014; American Psychological Association, 2017, American Psychological Association & APA Task Force on Psychological Assessment and Evaluation Guidelines, 2020). Users should be aware of the method employed in generating the scores and interpretations and be sufficiently familiar with the test to be able to evaluate its applicability to the purpose for which it will be used. The user should judge, for each test taker, the validity of the computerized test report based on the user's professional knowledge of the total context of testing and the test-taker's performance and characteristics. Clearly, the developers of computerized testing services and the clinicians who use them share responsibility for ensuring that the results are valid and are used appropriately.

AN ILLUSTRATIVE CASE

To illustrate the strategy just discussed, an actual case (Jeff) will now be considered, and a step-by-step analysis of the MMPI-2 protocol will be presented. As a practice exercise, readers can interpret Jeff's scores and then compare their interpretations with the ones presented in this section. All of Jeff's scores can be found in the Extended Score Report that is an appendix to this chapter.

Background Information

Jeff is a 24-year-old White man. He has never been married and lives with his older sister and her family. He graduated from high school with somewhat below-average grades. He did not get into trouble in school. He did not participate in sports or other school activities, and he did not have any close friends. He has never had a serious romantic relationship. Since completing high school, he has had several jobs in fast-food restaurants and service stations; and he currently is unemployed.

The MMPI-2 was administered to Jeff when he requested services at a local community mental health center. He was cooperative and completed the MMPI-2 in about 90 minutes. Jeff had not previously been involved with mental health services. He was referred to the mental health center by emergency room staff at a local hospital. Apparently, during a period of excessive drinking, he took a large number of aspirin. He was treated at the emergency room and released. Jeff admitted that he had been feeling increasingly upset and depressed lately. His sister had encouraged him to seek professional help, and she came with him for his intake appointment.

Test–Taking Attitude

Jeff completed the MMPI-2 in about an average amount of time for a mental health outpatient, indicating that he was neither excessively indecisive nor impulsive in responding to the items. He omitted no items, suggesting that he was cooperative and did not use this rather simple way of avoiding unfavorable self-statements (CNS = 0). The VRIN T score of 46 does not suggest random responding. The TRIN T score of 50 is not suggestive of all-true or all-false responding. As non-content-based invalid responding is not an issue, the next step is to determine whether there are any indications of over- or underreporting.

Consideration of overreporting begins with the F scale. Although Jeff's T score of 55 is slightly above the average in comparison to the normative sample, this score is unremarkable for people seeking outpatient mental health services. His F scale score is not high enough to suggest overreporting response set or any other approach to the test that would invalidate the protocol. His T score of 71 on F_B suggests that he endorsed items appearing later in the test booklet in the keyed direction more often than individuals in the normative sample; however, the score is not high enough to suggest invalidity. The F_p T score of 41 is below average and does not suggest overreporting; and his FBS T score of 59 suggests somewhat more than an average number of somatic complaints but not enough to suggest noncredible responding.

Next, we consider the possibility of underreporting response styles. Jeff's T score of 48 on the L scale is slightly below average, so we may infer that he was not claiming virtues and other positive characteristics that he does not really have. His S scale T score of 41 also is somewhat below average, indicating that he did not try to present himself as highly virtuous, responsible, and free of psychological problems. Jeff's T score of 41 on the K scale indicates that he was not defensive. In fact, he was somewhat self-critical in responding to the items, an approach that is common among persons seeking mental health services.

In summary, Jeff seems to have approached the MMPI-2 in an honest and open manner, admitting to some symptoms and problem behaviors. There are no indications that he engaged in non-content-based invalid responding; overreporting; or underreporting. Therefore, interpretation of other MMPI-2 scales assessing substantive content can be undertaken.

Adjustment Level

Several MMPI-2 scales are excellent indicators of experienced distress. Elevated scores on Clinical Scale 2 (T = 81), the DEP Content scale (T = 77), and RCd (T = 79) suggest Jeff is feeling depressed and demoralized. Elevated scores on Clinical Scale 7 (T = 77), the ANX Content scale (T = 80), and RC7 (T = 77) indicate he also may be experiencing considerable anxiety and may report difficulties with concentration and attention.

Overall mean elevation on the Clinical scales (excluding Scales 5 and 0) is a simple but meaningful index of the extent to which Jeff is not coping well with the demands of his life situation. Jeff's mean score of 63.8 (indicated as Profile Elevation on the Extended Score Report) suggests that he is coping less well than the average person and is likely to experience impairment in important aspects of functioning. Scores on several other MMPI-2 scales also are related to coping. Jeff's high scores on Welsh's A (T = 81) and RCd (T = 79) indicate that he is not coping very well. His very low score on the Es scale (T = 30) suggests that Jeff has limited psychological resources for coping with the demands of his life situation. A brief review of suicidal ideation and behavior indicators reveals that Jeff endorsed a single item on the DEP4 (Suicidal Ideation) Content Component scale (T = 62). He did not endorse any of the individual items containing explicit suicidal content. In summary, Jeff appears to be experiencing considerable emotional distress and is not coping very effectively. However, he is not currently reporting explicitly suicidal thinking.

Characteristic Traits and Behaviors

At this point in the interpretation, we want to generate as many inferences about Jeff as we possibly can from his MMPI-2 scores. A first step in trying to generate inferences is to determine if Jeff has a well-defined code type and, if he does, generate inferences based on the code type. It is best to start with the most complex code type for which interpretive information is available. Jeff's three highest scores are on Clinical Scales 2, 7, and 6 (in that order). Because there is not a 5-T-score point difference between scores on Scale 6 (his third-highest Clinical scale) and Scale 3 (his fourth-highest Clinical scale), a defined three-point code type does not exist. Thus, no inferences are made on the basis of the configuration of these three highest scales. However, there is a 9-T-score point difference between his scores on Scale 7 (his second-highest Clinical scale) and Scale 6 (his third highest Clinical scale). Thus, Jeff has a defined two-point code type comprised of Scales 2 and 7.

27/72 Code Type

This is a commonly occurring code type among mental health outpatients, and considerable information is available concerning its correlates. The two scales in the code type are quite elevated, and the code type is well defined. Therefore, we are confident that inferences based on the code type are likely to fit him well. Because the scales in the code type are quite elevated, we can make inferences both about symptoms and personality characteristics commonly associated with the code type.

Numerous inferences about Jeff can be made on the basis of the 27/72 code type. He is reporting symptoms of clinical depression that may include weight loss, slow personal tempo, and slowed thought processes. He seems to be extremely pessimistic about the world in general, and more specifically about the likelihood of overcoming his problems; and he tends to brood about his problems much of the time.

Jeff also is reporting symptoms of anxiety. He is likely to feel anxious, nervous, tense, high-strung, and jumpy. He worries excessively and is vulnerable to real and imagined threat. He tends to anticipate problems before they occur and to overreact to minor stress. Vague somatic symptoms and complaints of fatigue, tiredness, and exhaustion may be reported.

Jeff seems to have a strong need for achievement and for recognition of his accomplishments. He has high expectations for himself, and he feels guilty when he falls short of his goals. He tends to be indecisive and to harbor feelings of inadequacy, insecurity, and inferiority. He is likely to blame himself for the problems in his life. He tends to be rigid in his thinking and problem solving, and he is meticulous and perfectionistic in his daily activities. He may be very religious and moralistic.

Jeff tends to be rather docile and passive–dependent in his relationships. In fact, he often finds it difficult to be even appropriately assertive. He has the capacity for forming deep emotional ties; and in times of stress, he may become overly dependent and clingy. He is not aggressive or belligerent, and he tends to elicit nurturance and helping behavior from other people.

Clinical Scales
Next, the Clinical scale scores should be examined to determine what, if any, inferences are appropriate for each of them.

SCALE 1 (T = 57)
This is an average score, so no inferences would be made on the basis of this scale. Scores on the RC1 and the HEA Content scale are consistent with the average score on Scale 1.

SCALE 2 (T = 81)
Consistent with the two-point code type, this high score could suggest symptoms of depression. However, his high score on RCd and an average score on RC2 scale suggest that symptoms of clinical depression are less likely than an overall sense of dysphoria, dissatisfaction, and feelings of emotional turmoil.

SCALE 3 (T = 64)
This is an average score, so no inferences would be made on the basis of this scale.

SCALE 4 (T = 62)
This is an average score, so no inferences would be made on the basis of this scale.

SCALE 5 (T = 48)
This is an average score, so no inferences would be made on the basis of this scale.

SCALE 6 (T = 68)
Although this score represents a significant elevation, the score is not high enough to lead to inferences concerning psychotic symptoms and behavior. Rather, we would expect Jeff to be excessively sensitive and overly responsive to the opinions of others. He feels that he is getting a raw deal from life. He is suspicious and guarded in relationships. He tends to rationalize and blame others for difficulties and may be hostile,

resentful, and argumentative in relationships. He may appear to overemphasize rationality and to be moralistic and rigid in opinions and attitudes. Examination of the Harris–Lingoes subscales for Scale 6 is not helpful because all T scores are between 50 and 60. Observations that Jeff achieved T scores of 39 on the Bizarre Mentation (BIZ) Content scale, 52 on RC8, and 41 on RC6 reinforce the inference that Jeff is not likely to be experiencing psychotic symptoms. These average or be-low-average scores, along with the very high RCd scale score (T = 79), suggest that the high score on Scale 6 is to a large extent the product of Jeff's endorsement of many items in the scale having to do with personal distress.

SCALE 7 (T = 77)
The elevated score on Scale 7 indicates that he may feel overwhelmed by anxiety and fears. He is likely to have a pessimistic attitude about the future.

SCALE 8 (T = 56)
This is an average score, so no inferences would be made based on this scale.

SCALE 9 (T = 45)
This is an average score, so no inferences would be made based on this score.

SCALE 0 (T = 74)
This high score suggests that Jeff is socially introverted, shy, timid, reserved, and retiring. He is not likely to participate in many social activities; and when he does, he probably feels very insecure and uncomfortable. He is especially likely to feel un-comfortable around potential sexual partners. He may feel more comfortable alone or with a few close friends. Jeff lacks self-confidence and is likely to be described by others as cold, distant, and hard to get to know. He is quite troubled by lack of in-volvement with other people. He tends to be overcontrolled and is not likely to display feelings openly. He is submissive and compliant in interpersonal relationships and is overly accepting of authority. He is described as having a slow personal tempo. He also is described as cautious, conventional, and unoriginal in his approach to prob-lems; and he gives up easily when things are not going well. He is somewhat rigid and inflexible in attitudes and opinions, and he may have great difficulty making even minor decisions. He enjoys work and gets pleasure from productive personal achieve-ment. He tends to worry, to be irritable, and to feel anxious. Others describe him as moody, and he may experience episodes of depression characterized by lack of energy and lack of interest in the activities of daily living.

Examination of the Scale 0 subscales sometimes helps clarify the primary reasons for an elevation on Scale 0. Jeff's scores on two of the Scale 0 subscales are high. The T score of 74 on the Si1 (Shyness/Self-Consciousness) subscale indicates that he feels quite shy, embarrassed, and ill at ease around other people. The T score of 68 on the Si3 (Self/Other Alienation) subscale suggests that he has low self-esteem and feels unable to effect changes in his life. The absence of a high score (T = 58) on the Si2 (Social Avoidance) scale may mean that despite his social discomfort, Jeff is not totally avoiding social activities.

Restructured Clinical (RC) Scales

The RC scales of the MMPI-2 are more narrowly focused than their Clinical counterparts. These scales can provide important information about Jeff's symptoms. Additionally, as done above when making inferences based on Clinical Scale scores, differential patterns of elevation in the Clinical and RC scales can be helpful in narrowing the description of Jeff's symptoms, problems, and behaviors. Jeff has three RC scale scores equal to or greater than 65. We would next generate inferences based on each of these high RC scale scores.

DEMORALIZATION—RCD (T = 79)

This high score suggests that Jeff is reporting a great deal of overall emotional discomfort. He feels discouraged, generally demoralized, insecure, and pessimistic. He has a poor self-concept, expecting to fail in various aspects of his life. He feels helpless, overwhelmed, and incapable of coping with his current circumstances.

SOMATIC COMPLAINTS—RC1 (T = 48)

Because this is an average score, no inferences would be made on the basis of this scale.

LOW POSITIVE EMOTIONS—RC2 (T = 60)

Because this is an average score, no inferences would be made on the basis of this scale.

CYNICISM—RC3 (T = 41)

Because this is an average score, no inferences would be made on the basis of this scale.

ANTISOCIAL BEHAVIOR—RC4 (T = 68)

The moderately high score on this scale suggests that Jeff may find it difficult to conform to societal norms and expectations and may engage in some antisocial acts. He may be viewed by others as being antagonistic, angry, and argumentative. A history of conflictual family relationships and poor achievements is likely, and substance misuse should be considered.

IDEAS OF PERSECUTION—RC6 (T = 41)

Because this is an average score, no inferences would be made on the basis of this scale.

DYSFUNCTIONAL NEGATIVE EMOTIONS—RC7 (T = 77)

The high score on this scale suggests that Jeff is likely to have many negative emotional experiences, including anxiety, irritability, and other forms of aversive reactivity. He tends to ruminate and worry excessively, is sensitive to criticism, and feels guilty and insecure. He tends to be preoccupied about self-perceived failures. He may experience intrusive, unwanted ideation.

ABERRANT EXPERIENCES—RC8 (T = 52)

Because this is an average score, no inferences would be made on the basis of this scale.

HYPOMANIC ACTIVATION—RC9 (T = 47)

Because this is an average score, no inferences would be made on the basis of this scale.

Content Scales

The Content scales of the MMPI-2 are much more homogeneous than the Clinical scales and can be helpful in understanding Jeff's symptoms, problems, and behaviors. Jeff has eight Content scale scores equal to or greater than 65. We would next generate inferences based on each of these high Content scale scores.

ANXIETY—ANX (T = 80)

The very high score on this scale suggests that Jeff is feeling anxious, nervous, worried, and apprehensive. He may have problems concentrating, his sleep may be disturbed, and he may be uncomfortable making decisions. He also may report feeling that life is a strain and that he is pessimistic about things getting better. He lacks self-confidence and feels overwhelmed by the responsibilities of daily life.

FEARS—FRS (T = 57)

Because this is an average score, no inferences would be made based on this scale.

OBSESSIVENESS—OBS (T = 77)

The high score on this scale suggests that Jeff frets, worries, and ruminates about trivial things. He may engage in compulsive behaviors such as counting or hoarding. He has difficulty making decisions. He is rigid and dislikes change. He lacks self-confidence, lacks interest in things, and may feel dysphoric and despondent.

DEPRESSION—DEP (T = 77)

The high score on this scale indicates that Jeff is experiencing symptoms of depression. He feels sad, blue, and despondent; and he may cry easily. He feels fatigued and lacks interest in things. He feels pessimistic and hopeless. He may recently have been preoccupied with thoughts of death and suicide. He lacks self-confidence and often feels guilty. He feels lonely and empty much of the time. He may be expressing health concerns. Jeff had T scores greater than 65 for four of the five DEP Content Component scales. However, because differences between these four scales are not at least 10 T-score points, they are of little help in helping to focus our interpretation of the DEP scale score. It should be noted that Jeff endorsed only one item in the Suicidal Ideation (DEP4) content component scale, and that item did not have to do directly with suicide.

HEALTH CONCERNS—HEA (T = 51)

Because this is an average score, no inferences would be made based on this scale.

BIZARRE MENTATION—BIZ (T = 39)

Because this is a below average score, we would not expect Jeff to be experiencing psychotic symptoms.

ANGER—ANG (T = 70)

The high score on this scale suggests that Jeff feels angry and hostile much of the time. He may feel like swearing or smashing things and may at times have angry outbursts during which he is quite verbally aggressive. Others see him as irritable, grouchy, impatient, and stubborn. Although there is not a difference of 10 T-score points between the two ANG Content Component scales, we would note that the Explosive Behavior (ANG1) scale was eight points lower than the Irritability (ANG2) scale, suggesting that Jeff is not likely to act out angry feelings very readily.

CYNICISM—CYN (T = 41)

Because this is an average score, no inferences would be made based on this scale.

ANTISOCIAL PRACTICES—ASP (T = 47)

Because this is an average score, no inferences would be made based on this scale.

TYPE A PERSONALITY—TPA (T = 53)

Because this is an average score, no inferences would be made based on this scale.

LOW SELF-ESTEEM—LSE (T = 72)

Based on the high score on this scale, we would expect Jeff to have a very poor self-concept. He anticipates failure and gives up easily. He is overly sensitive to criticism and rejection. He is likely to be passive in relationships, and it may be difficult for him to accept compliments from others. He worries and frets a great deal, and he has difficulty making decisions. Because the Submissiveness (LSE2) Content Component scale is significantly more elevated than the Self-Doubt (LSE1) scale, greater emphasis would be placed on inferences having to do with passivity and submissiveness.

SOCIAL DISCOMFORT—SOD (T = 68)

The high score on this scale suggests that Jeff is shy and socially introverted. He would rather be alone than around other people. It is difficult for him to initiate conversations, and he dislikes parties and other group activities. Because the two SOD Content Component scale scores are not at least 10 points different from each other, these scores are not helpful in focusing the interpretation of the SOD scale.

FAMILY PROBLEMS—FAM (T = 44)

Because this is an average score, no inferences would be made based on this scale.

WORK INTERFERENCE—WRK (T = 81)

Jeff may be reporting some negative attitudes and characteristics that are likely to lead to poor work performance. He may have rather negative perceptions of coworkers. He may not be very confident about his career or vocational choices and feels that his family does not approve of his choices. However, because Jeff appears to be demoralized, we would be quite tentative in making such inferences.

NEGATIVE TREATMENT INDICATORS—TRT (T = 66)

The marginally elevated score of 66 on the TRT scale suggests that Jeff may have some characteristics that are likely to interfere with psychological treatment. Because the Low Motivation (TRT1) Content Component scale is 11 T-score points higher than the Inability to Disclose (TRT2) Content Component scale, the interpretation would focus more on the lack of motivation to change in treatment than on inability to disclose personal information in treatment. However, because other scores indicate that he is likely to be demoralized, inferences about treatment based on the TRT scale would be rather tentative.

Supplementary Scales

Jeff's scores on some of the Supplementary scales can be used to generate additional inferences about him.

ANXIETY—A (T = 81)

The very high score on this scale suggests that Jeff is likely to be experiencing considerable emotional turmoil, including anxiety and depression. In addition, he is not likely to be coping very well with the demands of his life situation.

REPRESSION—R (T = 65)

Because this score is only moderately high, not much emphasis should be placed on it in the interpretation of Jeff's MMPI-2. However, a score at this level indicates that Jeff tends to be passive in relationships. He may be described by others as slow, painstaking, unexcitable, and clear-thinking. He tends to be conventional and formal in his attitudes.

EGO STRENGTH—ES (T = 30)

Low scores on this scale tend to be associated with poor adjustment and limited psychological resources. In addition, Jeff is presenting himself as overwhelmed by and unable to respond to the demands of his life situation.

DOMINANCE—DO (T = 30)

The very low score on this scale suggests that Jeff is not very strong in face-to-face situations and is lacking in self-confidence.

RESPONSIBILITY—RE (T = 39)

This relatively low score likely reflects Jeff's lack of self-confidence and social discomfort.

COLLEGE MALADJUSTMENT—MT (T = 81)

Because Jeff is not a college student, this scale would not be interpreted.

POSTTRAUMATIC STRESS DISORDER SCALE—PK (T = 75)

The PK scale is useful only when we know that we are dealing with persons who have been exposed to traumatic stressors (such as combat experiences or sexual assault). Because we have no information suggesting that Jeff has been exposed to such stressors, we would make no inferences about him based on this scale. His high score likely is reflecting the emotional distress that has been inferred from other scales.

MARITAL DISTRESS—MDS (T = 51)

Because Jeff is not married, this scale would not be interpreted.

HOSTILITY—HO (T = 48)

Because this is an average score, no inferences would be made based on this scale.

OVERCONTROLLED-HOSTILITY—O-H (T = 35)

Because low scores on this scale are not interpreted, no inferences would be made.

MACANDREW ALCOHOLISM SCALE-REVISED—MAC-R (RAW SCORE = 23)

This is a borderline score on the MAC-R screening measure of alcohol and drug problems. The score is not high enough to permit us to have confidence in inferences about Jeff's use or misuse of substances.

ADDICTION ADMISSION SCALE—AAS (T = 70)

The high score on this scale indicates that in responding to the MMPI-2 items, Jeff acknowledged substance-related problems and behaviors associated with the use of substances. Additional information should be obtained from other sources included in the assessment about his patterns of substance use and misuse.

ADDICTION POTENTIAL SCALE—APS (T = 76)

Because of the conflicting research concerning the relationship between this scale and substance-related problems, no inferences would be made based on this scale.

MASCULINE GENDER ROLE-GM (T = 32) AND FEMININE GENDER ROLE-GF (T = 50)

There is not enough research to support making inferences based on these scales.

Personality Psychopathology Five (PSY-5) Scales

The PSY-5 scales can provide important information about Jeff's symptoms but also key personality traits related to maladaptive personality patterns. Jeff has two scale scores equal to or greater than 65 and one scale score equal to or less than 40. We would next generate inferences based on each of these PSY-5 scale scores.

AGGRESSIVENESS—AGGR (T = 33)

The low score on this scale suggests that Jeff is passive, submissive, and not very aggressive in interactions with other people.

PSYCHOTICISM—PSYC (T = 49)
Because this is an average score, no inferences would be made on the basis of this scale.

DISCONSTRAINT—DISC (T = 54)
Because this is an average score, no inferences would be made on the basis of this scale.

NEGATIVE EMOTIONALITY/NEUROTICISM—NEGE (T = 78)
The very high score on this scale suggests that Jeff has a predisposition toward negative affect, meaning he is likely to experience higher levels of negative emotions than other people. This disposition is likely to lead Jeff to focus on problematic features of incoming information, to worry, to be self-critical, to feel guilty, and to concoct worst-case scenarios. He is likely to experience anxiety, depression, and sad mood.

INTROVERSION/LOW POSITIVE EMOTIONALITY—INTR (T = 68)
The moderately high score on this scale suggests that Jeff has limited capacity to experience joy and positive engagement. He tends to be socially introverted and has a low need to achieve. His symptoms are likely to include depression, anxiety, and somatic complaints.

Resolving Inconsistent Inferences
A review of the inferences that were generated concerning Jeff's characteristic traits and behaviors indicates a striking consistency among them. However, several of the inferences appear to be somewhat inconsistent. It may be helpful to discuss how these apparent inconsistencies would be handled.

One of the inferences based on the 27/72 code type was that Jeff may express vague somatic concerns. However, average scores on other more specific indicators of somatic symptoms (Scales 1, RC1, HEA) suggest that somatic symptoms would not be a primary part of Jeff's presenting complaints.

Jeff's T score of 70 on the ANG Content scale led to inferences that he is angry and hostile much of the time, that he may have angry outbursts during which he is verbally aggressive, and that others may describe him as irritable and grouchy. Examination of the ANG Content Component scales is not particularly helpful because the two scales do not differ from each other by at least 10 T-score points. However, we would note that the ANG1 scale was eight points lower than the ANG2 scale. This difference is in the direction that would lead us to infer that Jeff is not very likely to express anger openly and directly. Review of Jeff's critical-item endorsements indicates that he admitted to feeling like smashing things and having a strong urge to do something harmful or shocking. He is often said to be hotheaded and easily angered. Based on all this information, we would conclude that Jeff probably harbors a great deal of anger and resentment that does not usually get expressed openly. However, he may occasionally vent the angry feelings in verbal outbursts.

On the basis of the 27/72 code type and the high score on Scale 0, it was inferred that Jeff has a strong need for achievement and is likely to enjoy work and get pleasure from productive personal achievement. A high score on the WRK Content scale led to the inference that Jeff lacks ambition and energy and may have attitudes and behaviors that would interfere with job performance. Because inferences based on code types are likely to be more accurate than those based on individual scales, and because there has been much more empirical research concerning the 27/72 code type and Scale 0 than concerning the WRK Content scale, we would have greater confidence in the inferences that Jeff has a strong need to achieve and is likely to enjoy work. We would also consider that the WRK scale often is high for persons like Jeff who are experiencing a great deal of emotional distress, regardless of their work performance. Background information about Jeff suggests that he has had a number of low-level jobs and that at least some were lost because of problems with supervisors. Thus, although we cannot resolve these somewhat inconsistent inferences, it appears that this would be an important area to explore in future assessment sessions or during therapy.

The 27/72 code type suggests that Jeff tends to be self-blaming, but the high score on Scale 6 led to an inference that he tends to blame others. Again, because we tend to have more confidence in inferences based on code types than those based on individual scales, we would probably describe Jeff as self-blaming. That the Scale 6 score was only moderately high (T = 68) also suggests that we should have more confidence in the inference that he is self-blaming. In addition, we know from Jeff's RCd scale score that his elevated Scale 6 score is likely to be due, in large part, to great personal distress.

The T score of 68 on the RC4 scale led to inferences of antisocial characteristics that can include difficulty conforming to societal norms, legal difficulties, and behaving aggressively toward others. However, Jeff's T scores of 62 on Scale 4 and 47 on the ASP Content scale are not consistent with these antisocial characteristics. There is no simple way to resolve these apparent inconsistencies. However, based on our analyses of these scales and the ANG elevation (above), we would expect that if Jeff has some problems with social conformity and acceptance of authority, he is not likely to act out in illegal ways.

Finally, Jeff's high scores on Scale 2, RCd, and the DEP Content scale would lead to concerns about suicidal ideation and perhaps intent. Because this obviously is a very serious issue, it should be mentioned in the interpretation. However, we would also want to note that examination of Jeff's critical-item endorsement indicates that he did not endorse any of the items dealing directly with suicidal ideation or behavior. Finally, we would need to flag this information as potentially discrepant from the background information we obtained—namely, that Jeff sought treatment after being treated by emergency room staff for ingesting a large number of aspirin while drinking alcohol excessively, suggesting a possible history of suicidal behavior. This potential discrepancy across sources would need to be considered during the integration of information gathered from the entire assessment process and suggests explicit exploration of Jeff's suicidality is indicated in future assessment or therapy sessions.

Integration of Inferences
Having dealt with apparent inconsistencies in inferences about Jeff, the next step would be to examine all the inferences concerning characteristic traits and behaviors

and to organize them into meaningful categories. Earlier in this chapter a list of possible categories was suggested.

SYMPTOMS

There is clear agreement from many aspects of the MMPI-2 protocol that Jeff is experiencing a great deal of emotional turmoil. He lacks energy and has lost interest in things going on around him. Life seems to be a strain for him, and he is pessimistic about things ever getting better for him. At times he may feel that life is not worthwhile; but in responding to the MMPI-2 items, he did not endorse the items dealing directly with suicidal ideation or behavior. Nonetheless, given the potential lethal consequences of mistaking Jeff's risk for suicide, additional information about his experience of suicidal thinking and behavior from sources other than the MMPI-2 is needed. This information could be gathered in additional assessment sessions or in initial stages of treatment and should aim to resolve the potential discrepancy in his report on the MMPI-2 about suicidal thinking and behavior and the reasons he sought treatment (i.e., ingesting sufficient amounts of alcohol and aspirin such that medical treatment was needed).

Jeff also appears to feel anxious, tense, and nervous. He is high-strung, jumpy, agitated, and apprehensive. He worries excessively and is vulnerable to real and imagined threat. He may have a sense of dread that something bad is going to happen to him. He is likely to be experiencing difficulties in concentrating and attending. His thinking may be obsessive and his behavior compulsive. He is likely to be quite indecisive, even about very trivial matters. Perceived lack of control over thoughts and emotions may cause him to fear that he is losing his mind. Jeff may report vague somatic concerns, but these are not likely to be central to his presenting complaints.

Jeff's high score on AAS indicates that he is openly admitting to misuse of alcohol or other drugs and may experience problems associated with this misuse. Clearly, additional information about substance use is needed, and this should be further explored in future assessment sessions or during therapy.

MAJOR NEEDS

Many of the inferences generated from Jeff's MMPI-2 scores suggest that he has very strong unfulfilled dependency needs. He is likely to be passive–dependent in relationships, and he worries about not being popular and socially accepted. Jeff seems to harbor above-average levels of anger and resentment. Most of the time he does not express these negative feelings directly. However, occasional verbal outbursts of anger may occur. Jeff also seems to have rather strong abasement needs. He often evaluates himself negatively and compares himself unfavorably with others. Jeff seems to have strong needs to achieve and to receive recognition for his accomplishments, but insecurity and fear of failure keep him from placing himself in many directly competitive situations.

PERCEPTIONS OF THE ENVIRONMENT

Jeff sees the world as a demanding place and feels incapable of responding to the demands of his daily life. He has a sense of dread that bad things are going to happen to him. He seems to feel that his needs are not met by others and that he is getting a raw deal from life. He views others with caution or even suspicion because he fears they will reject him.

REACTIONS TO STRESS

Jeff's MMPI-2 scores suggest that he feels poorly equipped to deal with stress. He is vulnerable to real and imagined threat, tends to anticipate problems before they occur, and often overreacts to minor stress. During times of increased stress, he may develop somatic symptoms and become increasingly clingy and dependent. Although he prefers to use denial and repression as defenses, these mechanisms do not seem to be working well for him now. As a result, he is overwhelmed with emotional turmoil. At times, Jeff may respond to stress by withdrawing into fantasy and daydreaming, and at other times he may seek escape from stress through the use of alcohol or other drugs.

Jeff appears to be a responsible, conscientious person. He is likely to be neat, organized, and persistent in his approach to problems. However, he is also likely to be quite cautious, conventional, and rigid. He is rather indecisive about most things in his life. He is a rather poor problem solver and often may show poor judgment. He tends to give up easily when faced with increasing stress.

SELF-CONCEPT

Jeff's MMPI-2 scores indicate that he has an extremely negative self-concept. He is plagued by feelings of inadequacy, insecurity, and inferiority. He is quite self-critical and often compares himself unfavorably with other people. He has high expectations for himself and feels guilty when he falls short of his goals. He blames himself for the problems in his life and feels hopeless and unable to effect life changes.

EMOTIONAL CONTROL

Jeff is likely to be emotionally overcontrolled much of the time. He tends to deny his impulses and is not likely to display feelings openly. He tends to emphasize rational rather than emotional aspects of situations. Although he is not likely to express anger and resentment openly most of the time, during occasional outbursts, these feelings may get expressed verbally. He is so emotionally uncomfortable at this time that he may cry easily.

INTERPERSONAL RELATIONSHIPS

Jeff is a shy, socially introverted person. Although he has the capacity to form deep emotional ties and very much wants to be involved with others, his poor self-concept causes him to feel quite uncomfortable in social situations. He is likely to avoid large gatherings and may feel most comfortable when with a few close friends. He is troubled by his limited interactions with other people, and he feels lonely much of the time. In relationships, Jeff is likely to be passive, submissive, and compliant. He is very unassertive and likely to make concessions to avoid confrontations.

Other people's perceptions of Jeff are quite variable. Sometimes he is seen as sentimental, peaceable, and soft-hearted; and he elicits nurturance and helping behavior from others. At other times, he is seen as moody, irritable, dull, and moralistic. His shyness may be misinterpreted by others as indicating that he is aloof, cold, and distant.

Jeff has ambivalent feelings about other people. He is drawn to them because they represent sources of gratification for his strong dependency needs. However, he also has negative perceptions of other people. He seems to view them as not being very understanding and supportive. He is quite sensitive to criticism, and his feelings are easily hurt. At times he can be rather blunt and harsh in social interactions. Jeff may have some negative attitudes about coworkers that are likely to interfere with productive work.

PSYCHOLOGICAL RESOURCES

Because the MMPI-2 scales tend to emphasize psychopathology and negative characteristics and because Jeff has many high scores on the scales, most of the inferences generated tend to be negative. However, a review of the inferences previously generated reveals a few that could be viewed as psychological resources. Although he often feels like a failure, Jeff has strong needs to receive recognition for his accomplishments. He is neat, meticulous, persistent, and reliable. He has the capacity for forming deep emotional ties. Others sometimes see him in positive ways (e.g., sensitive, kind, soft-hearted, and peaceable) and react to him in nurturant and helping ways.

Diagnostic Impressions

As was discussed earlier in this chapter, it is not possible to assign psychiatric diagnoses solely on the basis of psychological test data. The criteria for most diagnoses include information that cannot be obtained from psychological test data. However, we can make statements concerning the diagnoses that are most consistent with Jeff's MMPI-2 results.

The MMPI-2 data suggest that a diagnosis of generalized anxiety disorder should be considered. The 27/72 code type and high scores on Clinical scale 7, the RCd and RC7 scales, and the ANX Content scales supports this diagnosis. The 27/72 code type and a high score on the OBS Content scale indicate that a diagnosis of obsessive–compulsive disorder should be considered. The very high score on the AAS is consistent with substance use disorders, and more information about substance use should be obtained. The descriptions of symptoms and personality characteristics that were generated about Jeff are consistent with diagnoses of dependent and obsessive–compulsive personality disorders. There were also several indications of a depressive or dysthymic disorder in Jeff's profile. This includes high scores on Clinical Scale 2 and the DEP Content scale. However, given his high elevation on RCd and Welsh's A and lack of elevation on RC2, we can hypothesize these scores are more likely to reflect dysphoric affect than they are symptoms of clinical depression. As such, we would not likely consider including a depressive disorder in the diagnostic possibilities we outline in our interpretation.

Implications for Treatment

Many indicators in Jeff's MMPI-2 data suggest that he is in a great deal of emotional turmoil and is not likely to be meeting the responsibilities of daily life in an effective manner. Because of his intense distress, he is likely to be motivated for psychotherapy.

The 27/72 code type indicates that Jeff is likely to remain in treatment longer than most patients and can be expected to show slow positive change during treatment. However, there are indications of characteristics that are likely to interfere with effective therapy. He may not have the energy to participate effectively in traditional psychotherapy. His very low score on Es suggests that he has limited psychological resources that can be utilized in treatment. Based on the high score on Scale 7, we would expect that he will rationalize and intellectualize a great deal in therapy. He probably would be resistant to psychological interpretations and could come to express significant hostility toward a therapist. He seems to believe that he is helpless to change major aspects of his life. His rigidity and tendency to give up easily in stressful situations could also be liabilities in treatment.

As stated earlier, Jeff's scores on the substance use scales of the MMPI-2 indicate that he may have problems with alcohol or other drugs. If corroborating information supports the inferences concerning problematic substance use, a treatment plan should include a component intended to address these difficulties. Furthermore, the potentially discrepant information gathered in the background information and on the MMPI-2 about Jeff's experience of suicidal thinking and behavior should be explored. If this additional information suggests Jeff experiences these types of difficulties, treatment plans should likely include regular monitoring of his risk for suicide and interventions intended to lower this risk.

Summary

The preceding analysis of this single case is lengthy in its presentation because it is meant as a teaching–learning tool for the beginning MMPI-2 user. The experienced user would write a much briefer interpretation of the protocol. Specifically, the following is what we might write about Jeff in a clinic chart, to the referring source, or for his own psychotherapy notes.

The MMPI-2 protocol produced by Jeff appears to be valid. He likely paid attention to the content of the items and was not overly defensive in responding to the MMPI-2. He admitted to some attitudes and behaviors that are not typically endorsed by other people, but these admissions are seen as an accurate reporting of problems.

Jeff appears to be experiencing significant psychological problems. He is reporting a great deal of emotional distress. He feels overwhelmed and unable to respond to the demands of daily life. He is pessimistic about the future and at times may feel that life is not worthwhile. Jeff may report vague somatic symptoms and difficulties in concentrating and attending. His thinking may be obsessive and his behavior compulsive.

Jeff sees the world as a demanding place and feels that his needs are not being met by other people. Although he typically engages in denial and repression, these defenses do not seem to be working very well for him at this time.

Jeff has an extremely negative self-concept. He is plagued by feelings of inadequacy, insecurity, and inferiority. At times he may blame himself for the problems in his life, but at other times he tends to rationalize and blame others.

Although Jeff may be harboring feelings of anger and resentment, he typically does not express these feelings openly. However, he may have brief verbal outbursts of anger where he expresses his negative feelings toward others quite strongly.

Jeff is shy, timid, and socially introverted. Although he seems to want to be involved with other people and has the capacity to form deep emotional ties, he tends to withdraw from many social interactions in order to protect himself from the criticism and rejection that he has come to expect. In relationships, he is likely to be passive, submissive, and unassertive. He can be expected to make concessions to avoid unpleasant confrontations. He seems to have negative perceptions of other people, seeing them as neither understanding nor supportive of him.

Jeff's MMPI-2 data are consistent with diagnoses of generalized anxiety disorder and obsessive–compulsive disorder. His symptoms and personality characteristics are also consistent with diagnoses of dependent and obsessive–compulsive personality disorders. Additional information should be gathered about his use of alcohol and other substances to rule out the possibility of a substance use disorder. Additionally, though a possible suicide attempt led to his seeking treatment, he is not reporting suicidal ideation or behavior at this time. Additional information should be gathered to resolve this potential discrepancy.

Jeff is not coping very well with the demands of his life situation and would likely benefit from psychological treatment. Because of his intense psychological discomfort, he is likely to be receptive to psychotherapy. If his distress is so severe that it interferes with his ability to participate meaningfully in psychotherapy, a medical referral to evaluate the appropriateness of psychotropic medications should be considered. Although he is not likely to respond well to brief psychotherapy, he probably will stay in treatment longer than many patients and may show slow but steady progress. If corroborating information indicates that he has a problematic pattern of alcohol or other drug use, a component addressing these difficulties should be included in his treatment plan. Risk management for suicidal ideation and behavior may also be warranted if additional information suggests the events that led to his treatment in the emergency room, which precipitated his seeking treatment, were suicidal behaviors.

ADDITIONAL PRACTICE CASES

MMPI-2 data are presented for additional cases in the online supplementary materials for this text available at the Oxford University Press' website. These cases can be used to practice the various aspects of MMPI-2 interpretation and feedback that are described in this chapter. Please visit www.oup.com/he/graham6e to access these materials.

GIVING MMPI-2 FEEDBACK

Although most persons who take the MMPI-2 are interested in their test performance and many expect to receive feedback about their test results, often such feedback is not given or is not given in a comprehensive and systematic way. In addition to client expectations, there are other important reasons for routinely giving feedback about MMPI-2 results (Butcher, 1990b; S. E. Finn, 1996; Pope, 1992). In many circumstances clients have legal rights to information about their test results. Also, according to the Ethical Principles of Psychologists (American Psychological Association, 2017), psychologists have the professional responsibility to provide clients with information about test results in a manner that can be easily understood.

Giving feedback about MMPI-2 results to clients can be clinically beneficial. If handled well by clinicians, feedback can be a vehicle for establishing good rapport with clients. Feedback also can be helpful to clients in understanding why treatment is being recommended, suggesting possible problem areas to be explored in treatment, and identifying resources that can be utilized in treatment. In fact, some preliminary data suggest that receiving assessment feedback is associated with a significant decline in symptomatic distress and a significant increase in self-esteem (S. E. Finn & Tonsager, 1992; Newman & Greenway, 1997; Poston & Hanson, 2010). S. E. Finn (1996) developed detailed procedures for using MMPI-2 results as a therapeutic intervention. When the MMPI-2 is repeated during treatment, discussion of changes in results can help the client and therapist assess treatment progress and define additional treatment goals.

Valid and interpretable test results are more likely to be obtained if, prior to test administration, the examiner explains why the MMPI-2 is being administered, who will have access to the test results, and why it is in the client's best interest to cooperate with the testing. At this time, the examiner can also explain that the client will be given feedback about test results and will have an opportunity to ask general questions about the test and specific questions about test results. Clients often ask for a written report of test results and interpretations. In most cases, it is not a good idea to provide such a report because the clinician cannot be sure that the client will understand everything in the report. Instead, indicate that you will be willing to meet with the client after the testing has been completed, discuss the results, and give the client an opportunity to ask questions and make comments.

General Guidelines

1. Communicate in a manner that is easily understood by the client. Some clients will be able to understand rather complex and technical explanations, whereas others will require greatly simplified explanations.
2. Use vocabulary that the client can understand. Avoid psychological jargon. If you use psychological terms, take the time to explain exactly what they mean. Invite clients to ask you to explain terms they do not understand or find confusing.
3. Present both positive and negative aspects of the client's personality and functioning. Finding positive things to say may be rather difficult in the case of certain clients, but it is usually possible to do so. Clients are much more likely to accept interpretations if you maintain a balance between positive and negative characteristics.
4. Avoid terms such as "abnormal," "deviant," or "pathological." It is helpful to explain that most symptoms and negative characteristics are shared by most people but perhaps are not possessed by individuals to the same extent as by a particular client.
5. Do not overwhelm the client with a long list of adjectives. Instead, limit your interpretations to a few of the most important things you want the client to hear and understand, and explain each as fully as possible to ensure that the client understands what you are trying to communicate.

6. Encourage clients to make comments and ask questions about what you have said. This often provides additional information about clients and makes them feel that they are a part of the process.

7. Do not argue with clients or otherwise try to convince them that your interpretations are correct. This will increase their defensiveness and can jeopardize your future role as therapist or counselor.

8. When the discussion of the test results has been completed, ask the client to summarize the major points that have been covered. This will increase the likelihood that the client will remember what has been discussed and will give you an opportunity to clarify any misunderstandings the client might have about what was discussed.

General Explanation of the MMPI-2

To increase the likelihood that the client will have confidence in your interpretations and take the feedback seriously, you should indicate that the MMPI has been used by psychologists for more than 75 years, that there have been thousands of research studies concerning what MMPI scores mean, and that the test was revised and updated in 1989. You could also point out that the test is one of the most widely used psychological test in the world.

Before giving specific feedback about a client's MMPI-2 results, you should spend some time explaining in general how the test was developed and how it is interpreted. You may want to illustrate your explanation by referring to an MMPI-2 profile. It is a good idea not to use the client's own profile at this time. Clients may be so anxious about their own scores that it will be difficult for them to attend to what you are saying.

Scale Development

Typically, it is not very difficult to explain to clients how the MMPI-2 scales were developed. For most people, the empirical construction of the basic scales is easy to understand and makes sense. Understanding these procedures increases the client's confidence in the test and in your interpretations.

You should explain that the MMPI-2 is made up of a large number of statements to which true or false responses are given. The basic MMPI-2 scales were developed by comparing the item responses of a group of patients having specific kinds of problems (e.g., anxiety and depression) with the responses of persons who were not having any serious psychological problems. You should avoid mentioning that the groups were defined according to psychiatric diagnoses. If a client persists in asking what the scale abbreviations (e.g., Sc) stand for, you should give honest answers but emphasize that these labels are not important in the way that the MMPI-2 is used today. You should then point out that the client's responses were scored for each of these scales. It is helpful to show the client a profile sheet (not their own yet) and point out that each number at the top and bottom of the sheet corresponds to one of these original scales.

The Content scales of the MMPI-2 represent direct communication between the client and the clinician. High scores on any of these scales indicate that the client wants you to know about certain symptoms, problems, and characteristics. Because you may want to present scores on some of the Content scales to support inferences about a client, you should mention how these scales were developed. It probably will be sufficient to indicate that each of these scales is made up of items in the test with similar content. For example, the items in the ANX Content scale all have to do with various aspects of anxiety.

Norms

You should then indicate that the client's score on each of these scales is compared with scores of a large group of persons living in communities throughout the United States. Avoid referring to "normals" or "norms" because clients who have scores different from this group may label themselves as "abnormal." You can again refer to a profile sheet, indicating that most people obtain scores near the lower heavy black line on the profile sheet. If clients ask about the meaning of the numbers along the left or right sides of the profile (T scores), you should explain in very simple terms what they mean. Otherwise, it probably is best not to deal directly with the T scores. You can also point out that because scores above the upper heavy black line (T > 65) are rare, we tend to emphasize them in our interpretations. These high scores indicate the likelihood of problems similar to those of persons involved in the original development of the scales (e.g., anxiety and depression). Because the meaning of low scores is not very clear at this time, you can simply indicate that scores below the lower heavy black line (T = 50) indicate that the client is not likely to have problems similar to those of people involved in the development of these scales.

Validity Scales

You should emphasize that we can gain useful information about clients from their MMPI-2 results only if they have followed the test instructions (i.e., read each item and responded honestly as the item applies to them). Indicate that there are special MMPI-2 scales to help us determine if the instructions have been followed. Mention that these scales tell us if a person left too many items unanswered (CNS), responded to the items without really reading them (VRIN and TRIN), was defensive and denying (L, K, and S scales), or exaggerated problems and symptoms (F, F_B, F_P, FBS). You should spend more time explaining the Validity scales if the client's scores suggest that the results may be invalid or of questionable validity.

Sources of Interpretive Statements

After you are confident that the client understands how the scales were developed and what is meant by high scores, you should explain how interpretive inferences are made on the basis of these scores. Emphasize that the inferences are based on extensive study of persons who have obtained high scores on the various scales. For example, when we have studied persons who have had high scores on Scale 2, we have found that they reported feeling more depressed than persons scoring lower on Scale 2. You can also mention that such studies have been done concerning persons who obtain high scores on several of the scales at the same time (e.g., 2 and 7). In interpreting a specific client's scores, we infer that the client will have problems and characteristics similar to persons we have studied who have had similar scores. Clients often ask about the meaning of specific MMPI-2 items. You should acknowledge that their responses to such items are important because they represent something that the clients want us to know but that we tend to emphasize scale scores rather than individual item responses in our interpretations.

Organizing the Feedback

Once you are confident that the client has a basic understanding of how the MMPI-2 was developed and how it is interpreted, you are ready to present feedback about their specific results. There is no correct or incorrect way of organizing your feedback. However, you may find it helpful to organize it by using some of the categories described earlier in this chapter: (a) test-taking attitudes, (b) overall adjustment level, (c) characteristic traits and behaviors (e.g., symptoms, needs, self-concept, interpersonal relationships, psychological resources), and (d) treatment implications. Because diagnoses should only be assigned based on the totality of information collected in an assessment, we do not recommend addressing the category of inferences reflecting potential diagnoses in a feedback session.

Illustration

Assuming that a general explanation of the MMPI-2 has been given, we can illustrate the specific feedback that we might give to Jeff, the person whose MMPI-2 was interpreted previously. You will remember that Jeff is a 24-year-old man who took the MMPI-2 at a mental health center where he had been referred after emergency treatment following ingestion of a large number of aspirin.

After explaining how the MMPI-2 was developed and how it is interpreted generally, you could begin by pointing out to Jeff that he was very cooperative in completing the MMPI-2. He omitted no items, and his scores on the Validity scales suggest that he carefully read each item and responded to it honestly and thoughtfully as it applied to him. Therefore, you have confidence that his scores on the other scales will give an accurate picture of what he is like.

Next, you should indicate that he seems to be in a great deal of emotional turmoil. His high scores on several scales (Scale 2, RCd, DEP) indicate that he is likely to be dissatisfied with his current life situation; and his high scores on Scales 7, RC7, and ANX indicate that he is likely to feel anxious, tense, and nervous much of the time. You could add that he seems to be lacking in self-confidence (high scores on Scales 2 and 7 and on the LSE Content scale). High scores on Scale 0 and on the SOD Content scale suggest that he is shy, introverted, and uncomfortable around people that he does not know well.

You could point out that several scores suggest that he feels overwhelmed with the demands of his everyday life situation. The most important source of this inference is the very low score on the Es scale. You could explain that this means he feels he just does not know how to cope with everything that is happening in his life at this time. This may be an appropriate time to discuss potential discrepancies in information about suicidal behavior. You could ask Jeff to help you understand why he did not endorse any items related to experiencing suicidal thinking or behavior on the MMPI-2 when he sought treatment after being seen at the emergency room for ingesting a large number of aspirin. If he describes the past behavior as being related to suicidal intent, you could suggest incorporating suicide risk-management into treatment planning. If he denies the past behavior was intended to end his life, then a conversation regarding the motivation for those behaviors and how to prevent them in the future is likely warranted.

You probably then would want to point out that in his responses to items on AAS suggest he admitted to substance-related problems. You could speculate that he might ng alcohol or other drugs as a way of trying to handle some of the discomfort he is feeling. These concerns suggest additional substance use assessment is indicated. As such, this might be a good time to gather additional information from Jeff about his use of substances, likely using a motivational perspective. If he readily identifies his use as problematic, then you could encourage him to consider whether he would benefit from including treatment goals intended to address these types of difficulties or being involved with other programs designed to help individuals deal with substance use problems.

You could indicate that the high score on Scale 6 could mean that he sees the world as a rather demanding place and feels that he gets a raw deal from life. He may be somewhat suspicious and skeptical of the motives of other people. His high score on the ANG Content scale suggests that he is resentful of this perceived mistreatment.

Based on the inferences that have been made about psychological turmoil and feeling overwhelmed by the demands of everyday life, you might indicate that he probably is feeling the need for some professional psychological help. You could emphasize that when people are in so much turmoil, they generally are willing to get involved in treatment and often show positive changes as a result of treatment. However, you would probably want to add that the moderately high score on the TRT Content scale suggests that he may feel unable to bring about changes in his own life.

At this point, having described many of Jeff's problem areas and negative characteristics, you should balance the feedback by mentioning some positive aspects of his MMPI-2 results. You could point out that his high scores on Scales 2 and 7 indicate that he is likely to be a persistent, conscientious, and reliable person. These high scores, coupled with his high score on Scale 0, indicate that he has a strong need to achieve, probably enjoys work, and gets pleasure from productive personal achievement. You may also want to discuss that others often view him as having many positive qualities, such as being sensitive and kind, and provide reassurance that he can create and maintain meaningful relationships with others due to his capacity for forming deep emotional ties.

The reader will note that many of the inferences made about Jeff earlier in this chapter have not been addressed in the feedback session. In keeping with the recommendation made earlier in this section, feedback should be limited to a few of the most important things that you want to communicate to Jeff. Although you should have encouraged Jeff's questions and reactions throughout the feedback session, near the end of the session, you should ask very directly if he has any questions or comments about the feedback or any aspect of his MMPI-2 results. You would end the feedback session by having Jeff summarize what had been discussed, which would give you the opportunity to determine if he had misunderstood or misinterpreted some aspects of the feedback. If he had, you should carefully restate your interpretations and again ask Jeff to repeat what he heard.

If you were going to be Jeff's therapist or counselor, you might want to mention that you and he probably will discuss the MMPI-2 results again at various times during treatment. If you plan to readminister the MMPI-2 during treatment, you should mention this possibility to him and indicate that it will give you and him an opportunity to examine possible changes as treatment progresses.

CHAPTER APPENDIX

MMPI®-2

Minnesota Multiphasic Personality Inventory®-2

Extended Score Report

Name:	Jeff
ID Number:	
Age:	24
Gender:	Male
Date Assessed:	09/02/1998

ALWAYS LEARNING   PEARSON

MMPI-2 VALIDITY AND CLINICAL SCALES PROFILE

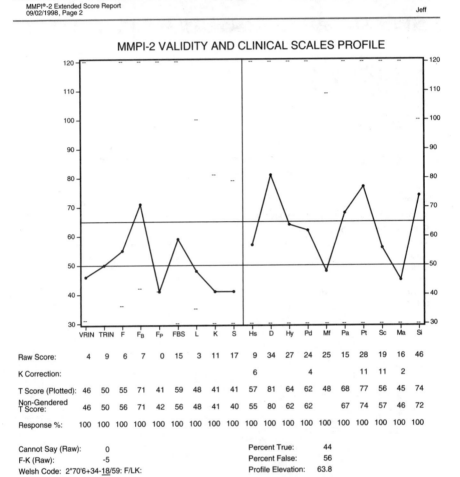

	VRIN	TRIN	F	F_B	F_p	FBS	L	K	S	Hs	D	Hy	Pd	Mf	Pa	Pt	Sc	Ma	Si
Raw Score:	4	9	6	7	0	15	3	11	17	9	34	27	24	25	15	28	19	16	46
K Correction:										6			4			11	11	2	
T Score (Plotted):	46	50	55	71	41	59	48	41	41	57	81	64	62	48	68	77	56	45	74
Non-Gendered T Score:	46	50	56	71	42	56	48	41	40	55	80	62	62		67	74	57	46	72
Response %:	100	100	100	100	100	100	100	100	100	100	100	100	100	100	100	100	100	100	100

Cannot Say (Raw): 0
F-K (Raw): -5
Welsh Code: 2"70'6+34-18/59: F/LK:

Percent True: 44
Percent False: 56
Profile Elevation: 63.8

The highest and lowest T scores possible on each scale are indicated by a "--".

For information on FBS, see Ben-Porath, Y. S., & Tellegen, A. (2006). The FBS: Current Status, a report on the Pearson web site (www.pearsonassessments.com/tests/mmpi_2.htm).

MMPI®-2 Extended Score Report
09/02/1998, Page 3

Jeff

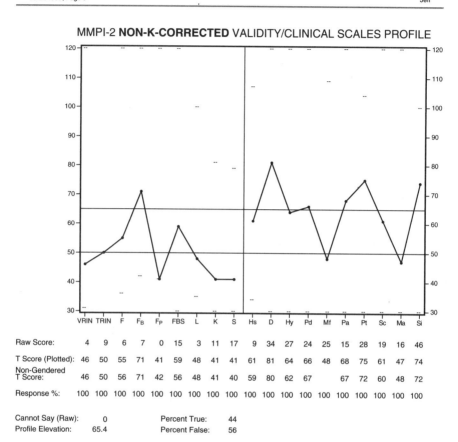

MMPI-2 **NON-K-CORRECTED** VALIDITY/CLINICAL SCALES PROFILE

	VRIN	TRIN	F	F$_B$	F$_P$	FBS	L	K	S	Hs	D	Hy	Pd	Mf	Pa	Pt	Sc	Ma	Si
Raw Score:	4	9	6	7	0	15	3	11	17	9	34	27	24	25	15	28	19	16	46
T Score (Plotted):	46	50	55	71	41	59	48	41	41	61	81	64	66	48	68	75	61	47	74
Non-Gendered T Score:	46	50	56	71	42	56	48	41	40	59	80	62	67		67	72	60	48	72
Response %:	100	100	100	100	100	100	100	100	100	100	100	100	100	100	100	100	100	100	100

Cannot Say (Raw):   0   Percent True: 44
Profile Elevation: 65.4   Percent False: 56

The highest and lowest T scores possible on each scale are indicated by a "--".

Non-K-corrected T scores allow interpreters to examine the relative contributions of the Clinical Scale raw score and the K correction to K-corrected Clinical Scale T scores. Because all other MMPI-2 scores that aid in the interpretation of the Clinical Scales (the Harris-Lingoes subscales, Restructured Clinical Scales, Content and Content Component Scales, PSY-5 Scales, and Supplementary Scales) are not K-corrected, they can be compared most directly with non-K-corrected T scores.

For information on FBS, see Ben-Porath, Y. S., & Tellegen, A. (2006). The FBS: Current Status, a report on the Pearson web site (www.pearsonassessments.com/tests/mmpi_2.htm).

MMPI®-2 Extended Score Report
09/02/1998, Page 4   Jeff

MMPI-2 RESTRUCTURED CLINICAL SCALES PROFILE

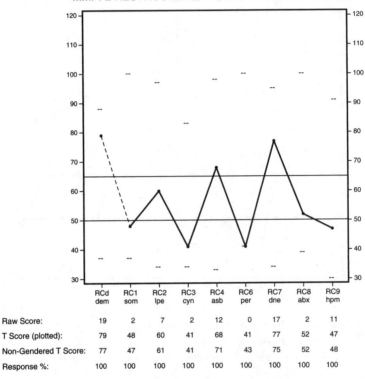

	RCd dem	RC1 som	RC2 lpe	RC3 cyn	RC4 asb	RC6 per	RC7 dne	RC8 abx	RC9 hpm
Raw Score:	19	2	7	2	12	0	17	2	11
T Score (plotted):	79	48	60	41	68	41	77	52	47
Non-Gendered T Score:	77	47	61	41	71	43	75	52	48
Response %:	100	100	100	100	100	100	100	100	100

The highest and lowest T scores possible on each scale are indicated by a "--".

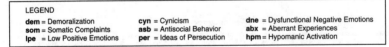

LEGEND

dem = Demoralization   **cyn** = Cynicism   **dne** = Dysfunctional Negative Emotions
som = Somatic Complaints   **asb** = Antisocial Behavior   **abx** = Aberrant Experiences
lpe = Low Positive Emotions   **per** = Ideas of Persecution   **hpm** = Hypomanic Activation

For information on the RC scales, see Tellegen, A., Ben-Porath, Y.S., McNulty, J.L., Arbisi, P.A., Graham, J.R., &
Kaemmer, B. 2003. The MMPI-2 Restructured Clinical (RC) Scales: Development, Validation, and Interpretation.
Minneapolis: University of Minnesota Press.

MMPI-2 CONTENT SCALES PROFILE

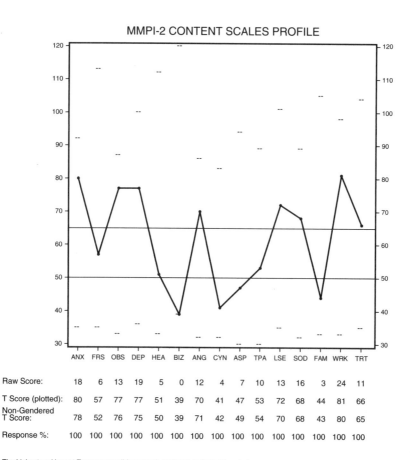

	ANX	FRS	OBS	DEP	HEA	BIZ	ANG	CYN	ASP	TPA	LSE	SOD	FAM	WRK	TRT
Raw Score:	18	6	13	19	5	0	12	4	7	10	13	16	3	24	11
T Score (plotted):	80	57	77	77	51	39	70	41	47	53	72	68	44	81	66
Non-Gendered T Score:	78	52	76	75	50	39	71	42	49	54	70	68	43	80	65
Response %:	100	100	100	100	100	100	100	100	100	100	100	100	100	100	100

The highest and lowest T scores possible on each scale are indicated by a "--".

MMPI®-2 Extended Score Report
09/02/1998, Page 6

Jeff

MMPI-2 SUPPLEMENTARY SCALES PROFILE

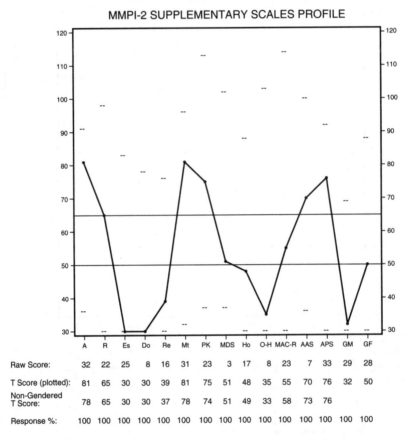

	A	R	Es	Do	Re	Mt	PK	MDS	Ho	O-H	MAC-R	AAS	APS	GM	GF
Raw Score:	32	22	25	8	16	31	23	3	17	8	23	7	33	29	28
T Score (plotted):	81	65	30	30	39	81	75	51	48	35	55	70	76	32	50
Non-Gendered T Score:	78	65	30	30	37	78	74	51	49	33	58	73	76		
Response %:	100	100	100	100	100	100	100	100	100	100	100	100	100	100	100

The highest and lowest T scores possible on each scale are indicated by a "--".

MMPI®-2 Extended Score Report
09/02/1998, Page 7

Jeff

MMPI-2 PSY-5 SCALES PROFILE

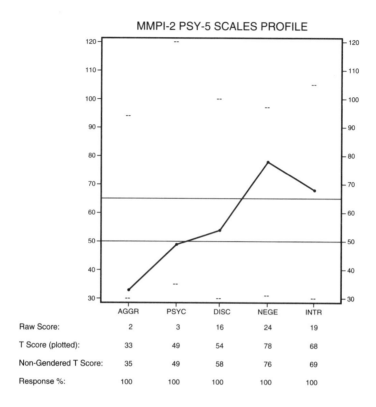

	AGGR	PSYC	DISC	NEGE	INTR
Raw Score:	2	3	16	24	19
T Score (plotted):	33	49	54	78	68
Non-Gendered T Score:	35	49	58	76	69
Response %:	100	100	100	100	100

The highest and lowest T scores possible on each scale are indicated by a "--".

ADDITIONAL SCALES
(to be used as an aid in interpreting the parent scales)

	Raw Score	T Score	Non-Gendered T Score	Resp %
Harris-Lingoes Subscales				
Depression Subscales				
Subjective Depression (D_1)	20	85	82	100
Psychomotor Retardation (D_2)	8	65	64	100
Physical Malfunctioning (D_3)	6	75	73	100
Mental Dullness (D_4)	8	77	76	100
Brooding (D_5)	5	68	65	100
Hysteria Subscales				
Denial of Social Anxiety (Hy_1)	0	30	30	100
Need for Affection (Hy_2)	8	55	55	100
Lassitude-Malaise (Hy_3)	13	97	94	100
Somatic Complaints (Hy_4)	2	48	46	100
Inhibition of Aggression (Hy_5)	2	40	39	100
Psychopathic Deviate Subscales				
Familial Discord (Pd_1)	2	51	51	100
Authority Problems (Pd_2)	5	60	64	100
Social Imperturbability (Pd_3)	0	30	30	100
Social Alienation (Pd_4)	5	56	55	100
Self-Alienation (Pd_5)	10	82	82	100
Paranoia Subscales				
Persecutory Ideas (Pa_1)	3	58	58	100
Poignancy (Pa_2)	3	55	54	100
Naivete (Pa_3)	6	56	55	100
Schizophrenia Subscales				
Social Alienation (Sc_1)	4	55	54	100
Emotional Alienation (Sc_2)	4	78	78	100
Lack of Ego Mastery, Cognitive (Sc_3)	3	60	61	100
Lack of Ego Mastery, Conative (Sc_4)	10	92	92	100
Lack of Ego Mastery, Defective Inhibition (Sc_5)	3	61	60	100
Bizarre Sensory Experiences (Sc_6)	2	51	50	100
Hypomania Subscales				
Amorality (Ma_1)	1	42	44	100
Psychomotor Acceleration (Ma_2)	8	63	64	100
Imperturbability (Ma_3)	0	30	30	100
Ego Inflation (Ma_4)	3	50	50	100
Social Introversion Subscales				
Shyness/Self-Consciousness (Si_1)	13	74	72	100
Social Avoidance (Si_2)	5	58	59	100
Alienation--Self and Others (Si_3)	11	68	67	100

MMPI®-2 Extended Score Report
09/02/1998, Page 9   Jeff

Content Component Scales	Raw Score	Non-Gendered		Resp %
		T Score	T Score	
Fears Subscales				
Generalized Fearfulness (FRS$_1$)	2	62	58	100
Multiple Fears (FRS$_2$)	4	54	50	100
Depression Subscales				
Lack of Drive (DEP$_1$)	7	79	77	100
Dysphoria (DEP$_2$)	4	74	69	100
Self-Depreciation (DEP$_3$)	6	83	84	100
Suicidal Ideation (DEP$_4$)	1	62	62	100
Health Concerns Subscales				
Gastrointestinal Symptoms (HEA$_1$)	0	44	44	100
Neurological Symptoms (HEA$_2$)	0	40	40	100
General Health Concerns (HEA$_3$)	4	72	72	100
Bizarre Mentation Subscales				
Psychotic Symptomatology (BIZ$_1$)	0	44	44	100
Schizotypal Characteristics (BIZ$_2$)	0	41	41	100
Anger Subscales				
Explosive Behavior (ANG$_1$)	4	64	67	100
Irritability (ANG$_2$)	7	72	71	100
Cynicism Subscales				
Misanthropic Beliefs (CYN$_1$)	1	36	37	100
Interpersonal Suspiciousness (CYN$_2$)	3	48	49	100
Antisocial Practices Subscales				
Antisocial Attitudes (ASP$_1$)	4	43	45	100
Antisocial Behavior (ASP$_2$)	3	59	64	100
Type A Subscales				
Impatience (TPA$_1$)	6	68	70	100
Competitive Drive (TPA$_2$)	3	50	51	100
Low Self-Esteem Subscales				
Self-Doubt (LSE$_1$)	5	64	64	100
Submissiveness (LSE$_2$)	6	83	79	100
Social Discomfort Subscales				
Introversion (SOD$_1$)	10	65	67	100
Shyness (SOD$_2$)	6	68	67	100
Family Problems Subscales				
Family Discord (FAM$_1$)	2	45	44	100
Familial Alienation (FAM$_2$)	1	49	50	100

	Raw Score	Non-Gendered T Score	T Score	Resp %
		T Score		
Negative Treatment Indicators Subscales				
Low Motivation (TRT$_1$)	5	71	69	100
Inability to Disclose (TRT$_2$)	3	60	61	100

Uniform T scores are used for Hs, D, Hy, Pd, Pa, Pt, Sc, Ma, the content scales, the content component scales, and the PSY-5 scales. The remaining scales and subscales use linear T scores.

NOTE:** The final pages of this report display any items that were skipped or unscorable as well as any endorsed items that are part of a critical responses or critical items list. These sections include both the item number and content. The final page of the report includes the test taker's item level responses to every test item. These pages are not displayed in this book in order to maintain test security; however, redacted sample reports are available on the Pearson Assessments' website.

CHAPTER 12

MMPI-2 RESTRUCTURED FORM (MMPI-2-RF)

THE MMPI-2-RF WAS PUBLISHED in 2008 and represented a substantial change to the instrument from previous versions of the MMPI. This is because the core scales comprising the MMPI-2-RF are the Restructured Clinical (RC) scales, not the original Clinical scales. As described in Chapter 7 of this book, Tellegen et al. (2003) developed the RC scales for two reasons. First, they aimed to remove a common demoralization element from the original Clinical scales. Second, they intended to construct scales that would assess the core clinical construct of each Clinical scale without also measuring demoralization. As noted in Chapter 7, research examining the RC scales suggests they have concurrent validity as good as or better than corresponding Clinical scales and better discriminant validity than the corresponding Clinical scales. Nonetheless, Ben-Porath and Tellegen (2008/2011) recognized that the RC scales did not measure all the important characteristics that could be assessed by MMPI-2 item pool. As such, after the RC scales were constructed, they began work on developing other scales that would reflect the substantive content of the MMPI-2 item pool in a psychometrically sound manner. The product of these efforts is the MMPI-2-RF.

The MMPI-2-RF's authors (Ben-Porath & Tellegen, 2008/2011) state that the MMPI-2-RF "is a revised, 338-item version of the MMPI-2 designed to provide an exhaustive and efficient assessment of clinically relevant variables measurable with the instrument's item pool" (p. 1). The MMPI-2-RF has 51 scales. The nine RC scales of the MMPI-2 are augmented by seven revised Validity scales, two new Validity scales, three new Higher-Order (H-O) scales, 23 new Specific Problems (SP) scales, two new Interest scales, and revised versions of the Personality Psychopathology Five (PSY-5) scales. Table 12.1 lists all 51 of the MMPI-2-RF scales.

TABLE 12.1 *MMPI-2-RF Scales*

Validity Scales	
VRIN-r	Variable Response Inconsistency
TRIN-r	True Response Inconsistency
F-r	Infrequent Responses
Fp-r	Infrequent Psychopathology Responses
Fs	Infrequent Somatic Responses
FBS-r	Symptom Validity
RBS	Response Bias Scale
L-r	Uncommon Virtues
K-r	Adjustment Validity
Higher-Order (H-O) Scales	
EID	Emotional/Internalizing Dysfunction
THD	Thought Dysfunction
BXD	Behavioral/Externalizing Dysfunction
Restructured Clinical (RC) Scales	
RCd	Demoralization
RC1	Somatic Complaints
RC2	Low Positive Emotions
RC3	Cynicism
RC4	Antisocial Behavior
RC6	Ideas of Persecution
RC7	Dysfunctional Negative Emotions
RC8	Aberrant Experiences
RC9	Hypomanic Activation
Specific Problems (SP) Scales	
Somatic/Cognitive Scales	
MLS	Malaise
GIC	Gastrointestinal Complaints
HPC	Head Pain Complaints
NUC	Neurological Complaints
COG	Cognitive Complaints
Internalizing Scales	
SUI	Suicidal/Death Ideation
HLP	Helplessness/Hopelessness
SFD	Self-Doubt
NFC	Inefficacy

	STW	Stress/Worry
	AXY	Anxiety
	ANP	Anger Proneness
	BRF	Behavior-Restricting Fears
	MSF	Multiple Specific Fears
Externalizing Scales		
	JCP	Juvenile Conduct Problems
	SUB	Substance Abuse
	AGG	Aggression
	ACT	Activation
Interpersonal Scales		
	FML	Family Problems
	IPP	Interpersonal Passivity
	SAV	Social Avoidance
	SHY	Shyness
	DSF	Disaffiliativeness
Interest Scales		
AES		Aesthetic–Literary Interests
MEC		Mechanical–Physical Interests
Personality Psychopathology Five (PSY-5) Scales		
AGGR-r		Aggressiveness–Revised
PSYC-r		Psychoticism–Revised
DISC-r		Disconstraint–Revised
NEGE-r		Negative Emotionality/Neuroticism–Revised
INTR-r		Introversion/Low Positive Emotionality–Revised

Note. Excerpted (Table 1.1) from *MMPI-2-RF Manual for Administration, Scoring, and Interpretation* by Yossef S. Ben-Porath and Auke Tellegen. Copyright © 2008, 2011 by the Regents of the University of Minnesota. Reproduced by permission of the University of Minnesota Press. All rights reserved. "Minnesota Multiphasic Personality Inventory-2-Restructured Form®" and "MMPI-2-RF®" are registered trademarks of the Regents of the University of Minnesota.

DEVELOPMENT OF THE MMPI-2-RF SCALES

Validity Scales

The MMPI-2-RF has nine Validity scales. Seven of these scales are revised versions of MMPI-2 Validity scales. Two—Infrequent Somatic Responses (Fs) and the Response Bias Scale (RBS)—are new Validity scales. As with the MMPI-2, the Cannot Say (CNS) index is also used as an indicator of response invalidity. All these indices were scored on the MMPI-2-RF when it was released in 2008 except RBS, which was added to the standard scoring of the MMPI-2-RF in 2011. Raw scores for these scales are converted to linear T scores (M = 50, SD = 10) based on responses of the MMPI-2-RF normative sample. The only exception is CNS, which is scored by simply counting the number of unanswered items and items answered both true and false.

Variable Response Inconsistency (VRIN-r) and True Response Inconsistency (TRIN-r) Scales

These scales were constructed using procedures very similar to those used in constructing the Variable Response Inconsistency (VRIN) and True Response Inconsistency (TRIN) scales of the MMPI-2 (see Chapter 3). However, some additional criteria were added to achieve greater independence of the two inconsistency measures.

The VRIN-r scale consists of 53 positively correlated item pairs. When scoring this scale, a point is assigned whenever a test taker responds to two items within a pair in an inconsistent manner. For example, if someone responds "true" when asked if they wake up fresh and rested most mornings, and then they respond "false" when asked if they generally sleep well, then one point would be assigned on the VRIN-r scale. The VRIN-r raw score is simply the number of inconsistencies identified in responses to the pairs of items. Raw scores are converted to linear T scores. Higher scores indicate a greater degree of inconsistent responding. Interpretive guidelines for the VRIN-r scale are presented later in this chapter.

The TRIN-r scale consists of 26 pairs of negatively correlated items for which either two true or two false answers to a pair of items indicate inconsistent responding. The TRIN-r raw score is the number of true–true responses to the item pairs minus the number of false–false answers to the item pairs. A higher difference score indicates a tendency to respond in an acquiescent, content-nonresponsive manner (yea-saying), whereas a lower difference score indicates a tendency to respond in a counter-acquiescent, content-nonresponsive manner (naysaying). Difference scores are converted to linear T scores, and T scores lower than 50 are reflected. For example, a T score of 40 is reflected as a T score of 60. Thus, TRIN-r T scores cannot be lower than 50. Higher T scores indicate non-content-based invalid responding of either an acquiescent or counter-acquiescent type, with the former being designated with the letter T and the latter with the letter F in scoring reports. Interpretive guidelines for the TRIN-r scale are presented later in this chapter.

Infrequent Responses (F-r) Scale

The F-r scale is a revised version of the Infrequency (F) scale of the MMPI-2. The F-r scale consists of 32 items that were endorsed in the keyed direction by 10% or fewer of both men and women in the MMPI-2 normative sample. Some items that met this criterion were not included in the F-r scale because they also appeared on other Validity scales assessing content-based invalid responding. Raw scores are converted to linear T scores, with higher scores indicating greater endorsement of items rarely answered in that manner by persons in the normative sample. Interpretive guidelines for the F-r scale are presented later in this chapter.

Infrequent Psychopathology Responses (Fp-r) Scale

Recognizing that persons with serious psychopathology tended to get higher scores on the F scale of the MMPI-2, Arbisi and Ben-Porath (1995) developed the Infrequency-Psychopathology (Fp) scale to identify invalid responding in settings where the base rate of serious psychopathology is high. They chose items for the Fp scale that were endorsed infrequently by persons in both the MMPI-2 normative sample and an inpatient psychiatric sample (see Chapter 3 for details). Subsequent research indicated that the Fp scale was quite effective in identifying persons who overreported when responding to the MMPI-2 items (e.g., Rogers et al., 2003). Thus, Ben-Porath and Tellegen (2008/2011) thought it important to include a revised version of Fp on the MMPI-2-RF.

The Fp-r scale retained 18 of the 27 items from the Fp scale of the MMPI-2 and added three items. Four Fp items that are also in the Lie (L) scale were deleted, as were three items that are included in the Fs scale. Two additional Fp items were dropped because analyses indicated that they did not function as effectively as other items in the scale, and three items not in the original Fp scale were added because they improved the effectiveness of the scale. Raw scores on Fp-r are converted to linear T scores. Higher scores on the resulting 21-item Fp-r scale suggest overreporting of psychopathology. Interpretive recommendations for this scale are presented later in this chapter.

Infrequent Somatic Responses (Fs) Scale

This scale was developed by Wygant et al. (2004) to identify the reporting of uncommon somatic symptoms. The 16 items in the Fs scale were endorsed by 25% or less of men and women in several large samples of medical patients. Ben-Porath and Tellegen (2008/2011) included Fs on the MMPI-2-RF to address the fact that test takers in some settings may be motivated to overreport somatic symptoms when being assessed for psychological reasons (e.g., personal injury evaluations). Raw scores on this scale are converted to linear T scores. Higher scores on Fs indicate a greater likelihood of noncredible reporting of somatic symptoms and complaints. Interpretive guidelines for this scale are presented later in this chapter.

Symptom Validity (FBS-r) Scale

This scale is an abbreviated version of the Symptom Validity Scale (FBS) of the MMPI-2. Ben-Porath and Tellegen (2008/2011) thought it was important to include a revised version of FBS on the MMPI-2-RF because some test takers are motivated to report noncredible somatic and cognitive symptoms (as opposed to psychological symptoms) during an assessment. Of the 43 items in the original FBS scale, 30 were included in FBS-r because they are part of the 338-item, MMPI-2-RF item pool. Raw scores on FBS-r are converted to linear T scores. Higher scores on this scale indicate the likelihood of noncredible reporting of somatic or cognitive difficulties. Interpretive recommendations for the FBS-r scale are presented later in this chapter.

Response Bias Scale (RBS)

Gervais et al. (2007) developed the 28-item RBS to identify persons who are overreporting cognitive symptoms and problems in forensic neuropsychological or disability assessment settings. Items in the scale were identified by comparing responses of persons who failed and passed performance validity tests. Subsequent research indicated scores on RBS were an effective method of identifying noncredible reporting of difficulties with memory (e.g., Gervais et al., 2008; Whitney et al., 2008). Because it appears to assess a unique type of noncredible responding when compared to other MMPI-2-RF Validity scales (Gervais et al., 2008), it was added to the standard scoring of the MMPI-2-RF in 2011 (Ben-Porath & Tellegen, 2008/2011). Raw scores on RBS are converted to linear T scores. Higher scores on the scale suggests overreporting of memory problems. Interpretive guidelines for the RBS are presented later in this chapter.

The Uncommon Virtues (L-r) and Adjustment Validity (K-r) Scales

These scales were developed to identify underreporting on the MMPI-2-RF. To create the underreporting scales, items in the Lie (L), Correction (K), Superlative Self-Presentation (S), and Wiggins Social Desirability (Wsd; an experimental MMPI-2 scale designed to measure of socially desirable responding) scales of the MMPI-2 were factor analyzed. Two distinct factors emerged, and two separate scales were developed by selecting items that loaded substantially on one factor but not on the other factor. The scale reflecting the first factor was labeled Uncommon Virtues (L-r) and consists of 14 items, 11 from the L scale and three from the Wsd scale. The scale reflecting the second factor was labeled Adjustment Validity (K-r), and all of its 14 items are from the K scale. Raw scores on the L-r and K-r scales are converted to linear T scores. Higher scores on these two scales suggest greater likelihood of underreporting of symptoms and problems (K-r) or the claiming of more virtuous behavior (L-r) than the average person. Interpretive guidelines for the L-r and K-r scales are presented later in this chapter.

Higher-Order (H-O) Scales

In creating the MMPI-2-RF Tellegen and Ben-Porath (2008/2011) aimed to develop a set of H-O scales that would capture the major dimensions of psychopathology represented in the MMPI-2-RF item pool and provide an organizational structure for the interpretation of its substantive scales. They created these scales using factor analyses of the RC scales in three clinical samples. These analyses yielded three consistent factors reflecting internalizing, externalizing, and psychosis-related difficulties. Scales were constructed to measure these three dimensions by correlating factor scores from these analyses with the 567 items in the MMPI-2 item pool. Most of the items in the Emotional /Internalizing (EID) scale come from RCd, RC2, and RC7; most of the items in the Thought Dysfunction (THD) scale come from RC6 and RC8; and most of the items in the Behavioral/Externalizing (BXD) scale come from RC4 and RC9. Thus, the H-O scales are analogous to dimensional forms of three commonly occurring MMPI-2 code types (27/72, 68/86, and 49/94). The three H-O scales also align closely with some of the higher-order dimensions identified in contemporary models of psychopathology—like the Hierarchical Taxonomy of Psychopathology (HiTOP; Kotov et al., 2021). Namely, EID aligns closely with HiTOP's Internalizing spectrum, THD aligns closely with the Thought Disorder spectrum, and BXD overlaps conceptually with both the Disinhibited Externalizing and Antagonistic Externalizing spectra (Sellbom, 2019). Interpretive guidelines for the Higher-Order scales are presented later in this chapter.

Restructured Clinical (RC) Scales

The nine RC scales of the MMPI-2-RF are identical to the RC scales of the MMPI-2. The construction and psychometric properties of these scales were discussed in Chapter 7 of this book. Interpretive guidelines for the RC scales were presented in Chapter 7 and are reprinted again later in this chapter.

Specific Problems (SP) Scales

Recognizing that the RC scales do not assess all the important clinical constructs represented in the MMPI-2 item pool, Ben-Porath and Tellegen (2008/2011) developed 23 SP scales. The SP scales were constructed to measure distinctive Clinical scale components not represented by the RC scales, RC scale facets warranting separate assessment, and other clinically significant attributes captured by the MMPI-2 item pool but not assessed by the RC scales.

The exact procedures used to construct each of the SP scales are not reported in Tellegen and Ben-Porath (2008/2011). However, the authors provide an overview of how the scales were constructed. It seems that initially, the authors relied on their own ideas about what additional constructs should be measured. Numerous item factor analyses were conducted to identify constructs and items to assess them. In the construction of each scale, efforts were made to minimize the contribution of demoralization to the scales (see Chapter 7). After a preliminary set of constructs had been identified, experts were asked to suggest additional constructs that could be assessed with the MMPI-2 item pool (beyond the RC scales, the PSY-5 scales, and the preliminary list of SP scales). Based on these suggestions and additional data analyses, a final set of 23 SP scales was established. A list of these scales can be found in Table 12.1. Interpretive guidelines for each of these scales are presented later in this chapter.

Interest Scales

The two Interest scales of the MMPI-2-RF were based on factor analyses of items in Clinical Scale 5 of the MMPI-2, which reflects interests that have been historically associated with stereotypical notions of masculinity and femininity. These analyses identified two relatively independent dimensions for which scales were developed. The first scale is labeled Aesthetic–Literary Interests (AES) and has seven items having to do with interest in writing, music, and theater. The second scale is labeled Mechanical–Physical Interests (MEC) and has nine items having to do with interest in fixing or building things, outdoor activities, and sports. Guidelines for the interpretation of the Interest scales are presented later in this chapter.

Personality Psychopathology Five (PSY–5) Scales

The PSY-5 scales of the MMPI-2-RF are revised versions of the MMPI-2 PSY-5 scales that were described in detail in Chapter 7. Recognizing the importance of assessing dimensions of personality that contribute to personality pathology, Ben-Porath and

Tellegen asked Harkness and McNulty to develop PSY-5 scales for the MMPI-2-RF (Ben-Porath, 2012). As noted in Chapter 7, these scales provide a conceptual link between the MMPI instruments and modern models of personality psychopathology—such as that represented in the DSM's Alternative Model for Personality Disorders (AMPD; American Psychiatric Association, 2013)—and dimensional models of psychopathology such as the HiTOP model (Kotov et al., 2021).

In creating versions of the PSY-5 for the MMPI-2-RF, Harkness and McNulty started with the 96 MMPI-2 PSY-5 items retained in the MMPI-2-RF item pool (Harkness, McNulty, et al., 2014). They then used internal consistency and external criterion information to revise each of the PSY-5 scales. They discarded 22 of the 96 carryover PSY-5 items that did not contribute to scale reliability and validity. They added 30 other items from the MMPI-2-RF item pool that improved scale reliability and validity. Some of these items were selected based on previous research in which lay persons selected MMPI-2 items that were judged to be associated with each PSY-5 scale, while other items were added to scales based on correlations between existing scales and other items in the MMPI-2-RF item pool. These procedures resulted in 104 items assessing the PSY-5 constructs. Additional details regarding the development of the PSY-5 scales for the MMPI-2-RF are reported in Harkness, McNulty, et al. (2014). The MMPI-2-RF PSY-5 scales are listed in Table 12.1, and interpretive guidelines are presented later in this chapter.

ADMINISTRATION AND SCORING

User Qualifications

As with the MMPI-2, the MMPI-2-RF is to be used only by persons with appropriate education and training in the use of clinical assessment instruments. The test distributor, Pearson Assessments, has established minimum qualifications for users of tests of this kind. Their website (pearsonassessments.com) provides details concerning these qualifications. Basically, users are to be adequately trained in the administration and interpretation of clinical assessment instruments. This training can be obtained through completion of degree programs or continuing education workshops.

Who Can Take the MMPI-2-RF?

To produce meaningful MMPI-2-RF results, the test taker must read well enough to understand the items and respond to them appropriately. The average Flesch–Kincaid reading level of all MMPI-2-RF items is 4.5, suggesting slightly less than a fifth-grade reading level is needed to complete the test. However, there are many MMPI-2-RF items that have a higher estimated reading level. As such, even for test takers who have the required reading skill, test users should be prepared to screen scored profiles carefully for indications of possible difficulties with comprehending the items, which can elevate scores on scales like CNS, VRIN-r, and TRIN-r. If the examiner has doubt about the reading ability of a test taker, a standardized test of reading comprehension should be administered. Sometimes persons with lower reading levels can meaningfully complete the MMPI-2-RF if it is administered using a standard audio version available from Pearson Assessments.

The MMPI-2-RF is intended for use with persons who are 18 years of age or older. The MMPI-A (Butcher et al., 1992) or MMPI-A-RF (Archer et al., 2016) should be used with persons who are younger than 18. Because both adolescent and adult versions of the MMPI were normed on 18-year-olds, clinicians must decide for each individual case whether to use an adult or adolescent version of the test with 18-year-olds. Ordinarily, the MMPI-A or MMPI-A-RF would be selected for 18-year-olds who are still in high school; and the MMPI-2, MMPI-2-RF, or MMPI-3 would be selected for 18-year-olds who are in college, working, or otherwise living a more independent lifestyle. The MMPI-2 was discussed in previous chapters and the MMPI-3 is discussed in Chapter 13. Adolescent versions of the MMPI are discussed in Chapters 14 and 15 of this book. There is no upper age limit to who can take the MMPI-2-RF.

The clinical condition of potential examinees is an important consideration in deciding who can take the MMPI-2-RF. Completion of the test is a challenging and tedious task for many individuals. Persons who are very depressed, anxious, or agitated often find the task quite difficult, as do many who have experienced cognitive injuries or decline. It may be desirable to break the testing session into several shorter periods for such individuals. Sometimes persons who are in great distress find it easier to complete the test if the items are presented by means of a standardized audio version available from Pearson Assessments.

Administration

As with the MMPI-2, the MMPI-2-RF should be administered in a professional way. The test is usually administered by means of either a printed booklet or computer software. When the booklet is used, responses are recorded on a separate answer sheet. When computerized administration is used, responses are recorded by pressing designated keys. The Pearson Assessments website (pearsonassessments.com) should be consulted to determine what test materials and software are available. Ben-Porath and Tellegen (2008/2011) indicate that booklet and answer sheet administration typically takes 35–50 minutes, and computer administration typically takes 25–35 minutes. For persons with borderline reading levels or with visual disabilities, a standardized audio version of the test is available. Reading items aloud to test takers is strongly discouraged because the practice deviates from the standardized procedures for test administration. Subtle changes in tone of voice or body language can affect responses. Either a qualified user or someone trained by a qualified user in test administration procedures should administer the test. The test should never be given to someone to take outside of a supervised setting.

Printed and computerized versions of the MMPI-2-RF are available in English, Spanish, and French for Canada through Pearson Assessments. Individuals who are interested in using the MMPI-2-RF in other languages should contact the University of Minnesota Press Test Division (https://www.upress.umn.edu/test-division).

Scoring

If the MMPI-2-RF was administered using the printed booklet and separate answer sheet, several scoring methods are available. Answer sheets can be mailed to Pearson Assessments and score or interpretive reports will be mailed back within 24–48 hours. Hand scoring can be accomplished using scoring templates and profile sheets available from the test distributor. Responses can also be entered by hand and then computer scored using computer software available from the test distributor. High-volume users can score the test efficiently by means of a scanner. If a computerized administration was used, responses are saved, and scoring is accomplished efficiently using the test distributor's software.

There are two primary types of reports available for the MMPI-2-RF offered by Pearson Assessments. First, they offer a *Score Report* that provides scores and profiles for all 51 MMPI-2-RF scales and has the option of providing mean data for various comparison groups (e.g., mental health outpatients, psychiatric inpatients, prisoners, medical conditions, substance abuse). A sample *Score Report* is appended to this chapter—the case (Jeff) was also interpreted in Chapter 11 of this book when the MMPI-2 interpretive strategy was discussed. Second, an *Interpretive Report* is also available. It provides scores and profiles for all 51 scales, as well as a narrative interpretation that identifies the source(s) from which each interpretative statement is derived. Like the Score Report, the Interpretative Report also has the option of reporting mean data for various comparison groups.

PSYCHOMETRIC CHARACTERISTICS

Normative Sample

The normative sample for the MMPI-2-RF is essentially the same as for the MMPI-2. Details concerning the MMPI-2 sample were reported in Chapter 1 of this book. However, only nongendered norms are available for the MMPI-2-RF. The non-gendered sample was created by combining data for all 1,138 men in the MMPI-2 sample and data from 1,138 women selected randomly from the 1,462 women in the MMPI-2 sample (Ben-Porath & Forbey, 2003). Having nongendered norms conforms to the provision in the Civil Rights Act of 1991 that prohibits consideration of sex in employment practices.

When the MMPI-2-RF was developed, the MMPI-2 norms were almost 20 years old. As such, Tellegen and Ben-Porath (2008/2011) compared MMPI-2-RF scores derived from a 1990 college student sample with scores of a similar college student sample tested with the MMPI-2-RF approximately 20 years later. They found that MMPI-2-RF scores generated from the two cohorts were essentially interchangeable, suggesting that it was appropriate to use the 1989 norms for the MMPI-2-RF. Detailed information about the MMPI-2-RF normative sample can be found in Ben-Porath and Tellegen (2008/2011).

Standard Scores

For most MMPI-2 scales, raw scores are converted to Uniform T scores (see Chapter 2). A primary advantage of Uniform T scores is that scores at a particular level have the same percentile meaning across scales. Thus, comparisons between scores on scales are easily made. Similarly, raw scores on most MMPI-2-RF scales are converted to Uniform T scores by means of the same procedures used with the

MMPI-2. Linear T scores are used for the Validity scales and the two Interest scales, however, because distributions of raw scores for these scales are not like those of the other MMPI-2-RF scales.

Reliability

Tables 3.2–3.6 in Tellegen and Ben-Porath (2008/2011) report test–retest coefficients, internal consistency coefficients (alpha), and estimates of standard error of measurement (SEM) for all the MMPI-2-RF scales for normative, mental health inpatient, and mental health outpatient samples. Internal consistency and test–retest estimates for the Validity scales vary across scales and samples, but they generally are much lower than those demonstrated for the substantive scales. This is to be expected because of the limited variability of these scales in samples where test takers are likely to be cooperative and to give credible responses. However, the SEM for each of the Validity scales is small enough to justify the kinds of interpretations discussed later in this chapter.

Test–retest reliability data were based on a combined gender subset (82 men and 111 women) of individuals from the MMPI-2 normative sample who completed the test twice with a median test–retest interval of 7 days. Test–retest reliability coefficients for the H-O scales tended to be in the .80 to .90 range. The lowest value was for the THD scale in the normative sample, where the base rate for this kind of serious psychopathology was very low.

Consistent with data reported in Chapter 7, temporal stability of the RC scales was generally good, ranging from .89 for RC4 to .64 for RC6. Again, the lower value for RC6 is likely due to the low base rate of this kind of serious psychopathology in the normative sample. Test–retest coefficients for the SP and Interest scales ranged from .54 to .93, with most values falling between .70 and .80 in the normative sample. Scales with more items tended to be more stable than scales with fewer items. It should be noted that some of the SP scales have as few as four or five items. Test–retest reliability coefficients for the revised PSY-5 scales were acceptable and ranged from .80 for Psychoticism (PSYC-r) to .93 for Disconstraint (DISC-r).

Internal consistency coefficients (alpha) for the H-O scales were quite high in the clinical samples, with typical values falling in the .80s and .90s. As expected, values were lower in the normative sample, likely due to restriction of range. As reported previously, the RC scales had good internal consistency, with values for the clinical samples generally in the .80s and .90s; and for the normative sample, in the .70s and .80s. As would be expected, the internal consistencies of the SP scales, which have fewer items than the H-O or RC scales, were lower than for the longer scales. Alpha coefficients for the SP scales varied from a low of .34 to a high of .86, with most values falling in the .60s and .70s in the normative sample. The SEMs for the SP scales were only slightly higher than the SEMs for the H-O and RC scales. Internal consistency coefficients (alpha) for the PSY-5 scales in the normative sample ranged from .69 for PSYC-r to .77 for Negative Emotionality/Neuroticism (NEGE-r). Corresponding values in clinical samples were slightly higher.

In summary, the internal consistency and temporal stability of the H-O, RC, and PSY-5 scales are good and comparable to those of other self-report scales.

The somewhat lower reliabilities of the SP and Interest scales suggest that test users should have more confidence in interpreting scores on these scales that are more elevated as opposed to those that are only marginally elevated.

Validity

Upon publication of the MMPI-2-RF, Tellegen and Ben-Porath (2008/2011; Tables A.1–A.136) included more than 50,000 correlations between MMPI-2-RF scale scores and external criteria for a variety of samples, including college students, community mental health center clients, psychiatric patients, individuals in substance use treatment, criminal defendants, and disability claimants. Criterion measures consisted of therapist ratings, intake information, record reviews, and other self-report instruments. The test authors based many of their interpretative recommendations on these correlational data. Subsequently, numerous studies investigating the validity of the test's scales have been published. When these studies are combined with the research that already existed on the RC and PSY-5 scales (previously summarized in Chapter 7), there exists a pool of several hundred publications that examine the validity of MMPI-2-RF's scales. The sections that follow briefly summarize validity data reported in Tellegen and Ben-Porath (2008/2011) as well as research published in professional journals.

Validity Scales

CANNONT SAY (CNS)

Ben-Porath and Tellegen (2008/2011) indicate that excessive item omissions are associated with lowered scores on some scales; and that when 15 or more total items are omitted, scores on some substantive scales may not accurately reflect characteristics of the test taker. The manual also indicates that scales can be interpreted when at least 90% of items from an individual scale are answered. This recommendation coincides with past research that demonstrated that little interpretive validity is lost when up to 10% of items in scales are omitted (Dragon et al., 2012).

NON-CONTENT-BASED INVALID RESPONDING SCALES (VRIN-r AND TRIN-r)

Ben-Porath and Tellegen (2008/2011) indicate that when VRIN-r T scores are between 70 and 79, substantive scales should be interpreted cautiously; when VRIN-r T scores are ≥ 80, the test taker likely responded to items so inconsistently that scores on other scales should not be interpreted. For the MMPI-2, several studies demonstrated that a T score of 80 on the VRIN scale was optimal for identifying random responding (Gallen & Berry, 1996; Paolo & Ryan, 1992). Given the similarity between the VRIN and VRIN-r scales, one would expect that the recommended T-score cutoff of 80 is also appropriate for the VRIN-r scale.

In a simulation study in which varying percentages of random responses were inserted into MMPI-2-RF protocols, Handel et al. (2010) demonstrated that the MMPI-2 VRIN scale and the MMPI-2-RF VRIN-r scale were similarly affected by the insertion of random responses. The external validity of RC scales was partially compromised when the VRIN and VRIN-r T scores were between 70 and 79;

when the T scores were ≥ 80, validity was compromised to an extent that the RC scales should not be interpreted. In a similar simulation study, Burchett et al. (2016) found that F-r, Fp-r, Fs, RBS, and L-r were elevated when VRIN-r T scores were ≥ 80; and that Fp-r and Fs were elevated for a small but meaningful number of cases when VRIN-r T scores were between 70 and 79. Thus, the results of these simulation studies support the interpretive guidelines for the VRIN-r scale as well as the recommended order for interpreting Validity scales reported in Ben-Porath and Tellegen (2008/2011).

Ben-Porath and Tellegen (2008/2011) recommend that a TRIN-r scale T score ≥ 80 be interpreted as indicating fixed (true or false) responding that invalidates the protocol. Research with the MMPI-2 indicated that the TRIN scale was sensitive to the random insertion true or false responses (Wetter & Tharpe, 1995). Given the similarity between the TRIN and TRIN-r scales, one would expect that the TRIN-r scale also is sensitive to fixed responding.

Handel et al. (2010) reported results of a simulation study in which varying percentages of true or false responses were inserted into MMPI-2-RF protocols. They found that TRIN-r scores became greater as the percentage of inserted true or false items increased. They also reported that the insertion of up to 10% true or false responses into the protocol did not affect the external validity of the RC scales. However, as percentages of inserted responses increased, the correlations between RC scales and external criteria were lower. Using a similar simulation technique, Burchett and colleagues (2016) found that TRIN-r T scores ≥ 80 resulted in elevations on F-r, Fp-r, Fs, RBS, and L-r. They also found that Fp-r and Fs were elevated in a small but meaningful number of cases where TRIN-r was moderately elevated in the "True" direction with T scores between 70 and 79. These studies support the interpretive guidelines given for the TRIN-r scale as well as the recommended order for Validity scale interpretation found in Ben-Porath and Tellegen (2008/2011).

OVERREPORTING SCALES (F–r, Fp–r, Fs, FBS–r, RBS)

As noted earlier, three of the overreporting scales of the MMPI-2-RF are revised versions of scales appearing on the MMPI-2 (F-r, Fp-r, and FBS-r). The MMPI-2-RF also has two Validity scales designed to identify overreporting that did not appear on the MMPI-2: Fs and RBS. Below we will review data from the MMPI-2-RF *Technical Manual* and research investigating the overreporting scales to describe what we know about the constructs assessed by these scales, as well as the effectiveness of cut scores on these scales for detecting different kinds of overreporting. Interpretive guidelines for each of the overreporting scales are summarized later in this chapter.

The F-r, Fp-r, and FBS-r scales appear to be very similar to their MMPI-2 counterparts. Tellegen and Ben-Porath (2008/2011) report correlations between the MMPI-2 and MMPI-2-RF versions of these Validity scales in several different settings. Correlations differed across settings; but in settings that showed sufficient variability in scores, the MMPI-2-RF and corresponding MMPI-2 scales were highly correlated. Thus, similar interpretations can probably be made for MMPI-2-RF overreporting scales. As noted in Chapter 3, research has consistently demonstrated that the F, Fp, and FBS scales of the MMPI-2 tend to be higher for persons who are overreporting symptoms and problems than for persons who give credible responses (Rogers et al., 2003). The research further indicates that the Fp scale is more sensitive to overreporting than the F scale in settings with a high base rate of severe psychopathology. The FBS scale seems to be most sensitive to exaggeration of cognitive and somatic symptoms (Ben-Porath et al., 2009).

Wygant et al. (2004) developed Fs to assess overreported somatic symptoms, and it was quickly incorporated into the MMPI-2-RF. Thus, most of what we know about this scale comes from empirical studies that broadly examine the overreporting scales. That literature will be reviewed later in this chapter. However, there were several studies examining what scores on RBS assessed prior to its incorporation into the MMPI-2-RF. Gervais et al. (2007) provided initial validation of the RBS after developing the scale by comparing different groups of individuals who passed or failed performance validity tests. Their results suggested that higher scorers on RBS were more likely to fail performance validity tests. False positive classification errors (i.e., concluding that honest responders are overreporting) were minimal, although false negative errors (i.e., concluding that overreporters responded honestly) were more common.

Subsequent research has supported the validity of the RBS in predicting overreporting of cognitive problems. Nelson et al. (2007) examined RBS scores of persons who were referred for neuropsychological evaluation in relation to cognitive complaints. The RBS was effective in differentiating between those who were presumed to have secondary gain versus those without secondary gain. Whitney et al. (2008) found the RBS to be more effective than other MMPI-2 Validity scales in predicting failure on the Test of Memory Malingering (TOMM; Tombaugh, 1997). Grossi and colleagues (2017) also evaluated the utility of the RBS in identifying individuals who failed the TOMM drawing from a sample of criminal defendants undergoing pretrial evaluations of competency to stand trial. They concluded the RBS achieved moderate classification accuracy and noted that the recommended cut scores maximize specificity (99%) but at the cost of reduced sensitivity (29%). Wygant et al. (2010) found mean scale scores on the RBS were much higher among participants who failed at least one performance validity test compared to those who passed those tests in both disability and criminal forensic samples. The RBS also demonstrated strong clinical utility in successfully classifying individuals using passing/failing performance validity tests as the classification criterion. Gervais et al. (2010) reported that the RBS was a better predictor of memory complaint scores than other MMPI-2-RF Validity scales. Importantly, there was no relationship between RBS scores and an objective measure of verbal memory. In sum, these research findings suggest that the RBS scores are an effective indicator for detecting overreported memory problems.

Since the MMPI-2-RF was released, there have been a sufficient number of studies conducted on its Validity scales to facilitate meta-analyses of the findings. The first of these meta-analyses was conducted by Ingram and Ternes (2016), who identified 24 published and unpublished studies that met their inclusion criteria. They reported overall effect sizes ranging from Hedge's $g = 1.08$ (FBS-r) to $g = 1.43$ (Fp-r), indicating very large mean score differences between overreporting and comparison samples across all five overreporting Validity scales (i.e., F-r, Fp-r, Fs, FBS-r, RBS). Ingram and Ternes identified several moderating variables that influenced the effect sizes reported for each scale. For example, most overreporting scales demonstrated effect sizes of about 1.5 when identifying overreporting in simulation studies, but they only demonstrated effect sizes of about 1.0 when identifying overreporting in studies using a known groups design. The only notable exception was FBS-r, which showed little difference between the two methodologies ($g = 1.12$ and 1.00, respectively). Although the specific moderators varied somewhat from scale to scale, Ingram and Ternes suggested clinicians might best account for these factors by comparing an individual's Validity scale scores with the mean scores from an appropriate clinical comparison sample. Specifically, if this comparison indicated the individual's score on any given scale was at least one standard deviation higher than the comparison group's mean score, they recommended clinicians give special consideration to possible overreporting—even in the case of only moderately elevated T scores.

In the second meta-analysis, Sharf and colleagues (2017) identified 29 studies that met their inclusion criteria and reported effect sizes for all five MMPI-2-RF overreporting Validity scales (i.e., F-r, Fp-r, Fs, FBS-r, and RBS) as well as L-r and K-r. They found effect sizes for the overreporting Validity scales ranging from $d = 0.77$ (FBS-r) to $d = 1.40$ (Fp-r) when comparing overreporting groups to nonclinical controls and effect sizes ranging from $d = 0.75$ (FBS-r) to $d = 1.35$ (Fp-r) when comparing overreporting groups to clinical comparison samples. Sharf et al. also reported effect sizes when comparing individuals who overreported psychiatric disorders, cognitive problems, and medical problems to appropriate clinical comparison samples. They found Fp-r ($d = 1.32$) and F-r ($d = 1.12$) were most effective at detecting overreported psychiatric problems, although Fs ($d = 1.05$) and RBS ($d = 0.95$) were only slightly less effective. For overreporting of cognitive impairments, Fs ($d = 0.89$), FBS-r ($d = 0.88$), RBS ($d = 0.88$), and F-r ($d = 0.75$) all demonstrated comparable results. Finally, for overreporting of medical problems, Fs ($d = 1.23$) and Fp-r ($d = 1.00$) demonstrated the largest effect sizes.

Sharf et al. (2017) included clinical utility estimates for each overreporting scale across all three overreporting domains (e.g., RBS estimates for overreporting of psychiatric and medical symptoms as well as overreporting of cognitive impairments). Results generally supported the utility of each scale for the domain it is intended to evaluate. Next, Sharf et al. examined the most common cut scores for each scale in their meta-analysis. Results were generally supportive of the cutoff scores recommended in the interpretive guidelines. For example, using a cut score of 100T or greater on F-r to identify feigned mental disorders resulted in a sensitivity of .71 and a specificity of .80, but using a cutoff of 120T resulted in a sensitivity of .51 and specificity of .93. Sharf and colleagues' cut scores analyses serve as an important reminder that higher cut scores are associated with increased scale specificity and decreased sensitivity, while lower cut scores are more appropriately conceptualized as "screeners" for possible overreporting because of their increased sensitivity but decreased specificity.

Since the publication of these two meta-analyses, several other studies have been published examining the overreporting Validity scales. The results from two of these studies were consistent with the meta-analytic findings (Jones, 2016; Sánchez et al., 2017). However, Ingram et al. (2020) found atypically small effect sizes ($g = .32$ [F-r] to $g = .73$ [RBS]) when detecting active-duty military members who were classified as possible malingerers due to failing at least one performance validity test.

In summary, research indicates the overreporting scales of the MMPI-2-RF are sensitive to various kinds of exaggerated or feigned symptom reports. Optimal cut scores differ somewhat from scale to scale, setting to setting, and according to the base rates of invalid responding. When available, clinicians may be well served to compare individual Validity scale scores to the mean scores of an appropriate clinical comparison sample. Scale scores greater than one standard deviation above the comparison group's mean should raise suspicion of overreporting. Many individual studies report sample-specific optimal cut scores, and we refer the interested reader to the references lists of the Ingram and Ternes (2016) and Sharf et al. (2017) meta-analyses to help identify specific studies that might closely match the context in which they are using the MMPI-2-RF. However, cut scores identified in most of these studies are generally consistent with the interpretive guidelines found in the test manual (Ben-Porath and Tellegen, 2008/2011). Thus, we recommend these guidelines, which are presented later in this chapter, should be followed in most cases.

Studies on Coaching.
As noted in Chapter 3, the possibility that individuals motivated to feign psychological disturbance when they complete the MMPI-2 could do so more effectively if they were coached, either by obtaining information about the symptoms of the disorder they want to simulate or about how the instrument identifies overreporting, has long been a concern. These same concerns apply to the MMPI-2-RF, and several studies have examined the impact that knowledge of psychiatric symptoms might have on the efficacy of MMPI-2-RF overreporting Validity scales. Marion et al. (2011) found that personal experience with PTSD or professional knowledge of schizophrenia and major depressive disorder did not help participants avoid detection as an over-reporter when they were instructed to feign one of those three conditions. Goodwin et al. (2013) asked mental health professionals to complete the MMPI-2-RF as if they suffered from PTSD. They too found that professional knowledge of psychiatric symptoms did not dramatically hinder the ability of the MMPI-2-RF's Validity scales to differentiate individuals who were overreporting from genuine patients. Finally, Lau et al. (2017) found similar results when participants were provided with detailed symptom coaching about Traumatic Brain Injury (TBI). Results indicated individuals who were coached and feigned TBI when responding to the instrument produced only slightly lower scores on FBS-r and RBS than participants who received no symptom coaching. Overall, these results suggest MMPI-2-RF overreporting scales are effective in detecting exaggerated or feigned symptoms, even when such reports are a product of symptom coaching.

Other researchers have examined the impact of providing test takers with information about MMPI-2-RF's Validity scales and how to avoid having overreporting detected by these scales. Sellbom and Bagby (2010) found that participants instructed to overreport symptoms of mental illness did produce lower Validity scale scores if they were provided with tips on how to avoid being identified by the MMPI-2-RF's Validity scales; however, the scales were still able to differentiate coached simulators from genuine patients. Sellbom and Bagby (2010) found Fp-r was especially effective at making this distinction (d = 1.36). In contrast, Lau et al. (2017) found that participants instructed to feign TBI and coached to avoid detection on performance validity tests also produced significantly lower scores on FBS-r and RBS compared to participants who were only provided with detailed symptom information about TBI. The disparate results from these two studies suggest additional research regarding the impact of coaching on MMPI-2-RF Validity scales is warranted. However, Olsen and Veltri (2019) provide an early hint at a more nuanced understanding of the impact of Validity scale coaching. In their study, Olsen and Veltri compared individuals instructed to feign schizophrenia, PTSD, and generalized anxiety disorder (GAD) who were uncoached to those who were coached on both symptoms and Validity scale scores. Their results indicated that successfully feigning schizophrenia was more difficult than feigning the other two disorders. They also found that coaching did not result in a statistically significant increase in valid profile rates for schizophrenia simulators, whereas it did for both PTSD and GAD. Finally, they found that the impact of Validity scale coaching was moderated by the specific disorder being feigned on F-r, Fs, and RBS at the mean score level. Taken in sum, the results from these three studies suggest to us that the impact of coaching likely differs depending on what kinds of symptoms are being overreported.

UNDERREPORTING SCALES (L–r, K–r)

As reviewed in Chapter 3, the MMPI-2 literature contains many studies indicating that the L scale is sensitive to underreporting. These findings were supported in a meta-analysis by Baer and Miller (2002) that compared findings across 14 studies and determined that the L scale is very sensitive to underreporting. Baer and Miller also concluded that optimal cutoff scores for determining underreporting that invalidates protocols are likely to vary from setting to setting, with somewhat higher scores needed in nonclinical settings where the base rate of underreporting is greater than in most clinical settings.

Ben-Porath and Tellegen (2008/2011) indicate that T scores between 70 and 79 on the L-r scale indicate an overly virtuous self-presentation and that scores on the substantive scales should be interpreted with caution because they may underestimate the problems assessed by the scales. The manual further recommends that when L-r scale T scores are ≥ 80, the absence of elevation on substantive scales is not interpretable. However, elevated scores on substantive scales are interpretable, but it should be recognized that the scores may underestimate the magnitude of the problems that they assess. The manual is silent concerning differential cutoff scores for clinical and nonclinical settings.

Sellbom and Bagby (2008) reported the results of two MMPI-2-RF underreporting studies. In one study, college students and patients with diagnoses of schizophrenia completed the MMPI-2 with instructions to underreport symptoms and problems; their L-r scale scores were compared with students who completed the test with standard instructions. As expected, both underreporting groups had higher L-r scale scores than the students who completed the MMPI-2-RF with standard instructions. In a second study, Sellbom and Bagby (2008) compared L-r scale scores of students who completed the test under standard instructions, students who completed the test with instructions to underreport problems, and parents who completed the test as part of child custody proceedings. As in the first study, both underreporting groups had higher L-r scale scores than the students who completed the test using standard instructions.

Crighton et al. (2017) used a simulation design to investigate the utility of L-r in identifying underreporting. They asked some college students to complete the test under standard instructions, while other college students were instructed to answer the test so as to appear very well adjusted. As expected, students instructed to underreport had much higher L-r scores than those who completed the test under standard instructions. Crighton and colleagues also inspected classification accuracies using several L-r cut scores and found T = 70 to be the most accurate. T. A. Brown and Sellbom (2020) also investigated underreporting using a simulation design with college students. They too found higher L-r scores among those instructed to underreport; however, they found cutoff scores of T = 70 and T = 80 on L-r to be equally accurate, with the higher cutoff showing improved specificity but decreased sensitivity compared to the lower score. Both studies also provide strong evidence to support the interpretive practice of using lower cutoff scores on L-r to raise concern about possible underreporting and higher cutoff scores as being more definitively indicative of underreporting due to extremely low false positive rates.

Several studies have investigated how holding traditional religious beliefs might impact scores on the L-r scale. Bridges and Baum (2013) found that outpatients who self-identified as Christian and were seeking services at a university mental health center had modestly higher mean L-r scores compared to test takers who did not endorse those beliefs. Bagby et al. (2020) reported similar results for test takers endorsing values grounded in Islam. They also found participants in their study who both engaged in positive impression management and endorsed traditional Muslim values had even higher L-r scores, although positive impression management was the more influential predictor of L-r scores. These studies support Ben-Porath and Tellegen's (2008/2011) recommendation to consider whether modest elevations on L-r may be the result of a test taker holding traditional values.

In summary, the L-r scale of the MMPI-2-RF is very similar to the L scale of the MMPI-2. Of the 14 items in the L-r scale, 11 items are also in the L scale. Research supports the sensitivity of the L-r scale to underreporting. There is also empirical support for the use of the tiered interpretive guidelines and cutoff scores reported in Ben-Porath and Tellegen (2008/2011), which are presented later in this chapter.

Chapter 3 reviews research concerning the use of the MMPI-2 K scale in identifying underreporting of symptoms and problems. Baer and Miller (2002) conducted a meta-analysis of 14 MMPI-2 underreporting studies and concluded that the K scale is effective in identifying persons who underreport symptoms and problems. They also concluded that optimal cutoff scores for identifying underreporting may differ from setting to setting. Recognizing that persons who complete the MMPI-2 in nonclinical settings (e.g., employment screening) generally have higher K scores, the MMPI-2 manual (Butcher et al., 2001) recommend different cutoff scores for clinical and nonclinical settings.

Ben-Porath and Tellegen (2008/2011) indicate that K-r scale T scores between 60 and 69 can indicate either very good psychological adjustment or underreporting of symptoms and problems. For individuals who are not especially well adjusted, scores in this range likely indicate underreporting; and scores on substantive scales should be interpreted with caution. The manual further indicates that K-r T scores ≥ 70 suggest underreporting to an extent requiring great caution in interpreting scores on substantive scales, since those scores are likely to reflect underestimation of test takers' actual symptoms and problems. As with the L-r scale, the manual is silent concerning the need for different cutoff scores for clinical and nonclinical settings.

In the same studies reported for the L-r scale, Sellbom and Bagby (2008) compared scores on the K-r scale of students who completed the MMPI-2 with standard instructions, students who completed the MMPI-2 with instructions to appear to be free of psychological problems, patients with diagnoses of schizophrenia who were instructed to avoid revealing their symptoms, and parents who completed the test as part of child custody proceedings. As was true for the L-r scale, all three underreporting groups had higher K-r scale scores than the standard instruction group. The authors did not address the issue of K-r scale cutoff scores for identifying underreporting. However, Sellbom and Bagby (2008) did demonstrate that, although the L-r and K-r scales are correlated, each identified unique variance in underreporting.

While investigating L-r, both Crighton et al. (2017) and T. A. Brown and Sellbom (2020) simultaneously investigated K-r. These studies demonstrated similar results for K-r to those reported for L-r. Mean K-r scores were higher for the groups of students instructed to underreport than they were for the groups of students completing the MMPI-2-RF under standard instructions. Both studies found T = 60 to be the single most efficient cutoff score for K-r, but also provided strong evidence supporting the practice of interpreting graduated K-r cutoff scores with increasing confidence. Interestingly, Crighton et al. and T. A. Brown and Sellbom also both found that L-r and K-r added incrementally to one another. These data support the general practice of using both scales to identify potential underreporting.

In summary, the MMPI-2 K and MMPI-2-RF K-r scales are very similar. In fact, all 14 items in the K-r scale are also in the K scale. Available evidence supports the general interpretive strategy and specific K-r cutoff scores presented in Ben-Porath and Tellegen (2008/2011) and included later in this chapter. Finally, while L-r and K-r both assess underreporting, they do assess related, yet distinct, aspects of this response style and are better able to identify underreporting when used conjointly.

Substantive Scales

The published literature examining the substantive scales of the MMPI-2-RF has accumulated rapidly since the publication of the test. One important aspect of this research has been the substantial body of work examining the construct validity of the MMPI-2-RF and how the constructs measured by its scales map onto contemporary models of psychopathology like HiTOP (Kotov et al., 2021) and the DSM-5's AMPD (American Psychiatric Association, 2013).

In Chapter 7, we reviewed how the RC and PSY-5 scales align with these contemporary models of psychopathology. There is evidence suggesting the other substantive scales of the MMPI-2-RF also align well with these models. For example, several studies using factor analysis to explore the internal structure of either the MMPI-2-RF scales by themselves (McNulty & Overstreet, 2014; Sellbom, 2017) or in conjunction with other instruments (Anderson, Sellbom, Ayearst, et al., 2015) have identified factor structures approximating the spectra level dimensions identified in the HiTOP. In another example, Sellbom et al. (2013) demonstrated strong convergence between MMPI-2-RF substantive scales and the six specific personality disorders proposed in the DSM-5's AMPD. In sum, the MMPI-2-RF has strong theoretical and empirical ties to contemporary models of psychopathology. We believe this is an important achievement, as clinicians and researchers alike can have confidence that specific constructs measured by the MMPI-2-RF align closely with those constructs investigated in the psychopathology literature. Interested readers are referred to Sellbom (2019) for a detailed review of this topic.

In terms of empirical correlates, for the most part, the research published since the release of the MMPI-2-RF has reported results that are congruent with those reported in the MMPI-2-RF's *Technical Manual* (Tellegen & Ben-Porath, 2008/2011). These studies have been conducted across a variety of settings, including outpatient samples (e.g., Haber & Baum, 2014; van der Heijden et al., 2013; Zahn et al., 2017), inpatient samples (e.g., Anderson, Sellbom, Ayearst, et al., 2015; Anderson, Sellbom, Pymont, et al., 2015; Moultrie & Engel, 2017), college student samples (e.g., Forbey et al., 2010; Franz et al., 2017), community samples (e.g., Anderson & Sellbom, 2021), correctional samples (e.g., Tylicki, Phillips, et al., 2020), forensic samples (e.g., Anderson, Sellbom, Pymont, et al., 2015; Anderson et al., 2018; Romero et al., 2017; Sellbom, 2016), veterans samples (e.g., Ingram et al., 2021), and medical samples (e.g., Marek, Anderson, et al., 2020; Marek, Ben-Porath, et al., 2020). This suggests the correlates providing a foundation for MMPI-2-RF interpretations generalize well across settings in which the test is commonly used. Below we will offer our general summary of the data reported in both Tellegen and Ben-Porath (2008/2011) and the research literature.[1] We will also highlight specific findings that extend what we know about the substantive scales and, hence, what we might conclude about a test taker when interpreting these scales.

HIGHER-ORDER (H-O) SCALES

In general, the correlations reported in Tellegen and Ben-Porath (2008/2011) and the reviewed studies published in peer-reviewed journals support both the convergent and discriminant validity of the H-O scales. Higher scores on the EID scale are associated with many aspects of emotional distress, including feeling overwhelmed, vulnerable, and helpless. Depression and, to some extent, anxiety, are prominent for high EID scale scorers. Patel and Suhr (2020) found EID scores were inversely correlated with client ratings of therapeutic alliance in a university-based psychology training

---

[1] In addition to correlates presented in Tellegen and Ben-Porath (2008/2011) and the specific studies cited below, the following sources were consulted in preparing descriptors of the MMPI-2-RF scales: Anderson et al., 2018; Anderson & Sellbom, 2021; Anderson, Sellbom, Ayearst, et al., 2015; Anderson, Sellbom, Pymont, et al., 2015; Forbey et al., 2010; Franz et al., 2017; Haber & Baum, 2014; Ingram et al., 2021; Marek, Anderson, et al., 2020; Marek, Ben-Porath, et al., 2020; Moultrie & Engel, 2017; Romero et al., 2017; Sellbom, 2016; Tylicki, Phillips, et al., 2020; van der Heijden et al., 2013; and Zahn et al., 2017.

clinic. Data presented in the MMPI-2-RF *Technical Manual* (Tellegen & Ben-Porath, 2008/2011) and published studies indicate higher scores on the EID scale are unrelated, or in some settings negatively related, to measures of externalizing behaviors such as getting in trouble with the law or problematic use of substances. Data from Tellegen and Ben-Porath (2008/2011) suggests in inpatient psychiatric settings, higher EID scale scores are meaningfully related to increased symptoms of psychotic disorders (e.g., delusions, hallucinations).

Correlates in the MMPI-2-RF *Technical Manual* (Tellegen & Ben-Porath, 2008/2011) and subsequently published studies indicate higher scores on the THD scale are associated with indicators of psychotic disorder. High scorers often receive psychotic diagnoses, and they may report auditory or visual hallucinations and delusions of persecution or grandeur. Sellbom, Bagby, et al. (2012) found EID and THD to be useful in differentiating between patients at a community clinic diagnosed with depression and schizophrenia, a result replicated by Lee et al. (2018) among psychiatric inpatients. In terms of discriminant validity, scores on THD do not appear to be strongly related to severe emotional distress or to externalizing behaviors, such as getting into trouble with the law or problematic use of substances (Tellegen & Ben-Porath, 2008/2011).

High scores on the BXD scale are associated with a wide variety of externalizing behaviors. Specifically, data in the MMPI-2-RF *Technical Manual* (Tellegen & Ben-Porath, 2008/2011) and subsequently published studies indicate higher scores are associated with having been in trouble at home, at work, and with the law and with histories of problematic substance use. Low tolerance for frustration and stormy interpersonal relationships are associated with higher scores. Several studies have indicated that high BXD scores are predictive of increased risk of failure to complete a full course of psychotherapy (Mattson et al., 2012; Patel & Suhr, 2020; Whitman et al., 2020) and appointment no-shows (Anestis et al., 2015; Patel & Suhr, 2020). In terms of discriminant validity, BXD scores are not related to many indicators of emotional distress, but some high scorers may report anxiety and depression (Tellegen & Ben-Porath, 2008/2011). Higher scores are not strongly related to symptoms of psychotic disorder.

McCord et al. (2017) conducted a unique study examining associations between MMPI-2-RF scores and physiological responsivity. Specifically, they measured the pupil dilation of college students while showing them emotionally evocative video clips. Consistent with their expectations, they found increased physiological arousability was associated with higher EID scores when the videos intended to elicit negative emotional reactions were viewed. They found that BXD scores were negatively correlated with arousability when the video clips contained angry or threatening stimuli. Overall, McCord et al. interpreted these results as supporting the construct validity of these scales, as they demonstrated associations consistent with prior basic research examining the role of physiological arousal in internalizing and externalizing syndromes.

In sum, research supports that the three H-O scales can provide broad, yet important information about the nature of problems that a test taker may be experiencing. These scales have meaningful connections to dimensions of psychopathology identified in modern models of psychopathology and can be linked to findings from basic psychopathology research. More precise inferences about test takers are based on substantive scales assessing narrower aspects of social, emotional, and behavioral functioning—including the RC, SP, Interest, and PSY-5 scales.

RESTRUCTURED CLINICAL (RC) SCALES

Because the RC scales of the MMPI-2-RF are identical to the RC scales of the MMPI-2, the validity data presented in Chapter 7 apply to the MMPI-2-RF RC scales. As noted in Chapter 7, since the publication of the RC scales (Tellegen et al., 2003), a sizable body of research literature has accumulated concerning their utility in a variety of settings and for a variety of purposes. That research indicates that the RC scale authors were largely successful in developing a set of scales that captured the core constructs of the original Clinical scales while reducing, but not eliminating, the effects of the demoralization that was present in the Clinical scales. External correlate data suggest that the RC scales have convergent validity that is equal to, or in some cases greater than, the original Clinical scales and considerably greater discriminant validity.

SPECIFIC PROBLEMS (SP) SCALES: SOMATIC/COGNITIVE SCALES

The five Somatic/Cognitive SP scales were developed to assess general preoccupation with poor health as well as presentation of more specific somatic symptoms and cognitive deficits. The Malaise (MLS) scale indicates the extent to which the test taker is presenting themself as being in poor health and debilitated by physical problems. The other four scales—Gastrointestinal Complaints (GIC), Head Pain Complaints (HPC), Neurological Complaints (NUC), and Cognitive Complains (COG)—focus on circumscribed symptoms and problems. Because of the brevity of the scales and the homogeneity of their item content, persons who obtain high scores on a scale are likely to have endorsed items consistent with the label of the scale. However, the pattern of correlations of each scale with external criterion measures (Tellegen & Ben-Porath, 2008/2011) indicates that anyone who scores high on any Somatic/Cognitive scale in a clinical setting also is likely to have the characteristics described for the MLS scale (e.g., feeling overwhelmed and unable to cope). Similar conclusions were reached by Gironda and Clark (2009), who examined MMPI-2-RF Somatic/Cognitive scales in two samples of patients in chronic pain programs. They also demonstrated that the Somatic/Cognitive scales added incrementally to the prediction of pain-specific outcome measures.

Other studies published after the MMPI-2-RF's release have expanded our understanding of the constructs assessed by the Somatic/Cognitive scales. Kremyar et al. (2020) reported that among college students, high MLS scores were closely associated with low quality of sleep and decreased physical activity. In contrast, they found that low MLS scores (T < 39) were associated with positive health indicators including high-quality sleep. Patel and Suhr (2020) found that higher scores on MLS and HPC were associated with lower client ratings of therapeutic alliance in a university-based, psychology training clinic. They also found COG was positively correlated with higher rates of clients not attending scheduled appointments.

Several other studies have focused specifically on examining the validity of scores on COG. Using a large sample (N = 1,741) of disability claimants evaluated in a private-practice setting, Gervais et al. (2009) explored relationships between scores on COG, objective measures of cognitive deficits, and self-reported cognitive deficits. Scores on COG were not significantly correlated with age or objective cognitive and memory measures and were only weakly correlated with education (r = .17). However, high COG scale scores were related to subjective reports of cognitive and memory problems. This relationship was present even when insufficient cognitive effort and symptom exaggeration were accounted for. Mattson and colleagues (2019) examined the relationship between COG scores and objective measures of cognitive deficits in a sample of combat-exposed veterans. At the zero-order level, they found COG was positively related to objective deficits. However, this relationship was fully mediated by PTSD symptomatology, such that once PTSD symptoms were accounted for, the relationship between objective cognitive test performance and COG scale scores was no longer significant. Overall, these studies suggest COG is likely an effective measure of perceived difficulties with cognition and memory but that higher scores are not necessarily indicative of decreased cognitive functioning.

SPECIFIC PROBLEMS (SP) SCALES: INTERNALIZING SCALES

The nine Internalizing SP scales address particular aspects of internalizing dysfunction inherent in elevations on broader scales in the internalizing domain, which include EID, RCd, RC2, and RC7. Suicidal/Death Ideation (SUI) inquires about suicidal thinking and behavior. Items in Helplessness/Hopelessness (HLP) have content related to negative beliefs about one's future; while Self-Doubt (SFD) items reflect having low confidence in one's self; and Inefficacy (NFC) reflects feelings of indecisiveness and inefficaciousness—or one's ability to affect change in one's life. Items on Stress/Worry (STW), Anxiety (AXY), and Anger Proneness (ANP) all assess experiences with excessive negative emotionality, reflecting experiences of excessive stress, anxiety, and anger, respectively. Behavior-Restricting Fears (BRF) and Multiple Specific Fears (MSF) both assess fearfulness, with BRF reflecting phobic avoidance and MSF reflecting a variety of different stimuli that may provoke acute threat responses.

The Internalizing SP scales are relatively short (4–9 items), and the content of items in each scale is quite homogeneous. Thus, persons who have elevated scores on a scale likely have endorsed items consistent with the label of the scale. As reported in Tellegen and Ben-Porath (2008/2011), the intercorrelations of the nine scales are relatively high. External correlate data indicate that the scales have relatively good convergent validity (i.e., they relate to criterion measures that are consistent with the purposes of the scale), but evidence of their discriminant validity is somewhat limited in that the scales are also generally correlated with a variety of other broader, internalizing kinds of symptoms. For example, most of the scales are also positively correlated with depression, anxiety, and other indicators of general emotional distress.

Several studies have examined the validity of the SUI scale. In 2014, Gottfried et al. reported the association between SUI scale scores and several criterion variables in an outpatient sample. They found SUI was strongly correlated with other self-report measures of suicidal ideation and behavior as well as past suicide attempts. Scores were also closely associated with clinician-ratings of suicide risk. Glassmire et al. (2016) examined the postdictive, concurrent, and predictive validity of the scale in a forensic inpatient setting. They found SUI was positively correlated with past suicide ideation and attempts as well as current suicidal ideation as reported via clinical interview. Perhaps most importantly, they found higher scores on SUI were predictive of future suicidal behavior (including both threats and attempts) over the course of one year. In fact, SUI was the only unique predictor of future suicidal behavior when it was evaluated in conjunction with demographic characteristics, history of suicidality, and concurrent suicidal ideation. In Glassmire et al.'s study, patients who endorsed even a single SUI item were more than five times as likely to engage in future suicidal behavior. Anestis and colleagues (2018) evaluated the MMPI-2-RF in the context of the interpersonal-psychological theory of suicide (IPTS; Joiner, 2005) in a mental health outpatient sample. They found high scores on SUI were strongly associated with increased scores on the factors of the IPTS—especially perceived burdensomeness—as well the strongest MMPI-2-RF correlate of self-reported suicidal ideation and clinician-rated suicide risk. S. N. Miller et al. (2019) found that SUI scores differentiated between psychiatrically hospitalized veterans who were depressed but had no evidence of suicidality, those who reported suicidal ideation during intake but had no history of suicide attempts, and those who reported a history of suicide attempts. Khazem et al. (2021) found that SUI scores were strongly associated with past-week suicidal ideation among veterans in a partial psychiatric hospitalization program. No other MMPI-2-RF scale added incrementally to SUI in accounting for past-week suicidal ideation. Furthermore, Khazem et al. found that SUI scores were only minimally influenced by possible underreporting (i.e., L-r ≥ 65T or K-r ≥ 60T) in their sample. Most recently, Whitman, Kremyar, and Ben-Porath (2021) reported that SUI was also strongly related to nonsuicidal self-injurious behavior. In sum, these results strongly support the validity of SUI and indicate scores may also be helpful in identifying individuals who are at risk for future suicidal thinking or behavior.

There have been several studies that have identified AXY as being strongly associated with experiencing posttraumatic stress and symptoms of PTSD. Arbisi et al. (2011) found AXY to be the only MMPI-2-RF scale to uniquely contribute to differentiating post-deployment National Guard soldiers who screened positive for PTSD from those who did not. Sellbom, Lee, et al. (2012) identified AXY as the SP scale most strongly and uniquely associated with symptoms of PTSD in a sample of disability claimants undergoing psycho-legal evaluation following exposure to non-combat-related traumatic events. Partially replicating these findings, Gottfried et al. (2016) found AXY was correlated with symptoms of posttraumatic stress among female inmates; however, they found Self-Doubt (SFD) was the best unique predictor of PTSD symptomatology among the SP scales.

Ben-Porath and Tellegen (2008/2011) noted potential treatment implications for MMPI-2-RF scales in the *MMPI-2-RF Administration, Scoring, and Interpretation Manual*. Patel and Suhr (2020) added to these second-order inferences when they demonstrated BRF scale scores were inversely related to client ratings of therapeutic alliance in a psychology training clinic.

SPECIFIC PROBLEMS (SP) SCALES: EXTERNALIZING SCALES

The four SP Externalizing scales deal with acting-out behavior, and each of the scales addresses specific manifestations of this behavior. Items in the Juvenile Conduct Problems (JCP) scale have to do with getting in trouble at school and with the law; items in the Substance Abuse (SUB) scale deal with the use and misuse of alcohol or other drugs; items in the Aggression (AGG) scale deal with anger and acting out in aggressive ways; and items in the Activation (ACT) scale describe periods of excessive energy and excitement. While some of the external correlates presented in Tellegen and Ben-Porath (2008/2011) are quite consistent with specific item content, all four Externalizing scales are also meaningfully related to a wide variety of acting-out behaviors. In other words, each scale seems to have good convergent validity, but generally the discriminant validity within the realm of externalizing behaviors is not as good. For example, scores on the AGG scale are significantly correlated with therapist ratings of angry resentment, but increased scores on the JCP and SUB scales also are related to higher ratings of angry resentment.

Tellegen & Ben-Porath (2008/2011) as well as subsequently published studies have indicated scores on SUB measure problematic alcohol and other illicit drug use. Thornton et al. (2020) extended these findings by asking pairs of college students to complete the MMPI-2-RF as well as self- and peer-report measures of general drug use and misuse of prescription stimulant medications. Results indicated SUB was strongly correlated with both misuse of prescription stimulant medication and general drug use—regardless of whether the criterion measure was self- or other-report. Interestingly, the other Externalizing SP scales were only moderately correlated with these same measures of substance use, offering some evidence of discriminant validity.

Scores on ACT are related to symptoms of hypomanic behavior, such as periods of accelerated speech and decreased need for sleep (Tellegen & Ben-Porath, 2008/2011). Sellbom, Bagby, and colleagues (2012) extended these findings by demonstrating scores on ACT were better able to differentiate patients at a community clinic diagnosed with bipolar disorder from those diagnosed with major depression.

Externalizing SP scales may also be useful in identifying individuals who are at risk for suicidal behavior when used in conjunction with scores on RCd or SUI. Stanley et al. (2018) examined a sample of psychiatric outpatients who self-reported a history of suicidal ideation. They found that an interaction between RCd and ACT differentiated individuals who had made a past suicide attempt from those who had not. The interaction was such that RCd elevations were only associated with past suicide attempts when ACT was also elevated. Anestis et al. (2018) and S. N. Miller et al. (2019) reported similar exacerbation of suicide risk when SUB was elevated in conjunction with SUI. Their results indicated similar elevation of risk when SUI and scales assessing broader externalizing constructs were elevated, including BXD, RC4, and DISC-r.

Several studies have reported some of the Externalizing SP scales are predictive of poor treatment outcomes. For example, Mattson et al. (2012) reported that higher JCP and AGG scores were independently correlated with failure to complete a drug court treatment program. Anestis et al. (2015) found that higher scores on JCP were a significant predictor of clients not attending scheduled appointments as well as premature termination of therapy at a university-based outpatient clinic. Similarly, Patel and Suhr (2020) reported that JCP and AGG scores were each positively correlated with increased appointment no-shows in their university-clinic sample.

SPECIFIC PROBLEMS (SP) SCALES: INTERPERSONAL SCALES

The five SP Interpersonal scales address test takers' relationships with other people. The Family Problems (FML) scale contains items assessing family closeness and conflict and is associated with having strong negative feelings about family members and high levels of family disagreement (Tellegen & Ben-Porath, 2008/2011). Lee and colleagues (2019) had romantic partners complete the MMPI-2-RF and markers related to the quality of their relationship. They found that FML was negatively correlated with self-ratings and partner ratings of both relationship satisfaction and general agreement about important issues.

As reported in Tellegen and Ben-Porath (2008/2011) and replicated in the peer-reviewed literature, all of the remaining Interpersonal scales (i.e., Interpersonal Passivity [IPP], Shyness [SHY], Social Avoidance [SAV], and Disaffiliativeness [DSF]) are correlated with external measures of introversion. However, each scale seems to be associated with a particular aspect of introversion. The IPP scale is related to low assertiveness, the SHY scale is related to social reticence and anxiety, the SAV scale is related to low gregariousness, and the DSF scale is related to interpersonal coldness and low social closeness. Scores on all these scales also are positively related to indicators of emotional distress (e.g., anxiety, depression). Patel and Suhr (2020) reported that client ratings of therapeutic alliance were inversely correlated with IPP and SHY scores in a psychology training clinic.

Ayearst et al. (2013) further explored the different aspects of introversion captured by IPP, SHY, SAV, and DSF by comparing these scales to several other well-validated measures of interpersonally based personality traits (e.g., dominance and warmth) and social functioning. They found IPP was associated with an interpersonally warm manifestation of passivity; while SHY, SAV, and DSF each reflected increasingly colder interpersonal passivity. They also found that SHY was associated with neuroticism to a greater extent than the other interpersonal scales.

INTEREST SCALES

As stated earlier in this chapter, all the items in the two MMPI-2-RF Interest scales are from Clinical Scale 5 of the MMPI-2. Persons scoring higher on Aesthetic–Literary Interests (AES) are reporting interest in occupations and activities that are aesthetic or literary in nature, whereas high scorers on the Mechanical–Physical Interests (MEC) scale are reporting interest in occupations and activities that are mechanical or physical in nature. The two Interest scales are not meaningfully correlated with each other.

Examination of external correlates reported in Tellegen and Ben-Porath (2008/2011) for the two scales indicates that neither scale is meaningfully related to serious psychopathology. Men who score higher on the AES scale are described by others as not having stereotypically masculine interests and as rejecting a traditional masculine gender role. Men and women who score higher on the AES scale are also seen as conscientious, optimistic, and open to experience. Both men and women who score high on the MEC scale are described by others as having stereotypically masculine interests. Men scoring higher on the MEC scale are described as not rejecting a traditional masculine gender role, whereas higher scoring women are described as rejecting a traditional feminine gender role.

PERSONALITY PSYCHOPATHOLOGY-FIVE SCALES (PSY-5)

Examination of correlations between the original MMPI-2 PSY-5 scales and the MMPI-2-RF PSY-5 scales and external criterion measures reported in Tellegen and Ben-Porath (2008/2011) suggests that the original and revised scales are associated with essentially the same test-taker characteristics. Harkness, McNulty, et al. (2014) provided additional data examining the congruence between these two sets of scales as well as further exploring the construct validity of the MMPI-2-RF PSY-5 scales (see Chapter 7 for additional details). As such, the validity data presented in Chapter 7 are generally applicable to the MMPI-2-RF PSY-5 scales as well. Interpretive guidelines for the PSY-5 scales are presented later in this chapter.

Setting-Specific Applications

The validity data summarized in the previous section covers research examining the use of the MMPI-2-RF as a measure of psychopathology and personality. The utility of the test for this purpose applies broadly to any setting where the context of the evaluation includes consideration of psychopathology, even if the setting itself is not primarily focused on mental health. However, since its publication, there have also been numerous studies examining the validity of the MMPI-2-RF for other setting-specific purposes. For example, a body of literature has developed exploring the utility of the test for uses like presurgical screenings for bariatric surgery candidates. Although these literatures both draw from and inform the validity of the MMPI-2-RF for measuring personality and psychopathology, these applications extend the use of the test beyond the data we have reviewed here. Reviewing the literature on the validity and utility of the MMPI-2-RF in these setting-specific purposes is beyond the scope of this chapter. We refer the interested reader to the following resources to serve as a starting place for better understanding the strengths and limitations of using the MMPI-2-RF in these specialized contexts. For general behavioral health applications, we recommend Marek and Ben-Porath (2017). For police and other public safety screening, we recommend Corey and Ben-Porath (2018). For forensic applications, we recommend Sellbom and Wygant (2018).

INTERPRETATION

Interpretive Guidelines

In the sections that follow, interpretive guidelines are offered for the Validity and substantive scales of the MMPI-2-RF. The suggested interpretations for the Validity scales are based on the guidelines offered by Ben-Porath and Tellegen (2008/2011), which—as reviewed earlier in this chapter—have been largely supported by subsequent empirical work. The suggested interpretations for the substantive scales are based on guidelines suggested in the interpretive manual, our examination of the empirical correlate data presented in the technical manual, and other research that has been reported since the MMPI-2-RF was published in 2008. Inferences generated from the technical manual emphasize correlations between scales and criterion measures that were of at least a small effect size ($r \geq$ .20; Cohen, et al., 2002).

As with the scales of the MMPI-2, inferences based on substantive scales should be treated as hypotheses that are to be compared with other information available about test takers (e.g., interview, other tests, behavioral observations). Clinical interpretation is generally recommended when $T \geq 65$. Scores much higher than 65T suggest a greater likelihood that the listed descriptors will apply to a test taker and that listed symptoms will be more severe than those associated with less elevated scores. Interpretation of low scores, demarcated at $T < 39$, is recommended in the interpretive manual for some MMPI-2-RF scales. There is some research available to guide interpretation of low scores (e.g., Kremyar et al., 2020; J. T. Hall, Lee, et al., 2021). The interpretive guidelines presented in this chapter for low scores are based on information in Ben-Porath and Tellegen (2008/2011), negative correlations between scales and external criterion measures presented in Tellegen and Ben-Porath (2008/2011), and the published empirical studies.

Interpretive Guidelines for Validity Scales

Cannot Say (CNS)

When the test taker omits fewer than 15 items, the protocol is interpretable. However, when 15 or more items are omitted, caution is indicated in the interpretation of the substantive scales because the omission of items tends to lead to lower scores on these scales. One should always examine the percentage of items omitted from each scale. If more than 10% of items are omitted from a scale, the scale should not be interpreted. This information is readily available in MMPI-2-RF score and interpretive reports.

Variable Response Inconsistency (VRIN-r) Scale

HIGH SCORES (T ≥ 70)

Scores at this level indicate that the test taker responded in an inconsistent manner. T scores between 70 and 79 suggest that the protocol should be interpreted with caution. When T scores are ≥ 80, inconsistent responding is so pervasive that the protocol should not be interpreted.

AVERAGE SCORES (T = 39–69)

The test taker responded in a consistent manner, and the protocol is interpretable.

LOW SCORE (T = 30–38)

The test taker was remarkably consistent, and perhaps overly cautious, in responding; but the protocol is interpretable.

True Response Inconsistency (TRIN-r) Scale

HIGH SCORES (T ≥ 70)

High scores on this scale indicate that the test taker responded in an inconsistent manner with fixed responding. When a designation of T is associated with the score, the fixed responding is likely to be yea-saying, whereas a designation of F associated with the score indicates that the fixed responding is likely to be naysaying. T scores between 70 and 79 indicate a tendency toward fixed responding, and the protocol should be interpreted with caution. When T scores are ≥ 80, the fixed responding is pervasive enough that the protocol should not be interpreted.

AVERAGE SCORES (T = 50–69)

Scores in this range indicate that there is no evidence of fixed responding, and the protocol is interpretable.

Infrequent Responses (F-r) Scale

T = 120

Scores at this level indicate that the test taker has reported a large number of symptoms that are rarely endorsed by most individuals. The VRIN-r and TRIN-r scales should be consulted to determine whether F-r scale scores are the product of non-content-based invalid responding. If evidence of this response style is not found, then the scores likely represent an attempt on the part of the test taker to appear to have much more severe psychopathology or distress than is actually the case. Protocols with F-r scale scores at this level should be considered invalid and should not be interpreted.

T = 100–119

Scores at this level may indicate non-content-based invalid responding, severe emotional distress, or overreporting. Check the VRIN-r and TRIN-r scales. If these scales are not at acceptable levels, the protocol should be considered invalid and should not be interpreted. If these scores are at acceptable levels, it is important to determine whether the F-r scale scores are reflecting severe psychopathology or overreporting. For individuals for whom there is neither history nor any current indication of serious dysfunction, scores at this level likely indicate overreporting, and the protocol should not be interpreted. For individuals with a history or current indications of serious dysfunction, the scores at this level should be interpreted as reflecting genuine psychopathology, and the protocol can be interpreted. Protocols with F-r scale scores at this level are more likely to reflect genuine psychopathology if the Fp-r scale is at an acceptable level (see later).

T = 90–99

Scores at this level are to be interpreted similarly to T scores between 110 and 119, except the likelihood of overreporting is less than at the higher levels.

T = 79–89

Inconsistent responding or overreporting of symptoms is possible at this level, but scores are more likely to be reflective of serious psychopathology, especially if the Fp-r scale score is at an acceptable level (see later). The protocol can be interpreted but with the caution that scores may to some extent overestimate the severity of symptoms and problems.

T < 79

When scores are at this level, there is no evidence of significant overreporting, and the protocol can be interpreted.

Infrequent Psychopathology Responses (Fp-r) Scale

T ≥ 100

Scores at this level indicate an invalid protocol that should not be interpreted because the test taker has endorsed many very rare symptoms. Scores at this level can result from non-content-based invalid responding (check VRIN-r and TRIN-r) or from the test taker overreporting severe psychological symptoms and problems in order to appear more maladjusted than is really the case.

T = 80–99

Scores at this level can indicate non-content-based invalid responding (check VRIN-r and TRIN-r). For individuals with histories or current corroborating evidence of severe dysfunction, scores at this level likely reflect genuine psychopathology. For those without histories or corroborating evidence of severe dysfunction, scores at this level likely reflect overreporting.

T = 70–79

Scores at this level may indicate non-content-based invalid responding (check VRIN-r and TRIN-r), overreporting, or genuine psychopathology. Scores should be interpreted similarly to those at the 80–99 level, except at this level the likelihood of genuine psychopathology is greater than at the higher levels.

T < 70

There is no evidence of overreporting that would compromise protocol validity.

Infrequent Somatic Responses (Fs) Scale

T ≥ 100

Scores at this level indicate overreporting of somatic symptoms rarely described by persons with genuine medical problems. The scores may result from non-content-based invalid responding (check VRIN-r and TRIN-r). If these scales are at acceptable levels, the Fs scores are likely to reflect overreporting of physical complaints; and scores on the somatic substantive scales (i.e., RC1 and Somatic/Cognitive SP scales) should be interpreted with considerable caution if at all.

T = 80–99

Scores at this level indicate possible overreporting of somatic symptoms either as a product of non-content-based invalid responding (check VRIN-r and TRIN-r) or as indicating an effort to appear to have more somatic problems than is actually the case. In individuals with no histories or corroborating evidence of physical health problems, scores at this level likely represent overreporting of somatic symptoms, and scores on RC1 and the Somatic/Cognitive SP scales should only be interpreted with caution.

T < 80

There is no evidence of overreporting of somatic symptoms, and scores on the somatic substantive scales can be interpreted.

Symptom Validity (FBS-r) Scale

T ≥ 100

Scores at this level suggest that the test taker has reported a very unusual combination of symptoms that likely reflects noncredible reporting of somatic or cognitive symptoms. Because scores at this level can result from non-content-based invalid responding, check the VRIN-r and TRIN-r scales. If this type of responding can be ruled out, scores on RC1 and the Somatic/Cognitive SP scales should be interpreted with great caution if at all.

T = 80–99

Scores at this level indicate possible reporting of unusual combinations of somatic or cognitive symptoms. Because scores at this level can be the product of non-content-based invalid responding, check the VRIN-r and TRIN-r scales. If this type of responding can be ruled out, FBS-r scores may reflect credible reporting of serious somatic problems or cognitive deficits. Alternatively, they may reflect the test taker overreported these kinds of symptoms in order to appear to have medical or neurological problems that do not exist or to exaggerate genuine symptoms. Scores on the RC1 scale and the Somatic/Cognitive SP scales should only be interpreted with caution.

T < 80

When scores are at this level, there is no evidence of significant overreporting of somatic or cognitive symptoms, and scales that assess such symptoms can be interpreted.

Response Bias Scale (RBS)

T ≥ 100

Scores at this level suggest the test taker has reported a highly unusual combination of symptoms closely associated with noncredible memory problems. The VRIN-r and TRIN-r scales should be reviewed to rule out non-content-based invalid responding. The only other cause sufficient to explain RBS scores at this level of elevation is overreporting. Thus, scores on the COG scale should be interpreted with great caution if at all.

T = 80–99

Scores at this level indicate that unusual combinations of symptoms often associated with noncredible memory complaints were endorsed. If non-content-based invalid responding can be ruled out (see VRIN-r and TRIN-r), then RBS scores at this level of elevation may result from credible reporting of symptoms in a test taker experiencing severe emotional distress. Alternatively, RBS scores of this magnitude may reflect symptom exaggeration, which will lead the COG scale to overestimate the severity and scope of memory problems. As such, scores on COG should be interpreted with caution.

T < 80

When scores are at this level, there is no evidence of significant overreporting, and the COG scale can be interpreted normally.

Uncommon Virtues (L-r) Scale

T ≥ 80

Scores at this level indicate that test takers have presented themselves in an overly positive and virtuous manner. Since scores at this level can be a product of non-content-based invalid responding, the VRIN-r and TRIN-r scales should be examined. If this response style is ruled out, then elevated scores on substantive scales can be interpreted but only cautiously, as the test taker is likely to have engaged in underreporting. The observed scores may underestimate problems assessed by those scales. Substantive scales that are not elevated, including those occurring in the interpretable low score range, are uninterpretable. This is because the magnitude of the score may reflect the absence of the difficulty assessed by the scale or the impact of underreporting.

T = 70–79

Scores at this level indicate that the test taker likely presented themselves in a very positive way. Because the score may be the product of non-content-based invalid responding, check the VRIN-r and TRIN-r scales. If this response style is not indicated, scores on substantive scales should be interpreted with caution, as the test taker may have engaged in underreporting. The absence of elevations on substantive scales is uninterpretable, and elevated scores on substantive scales may underestimate the problems assessed by the scales. Scores at this level may also indicate someone with an upbringing that strongly stressed traditional values.

T = 65–69

Scores at this level may be the product of non-content-based invalid responding (check VRIN-r and TRIN-r) or an effort by test takers to present themselves in an unrealistically favorable light. If non-content-based invalid responding is ruled out, substantive scores can be interpreted but only cautiously, as elevated scores will likely underestimate problems assessed by those scales. Substantive scales that are not elevated are uninterpretable. Scores at this level may also indicate that the test takers were raised in a very traditional way.

T < 65

When scores are at this level, there is no evidence of significant underreporting, and substantive scales can be interpreted.

Adjustment Validity (K–r) Scale

T ≥ 70

Scores at this level indicate that the test taker has presented themselves as remarkably well adjusted. Because scores at this level can be a product of non-content-based invalid responding, check the VRIN-r and TRIN-r scales. If this kind of responding can be ruled out, interpretation should proceed with considerable caution, as the score on K-r likely represents an attempt by the test taker to present themselves as much better adjusted than they really are. If elevated, then substantive scales can be interpreted, but they are likely to understate the problems assessed by those scales. Scales that are not elevated, including those in the interpretable low score range, should not be interpreted. This is because the unelevated scale score may reflect the absence of problems or the effect of underreporting.

T = 66–69

Because scores at this level can be a product of non-content-based invalid responding, check the VRIN-r and TRIN-r scales. If this response style can be ruled out, K-r scores may reflect either underreporting of symptoms and problems or very good psychological adjustment. For persons for whom there is no corroborating evidence of good psychological adjustment, the absence of elevation on substantive scales is uninterpretable. Elevations on substantive scales may underestimate the problems assessed by those scales, but they can be interpreted.

T = 60–65

Scores at this level indicate possible underreporting of symptoms and problems. Non-content-based invalid responding should be ruled out by checking the VRIN-r and TRIN-r scales. If this response style is ruled out, for persons for whom there is corroborating evidence of poor adjustment, absence of elevations on substantive scales should be interpreted with caution. Elevated scores on substantive scales may underestimate the problems assessed by those scales. Scores at this level are common among persons who complete the MMPI-2-RF in nonclinical settings (e.g., custody evaluations, pre-employment screening).

T < 60

When scores are at this level, there is no evidence of significant underreporting, and scores on substantive scales may be interpreted.

Interpretive Guidelines for Higher–Order (H–O) Scales

The H-O scales reflect problems in feeling, thinking, and behaving and are intended to provide a broad overview of the types of difficulties a test taker may be experiencing. More extremely elevated scores on these scales can reflect symptom severity but can also reflect the breadth of symptoms within the domain a test taker is reporting.

The absence of elevation on a H-O scale could mean either that a test taker is reporting no difficulties within that domain or a very circumscribed set of difficulties. In the latter circumstance, these narrower difficulties are likely to be captured by scales lower in the MMPI-2-RF hierarchy, such as the RC or SP scales.

Emotional/Internalizing Dysfunction (EID)

This scale is comprised of 41 items reflecting a variety of emotional difficulties that tend to characterize internalizing dysfunctions. Scores on EID are associated with the internalizing dimension in structural models of psychopathology.

High scores (T ≥ 65) indicate persons who

1. are experiencing a great deal of emotional turmoil (when T score ≥ 80, the distress is likely to be perceived as a crisis)
2. feel overwhelmed by their life situations
3. feel vulnerable, helpless, and unable to cope
4. have depression as a prominent presenting problem
5. are likely to feel sad and blue
6. lack energy and motivation to get things done
7. may have suicidal ideation and histories of suicide behavior
8. report anxiety
9. present somatic complaints
10. are likely to have obsessive thoughts
11. have difficulty concentrating
12. may feel mistreated
13. tend to be dissatisfied in their romantic relationships
14. feel angry
15. should be evaluated for depressive, anxiety, and somatic symptom disorders
16. are likely to be motivated for treatment because of emotional turmoil
17. likely view the working alliance with their therapist as weak

Low scores (T < 39) indicate individuals who report a better than average level of emotional adjustment.

Thought Dysfunction (THD)

This scale is comprised of 26 items reflecting thought dysfunction, such as unusual perceptual experiences and odd beliefs that may suggest delusions. This scale reflects the thought disorder dimension in quantitative models of psychopathology.

High scores (T ≥ 65) indicate individuals who

1. have reported symptoms of thought dysfunction
2. may experience auditory or visual hallucinations
3. may have delusions of grandeur or persecution
4. may engage in magical thinking
5. feel that life is a strain
6. report somatic complaints
7. feel depressed

8. are suspicious and untrusting
9. have low frustration tolerance
10. sometimes act aggressively toward others
11. do not communicate effectively
12. do not make good impressions on other people
13. do not seem motivated to work or achieve
14. may have problems with the law dating back to adolescence
15. should be evaluated for psychotic spectrum disorders (e.g., schizophrenia, delusional disorder)
16. should be evaluated for antipsychotic medications
17. may require treatment in a structured environment

Low scores (T < 39) on this scale are not interpreted.

Behavioral/Externalizing Dysfunction (BXD)

This scale is comprised of 23 items reflecting externalizing tendencies, such as substance use and antisocial behaviors. This scale reflects both disinhibited and antagonistic externalizing dimensions in quantitative models of psychopathology.

High scores (T ≥ 65) indicate persons who

1. report engaging in a wide variety of externalizing behaviors that have gotten them into difficulties
2. may have histories of arrests and convictions dating back to adolescence
3. may misuse alcohol and other substances
4. are aggressive in relationships
5. have low frustration tolerance
6. often show poor judgment
7. are cynical and untrusting
8. often feel that they have been mistreated
9. have histories of problems in school, at home, and at work
10. are narcissistic, selfish, and self-indulgent
11. typically do not report great emotional distress but may report some symptoms of anxiety and depression
12. often are given Cluster B personality disorder or substance use disorder diagnoses
13. typically are not interested in changing but may agree to treatment to avoid negative consequences
14. need to develop better self-control
15. may terminate treatment prematurely

Low scores (T < 39) indicate persons who report higher than average levels of behavioral constraint. They are unlikely to engage in externalizing, acting-out behaviors.

Interpretive Guidelines for Restructured Clinical (RC) Scales

As discussed earlier in this chapter, the RC scales of the MMPI-2-RF are identical to the RC scales of the MMPI-2. Thus, the interpretive guidelines reported in Chapter 7 of this book apply to the MMPI-2-RF RC scales and are reprinted here for your convenience.

Demoralization (RCd)

The RCd scale reflects the pleasantness–unpleasantness (also known as the happiness–unhappiness) dimension from Tellegen and colleagues' (1999a; 1999b) model of mood and affect and is associated with the "distress" dimension of internalizing psychopathology posited in recent quantitative models of psychopathology. Scores on RCd provide an indication of the overall emotional discomfort and turmoil a person is experiencing. High scorers (T ≥ 65) on this scale are likely also to have high scores on other RC, SP, and PSY-5 scales—especially those that have strong affective components.

Very high scores (T ≥ 80) on the RCd scale indicate persons who

1. are experiencing significant emotional turmoil
2. report feeling depressed
3. report being anxious and unable to concentrate
4. report somatic complaints that may increase in times of stress
5. feel overwhelmed by the demands of their life situations
6. feel incapable of coping with their current life circumstances
7. may be experiencing suicidal thinking or engaging in suicide-related behavior
8. should be evaluated for suicide risk (particularly if RC9 is ≥ 65)
9. should be evaluated for disorders characterized by high levels of dysphoric affect such as depressive, generalized anxiety, and trauma-related disorders
10. may be motivated for treatment because of emotional distress
11. need intervention to relieve emotional distress
12. are at risk for poor treatment outcomes

High scores (T = 65–79) indicate persons who

1. feel sad and unhappy
2. feel anxious much of the time
3. are dissatisfied with their life situations
4. have poor self-concepts and feel like failures
5. have low self-efficacy and view themselves as unworthy and incapable
6. react poorly to stress
7. tend to imagine the worst possible outcomes for actions or events
8. respond to negative events with internal, global, and stable attributions
9. are pessimistic about their lives getting better
10. may engage in excessive reassurance seeking

Low scores (T < 39) indicate persons who report a greater than average level of morale and life satisfaction.

Somatic Complaints (RC1)

Items on RC1 inquire about an individual's general sense of physical well-being and specific somatic difficulties and reflect a broad somatoform construct similar to that posited in dimensional models of psychopathology. The cardinal feature of high scores (T ≥ 65) on the RC1 scale is somatic preoccupation.

High scores on the RC1 scale indicate persons who

1. report multiple somatic complaints including gastrointestinal problems, head pain, and neurological symptoms
2. have increased somatic symptoms in times of stress
3. are quite resistant to considering psychological factors that may be related to somatic symptoms
4. are at risk for terminating therapy before goals are met
5. if physical explanations for their somatic symptoms can be ruled out, they should be further evaluated for somatoform disorders

Low scores (T < 39) indicate persons who report a sense of physical well-being. Specifically, low scores on RC1 indicate people who are likely to describe having fewer medical and physical difficulties than is typical.

Low Positive Emotions (RC2)

Items on RC2 ask about the test-taker's experience of positive emotions, social engagement, and interest and ability to engage in activities. The RC2 scale reflects the positive affect dimension of the Tellegen and colleagues' (1999a; 1999b) model of mood and affect. It has conceptual connections to the internalizing and social detachment spectra described in dimensional models of psychopathology. Scores on this scale are intended to reflect the test taker's low capacity for positive emotional experiences, a core component of depressive syndromes (i.e., anhedonia).

High scores (T ≥ 65) on the RC2 scale indicate persons who

1. lack positive emotional experiences in life
2. have deficits in their ability to experience joy and happiness (anhedonia)
3. are unhappy and demoralized
4. lack energy to handle demands of their life situations
5. find it difficult to take charge, make decisions, and get things done
6. tend to be introverted, passive, and withdrawn in social situations
7. often feel bored and isolated
8. are pessimistic
9. have low expectations of success and are not likely to place themselves in competitive situations
10. may meet criteria for Major Depression or other depressive disorders
11. should be evaluated for disorders characterized by social withdrawal or avoidance, such as social anxiety disorder
12. should be evaluated for antidepressant medications
13. may have difficulty engaging in treatment because of low positive emotionality
14. are at risk for terminating therapy before goals are met
15. if T ≥ 75, may need inpatient treatment for depression

Low scores (T < 39) on the RC2 scale indicate persons who

1. report a high level of psychological well-being
2. are likely to be satisfied with their life

3. report a wide range of emotionally positive experiences
4. report feeling confident and energetic
5. have high levels of positive affect
6. have positive self-esteem
7. are extraverted and socially engaged
8. are optimistic about the future

Cynicism (RC3)

The MMPI-2's Clinical Scale 3 has two major components—somatic complaints and avowal of excessive trust of others. As mentioned in Chapter 7, during development of the RC scales, the somatic complaint component was assigned to the RC1 scale. The RC3 scale assesses the second component but is scored in the opposite direction from Scale 3. Thus, RC3 reflects cynical (as opposed to naïve) beliefs about others.

High scores (T ≥ 65) indicate persons who

1. have cynical beliefs
2. see other people as untrustworthy, uncaring, and concerned only about themselves
3. may be hostile or manipulative when interacting with other people
4. feel alienated from others
5. need help in developing interpersonal trust
6. may have difficulty engaging in therapy or forming therapeutic relationships
7. are at risk for negative treatment outcomes

Low scores (T < 39) on the RC3 scale indicate persons who

1. disavow cynical beliefs
2. see others as well-intentioned and trustworthy
3. may be naive, gullible, and overly trusting of others

Antisocial Behavior (RC4)

The RC4 scale assesses antisocial characteristics and reflects both the antagonistic and disinhibited aspects of externalizing tendencies reflected in dimensional models of psychopathology.

High scores (T ≥ 65) on the RC4 scale indicate persons who

1. report histories of antisocial behaviors
2. find it difficult to conform to societal norms and expectations
3. are likely to have been in trouble with the law
4. are at increased risk for problematic substance use
5. behave aggressively toward other people
6. are critical, argumentative, and antagonistic
7. have conflictual relationships with other people
8. may have significant family problems
9. should be evaluated for Cluster B Personality Disorders
10. are not likely to be motivated for treatment

11. may not be very compliant in treatment
12. may be at risk for not completing recommended treatments
13. need help in developing better self-control

Low scores (T < 39) on the RC4 scale indicate persons who report higher than average levels of behavioral constraint. Individuals achieving low scores on RC4 are likely to be overcontrolled.

Ideas of Persecution (RC6)

Items on RC6 inquire about an individual's beliefs about others wanting to harm them and perceptions of being persecuted. Scores on RC6 reflect aspects of a liability toward thought dysfunction described in dimensional models of psychopathology. However, it is important to note that elevations on this scale do not necessarily indicate the presence of thinking that is delusional in nature. Elevations can occur in individuals who are suspicious and cautious around people for other reasons (e.g., as a result of traumatic experiences).

High scores (T ≥ 65) indicate persons who

1. feel targeted, controlled, or victimized by others
2. are suspicious of the motivation of others
3. have difficulty in forming relationships
4. may have difficulty forming therapeutic relationships
5. if T ≥ 80, may indicate paranoid delusions or hallucinations
6. if T ≥ 80, should be evaluated further for schizophrenia and other psychotic spectrum disorders, including Cluster A personality disorders

Low scores on this scale are not interpreted.

Dysfunctional Negative Emotions (RC7)

The RC7 scale reflects the negative affect dimension of the Tellegen and colleagues (1999a; 1999b) model of mood and affect and is associated with the "fear" dimension of internalizing psychopathology described in dimensional models of psychopathology. Items on RC7 assess the test-taker's experience of negative emotions such as anxiety, anger, and fear. Given the negative emotions reflected in RC7, test takers with high scores on this scale will also frequently report experiencing demoralization. However, while these experiences are correlated, negative emotionality is distinct from demoralization, which tends to pervade many different kinds of psychopathology.

High scores (T ≥ 65) on the RC7 scale indicate persons who

1. report negative emotional experiences including anxiety, fear, and irritability
2. worry excessively
3. experience intrusive ideation
4. report feeling sad and unhappy
5. are insecure and excessively sensitive to perceived criticism
6. are self-critical and guilt-prone
7. ruminate and brood about perceived failures

8. should be evaluated for disorders related to fearfulness (i.e., phobias, social anxiety, and obsessive–compulsive disorders), trauma-related disorders, and Cluster C Personality disorders
9. may be motivated for treatment because of emotional distress
10. are at risk for terminating therapy before goals are met
11. should be evaluated for anxiolytic medications

Low scores (T < 39) on the RC7 scale indicate persons who report below-average levels of negative emotional experiences.

Aberrant Experiences (RC8)

Items on RC8 inquire about the test-taker's experience of unusual thinking and perceptual experiences. It assesses sensory, perceptual, cognitive, and motor disturbances suggestive of psychotic disorders. Scores on RC8 reflect aspects of a liability toward thought dysfunction described in dimensional models of psychopathology.

High scores (T ≥ 65) on the RC8 scale indicate persons who

1. report unusual sensory, perceptual, cognitive, or motor experiences
2. may experience hallucinations or delusions
3. may experience bizarre sensory experiences
4. have impaired reality testing
5. may report feeling anxious or depressed
6. have impaired occupational and interpersonal functioning
7. may be experiencing subclinical levels of thought disturbance that reflect a vulnerability to psychotic disorders
8. in mental health settings should be evaluated further for psychosis spectrum disorders, including Schizophrenia
9. may require treatment in structured settings
10. should be evaluated for antipsychotic medications
11. may find it difficult to participate appropriately in treatment because of disordered thinking

Low scores on the RC8 scale are not interpreted.

Hypomanic Activation (RC9)

Items on RC9 have content reflecting experiences often associated with hypomanic activation, such as excessive energy and movement and racing thoughts. In this way, RC9 reflects aspects of the mania subfactor in dimensional models of psychopathology, which is linked to both internalizing and thought disorder spectra. Items on this scale also inquire about impulsive risk-taking and excitement-seeking behaviors, which can occur during hypomanic episodes. Thus, in many samples, items on RC9 reflect disinhibited aspects of the externalizing spectrum identified in dimensional models of psychopathology.

High scores (T ≥ 65) on the RC9 scale indicate persons who

1. experience racing thoughts
2. experience high energy levels
3. have heightened mood

4. are irritable and aggressive
5. show poor impulse control
6. may engage in antisocial behaviors
7. may misuse substances
8. are sensation seekers and risk takers
9. should be evaluated further for bipolar disorders
10. may find appropriate participation in treatment difficult because of excessive behavioral activation
11. should be evaluated for mood-stabilizing medications
12. if T ≥ 75, may experience manic episodes

Low scores (T < 39) on the RC9 scale indicate persons who have below-average levels of activation and engagement with their environments. Individuals with low scores on RC9 are likely to experience low energy levels and be withdrawn from their environment. They should be evaluated for depressive disorders, especially if scores on RC2 are also elevated.

Interpretive Guidelines for Specific Problems (SP) Scales

Somatic/Cognitive Specific Problems (SP) Scales
The Somatic/Cognitive SP scales assess somatic and cognitive concerns a test taker may have. Scores on these scales can be of assistance in determining what kind of specific physical difficulties a test taker may report, either in the context of an elevated score on RC1 or when interpreting isolated SP scale elevations.

Malaise (MLS)
This scale is comprised of eight items assessing the test taker's beliefs about their physical health and functioning.
High scores (T ≥ 65) indicate individuals who

1. report feelings of ill health and fatigue that may interfere with work and other activities
2. have vague somatic complaints
3. tend to experience poor sleep
4. have low levels of physical activity
5. feel sad and depressed
6. feel unable to deal with stressors in their life situations
7. are pessimistic about the likelihood of their lives getting better
8. may feel angry much of the time
9. feel mistreated by others
10. should be evaluated for depressive and somatic symptom disorders
11. may be unwilling or unable to participate in treatment because of malaise
12. likely view the working alliance with their therapist as weak

Low scores (T < 39) indicate persons who report a general sense of physical well-being. Individuals with low scores are likely to experience high-quality sleep and engage in behaviors that promote good health.

Gastrointestinal Complaints (GIC)

This scale is comprised of five items assessing the test taker's experience of gastrointestinal difficulties.

High scores (T ≥ 65) indicate individuals who

1. report gastrointestinal complaints (e.g., nausea, vomiting)
2. may report manifestations of depression (e.g., sad mood, decreased energy, suicidal ideation)
3. often are given depressive disorder diagnoses
4. should be evaluated for somatic symptom disorder if physical explanations for somatic symptoms can be ruled out
5. may benefit from learning stress reduction techniques

Low scores (T < 39) on this scale are not interpreted.

Head Pain Complaints (HPC)

This scale consists of six items assessing the test-taker's experience of headaches and other head-related pain.

High scores (T ≥ 65) indicate individuals who

1. report head or neck pain
2. experience increased pain during times of stress
3. may lack energy
4. feel overwhelmed by the demands of their life situations
5. tend to feel sad and depressed
6. in mental health settings, often are given depressive disorder diagnoses and treated with antidepressant medications
7. should be considered for somatic symptom disorder if physical explanations for the reported pain can be ruled out
8. may benefit from learning pain management techniques

Low scores (T < 39) on this scale are not interpreted.

Neurological Complaints (NUC)

This scale is comprised of 10 items. Its contents reflect the test-taker's experience of difficulties that could be the result of neurological or psychological difficulties, such as unexplained numbness, dizziness, and involuntary movements.

High scores (T ≥ 65) indicate persons who

1. report problems with motor control (e.g., balance, dizziness, paralysis)
2. in mental health settings, may report feeling depressed and anxious
3. do not cope well with stress
4. lack energy to meet the demands of everyday life
5. should be considered for somatic symptom disorder if physical explanations for somatic symptoms can be ruled out
6. may benefit from medical or behavioral management of symptoms if a physical origin of neurological complaints has been established

Low scores (T < 39) on this scale are not interpreted.

Cognitive Complaints (COG)

This scale is comprised of 10 items assessing a test-taker's perception that they are experiencing difficulties with cognition, including problems with memory.

High scores (T ≥ 65) indicate persons who

1. report problems with memory and concentration
2. do not cope well with stress
3. often feel inadequate and inferior
4. sometimes report perceptual aberrations or strange thoughts
5. in mental health settings, may report feeling anxious and depressed
6. should be referred for neurological evaluation
7. should be considered for somatic symptom disorder if physical explanations for the cognitive problems can be ruled out
8. in mental health settings, may be at increased risk for missing appointments

Low scores (T < 39) on this scale are not interpreted.

Internalizing Specific Problems (SP) Scales

These scales reflect narrow manifestations of internalizing symptoms. They represent facets of problems described by EID (all Internalizing SP scales), RCd (SUI, HLP, SFD, NFC), and RC7 (STW, AXY, ANP, BRF, MSF). They can be interpreted in the context of elevations on these broader scales, but also in isolation.

Suicidal/Death Ideation (SUI)

This scale is comprised of five items reflecting thoughts of death and suicide, as well as past suicidal behavior. Elevated scores on this scale signal the need for a more comprehensive evaluation of the individual's risk for suicide.

High scores (T ≥ 65) indicate persons who

1. report suicidal ideation or histories of suicide attempts
2. should be thoroughly evaluated for suicide risk
3. are at an increased risk for suicide attempt; this risk is further increased if BXD, RC4, RC9, JCP, AGGR-r, or DISC-r are also elevated (T ≥ 65); or if MSF or IPP are low (T < 39)
4. feel quite depressed
5. feel overwhelmed and helpless
6. feel pessimistic about the likelihood of their lives getting better
7. may report anxiety, rumination, and specific fears
8. often receive diagnoses of depressive disorders and are treated with antidepressant medications

Low scores (T < 39) on this scale are not interpreted.

Helplessness/Hopelessness (HLP)

This scale consists of five items assessing the test-taker's experience of hopelessness and their beliefs about the likelihood their lives could be improved.

High scores (T ≥ 65) indicate persons who

1. are expressing unhappiness with their lives
2. feel that they cannot make significant changes in their lives
3. are pessimistic about the likelihood of their lives getting better
4. experience a great deal of emotional turmoil
5. feel depressed
6. feel inadequate and inferior
7. feel angry because of perceived mistreatment by others
8. are suspicious of the motives of others
9. may see suicide as the only solution to their problems
10. often have histories of suicide attempts
11. often receive depressive disorder diagnoses and are treated with antidepressant medications
12. may benefit from treatment to increase feelings of hope

Low scores (T < 39) on this scale are not interpreted.

Self-Doubt (SFD)

This scale is composed of four items reflecting the test taker's low self-confidence and esteem.

High scores (T ≥ 65) indicate persons who

1. report lack of self-confidence
2. report feelings of uselessness
3. feel inferior to other people
4. feel sad and depressed
5. may have suicidal ideation and histories of suicide attempts
6. report anxiety, obsessiveness, and rumination
7. feel that they get a raw deal from life
8. feel angry and resentful about perceived mistreatment
9. in mental health settings, often receive depressive disorder diagnoses and are treated with antidepressant medications
10. may benefit from treatment to increase self-esteem

Low scores (T < 39) on this scale are not interpreted.

Inefficacy (NFC)

This scale is comprised of nine items reflecting whether test takers view themselves as decisive and as having the capacity to deal effectively with difficult situations.

High scores (T ≥ 65) indicate persons who

1. report being very indecisive
2. try to avoid making difficult decisions in life
3. are not very self-reliant
4. may experience depression and anxiety

5. feel insecure and inadequate
6. give up easily
7. may benefit from treatment to decrease indecisiveness

Low scores (T < 39) on this scale indicate persons who are efficacious and decisive in stressful situations.

Stress/Worry (STW)

This scale is comprised of seven items reflecting the test-taker's experience of excessive worry and difficulties arising from that worry.

High scores (T ≥ 65) indicate persons who

1. feel anxious and worried about many things
2. feel there is much to do and little time to do it
3. feel overwhelmed
4. do not cope well with stress
5. may develop somatic symptoms when stress levels increase
6. in mental health settings, may be depressed and anxious
7. may experience suicidal ideation
8. often feel like failures
9. are pessimistic about the future
10. may benefit from learning stress management techniques

Low scores (T < 39) indicate persons who report below-average levels of stress and worry.

Anxiety (AXY)

This scale is comprised of five items reflecting the test-taker's experience of anxiety and related difficulties.

High scores (T ≥ 65) indicate persons who

1. report frequent and pervasive feelings of anxiety, dread, and fear
2. experience intrusive ideation
3. have difficulty concentrating
4. experience nightmares and disturbed sleep
5. feel depressed
6. may have suicidal ideation
7. report somatic complaints
8. do not cope well with stress
9. feel overwhelmed by the demands of their lives
10. are pessimistic about the likelihood of things getting better
11. may be experiencing posttraumatic distress
12. should be evaluated for anxiety disorders, especially trauma- and other stress-related disorders
13. should be evaluated for anxiolytic medications

Low scores (T < 39) on this scale are not interpreted.

Anger Proneness (ANP)

This scale consists of seven items assessing experiences and expressions of anger.

High scores (T ≥ 65) indicate individuals who

1. report having a low frustration tolerance
2. are impatient and easily irritated
3. do not cope well with stress and feel that life is a strain
4. may report anxiety, depression, and somatic symptoms
5. may have histories of school problems and juvenile delinquency
6. may benefit from learning anger management techniques

Low scores (T < 39) on this scale are not interpreted.

Behavior-Restricting Fears (BRF)

This scale is comprised of nine items reflecting the test-taker's restriction of their activities in- and outside of the home due to fearfulness.

High scores (T ≥ 65) indicate persons who

1. report several specific fears that restrict normal activities in- and outside the home
2. feel uneasy when away from home
3. may express fear of darkness, dirt, money, or pointed objects
4. report feeling generally anxious and depressed
5. may report somatic complaints
6. are seen by others as socially awkward and not very self-reliant
7. do not cope well with stress
8. are not achievement oriented
9. should be evaluated for anxiety disorders, particularly agoraphobia
10. likely view the working alliance with their therapist as weak

Low scores (T < 39) on this scale are not interpreted.

Multiple Specific Fears (MSF)

This scale is comprised of nine items reflecting fears of specific things or environments.

High scores (T ≥ 65) indicate persons who

1. report having multiple fears
2. report fear of natural events (e.g., windstorms, earthquakes)
3. report fear of animals (e.g., snakes, spiders)
4. tend to feel anxious and depressed
5. may report somatic complaints
6. do not cope well with stress
7. do not engage in risky behaviors
8. are not achievement oriented
9. lack energy
10. are pessimistic about the future

11. in inpatient mental health settings, may report magical thinking, hallucinations, or other symptoms of psychosis
12. in substance use treatment settings, tend to have more severe substance-related difficulties
13. may benefit from behavioral approaches to fear reduction

Low scores (T < 39) indicate persons who report a lower-than-average number of fears.

Externalizing Specific Problems (SP) Scales

These scales are intended to help identify specific manifestations of externalizing symptoms. They reflect facets of BXD (all Externalizing SP scales), RC4 (JCP & SUB), and RC9 (AGG & ACT), but can be interpreted even in the absence of elevations on these broader scales.

Juvenile Conduct Problems (JCP)

This scale is comprised of six items assessing a test-taker's history of engaging in acting-out and antisocial behaviors as a child or adolescent.

High scores (T ≥ 65) indicate persons who

1. report school difficulties including behavior problems and truancy
2. may report having stolen things when young
3. have histories of acting out both as adolescents and adults
4. are likely to have histories of trouble with the law
5. are likely to have histories of problematic use of alcohol and other substances
6. show poor judgment
7. are emotionally labile
8. may act out in aggressive ways
9. tend to have problems with authority figures
10. have stormy relationships, especially with family members
11. tend to blame their family for their difficulties
12. do not report many internalizing symptoms, but in mental health settings may report feeling anxious and depressed
13. often are given diagnoses of antisocial personality disorder or substance use disorders
14. are not likely to be motivated for treatment
15. are at increased risk for missing treatment appointments
16. may be at increased risk for not completing a recommended course of treatment

Low scores (T < 39) on this scale are not interpreted.

Substance Abuse (SUB)

This scale consists of seven items asking a test taker about their use of alcohol or other drugs as well as problems that may have arisen because of this use.

High scores (T ≥ 65) on this scale indicate persons who

1. are openly acknowledging use of alcohol, marijuana, or other substances
2. report using substances in order to relax
3. are likely to have a pattern of risky or problematic use of alcohol or other drugs, including prescription medications
4. tend to have problems with authority figures
5. may be physically aggressive at times
6. tend to be argumentative and provocative
7. have stormy interpersonal relationships
8. have difficulty trusting others
9. in mental health settings, may feel depressed
10. often receive substance use disorder diagnoses
11. should be more thoroughly evaluated for substance-related difficulties
12. may benefit from participating in a substance use treatment program

Low scores on SUB are not interpreted because they could indicate either absence of substance use or denial of existing substance use and related difficulties.

Aggression (AGG)
This scale is composed of nine items reflecting the test-taker's engagement in aggressive behavior as well as attitudes they endorse that may support acting in an aggressive manner.

High scores (T ≥ 65) indicate persons who

1. report feeling angry
2. report acting out in aggressive ways toward other people
3. acknowledge breaking things and hurting other people in fights
4. experience pleasure from making other people afraid of them
5. are cynical and suspicious of the motives of others
6. may have histories of violent behavior
7. tend to have problems with authority figures
8. are seen by others as antisocial
9. tend to have histories of misbehavior in school
10. have had difficulties with the law
11. tend to have a risky or problematic pattern of alcohol or other substance use
12. may report physical problems
13. may feel sad and anxious
14. may have underlying feelings of inadequacy
15. may benefit from learning anger management techniques
16. may be at increased risk for missing treatment appointments or for not completing a recommended course of treatment

Low scores (T < 39) indicate individuals who report below-average levels of aggressive behavior.

Activation (ACT)

This scale is comprised of eight items assessing a test-taker's level of excitation and energy.

High scores (T ≥ 65) indicate persons who

1. describe periods of excessive energy and excitement
2. report they have difficulty controlling their thoughts, speech, or behavior at times
3. may have histories of mood swings and hypomanic behavior
4. have periods of accelerated speech and decreased need for sleep
5. may have histories of substance misuse and juvenile delinquency
6. in inpatient settings, may show evidence of magical thinking, perceptual aberrations, or hallucinations
7. if T > 80, should be evaluated for bipolar disorder
8. may benefit from mood-stabilizing medications

Low scores (T < 39) indicate persons who report below-average levels of energy and activation.

Interpersonal Specific Problems (SP) Scales

The Interpersonal SP Scales provide information about the test-taker's interpersonal functioning. The Interpersonal Scales assess an independent domain of functioning that also includes RC3.

Family Problems (FML)

This scale is comprised of 10 items reflecting the test-taker's experience of negative family relationships, including having conflict and a perceived lack of support. High scores should be contextualized using information from other parts of the assessment. This is because scores on FML do not tell us whether the negative relationships are occurring within the test-taker's family of origin, their current family, or both.

High scores (T ≥ 65) indicate persons who

1. report having negative attitudes toward their families
2. describe conflicts with their families
3. do not feel supported by their families
4. report being mistreated, and even abused, by their families
5. may be in a romantic relationship marked by mutual dissatisfaction and frequent disagreement over important issues
6. tend to have histories of juvenile delinquency and substance misuse
7. in mental health settings, may feel depressed, anxious, helpless, and hopeless
8. in mental health settings, may experience suicidal ideation
9. may benefit from having family members involved in treatment

Low scores (T < 39) indicate persons who report comparatively conflict-free family environments, past and present.

Interpersonal Passivity (IPP)

This scale consists of 10 items assessing how willing and able a test taker is to assert themselves in interpersonal contexts.

High scores (T ≥ 65) indicate persons who

1. describe themselves as passive and unassertive in interpersonal situations
2. report that they do not express opinions or feelings strongly
3. have difficulty making decisions
4. do not want to be in positions of leadership
5. are seen by others as passive and submissive
6. are not achievement or power oriented
7. are introverted
8. feel insecure
9. may describe low sex drive and feelings of sexual inadequacy
10. in mental health settings, tend to report feeling depressed and having suicidal ideation
11. should be evaluated for disorders involving passive, submissive behaviors (e.g., dependent personality disorder)
12. may benefit from treatment to reduce passive, submissive behaviors
13. likely view the working alliance with their therapist as weak

Low scores (T < 39) indicate persons who describe themselves as

1. having strong opinions
2. standing up for themselves
3. being assertive and direct
4. being able to lead others

Social Avoidance (SAV)

This scale is comprised of 10 items inquiring about the test-taker's lack of enjoyment and engagement in social situations, such as dances and parties.

High scores (T ≥ 65) indicate persons who

1. describe themselves as being socially awkward
2. do not like being in social situations involving many people
3. are seen by others as introverted, interpersonally cool, and shy
4. lack self-confidence and feel like failures
5. feel hopeless and helpless
6. do not make good first impressions
7. tend to be passive in relationships
8. in mental health settings may report anxiety, depression, and somatic complaints
9. may benefit from treatment to reduce social avoidance

Low scores (T < 39) indicate persons who report enjoying social situations and events.

Shyness (SHY)

This scale consists of seven items assessing shyness including how uncomfortable and anxious the test taker is when interacting with others.

High scores (T ≥ 65) indicate persons who

1. report being shy, easily embarrassed, and uncomfortable around other people
2. tend to be socially anxious
3. find it difficult to interact with other people, especially those they do not know well
4. are seen by others as socially awkward and passive in relationships
5. are self-doubting and self-degrading
6. may be in considerable emotional turmoil
7. do not react well to stress
8. in mental health settings, may report anxiety, depression, and health concerns
9. should be evaluated for social anxiety disorder (social phobia)
10. likely view the working alliance with their therapist as weak

Low scores (T < 39) indicate persons who report little or no social anxiety.

Disaffiliativeness (DSF)

This scale is comprised of six items reflecting asocial tendencies and a dislike of interpersonal relationships.

High scores (T ≥ 65) indicate persons who

1. report that they prefer being alone rather than around other people
2. report that they do not want to hear other people's opinions
3. report that they do not want to talk with other people about their problems
4. tend to be interpersonally cold and callous
5. are seen by others as introverted and uncomfortable in social situations
6. are observed by others to lack close relationships
7. in mental health settings, are likely to be experiencing a great deal of emotional turmoil including anxiety, depression, and somatic symptoms
8. feel that life is a strain
9. are pessimistic about the likelihood of things getting better
10. may have difficulty developing therapeutic alliances

Low scores (T < 39) on this scale are not interpreted.

Interpretive Guidelines for Interest Scales

The Interest scales provide information about the types of activities a test taker reports enjoying. These scales assess an independent domain of functioning and high scores are not likely to reflect psychopathology. Low scores on both scales reflect a general lack of interests that may be suggestive of anhedonia, especially in combination with elevations on RC2.

Aesthetic–Literary Interests (AES)

This scale is comprised of seven items reflecting a test-taker's interest in aesthetic and literary activities (e.g., writing, music, theater).

High scores (T ≥ 65) indicate persons who

1. report an above-average interest in activities or occupations that are aesthetic or literary in nature
2. are seen by others as not having stereotypically masculine interests
3. in mental health settings, are more likely to have symptoms of internalizing disorders and less likely to have symptoms of externalizing disorders

Low scores (T < 39) indicate persons who report little interest in activities or occupations of an aesthetic or literary nature.

Mechanical–Physical Interests (MEC)

This scale is comprised of nine items reflecting a test-taker's interest in activities and occupations that involve mechanics or physical activity (e.g., sports, auto mechanics, being an outdoors person).

High scores (T ≥ 65) indicate persons who

1. report an above-average interest in activities or occupations of a mechanical or physical nature
2. in clinical settings are more likely to report symptoms of externalizing disorders and less likely to report symptoms of internalizing disorders

Low scores (T < 39) indicate persons who report little interest in activities or occupations of a mechanical or physical nature.

Interpretive Guidelines for the Personality Psychopathology Five (PSY–5) Scales

As detailed in Chapter 7, the PSY-5 Scales were intended to assess adaptive and maladaptive manifestations of personality characteristics (Harkness, McNulty, & Ben-Porath, 1995). The versions of these scales scored on the MMPI-2 and MMPI-2-RF are largely equivalent (Harkness, McNulty, et al., 2014). As such, interpretative statements presented in Chapter 7 for the PSY-5 can be applied to understanding and interpreting MMPI-2-RF versions of these scales. These interpretative statements from Chapter 7 are provided below, but we have also included additional interpretations suggested by the empirical correlates presented in Tellegen and Ben-Porath (2008/2011).

Aggressiveness (AGGR-r)

The AGGR-r scale consists of 18 items reflecting individual differences in offensive and instrumental aggression. The construct assessed by this scale aligns with the antagonism domain trait proposed in the AMPD and the antagonistic externalizing spectrum in the HiTOP model. Both high and low scores on this scale are interpreted.

High scores (T ≥ 65) on the AGGR-r scale indicate persons who

1. report they are interpersonally dominant, assertive, and aggressive
2. report a history of physical fights
3. are likely to be both verbally and physically aggressive
4. may use aggression to dominate and control others
5. may enjoy intimidating other people
6. may react aggressively when provoked or in response to threats
7. have histories of behavioral problems in school
8. have histories of arrests
9. may have histories of assaulting or physically abusing others
10. if male, often have histories of committing domestic violence
11. are extroverted
12. are domineering and overbearing in relationships
13. have unrealistic self-appraisals
14. indicate that they are self-confident and would be good leaders of other people
15. are narcissistic
16. in clinical or forensic settings, tend to have diagnoses of antisocial personality disorder
17. in forensic settings, may exhibit traits consistent with psychopathy
18. in treatment may attempt to control and dominate therapists
19. in treatment may benefit from discussion of the costs and benefits of their aggressiveness
20. may benefit from learning anger control techniques

Low scores (T < 39) indicate persons who

1. report being interpersonally passive and submissive
2. are likely to be less aggressive than the average person
3. are introverted
4. are conforming

Psychoticism (PSYC-r)

This scale consists of 26 items describing a disconnection from consensual reality, feelings of alienation, and unrealistic expectations of harm. PSYC-r aligns with the AMPD domain trait of the same name as well as the thought disorder spectrum in the HiTOP model. Low scores are not interpreted for this scale.

High scores (T ≥ 65) on the PSYC-r scale indicate persons who

1. report unusual thought processes or perceptual experiences
2. are experiencing a disconnection from reality
3. may experience unshared beliefs or unusual perceptual experiences
4. may have bizarre, disoriented, or circumstantial thinking
5. may report delusions of reference
6. have an unrealistic expectation of harm that may rise to the level of a delusion

7. in inpatient settings, may receive psychotic diagnoses and be treated with antipsychotic medications
8. display symptoms of demoralization (e.g., depression, hopelessness)
9. feel that life is a strain
10. do not cope well with the demands of their life situations
11. may develop somatic symptoms at times of increased stress
12. feel alienated
13. have few or no friends
14. have poor work histories
15. are not very achievement oriented
16. should be evaluated for psychotic spectrum disorders and Cluster A personality disorders (i.e., paranoid, schizoid, and schizotypal personality disorders)
17. in therapy may benefit from frequent opportunities to engage in reality checking

Disconstraint (DISC-r)

The DISC-r scale is comprised of 20 items measuring differences in disinhibitory traits such as self-control and risk-taking. It most closely aligns with the HiTOP model's disinhibited externalizing spectra and the AMPD's disinhibition domain trait. Both high and low scores are interpreted for this scale.

High scores (T ≥ 65) on the DISC-r scale indicate persons who

1. report various manifestations of poorly constrained, undercontrolled behavior
2. are impulsive and lack self-control
3. show poor judgment
4. take physical risks
5. are easily bored by routine and seek out excitement
6. are nonconforming and rebellious
7. are less bound by traditional moral constraints
8. are narcissistic and overvalue their own worth
9. report family problems
10. often have histories of school problems and arrests
11. often have histories of problematic substance use
12. in forensic settings, tend to have histories of violence and antisocial personality disorder diagnoses
13. in treatment may benefit from exploring more constructive ways to satisfy needs for novelty, excitement, and risk-taking
14. are not likely to be motivated for treatment and may be at risk for non-adherence
15. may benefit from learning better impulse control

Low scores (T < 39) on the DISC-r scale indicate persons who

1. report overly constrained behavior
2. are self-controlled and not impulsive
3. do not take many physical risks

4. have high tolerance for boredom
5. are seen by others as dependable, conscientious, and agreeable
6. tend to follow rules and laws
7. are passive and submissive in relationships
8. may respond better to structured treatment approaches

Negative Emotionality/Neuroticism (NEGE-r)

This scale captures a predisposition to experience negative emotions (e.g., fear, anxiety) and fixate on problematic features of incoming information. It is comprised of 20 items and aligns with the internalizing spectrum from the HiTOP model and the AMPD's negative affectivity domain trait. Low scores on NEGE-r are not interpreted.

High scores (T ≥ 65) on the NEGE-r scale indicate persons who

1. report overwhelming negative emotions
2. have a predisposition to experience negative affect
3. focus on problematic features of incoming information
4. concoct worst-case scenarios
5. feel anxious much of the time
6. worry excessively about many things
7. may realize their anxiety and worry are not justified
8. feel guilty
9. are self-critical
10. feel insecure, inadequate, and inferior
11. hold dysfunctional beliefs about themselves and their relationships
12. may have few or no friends
13. are pessimistic
14. may report feeling sad or blue
15. are irritable and easily angered
16. are not very achievement oriented
17. in clinical settings, may have histories of suicide attempts
18. in clinical settings, often receive diagnoses of depression or dysthymia
19. may report somatic symptoms, especially in times of stress
20. should be evaluated for anxiety and depressive disorders
21. should be evaluated for anxiolytic medications
22. may be motivated for treatment because of emotional distress
23. may benefit from therapy designed to identify and deal with their tendencies to process information in ways that produce negative emotional responses

Introversion/Low Positive Emotionality (INTR-r)

INTR-r is comprised of 20 items that assess individual differences in the capacity to experience positive emotions (e.g., joy) and engage with one's environment, including socially. Conceptually, it is congruent with the construct named detachment in both the AMPD and HiTOP models. Both high and low scores on this scale are interpreted.

High scores (T ≥ 65) on the INTR-r scale indicate persons who

1. report a lack of positive emotional experiences
2. report avoiding social situations
3. seem to have little capacity to experience joy and pleasure
4. feel sad and depressed
5. lack energy to get things done
6. have low need to achieve
7. have a poor self-concept and feel that they are failures
8. feel overwhelmed and that life is a strain
9. feel hopeless and pessimistic about the likelihood of their lives getting better
10. do not cope well with stress
11. report somatic symptoms that may increase during times of stress
12. are socially introverted
13. are socially awkward
14. are very sensitive to criticism
15. often feel anxious
16. in clinical settings, tend to have diagnoses of depression
17. in clinical settings, may have histories of suicide attempts
18. should be evaluated for Cluster C personality disorders (i.e., avoidant, dependent, obsessive–compulsive)
19. should be evaluated for antidepressant medications
20. may have difficulty engaging in therapy because of lack of positive emotions
21. tend to show little emotional response in therapy

Low scores on the INTR-r scale (T < 39) indicate persons who

1. report feeling energetic and having many positive emotional experiences
2. have the capacity to experience joy and pleasure
3. are extroverted and sociable
4. have lots of energy
5. cope well with stress
6. are achievement oriented
7. if scores are very low, may exhibit symptoms of hypomania
8. are likely to be quite emotionally responsive in therapy

Interpretive Strategy

The MMPI-2-RF's authors have suggested a strategy for interpreting MMPI-2-RF protocols (Ben-Porath, 2012; Ben-Porath & Tellegen, 2008/2011). The first step is to examine the Validity scales to determine whether interpretation of the substantive scales is warranted. If Validity scale scores suggest that the test taker approached the test in an invalid manner (e.g., omitted items, responded without considering item content, overreported, underreported), no further consideration is given to other MMPI-2-RF substantive scale scores. However, sometimes Validity scale scores provide some evidence an invalidating response style is present, but not to an extent that would invalidate the protocol. In these cases, substantive scales are interpreted, but caution is advised, as they may over- or underestimate the test-taker's difficulties. Guidelines for interpreting Validity scales are presented in Ben-Porath and Tellegen (2008/2011) and were summarized earlier in this chapter.

If a protocol is deemed valid and interpretable, the substantive scales are then interpreted. Inferences are made first about general areas of dysfunction (i.e., somatic/cognitive, emotional, thought, and behavioral) and then about more specific aspects of dysfunction. Six areas are addressed: (a) somatic/cognitive dysfunction, (b) emotional dysfunction, (c) thought dysfunction, (d) behavioral dysfunction, (e) interpersonal functioning, and (f) interests. Specific MMPI-2-RF scales are interpreted within each of these areas, and interpretations are hierarchical in nature—moving from scales that offer the broadest information to those that offer the narrowest information. If appropriate to the context, two additional areas can then be considered: diagnostic and treatment considerations. Inferences for these areas are based on scores from all MMPI-2-RF scales.

The H-O, RC, SP, and PSY-5 scales for each of the areas of dysfunction are listed in Table 12.2. The H-O scales allow inferences about general areas of dysfunction (i.e., emotional, thought, and behavioral). There are RC scales associated with each H-O scale that allow inferences about narrower aspects of dysfunction suggested by elevated scores on the H-O scales. Likewise, there are SP scales associated with the RC scales that permit inferences about even more specific facets of dysfunction suggested by elevations on RC scales.

When presenting MMPI-2-RF results, four areas (i.e., somatic/cognitive, emotional, thought, and behavioral dysfunction) are addressed in the order of their prominence in the MMPI-2-RF protocol. This allows the interpretation to give a general idea of the most salient problems that the test taker is likely to have. Prominence is identified using scores from RC1 for the somatic/cognitive area and the three H-O scales for the emotional (EID), thought (THD), and behavioral (BXD) dysfunction areas. Start the interpretation with the area having the highest T score. Generate inferences based on that score and then for all the scales under it in the MMPI-2-RF hierarchy. Next, repeat this process for the remaining areas by order of elevation.

Within each of these four domains, interpretation of scales should proceed from those that reflect the broadest to narrowest aspects of the test-taker's functioning. Inferences based on the RC scales typically will be more specific than those based on the H-O scale. Inferences based on the SP scales will be more focused than those based on the H-O and RC scales. In practice, this means if the highest score is for an H-O scale, we would interpret this scale, then the RC scales associated with it (i.e., RCd, RC2, and RC7 for EID; RC6 and RC8 for THD; and RC4 and RC9 for BXD). When interpreting elevated RC scales within a domain, generate inferences about the RC scale and then examine and interpret SP scales that are facets of the RC scale, making inferences about scales with T scores ≥ 65. If there are no elevated scores for the RC scales associated with the H-O scale, then go directly to the SP scales associated with that domain and interpret any scales with T scores ≥ 65. Relevant PSY-5 scales should also be interpreted at this point (i.e., INTR-r and NEGE-r for EID, PSYC-r for THD, and AGGR-r and DISC-r for BXD).

TABLE 12.2 *Recommended Structure and Sources of Information for MMPI-2-RF Interpretation*

Topic	MMPI-2-RF Sources
1. Protocol Validity	
a. Content Non-Responsiveness	CNS, VRIN-r, TRIN-r
b. Overreporting	F-r, Fp-r, Fs, FBS-r, RBS
c. Underreporting	L-r, K-r
2. Substantive Scale Interpretation	
a. Somatic/Cognitive Dysfunction	1. RC1, MLS, GIC, HPC, NUC, COG
b. Emotional Dysfunction	1. EID
	2. RCd, SUI, HLP, SFD, NFC
	3. RC2
	4. RC7, STW, AXY, ANP, BRF, MSF
	5. NEGE-r, INTR-r
c. Thought Dysfunction	1. THD
	2. RC6
	3. RC8
	4. PSYC-r
d. Behavioral Dysfunction	1. BXD
	2. RC4, JCP, SUB
	3. RC9, AGG, ACT
	4. AGGR-r, DISC-r
e. Interpersonal Functioning	1. FML, RC3, IPP, SAV, SHY, DSF
f. Interests	1. AES, MEC
g. Diagnostic Considerations	Most substantive scales
h. Treatment Considerations	All substantive scales

Note. Excerpted (Table 5.1) from *MMPI-2-RF Manual for Administration, Scoring, and Interpretation* by Yossef S. Ben-Porath and Auke Tellegen. Copyright © 2008, 2011 by the Regents of the University of Minnesota. Reproduced by permission of the University of Minnesota Press. All rights reserved. "Minnesota Multiphasic Personality Inventory-2-Restructured Form®" and "MMPI-2-RF®" are registered trademarks of the Regents of the University of Minnesota.

The somatic/cognitive domain is not associated with an H-O scale, instead having its order in the interpretation guided by scores on RC1. Thus, when interpreting scales in this domain, interpret the RC1 scale first, followed by the SP scales associated with RC1. In some cases, it may be appropriate to interpret scales in the somatic/cognitive domain immediately after the emotional dysfunction domain. Data presented in Tellegen and Ben-Porath (2008/2011) suggest scales within these two domains are highly correlated in non-medical settings. We advise this deviation from the standard interpretation guidelines when (a) the test is being used in a non-medical context, (b) emotional dysfunction is a prominent part of the profile, and (c) only a few somatic/cognitive scales are elevated.

Notably, a test-taker's protocol may not always have elevated scores at all levels of the MMPI-2-RF hierarchy. In these cases, interpretation should begin at the level of the hierarchy where T score elevations (i.e., T ≥ 65) occur. For example, if there are no H-O scales with T scores ≥ 65, start interpreting the substantive scales by considering the highest RC scale score and its associated SP scales. If no RC scales have T scores ≥ 65, go directly to the SP scales, starting with the scale that has the highest T score.

After interpretation of these first four domains is complete, then the interpersonal dysfunction and interests domains are interpreted. The interpersonal dysfunction domain includes information from RC3 and the Interpersonal Functioning SP scales. Ben-Porath and Tellegen (2008/2011) recommend the interpretation for the interpersonal dysfunction domain be ordered in the following way: FML, RC3, IPP, SAV, SHY, and DSF. For the interests domain, AES and MEC, the order of interpretation is not prescribed.

If the assessment context warrants their inclusion, once all scales that are elevated within the areas of dysfunction have been interpreted, diagnostic and treatment implications should be considered. Most of the substantive scales provide information about diagnostic impressions and treatment considerations. Ben-Porath and Tellegen (2008/2011) indicated that inferences provided in the test's manuals about diagnostic considerations are based in part on empirical data and are in part inferential. Many of these inferences have been supported in the empirical research reviewed earlier in this chapter. Ben-Porath and Tellegen (2008/2011) also stated that inferences about treatment from the instrument's manual were not based on empirical data but rather were second-order inferences. As noted earlier in this chapter, a growing body of research has supported some of these inferences, as well as added to what we know about the treatment implications of MMPI-2-RF scale scores.

Ben-Porath and Tellegen (2008/2011) note that the MMPI-2-RF score and interpretive reports list "critical responses" given by test takers. Specifically, seven MMPI-2-RF substantive scales—SUI, HLP, AXY, RC6, RC8, SUB, and AGG—were identified as having critical item content that may require immediate attention and follow-up. Items answered in the scored direction are examined for scales for which T scores are ≥ 65. Ben-Porath and Tellegen indicate that the critical responses should be used to guide follow-up interviews with test takers rather than being incorporated into the interpretation of the test protocol. This is due to problems with the reliability and validity of responses provided to single items. We agree with this recommendation.

In addition to the MMPI-2-RF manual's table reprinted here as Table 12.2, there are several other tools available to help you organize and complete your test interpretation following Ben-Porath and Tellegen's (2008/2011) structured approach. First, the MMPI-2-RF Score Report and MMPI-2-RF Interpretive Report include a page titled "MMPI-2-RF T Scores (By Domain)" where all the scale scores are reported and organized using the clusters displayed in Table 12.2. Second, on Pearson Assessments' website (https://www.pearsonassessments.com/content/dam/school/global/clinical/us/assets/MMPI-2-RF/mmpi-2-rf-interpretation-worksheet.pdf), you can find a fillable form pdf titled "MMPI-2-RF Interpretation Worksheet." This worksheet also organizes the MMPI-2-RF scales by domain using the same scheme found in the manual. We recommend using the worksheet to record all the interpretive statements by domain as you generate them for each scale. The worksheet can thus serve as a working draft from which you will then draw interpretive inferences as you edit, consolidate, refine, and reorganize your formal test interpretation and turn it into a final product.

Illustrative Case

It may be instructive to apply the preceding strategy to the scores for the illustrative case (Jeff) appended to this chapter. Readers should note that this is the same case discussed in Chapter 11 in relation to the MMPI-2 interpretive strategy. Additional MMPI-2-RF protocols for readers to practice interpretation with are included in the supplemental materials available for this book on the publisher's website. Please visit www.oup.com/he/graham6e to access these materials.

Examination of Jeff's Validity scale scores indicates that he approached the test in an appropriate manner and that the substantive scales are interpretable. He omitted only one item, and he appears to have answered items after considering their content (VRIN-r T = 43; TRIN-r T = 57 in true direction). He was not at all defensive (L-r T = 42; K-r T = 38), and there was no evidence of overreporting (F-r T = 70; Fp-r T = 51; Fs T = 50; FBS-r T = 58; RBS T = 76).

Next, we examine scores on the indicators of prominence for the four dysfunction areas in the interpretative strategy (i.e., Somatic/Cognitive, Emotional, Behavioral, and Thought Dysfunctions), which include the H-O and RC1 scale scores. Because his highest score is on the EID scale, and because that scale's score is T ≥ 65, we would infer that he is reporting significant signs of emotional dysfunction. We then interpret the RC scales associated with EID—RCd, RC2, and RC7—in order of elevation, followed by their associated SP and PSY-5 scales. Interpretation of these scales will give a more specific picture of Jeff's symptoms and problems.

In this case, we would begin with Jeff's T score of 77 on RCd, as it is the RC scale associated with EID that has the highest elevation. The RCd scale T score of 77 suggests that Jeff is reporting feeling sad, unhappy, and dissatisfied with his current life situation. The SP scales associated with RCd are interpreted next. The T scores above 65 on the NFC and SFD scales suggest that Jeff is reporting that he lacks self-confidence and feels useless. He also is reporting being indecisive, inefficacious, and incapable of coping with his current difficulties. Empirical correlates associated with elevated scores on the NFC and SFD scales indicate that Jeff feels insecure and inferior and that he engages in self-degrading and intropunitive behaviors. Further, he has difficulty dealing with small inconsequential matters. He is not very self-reliant and tends to be passive in relationships.

After interpreting RCd and its associated SP scale, we move to the other emotional dysfunction RC scales, RC2 and RC7. The RC7 scale has the second highest RC scale score in this domain, so we would interpret it next. The elevated score on RC7 (T = 75) suggests that Jeff is reporting negative emotional experiences including anxiety, anger, and fear. This is consistent with the NEGE-r T score of 77, which indicates that Jeff likely has a disposition to experience these types of emotions. T scores greater than 65 on the STW, ANP, and NEGE-r scales indicate that Jeff is reporting multiple problems involving stress and worry, including pre-occupation with disappointments, difficulties, and time pressure. He also may be reporting specific worries about misfortune and finances. The ANP scale T score of 80 indicates that Jeff is reporting that he gets upset easily, is impatient with others, becomes easily angered, and sometimes even is overcome with anger. Empirical correlates of these SP and PSY-5 scales are consistent with Jeff's self-report. He is likely to be stress reactive and worry prone, and he may engage in obsessive rumination. He tends to feel angry and irritable, has a temper, and is likely to be argumentative. He is also likely to feel anxious and insecure, and he may worry excessively and experience intrusive ideation. He may be self-critical and guilt-prone. Having interpreted RC7 and its associated scales, we then turn to examining RC2. Because the RC2 and INTR-r scale T scores are not greater than 65, no inferences are made based on these scales.

Because Jeff was evaluated in a non-medical context and had prominent emotional dysfunction indicated in his MMPI-2-RF profile, we would next consider interpreting the somatic/cognitive domain scales. Given his only significant elevation in this domain is on MLS (T = 87), we would proceed with interpreting this domain next. The very high score on MLS indicates that Jeff reported that feelings of ill health interfere with work and other activities. He may feel weak and tired and lack energy for the activities of everyday life. Persons with elevated MLS scale scores may or may not report specific somatic or cognitive complaints. The absence of significant elevation on the GIC, HPC, and NUC scales suggests that Jeff is not presenting multiple somatic complaints. However, his T score on COG is approaching 65 (T = 64); thus, we would want to consider that Jeff may report experiencing some difficulties with cognition, such as problems with concentration or memory. This is consistent with his report of difficulties with stress and worry, so we would make a note to further explore his experience of these types of difficulties in future interactions.

The next highest H-O scale score is for BXD, which has a T score of 65. Because the score is at the recommended cut score (T ≥ 65), inferences can be made based on the scale; but one should have less confidence in the inferences than would be warranted if the score were higher. The BXD scale score suggests that Jeff reported externalizing, acting-out behavior, which may have gotten him into difficulties.

The RC scales associated with the BXD scale are RC4 and RC9. The RC4 T score of 71 is higher than the RC9 T score of 48, so we would interpret RC4 first. Jeff's score on RC4 suggests he reported a history of antisocial behavior. Next, we examine the SP scales associated with RC4. The JCP T score of 63 is not high enough to warrant interpretation. The SUB T score of 69 indicates that Jeff reported past and current substance use. He may be prone to problematic or risky use of alcohol or other substances. Having interpreted RC4 and its associated SP scales, we would then turn to RC9. Because Jeff's RC9 scale T score is 48, no inferences are generated based on this scale. However, we would still examine scores on the SP and PSY-5 scales associated with RC9 (AGG, ACT, AGGR-r, and DISC-r). Because T scores on these scales are not greater than 65, no interpretations are made.

Because Jeff's remaining H-O scale T score (THD) is only 39, no interpretation is appropriate. Likewise, there are no significant elevations for either of the RC scales (RC6, RC8) associated with THD. The PSY-5 scale associated with the THD scale (PSYC-r) has a T score of 47, so this scale is not interpreted.

We next turn to interpretations within the interpersonal dysfunction domain. The RC3, FML, SAV, and DSF scales are not interpreted because their T scores are below 65. The IPP T score of 74 indicates that Jeff reported being unassertive, passive, and submissive in interpersonal relationships, characteristics that are consistent with others' perceptions of him. The T score of 75 on the SHY scale indicates that Jeff reported being shy, uncomfortable, and easily embarrassed around others. Empirical correlates of the SHY scale indicate that others see Jeff as introverted, inhibited, anxious, and nervous in social situations.

We next consider scales within the interests domain. Jeff's T score of 39 on AES indicates that he reported below-average interest in activities or occupations of an aesthetic or literary nature. His T Score of 52 on the MEC scale indicates that he reported an average interest in activities or occupations of a mechanical or physical nature.

Because it is appropriate for the context in which Jeff was evaluated, we next examine all of Jeff's scores to determine whether there is evidence to suggest that specific mental disorders should be considered. Jeff's scores on internalizing and somatic/cognitive domain scales suggest several internalizing diagnoses should be considered. The high scores on RCd (T = 77) and SFD (T = 76) suggest he should be evaluated for depressive disorders, although anhedonia and other vegetative symptoms may not be prominent given his score on RC2 was not clinically elevated (T = 61). The MLS (T = 87) scale score indicates that Jeff reported that feelings of ill health interfere with work and other activities. If physical origins for his health concerns can be ruled out, further evaluation for somatic symptom disorder is indicated. His scores on the RC7 (T = 75), STW (T = 81), and SHY (T = 75) scales suggest that anxiety disorder diagnoses should be considered (e.g., obsessive–compulsive, social anxiety, and generalized anxiety disorders). Jeff's scores also indicate further evaluation for several personality disorder diagnoses related to negative emotions such as anxiety. Specifically, his scores on the NEGE-r (T = 77) scale and the IPP scale (T = 74) suggest that he should be evaluated further for Cluster C personality disorders (i.e., avoidant, dependent, obsessive–compulsive).

Jeff's BXD scale T score of 65 is only marginally elevated, but it raises the possibility of externalizing disorders, including antisocial behavior and substance use disorders. His RC4 scale score of 71 reinforces this notion. The absence of elevations on the RC9, DISC-r, and AGGR-r scales and all but one of the SP scales associated with BXD helps refine our interpretation. Namely, the significant elevation on the SUB scale (T = 69) suggests the primary factor leading to elevations on the BXD and RC4 scales is his acknowledged substance use, not antisocial behavior disorders. Thus, we would recommend Jeff be further evaluated for a substance use disorder.

Finally, we examine Jeff's scores again to determine whether inferences concerning treatment are warranted. T scores ≥ 65 on the EID, RCd, RC7, and NEGE-r scales suggest that Jeff is likely to be motivated for treatment because of his high level of emotional distress. However, a T score of 65 on the BXD scale indicates that he might not be internally motivated for treatment. Because his BXD scale score is considerably lower than the EID, RC7, and NEGE-r scale scores, we would emphasize the motivation because of emotional turmoil aspect of these interpretations.

Several scores suggest characteristics that may interfere with effective treatment. An elevated score on the MLS scale (T = 87) indicates general fatigue and pessimism about the likelihood of things getting better that may make it difficult for Jeff to actively engage in the therapy process. An elevated score on the RC4 scale (T = 71) and a moderately elevated score on the BXD scale (T = 65) raise the possibility of noncompliance in treatment. Jeff's indecisiveness (NFC = 80) may interfere with establishing goals in therapy.

Scores on several scales suggest potential targets for treatment. Relief of psychological distress as a target is suggested by elevated T scores on the RCd (T = 77) and RC7 (T = 75) scales. The T score of 77 on the NEGE-r scale suggests that Jeff should be evaluated for anxiolytic medications. The SFD scale T score of 76 suggests that low self-esteem and self-doubt may be appropriate targets. Shyness in social situations is suggested as a treatment target by the SHY scale T score of 69. Stress management is suggested by the T score of 81 on the STW scale. Reduction of passive, submissive behaviors as a target is suggested by the T score of 74 on the IPP scale. Helping Jeff develop better self-control is suggested by elevated scores on the RC4 (T = 71) and BXD (T = 65) scales. Anger management is suggested by Jeff's T score of 80 on the ANP scale. Jeff's T score of 69 on the SUB scale indicates that a detailed substance use evaluation is indicated.

The last thing we would do is inspect the critical responses identified in Jeff's MMPI-2-RF report to determine what types of follow-up information might need to be gathered in future interactions. Of the seven scales for which critical responses should be examined if T scores are ≥ 65, Jeff had an elevated score on only one scale, SUB (T = 69). His responses to items in this scale indicate that he acknowledged use of marijuana and excessive use of alcohol. He further indicated that he sometimes takes drugs or sleeping pills that were not ordered by doctors. He stated directly that he has an alcohol or drug problem. These responses would prompt follow-up questions and quite probably a detailed evaluation for substance-related difficulties.

In summary, Jeff appears to have approached the MMPI-2-RF in a valid manner. He responded to items with regard to their content, was not defensive, and did not overreport symptoms and problems. His problems are predominantly internalizing in nature. He seems to be experiencing a great deal of emotional distress. He likely feels overwhelmed by the demands of his life situation and believes that he cannot do anything to make things better. His symptoms likely include feelings of ill health, anxiety, and, to a lesser extent, depressed mood. He worries excessively about inconsequential things, and he may ruminate about perceived failures in his life. Jeff tends to be irritable and easily upset, and he may not control his anger effectively at times. Jeff openly acknowledges that he uses alcohol and marijuana excessively; and this use may be an attempt to dampen high levels of unpleasant, negative emotions. Jeff has a poor self-concept, lacks self-confidence, and expects to fail in life. He is likely to be passive and dependent in relationships and to feel shy, anxious, and awkward in social situations.

Jeff is likely to be motivated for treatment because of the psychological distress that he is experiencing. However, there are factors that may interfere with effective treatment. He may lack the energy to actively participate in the therapy process, and he may not adhere to treatment recommendations. His indecisiveness may make it difficult to establish treatment goals. He is pessimistic about being able to make changes that will lead to improvements in his life.

A primary focus of treatment should be to reduce his psychological distress. This may be accomplished by referring him for an evaluation to examine whether he would benefit from anxiolytic and antidepressant medications. Interventions intended to assist him develop stress management techniques are also likely to be helpful. Reduction of passive–dependent behaviors and increasing self-esteem are also important goals. Developing better self-control, especially in terms of expressing anger, are also likely to be appropriate treatment targets. Jeff's open acknowledgment of substance use indicates that a thorough evaluation of his use of alcohol and other drugs, as well as problems associated with this use, is warranted; and he may benefit from treatment focused on reducing or ceasing his use of substances.

CLOSING COMMENTS

As mentioned at the beginning of this chapter, the MMPI-2-RF represents a substantial change to the MMPI family of instruments and was intended to address several long-standing criticisms of the MMPI-2. Since the MMPI-2-RF was released in 2008, a substantial body of research has emerged that guides our understanding of the scales and the constructs they assess. This research suggests MMPI-2-RF scale scores have strong psychometric properties that generalize across a wide variety of settings, allowing us to have confidence the key features captured in MMPI-2-RF scales are reflected in the assessment contexts in which the test is most used. These studies also provide strong evidence of the construct validity of MMPI-2-RF substantive scales and directly link test results to contemporary models of personality and psychopathology. Nonetheless, there are two potential issues with the MMPI-2 that remain unaddressed by the MMPI-2-RF: a dated normative sample that is unrepresentative of the diverse people being evaluated with the instrument, and little or no direct assessment of several important constructs relevant to current mental health practice. These limitations were addressed in the most recently developed, adult version of the MMPI—the MMPI-3—which we review in Chapter 13. There, we provide not only an overview of the development, use, and interpretation of the MMPI-3, but we also discuss factors clinicians might consider for and against adopting each version of the MMPI available for use with adults.

CHAPTER APPENDIX

Minnesota Multiphasic
Personality Inventory-2
Restructured Form®

Score Report

MMPI-2-RF®

Minnesota Multiphasic Personality Inventory-2-Restructured Form®

Yossef S. Ben-Porath, PhD, & Auke Tellegen, PhD

Name:	Jeff
ID Number:	
Age:	24
Gender:	Male
Marital Status:	Not reported
Years of Education:	Not reported
Date Assessed:	09/02/1998

ALWAYS LEARNING   **PEARSON**

MMPI-2-RF Validity Scales

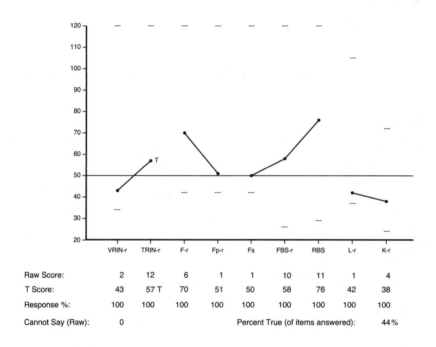

	VRIN-r	TRIN-r	F-r	Fp-r	Fs	FBS-r	RBS	L-r	K-r
Raw Score:	2	12	6	1	1	10	11	1	4
T Score:	43	57 T	70	51	50	58	76	42	38
Response %:	100	100	100	100	100	100	100	100	100

Cannot Say (Raw):   0   Percent True (of items answered):   44%

The highest and lowest T scores possible on each scale are indicated by a "---"; MMPI-2-RF T scores are non-gendered.

VRIN-r Variable Response Inconsistency	Fs Infrequent Somatic Responses	L-r Uncommon Virtues
TRIN-r True Response Inconsistency	FBS-r Symptom Validity	K-r Adjustment Validity
F-r Infrequent Responses	RBS Response Bias Scale	
Fp-r Infrequent Psychopathology Responses		

MMPI-2-RF Higher-Order (H-O) and Restructured Clinical (RC) Scales

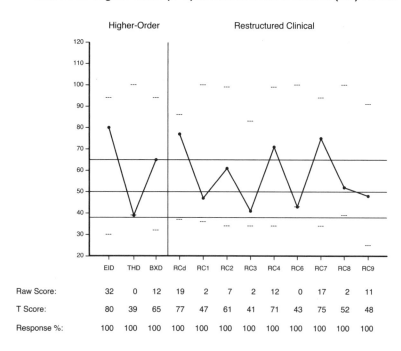

	EID	THD	BXD	RCd	RC1	RC2	RC3	RC4	RC6	RC7	RC8	RC9
Raw Score:	32	0	12	19	2	7	2	12	0	17	2	11
T Score:	80	39	65	77	47	61	41	71	43	75	52	48
Response %:	100	100	100	100	100	100	100	100	100	100	100	100

The highest and lowest T scores possible on each scale are indicated by a "---"; MMPI-2-RF T scores are non-gendered.

EID Emotional/Internalizing Dysfunction	RCd Demoralization	RC6 Ideas of Persecution
THD Thought Dysfunction	RC1 Somatic Complaints	RC7 Dysfunctional Negative Emotions
BXD Behavioral/Externalizing Dysfunction	RC2 Low Positive Emotions	RC8 Aberrant Experiences
	RC3 Cynicism	RC9 Hypomanic Activation
	RC4 Antisocial Behavior	

MMPI-2-RF Somatic/Cognitive and Internalizing Scales

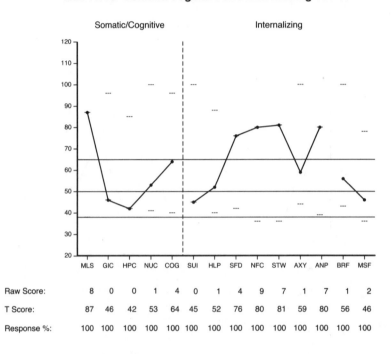

	MLS	GIC	HPC	NUC	COG	SUI	HLP	SFD	NFC	STW	AXY	ANP	BRF	MSF
Raw Score:	8	0	0	1	4	0	1	4	9	7	1	7	1	2
T Score:	87	46	42	53	64	45	52	76	80	81	59	80	56	46
Response %:	100	100	100	100	100	100	100	100	100	100	100	100	100	100

The highest and lowest T scores possible on each scale are indicated by a "---"; MMPI-2-RF T scores are non-gendered.

MLS	Malaise	SUI	Suicidal/Death Ideation	AXY	Anxiety
GIC	Gastrointestinal Complaints	HLP	Helplessness/Hopelessness	ANP	Anger Proneness
HPC	Head Pain Complaints	SFD	Self-Doubt	BRF	Behavior-Restricting Fears
NUC	Neurological Complaints	NFC	Inefficacy	MSF	Multiple Specific Fears
COG	Cognitive Complaints	STW	Stress/Worry		

MMPI-2-RF Externalizing, Interpersonal, and Interest Scales

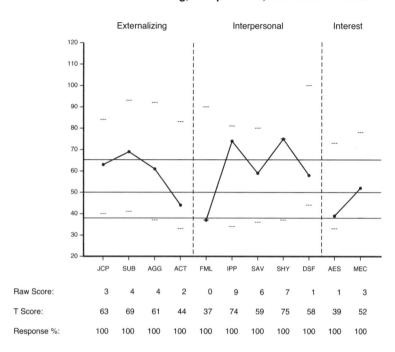

The highest and lowest T scores possible on each scale are indicated by a "---"; MMPI-2-RF T scores are non-gendered.

JCP Juvenile Conduct Problems	FML Family Problems	AES Aesthetic-Literary Interests
SUB Substance Abuse	IPP Interpersonal Passivity	MEC Mechanical-Physical Interests
AGG Aggression	SAV Social Avoidance	
ACT Activation	SHY Shyness	
	DSF Disaffiliativeness	

MMPI-2-RF PSY-5 Scales

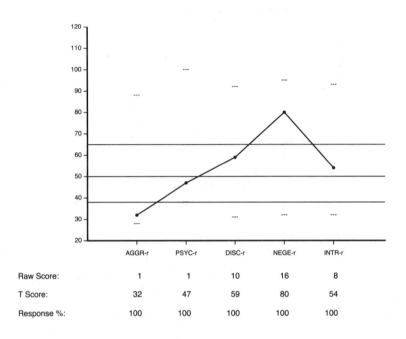

	AGGR-r	PSYC-r	DISC-r	NEGE-r	INTR-r
Raw Score:	1	1	10	16	8
T Score:	32	47	59	80	54
Response %:	100	100	100	100	100

The highest and lowest T scores possible on each scale are indicated by a "---"; MMPI-2-RF T scores are non-gendered.

AGGR-r   Aggressiveness-Revised
PSYC-r   Psychoticism-Revised
DISC-r   Disconstraint-Revised
NEGE-r   Negative Emotionality/Neuroticism-Revised
INTR-r   Introversion/Low Positive Emotionality-Revised

MMPI-2-RF T SCORES (BY DOMAIN)

PROTOCOL VALIDITY

Content Non-Responsiveness

0	43	57 T
CNS	VRIN-r	TRIN-r

Over-Reporting

70	51		50	58	76
F-r	Fp-r		Fs	FBS-r	RBS

Under-Reporting

42	38
L-r	K-r

SUBSTANTIVE SCALES

Somatic/Cognitive Dysfunction

47	87	46	42	53	64
RC1	MLS	GIC	HPC	NUC	COG

Emotional Dysfunction

80		77	45	52	76	80		
EID		RCd	SUI	HLP	SFD	NFC		
		61	54					
		RC2	INTR-r					
		75	81	59	80	56	46	80
		RC7	STW	AXY	ANP	BRF	MSF	NEGE-r

Thought Dysfunction

39		43
THD		RC6
		52
		RC8
		47
		PSYC-r

Behavioral Dysfunction

65		71	63	69		
BXD		RC4	JCP	SUB		
		48	61	44	32	59
		RC9	AGG	ACT	AGGR-r	DISC-r

Interpersonal Functioning

37	41	74	59	75	58
FML	RC3	IPP	SAV	SHY	DSF

Interests

39	52
AES	MEC

Note. This information is provided to facilitate interpretation following the recommended structure for MMPI-2-RF interpretation in Chapter 5 of the MMPI-2-RF Manual for Administration, Scoring, and Interpretation, which provides details in the text and an outline in Table 5-1.

NOTE**: The final pages of this report display any items that were skipped or unscorable as well as any endorsed items that are part of a critical responses or critical items list. These sections include both the item number and content. The final page of the report includes the test taker's item level responses to every test item. These pages are not displayed in this book in order to maintain test security; however, redacted sample reports are available on the Pearson Assessments' website.

CHAPTER 13

MMPI-3

THE MMPI-3 (Ben-Porath & Tellegen, 2020a; 2020b) is the latest addition to the MMPI family of psychological assessment instruments. The MMPI-3 is a 335-item, true–false inventory that measures psychological constructs relevant to the assessment of personality and psychopathology. Ben-Porath and Tellegen indicated that the MMPI-3 was developed to improve on earlier versions of the test (i.e., MMPI-2 and MMPI-2-RF) by developing several new scales reflecting clinically important constructs not assessed by previous versions of the instrument and by basing scores on up-to-date normative data more representative of today's U.S. population. Toward these ends, Ben-Porath and Tellegen refined and expanded the MMPI-2-RF item pool. Then, using MMPI-2-RF scales as a model, they revised existing MMPI-2-RF scales and developed new scales for the MMPI-3. They provided initial validation evidence for MMPI-3 scales in a variety of samples reflecting contexts in which the MMPI is frequently used. Finally, they collected new norms intended to be demographically representative of the U.S. population based on 2020 census projections.

The product of these efforts is the MMPI-3 (Ben-Porath & Tellegen, 2020a; 2020b; 2020c). The MMPI-3 has 52 scales, including 10 Validity and 42 substantive scales. Like the MMPI-2-RF, most MMPI-3 scales are arranged hierarchically, with the widest perspectives provided by Higher-Order (H-O) scales, mid-level measurement provided by Restructured Clinical (RC) scales, and the narrowest measurement provided by Specific Problems (SP) scales. Revised Personality Psychopathology-Five (PSY-5) scales are adjacent to this hierarchy and provide assessment of maladaptive traits. Many of the scales are iterations of scales from the MMPI-2-RF, and several are entirely new to the MMPI-3. Table 13.1 lists all the MMPI-3 scales. The MMPI-3 also has two new normative samples, one for U.S. English speakers and one for U.S. Spanish speakers. Finally, there is a set of critical responses reflecting item endorsements that warrant attention.

TABLE 13.1 *MMPI-3 Scales*

Validity Scales	
CRIN	Combined Response Inconsistency
VRIN	Variable Response Inconsistency
TRIN	True Response Inconsistency
F	Infrequent Responses
Fp	Infrequent Psychopathology Responses
Fs	Infrequent Somatic Responses
FBS	Symptom Validity Scale
RBS	Response Bias Scale
L	Uncommon Virtues
K	Adjustment Validity
Higher-Order (H-O) Scales	
EID	Emotional/Internalizing Dysfunction
THD	Thought Dysfunction
BXD	Behavioral/Externalizing Dysfunction
Restructured Clinical (RC) Scales	
RCd	Demoralization
RC1	Somatic Complaints
RC2	Low Positive Emotions
RC4	Antisocial Behavior
RC6	Ideas of Persecution
RC7	Dysfunctional Negative Emotions
RC8	Aberrant Experiences
RC9	Hypomanic Activation
Specific Problems (SP) Scales	
Somatic/Cognitive SP Scales	
MLS	Malaise
NUC	Neurological Complaints
EAT	Eating Concerns
COG	Cognitive Complaints

Internalizing SP Scales

SUI	Suicidal/Death Ideation
HLP	Helplessness/Hopelessness
SFD	Self-Doubt
NFC	Inefficacy
STR	Stress
WRY	Worry
CMP	Compulsivity
ARX	Anxiety-Related Experiences
ANP	Anger Proneness
BRF	Behavior-Restricting Fears

Externalizing SP Scales

FML	Family Problems
JCP	Juvenile Conduct Problems
SUB	Substance Abuse
IMP	Impulsivity
ACT	Activation
AGG	Aggression
CYN	Cynicism

Interpersonal SP Scales

SFI	Self-Importance
DOM	Dominance
DSF	Disaffiliativeness
SAV	Social Avoidance
SHY	Shyness

Personality Psychopathology Five (PSY-5) Scales

AGGR	Aggressiveness
PSYC	Psychoticism
DISC	Disconstraint
NEGE	Negative Emotionality/Neuroticism
INTR	Introversion/Low Positive Emotionality

DEVELOPMENT OF THE MMPI-3

MMPI-3 Items

The 335 items comprising the MMPI-3[1] were selected from a larger pool of items that included the 338 MMPI-2-RF items—of which 39 were rewritten to correct awkward language or simplify content—and 95 trial items that were candidates for inclusion in the final inventory. Data were collected to ensure the comparability of the original 39 items and their rewritten versions. The 95 trial items included content judged to be inadequately represented in the MMPI-2-RF scales. The test authors thought including these items on the instrument could improve the psychometric properties of existing MMPI-2-RF scales as well as facilitate the development of new scales. These 433 candidate items—along with a survey collecting information about test takers' biographical characteristics—constituted the MMPI-2-RF–Expanded Form (MMPI-2-RF-EX). The MMPI-2-RF-EX was used to collect data from MMPI-3 normative, development, and validation samples (described later in this chapter). The test authors also explored using a four-option response format and found this modification had no clear advantage over the true–false format used in other MMPI instruments. The content of MMPI-3 items can be found in Appendix A of the MMPI-3 *Manual for Administration, Scoring and Interpretation* (Ben-Porath & Tellegen, 2020a).

Samples Used for MMPI-3 Scale Development and Validation

To obtain the data needed to develop and examine the psychometric properties of MMPI-3 scales, the MMPI-3 authors and their associates collected test data and collateral information from the following groups: (a) community mental health center outpatients, (b) private practice outpatients, (c) spinal cord injury patients, (d) disability claimants, (e) police candidates, (f) prison inmates, and (g) college students. Some of these data were used in the process of developing scales for the MMPI-3, which included both refining existing MMPI-2-RF scales to improve their psychometric properties and creating new scales that reflected constructs not well assessed by the MMPI-2-RF. For substantive scale development processes, analyses were conducted in a composite development sample of 1,000 adults with valid MMPI-2-RF profiles tested in mental health (n = 434), medical (n = 366), and college (n = 200) settings. There were 500 men and 500 women who had an average age of 36.95 (SD = 17.4) years in this composite development sample, most of whom identified as White. The test authors included individuals from a wide range of settings in the composite development sample in an effort to obtain item response variability adequate for scale development analyses.

Separate sets of data were used to develop the MMPI-3 Validity scales. For development of Validity scales intended to assess non-content-based invalid responding, a large sample that reflected variability in responding to candidate MMPI-3 items was needed because these scales are derived by looking at item intercorrelations. As such,

---

[1] Information concerning development of the MMPI-3 is based on material presented in the MMPI-3 manuals (Ben-Porath & Tellegen, 2020a, 2020b).

the composite inconsistency scale development sample included 2,644 individuals tested in pre-employment evaluations (n = 1,402), at intake to a mental health center (n = 538), or as part of their medical care (n = 704). The MMPI-2-RF Infrequent Responses (F-r) scale was updated for inclusion in the MMPI-3 using a sample of 1,143 men and 1,242 women who were tested as part of the normative data collection efforts (described later). Other MMPI-2-RF overreporting and underreporting scales were refined using data from individuals completing the tests' items in mental health (N = 756), medical (N = 891), and public safety evaluation (N = 3,069) contexts. All of these samples were predominantly comprised of middle-aged adults who identified as White. Additional details can be found in Table 2-1 of Ben-Porath and Tellegen (2020b).

Data from the various samples were also used to provide initial information about the psychometric properties of MMPI-3 scale scores. Broadly, unless analyses precluded their exclusion (e.g., examination of overreporting indices), data in these samples were screened for invalid responding using MMPI-2-RF and MMPI-3 Validity scale scores to reduce erroneous conclusions. Reliability analyses were conducted using data from the MMPI-3 normative sample (N = 1,620) in a subset of individuals from the normative sample who completed the test on two occasions approximately 8 days apart (N = 275) and in a sample of individuals assessed at intake to a community mental health facility (N = 791). Scales assessing non-content-based invalid responding were examined using simulation data based on item responses from a subset of 1,492 individuals in the MMPI-3 normative sample. Overreporting Validity scales were examined in two samples of college students instructed to respond to the MMPI-2-RF-EX as if they had problems and difficulties they did not have (N = 558 and N = 204, respectively). Similarly, MMPI-3 scales intended to assess underreporting were examined in a large sample of college students instructed to respond to the test as if they were extremely well-adjusted (N = 561). Finally, eight additional samples who completed the MMPI-2-RF-EX and had collateral information available were used to examine empirical correlates of MMPI-3 scales. This included individuals tested at intake to a community mental health center (N = 315) or as part of their services at an outpatient private practice (N = 359), and those who were spine surgery/stimulator candidates (N = 546), disability claimants (N = 404), or police candidates (N = 1,513 and N = 164). Empirical correlates were also investigated in samples of male prison inmates (N = 448) and college students (N = 1,546). More information about each of these samples is available in Table 3-1 of Ben-Porath and Tellegen (2020b). Reliability and external correlate findings are described later in this chapter.

MMPI-3 Scale Development

Validity Scales
The MMPI-3 has 10 Validity scales. As with other MMPI instruments, these scales were designed to determine the extent to which test takers followed the standard test instructions to indicate whether an item applies to them. All the MMPI-3 Validity scales are revised versions of scales appearing on the MMPI-2-RF, development of

which is described in Chapter 12. The exception is Combined Response Inconsistency (CRIN), which is a new scale. Raw scores for all Validity scales are transformed to linear T scores ($M = 50$, $SD = 10$) based on responses of the MMPI-3 normative sample. In addition, as with previous versions of the MMPI, Cannot Say (CNS) is used as an index of nonresponding. Scores on CNS are simply the number of MMPI-3 items unanswered or answered as both true and false. A list of the MMPI-3 Validity scales is provided in Table 13.1, and guidelines for interpreting the Validity scales are presented later in this chapter.

VARIABLE RESPONSE INCONSISTENCY (VRIN), TRUE RESPONSE INCONSISTENCY (TRIN), AND COMBINED RESPONSE INCONSISTENCY (CRIN) SCALES

The MMPI-3's VRIN, TRIN, and CRIN scales assess non-content-based invalid responding. Two of these scales (VRIN and TRIN) are revised versions of the corresponding MMPI-2 and MMPI-2-RF scales and were constructed in a manner similar to their MMPI-2-RF counterparts. The CRIN scale is new to the MMPI-3 and is a composite of the item pairs that make up VRIN and TRIN.

The VRIN scale has 53 pairs of items where each item has similar content. The VRIN scale raw score is the number of item pairs where the person taking the test answers the two items in a manner such that the responses contradict one another, thus suggesting that the content of the items was not considered (e.g., random responding). Raw scores are transformed to linear T scores, and higher scores reflect a greater likelihood that the test taker responded inconsistently to items.

The TRIN scale assesses the extent to which a test taker responded to test items with an all true or all false response set. The TRIN scale consists of 33 pairs of items where the content of each item in the pair is reversed from the other item. The raw score is the number of item pairs endorsed "true-true" minus the number of item pairs endorsed "false-false." To prevent scores from being negative, a constant of 13 raw score points is added to this total. A higher difference score indicates a tendency to respond in an acquiescent manner (yea-saying). A lower difference score indicates a tendency to respond in a counter-acquiescent manner (naysaying). Raw difference scores are transformed to linear T scores, and T scores less than 50 are reflected. Higher T scores indicate non-content-based fixed responding of either an acquiescent (indicated by the letter T after the score) or counter-acquiescent (indicated by the letter F after the score) type.

The new CRIN scale is intended to assess overall response inconsistency. This scale is made up of all 86 item pairs from the VRIN and TRIN scales. An elevated CRIN score indicates that the test taker intermittently engaged in random responding and fixed responding but not to an extent that the VRIN or TRIN scales are elevated. Raw scores on CRIN are calculated by summing the number of inconsistent responses to VRIN item pairs, the number of true-true responses to TRIN item pairs, and the number of false-false responses to TRIN item pairs. Raw scores are converted to linear T scores, and higher scores indicate a greater degree of non-content-based invalid responding.

INFREQUENT RESPONSES (F), INFREQUENT PSYCHOPATHOLOGY RESPONSES (Fp), INFREQUENT SOMATIC RESPONSES (Fs), SYMPTOM VALIDITY (FBS), AND RESPONSE BIAS (RBS) SCALES

Five MMPI-3 scales are available to assess the extent to which test takers overreported problems and symptoms. Three of these scales—F, Fp, and Fs—were refined from their MMPI-2-RF counterparts during the scale development process. Broadly, these scales are comprised of items that are infrequently endorsed by test takers in certain contexts. As such, they are often referred to as "infrequency scales." The F scale is a revised version of the corresponding Infrequency (F) and Infrequent Responses (F-r) scales scored on the MMPI-2 and MMPI-2-RF. The MMPI-3 F scale has 35 items endorsed by no more than 15% of the persons who completed the MMPI-3 as part of the normative sample data collection. Some items that met this criterion were not included on the F scale because they were assigned to the other infrequency scales, Fp and Fs. The MMPI-3 Fp scale is an updated version of the Infrequent Psychopathology Responses (Fp-r) scale of the MMPI-2-RF. The 21 items in the Fp scale were endorsed by no more than 20% of a composite mental health sample of 301 men and 455 women. As was the case with the MMPI-2-RF, the Fp scale is intended to detect overreporting in settings where the base rate for psychopathology is higher than in the general population. The MMPI-3 Fs scale is a revised version of the MMPI-2-RF Fs scale. It is intended to identify overreporting in settings where reports of somatic symptoms are higher than in the general population. The 16 items in the revised MMPI-3 Fs scale endorsed by no more than 25% of a composite medical sample of 373 men and 572 women. For each of the infrequency scales, raw scores are converted to linear T scores; and elevated scores indicate the endorsement of problems and symptoms to a greater extent than expected in that setting.

The remaining two scales intended to assess overreporting—FBS and RBS—are identical to versions of those scales found in the MMPI-2-RF. The FBS has 30 items, originally selected because they were endorsed by persons judged to be overreporting somatic and cognitive symptoms. The RBS is composed of 28 items that were answered differently by persons who passed and failed performance validity tests. Elevated T scores on FBS or RBS suggest overreporting of cognitive and somatic problems.

UNCOMMON VIRTUES (L) AND ADJUSTMENT VALIDITY (K) SCALES

Two MMPI-3 Validity scales are intended to detect persons who are underreporting problems and symptoms. The 14-item, MMPI-3 L scale is a modified version of the Uncommon Virtues (L-r) scale of the MMPI-2-RF. Items in the scored direction indicate an attempt to present oneself in a favorable light by denying minor faults and shortcomings that most people acknowledge. The 14-item, MMPI-3 K scale is a modified version of the MMPI-2-RF Adjustment Validity (K-r) scale. Individuals with elevated scores on this scale are claiming to be better adjusted than the average person. They may be presenting an inaccurate picture of themselves; or they may, in fact, be better adjusted than the average person. Elevated scores on either or both these scales suggest caution is required when interpreting scores on the substantive scales.

The MMPI-3 L and K scales were both derived using their MMPI-2-RF counterpart as a base. For L, Ben-Porath and Tellegen (2020b) examined the frequency with which individuals who took the test as part of a public safety, pre-employment evaluation ($N = 3,069$) endorsed items on the MMPI-2-RF L-r scale. They then created a provisional version of the L scale using items from L-r that they perceived as not being too frequently endorsed (< 40%). For K, they created a provisional version of the scale using items from K-r, but they excluded one item with content they deemed better fit the construct assessed by L. Then, in the same pre-employment evaluation sample, they examined correlations of the provisional versions of L and K with other items in the MMPI-3 item pool. Items the test authors judged as being sufficiently associated with the provisional scale and as having content relevant to the construct assessed by that scale were added to it.

Substantive Scales

In addition to the Validity scales, the MMPI-3 has 42 substantive scales intended to assess important aspects of a test-taker's functioning. These scales are presented in their scale families in Table 13.1.

Most MMPI-3 substantive scales were developed using their MMPI-2-RF counterparts as a baseline. Details concerning development of MMPI-3 scales can be found in Chapter 2 of the *MMPI-3 Technical Manual* (Ben-Porath & Tellegen, 2020b). Broadly, the same general procedures were used in refining each of the existing MMPI-2-RF substantive scales for their inclusion on the MMPI-3. These procedures began by examining whether a scale could be revised to improve its distinctiveness. This was accomplished through an iterative process of inspecting a scale's psychometric properties after deletion of items scored on the MMPI-2-RF version of the scale and after considering the potential addition of items from the 95 trial items. Psychometric properties considered included internal consistencies, corrected item-total correlations, and intercorrelations with other scales. Ben-Porath and Tellegen (2020b) inspected potential item additions and deletions to judge whether their content was relevant to the construct the scale was intended to assess. They also examined various extratest criterion correlations of the preliminary MMPI-3 scales and compared them to the same correlates for their MMPI-2-RF predecessor scales using data from 200 college students included in the larger development sample.

Additionally, several potential new SP scales were created during the test development process. These scales were intended to assess clinically important constructs that were not adequately assessed by the MMPI-2-RF (e.g., eating concerns). Ben-Porath and Tellegen began by identifying subsets of the 95 trial items that assessed similar content. These items sets were treated as seed scales to which additional items in the MMPI-3 item pool could be added to or removed from based on their correlations with one another in the development sample. They then inspected the correlations of preliminary new SP scales and external criteria in the college development subsample. Preliminary scales with poor evidence supporting convergent and discriminant validity were not included on the MMPI-3. It appears it was at this time decisions about not carrying over some scales scored on the MMPI-2-RF to the MMPI-3 were made as well. The MMPI-2-RF Interest Scales and several MMPI-2-RF SP scales (i.e., Gastrointestinal Complaints [GIC], Head Pain Complaints [HPC], and Multiple Specific Fears [MSF]) are not included on the MMPI-3. Additional details about the types of scales developed for the MMPI-3 are provided next.

HIGHER ORDER (H-O) SCALES

As noted in Chapter 12, the three H-O scales—Emotional/Internalizing Dysfunction (EID), Thought Dysfunction (THD), and Behavioral/Externalizing Dysfunction (BXD)—were developed for the MMPI-2-RF to assess the major dimensions reflecting problems in feeling, thinking, and behaving identified in factor analyses of the instrument's scales and items. These three scales are available for the MMPI-3 in revised form. Comprised of 42 items, the EID scale deals with the overall level of emotional difficulties a test taker is experiencing. Its items assess anxiety, depression, and other negative emotions. It is related most strongly to the RCd (Demoralization), RC2 (Low Positive Emotions), and RC7 (Dysfunctional Negative Emotions) scales. THD is a 27-item scale that includes content associated with delusions, hallucinations, and other aspects of disordered thinking. It is related most strongly to RC6 (Ideas of Persecution) and RC8 (Aberrant Experiences). Finally, BXD is a 24-item scale that serves as an overall measure of behavioral acting out. It is related most strongly to RC4 (Antisocial Behavior) and RC9 (Hypomanic Activation).

RESTRUCTURED CLINICAL (RC) SCALES

As described in Chapter 7, the RC scales were first developed for the MMPI-2 and carried over without change to the MMPI-2-RF (Ben-Porath & Tellegen, 2008/2011). A major reason for developing the original RC scales was to deal with high correlations between Clinical scale scores on the MMPI-2 due to the inclusion in each Clinical scale of a general factor that Tellegen et al. (2003) called "demoralization." Scales were developed to measure this general factor and the constructs reflected in seven Clinical scales with the demoralization factor reduced or removed. The complex psychometric and statistical procedures used in developing the original RC scales have been reported elsewhere (see Chapter 7 or Tellegen et al., 2003).

Using the item analytic procedures described earlier in this chapter, the MMPI-3 authors created updated versions of the RC scales for the MMPI-3. The RC scales and their abbreviations are listed in Table 13.1. Notably, there is not a RC3 scale in the MMPI-3. Based on associations of RC3 scores with external criteria (Sellbom, 2020), the test authors decided that the scale should instead be considered a SP scale, which they labeled Cynicism (CYN). This scale will be discussed later in the chapter.

On the MMPI-3, RCd consists of 17 items measuring emotional distress and general unhappiness and dissatisfaction. The 21 items of RC1 (Somatic Complaints) tap into diffuse reports of physical health problems. A lack of positive emotional experiences is captured by RC2 (14 items). RC4 measures antisocial behaviors and attitudes and is comprised of 14 items. RC6 has 14 items that serve as markers of concerns that other people are a threat or may cause the test taker harm. The 19 items in RC7 are indicators of negative emotional experiences such as fear, anxiety, and anger; while RC8 measures unusual thoughts and perceptions (18 items). Finally, RC9 is made up of 15 items associated with heighted energy and mood as well as a tendency to behave in thrill-seeking and impulsive ways.

SPECIFIC PROBLEMS (SP) SCALES

There are 26 SP scales on the MMPI-3, which are grouped according to the kinds of problems assessed (i.e., somatic/cognitive; internalizing; externalizing; and interpersonal). Some of these scales were carried over unchanged from the MMPI-2-RF, and others are revised versions of MMPI-2-RF scales developed using the procedures described earlier. As also noted in our overview of scale development procedures, several additional SP scales were created specifically for the MMPI-3.

There are four scales in the Somatic/Cognitive SP scales group, all of which reflect aspects of the somatization construct captured by RC1. The Neurological Complaints (NUC) scale on the MMPI-3 is identical to its MMPI-2-RF counterpart. This is a 10-item scale whose content includes dizziness, paralysis, and other symptoms that could be indicative of neurological disorders. The Malaise (MLS) and Cognitive Complaints (COG) scales were carried over from the MMPI-2-RF as well, but in slightly revised forms. MLS is a seven-item scale with higher scores reflecting reports of poor health and feelings of fatigue. COG is an 11-item scale that assesses problems with concentration and memory. The Eating Concerns (EAT) scale is new to the MMPI instruments and was constructed because no existing scales adequately assessed behaviors specifically associated with eating problems. EAT is a five-item scale having to do with binging, purging, and body image.

There are 10 Internalizing SP scales. They reflect narrower aspects of the constructs reflected in the RCd and RC7 scales; six of these scales are slightly revised versions of MMPI-2-RF scales: Suicidal/Death Ideation (SUI); Helplessness/Hopelessness (HLP); Self Doubt (SFD); Inefficacy (NFC); Anger Proneness (ANP); and Behavior-Restricting Fears (BRF). The SUI scale has seven items related to thoughts of death and suicide as well as past suicide attempts. The MMPI-3 version of this scale contains a larger proportion of items directly asking the test taker about their experiences of suicidal thinking and behavior than its MMPI-2-RF counterpart. The HLP scale has seven items expressing beliefs that one cannot solve problems or accomplish goals. The SFD scale has seven items dealing with lack of self-confidence and feelings of uselessness. NFC consists of nine items having to do with indecisiveness and difficulty in starting tasks. ANP is a 12-item scale whose content includes various manifestations of anger and impatience with other people. There are seven items in the BRF scale, which reflect fears that keep one from engaging in everyday kinds of behaviors.

Three of the Internalizing SP scales are substantially revised versions of scales in the MMPI-2-RF. The 15 items in the Anxiety-Related Experiences (ARX) scale include many forms of anxiety (e.g., panic, dread). This scale is intended to replace the MMPI-2-RF Anxiety (AXY) scale and has items assessing a wider variety of anxiety-related difficulties than its predecessor. The MMPI-2-RF Stress and Worry (STW) scale was divided into the Stress (STR) and Worry (WRY) scales of the MMPI-3. The six items in the STR scale report feeling nervous and easily stressed. The WRY scale has seven items having to do with excessive worry and preoccupation with one's own thoughts.

The Compulsivity (CMP) scale is a new Internalizing SP scale developed for the MMPI-3. This scale's eight items address a desire for orderliness, feeling nervous when things are out of order, and repeating some behaviors over and over. The characteristics captured in CMP were not well assessed by previous versions of the MMPI, and Ben-Porath and Tellegen (2020a; 2020b) deliberately included items targeting this construct on the MMPI-2-RF-EX.

There are seven Externalizing SP scales. They encompass much of the content of the RC4 and RC9 scales. One of these scales, Activation (ACT) is identical to its MMPI-2-RF counterpart. The eight-item ACT scale includes reports of symptoms consistent with hypomanic/manic episodes and current high energy levels. Three of these scales are slightly revised versions of Externalizing SP scales scored on the MMPI-2-RF. The seven items in the Juvenile Conduct Problems (JCP) scale cover acts of juvenile delinquency as well as current acting-out behaviors. If JCP is the only behavioral dysfunction scale elevated, it may be an acknowledgement by the test taker that they engaged in acting out as a youth but do not engage in current acting-out behavior. The Substance Abuse (SUB) scale has nine items having to do with present and past use of substances, especially alcohol. The Aggression (AGG) scale consists of six items describing physically aggressive behavior and a callous attitude about engaging in such behavior.

The Externalizing SP scales also include the Family Problems (FML) and CYN scales. FML contains 10 items addressing negative experiences with family and negative perceptions of family members. CYN is a revised version of the MMPI-2-RF RC3 scale. It has 13 items reflecting beliefs that other people have bad intentions and should not be trusted. Slightly different versions of both of these scales were scored on the MMPI-2-RF but were organized into different domains. They were moved to the externalizing domain for the MMPI-3 because they have strong positive associations with antagonistic traits (Sellbom, 2020).

The Externalizing SP scales also include one new scale, Impulsivity (IMP). The six items in IMP include reports of problematic impulsivity and hyperactivity. These characteristics captured in IMP were not well assessed by previous versions of the MMPI, despite their clinical relevance. As such, Ben-Porath and Tellegen (2020a; 2020b) deliberately included items targeting this construct on the MMPI-2-RF-EX.

Finally, there are five Interpersonal SP scales on the MMPI-3. Several of these scales are identical to or are slight revisions to MMPI-2-RF Interpersonal SP scales. The Dominance (DOM) scale is a revision of the Interpersonal Passivity (IPP) scale of the MMPI-2-RF with a reversal of the scoring key and a new label. The nine items in this scale describe being assertive, having strong opinions, and feeling confident in accepting leadership roles. Scores on DOM are positively related to measures of externalizing antagonistic psychopathology, but it was identified as an Interpersonal SP scale because it more strongly reflects interpersonal difficulties (Sellbom, 2020). The seven-item Disaffiliativeness (DSF) scale includes items reflecting an expression of dislike of people, preferring to be alone instead of involved with others, and never having close relationships. Social Avoidance (SAV) is a nine-item revision tapping into dislike for social situations and avoidance of social events. The seven-item

Shyness (SHY) scale is identical to the MMPI-2-RF scale with the same name. Its item content focuses on social anxiety, including feeling uncomfortable and easily embarrassed around other people.

The Self-Importance (SFI) Interpersonal SP scale is new to the MMPI-3. The construct assessed by this scale was one specifically targeted by Ben-Porath and Tellegen (2020a; 2020b) and included among the 95 new trial items for the MMPI-3. This scale's 10 items express the belief that one is an extraordinary person with special talents and abilities that other people do not have.

PERSONALITY PSYCHOPATHOLOGY FIVE (PSY-5) SCALES

The PSY-5 scales were developed originally by Harkness and McNulty for inclusion in the MMPI-2 (Harkness, McNulty, & Ben-Porath, 1995) and later revised for the MMPI-2-RF (Harkness, McNulty, et al., 2014). The PSY-5 scales measure constructs posed by Harkness and McNulty (1994) to account for important features of both normal and abnormal personality. The PSY-5 constructs and the original scales developed to assess them are described in detail in Chapter 7 of this book and in a monograph published by the University of Minnesota Press (Harkness et al., 2002).

Harkness and McNulty were asked once again by the test authors to revise the PSY-5 scales for inclusion on the MMPI-3 (Ben-Porath & Tellegen, 2020a; 2020b). They used the same general procedures described earlier in this chapter for other MMPI-3 substantive scale revisions, but they began with only the items that had already been retained from the MMPI-2-RF-EX after the other MMPI-3 scales had been developed by Ben-Porath and Tellegen. The 15-item Aggressiveness (AGGR) scale focuses on assertive and aggressive behavior intended to get what one wants rather than such behavior in reaction to the aggressive behavior of others. The 20-item Psychoticism (PSYC) scale includes experiences associated with thought disorder. The 18-item Disconstraint (DISC) scale focuses on poor impulse control, acting out, and sensation seeking. The 15-item Negative Emotionality/Neuroticism (NEGE) scale assesses a tendency to experience negative emotions such as anxiety, insecurity, and worry. The 14-item Introversion/Low Positive Emotionality (INTR) scale describes avoidance of social situations and deficiencies in experiencing joy and other positive emotions.

ADMINISTRATION AND SCORING

User Qualifications

As with all MMPI instruments, the MMPI-3 is to be used only by persons with appropriate education and training in the use of clinical assessment instruments. The test distributor has established minimum qualifications for users of tests of this kind. Their website (pearsonassessments.com) provides details concerning these qualifications. Basically, users are to be adequately trained in the administration and interpretation of clinical assessments. The training can be obtained through completion of degree programs or continuing education workshops.

Who Can Take the MMPI-3?

To produce meaningful MMPI-3 results, the test taker must read well enough to understand the items and respond to them appropriately. The average Flesch-Kincaid reading level of all MMPI-3 items is 4.5 (Ben-Porath & Tellegen, 2020a), suggesting slightly less than a fifth-grade reading level is needed to complete the test. However, there are many individual MMPI-3 items that have a higher estimated reading level. As such, even for test takers who have the required average reading skill, test users should be prepared to screen scored profiles carefully for indications of possible difficulties with comprehending the items, which can elevate scores on scales like CNS, VRIN, TRIN, and CRIN. If the examiner has concerns about the reading ability of a test taker, then a standardized test of reading comprehension should be administered. Sometimes persons with lower reading levels can meaningfully complete the MMPI-3 if it is administered using a standardized audio version available from Pearson Assessments.

The MMPI-3 is intended for use with persons who are 18 years of age or older. The MMPI-Adolescent (MMPI-A; Butcher et al., 1992) or MMPI-A-Restructured Form (MMPI-A-RF; Archer et al., 2016) should be used with persons who are younger than 18. Because all versions of the MMPI (adolescent and adult) were normed on 18-year-olds, clinicians must decide for each individual case whether it is more appropriate to use an adult or adolescent version of the test with 18-year-olds. Ordinarily, the MMPI-A or MMPI-A-RF would be selected for 18-year-olds who are still in high school; and the MMPI-2, MMPI-2-RF, or MMPI-3 would be selected for 18-year-olds who are in college, working, or otherwise living a more independent lifestyle. Adolescent versions of the MMPI are discussed in Chapters 14 and 15 of this book. The MMPI-2 and MMPI-2-RF were discussed in Chapters 1 – 12. Information to guide decisions on whether to use the MMPI-2, MMPI-2-RF, or MMPI-3 is discussed later in this chapter. There is no upper age limit to who can take the MMPI-3.

The clinical condition of potential examinees is an important consideration in deciding who can take the MMPI-3. Completion of the test is a challenging and tedious task for many individuals. Persons who are very depressed, anxious, or agitated often find the task quite difficult, as do many who have experienced cognitive injuries or decline. Frequently it is possible to break the testing session into several shorter periods for such individuals. Sometimes persons who are in great distress find it easier to complete the test if the items are presented by means of a standardized audio version available from Pearson Assessments.

Administering the MMPI-3

The MMPI-3 is a well-standardized instrument, assuring that differences in test results are due to differences in test takers and not due to the way the test is administered. Approved administration methods for the MMPI-3 include a pencil/paper version where the test takers read items from a printed booklet and mark their responses on an answer sheet and a computerized version that uses Q-Local or Q-Global software available from Pearson Assessments. For persons of average or above-average intelligence, without complicating factors—such as limited reading ability or significant emotional distress—the computerized testing time typically is 25–35 minutes. Pencil/paper administrations typically take 35–50 minutes. For persons with reading difficulties or other complicating factors, the testing time may be appreciably longer. A standardized audio version of the test is available for test takers with difficulties that preclude reading the items from a test booklet or computer screen. We discourage reading items aloud to test takers, as this practice deviates from standardized administration procedures and could impact the test-taker's responses. The MMPI-3 should always be administered by someone trained in test administration in a supervised setting. Additional information about appropriate test administration is available in Chapter 2.

Printed and computerized versions of the MMPI-3 are available in English, Spanish, and French for Canada. Individuals who are interested in using the MMPI-3 in other languages should contact the University of Minnesota Press Test Division (https://www.upress.umn.edu/test-division).

Scoring the MMPI-3

There are several options for scoring the MMPI-3. Computer scoring is available for the MMPI-3, and it has the advantage of being accurate, efficient, and reliable. If the test has been completed using Q-Local or Q-Global systems, responses are immediately processed, yielding scores and profiles for all of the MMPI-3 scales. If a pencil/paper form was used, hand scoring is also available using scoring templates and profile sheets. We do not recommend hand scoring, as this process is not very efficient and is more prone to errors than computer scoring. Scoring the TRIN, VRIN, and CRIN scales is especially complex, so special care should be taken when hand scoring these scales. One can also use a scanner or keyboard to input responses recorded on the answer sheet into the Q-Local or Q-Global scoring and reporting systems available from Pearson Assessments. Test users also have the option of mailing answer sheets to Pearson for computer scoring.

If the MMPI-3 has been administered using the Q-local or Q-global systems—or has been administered using the pencil/paper version, and the responses were later entered into the computerized systems—then there are several report options available. *The User's Guide for the Score and Interpretive Reports* (Ben-Porath & Tellegen, 2020c) provides useful information concerning the use of these reports. The standard report is titled *The MMPI-3 Score Report*, and it presents raw scores and T scores for all the scales, along with profiles of the scores. It also includes an option to add the mean scores for specific comparison groups of interest (e.g., police officer candidates, community mental health outpatients, male prison inmates). These comparison-group data were largely drawn from the validation samples collected as part of the test development process. They allow the test taker to be compared to not just individuals in the normative sample but also individuals tested in similar contexts. A sample *MMPI-3 Score Report* can be found in the appendix to this chapter.

In addition to the *MMPI-3 Score Report*, two interpretive reports are available from Pearson Assessments (Ben-Porath & Tellegen, 2020c). The most general is the *MMPI-3 Interpretive Report for Clinical Settings*. This report includes all the information in the score report as well as an interpretation of that information by the test authors that identifies the source from which each interpretive statement is derived. The other interpretive report is the *Police Candidate Interpretive Report*. This report offers a summary of a test-taker's MMPI-3 scores and an empirically sourced interpretation of how these scores may be reflected in their performance as a police officer. Users interested in any of these reports should contact Pearson Assessments for more details.

PSYCHOMETRIC CHARACTERISTICS

MMPI-3 Norms

English Language Norms

A major reason for developing the MMPI-3 was to establish contemporary norms that are demographically representative of the United States. The MMPI-2-RF-EX, which was described earlier in this chapter, was used to collect normative data. Data collection was carried out in 2017 and 2018 by EurekaFacts, a social science research firm experienced in this type of project. Research participants were solicited utilizing social media, general advertisements, community organizations, and direct solicitation of individuals in existing databases. Guidelines were given to the firm to ensure that participants represented projected 2020 United States census data. Those who expressed interest in participating were screened by telephone to determine if their inclusion would be consistent with target goals. A total of 2,383 individuals were tested, with 98% completing the MMPI-2-RF-EX on computer tablets. Individuals who completed the testing were paid $50.00 each. Data from some test takers was excluded due to their scores on MMPI-2-RF indicators of non-content-based invalid responding (i.e., CNS > 17, VRIN-r or TRIN-r > 79T) and overreporting (i.e., F-r = 120 and Fp-r > 99). After these exclusionary criteria were applied, 2,008 individuals remained. A total of 1,620 (810 women and 810 men) were selected from these remaining individuals to compose the MMPI-3 normative sample based on their demographic characteristics. This selection was done to facilitate the final normative sample approximating the proportions of individuals of varying ages, educational levels, and racial and ethnic identification observed in the U.S. population based on the projected 2020 census.

Chapter 2 of the *MMPI-3 Technical Manual* (Ben-Porath & Tellegen, 2020b) includes more details about normative data collection and summarizes demographic information for the individuals comprising the MMPI-3 normative sample. Broadly, data were collected from community residents in nine areas of the United States. The combined sample of men and women was 60.3% White, 14.0% Hispanic/ Latinx, 12.4% Black/African American, 5.1% Asian, 4.5% Mixed Race, and 3.7% Other.[2] Ben-Porath and Tellegen (2020a; 2020b) noted that individuals identifying

---

[2] Ben-Porath and Tellegen (2020a, 2020b) use slightly different labels in tables and text describing the normative sample (e.g., Table 3-1 in the administration manual). Y. S. Ben-Porath (personal communication, November 2021) indicated these labels were abbreviated versions of the ethnic and racial origins reflected in the MMPI-2-RF-EX Biographical Data Sheet (see Appendix A of Ben-Porath & Tellegen, 2020b). To ensure full representation of the normative samples' identities, we have elected to use the broader labels from the Biographical Data Sheet. There is no description of the proportion of individuals who identified as "American Indian or Alaska Native" or "Native Hawaiian or Pacific Islander," as these individuals were reported as part of the "other" identification.

as Hispanic/Latinx underrepresent the proportion of individuals in the population with this identity in the projected 2020 census data (14.0% in MMPI-3 normative sample vs. 16.8% projected for the 2020 census). They attributed this to the fact that many Hispanic/Latinx individuals screened for inclusion did not speak English fluently enough to complete the MMPI-2-RF-EX in English, thus emphasizing the importance of the concurrent development of the MMPI-3 in Spanish as well as the development of the U.S. Spanish-language norms (described later in this chapter).

Concerning age, 21.6% of the MMPI-3 normative sample were between the ages of 18 and 29 years; 55.7% were between 30 and 59 years; 20.6% were between 60 and 79 years; and 2.1% were 80 years or older. Ben-Porath and Tellegen (2020a; 2020b) noted that the normative sample underrepresented individuals in the 60–79 and 80+ years categories. They thought the more severe underrepresentation of individuals who were 80+ may not be too concerning, given MMPI instruments are used infrequently with individuals in this age range. Nonetheless, further research on this issue and the impact of this underrepresentation on test interpretation for older test takers may be warranted.

Educational levels of individuals in the normative sample were "No High School or GED" (8.6%), "High School or GED" (29.0%), "Some College" (27.7%), and "Bachelor's Degree or Higher" (34.8%). The test's authors indicated there was slight underrepresentation of individuals in the lowest education level and slight overrepresentation in the highest level when the MMPI-3 normative sample proportions were compared to projections for the 2020 census (Ben-Porath & Tellegen, 2020a; 2020b). The underrepresentation of individuals at the lowest education level was due, in part, to this group producing more invalid test results. This pattern of over- and underrepresentation was similarly present in MMPI-2 norms and was demonstrated to have little impact on test interpretation (Schinka & LaLone, 1997). Thus, we suspect this deviation from census projections will not affect MMPI-3 test interpretation. Nonetheless, it may also be an area for future research.

No test normative samples match census data exactly. However, the test authors conclude, and we agree, that the MMPI-3 norms represent an acceptably close approximation of the U.S. population and, in this regard, reflect a dramatic improvement over the MMPI-2 and MMPI-2-RF norms. As is true for the MMPI-2-RF, only nongendered norms are available for the MMPI-3. Using nongendered norms conforms to the provision in the Civil Rights Act of 1991 that prohibits consideration of sex in employment practices.

U.S. Spanish Language Norms

A normative sample for U.S. Spanish speakers was developed concurrently to the English-language norms (Ben-Porath et al., 2020). The Spanish translation efforts began as soon as the MMPI-2-RF-EX was developed. The MMPI-2-RF-EX items underwent a translation–back translation process with a special emphasis on ensuring a "pan-Spanish" translation to facilitate use of the test by any Spanish speaker regardless of dialect (for details, see Ben-Porath et al., 2020).

Data collection using the Spanish-language MMPI-2-RF-EX was also completed by EurekaFacts using the same recruitment strategies and data collection procedures previously described. Monolingual Spanish speakers were recruited to develop

Spanish-language norms for the MMPI-3. Bilingual Spanish/English speakers were also recruited to examine item comparability across the Spanish and English forms. One item initially selected for inclusion on the MMPI-3 was replaced because of poor comparability between the English and Spanish translations.

A total of 655 individuals completed the Spanish-language MMPI-2-RF-EX in Dallas, TX; Washington, DC; Miami, FL; and San Diego, CA, as part of the Spanish-language normative data collection project. Valid test results were obtained for 585 individuals. All the men from this group ($n = 275$) as well as 275 women randomly selected (out of $n = 310$) comprise the 550 individuals who make up the Spanish-language normative sample. Chapter 2 of the *MMPI-3 Manual Supplement for the U.S. Spanish Translation* (Ben-Porath et al., 2020) provides additional details about normative data collection and summarizes demographic information for the MMPI-3 Spanish-language normative individuals.

Concerning age, 24.4% of Spanish-language normative individuals were between the ages of 18 and 29 years; 63.3% were between 30 and 59 years; 12.4% were between 60 and 79 years; and no members of the sample were 80 years or older. Educational levels of Spanish-language normative individuals were "No High School or GED" (22.7%), "High School or GED" (27.5%), "Some College" (27.8%), and "Bachelor's Degree or Higher" (22.0%).

Chapter 2 of the *MMPI-3 Manual Supplement for the U.S. Spanish Translation* (Ben-Porath et al., 2020) includes a table displaying the mean scale scores and standard deviations for men and women from the Spanish-language normative sample if their tests had been scored using the MMPI-3 English-language norms. These results show that for a majority of the scales, the group-level differences between using the two sets of norms are unlikely to be clinically significant. However, there were a meaningful number of scales where this difference was substantial for men, women, or both (i.e., CRIN, TRIN, Fp, RBS, L, BXD, RC4, RC9, MLS, BRF, JCP, SUB, IMP, and DISC). As a result, the test authors recommend—and we agree—that the Spanish-language translation of the MMPI-3 should only be scored using the Spanish-language norms.

Standard Scores

Raw scores for substantive scales are converted to Uniform T (UT) scores by comparing the raw scores to scores for the normative sample. The use of UT scores assures that the same T scores on different substantive scales represent the same percentile rank. More details about the use of UT scores can be found in Chapter 2 of this book, or in Chapter 3 of the *MMPI-3 Manual for Administration, Scoring, and Interpretation* (Ben-Porath & Tellegen, 2020a). As with the MMPI-2 and MMPI-2-RF, raw scores on the Validity scales are not converted to UT scores. Rather, because the distributions of raw scores for the Validity scales are different from substantive scale distributions, Validity scale raw scores are converted to linear T scores.

Reliability

Tables 3.2–3.6 of the *MMPI-3 Technical Manual* (Ben-Porath & Tellegen, 2020b) present test–retest, internal consistency, and standard errors of measurement (SEMs) for all the MMPI-3 scales for the normative and outpatient mental health samples.

Test–retest reliability was determined using scores of 123 men and 152 women from the English language normative sample who were tested a second time after a median interval of 8 days. The test–retest reliability values varied across Validity scales, with the consistency scales (VRIN, TRIN, and CRIN) being less reliable than the overreporting (F, Fp, Fs, FBS, and RBS) and underreporting (L, K) scales. Test–retest correlations for the consistency scales ranged from .47 to .65, while the test–retest coefficients for the overreporting and underreporting scales ranged from .73 to .87. Internal consistency values for the Validity scales ranged from .31 to .78 for the normative sample and from .23 to .83 for the outpatient mental health sample. Generally, these internal consistency and test–retest estimates for the Validity scales vary across scales and samples, and they typically are much lower than those demonstrated for the substantive scales (described below). This is to be expected because of the limited variability of these scales in samples where test takers are likely to be cooperative and to give credible responses. However, the SEMs for the Validity scales are small enough that the interpretive recommendations in the *MMPI-3 Manual for Administration, Scoring, and Interpretation* (Ben-Porath & Tellegen, 2020a) seem justified.

For the substantive scales, test–retest reliability coefficients for the H-O scales were very strong, with all estimates for EID and BXD ≥ .90. The test–retest values were somewhat lower but still good for THD among both the normative sample of men and women (r_{tr} = .76 and .81, respectively). THD having the lowest test–retest reliability estimates is unsurprising given the base rate for this kind of serious psychopathology is very low in the general population. Temporal stability of the RC scales was also very good, ranging from .94 for RC4 to .81 for RC6 (median r_{tr} = .85). Test–retest coefficients for the SP scales ranged from .68 (EAT) to .94 (SUB; median r_{tr} = .84). Scales with more items tended to be more stable than scales with fewer items. Test–retest reliability coefficients for the MMPI-3's PSY-5 scales were acceptable and ranged from .72 for PSYC (normative sample men) to .93 for DISC (normative sample men), with a median value of .87.

Internal consistency coefficients (alpha) for the H-O scales were quite high in the clinical samples, with values ranging from .79 (THD) to .92 (EID; median α = .85). As expected, values were slightly lower in the normative sample likely due to restriction of range (range α = .76 [THD] to .92 [EID]; median α = .83). The RC scales had good internal consistency, with values for the clinical samples ranging from .76 (RC4) to .93 (RCd; median α = .82) and for the normative sample from .69 (RC8) to .89 (RCd; median α = .78). As would be expected, the internal consistencies of the SP scales, which have fewer items than the H-O or RC scales, were lower than for the longer scales. Alpha coefficients for the SP scales varied from a low of .40 (BRF) to a high of .89 (ANP), with 90% of the values falling between .62 and .85 across the normative and clinical samples combined. Internal consistency coefficients (alpha) for the PSY-5 scales in the normative sample ranged from .67 for PSYC to .88 for DISC; and in the clinical sample, they ranged from .72 (PSYC) to .90 (INTR).

The SEMs for the H-O, RC, and PSY-5 scales in both the normative and outpatient mental health samples tended to be small, ranging from 3 to 5 points for the H-O scales, 3 to 6 points for the RC scales, and 3 to 6 points for the PSY-5 scales. Despite evidence of the SP scales having lower test–retest and internal consistency reliability,

SEMs for the SP scales were largely similar to those reported for the H-O, RC, and PSY-5 scales, with the SEM estimates ranging from 2 to 8 points. The lone exception was BRF, which had an unusually large SEM in the sample of outpatient women (SEM = 10), although the SEM estimates for BRF in other samples ranged from 4 to 8. Overall, these data suggest observed T scores are likely to be relatively precise measures of test takers' true standings on the constructs assessed by these scales.

In summary, the internal consistency and temporal stability of the H-O, RC, and PSY-5 scales are good and comparable to those of other self-report scales. The somewhat lower reliabilities of the SP scales suggest that test users should have more confidence in interpreting scores on SP scales with higher elevations as opposed to those that are only marginally elevated.

Validity

In the sections that follow, we briefly review and summarize MMPI-3 validity data from three general sources. First, Ben-Porath and Tellegen (2020b) published more than 36,000 unique correlations in the *MMPI-3 Technical Manual* (Appendixes B, D, and E) between MMPI-3 scale scores and external criteria in a variety of samples including community mental health center outpatients, private practice outpatients, spine surgery/spinal cord stimulator patients, forensic disability claimants, prison inmates, police officer candidates, and college students. Criterion measures consisted of therapist ratings, intake information, record reviews, and other self-report instruments. These samples reflect contexts in which the MMPI family of instruments are frequently used except for the college students, who were included because they could be administered a wide variety of criterion measures that would not be feasible in other settings (Ben-Porath & Tellegen, 2020b). Second, because most the scales on the MMPI-3 are revised versions of scales that existed on the MMPI-2-RF, we review how similar each MMPI-3 scale is to its predecessor. For scales that are very similar, we draw on MMPI-2-RF research to help evaluate their validity. Finally, we review several studies investigating the validity of the test's scales that have already been published in peer-reviewed journals.

Validity Scales

CANNOT SAY (CNS) SCORE
Ben-Porath and Tellegen (2020a) indicate that excessive item omissions are associated with lowered scores on some scales such that those scores may not accurately reflect characteristics of the test taker. The manual indicates that scales can be interpreted when at least 90% of items from that scale are answered. This recommendation draws on research on the MMPI-2 and MMPI-2-RF that demonstrated that little interpretive validity is lost when up to 10% of a scale's items are omitted (Dragon et al., 2012).

NON–CONTENT-BASED INVALID RESPONDING SCALES (CRIN, VRIN, TRIN)
As previously described, the CRIN scale is new to the MMPI-3 and serves as a marker of intermittent, non-content-based invalid responding. Ben-Porath and Tellegen (2020a) recommend that the entire protocol is uninterpretable when CRIN T scores are ≥ 80. They recommend cautious interpretation of all content-based Validity

scales, as well as all substantive scales, when CRIN T scores are moderately elevated (i.e., 70–79). While these cut-score recommendations need empirical study, Ben-Porath and Tellegen (2020b) provide some preliminary empirical support for CRIN cut-scores using a simulation study. Using the normative sample, they randomly selected and replaced 70% of the individual item responses for each participant. Half of the time, each individual item was replaced with a "True" response; and half of the time, it was replaced with a "False" response. The correlation between CRIN and the MMPI-2-RF's VRIN-r scale was $r = .89$. The same procedure was repeated two more times, once where a "True" response was inserted each time and once where a "False" response was always inserted. Under these conditions, CRIN was strongly positively correlated with the MMPI-2-RF's TRIN-r scale in the former ($r = .91$) and negatively correlated in the latter ($r = -.72$). These simulation studies follow a methodology utilized by Handel and colleagues (2010) to evaluate the sensitivity of VRIN-r and TRIN-r to random and fixed non-content-based responding. Extrapolating from the Handel et al. data, the correlations presented by Ben-Porath and Tellegen (2020b) offer preliminary support for their interpretive recommendations for CRIN, although to a somewhat lesser degree in the case of a fixed, false-response style (i.e., nonacquiescence).

Ben-Porath and Tellegen (2020b) indicate that when VRIN T scores are between 70 and 79, scores on the other scales should be interpreted cautiously; when VRIN T scores are ≥ 80, the test taker likely responded to items so inconsistently that scores on other scales should not be interpreted. These recommendations are identical to those provided for the MMPI-2-RF VRIN-r scale, which are well-supported by past research (i.e., Burchett et al. 2016; Handel et al., 2010). Nonetheless, these cut scores need empirical study, as less than half (24 of 53) of the MMPI-2-RF VRIN-r item pairs were retained for use with the MMPI-3. However, the random responding simulation data provided in the *Technical Manual* (Ben-Porath & Tellegen, 2020b) offer support that VRIN measures inconsistent responding in a manner similar to its predecessors. Namely, after using the random responding simulation procedure, Ben-Porath and Tellegen (2020b) calculated a correlation of $r = .88$ between VRIN and the MMPI-2-RF's VRIN-r scale.

Ben-Porath and Tellegen (2020b) recommend that a TRIN scale T score ≥ 80 be interpreted as indicating fixed (true or false) responding that invalidates the protocol, with T scores ranging from 70 to 79 indicating that other scales should be interpreted cautiously. Again, these recommendations are aligned with the MMPI-2-RF research literature (Burchett et al., 2016; Handel et al., 2010). However, only 16 of the 33 MMPI-3 TRIN scale item pairs were carried over from its predecessor scale, meaning these cut scores likely need to be empirically investigated. The "True" and "False" fixed responding simulation data demonstrates an extremely high correlation between the two versions of the TRIN scale ($r = .96$ and .95, respectively; Ben-Porath & Tellegen, 2020b), indicating TRIN and TRIN-r assess a highly similar construct.

OVERREPORTING SCALES (F, Fp, Fs, FBS, RBS)

The F, Fp, and Fs scales are revisions of their MMPI-2-RF counterparts, sharing 74%, 81%, and 81% of their items with their predecessor scales, respectively (Ben-Porath

& Tellegen, 2020b). The criteria used to guide item changes to each of these scales (summarized previously in this chapter) were nearly identical to those criteria used to construct the MMPI-2-RF versions of the scales. Given these high rates of item continuity as well as the similarity in scale construction practices, it is little surprise that these scales are very similar to their predecessors. In four samples with sufficient variability on the overreporting validity scales (two simulation samples and two forensic disability samples), Ben-Porath and Tellegen (2020b) reported extremely high correlations between the MMPI-3 and MMPI-2-RF versions of these scales, with values ranging from $r = .84$ to .99 (median $r = .95$). FBS and RBS were carried over unchanged to the MMPI-3.

Given the similarities between the MMPI-3 and MMPI-2-RF overreporting Validity scales, we expect interpretations made for a specific MMPI-2-RF scale are also appropriate for its MMPI-3 counterpart. In Chapter 12, we reviewed the validity research supporting the use of the MMPI-2-RF versions of these scales. Applying this research to the MMPI-3, it suggests the overreporting scales of the MMPI-3 are sensitive to overreporting of various kinds. Optimal cutoff scores will likely shift from setting to setting. However, the various cut scores in the MMPI-2-RF literature are generally consistent with the interpretive guidelines found in the MMPI-3 manual (Ben-Porath & Tellegen, 2020a).

Whitman, Tylicki, and Ben-Porath (2021) employed a simulation design to examine the effectiveness of the MMPI-3 overreporting Validity scales. They instructed college students to feign "serious mental health problems" to avoid incarceration for a crime. Their results revealed the feigning group produced mean scale scores that were much larger than those produced by a group completing the test under standard instructions. Cohen's d effect size estimates ranged from 2.35 (FBS) to 5.56 (Fp). Given these extreme differences, it is no surprise that classification accuracies were near perfect using the recommended cut scores. For example, using a cut score of 100T for Fp resulted in a sensitivity of .97, specificity of .99, and hit rate of .98. The effect sizes reported by Whitman, Tylicki, and Ben-Porath are much larger than those typically found in the MMPI simulation literature, perhaps as a result of the specific simulation procedure employed. Thus, additional research, employing both simulation and known-groups designs, is needed to provide greater certainty regarding the classification accuracy of the MMPI-3 overreporting scales.

Tylicki, Gervais, and Ben-Porath (2020) examined the utility of the MMPI-3 overreporting validity scales in a non-head injury, forensic disability sample. They used both performance validity tests (PVT) and non-MMPI symptom validity tests as their criterion measures. Their results indicate that RBS consistently demonstrated the largest difference in mean scores between those who passed a PVT versus those who failed a PVT (Cohen's d ranging from .71 to 1.01 across four different PVTs; *median* = .82). They also used the Slick et al. (1999) criteria for malingered neurocognitive dysfunction (MND) to identify groups of Probable/Definite MND, Possible MND, and Incentive Only. Cohen's d effect sizes greater than 1.00 were produced by every overreporting validity scale except Fp when differentiating Probable/Definite MND from Incentive Only participants, with RBS ($d = 1.34$) and Fs ($d = 1.30$) producing the largest effects. As expected, effect sizes were smaller when differentiating participants in the Possible MND group from those in the Incentive Only group; however, F and Fs still demonstrated large effects (d = .85 and .79, respectively). Finally, Tylicki, Gervais, and Ben-Porath examined the classification accuracies of the overreporting scales at the cut scores recommended in the manual (Ben-Porath & Tellegen, 2020a) and found the scales performed as would be expected—with higher cut scores demonstrating excellent specificity at the expense of decreased sensitivity, while lower cut scores improved sensitivity but decreased specificity.

In sum, preliminary research using the MMPI-3 overreporting Validity scales suggests they function as expected in detecting overreporting symptoms. It appears these scales are similar enough to their MMPI-2-RF counterparts to allow us to extrapolate from that body of research. Until additional research suggests otherwise, we recommend using the interpretive guidelines presented in the MMPI-3 manual (Ben-Porath & Tellegen, 2020a) and included later in this chapter.

UNDERREPORTING SCALES (L, K)

The L scale of the MMPI-3 is very similar to the L-r scale of the MMPI-2-RF. Of the 14 items in the L scale, 12 are also in the L-r scale. Ben-Porath and Tellegen (2020b) report correlations between the L and L-r scales were extremely strong in a sample of college students instructed to underreport (r = .98) as well as men and women who were candidates for public safety jobs (r = .95 and .93, respectively). These data suggest the two scales are nearly identical, and the validity research conducted on the L-r scale is applicable to its MMPI-3 counterpart. This research was summarized in Chapter 12 and indicated the L-r scale is sensitive to underreporting. It was also generally supportive of the interpretive guidelines for L-r, which Ben-Porath and Tellegen (2020a) carried over to the MMPI-3.

The MMPI-3 K scale carries over eight of its 14 items from the MMPI-2-RF K-r scale, from which it is derived. Ben-Porath and Tellegen (2020b) report very high correlations between these two scales in college students simulating underreporting (r = .93) as well as men (r = .88) and women (r = .87) undergoing public safety pre-employment evaluations. These data indicate K is very similar to K-r and support applying the research summarized in Chapter 12 for K-r being applied to K. That evidence also supports the strategy and guidelines Ben-Porath and Tellegen (2020a) suggest for interpreting the K scale (reviewed later in this chapter).

Whitman, Tylicki, and Ben-Porath (2021) provided an initial examination of the MMPI-3 underreporting scales using a simulation methodology. They instructed a group of college students to present themselves as well-adjusted and virtuous while completing the MMPI-3 to obtain a desirable job. Extremely large mean group differences were found between the underreporting simulators and a comparison group of college students who completed the test under standard instructions for both L (d = 2.19) and K (d = 2.03). Classification accuracy analyses supported Ben-Porath and Tellegen's (2020a) recommended cut scores and demonstrated the expected patterns of utility, with high cut scores maximizing specificity and lower cut scores emphasizing sensitivity.

In summation, initial research investigating L and K as well as comparisons with the MMPI-2-RF L-r and K-r scales suggest the MMPI-3 underreporting scales do indeed detect underreporting tendencies by test takers. We anticipate new research will further inform interpretation of the MMPI-3 L and K scales; but until that time, we recommend following Ben-Porath and Tellegen's (2020a) guidelines, which we review later in this chapter.

Substantive Scales

Given its very recent publication, the validity literature examining the MMPI-3— apart from the extensive set of correlates presented by Ben-Porath and Tellegen (2020b) in the *Technical Manual*—is limited. Several studies have presented correlations with other self-report instruments among college students (J. T. Hall, Menton, & Ben-Porath, 2021; Kremyar & Lee, 2021). Those results were generally indicative of strong convergent and discriminant validity across the substantive scales. Whitman, Tylicki, Mascioli, et al. (2021) used a record review form to examine MMPI-3 correlates in an outpatient neuropsychology clinic. They too reported correlates that consistently support the construct validity of the various substantive scales of the MMPI-3.

Below, we briefly summarize the validity research on the MMPI-3 substantive scales. We base these summaries on reviews of how similar the MMPI-3 substantive scales are to their MMPI-2-RF predecessors, the validity data reported in Ben-Porath and Tellegen (2020b), and validity data reported in the research literature. We provide greater detail in reviewing the validity data examining scales new to the MMPI-3 in comparison to those carried over from the MMPI-2-RF.

HIGHER ORDER (H-O) SCALES

The H-O scales of the MMPI-3 are very similar to their MMPI-2-RF predecessors. Ben-Porath and Tellegen (2020b) report that 90% of EID items overlap across the two tests, as do 85% and 75% of THD and BXD items, respectively. The test authors also report MMPI-3/MMPI-2-RF scale intercorrelations separately for men and women in both the normative sample and a composite outpatient mental health sample. The MMPI-3 H-O scales correlated so strongly with their MMPI-2-RF counterparts in each instance (r = .93–.99) that we believe it reasonable to consider these scales act as alternate forms of one another. Research using the MMPI-2-RF broadly supports both the convergent and discriminant validity of the H-O scales (see Chapter 12 for additional details).

Initial research exploring the MMPI-3's EID scale also supports its convergent and discriminant validity. Ben-Porath and Tellegen (2020b) demonstrated that EID scale scores tend to be positively correlated with a variety of markers of emotional distress as well as the types of thoughts, behaviors, and physiological symptoms common among internalizing manifestations of psychopathology. EID scale scores are unrelated, or sometimes negatively related, to externalizing behaviors like aggressive or antisocial behaviors and substance use.

Ben-Porath and Tellegen (2020b) did not include data from an inpatient sample in their examination of empirical correlates, a sample that likely would have allowed for the best examination of the types of difficulties THD is intended to assess. However, based on MMPI-2-RF research, we have confidence that higher scores on the THD scale are associated with psychotic symptoms. Furthermore, in the empirical correlates in other clinical and nonclinical samples presented by Ben-Porath and Tellegen (2020b), THD is correlated with delusional thinking, use of antipsychotic medication, magical thinking, and persecutory beliefs. Additionally, these data suggest THD also has strong discriminant validity. Although THD is positively correlated with some externalizing markers like hostility and reactive anger, as well as some internalizing markers associated with traumatic stress (e.g., dissociative symptoms), these correlates appear limited to phenomena that are consistent with psychopathology research and common clinical presentations. For example, hostility and reactive anger—while typically considered markers of antagonistic externalizing forms of psychopathology—are correlated with THD, given that people experiencing persecutory thinking may often be mistrustful and lash out at others.

Ben-Porath and Tellegen (2020b) report a variety of externalizing correlates of BXD. Higher scores are associated with behaviors like substance use, risk-taking/thrill-seeking, aggression, and antisocial behavior. BXD is also positively correlated with anger, impulsivity, and hostility. BXD scores are largely unrelated to indicators of emotional distress, thought disorder, and somatic/cognitive complaints.

In summary, the three H-O scales provide information about the broad kinds of problems a test taker is experiencing. More specificity in the kinds of inferences a test user can make will require examination of the more narrowly designed substantive scales (i.e., RC and SP scales).

RESTRUCTURED CLINICAL (RC) SCALES

As mentioned in Chapter 7, we believe the MMPI-3 RC scales are generally equivalent to the RC scales on the MMPI-2/MMPI-2-RF; thus, validity research examining these scales using any version of the adult MMPI instruments applies to the versions of these scales found on the other adult MMPI instruments. However, the MMPI-3's RC scales are not identical to the predecessor RC scales found on the MMPI-2 and MMPI-2-RF. Except for RC8, the MMPI-3 RC scales are much shorter, having 18% to 46% fewer items (median = 22%). Each MMPI-3 RC scale also includes items that were not part of the MMPI-2-RF RC scales. Item additions range from as few as one new item (RC1) to as many as five new items (RC6, RC7, and RC9). Nonetheless, the MMPI-2-RF/MMPI-3 RC scale intercorrelations presented by Ben-Porath and Tellegen (2020b) were $r \geq .90$ in every instance across four different samples (i.e., normative sample men and women as well as composite outpatient men and women) except for RC6 (normative sample men, $r = .88$) and RC9 (normative sample men, $r = .82$, women, $r = .80$; composite outpatient men, $r = .80$, women, $r = .77$). However, given the RC6 intercorrelations were exceptionally strong among normative sample women ($r = .90$) and composite outpatient men and women ($r = .92$ and .91, respectively), we feel comfortable concluding that RC6 as well as the other RC scales are best considered alternate forms across the MMPI-2-RF and MMPI-3. We recommend interested readers review Chapter 7 to learn more about the validity evidence supporting interpretation of these scales.

RC9 deserves more careful inspection given the relatively weaker scale intercorrelations between the two MMPI instruments. When we examined the validity correlate data presented by Ben-Porath and Tellegen (2020b) regarding RC9, we found the most consistent and strong correlates to be those associated with the construct of hypomanic activation. Namely, scores on RC9 were positively correlated with impulsivity, substance use, anger and irritability, thrill-seeking/sensation-seeking behaviors, heightened levels of activity, self-injurious behavior, manic symptoms, aggression, affective instability, egocentricity, and diagnoses of bipolar disorder. Ben-Porath and Tellegen (2020b) also present side by side comparisons of the same external correlates for both the MMPI-3 and MMPI-2-RF versions of the same scale. A review of these correlates revealed any differences in the observed magnitude of associations rarely reached a small effect size ($r \geq .10$; Cohen et al., 2002), leaving us to conclude, for now, that the MMPI-3 RC9 scale is also equivalent to its predecessor.

SPECIFIC PROBLEMS (SP) SCALES: SOMATIC/COGNITIVE SCALES

Three of the four Somatic/Cognitive SP scales were carried over from the MMPI-2-RF. The fourth scale, EAT, was developed to cover important psychopathology content not included on previous MMPI instruments. The NUC scale remains unchanged from the MMPI-2-RF, while MLS and COG were both revised—with a single new item for MLS and six (of 11) new items for COG. Intercorrelations between the MMPI-2-RF and MMPI-3 versions of these scales range from $r = .92$ to .94 for MLS and $r = .87$ to .89 for COG. Review of external correlates suggest these three scales function as they did on the MMPI-2-RF (Ben-Porath & Tellegen, 2020b). Scores on MLS correlated with criteria indicating the test taker sees themselves as having poor health and sees their physical problems as severely limiting their functioning and quality of life. NUC is associated with a variety of neurological problems including dizziness and numbness, whereas COG indicates subjective reports of problems with memory and concentration. External correlates also reveal that all three of these scales are associated with poor stress tolerance and other diffuse internalizing difficulties (e.g., depressed mood).

The external correlates Ben-Porath and Tellegen (2020b) presented for EAT suggest this is a promising indicator of behavior associated with disordered eating. These correlates included periods of excessive eating, having a history of dieting, eating to cope with emotional distress, and a tendency to ignore bodily signs of hunger or satiation. EAT scores were also correlated with concerns about body image or shape as well as concerns about weight. Finally, Ben-Porath and Tellegen reported EAT was positively correlated with self- and other-report of self-injurious behavior.

Vaňousová et al. (2021) administered several self-report measures of behaviors related to eating disorders to college students and found similar results to those reported by Ben-Porath and Tellegen (2020b). Scores on EAT were predictive of a wide variety of relevant phenomena including binge eating, purging and restrictive eating, and body dissatisfaction and weight concerns—but not excessive exercise and muscle building. Whitman, Tylicki, Mascioli, et al. (2021) reported EAT scores were correlated with being assigned an eating disorder diagnosis and prior psychiatric hospitalization among outpatients at a neuropsychological clinic. Finally, Marek et al. (2021) examined EAT scale scores in a postoperative bariatric surgery sample. They observed EAT was positively correlated with a self-report measure of eating, shape, and weight concerns. EAT scores were also positively correlated with gaining back more of the weight initially lost after bariatric surgery approximately 5 years post-procedure.

SPECIFIC PROBLEMS (SP) SCALES: INTERNALIZING SCALES

There are 10 Internalizing SP scales, one of which—CMP—is new to the MMPI-3. The rest are revised versions of their MMPI-2-RF counterparts. Almost all the Internalizing SP scales on the MMPI-3 are longer than those found in the MMPI-2-RF, with the exception of STR and BRF. However, the scales remain relatively short (6–15 items), and the content of items in each scale continues to be quite homogeneous. Ben-Porath and Tellegen (2020b) report MMPI-2-RF/MMPI-3 intercorrelations of $r \geq .80$ for each scale in all four samples, with the only exceptions being STR (normative men, $r = .74$; women, $r = .79$; composite outpatient women, $r = .77$) and ARX (normative men, $r = .75$). STR and ARX were two scales intentionally targeted by Ben-Porath and Tellegen (2020b) for content revision; thus, it is of little surprise that they demonstrate weaker correlations with their predecessors. Both scales will benefit from future research to better explore their construct validity and inform their interpretation. Otherwise, we believe interpretations of these scales can generally rely on the validity research conducted on the MMPI-2-RF versions of these scales (see Chapter 12).

In general, test takers who elevate the Internalizing SP scales have endorsed items consistent with the label of the scale. External correlate data suggest the scales have strong convergent validity, but their discriminant validity within the internalizing symptom domain is limited. Namely, each scale is related to internalizing measures reflecting constructs specific to the scale; however, most of these scales are also correlated with markers of general emotional distress and other broad markers of internalizing symptoms.

The CMP scale is intended to assess compulsive behavior, and high scores indicate the test taker endorsed items related to living an orderly and organized life, engaging in repetitive behaviors, and experiencing emotional discomfort when they are required to deviate from their general lifestyle and habits. The external correlates provided by Ben-Porath and Tellegen (2020b) demonstrate CMP scores are associated with a tendency to engage in compulsive or ritualistic behaviors (e.g., cleaning, counting, checking). High CMP scores are also correlated with a tendency to be perfectionistic, rigid, and inflexible as well as consistently having unrealistic concerns about one's personal health and safety. Interestingly, across several studies, CMP has demonstrated only weak relations with measures of anxiety and emotional distress (Ben-Porath & Tellegen, 2020b; J. T. Hall, Menton, & Ben-Porath, 2021; Kremyar & Lee, 2021; Whitman, Tylicki, Mascioli, et al., 2021), suggesting it has stronger discriminant validity than other Internalizing SP scales.

SPECIFIC PROBLEMS (SP) SCALES: EXTERNALIZING SCALES

Six of the seven Externalizing SP scales of the MMPI-3 were also found on the MMPI-2-RF. The seventh, IMP, is an entirely new scale. Of those scales that were carried over from the MMPI-2-RF, AGG was the most significantly revised. The six items of the AGG scale all appeared on the MMPI-2-RF version; however, the MMPI-3 AGG scale dropped the other three items that appeared on the original. The remainder of the Externalizing SP scales are identical to or are near facsimiles of versions found on the MMPI-2-RF. Specifically, ACT remains unchanged from its MMPI-2-RF counterpart. FML, JCP, and CYN (formerly RC3) each have only a single item not found on their predecessor. The MMPI-3 SUB scale has three unique items compared to its MMPI-2-RF counterpart. Given this degree of similarity, it is not surprising that the scale intercorrelations between the MMPI-2-RF scales and their MMPI-3 versions are extremely high, with all correlations equal to or greater than .93 in all four samples reported in the manual (Ben-Porath & Tellegen, 2020b).

Thus, it is our view that the Externalizing SP scales of the MMPI-3 act as alternate forms of their predecessor scales. As such, prior validity research conducted on the MMPI-2-RF scales can be applied to these scales as well (see Chapter 12 for details). This work has identified a number of external correlates for each of these scales that are consistent with their intended focus (e.g., SUB scale scores are correlated with a variety of indicators dealing with the use and misuse of alcohol and other drugs). However, each of these scales is also correlated with a variety of other acting-out behaviors. In other words, while each scale has demonstrated strong convergent validity, the evidence for discriminant validity between different manifestations of externalizing psychopathology is weaker.

The new IMP scale consists of six items measuring impulsive behaviors. Test takers who elevate the IMP scale are reporting a tendency to act impulsively. They also endorse items indicative of frequent feelings of regret and the experience of negative consequences resulting from their impulsive actions. Ben-Porath and Tellegen (2020b) reported a number of external correlates of IMP scores supportive of its convergent validity, including a tendency to violate social norms and expectations as a result of poor behavioral control, having an increased number of impulsive actions during periods of strong emotions, difficulty controlling angry impulses, and a tendency to act without thinking through the potential consequences. Other correlates include a tendency to engage in thrill- and sensation-seeking behaviors and difficulties completing things that were started. Mental health care professionals were more likely to rate clients with high IMP scores as being impulsive as well as to identify them as engaging in higher rates of substance use. Furthermore, these clients were more likely to be diagnosed with ADHD, bipolar disorder, and substance-related disorders.

Initial evidence from published studies supports IMP as a measure of impulsive behavior. In J. T. Hall, Menton, and Ben-Porath's (2021) college student sample, IMP scores were correlated with other self-report scales measuring impulsivity, disinhibition, low self-control, lack of planning, and low dependability. It was also correlated with a history positive for mania and decreased frequency of medically related presenting problems in the outpatient neuropsychological sample investigated by Whitman, Tylicki, Mascioli, et al. (2021).

SPECIFIC PROBLEMS (SP) SCALES: INTERPERSONAL SCALES.
Three of the five SP Interpersonal scales on the MMPI-3—DSF, SHY, and SAV—have direct counterparts on the MMPI-2-RF. Another Interpersonal scale, DOM, is a reverse-keyed descendent of the MMPI-2-RF's IPP scale. The SFI scale is a newly created scale designed to measure beliefs that one is an extraordinary person. The MMPI-3's SHY scale is identical to the MMPI-2-RF scale, while the SAV scale

retained all but a single item from the MMPI-2-RF and is otherwise unchanged. All but a single item on DOM appeared on the MMPI-2-RF's IPP scale. DSF is the scale that underwent the greatest revision. Three items from the original DSF scale were dropped, and three were retained. An additional four items were added to the MMPI-3's DSF, bringing it to a total of seven items. As expected, the intercorrelations between the MMPI-3 and MMPI-2-RF versions of these scales are very high across all four comparison samples (all correlations were $r \geq |.96|$) except for DSF (Ben-Porath & Tellegen, 2020b). Despite the dramatic item changes, even DSF correlated highly across the two versions of the instrument in both the normative (men, $r = .74$; women, $r = .77$) and composite outpatient samples (men, $r = .81$; women, $r = .82$). However, the lesser magnitude of the DSF intercorrelations suggests to us that additional empirical research is needed to better illuminate the convergent and discriminant validity of this MMPI-3 scale.

Given these similarities, we generally believe the research exploring the validity of these scales on the MMPI-2-RF can be safely applied to the MMPI-3 Interpersonal SP scales (see Chapter 12). In short, the DOM scale is related to assertiveness, the SHY scale measures social anxiety, SAV is related to low gregariousness, and the DSF scale is related to low warmth and a strong preference for being alone. Scores on all of these scales are also somewhat positively related to emotional internalizing symptoms (e.g., depressed mood, anxiety). The exception is DOM, which demonstrates an expected pattern of negative associations with criterion assessing these types of difficulties.

The new SFI scale consists of 10 items measuring beliefs about the self being extraordinary. Elevated scores on SFI indicate the test taker reports having skills, talents, ideas, or abilities that make them special and important. They also see themselves as self-confident and well-suited for taking on leadership roles. Some of the external correlates identified by Ben-Porath and Tellegen (2020b) include high self-esteem, a tendency to be self-reliant, and a general sense of superiority that may be grandiose. Other correlates include a tendency to be authoritative, confident, determined, and ambitious. High scorers on SFI tend to be both interpersonally warm and dominant, although they may be seen as arrogant, vain, or narcissistic. SFI is also correlated positively with extraversion, optimism, and persistence. Finally, SFI scores are inversely correlated with both self-report and therapist ratings of internalizing symptoms; and, in mental health settings, high scorers are rarely diagnosed with depressive disorders.

Several published studies have also examined the validity of SFI scores. In an outpatient neuropsychological sample, Whitman, Tylicki, Mascioli, et al. (2021) found SFI was negatively correlated with presenting with emotional problems, a history of suicidal ideation, and diagnosis with a depressive disorder. Among college students, J. T. Hall, Menton, and Ben-Porath (2021) found that SFI scale scores were positively correlated with self-report instruments measuring positive emotionality, positive self-evaluations, grandiose narcissism, a sense of being competent, a sense of being likable, social potency, and emotion regulation. They also found SFI was negatively correlated with self-reported social concerns. Sellbom (2021) investigated the relationship of SFI with self-report measures of narcissistic personality disorder and grandiose narcissism using a college student sample. He found SFI to be strongly correlated with grandiose narcissism, but it was only modestly correlated with self-reported symptoms of narcissistic personality disorder. This latter finding is not surprising given these symptoms reflect both vulnerable and grandiose narcissism.

Whitman and Ben-Porath (2021) administered self-report instruments measuring self-esteem, self-competence, self-liking, positive self-evaluation, sense of superiority, self-sufficiency, and narcissism to three college student samples to better understand the construct overlap between the SFI and SFD scales. They found that while both MMPI-3 scales were correlated with all the external criteria, the SFI and SFD scales also added incrementally to each other in predicting most of the criterion variables. Higher scores on SFI were especially strongly related to positive self-evaluation, grandiose narcissism, and a sense of superiority. Higher scores on SFD were more strongly related to vulnerable narcissism, and demonstrated strong, negative associations with liking oneself and general self-esteem. The scales were roughly equally useful in predicting self-competence and self-sufficiency, although they still added incrementally to one another.

In sum, early research suggests that SFI is a strong marker of self-confidence, grandiosity, social potency, competency, self-esteem, and a general sense of superiority. It also reflects a sort of invulnerability to demoralization. Initial data also suggests that while SFI and SFD both reflect aspects of self-esteem, they do measure substantively different constructs.

PERSONALITY PSYCHOPATHOLOGY FIVE (PSY–5) SCALES

In Chapter 7, we shared our opinion that the MMPI-3 PSY-5 scales are generally equivalent to the PSY-5 scales found on the MMPI-2 and MMPI-2-RF. However, the MMPI-3's PSY-5 scales are not identical to their predecessors. Like the RC scales, the MMPI-3 PSY-5 scales are much shorter, having from 10% to 30% fewer items (median = 23%). The AGGR, PSYC, and INTR scales each include two new items that did not appear on their MMPI-2-RF predecessors, while DISC and NEGE each added eight items. Once again, despite these changes, the MMPI-2-RF/MMPI-3 PSY-5 scale intercorrelations presented by Ben-Porath and Tellegen (2020b) were remarkably high. These correlations were $r \geq .83$ for every scale in each of the examined samples. A review of the side by side external correlates for both the MMPI-3 and MMPI-2-RF PSY-5 scales further demonstrates that these scales are assessing largely the same constructs. The differences between the PSY-5 scales from the two instruments and their external correlates rarely reached a small effect size ($r \geq .10$; Cohen et al., 2002) in terms of magnitude. The only consistent differences in correlate patterns were that (a) the MMPI-3 DISC scale was more strongly related to markers of substance use than its MMPI-2-RF counterpart, and (b) the MMPI-3 NEGE scale was more strongly related to symptoms associated with anxiety and panic while being less strongly related to anger, aggression, and hostility when compared to its MMPI-2-RF counterpart. Overall, these results suggest that the validity data presented in Chapter 7 are generally applicable to the MMPI-3's PSY-5 scales as well. We recommend interested readers review that chapter to learn more about the validity evidence supporting interpretation of these scales. Interpretive guidelines for the PSY-5 scales are presented later in this chapter.

INTERPRETATION

Interpretive Guidelines

In the sections that follow, interpretive guidelines are offered for the Validity and substantive scales of the MMPI-3. The suggested interpretations for the Validity scales are based entirely on the guidelines offered by Ben-Porath and Tellegen (2020a). The suggested interpretations for the substantive scales are based on guidelines suggested in the test manual (Ben-Porath & Tellegen, 2020a), these authors' examination of the empirical correlate data presented in the technical manual (Ben-Porath & Tellegen, 2020b), research reported since the MMPI-3 was published in 2020, and—when psychometrically supported—research conducted on MMPI-2-RF scales that were carried over to the MMPI-3. Inferences generated from the technical manual were based on correlations between scales and criterion measures of at least a small to medium effect size ($r \geq .20$; Cohen et al., 2002). For H-O, RC, and PSY-5 scales, we have also offered information about a scales' connections with theoretical models of mood, psychopathology, or personality. Detailed information about these connections, and the research that supports them, can be found in Chapters 7 and 12. Finally, because interpretation of the SP scales is driven to a larger extent by content-based interpretations than the broader MMPI-3 substantive scales, we have summarized item content in greater detail for the SP scales.

As with the scales on other versions of the MMPI, inferences based on substantive scales should be treated as hypotheses to be compared and synthesized with other information available about the test taker (e.g., interviews, other tests, behavioral observations). T scores of 65 are considered clinically interpretable. T scores much higher than 65 suggest greater likelihood that the listed descriptors will apply to a test taker and that listed symptoms will be more severe than those associated with less elevated scores. Low scores are defined as those where $T < 39$. Although the interpretation of low scores on some MMPI-3 scales is recommended in the interpretive manual, little research is available that is specific to interpretation of low scores. The interpretive guidelines presented in this chapter for low scores are based on information in Ben-Porath and Tellegen (2020a), on negative correlations between scales and external criterion measures presented in Ben-Porath and Tellegen (2020b), and on relevant research conducted on MMPI-2-RF low scores.

Interpretive Guidelines for Validity Scales

Cannot Say (CNS)

When items are omitted, caution is needed during scale interpretation because the omission of items tends to artificially lower scores. Thus, the impact of item omission is best evaluated on a scale-by-scale basis. One should always examine the percentage of items omitted from each individual scale. If more than 10% of items are omitted from a single scale, then an absence of elevation (including those reflecting a low score) on that scale should not be interpreted. If a scale is elevated despite having 10% or more of its items omitted, then the degree of elevation may reflect an underestimate of any phenomena measured by that scale. The percentage of items omitted from each scale is readily available in MMPI-3 score reports and interpretive reports.

Combined Response Inconsistency (CRIN)

VERY HIGH SCORES (T ≥ 80)

Elevations on this scale indicate the test taker engaged in excessive, non-content-based invalid responding. When T scores are ≥ 80, non-content-based invalid responding is so pervasive that the protocol should not be interpreted.

HIGH SCORES (T = 70–79)

T scores between 70 and 79 indicate the test taker responded in a somewhat invalidating manner due to disregarding item content. Scores at this level suggest the protocol should be interpreted with caution.

AVERAGE SCORES (T = 39–69)

Average scores indicate the test taker responded in a consistent manner, and the protocol is interpretable.

LOW SCORE (T = 30–38)

Low scores indicate the test taker was remarkably consistent, and perhaps overly cautious, in responding, but the protocol is interpretable.

Variable Response Inconsistency (VRIN)

VERY HIGH SCORES (T ≥ 80)

Elevations on this scale indicate the test taker responded in a non-content-based invalid manner by engaging in inconsistent responding. When T scores are ≥ 80, inconsistent responding is so pervasive that the protocol should not be interpreted.

HIGH SCORES (T = 70–79)

Scores at this level indicate the test taker responded in a somewhat inconsistent manner. T scores between 70 and 79 suggest the protocol should be interpreted with caution.

AVERAGE SCORES (T = 39–69)

Average scores indicate the test taker responded in a consistent manner, and the protocol is interpretable.

LOW SCORES (T = 30–38)

Low scores indicate the test taker was remarkably consistent, and perhaps overly cautious, in responding; but the protocol is interpretable.

True Response Inconsistency (TRIN)

VERY HIGH SCORES (T ≥ 80)

Elevations on this scale indicate the test taker responded in a non-content-based invalid manner by engaging in fixed responding. When a designation of "T" is associated with the score, the fixed responding is likely to be yea-saying (i.e., acqui-escent responding) whereas a designation of "F" associated with the score indicates that the fixed responding is likely to be naysaying (i.e., nonacquiescent responding). When T scores are ≥ 80, the fixed responding is pervasive enough that the protocol should not be interpreted.

HIGH SCORES (T = 70–79)
T scores between 70 and 79 indicate a tendency toward fixed responding, and the protocol should be interpreted with caution.

AVERAGE SCORES (T = 50–69)
Scores in the average range indicate there is no evidence of fixed responding, and the protocol is interpretable.

Infrequent Responses (F)

T ≥ 100
Scores at this level indicate the test taker reported a large number of symptoms rarely endorsed by most individuals, even those experiencing severe psychopathology. The CRIN, VRIN, and TRIN scales should be consulted to determine whether F scale scores are the product of non-content-based invalid responding. If these scales are not elevated, then the F scale scores likely represent an attempt on the part of the test taker to appear to have much more severe psychopathology or distress than is actually the case. Protocols with F scale scores at this level should be considered invalid and should not be interpreted.

T = 90–99
Scores at this level may indicate non-content-based invalid responding, severe psychopathology, or overreporting. Check the CRIN, VRIN, and TRIN scales. If these scales are not at acceptable levels, then the protocol should be considered invalid and should not be interpreted. If these scores are at acceptable levels, then it is important to determine whether the F scale score reflects severe psychopa-thology or overreporting. For individuals for whom there is neither history nor any current indication of serious dysfunction, scores at this level likely indicate overreporting, and the protocol should not be interpreted. For individuals with a history or current indications of serious dysfunction, the scores at this level should be interpreted as reflecting genuine psychopathology, and the protocol can be interpreted. Protocols with F scale scores at this level are more likely to reflect genuine psychopathology if the Fp scale is at an acceptable level (see later in this chapter).

T = 80–89
Scores at this level are interpreted similarly to T scores between 90 and 99, except the likelihood of overreporting is less than at the higher levels.

T = 75–79

Non-content-based invalid responding or overreporting of symptoms is possible at this level, but scores are more likely to be reflective of serious psychopathology, especially if the Fp scale score is at an acceptable level (see later in this chapter). The protocol can be interpreted, but with the caution that scores may to some extent overestimate the severity of symptoms and problems.

T < 75

When scores are at this level, there is no evidence of significant overreporting, and the protocol can be interpreted.

Infrequent Psychopathology Responses (Fp)

T ≥ 100

Scores at this level indicate an invalid protocol that should not be interpreted because the test taker has endorsed many very rare symptoms—symptoms that are infrequently endorsed by those struggling with severe psychopathology. Scores at this level can result from non-content-based invalid responding (check CRIN, VRIN, and TRIN) or from overreporting of severe psychological symptoms.

T = 80–99

Scores at this level may indicate non-content-based invalid responding (check CRIN, VRIN, and TRIN to rule this out). In cases where the Fp score is due to non-content-based invalid responding, the test should not be interpreted. For individuals with histories or current corroborating evidence of severe dysfunction, Fp scores at this level likely reflect genuine psychopathology, although there should be some caution exercised during interpretation of the test, as scores may overestimate the severity and extent of problems. For those without histories or corroborating evidence of severe dysfunction, scores at this level likely reflect overreporting. In this latter instance, the protocol should be considered invalid.

T = 70–79

Scores at this level may indicate non-content-based invalid responding (rule out using CRIN, VRIN, and TRIN), overreporting, or genuine psychopathology. Fp scores should be interpreted similarly to those at the 80–99 level; except at this level, the likelihood of genuine psychopathology is greater than at the higher Fp scores.

T < 70

With these scores, there is no evidence of overreporting that would compromise protocol validity.

Infrequent Somatic Responses (Fs)

T ≥ 100

Scores at this level indicate the overreporting of somatic symptoms rarely described by persons with genuine medical problems. The scores may result from non-content-based invalid responding (check CRIN, VRIN, and TRIN). If these scales are at acceptable levels, then the Fs score likely reflects overreporting of physical complaints; and scores on the somatic substantive scales (i.e., RC1 and the Somatic/Cognitive SP Scales) should be interpreted with considerable caution if at all.

T = 80–99

Scores at this level indicate possible overreporting of somatic symptoms once non-content-based invalid responding has been ruled out (review CRIN, VRIN, and TRIN). In individuals with no history or corroborating evidence of physical health problems, scores at this level likely represent overreporting of somatic symptoms; and scores on RC1 and the Somatic/Cognitive SP Scales should be interpreted very cautiously. Among test takers with substantial medical problems, these scores may reflect the credible report of symptoms; but they may also be the result of some degree of overreporting. Thus, the substantive scale interpretations associated with somatic concerns may overestimate the extent or severity of those problems.

T < 80

At this level of scores, there is no evidence of overreporting of somatic symptoms, and scores on the substantive scales can be interpreted.

Symptom Validity Scale (FBS)

T ≥ 90

Scores at this level suggest test takers have reported a very unusual combination of symptoms closely associated with noncredible reporting of somatic and cognitive symptoms. Because scores at this level can result from non-content-based invalid responding, first check the CRIN, VRIN, and TRIN scales. If non-content-based invalid responding can be ruled out, then scores on RC1 and the Somatic/Cognitive SP Scales should be interpreted with great caution if at all.

T = 78–89

Scores at this level indicate the endorsement of unusual combinations of somatic and cognitive symptoms often associated with noncredible reporting of these problems. If non-content-based invalid responding can be ruled out (see CRIN, VRIN, and TRIN), then these FBS scores may result from credible reporting of serious somatic problems among those test takers with substantial medical problems. However, those problems may also be somewhat exaggerated and may result in the somatic and cognitive substantive scales overestimating the severity and scope of problems. Regardless, scores on the RC1 scale and the Somatic/Cognitive SP Scales should be interpreted with caution.

T < 78

When scores are at this level, there is no evidence of significant overreporting of somatic and cognitive symptoms; and scales that assess such symptoms can be interpreted.

Response Bias Scale (RBS)

T ≥ 90
Scores at this level suggest test takers have reported a very unusual combination of symptoms closely associated with the report of noncredible memory problems. The CRIN, VRIN, and TRIN scales should be reviewed to rule out non-content-based invalid responding. The only other cause sufficient to explain RBS scores of this elevation is overreporting. Thus, scores on the COG scale should be interpreted with great caution if at all.

T = 75–89
Scores at this level indicate that unusual combinations of symptoms often associated with noncredible memory complaints were endorsed. If non-content-based invalid responding can be ruled out (see CRIN, VRIN, and TRIN), then these RBS scores may result from credible reporting of symptoms among those test takers experiencing severe emotional distress. However, RBS scores of this magnitude may also be caused by symptom exaggeration and thus may result in the COG scale overestimating the severity and scope of memory problems. Regardless, scores on the COG scale should be interpreted with caution.

T < 75
When scores are at this level, there is no evidence of significant overreporting; and the COG scale may be interpreted.

Uncommon Virtues (L)

T ≥ 80
Scores at this level indicate that test takers have presented themselves in an overly positive and virtuous manner to such an extent that scores on substantive scales are likely to have been substantially lowered. Since L scale scores at this level can be a product of non-content-based invalid responding, the CRIN, VRIN, and TRIN scales should be examined. If those indicators are not elevated, then the absence of substantive scale elevations as well as low scores on all substantive scales are uninterpretable. Elevated scores on all substantive scales may underestimate the severity and extent of problems assessed by those scales.

T = 70–79
Scores at this level indicate that test takers likely presented themselves in a very positive way. Because the scores may be the product of non-content-based invalid responding, first check the CRIN, VRIN, and TRIN scales. If no evidence of non-content-based invalid responding is found, then the scores on all substantive scales should be interpreted only with great caution. The absence of elevations as well as low scores on all substantive scales may not reflect a true absence of the phenomena measured by the scale. Likewise, elevated scores on substantive scales may underestimate the problems assessed by the scales. Scores

at this level may also result, in part, from an upbringing that strongly stressed traditional values.

T = 65–69
Scores at this level may be the product of non-content-based invalid responding (check CRIN, VRIN, and TRIN) or an effort by test takers to present themselves in an unrealistically favorable light. Scores at this level may also indicate that the test taker was raised in a very traditional way. Interpretations of all substantive scales should be made utilizing the same cautions exercised for the previous score range (T = 70–79).

T < 65
When scores are at this level, there is no evidence of significant underreporting; and substantive scales can be interpreted normally.

Adjustment Validity (K)

T ≥ 70
Scores at this level indicate that test takers have presented themselves as unusually psychologically well-adjusted—to such an extent as to be rarely found in the general population. Because scores at this level can be a product of non-content-based invalid responding, check the CRIN, VRIN, and TRIN scales. Once non-content-based invalid responding has been ruled out, then interpretation should proceed only with considerable caution. The scores on all substantive scales likely represent an attempt on the part of the test taker to present themselves as much better adjusted than they really are. The absence of elevations as well as low scores on all substantive scales are uninterpretable. Elevated substantive scale scores likely understate the problems assessed by those scales.

T = 66–69
Because scores at this level can be a product of non-content-based invalid responding, first check the CRIN, VRIN, and TRIN scales. If non-content-based invalid responding can be ruled out, then scores may reflect either underreporting of symptoms and problems or very good psychological adjustment. For persons for whom there is no corroborating evidence of good psychological adjustment, an absence of elevation on substantive scales is uninterpretable. Elevations on substantive scales may underestimate the problems assessed by those scales.

T = 60–65
Scores at this level indicate possible underreporting of symptoms and problems. Non-content-based invalid responding should be ruled out by checking the CRIN, VRIN, and TRIN scales. For persons for whom there is corroborating evidence of poor adjustment, the absence of elevations on substantive scales should be interpreted with caution. Elevated scores on substantive scales may underestimate the problems assessed by those scales. Scores at this level are common among persons who complete the MMPI-3 in nonclinical settings (e.g., custody evaluations, pre-employment screening).

T < 60

When scores are at this level, there is no evidence of significant underreporting; and scores on substantive scales may be interpreted normally.

Interpretive Guidelines for Higher–Order (H–O) Scales

The H-O Scales provide a broad overview of dysfunction and problems in feeling, thinking, and behaving. Elevated scores result from symptom severity but also reflect wide-ranging symptom manifestations. As noted in more detail in Chapter 12, the H-O scales closely align with some of the spectra dimensions described in the Hierarchical Taxonomy of Psychopathology (HiTOP; Kotov et al., 2021). An absence of elevation on a H-O scale does not necessarily mean the test taker is reporting no problems in that domain. The RC Scales and SP Scales should still be inspected to identify more circumscribed problems.

Emotional/Internalizing Dysfunction (EID)

The EID scale provides a broad overview of emotional functioning and symptoms common to internalizing forms of psychopathology. This scale can be linked to the internalizing dimension reflected in recent quantitative models of psychopathology.

High scores (T ≥ 65) indicate persons who

1. are experiencing a great deal of emotional turmoil (when T score ≥ 80, the distress is likely to be perceived as a crisis)
2. feel overwhelmed by their life situations
3. feel vulnerable, helpless, and unable to cope
4. have depressed or anxious mood as a prominent presenting problem
5. are likely to feel sad and blue
6. may feel angry
7. are likely to have diminished experiences of positive emotions such as joy and happiness (i.e., anhedonia)
8. frequently feel overwhelmed by, and are often unable to cope adequately with, their emotions
9. likely worry excessively and engage in ruminative thinking
10. likely experience difficulty concentrating
11. may experience suicidal ideation and have histories of suicide attempts
12. lack energy and motivation to get things done
13. may present somatic complaints
14. may experience panic attacks
15. likely feel lonely, interpersonally inadequate, and mistreated by others
16. may fear that others will reject them or judge them harshly because of their emotional turmoil
17. in mental health settings, may have histories of psychiatric hospitalization
18. in mental health settings, are often diagnosed with depressive disorders
19. should be evaluated for internalizing disorders (e.g., depressive disorders, anxiety disorders, trauma- and stressor-related disorders, eating disorders)
20. are likely to be motivated for treatment because of emotional turmoil

Low scores (T < 39) indicate individuals who report a better than average level of emotional adjustment.

Thought Dysfunction (THD)

THD provides an overview of cognitive and sensory problems that fall within the spectrum of thought disorder, including delusions and hallucinations. The construct assessed by this scale can be conceptually linked to the thought dysfunction spectra identified in structural models of psychopathology.

High scores (T ≥ 65) indicate individuals who

1. have reported symptoms of thought dysfunction
2. may experience auditory or visual hallucinations
3. may have delusions of grandeur or persecution
4. may engage in magical thinking
5. are suspicious and untrusting
6. may experience intrusive thoughts
7. may experience referential thinking
8. feel that life is a strain
9. have low frustration tolerance
10. sometimes act aggressively toward others
11. should be evaluated for psychotic spectrum disorders (e.g., schizophrenia, delusional disorder)
12. should be evaluated for antipsychotic medications
13. may require treatment in a structured environment

Low scores (T < 39) on this scale are not interpreted.

Behavioral/Externalizing Dysfunction (BXD)

This H-O scale identifies broad manifestations of externalizing psychopathology, especially general patterns of undercontrolled behavior. This scale aligns with the broad externalizing dimension reflecting both tendencies toward antagonism and disinhibition identified in quantitative models of psychopathology.

High scores (T ≥ 65) indicate persons who

1. report engaging in a wide variety of externalizing behaviors that have gotten them into difficulties
2. may have histories of arrests and convictions dating back to adolescence
3. may have a problematic pattern of using alcohol and other substances
4. often act impulsively without carefully considering the consequences of their actions
5. have histories of problems in school, at home, and at work
6. more frequently engage in risk-taking and thrill-seeking behaviors
7. are irresponsible and unreliable
8. are rebellious and regularly violate norms and expectations
9. have low frustration tolerance
10. often show poor judgment

11. are aggressive in relationships
12. often feel that they have been mistreated and blame others for their problems
13. may seek to manipulate and exploit others
14. typically, do not report emotional distress other than anger, but may report some limited symptoms of anxiety and depression
15. in mental health settings, are often diagnosed with substance-related and addictive disorders
16. should be evaluated for externalizing disorder diagnoses (e.g., Cluster B personality disorders, substance use disorders)
17. typically, are not interested in changing but may agree to treatment to avoid negative consequences
18. need to develop better self-control
19. may terminate treatment prematurely

Low scores (T < 39) indicate persons who

1. report higher than average levels of behavioral constraint
2. are unlikely to engage in externalizing, acting-out behaviors

Interpretive Guidelines for Restructured Clinical (RC) Scales

The RC Scales represent more narrowly defined manifestations of psychopathology than are captured by the H-O Scales. The RC Scales do not measure syndromes (i.e., diagnoses) but instead tap into clusters of related symptoms that can be used by clinicians in case conceptualization, diagnostic evaluation, treatment planning, and ongoing assessment to better understand the test taker's current functioning. As discussed earlier in this chapter, the RC scales of the MMPI-3 are very similar to the RC Scales developed for the MMPI-2/MMPI-2-RF. Additional theoretical and empirical details about these scales, including their connections with models of mood, psychopathology, and personality, can be found in Chapter 7.

Demoralization (RCd)

The RCd scale reflects the pleasantness–unpleasantness (also known as the happiness–unhappiness) dimension from Tellegen and colleagues' (1999a; 1999b) model of mood and affect and is associated with the "distress" dimension of internalizing psychopathology posited in recent quantitative models of psychopathology. Scores on RCd provide an indication of the overall emotional discomfort and turmoil a person is experiencing.

Very high scores (T ≥ 74) on the RCd scale indicate persons who

1. are experiencing significant emotional turmoil
2. report feeling depressed
3. report being anxious and unable to concentrate
4. report somatic complaints that may increase in times of stress
5. feel overwhelmed by the demands of their life situations
6. feel incapable of coping with their current life circumstances

7. frequently feel overwhelmed by, and unable to cope adequately with, their emotions
8. may be experiencing suicidal thinking or engaging in suicide-related behavior
9. in mental health settings, are often diagnosed with depressive disorders
10. should be evaluated for suicide risk (particularly if SUI is > 65)
11. should be evaluated for disorders characterized by high levels of dysphoric affect such as depressive, anxiety, and trauma- and stressor- related disorders
12. may be motivated for treatment because of emotional distress
13. need intervention to relieve emotional distress
14. are at risk for poor treatment outcomes

High scores (T = 65–73) indicate persons who

1. feel sad and unhappy
2. feel anxious much of the time
3. are dissatisfied with their life situations
4. have poor self-concepts and feel like failures
5. have low self-efficacy and view themselves as unworthy and incapable
6. react poorly to stress
7. tend to imagine the worst possible outcomes for actions or events
8. respond to negative events with internal, global, and stable attributions
9. are pessimistic about their lives getting better
10. may engage in excessive reassurance seeking

Low scores (T < 39) indicate persons who report a greater than average level of morale and life satisfaction.

Somatic Complaints (RC1)

Items on RC1 inquire about an individual's general sense of physical well-being and specific somatic difficulties and reflect a broad somatoform construct similar to that posited in dimensional models of psychopathology. The cardinal feature of high scorers (T ≥ 65) on the RC1 scale is somatic preoccupation.

High scores on the RC1 scale indicate persons who

1. report multiple somatic complaints, including gastrointestinal problems, pain, and neurological symptoms
2. have increased somatic symptoms in times of stress
3. likely present with pain complaints
4. often present with symptoms of neurological dysfunction
5. may present with cognitive dysfunction
6. may experience symptoms consistent with depressive, anxiety, and trauma- and stressor-related disorders, especially physiological symptoms
7. may experience fear of the physiological symptoms of anxiety
8. are quite resistant to considering psychological factors that may be related to somatic symptoms
9. in mental health settings, are likely to have a history of chronic pain or other chronic medical conditions

10. in mental health settings, are often diagnosed with somatic symptom and related disorders
11. are at risk for terminating therapy before goals are met
12. if physical explanations for their somatic symptoms can be ruled out, should be further evaluated for somatic symptom disorders

Low scores (T < 39) indicate persons who report a sense of physical well-being. Specifically, low scores on RC1 indicate people who are likely to describe having fewer medical and physical difficulties than is typical.

Low Positive Emotions (RC2)

Items on RC2 ask about the test-taker's experience of positive emotions, social engagement, and interest and ability to engage in activities. This scale reflects the positive affect dimension of the Tellegen and colleagues (1999a; 1999b) model of mood and affect and aspects of the liabilities toward internalizing difficulties and interpersonal detachment described in dimensional models of psychopathology. Scores on RC2 are intended to reflect the test-taker's lack of capacity for positive emotional experiences, a core component of depressive syndromes (i.e., anhedonia).

High scores (T ≥ 65) on the RC2 scale indicate persons who

1. lack positive emotional experiences in life
2. have deficits in their ability to experience joy and happiness (anhedonia)
3. are unhappy and demoralized
4. lack energy to handle demands of their life situations
5. find it difficult to take charge, make decisions, and get things done
6. tend to be introverted, passive, and withdrawn in social situations
7. often feel bored and isolated
8. are pessimistic
9. have low expectations of success and are not likely to place themselves in competitive situations
10. in mental health settings, are often diagnosed with depressive disorders
11. may meet criteria for major depressive disorder or other depressive disorders
12. should also be evaluated for disorders characterized by social withdrawal or avoidance, such as social anxiety disorder
13. should be evaluated for antidepressant medications
14. may have difficulty engaging in treatment because of low positive emotionality
15. are at risk for terminating therapy before goals are met
16. if T ≥ 75, may need inpatient treatment for depression

Low scores (T < 39) on the RC2 scale indicate persons who

1. report a high level of psychological well-being
2. are likely to be satisfied with their life
3. report a wide range of emotionally positive experiences
4. report feeling confident and energetic
5. have high levels of positive affect
6. have positive self-esteem

7. are extraverted and socially engaged
8. are optimistic about the future

Antisocial Behavior (RC4)

RC4 measures antisocial characteristics and reflects both the antagonistic and disinhibited aspects of externalizing tendencies reflected in dimensional models of psychopathology.

High scores (T ≥ 65) on the RC4 scale indicate persons who

1. report histories of antisocial behaviors
2. tend to be rebellious and find it difficult to conform to societal norms and expectations
3. are likely to have been in trouble with the law
4. are at increased risk for problematic substance use
5. more frequently engage in reckless, risk-taking, and thrill-seeking behaviors
6. behave aggressively toward other people
7. are critical, argumentative, and antagonistic
8. have conflictual relationships with other people
9. may have significant family problems
10. in mental health settings, are often diagnosed with substance-related and addictive disorders
11. should be evaluated for externalizing disorder diagnoses (e.g., Cluster B personality disorders, substance use disorders)
12. are not likely to be motivated for treatment
13. may not be compliant in treatment
14. may be at risk for not completing recommended treatments
15. need help in developing better self-control

Low scores (T < 39) on the RC4 scale indicate persons who report higher than average levels of behavioral constraint and deny any history of antisocial behavior.

Ideas of Persecution (RC6)

Items on RC6 inquire about an individual's beliefs about others wanting to harm them. Scores on RC6 reflect aspects of a liability toward thought dysfunction described in dimensional models of psychopathology. However, it is important to note that elevations on this scale do not necessarily indicate the presence of thinking that is delusional in nature. Elevations can occur in individuals who are suspicious and cautious around people for other reasons (e.g., as a result of traumatic experiences).

High scores (T ≥ 65) indicate persons who

1. feel targeted, controlled, or victimized by others
2. are suspicious of the motivation of others
3. have difficulty trusting others
4. may seem hostile and act out aggressively because of beliefs that others are attempting to harm them
5. often have difficulty forming close relationships
6. may have difficulty forming therapeutic relationships

7. if T ≥ 80, may indicate paranoid delusions or hallucinations
8. if T ≥ 80, should be evaluated further for schizophrenia spectrum and other psychotic disorders, including Cluster A personality disorders

Low scores on this scale are not interpreted.

Dysfunctional Negative Emotions (RC7)

The RC7 scale reflects the negative affect dimension of Tellegen and colleagues' (1999a; 1999b) model of mood and affect and is associated with the "fear" dimension of internalizing psychopathology described in dimensional models of psychopathology. Items on RC7 assess the test-taker's experience of negative emotions such as anxiety, anger, and fear. Given the negative emotions reflected in RC7, test takers with high scores on this scale will also frequently report experiencing demoralization. However, while these experiences are correlated, negative emotionality is distinct from demoralization, which tends to pervade many different kinds of psychopathology.

High scores (T ≥ 65) on the RC7 scale indicate persons who

1. report negative emotional experiences including anxiety, fear, and irritability
2. worry excessively
3. experience intrusive ideation
4. report feeling sad and unhappy
5. are insecure and excessively sensitive to perceived criticism
6. are self-critical and guilt-prone
7. ruminate and brood about perceived failures
8. frequently feel unable to cope with their emotions
9. often feel unable to cope adequately with stress and are frequently overwhelmed by it
10. may fear that others will reject them or judge them harshly because of their negative emotions
11. in mental health settings, are often diagnosed with anxiety disorders, trauma- and stressor-related disorders, and depressive disorders
12. should be evaluated for disorders related to fearfulness (i.e., phobias, social anxiety, and obsessive-compulsive and related disorders), trauma- and stressor-related disorders, and Cluster C personality disorders
13. may be motivated for treatment because of emotional distress
14. are at risk for terminating therapy before goals are met
15. should be evaluated for anxiolytic medications

Low scores (T < 39) on the RC7 scale indicate persons who report below average levels of negative emotional experiences.

Aberrant Experiences (RC8)

Items on RC8 inquire about the test-taker's experience of unusual thinking and perceptual experiences. Scores on RC8 reflect aspects of a liability toward thought dysfunction described in dimensional models of psychopathology.

High scores (T ≥ 65) on the RC8 scale indicate persons who

1. report unusual sensory, perceptual, cognitive, or motor experiences
2. may experience hallucinations or delusions
3. may experience bizarre sensory experiences
4. have impaired reality testing
5. may frequently experience intrusive thoughts
6. may report dissociative experiences
7. tend to be prone to becoming engrossed in daydreams or other internal experiences
8. often have impaired occupational and interpersonal functioning
9. may be experiencing subclinical levels of thought disturbance that reflect a vulnerability to psychotic disorders
10. in mental health settings, should be evaluated further for schizophrenia spectrum and other psychotic disorders
11. may require treatment in structured settings
12. should be evaluated for antipsychotic medications
13. may find it difficult to participate appropriately in treatment because of disordered thinking

Low scores on the RC8 scale are not interpreted.

Hypomanic Activation (RC9)

RC9 items reflect impulsive actions, sensation-seeking/thrill-seeking tendencies, elevated mood, and increased energy. In this way, RC9 reflects aspects of the mania subfactor in dimensional models of psychopathology, which is linked to both internalizing and thought disorder spectra. However, because this scale has items assessing impulsive and sensation- and thrill-seeking tendencies—in samples with a low base rate of severe mental disorders, RC9 scores seem to be better conceptualized as capturing the disinhibited aspects of the externalizing spectrum identified in dimensional models of psychopathology.

High scores (T ≥ 65) on the RC9 scale indicate persons who

1. experience racing thoughts
2. experience high energy levels
3. have heightened mood
4. show poor impulse control
5. may engage in antisocial behaviors
6. may have a problematic pattern of substance use
7. are sensation seekers and risk takers
8. may be irritable and aggressive
9. in mental health settings, are often diagnosed with bipolar and related disorders
10. should be evaluated further for bipolar and related disorders
11. may find appropriate participation in treatment difficult because of excessive behavioral activation

12. should be evaluated for mood-stabilizing medications
13. if T ≥ 75, may experience manic episodes

Low scores (T < 39) on the RC9 scale indicate persons who have below average levels of activation and engagement with their environments. Individuals with low scores on RC9 are likely to experience low energy levels and be withdrawn from their environment. They should be evaluated for depressive disorders, especially if scores on RC2 are also elevated.

Interpretive Guidelines for Specific Problems (SP) Scales

Somatic/Cognitive Specific Problems (SP) Scales

These scales can be used to identify the general subcategories of somatic and cognitive symptoms reported by the test taker. They may be useful in helping to clarify RC1 elevations as well as in identifying more isolated somatic and cognitive complaints.

MALAISE (MLS)

The MLS scale consists of items measuring the test-taker's sense of overall poor physical health.

High scores (T ≥ 65) indicate individuals who

1. report feelings of poor overall physical health
2. report experiencing fatigue and unsatisfactory sleep
3. often have vague somatic complaints
4. may feel their poor health interferes with work and other activities
5. often feel sad and depressed
6. feel unable to deal with stressors
7. are pessimistic about the likelihood of their lives getting better
8. may present with symptoms of neurological dysfunction
9. in mental health settings, are often diagnosed with depressive disorders
10. should be evaluated for depressive disorders
11. if physical explanations for their somatic symptoms can be ruled out, should be further evaluated for somatic symptom and related disorders
12. may be unwilling or unable to participate in treatment because of malaise

Low scores (T < 39) indicate persons who report a general sense of physical well-being.

NEUROLOGICAL COMPLAINTS (NUC)

The items on NUC represent a series of vague physical complaints (e.g., numbness, dizziness, trembling) sometimes associated with neurological dysfunction.

High scores (T ≥ 65) indicate persons who

1. report vague neurological problems with motor control (e.g., balance, dizziness, paralysis)
2. likely experience other somatic complaints
3. do not cope well with stress

4. if physical explanations for their somatic symptoms can be ruled out, should be further evaluated for somatic symptom and related disorders
5. may benefit from medical or behavioral management of symptoms if physical origin of neurological complaints has been established
6. may be unwilling to participate in psychological treatment due to generally rejecting psychological explanations for symptoms or course of recovery

Low scores on this scale are not interpreted.

EATING CONCERNS (EAT)

The EAT scale items ask about three types of problematic eating behaviors that may be associated with eating disorders. These include items asking about binge eating behaviors, purging behaviors, and restrictive eating.

High scores (T ≥ 65) indicate persons who

1. report engaging in problematic eating behaviors including binging, purging, or restrictive eating
2. likely have experienced episodes where they engaged in excessive eating and lost control over their eating
3. often are concerned about their body image, shape, or weight
4. often have a history of dieting
5. may use eating as a means of coping with emotional distress
6. may disregard or not pay attention to bodily signs of being hungry or full
7. may have previously engaged in self-injurious behavior
8. in mental health settings, are often diagnosed with feeding and eating disorders
9. should be evaluated for feeding and eating disorder diagnoses

Low scores on this scale are not interpreted.

COGNITIVE COMPLAINTS (COG)

The COG scale consists of items asking about a variety of cognitive problems including difficulty focusing, maintaining attention, and recalling memories.

High scores (T ≥ 65) indicate persons who

1. report problems with attention, concentration, and memory
2. do not cope well with stress
3. often feel inadequate and inferior
4. tend to give up easily in response to challenges or failure
5. may fear that their cognitive problems are signs they are "going crazy" or "losing my mind"
6. in mental health settings, may report feeling anxious and depressed
7. may require neuropsychological or neurological evaluation
8. if neuropsychological/neurological conditions can be ruled out, and these cognitive symptoms are not well accounted for by internalizing disorders (e.g., depressive disorders, trauma- and stressor-related disorders), then they should be further evaluated for somatic symptom and related disorders

Low scores on this scale are not interpreted.

Internalizing Specific Problems (SP) Scales

These scales can be used to identify specific manifestations of the internalizing symptoms reported by the test taker. They may be useful in helping to clarify RCd (i.e., SUI, HLP, SFD, NFC) and RC7 (i.e., STR, WRY, CMP, ARX, ANP, BRF) elevations as well as in identifying more isolated internalizing difficulties.

SUICIDAL/DEATH IDEATION (SUI)

The SUI scale is comprised of items reflecting suicidality—including suicidal thinking, intent, planning, and past attempts—as well as items about thoughts or wishes about being dead. We concur with the recommendation found in the MMPI-3 manual to interpret SUI using a cut score of T ≥ 58. Thus, endorsing even a single item on SUI will result in an interpretable score. We recommend this approach because it maximizes scale sensitivity and best aligns with our recommendation to use SUI as a brief screening measure of suicidality. We also recommend a thorough suicide assessment for any test taker who elevates the SUI scale.

High scores (T ≥ **58**) indicate persons who

1. report suicidal ideation or histories of suicide attempts
2. should receive a detailed suicide assessment
3. feel quite depressed
4. feel overwhelmed and helpless
5. feel hopeless and pessimistic about the likelihood of their lives getting better
6. in mental health settings, may have histories of psychiatric hospitalization
7. should be evaluated for internalizing disorders (e.g., depressive disorders, anxiety disorders, trauma- and stressor-related disorders, eating disorders)
8. may require interventions to reduce suicide risk

Low scores on this scale are not interpreted.

HELPLESSNESS/HOPELESSNESS (HLP)

The item content of the HLP scale reflects a hopeless, pessimistic viewpoint and sense that nothing can be done to change the self or the situation.

High scores (T ≥ 65) indicate persons who

1. are expressing unhappiness with their lives
2. feel that they cannot make significant changes in their lives
3. are pessimistic about the likelihood of their lives getting better
4. experience depressed mood and a sense of despair
5. often see themselves as inadequate and inferior
6. tend to give up easily in response to challenges or failure
7. often feel they lack adequate support from others, sometimes leading to distrust, resentment, or feelings of hostility.
8. may see suicide as the only solution to their problems
9. should be evaluated for depressive disorders (or other internalizing disorders)
10. may benefit from treatment to increase feelings of hope

Low scores on this scale are not interpreted.

SELF-DOUBT (SFD)

The SFD item content represents low self-confidence and negative appraisals of self-worth, one's abilities, and one's usefulness as well as a sense that one is a weight or drag upon others.

High scores (T ≥ 65) indicate persons who

1. report lack of self-confidence
2. report feelings of uselessness
3. report feeling inferior to other people
4. feel sad, depressed, and hopeless
5. may have suicidal ideation
6. may experience anxiety
7. often ruminate
8. frequently feel unable to cope with their emotions
9. have low self-esteem
10. often experience uncertainty and awkwardness in interpersonal interactions, sometimes leading to distress in or withdrawal from relationships
11. may feel they lack adequate support from others, sometimes leading to distrust, resentment, or feelings of hostility
12. in mental health settings, may have histories of psychiatric hospitalization
13. in mental health settings, are often diagnosed with depressive disorders
14. should be evaluated for internalizing disorders, especially depressive disorders and social anxiety disorder
15. may benefit from treatment to increase self-esteem

Low scores on this scale are not interpreted.

INEFFICACY (NFC)

Item content on the NFC scale focuses on indecisiveness and a sense of being ineffectual, especially in the face of adversity.

High scores (T ≥ 65) indicate persons who

1. report being very indecisive
2. try to avoid making difficult decisions in life
3. are not very self-reliant
4. give up easily
5. feel insecure and inadequate
6. may experience depression and anxiety
7. likely worry and ruminate
8. often feel unable to cope with their emotions
9. often have a pessimistic outlook
10. typically struggle to cope effectively with stress
11. tend to be interpersonally passive
12. in mental health settings, are often diagnosed with depressive disorders
13. may feel they lack adequate support from others, sometimes leading to distrust, resentment, or feelings of hostility
14. may benefit from treatment to decrease indecisiveness

Low scores (T < 39) on this scale indicate persons who are efficacious and decisive in stressful situations. They are likely to be independent and interpersonally assertive.

STRESS (STR)

The STR scale item content is primarily focused on the subjective experience of stress and general nervousness as well as perceptions of one's ability to manage stress.

High scores (T ≥ 65) indicate persons who

1. report experiencing a great deal of stress
2. report being overwhelmed by and unable to adequately cope with the stress they are experiencing
3. report frequently feeling nervous
4. experience anxious and depressed mood
5. often feel unable to cope with their emotions
6. likely worry and ruminate
7. likely experience bodily symptoms of anxiety, which may include panic-like symptoms
8. often have a pessimistic outlook
9. tend to be moderately introverted
10. may feel interpersonally isolated and believe they lack adequate social support
11. may fear others will reject them or judge them harshly for not being able to better manage their emotions and stress
12. in mental health settings, are often diagnosed with anxiety disorders and depressive disorders
13. should be evaluated for trauma- and stressor-related disorders, anxiety disorders, and depressive disorders
14. may benefit from treatment focused on stress management

Low scores (T < 39) on this scale indicate persons who are experiencing below-average levels of stress and are effectively managing any stress they do experience.

WORRY (WRY)

The item content of the WRY scale almost exclusively reflects reports of a tendency to worry about a great many things (i.e., a generalized pattern of worry). Some items also focus on struggling to set aside feelings of disappointment.

High scores (T ≥ 65) indicate persons who

1. report frequently worrying about many different things
2. feel anxious and uneasy
3. also experience frequent sadness and, to a lesser extent, irritability and anger
4. feel unable to cope with their emotions
5. likely feel overwhelmed by their worries and hopeless for the future
6. often feel unable to cope with stress
7. likely experience physiological symptoms of anxiety, which may include panic attack symptoms
8. often feel uncertain in their relationships, sometimes leading to distrust, resentment, or feelings of hostility

9. likely fear others will reject them or judge them harshly for their inability to better manage their anxiety and worry
10. in mental health settings, are often diagnosed with anxiety disorders, trauma- and stressor-related disorders, and depressive disorders
11. should be evaluated for anxiety disorders, trauma- and stressor-related disorders, and depressive disorders
12. may benefit from treatment focused on their tendency to worry

Low scores (T < 39) indicate persons who report below-average levels of worry.

COMPULSIVITY (CMP)

The items of the CMP scale can be rationally sorted into two major content clusters. The first cluster describes a tendency to be rigidly ordered, organized, and focused. The second cluster has items related to engaging in repetitive behaviors (e.g., checking, counting).

High scores (T ≥ 65) indicate persons who

1. report living a very orderly and organized life as well as experiencing emotional discomfort when they deviate from this way of living
2. report a tendency to engage in repetitive behaviors
3. often engage in compulsive behaviors such as cleaning, counting, checking, or other ritualistic behaviors
4. are typically rigid and inflexible
5. may be perfectionistic
6. may express unrealistic concerns about their health or personal safety
7. should be evaluated for obsessive–compulsive and related disorders as well as other disorders characterized by compulsive or rigidly perfectionistic behaviors

Low scores on this scale are not interpreted.

ANXIETY–RELATED EXPERIENCES (ARX)

The items on the ARX scale ask about several different manifestations of anxiety. This includes feeling anxious or fearful as well as extreme cognitive and physiological experiences associated with these feelings such as intrusive memories, nightmares, physiological reactivity, and a heightened startle response.

High scores (T ≥ 65) indicate persons who

1. report frequent and pervasive feelings of anxiety, dread, and fear
2. experience intrusive memories
3. experience physiological symptoms of anxiety and startle easily
4. frequently experience nightmares and disturbed sleep
5. often feel depressed, sad, or hopeless
6. feel unable to cope with their emotions
7. are often fearful about having future episodes of anxiety and fear
8. likely experience panic attacks
9. may experience dissociative symptoms
10. may seek to avoid thoughts and external reminders of traumatic experiences

11. do not cope well with stress
12. feel overwhelmed by the demands of their lives
13. may view ambiguous situations or innocuous interactions with others as potentially threatening
14. may have difficulty concentrating
15. likely feel unsupported or uncertain in their relationships, sometimes leading to distrust, resentment, or feelings of hostility
16. likely fear that others will reject them or judge them harshly for their inability to better manage their anxiety and fear
17. in mental health settings, often are diagnosed with anxiety disorders and trauma- and stressor-related disorders
18. should be evaluated for anxiety disorders and trauma- and stressor-related disorders
19. should be evaluated for anxiolytic medications

Low scores (T < 39) indicate persons who report below-average levels of anxiety-related experiences.

ANGER PRONENESS (ANP)

Items on ANP reflect frequent and intense episodic anger, general irritability, and low frustration tolerance.

High scores (T ≥ 65) indicate individuals who

1. report frequently experiencing anger
2. report having a low frustration tolerance
3. are impatient and easily irritated
4. tend to be argumentative and express their anger through acts of verbal, and possibly physical, aggression
5. typically find it difficult to cope effectively with their anger and may act on angry impulses
6. may experience violent thoughts
7. may report symptoms of anxiety and depression
8. in mental health settings, may present with or be diagnosed with emotion-centric disorders (e.g., anxiety disorders, depressive disorders)
9. may benefit from learning anger management techniques

Low scores on this scale are not interpreted.

BEHAVIOR-RESTRICTING FEARS (BRF)

Most of the items on the BRF scale asks about fearfulness associated with specific situations or behaviors that are typically considered everyday kinds of experiences (e.g., fearing the dark). Some items also reflect engagement in avoidance behaviors due to the experience of fear.

High scores (T ≥ 65) indicate persons who

1. report multiple specific fears that restrict normal activities inside and outside the home
2. may report feeling anxious or fearful when away from home

3. may express fear of darkness, dirt, small spaces, or pointed objects
4. may experience symptoms of agoraphobia
5. in mental health settings, may report feeling generally anxious and depressed or report experiencing panic attacks
6. should be evaluated for anxiety disorders, particularly agoraphobia

Low scores on this scale are not interpreted.

Externalizing Specific Problems (SP) Scales

These scales can be used to identify specific manifestations of the externalizing symptoms reported by the test taker. They may be useful in helping to clarify RC4 (i.e., FML, JCP, SUB) and RC9 (i.e., IMP, ACT, AGG, CYN) elevations as well as identify more circumscribed externalizing difficulties.

FAMILY PROBLEMS (FML)

The FML scale items reflect experiences of family discord and feeling unsupported and unappreciated by family. Some items on the scale reflect very intense negative emotions directed toward family (e.g., fear, hatred). Because of item wording, it is not possible to tell whether the test taker is describing their current family, their family of origin, or both. As such, elevations on this scale may signal the need for additional assessment.

High scores (T ≥ 65) indicate persons who

1. report having negative experiences with and negative attitudes toward their families
2. describe conflicts with their families
3. do not feel supported by their families
4. frequently have experienced chaotic and dysfunctional family life marked by tumultuous relationships
5. frequently blame family for their problems
6. may report being mistreated, and even abused, by their families
7. may feel unsupported or uncertain in their relationships, sometimes leading to distrust, resentment, or feelings of hostility
8. in mental health settings, may feel depressed, anxious, helpless, and hopeless
9. in mental health settings, may report experiencing suicidal ideation
10. when histories of abuse are present, should be evaluated for trauma- and stressor-related disorders as well as other internalizing disorders
11. may benefit from treatment addressing family conflict and poor quality of family relationships, and, if appropriate, having family members involved in treatment

Low scores (T < 39) indicate persons who report comparatively conflict-free family environments, past and present.

JUVENILE CONDUCT PROBLEMS (JCP)

The JCP scale items reflect a history of having experienced behavioral and disciplinary problems in school and having engaged in illegal activity as a juvenile. The items focus exclusively on historical behaviors; and all but one explicitly refer to youth, adolescence, or school to provide the context for the test taker. Scores on JCP are correlated with suicidality; and, although there is not a clear connection between JCP and current suicidality, we recommend carefully reviewing and evaluating suicidality using other sources of information when scores on this scale are elevated.

High scores (T ≥ 65) indicate persons who

1. report past school difficulties, including behavior problems and truancy
2. may report having stolen things when young
3. frequently have histories of acting out both as adolescents and adults
4. frequently have histories of trouble with the law
5. frequently have histories of using, and often misusing, alcohol and other substances
6. are likely to be impulsive
7. tend to have problems with authority figures
8. are likely to frequently violate social norms and expectations
9. may act out in aggressive ways
10. in mental health settings, may have a history of suicide attempts
11. in mental health settings, often are given diagnoses of antisocial personality disorder or substance-related disorders
12. are not likely to be motivated for treatment
13. are at increased risk for missing treatment appointments
14. may be at increased risk for not completing a recommended course of treatment

Low scores on this scale are not interpreted.

SUBSTANCE ABUSE (SUB)

Item content of the SUB scale includes questions regarding the use of alcohol, marijuana, and other substances as well as problems associated with this use. Some items are worded in such a manner as to suggest present behaviors, while other items refer to past behaviors. As such, elevated scores on this scale suggest the need for additional assessment of the test-taker's use of substances.

High scores (T ≥ 65) on this scale indicate persons who

1. are openly acknowledging use and possible problematic use of alcohol, marijuana, or other substances
2. may report misusing prescription medications
3. may report using substances to relax
4. may have a history of substance use problems
5. often are rebellious and have problems with authority figures
6. are likely to often violate social norms and expectations
7. may engage in risky, thrill-seeking behavior
8. may at times be physically aggressive
9. in mental health settings, are often diagnosed with substance-related disorders
10. should receive a detailed substance use evaluation
11. may benefit from treatment for substance-related difficulties

Low scores on this scale are not interpreted.

IMPULSIVITY (IMP)

As suggested by its name, the items of the IMP scale reflect a tendency to act impulsively including struggling to control one's impulses, frequently acting without thinking things through, and experiencing regret or consequences due to acting impulsively.

High scores (T ≥ 65) indicate persons who

1. report they often act impulsively
2. report feeling regret or experiencing negative consequences because of their impulsive actions
3. may report experiencing a great deal of difficulty controlling their impulses
4. often have trouble controlling their behavior, and, as a result, are more likely to violate social norms and expectations
5. are especially prone to acting impulsively when they experience strong positive or negative emotions
6. may have trouble controlling angry impulses, and, as a result, are often seen by others as angry, irritable, or aggressive
7. often act before carefully thinking through the situation
8. may engage in thrill-seeking behavior
9. may tend to not see things through to the end
10. in mental health settings, are more likely to use alcohol and other substances
11. in mental health settings, are more likely to have historic or concurrent diagnoses of ADHD, substance-related disorders, or bipolar and related disorders
12. should be evaluated for disorders where poor impulse control is a core symptom such as disruptive, impulse-control, and conduct disorders
13. may benefit from treatment focused on improving impulse control

Low scores (T < 39) indicate persons who report below average levels of impulsive behavior.

ACTIVATION (ACT)

Items on the ACT scale primarily reflect the experience of elevated, elated, or labile moods. Other items reflect symptoms common to hypomanic/manic episodes such as racing thoughts, pressured speech, and a decreased need for sleep.

High scores (T ≥ 65) indicate persons who

1. describe periods of excited and elated mood
2. may report that they have excessive energy and decreased need for sleep at times
3. may report difficulty controlling their thoughts, speech, or behavior
4. may have histories of mood swings
5. may have histories of hypomanic or manic episodes
6. may appear impulsive or have a heightened level of activity
7. in mental health settings, often are diagnosed with bipolar and related disorders
8. should be evaluated for bipolar and related disorders
9. may benefit from mood-stabilizing medications

Low scores (T < 39) indicate persons who report below average levels of energy and activation.

AGGRESSION (AGG)

The items on the AGG scale reflect a tendency to engage in physical aggression including acting on angry impulses, intimidating others, and seeking to retaliate against others when they feel wronged.

High scores (T ≥ 65) indicate persons who

1. report acting out in aggressive ways toward other people
2. report a tendency to act upon their angry impulses
3. acknowledge breaking things and hurting other people in fights
4. experience pleasure from making other people afraid of them
5. are often angry and irritable
6. frequently view aggression as the best means to resolve interpersonal disputes
7. may have violent thoughts and histories of violent behavior
8. are seen by others as antisocial
9. tend to be somewhat self-centered and manipulative
10. tend to have problems with authority figures
11. tend to be moderately impulsive
12. likely use alcohol and other substances in a manner that may be problematic
13. may require a violence risk assessment
14. may benefit from learning anger management techniques
15. may be at increased risk for missing treatment appointments or for not completing a recommended course of treatment

Low scores on this scale are not interpreted.

CYNICISM (CYN)

Items on the CYN scale express a general mistrust of the honesty, motivations, and intentions of others. Some items suggest people are inherently selfish and are primarily motivated to serve their own interests. Other items explicitly state people are dishonest, foolish, incompetent, or manipulative.

High scores (T ≥ 65) indicate persons who

1. report holding cynical beliefs
2. see other people as untrustworthy, uncaring, and concerned only about themselves
3. may frequently be hostile or resentful when interacting with other people
4. have great difficulty forming trusting relationships
5. tend to easily become angry
6. are often dissatisfied with treatment providers
7. may have difficulty engaging in therapy or forming therapeutic relationships
8. are at risk for negative treatment outcomes

Low scores (T < 39) on the CYN scale indicate persons who

1. disavow cynical beliefs
2. see others as well-intentioned and trustworthy
3. may be naive, gullible, and overly trusting of others

Interpersonal Specific Problems (SP) Scales

The primary purpose of the Interpersonal SP Scales is to illuminate various styles of engagement with other people. Unlike the other SP Scales, the Interpersonal Scales are not situated within the MMPI-3 hierarchy of symptom specificity. Instead, the information provided by these scales can be combined with information gleaned from all other MMPI-3 scales to build a more complete understanding of how the test taker views and interacts with others.

SELF-IMPORTANCE (SFI)

Most of the SFI scale items reflect the general belief that one is an extraordinary person.
High scores (T ≥ 65) indicate persons who

1. report being extraordinary people
2. report having skills, talents, ideas, or abilities that make them special and important
3. report being self-confident and especially well-suited for leadership roles
4. are self-reliant
5. have high self-esteem
6. tend to have a sense of superiority
7. may be grandiose and narcissistic
8. are typically authoritative, confident, determined, and ambitious
9. tend to be both interpersonally warm and dominant
10. at times, are likely seen by others as arrogant, vain, or narcissistic
11. tend to be somewhat extroverted
12. are generally optimistic and persistent
13. tend to experience very few internalizing symptoms
14. in mental health settings, are rarely diagnosed with depressive disorders

Low scores (T < 39) indicate persons who do not see themselves as possessing any special skills or abilities. They view themselves as ordinary or unremarkable at best.

DOMINANCE (DOM)

The item content of the DOM scale reflects a tendency to be assertive during interpersonal interactions. Most items describe a direct communication style, including a tendency to readily assert one's opinions and perspectives. Other items reflect beliefs about being a strong leader and enjoying such roles.
High scores (T ≥ 65) indicate persons who

1. hold and assert strong opinions
2. report standing up for themselves
3. describe their communication style as direct and assertive
4. enjoy taking on leadership roles and see themselves as capable leaders

5. often assume dominant roles during interpersonal interactions
6. tend to be seen by others as authoritative, determined, and ambitious but may also be viewed as verbally aggressive, rude, unkind, or even hostile
7. are likely to be extroverted
8. tend to experience few internalizing symptoms

Low scores (T < 39) indicate persons who

1. describe themselves as passive and unassertive in interpersonal situations
2. report that they do not express opinions or feelings strongly
3. do not want to be in positions of leadership
4. are seen by others as passive and submissive
5. are not achievement or power oriented
6. are introverted
7. should be evaluated for disorders involving passive, submissive behaviors (e.g., dependent personality disorder)
8. may benefit from treatment to reduce passive, submissive behaviors

DISAFFILIATIVENESS (DSF)

Item content on the DSF scale primarily suggests a strong preference for and increased sense of happiness when alone. A secondary emphasis of item content reflects a tendency to avoid becoming close with other people.

High scores (T ≥ 65) indicate persons who

1. report that they prefer being alone rather than around other people
2. report that they feel happier when they are by themselves
3. report that they do not want to be close to others
4. are interpersonally detached and socially withdrawn
5. tend to have difficulty trusting others
6. are seen by others as introverted and lacking in interpersonal warmth
7. are observed by others to have no close relationships
8. may report that their childhoods were marked by isolation or interpersonal conflict
9. may be more likely to report emotional/internalizing symptoms like social phobia, depressed mood, and anhedonia
10. should be evaluated for disorders characterized by interpersonal detachment
11. may have difficulty developing therapeutic alliances

Low scores on this scale are not interpreted.

SOCIAL AVOIDANCE (SAV)

Most SAV scale items reflect disavowal of a tendency to seek out and enjoy social gatherings. Item content is especially focused on dislike of larger social gatherings; but some items also tap into denial of having an interest in meeting new people and making new friends.

High scores (T ≥ 65) indicate persons who

1. report they do not enjoy social situations, especially those involving many people
2. report they do not enjoy meeting strangers or making new friends
3. are socially withdrawn and isolated
4. are introverted and may be shy
5. tend to be socially awkward and may lack interpersonal warmth
6. may report that their childhoods were marked by isolation or interpersonal conflict
7. tend to be somewhat passive in relationships
8. often struggle to identify interests or hobbies
9. are likely to experience symptoms of social phobia as well as increased anhedonia, depression, and anxiety
10. may benefit from treatment to reduce social avoidance

Low scores (T < 39) indicate persons who report enjoying social situations and crowded events as well as meeting new people and making new friends.

SHYNESS (SHY)

The SHY scale items can be rationally divided into two different clusters. The first cluster represents a tendency to experience uncomfortable emotions when engaging with others. The second grouping reflects a general reluctance to speak to others.

High scores (T ≥ 65) indicate persons who

1. report being shy, easily embarrassed, and emotionally uncomfortable around other people
2. report it is difficult to interact with other people, especially with those whom they do not know well
3. are socially anxious
4. are typically seen by others as socially awkward and lacking in interpersonal warmth
5. are observed by others to be passive in relationships
6. are introverted and socially withdrawn
7. tend to feel ashamed and insecure
8. often feel unable to effectively cope with their anxiety
9. are more likely to experience anxiety, depression, and anhedonia
10. in mental health settings, are more likely to be diagnosed with anxiety or depressive disorders
11. should be evaluated for social anxiety disorder (social phobia)
12. may benefit from treatment focused on reducing and managing anxiety during social interactions

Low scores (T < 39) indicate persons who report little or no social anxiety.

Interpretive Guidelines for Personality Psychopathology 5 (PSY-5) Scales

As detailed in Chapter 7, the PSY-5 Scales assess broad personality dimensions—encompassing both adaptive and maladaptive manifestations—useful in clinical practice (Harkness, McNulty, & Ben-Porath, 1995). The traits captured by the PSY-5 closely align with the Alternative DSM-5 Model for Personality Disorders (AMPD), a dimensional model of personality dysfunction described in Section III of the Diagnostic and Statistical Manual of Mental Disorders (DSM-5; American Psychiatric Association, 2013). The PSY-5 traits also closely align with several spectra-level dimensions described in the HiTOP model (Kotov et al., 2021).

Because the MMPI-3's PSY-5 Scales are very similar to the scales developed for the MMPI-2 and MMPI-2-RF, the interpretative guidelines offered here are similar to those found in Chapter 7. Any differences in recommendations are based on these authors' examination of the research conducted on the MMPI-3's version of these scales. These recommendations also follow the guidance for interpreting low PSY-5 scores found in the MMPI-3 manual, which states that low scores (T < 39) are interpretable for all the scales except PSYC (Ben-Porath & Tellegen, 2020a).

Aggressiveness (AGGR)

The AGGR scale largely captures individual differences in interpersonal assertiveness and dominance. Higher scores are indicative of a tendency to engage in offensive and instrumental aggression and may include enjoyment of intimidating others. This trait aligns with the antagonism domain trait proposed in the AMPD and the antagonistic externalizing spectrum in the HiTOP model. Both high and low scores are interpreted for this scale.

High scores (T ≥ 65) on the AGGR scale indicate persons who

1. report being interpersonally dominant and assertive to such an extent that they are confrontational and willing to act aggressively to accomplish their goals
2. are both verbally and physically aggressive
3. likely use aggression to dominate and control others
4. may enjoy intimidating other people
5. may react aggressively when provoked
6. may have histories of arrests, behavioral problems in school, and other acting out and antisocial behaviors
7. are more likely to engage in thrill-seeking behavior
8. are likely seen by others as angry, hostile, and irritable
9. if male, are at an increased likelihood of having a history of committing acts of domestic violence
10. in clinical or forensic settings, tend to have diagnoses of antisocial personality disorder
11. in forensic settings, may exhibit traits consistent with psychopathy
12. in treatment, may attempt to control and dominate therapists
13. in treatment, may benefit from discussion of the costs and benefits of their aggressiveness

Low scores (T < 39) indicate persons who are passive, submissive, and not very aggressive in interactions with other people.

Psychoticism (PSYC)

The PSYC scale identifies disconnection from reality, feelings of alienation, and unrealistic expectations of harm. PSYC aligns with the AMPD domain trait of the same name as well as the thought disorder spectrum in the HiTOP model. Low scores are not interpreted for this scale.

High scores (T ≥ 65) on the PSYC scale indicate persons who

1. report experiences suggesting a disconnection from a shared reality
2. report improbable expectations that others wish to harm them, which may be delusional in nature
3. likely hold unshared beliefs or have unusual sensory or perceptual experiences
4. may experience delusions of reference
5. may have bizarre, disoriented, or circumstantial thinking
6. in outpatient mental health settings, are more likely to report experiencing delusional thinking, frequent nightmares, and intrusive thoughts
7. in outpatient mental health settings, are more likely to report a history of taking antipsychotic medications
8. in outpatient mental health settings, may be diagnosed with a variety of conditions including those where unusual thinking, unrealistic expectations of harm, or unusual sensory/perceptual experiences are not primary symptoms (e.g., trauma- and stressor-related disorders, bipolar and related disorders)
9. should be evaluated further for schizophrenia spectrum and other psychotic disorders as well as Cluster A personality disorders
10. in therapy, may benefit from frequent opportunities to engage in reality checking

Disconstraint (DISC)

The DISC scale measures differences in self-control, risk-taking behaviors, and tendencies to follow rules and expectations. It most closely aligns with the HiTOP model's disinhibited externalizing spectra and the AMPD's disinhibition domain trait. Both high and low scores are interpreted for this scale.

High scores (T ≥ 65) on the DISC scale indicate persons who

1. report they have often engaged in externalizing behaviors such as substance use, problematic behavior in school, and breaking the law
2. report they often act impulsively
3. are impulsive and lack self-control
4. often have histories of problematic substance use
5. tend to take physical risks
6. typically, are easily bored by routine and seek out excitement
7. tend to be rebellious
8. are less bound by traditional moral constraints
9. often have histories of school problems and arrests

10. may have a history of engaging in self-injurious behavior
11. in forensic settings, tend to have histories of violence and antisocial personality disorder diagnoses
12. in mental health settings, tend to have diagnoses of substance-related and other addictive disorders
13. in treatment, may benefit from exploring more constructive ways to satisfy needs for novelty, excitement, and risk-taking

Low scores (T < 39) on the DISC scale indicate persons who

1. are very self-controlled and not impulsive
2. do not take many physical risks
3. have high tolerance for boredom
4. tend to follow rules and laws
5. have little or no history of substance use
6. may respond better to structured treatment approaches

Negative Emotionality/Neuroticism (NEGE)

The NEGE scale captures a predisposition to experience negative emotions (e.g., fear, anxiety) and fixate on problematic features of incoming information. The internalizing spectrum from the HiTOP model and the AMPD's negative affectivity domain trait demonstrate considerable conceptual overlap with NEGE. Both high and low scores on this scale are interpreted.

High scores (T ≥ 65) on the NEGE scale indicate persons who

1. report frequently experiencing anxiety and worry
2. have a predisposition to experience negative affect
3. are very anxious
4. worry excessively
5. tend to focus on problematic features of incoming information
6. often concoct worst-case scenarios
7. are typically self-critical
8. frequently feel guilty or ashamed
9. often report feeling sad or blue
10. are likely pessimistic
11. often feel overwhelmed by and unable to cope effectively with their emotions
12. are often fearful they may experience overwhelming negative emotions in the future
13. typically feel incapable of coping adequately with stress and quickly become overwhelmed by it
14. tend to hold dysfunctional beliefs about themselves and their relationships
15. likely fear that others will reject them or judge them harshly for their inability to better manage their negative emotions
16. may have few or no friends
17. may report somatic symptoms
18. are often not very achievement oriented

19. in clinical settings, may have histories of suicide attempts
20. in clinical settings, may present with or have a history of experiencing panic attacks
21. in clinical settings, often receive diagnoses of internalizing disorders including depressive disorders, anxiety disorders, and trauma- and stressor-related disorders
22. may benefit from therapy designed to identify and deal with their tendencies to process information in ways that produce negative emotions

Low scores on the NEGE scale (T < 39) indicate persons who report they are rarely anxious, worried, or fearful.

Introversion/Low Positive Emotionality (INTR)

The INTR scale detects individual differences in the capacity to experience positive emotions (e.g., joy) and engagement, including social engagement. Conceptually, it is congruent with the construct named detachment in both the AMPD and HiTOP model. Both high and low scores on this scale are interpreted.

High scores (T ≥ 65) on the INTR scale indicate persons who

1. report being introverted and socially disengaged
2. report rarely experiencing positive emotions
3. have little capacity to experience joy and pleasure
4. are introverted and very socially withdrawn
5. have trouble identifying hobbies or activities that interest them
6. tend to not be very achievement oriented
7. likely strike others as interpersonally disengaged, aloof, and cold
8. are often pessimistic about the future
9. may report feeling sad, blue, depressed, or anxious
10. may report somatic symptoms
11. in clinical settings, tend to have diagnoses of depressive disorders
12. in clinical settings, may have histories of suicide attempts
13. tend to show little emotional response in therapy

Low scores on the INTR scale (T < 39) indicate persons who

1. are extraverted and very sociable
2. have the capacity to experience joy and pleasure
3. have lots of energy
4. are likely to be quite emotionally responsive in therapy

Interpretive Strategy

The MMPI-3's authors have suggested a strategy for interpreting MMPI-3 protocols (Ben-Porath & Tellegen, 2020a). The first step is to examine the Validity scales to determine whether interpretation of the substantive scales is warranted. If Validity scale scores suggest that the test taker approached the test in an invalid manner (e.g., omitted items, responded without regard to item content, overreported, underreported), then no further consideration is given to other MMPI-3 scores. However, sometimes

Validity scale scores suggest some degree of response distortion but not to an extent that would invalidate the protocol. In these cases, the substantive scales are interpreted, but caution is advised. Guidelines for interpreting Validity scales are presented in Ben-Porath and Tellegen (2020a) and were summarized earlier in this chapter.

If a protocol is deemed valid and interpretable, the substantive scales are then interpreted. The interpretation of these scales is hierarchical in nature. Inferences are made first about general areas of dysfunction (e.g., emotional) and then about more specific symptoms and problems within that area. Five broad areas are addressed: (a) somatic/cognitive dysfunction, (b) emotional dysfunction, (c) thought dysfunction, (d) behavioral dysfunction, and (e) interpersonal functioning. These five areas closely align with the broader clusters identified by many contemporary models of psychopathology (e.g., the spectra level of the HiTOP). If appropriate to the context of the assessment in which the MMPI-3 is administered, then two additional types of interpretations are made—inferences dealing with diagnostic and treatment considerations.

The H-O, RC, SP, and PSY-5 scales for each of the areas of dysfunction are listed in Table 13.2. The H-O scales allow broad inferences about three general domains of dysfunction (i.e., emotional, thought, and behavioral). There are RC scales associated with each H-O scale that allow inferences about more specific aspects of dysfunction within each of those broad domains. Likewise, there are SP scales associated with some of the RC scales that permit inferences about even more specific facets of dysfunction.

Interpretation of the substantive scales begins with the broadest domains of dysfunction and the three H-O scales associated with those domains—EID for emotional, THD for thought, and BXD for behavioral. Interpretation of these areas is completed based on the order of their prominence in the MMPI-3 protocol. Begin your interpretation with the H-O scale having the highest T score. If that T score is ≥ 65, then you generate inferences based on the interpretive guidelines for that scale score. This provides you with a general idea of the most salient problems the test taker is likely to have. You next examine each RC scale associated with the H-O scale you just interpreted (i.e., RCd, RC2, and RC7 for EID; RC6 and RC8 for THD; and RC4 and RC9 for BXD). If the T score for any given RC scale is ≥ 65, then you generate inferences about the RC scale based on its interpretive guidelines. Next, examine and interpret all the SP scales that are facets of the RC scales you just reviewed. Again, you will make inferences about all scales with T scores ≥ 65 using each scale's interpretive guidelines. You will find that inferences based on the RC scales typically will be more specific than those based on the H-O scales; and, likewise, inferences based on the SP scales will be more specific than those based on the RC scales. If there are no elevated scores for the RC scales associated with the target H-O scale, then go directly to the SP scales associated with that general area of dysfunction and interpret any scales with T scores ≥ 65. Finally, relevant PSY-5 scales with T scores ≥ 65 should also be interpreted (i.e., INTR and NEGE for EID, PSYC for THD, DISC for BXD). After interpreting all the scales with high scores within the domain, then you should review and make interpretations for any scales with interpretable low scores (T < 39) in that domain.

TABLE 13.2 *Recommended Structure and Sources of Information for MMPI-3 Interpretation*

Topic	MMPI-3 Sources
1. Protocol Validity	
a. Content Non-Responsiveness	CNS, CRIN, VRIN, TRIN
b. Overreporting	F, Fp, Fs, FBS, RBS
c. Underreporting	L, K
2. Substantive Scale Interpretation	
a. Somatic/Cognitive Dysfunction	1. RC1, MLS, NUC, EAT, COG
b. Emotional Dysfunction	1. EID
	2. RCd, SUI, HLP, SFD, NFC
	3. RC2
	4. RC7, STR, WRY, CMP, ARX, ANP, BRF
	5. NEGE, INTR
c. Thought Dysfunction	1. THD
	2. RC6
	3. RC8
	4. PSYC
d. Behavioral Dysfunction	1. BXD
	2. RC4, FML, JCP, SUB
	3. RC9, IMP, ACT, AGG, CYN
	4. DISC
e. Interpersonal Functioning	1. SFI, DOM, DSF, SAV, SHY
	2. AGGR
f. Diagnostic Considerations	Most substantive scales
h. Treatment Considerations	All substantive scales

Note. Excerpted (Table 5-1) from *MMPI-3 Manual for Administration, Scoring, and Interpretation* by Yossef S. Ben-Porath and Auke Tellegen. Copyright © 2020 by the Regents of the University of Minnesota. Reproduced by permission of the University of Minnesota Press. All rights reserved. "MMPI" and "Minneosota Multiphasic Persaonlity Inventory" are registered trademarks of the Regents of the University of Minnesota.

By working from the broadest symptom level to the narrowest, you should be able to refine your interpretation of the protocol by emphasizing those specific symptoms, problems, and patterns of behavior that are best supported by the test data. Of course, all MMPI-3 interpretations should be treated as working hypotheses until they are supported or refuted by other extratest data about the test taker.

After completing the interpretation of all scales associated with the most prominent area of dysfunction, then you should return to the H-O scale with the next highest T score and repeat the process we just described. Once that is completed, then you repeat the process again for the area with the third highest H-O score. Finally, interpret the somatic/cognitive domain. Begin with RC1, and then move to the Somatic/Cognitive SP scales. There is one exception to this process. If the EID scale T score is ≥ 65, then interpretation of the scales in the emotional dysfunction domain should be immediately followed by the interpretation of all scales in the somatic/cognitive area (i.e., RC1, MLS, NUC, EAT, COG). This is because the somatic/cognitive domain is linked both theoretically and empirically to the emotional/internalizing domain. Thus, it can be important to the test interpretation and the broader case conceptualization to consider somatic/cognitive symptoms in conjunction with emotional/internalizing symptoms when the latter are strongly present.

If at any time in the interpretive process you reach a point where there are no H-O scales with T scores ≥ 65, then you interpret the domain by considering its highest RC scale score and its associated SP scales. Keep repeating this process until all the scales have been interpreted. If no RC scales have T scores ≥ 65, then go directly to the SP scales. In these circumstances, you start with the SP scale that has the highest T score, then interpret all the other interpretable SP scales in the same cluster. Again, keep repeating this process until all the scales have been interpreted.

Next, examine the Interpersonal Functioning scales. Often, your interpretation of the other four domains of functioning will include some sense of how the test taker functions interpersonally. However, the Interpersonal SP scales focus specifically on a variety of aspects of interpersonal functioning. Thus, inferences based on these scales will further refine your understanding of how the test taker typically interacts with others. Beginning with the highest score, interpret each of these SP scales with T ≥ 65. Once you have interpreted all the elevated Interpersonal scales, then review and generate additional inferences based on any of these scales with interpretable low scores (i.e., T < 39).

All the substantive scales (H-O, RC, SP, and PSY-5) are potential sources of information about diagnostic impressions and treatment implications. Ben-Porath and Tellegen (2020a) indicated that inferences about diagnostic considerations are based in part on empirical data and are in part inferential. They also stated that inferences about treatment are not based on empirical data.

Ben-Porath and Tellegen (2020a) do not offer any recommendations regarding item-level interpretation. Both the MMPI-3 Score Report and the MMPI-3 Interpretive Report provide item-level responses for "unscorable responses" and "critical responses" given by test takers. Seven MMPI-3 substantive scales—SUI, HLP, ARX, RC6, RC8, SUB, and AGG—were identified as having critical item content that may require immediate attention and follow-up. Items answered in the keyed direction are provided for any of these seven scales for which T scores are ≥ 65 (except SUI, for which all items endorsed in the keyed direction are listed regardless of scale elevation).

We believe critical item responses (and to a lesser extent unscorable items) are best used to help identify areas in need of follow-up assessment or prompt intervention. We caution against overinterpreting individual item responses, as they are unreliable. It is very easy for a test taker to incorrectly mark their response to a single item or to interpret a single item in an unusual manner.

In addition to the MMPI-3 manual's table reprinted here as Table 13.2, there are several other tools available to help you organize and complete your test interpretation following Ben-Porath and Tellegen's (2020a) structured approach. First, the MMPI-3 Score Report and MMPI-3 Interpretive Report include a page titled "MMPI-3 T Scores (By Domain)" where all the scale scores are reported and organized using the clusters displayed in Table 13.2. Second, on Pearson Assessments' website, you can find a fillable form pdf titled "MMPI-3 Interpretation Worksheet" (www.pearsonassessments.com/content/dam/school/global/clinical/us/assets/mmpi-3/mmpi-3-interpretation-worksheet.pdf). This worksheet also organizes the MMPI-3 scales by domain using the same scheme found in the manual. We recommend using the worksheet to record all the interpretive statements by domain as you generate them for each scale. The worksheet can thus serve as a working draft from which you will then draw interpretive inferences as you edit, consolidate, refine, and reorganize your formal test interpretation and turn it into a final product.

ILLUSTRATIVE CASE

To illustrate the strategy just discussed, the case of Janelle will now be considered, and a step-by-step analysis of the MMPI-3 protocol will be presented. As a practice exercise, readers can first interpret Janelle's scores and then compare their interpretations with the ones presented in this section. All of Janelle's scores can be found in the MMPI-3 Score Report appended to this chapter. Additional MMPI-3 cases for practice interpretation are available in an online supplement hosted by Oxford Press, the publisher of this book. Please visit www.oup.com/he/graham6e to access these materials.

Background Information

Janelle is a 24-year-old White female. She has never been married and lives alone. She graduated from college with a bachelor's degree in business with somewhat above average grades. Janelle tends not to join in social activities and has few friends. Her best friend from high school was also her closest friend and roommate in college. Janelle had a serious boyfriend in high school, but none of her subsequent romantic relationships lasted more than a few months. She has not been in a romantic relationship in close to 2 years. Since graduating from college, Janelle has taken a job as a truck dispatcher in a small city close to her home town. She was initially told the position would be temporary and that she would eventually be promoted to office manager. However, she has been in that position for over 2 years now, and the office manager position was filled by a different person who was hired shortly after her.

The MMPI-3 was administered to Janelle as part of routine intake procedures after she was referred to a local community mental health center by her primary care physician. In her last appointment with the physician, she requested a prescription for antidepressant medication and for information about where to obtain therapy. Janelle screened positive for depression and anxiety. She denied any suicidal ideation or history at that time.

Janelle was cooperative with the intake interview and testing. She completed the MMPI-3 in about 45 minutes. Janelle had previously been treated for depression—receiving both psychotherapy and a prescription for antidepressant medication—at age 18 and again at age 22. Janelle shared currently feeling stuck in her life. She has been feeling increasingly anxious and depressed over the last 3 months. She characterized herself as introverted, but she has begun to spend more time alone and has no meaningful friendships. She also described feeling criticized by her family. Recently, she has begun feeling very anxious while making her dispatch calls and experienced a panic attack before one of the calls. She thought part of her anxiety was a result of her supervisor expressing dissatisfaction with the quality and quantity of her work.

Protocol Validity

Examination of Janelle's Validity scale scores indicates that she approached the test in an appropriate manner and that the substantive scales are interpretable. She omitted no items and attended appropriately to item content (CRIN, T = 51; VRIN, T = 51; TRIN, T = 60, in true direction). The F scale T score was significantly elevated (T = 81). However, this F score likely indicates genuine emotional distress and psychopathology given Janelle's increasingly strong symptoms, her recent impairment in daily activity, and the absence of any elevations on the other overreporting scales, most importantly Fp (T = 58). There was no evidence of underreporting on Janelle's MMPI-3 (L, T = 56; K, T = 38).

Substantive Scales—Emotional Dysfunction

We begin interpretation of the substantive scales by examining her H-O scale scores. Because her highest score is on the EID scale (T = 81) and because that scale is elevated, we would infer Janelle is reporting significant signs of emotional dysfunction and begin our interpretation by reviewing the interpretive guidelines provided earlier in this chapter for EID.

Janelle's score on EID is extremely elevated (T = 81) and indicates that she is not only experiencing strong emotional turmoil, but that it has become strong enough that she perceives herself as being in a state of crisis. She is overwhelmed by depressed and anxious moods as well as her current life circumstances. She may also be experiencing non-mood symptoms related to her emotional distress like suicidal thinking and lack of energy. Janelle feels unable to cope adequately and likely worries things are only going to get worse for her. Finally, she probably feels lonely and unsupported by others. She may even fear that others will reject her or judge her harshly for being in such strong emotional distress.

We next review the RC scales associated with EID—RCd (T = 77), RC2 (T = 65), and RC7 (T = 78). All of the scores are elevated, revealing that Janelle's emotional dysfunction is diffuse—which is consistent with her very high score on EID. Interpretation of the RC scales will provide greater details regarding her symptoms and problems.

Because RC7 is the highest score (T = 78), we infer Janelle frequently experiences strong negative emotions and begin our interpretation there. Emotionally, Janelle frequently experiences anxiety, fear, and other distressing feelings. She worries excessively and experiences unwanted negative thinking even when she tries to focus her attention elsewhere. She is self-critical, guilt-prone, and tends to ruminate over her mistakes and failures. She feels unable to cope with her emotions and is frequently overwhelmed by stress. Janelle is insecure and extremely sensitive to the judgments and criticisms of others. The Internalizing SP scales associated with dysfunctional negative emotions help us to better understand Janelle's specific symptoms and problems. These scales are STR (T = 68), WRY (T = 72), CMP (T = 69), ARX (T = 73), ANP (T = 51), and BRF (T = 91). We work from highest to lowest to generate inferences from each of these scales except for ANP, which does not warrant interpretation since it is not clinically elevated.

Janelle's BRF score (T = 91) is extremely elevated and means that she is experiencing many specific fears that are interfering with her daily activities both within and outside the home. She is fearful and anxious when she is not at home and may be experiencing panic attacks and symptoms of agoraphobia. The ARX score of 73 supports previous inferences that Janelle frequently experiences anxiety, dread, and fear. It suggests she experiences intrusive thinking that may include unwanted memories. Janelle likely also has a sensitive startle response, nightmares, and disturbed sleep. Janelle is probably fearful she will experience future episodes of strong anxiety and fear. Janelle's elevated score on WRY (T = 72) reaffirms previous inferences that she worries about a variety of things and feels overwhelmed, anxious, and uneasy. It also again suggests she is uncertain in her relationships and adds that her fear of rejection by others may be related to her inability to control her cycles of anxiety and worry. Her CMP score (T = 69) suggests that she is orderly and organized; she probably performs some repetitive behaviors; and she is likely perfectionist, rigid, and inflexible. Finally, her STR score of 68 further supports what we have seen inferred on other scales—Janelle is experiencing high levels of stress and is overwhelmed by it. She has exceeded her capacity to cope with her stress and is pessimistic that things will change.

Next, we move to interpret the second-highest RC scale in the emotional dysfunction domain, RCd. Janelle's T score of 77 on this scale suggests that she is reporting feeling deeply sad and unhappy. She is overwhelmed by and unable to cope with her current life situation. There are a variety of other symptoms often experienced by individual's with RCd scores as high as Janelle's, many of which we have already identified based on the scales we have already interpreted. However, most importantly, we need to attend to the increased likelihood of suicidality associated with RCd scores of this magnitude. This potential risk for suicide can be further delineated by examining the SP scales associated with RCd, which is where we turn our attention to next.

The SP scales associated with RCd are all elevated (SUI, T = 65; HLP, T = 69; SFD, T = 78; NFC, T = 72). Janelle's elevated SFD score indicates that she has no confidence in herself, sees herself as useless, and believes she is inferior to others. People with scores this high typically have very low self-esteem and frequently experience uncertainty and awkwardness during interpersonal interactions, which may lead to them withdrawing from interpersonal relationships. Janelle's responses to NFC scale items reveal that she is indecisive and tends to avoid making difficult decisions. Because of feelings of insecurity and inadequacy, she is not very self-reliant and gives up easily in the face of adversity. A HLP score of 69T suggests Janelle feels incapable of making meaningful change and is pessimistic that her life will improve. Finally, Janelle's elevated score on SUI reveals that she has endorsed suicidal ideation or a history of suicide attempts. Anytime SUI is elevated (T ≥ 58), it is important to conduct a detailed suicide assessment. Janelle's case is no exception, especially because she has elevated several other MMPI-3 scales empirically associated with increased suicidality (i.e., EID, RCd, HLP, SFD, NEGE, INTR, FML).

Next, RC2 is interpreted (T = 65). Janelle's score on this scale indicates she reports having few positive emotional experiences in her life. She may also have a deficit in her ability to experience joy and happiness. She likely often feels bored and isolated. She may have low expectations for her own success, and she likely tries to avoid competitive situations. Janelle is probably somewhat introverted, passive, and socially withdrawn. There are many additional inferences associated with an elevated RC2 scale, but they have already been identified based on other scale scores. Thus, her score on this scale also strengthens our confidence in many of these earlier inferences (e.g., unhappy, difficulty making decisions, pessimistic).

Finally, the PSY-5 scales associated with the internalizing domain, NEGE (T = 76) and INTR (T = 69), are interpreted. Janelle's NEGE score provides additional support for many previously generated inferences associated with negative affect, especially that Janelle is likely experiencing strong anxiety and excessive worry. Similarly, her INTR score provides additional support for inferences about the likelihood that Janelle is introverted, socially withdrawn, and experiencing a lack of positive emotional experiences.

There are no interpretable low scores in the emotional/internalizing domain, so we move to the next domain.

Somatic/Cognitive Dysfunction

Because the EID scale T score was ≥ 65, we now interpret scores for scales in the Somatic/Cognitive domain. Because Janelle's RC1 scale (T = 55) is not elevated, we turn immediately to the Somatic/Cognitive SP scales. Her MLS T score of 68 indicates Janelle believes she has poor overall physical health, often feels fatigued, and experiences poor sleep. These symptoms likely interfere with her work and other daily activities. She may also experience a variety of vague somatic complaints, especially at times of increased emotional turmoil or stress. Janelle may be somewhat preoccupied with her poor health and is pessimistic about it improving. The remaining Somatic/Cognitive scales are neither elevated nor have interpretable low scores (NUC, T = 47; EAT, T = 56; COG, T = 57), so we move to the next domain.

Thought Dysfunction and Behavioral Dysfunction

Neither of the remaining H-O scores are elevated (THD, T = 53; BXD, T = 46), so we move to examining all of the remaining RC scales. Again, none of these scales is elevated, nor are there interpretable low scores (RC 4, T = 50; RC6, T = 63; RC8, T = 52; RC9, T = 39). So, we review all the SP scales in the behavioral dysfunction domain. First, we interpret any elevated scales beginning with the highest, then we will interpret any low scores.

The only interpretable SP scale is FML (T = 70). Janelle's FML score means she is reporting negative experiences with and attitudes toward her family. She does not feel supported by them, and she may not trust them or may resent them as a result. Janelle's family is likely to be full of conflict, and she is likely to blame them for her problems. Tumultuous relationships with family members were likely a hallmark of her childhood, and her family life may have been chaotic and dysfunctional.

Finally, we review the PSY-5 scales from these two domains, PSYC (T = 47) and DISC (T = 48), but we draw no inferences from them because they are not clinically elevated.

Interpersonal Functioning

We finish our interpretation of Janelle's substantive scales by turning to the Interpersonal Functioning scales. A quick review reveals that all of these scales are interpretable except DSF (T = 58). We begin with the elevated scales (SHY, T = 77; SAV, T = 71). Janelle's SHY scale score reveals she is shy, easily embarrassed, and emotionally uneasy around others. She finds it difficult to interact with others, especially people she does not know well, and she is likely to be socially withdrawn. Janelle experiences social anxiety and is likely viewed by other people as socially awkward, passive, and interpersonally cool. She often feels ashamed and insecure about her interpersonal interactions. Her SAV scale adds to this understanding by indicating that she does not enjoy social situations, especially those situations involving lots of people or requiring her to meet strangers or make new friends. Janelle is not only socially withdrawn, but she may be so withdrawn as to be socially isolated. She may struggle to identify hobbies or other interests. Her childhood may have been marked by social isolation or interpersonal conflict.

Next, we review the Interpersonal Functioning scales with low scale scores. Her DOM scale score (T = 27) indicates that Janelle is very interpersonally passive and unassertive. She rarely expresses her opinions or feelings and avoids leadership positions. She is not likely to be achievement oriented and does not seek to be in positions of power or authority. Janelle's SFI scale score (T = 37) indicates that she does not see herself as possessing any special skills or abilities. Instead, she views herself as ordinary at best.

Finally, we turn to the PSY-5 scale placed in the Interpersonal domain, AGGR. Janelle's score on this scale again suggests she is interpersonally passive and submissive (AGGR, T = 28). She is very unlikely to be aggressive, or even assertive, in her interactions with others.

Diagnostic Considerations

We next examine Janelle's substantive scale scores to identify any specific diagnoses that should be evaluated. As a reminder, the MMPI-3 is not a diagnostic test; however, it does provide us with information about Janelle's symptoms and functioning, and thus the MMPI-3 serves as one source of information used in a thorough diagnostic evaluation.

Janelle's scores on EID and most of the emotional dysfunction RC, SP, and PSY-5 scales suggest that several internalizing diagnoses should be considered—depressive disorders, anxiety disorders, and trauma- and stressor-related disorders. Some specific disorders within those categories worthy of extra attention based on MMPI-3 results include Major Depressive Disorder (RC2, INTR, HLP, SFD, NFC); Social Anxiety Disorder (RC2, INTR, SFD, SAV, SHY); Agoraphobia (ARX, BRF); and PTSD (ARX). In addition, her scores on RC7, NEGE, and CMP suggest obsessive–compulsive and related disorders should be evaluated.

Several scales also suggest Janelle should be evaluated for Cluster C personality disorders (RC7, NEGE) including Avoidant (RC2, INTR, SAV, SHY), Dependent (NFC, DOM), and Obsessive–Compulsive (RC7, CMP) personality disorders. Using the DSM-5's AMPD, the scores on NEGE and INTR suggest consideration of Personality Disorder-Trait Specified for Negative Affectivity or Detachment.

Finally, if Janelle's concerns related to her view of poor physical health are not better accounted for by physical explanations or her symptoms of emotional dysfunction, then she should be evaluated for somatic symptom and related disorders based on her MLS scale score.

Treatment Considerations

Finally, we examine Janelle's substantive scale scores one final time to determine whether inferences concerning treatment are warranted. Most of these inferences are higher-order inferences. This means that they are not drawn from empirical literature specific to the MMPI-3 scale scores. Instead, these inferences are based on our general understanding of psychopathology and psychotherapy as well as our specific understanding of Janelle's case. Thus, we must acknowledge that these inferences do not come from research specific to the MMPI-3 but instead represent our best clinical judgement as we apply the test data to her treatment. Regardless, these higher-order inferences should be made with less confidence and represent hypotheses that we would collaboratively explore with Janelle during treatment planning.

Janelle is overwhelmed by the strong emotional turmoil and distress (EID, RCd, RC7) she has been experiencing. As a result, she is likely motivated to seek treatment and find relief. Some of her test results raise concerns that she may be at risk for poor treatment outcomes (RCd), possibly due to being at an increased risk for prematurely ending therapy before her treatment goals are met (RC2, RC7). She may have trouble engaging in psychotherapy because of her low positive emotionality (RC2); and she will almost certainly experience insecurity, social anxiety, and fear of being judged harshly early in the therapeutic relationship (EID, RC7, STR, WRY, ARX, NEGE, SAV, SHY). Janelle is at risk for being overly passive during therapy (RC2, NFC, DOM, SAV, SHY, AGGR) and may struggle with indecisiveness when establishing treatment goals (NFC). Furthermore, she generally feels incapable of making meaningful change in her life and believes her situation is hopeless (EID, RCd, SUI, HLP, SFD, NFC, WRY, ARX, FML). Finally, Janelle is likely to be unwilling or unable to attend sessions at times because of her general malaise (MLS).

It will be important for Janelle's therapist to skillfully attend to these negative treatment indicators. Her therapist will need to work carefully early in the relationship to alleviate Janelle's interpersonal concerns and establish a strong therapeutic alliance. Her therapist will also need to attend to Janelle's tendency to be passive and ensure she is a full and active participant in treatment to build a truly collaborative treatment plan and therapeutic relationship. Finally, Janelle's therapist will need to anticipate and proactively address her tendency to miss sessions because of her poor health as well as her risk for terminating therapy prematurely.

Janelle's MMPI-3 results identify several potential treatment targets. However, there are several concerns requiring additional assessment prior to treatment planning. First, Janelle needs to undergo a thorough suicide assessment (RCd, SUI). Identification of her suicide risk factors, protective factors, and overall suicide risk should also generate strategies for mitigation, intervention, and ongoing assessment to be incorporated into her overall treatment plan. Next, Janelle's results indicate she may be experiencing PTSD (ARX), OCD (RC7, CMP), and agoraphobia (ARX, BRF). Additional assessment of these disorders is needed prior to developing her treatment plan. Other potential targets for intervention identified by the MMPI-3 include relief of emotional distress (RCd); identifying and reducing her tendency to process information in an anxiety-evoking manner (NEGE); increasing hope (HLP); improving self-esteem (SFD); reducing indecisiveness (NFC); stress management (STR); reducing worry (WRY); increasing assertiveness (DOM, AGGR); reducing social withdrawal and social anxiety (SAV, SHY); and addressing family conflict and strained family relationships (FML).

Overall, Janelle is a good candidate for treatment given her current emotional distress. Once her assessment is complete, her therapist will need to work deliberately with her to build a strong and collaborative therapeutic relationship. Some of the first tasks in therapy will include implementation of a plan for intervention, mitigation, and ongoing assessment of suicidality—increasing her hope for meaningful change and reducing her level of emotional distress. Additional targets for intervention should be identified in close collaboration with Janelle. Her treatment plan and goals may need to be revisited on a regular basis depending on her changing needs and response to treatment interventions. Janelle may also benefit from a referral for pharmacotherapy if she is not already receiving this type of treatment from her physician.

Critical Responses

We have now completed our interpretation of the MMPI-3. However, before we summarize the case, we first review Janelle's critical responses. Because these are her responses to single items, we refrain from drawing inferences based only on her responses. Instead, we use this item-level information to identify any areas of additional inquiry or immediate action we need to take.

Of the seven scales for which critical responses should be examined if T scores are ≥ 65, Janelle has elevated scores on three of them (SUI, HLP, and ARX). A review of these items (exact content withheld here for test security purposes) shows that Janelle revealed she has made a suicide attempt in the past. She is also currently experiencing thoughts about death, which are not explicitly suicidal. In addition, Janelle endorsed a handful of items that are expressions of hopelessness that her life will improve. These critical responses further support our earlier identification of the need to conduct a full suicide assessment with Janelle.

A second set of items, from the ARX scale, identify several specific anxiety-related symptoms Janelle has been experiencing. These symptoms include a heightened startle response, panic symptoms, and unwanted re-experiencing of past events. Taken together, these items suggest a detailed evaluation of trauma- and stressor-related disorders as well as anxiety disorders—beginning with PTSD and panic disorder—is warranted.

Summary

Janelle appears to have approached the MMPI-3 in a valid manner. She attended appropriately to item content, was not defensive, and did not overreport symptoms and problems. Her problems primarily lie within the internalizing spectrum of psychopathology. Janelle has been experiencing such strong emotional distress that she has reached a crisis state. She is overwhelmed by her current life situation and feels unable to cope adequately any longer. She may be at an increased risk for suicide and should receive a thorough suicide assessment. Janelle has little confidence in herself and believes there is nothing she can do to improve her situation. Her anxiety and fear are overwhelming her. She is experiencing anticipatory fear and worry focused on situations that are likely to activate strong negative emotions. She is engaging in avoidance behaviors that are negatively impacting her relationships, her work, and other activities of daily living. Janelle is also reporting ruminative thinking, panic attack-like symptoms, intrusive thoughts, fears of everyday kinds of situations, and a general reluctance to leave her home. Janelle reports a general sense of poor health that may be closely associated with her emotional distress and is likely contributing to her impaired level of functioning.

Janelle is also reporting interpersonal distress, dysfunction, and detachment. She experiences a great deal of social anxiety, becomes distressed when meeting new people, and avoids social gatherings whenever possible. She is extremely passive in her interpersonal relationships and rarely asserts herself or even expresses her opinion. She sees herself as unremarkable and views others as being superior to her. Janelle also reports dysfunctional and nonsupportive relationships with her family. Again, her interpersonal functioning is probably closely connected to her emotional distress and is certainly contributing to her functional impairments.

Janelle is likely motivated for treatment because of her strong psychological distress. However, there are several factors that may interfere with effective treatment. Janelle may have trouble engaging in therapy due to her low positive emotionality and because of her interpersonal insecurity, social anxiety, and fear of being judged harshly by the therapist. Her tendency to be extremely passive and indecisive may weaken the quality of collaboration within the therapeutic relationship. Her hopelessness regarding the possibility for making meaningful change in her life as well as her general malaise may also interfere with her engagement in therapy. Finally, she is at increased risk for premature termination.

Janelle's therapist will need to work deliberately to establish a strong therapeutic alliance and a collaborative partnership. Early targets for therapeutic intervention include reducing her emotional distress and increasing her hope for meaningful change. Other early therapeutic goals may be determined by additional assessment findings (i.e., follow-up assessment of suicidality, PTSD, OCD, and agoraphobia). Later goals in therapy should be developed collaboratively with Janelle and may include the fear and worry symptoms impairing her daily functioning; stress management; family dysfunction; and her interpersonal shyness, avoidance, and extreme passivity. Janelle may also benefit from a referral for pharmacotherapy if she is not already receiving treatment from her physician.

MMPI-3 VERSUS MMPI-2/MMPI-2-RF

Clinicians working with adults are now faced with choosing between three MMPI instruments. There are many general considerations when selecting an appropriate instrument in a specific evaluation context. Addressing these considerations is beyond the scope of this chapter, and we refer the reader to the *APA Guidelines for Psychological Assessment and Evaluation* (American Psychological Association & APA Task Force on Psychological Assessment and Evaluation Guidelines, 2020) and the Standards for Educational and Psychological Testing (American Educational Research Association, American Psychological Association, & National Council on Measurement in Education, 2014) for general guidance related to selecting and using psychological tests. However, there are also some specific considerations for selecting from among the three MMPI instruments we can address. Broadly, as we see it, there are two related questions a test user must consider when deciding which MMPI instrument to use: (a) which instrument(s) are appropriate and useful for answering the questions relevant to this evaluation? (b) Do I have the necessary competencies to use the test that best addresses the referral question?

Regarding the first question, there are several issues the test user must consider in determining which MMPI instrument is appropriate and useful. In general, one must evaluate the psychometric properties of the test for the purpose to which you are applying it. We have extensively reviewed the psychometric properties for all the MMPI instruments in this book, but we will make a few brief comparisons here.

The first, and most important, psychometric difference between these tests that the test user must consider is the normative sample. The ability of a test-taker's scores to accurately describe their standing on the assessed characteristics is in part determined by how well the test taker is represented by a test's normative sample. To the extent that an individual is not well represented, their scores will provide less accurate descriptions of their functioning. Given this, the MMPI-3 normative samples are a significant improvement over the normative sample used for the MMPI-2 and MMPI-2-RF in three key ways. First, there are separate U.S. norms for the English and Spanish versions of the test. We recommend using the MMPI-3 Spanish translation for U.S. Spanish speakers over the Spanish translations of the other adult MMPI instruments because of the Spanish-language normative sample. This is because the Spanish-language norms provide a more representative normative group for these individuals than what is available for the MMPI-2 and MMPI-2-RF, which use the same normative sample regardless of language of administration. Second, given the changing demographic constellation of the United States over the past 40 years, we cannot be confident the norms used for the MMPI-2 and MMPI-2-RF are representative of the diverse individuals being assessed with a MMPI instrument. However, the demographics of the MMPI-3 normative samples closely match the projected 2020 census. Thus, we recommend using the MMPI-3 normative samples to better ensure appropriate comparisons are being made. Third, over the past 40 years, how people tend to respond to specific test items has changed. The reasons for these changes are not known, but the consequences are demonstrated in data suggesting that about one in four MMPI-3 scales differs by five or more T score points when the MMPI-3 normative sample mean scores are calculated using the MMPI-2-RF normative sample (Ben-Porath & Tellegen, 2020b). This leads us to think the responses provided by the individuals comprising the MMPI-3 normative sample may better capture how people currently being tested are likely to respond to the test's items, and hence we recommend administration of the MMPI-3.

In terms of other psychometric properties, the MMPI-2, MMPI-2-RF, and MMPI-3 are all well standardized and demonstrate appropriate reliability. The validity data supporting the use of the MMPI-2 and MMPI-2-RF for the general purpose of measuring clinically relevant manifestations of personality and psychopathology is substantial and represents one of the most important strengths of the MMPI instruments. Given how similar the MMPI-3 scales are to their MMPI-2-RF counterparts, we concluded previously in this chapter that MMPI-2-RF validity research generally applies to those scales carried over to the MMPI-3. As a result, the MMPI-3 also demonstrates substantial validity for the purpose of measuring personality and psychopathology. One important exception to this generalization is specific to those scales that are new to the MMPI-3. Initial validity evidence for these scales is promising, but further empirical investigation is warranted. As a result, we view all three instruments as demonstrating general equivalence in terms of standardization, reliability, and validity. Test users will need to reevaluate reliability and validity of each of these instruments if they intend to use them for purposes other than general clinical applications.

Finally, we turn to questions related to clinician competencies in using the MMPI-2, MMPI-2-RF, and MMPI-3. Our assumption in writing this book is that competent use of each of these instruments has some degree of overlap but also requires unique education and training specific to the instrument. We explicitly structured the book to recognize these overlapping and distinct competencies, and we attempted to provide the user with a relatively straightforward method for developing the basic competencies necessary to use each instrument in the MMPI family. Of course, users will need to refer back to this text as well as pursue additional training and professional development to enhance their mastery of MMPI interpretation regardless of which instrument they use.

In summary, we believe the MMPI-3 will replace both the MMPI-2 and MMPI-2-RF in the coming years due primarily to the updated norms and secondarily because of the enhanced content coverage. Therefore, our advice for most readers would be to begin developing the skills needed to engage in evidence-based use of the MMPI-3 while continuing to use the MMPI-2 and MMPI-2-RF until you are prepared to make the transition. The only exception we see to this general guidance might be when the test is being used in contexts or for specific applications where the MMPI-3 has not yet been empirically evaluated but the MMPI-2 or MMPI-2-RF have.

CHAPTER APPENDIX

Minnesota Multiphasic Personality Inventory®-3

Score Report

MMPI®-3
Minnesota Multiphasic Personality Inventory®-3
Yossef S. Ben-Porath, PhD, & Auke Tellegen, PhD

ID Number:	Janelle
Age:	24
Gender:	Female
Marital Status:	Not reported
Years of Education:	Not reported
Date Assessed:	08/16/2021

ALWAYS LEARNING

PEARSON

MMPI-3 Validity Scales

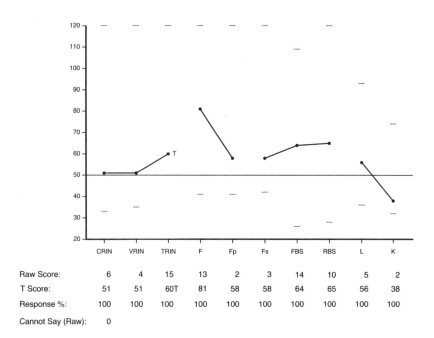

	CRIN	VRIN	TRIN	F	Fp	Fs	FBS	RBS	L	K
Raw Score:	6	4	15	13	2	3	14	10	5	2
T Score:	51	51	60T	81	58	58	64	65	56	38
Response %:	100	100	100	100	100	100	100	100	100	100

Cannot Say (Raw):   0

The highest and lowest T scores possible on each scale are indicated by a "---"; MMPI-3 T scores are non-gendered.

CRIN Combined Response Inconsistency	F Infrequent Responses	L Uncommon Virtues
VRIN Variable Response Inconsistency	Fp Infrequent Psychopathology Responses	K Adjustment Validity
TRIN True Response Inconsistency	Fs Infrequent Somatic Responses	
	FBS Symptom Validity Scale	
	RBS Response Bias Scale	

MMPI®-3 Score Report
08/16/2021, Page 3

Janelle

MMPI-3 Higher-Order (H-O) and Restructured Clinical (RC) Scales

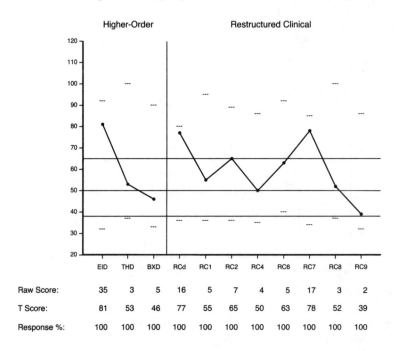

	EID	THD	BXD	RCd	RC1	RC2	RC4	RC6	RC7	RC8	RC9
Raw Score:	35	3	5	16	5	7	4	5	17	3	2
T Score:	81	53	46	77	55	65	50	63	78	52	39
Response %:	100	100	100	100	100	100	100	100	100	100	100

The highest and lowest T scores possible on each scale are indicated by a "---"; MMPI-3 T scores are non-gendered.

EID Emotional/Internalizing Dysfunction	RCd Demoralization	RC6 Ideas of Persecution
THD Thought Dysfunction	RC1 Somatic Complaints	RC7 Dysfunctional Negative Emotions
BXD Behavioral/Externalizing Dysfunction	RC2 Low Positive Emotions	RC8 Aberrant Experiences
	RC4 Antisocial Behavior	RC9 Hypomanic Activation

MMPI-3 Somatic/Cognitive Dysfunction and Internalizing Scales

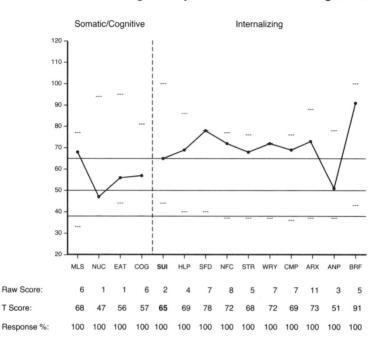

	MLS	NUC	EAT	COG	SUI	HLP	SFD	NFC	STR	WRY	CMP	ARX	ANP	BRF
Raw Score:	6	1	1	6	2	4	7	8	5	7	7	11	3	5
T Score:	68	47	56	57	65	69	78	72	68	72	69	73	51	91
Response %:	100	100	100	100	100	100	100	100	100	100	100	100	100	100

The highest and lowest T scores possible on each scale are indicated by a "---"; MMPI-3 T scores are non-gendered.

MLS	Malaise	SUI	Suicidal/Death Ideation	WRY	Worry
NUC	Neurological Complaints	HLP	Helplessness/Hopelessness	CMP	Compulsivity
EAT	Eating Concerns	SFD	Self-Doubt	ARX	Anxiety-Related Experiences
COG	Cognitive Complaints	NFC	Inefficacy	ANP	Anger Proneness
		STR	Stress	BRF	Behavior-Restricting Fears

MMPI-3 Externalizing and Interpersonal Scales

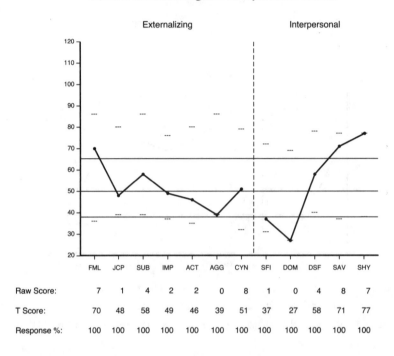

	FML	JCP	SUB	IMP	ACT	AGG	CYN	SFI	DOM	DSF	SAV	SHY
Raw Score:	7	1	4	2	2	0	8	1	0	4	8	7
T Score:	70	48	58	49	46	39	51	37	27	58	71	77
Response %:	100	100	100	100	100	100	100	100	100	100	100	100

The highest and lowest T scores possible on each scale are indicated by a "---"; MMPI-3 T scores are non-gendered.

FML	Family Problems	ACT	Activation	SFI	Self-Importance
JCP	Juvenile Conduct Problems	AGG	Aggression	DOM	Dominance
SUB	Substance Abuse	CYN	Cynicism	DSF	Disaffiliativeness
IMP	Impulsivity			SAV	Social Avoidance
				SHY	Shyness

MMPI-3 PSY-5 Scales

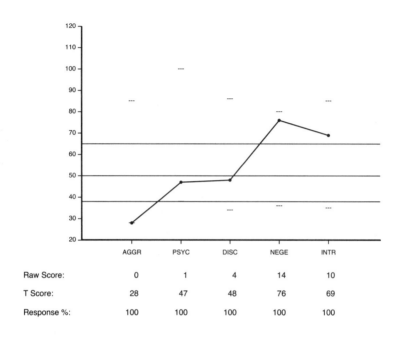

	AGGR	PSYC	DISC	NEGE	INTR
Raw Score:	0	1	4	14	10
T Score:	28	47	48	76	69
Response %:	100	100	100	100	100

The highest and lowest T scores possible on each scale are indicated by a "---"; MMPI-3 T scores are non-gendered.

AGGR   Aggressiveness
PSYC   Psychoticism
DISC   Disconstraint
NEGE   Negative Emotionality/Neuroticism
INTR   Introversion/Low Positive Emotionality

MMPI-3 T SCORES (BY DOMAIN)

PROTOCOL VALIDITY

Content Non-Responsiveness

0	51	51	60 T
CNS	CRIN	VRIN	TRIN

Over-Reporting

81	58		58	64	65
F	Fp		Fs	FBS	RBS

Under-Reporting

56	38
L	K

SUBSTANTIVE SCALES

Somatic/Cognitive Dysfunction

55	68	47	56	57
RC1	MLS	NUC	EAT	COG

Emotional Dysfunction

81					
EID					

77	65	69	78	72
RCd	SUI	HLP	SFD	NFC

65	69
RC2	INTR

78	68	72	69	73	51	91	76
RC7	STR	WRY	CMP	ARX	ANP	BRF	NEGE

Thought Dysfunction

53
THD

63
RC6

52
RC8

47
PSYC

Behavioral Dysfunction

46
BXD

50	70	48	58
RC4	FML	JCP	SUB

39	49	46	39	51
RC9	IMP	ACT	AGG	CYN

48
DISC

Interpersonal Functioning

37	27	28	58	71	77
SFI	DOM	AGGR	DSF	SAV	SHY

Note. This information is provided to facilitate interpretation following the recommended structure for MMPI-3 interpretation in Chapter 5 of the *MMPI-3 Manual for Administration, Scoring, and Interpretation*, which provides details in the text and an outline in Table 5-1.

NOTE:** The final pages of this report display any items that were skipped or unscorable as well as any endorsed items that are part of a critical responses or critical items list. These sections include both the item number and content. The final page of the report includes the test taker's item level responses to every test item. These pages are not displayed in this book in order to maintain test security; however, redacted sample reports are available on the Pearson Assessments' website.

CHAPTER 14

ASSESSING ADOLESCENTS: THE MMPI-A

ALTHOUGH THE ORIGINAL MMPI was intended for use with adults, it quickly became popular as an instrument for assessing adolescents (e.g., Hathaway & Monachesi, 1963). Results of a survey by Archer et al. (1991) indicated that the MMPI was the most widely used objective instrument for assessing adolescents. However, significant concerns were expressed about using the MMPI with adolescents because it had been developed with and normed on adults (e.g., Archer, 1987; Williams, 1986). Some of the items in the MMPI were irrelevant or inappropriate for many adolescents (e.g., worry about money and business, satisfactory sex life). Additionally, the MMPI had very few items dealing with experiences unique to adolescence (e.g., school, peer-group issues). Moreover, several studies demonstrated that the use of the adult MMPI norms overpathologized adolescent test takers (Archer, 1984, 1987; Klinge et al., 1978). Norms were developed for use with younger persons (Marks et al., 1974). Some studies indicated that the use of these adolescent norms seemed to underpathologize adolescents experiencing psychological difficulties assessed in clinical settings (Archer et al., 1986; Klinge & Strauss, 1976), whereas other research supported the notion that scores based on these adolescent norms more accurately portrayed the clinical status of adolescents in a variety of clinical settings (e.g., Wimbish, 1984).

Another concern in using the MMPI with adolescents was the source of interpretive statements about scores and configurations of scores of adolescents. Should only descriptors developed specifically for adolescents be used, or could those developed based on adult data also be used? Several studies suggested that the use of adult descriptors resulted in more accurate descriptions of adolescents (Ehrenworth & Archer,

1985; Lachar et al., 1976). Other studies (e.g., Wimbish, 1984) concluded that the most accurate inferences about adolescents came from the use of adolescent-based descriptors.

Based on these and other concerns, the committee responsible for developing the MMPI-2 decided to develop a separate instrument, the MMPI-A, specifically for use with adolescents between the ages of 14 and 18 (Butcher et al., 1992). Initial reviews of the MMPI-A were quite positive. Claiborn (1995) concluded that "the MMPI-A is an impressive inventory, sure to become a preeminent tool for assessing adolescent psychopathology. Its flaws are relatively minor, correctable, and enormously outweighed by the strength of the inventory" (p. 628). Lanyon (1995) observed that "in surveying the available test instruments for assessing psychopathology in adolescents, the MMPI-A would appear to have no serious competition" (p. 239).

The MMPI-A was also quickly adopted for use in psychological evaluations. Archer and Newsom (2000) surveyed 346 psychologists who worked with adolescent clients to determine their use of psychological tests. Results indicated that the MMPI-A was the fifth most frequently used test. Although the Wechsler Intelligence Scales, the Rorschach, the sentence completion tests, and the Thematic Apperception test were more frequently used, the MMPI-A was the most frequently used self-report instrument. A review conducted by Baum and colleagues (2009) identified 277 studies on MMPI-A scales conducted in a variety of settings, highlighting the research base supporting use of the MMPI-A.

WHO CAN TAKE THE MMPI-A?

As stated previously and in Chapter 9 of this book, the MMPI-A is intended for use with adolescents between the ages of 14 and 18. Because both the MMPI-2 and the MMPI-A can be used with 18-year-olds, clinicians must decide which version is most appropriate for each 18-year-old. Generally, it is advisable to use the MMPI-2 for mature 18-year-olds who are in college or otherwise living independently of their parents or caregivers. Use of the MMPI-A is recommended for 18-year-olds who have not adopted independent lifestyles.

These recommendations are based on research examining whether MMPI-A or MMPI-2 norms better represent the functioning of 18-year-olds. Shaevel and Archer (1996) conducted a study in which raw scores of 18-year-olds were plotted on both MMPI-A and MMPI-2 norms. The MMPI-A norms yielded higher T scores for the L and K scales and lower T scores for most of the Clinical scales. In some cases, the differences were as large as 15 T-score points. The authors recommended that both the MMPI-A and MMPI-2 norms be used for 18-year-olds in which no clear indicators in their life situations suggest that one or the other form should be used. Because no extratest data were available for these adolescents, we cannot know which set of scores (MMPI-A or MMPI-2) more accurately reflected their actual characteristics. However, Osberg and Poland (2002) also compared scores of 18-year-old students derived from MMPI-2 norms and MMPI-A norms. Consistent with the Shaevel and Archer study, scores based on the MMPI-2 norms yielded higher scores on most scales. Using information from a symptom checklist as a criterion measure, Osberg and Poland concluded that the MMPI-A norms better represented the psychological status of participants.

The MMPI-A manual (Butcher et al., 1992) indicates that adolescents younger than 14 years of age are likely to have difficulty responding meaningfully to the test items. Thus, the official MMPI-A norms do not include adolescents younger than 14. However, Archer (1992b) published norms for 13-year-olds and opined that many adolescents of this age should be able to complete the MMPI-A validly, so long as they can read and comprehend the test's items. The MMPI-A manual (Butcher et al., 1992) indicates that a seventh-grade reading level is required to understand items in the test.

DEVELOPMENT OF THE MMPI-A

Rationale

Because of concerns about using an adult instrument with adolescents, concurrently with the development of the MMPI-2, data were collected that later would be used to develop the MMPI-A, a version of the test designed specifically for use with adolescents (Butcher et al., 1992). Although there are marked similarities between the MMPI-A and MMPI-2, there also are some important differences.

Development of the MMPI-A Booklet

Development of the MMPI-A[1] began by creating an experimental form (Form TX) that contained the 550 items from the original MMPI with some items rewritten to eliminate awkward and archaic language as well as new items assessing treatment compliance, attitudes toward changing one's own behavior, treatment-related characteristics, and problems with alcohol and drugs. In addition, items were added dealing with adolescent-specific concerns (e.g., school behavior, attitudes toward teachers, peer-group influences, eating problems, and relationships with parents and other adults).

Based on several criteria, items from the experimental form were selected for inclusion in the MMPI-A, which consists of 478 items. Most of the items scored on the standard MMPI scales were included (see Table 14.1). Items were also included that were needed to score some of the more promising supplementary scales and newly developed adolescent Content scales. However, several items were eliminated because they were judged to be inappropriate for adolescents or had objectionable item content. Additionally, to keep the length of the MMPI-A as brief as possible, some items that were scored only on Scales 5 and 0 were eliminated.

Because of data indicating that the original MMPI's F (Infrequency) scale did not work well with adolescents, the scale was significantly modified. The problem had been that even adolescents in nonclinical samples who were known to be taking the test in a valid manner tended to produce high F scale scores. Careful analysis indicated that many of the standard F scale items were not endorsed as infrequently by

---

[1] Unless otherwise indicated, information concerning the development of the MMPI-A was abstracted from C. L. Williams et al. (1992) and Butcher et al. (1992).

TABLE 14.1 *Number of Items in the Basic Scales of the MMPI and MMPI-A*

Scale	Number of Items	
	MMPI	MMPI-A
L	15	14
F	64	66
K	30	30
1 (Hs)	33	32
2 (D)	60	57
3 (Hy)	60	60
4 (Pd)	50	49
5 (Mf)	60	44
6 (Pa)	40	40
7 (Pt)	48	48
8 (Sc)	78	77
9 (Ma)	46	46
0 (Si)	70	62

Note. Excerpted from *Minnesota Multiphasic Personality Inventory®-Adolescent (MMPI®-A) Manual for Administration, Scoring and Interpretation* by James N. Butcher, Carolyn L. Williams, John R. Graham, Robert P. Archer, Auke Tellegen, Yossef S. Ben-Porath, and Beverly Kaemmer. Copyright © 1992 by the Regents of the University of Minnesota. Reproduced by permission of the University of Minnesota Press. All rights reserved. "MMPI®" and "Minnesota Multiphasic Personality Inventory®" are registered trademarks of the Regents of the University of Minnesota.

adolescents as they were by adults. The version of the F scale scored on the MMPI-A includes 66 items that were endorsed in the keyed direction by no more than 20% of the boys and girls in the adolescent normative sample. Only 37 of the 64 original F scale items also are in the MMPI-A F scale. Further, the MMPI-A F scale was divided into two parts: F1 consists of items in the first part of the test booklet, and F2 consists of items in the latter part of the test booklet.

After the 478 items were selected for the MMPI-A booklet, several items were rewritten to correct wording carried over from the MMPI that was not appropriate for adolescents. Items were changed from past to present or present perfect tense. Several studies have demonstrated that the rewritten items are essentially equivalent to the original ones (Archer & Gordon, 1994; C. L. Williams et al., 1994).

MMPI-A Norms

There are 805 boys and 815 girls in the MMPI-A normative sample. They were solicited randomly from schools in seven states throughout the United States. They ranged in age from 14 to 18 years. Some preliminary data were collected for 13-year-olds, but because later analyses indicated that these younger persons had considerable difficulty completing the experimental form, they were eliminated from the sample (Butcher et al., 1992). Data presented in the MMPI-A manual (Butcher et al., 1992) indicate that the normative sample is approximately representative of the 1980 U.S. population in terms of race and ethnicity. Most of the adolescents in the normative sample were living with both of their biological parents, and their parents tended to have higher levels of education than was typical in the 1980 U.S. census data.

The MMPI-A manual (Butcher et al., 1992) does not present data separately for the racial and ethnic groups represented in the normative sample. However, using large samples of nonclinical adolescents from the MMPI-A normative sample and adolescents from outpatient and inpatient treatment facilities, Schinka et al. (1998) found that MMPI-A scores were not meaningfully influenced by age, sex, or ethnic identity.

Negy and colleagues (1997) reported data for 120 Mexican American adolescents in Texas. Their scores were remarkably similar to those of the MMPI-A normative sample. Negy et al. also reported that MMPI-A scores were related to socioeconomic status (SES) and level of acculturation, suggesting that Mexican American adolescents of lower SES or with lower levels of acculturation to the dominant U.S. culture could be disadvantaged on the test. However, they cautioned that it is also possible that adolescents of lower SES or acculturation experience more psychopathology than those of higher SES and greater levels of acculturation. Clearly, additional data are needed to address these issues.

Gumbiner (1998) reported MMPI-A data for very small groups of nonclinical Hispanic boys (*n* = 30) and girls (*n* = 17). The boys had higher mean scores than the boys in the MMPI-A normative sample. The girls' scores were at or slightly below average on most scales when compared to the girls in the MMPI-A normative sample. These results are difficult to interpret for several reasons. First, the samples are quite small. Second, the SES of the Hispanic adolescents was much lower than that of the individuals who comprise the normative sample. Third, no extratest data were presented to determine if the differences between scores of the Hispanic boys and the boys in the normative sample represent test bias or accurately reflect real differences in conceptually relevant characteristics.

Gómez et al. (2000) found that African- and Mexican American boys who were first-time criminal offenders did not differ significantly on MMPI-A scales and that mean scores for both groups were not much different from those of the MMPI-A normative sample. In a sample of adolescents who had been adjudicated delinquent, Cashel et al. (1998) found that Anglo-American boys scored significantly higher than African American and Hispanic boys on Scales 4 and 9. However, as has been the case with many studies of this kind, no extratest data were examined to determine if these MMPI-A score differences were related to differences in conceptually relevant extratest characteristics.

Using the standard Mexican version of the MMPI-A, Lucio et al. (2002) determined the extent to which the F, F1, and F2 scales and the F Minus K Index (F-K Index) were able to discriminate between nonclinical Mexican adolescents who were instructed to appear to have serious emotional problems from Mexican adolescents in outpatient mental health treatment who completed the MMPI-A with standard instructions. They found that the three F scales and the F-K Index all effectively differentiated the groups. Results, including optimal cut scores, were similar to previously reported data for adolescents from the U.S.

Very little is known about the use of the MMPI-A with adolescents of other racial or ethnic backgrounds. The study by Schinka et al. (1998) discussed earlier suggested that racial and ethnic background did not have a meaningful effect on MMPI-A scores. However, these authors could find no published research concerning the use of the English-Language MMPI-A with persons of Asian American or Native American backgrounds.

Historically, MMPI adolescent norms differed by age levels. However, for the MMPI-A, only one set of norms is presented for boys and another for girls. This is because data analyses conducted during the test's development indicated that there were only minor differences between age groups within the MMPI-A normative sample. To maintain consistency with the MMPI-2, raw scores on the eight Clinical scales (1, 2, 3, 4, 6, 7, 8, 9), the Content and Content Component scales, and the Personality Psychopathology Five (PSY-5) scales are transformed to Uniform T (UT) scores using the same procedures developed for the MMPI-2. The rationale for the use of UT scores and the procedures used to develop them are discussed in the MMPI-A manual (Butcher et al., 1992) and were described in Chapter 2 of this book. Scores on all other scales are transformed to linear T scores.

Compared with scores based on the adolescent norms Marks et al. (1974) collected for the MMPI, the MMPI-A norms yield significantly lower T scores for most of the Clinical scales. Janus et al. (1996) found that some of these differences in scores for adolescent psychiatric patients were greater than the five T-score point difference often used as a criterion for clinical meaningfulness. However, Janus et al. determined that interpretive descriptions based on code types resulting from the norms of Marks et al. and MMPI-A norms were not differentially accurate (as determined by members of the treatment staff).

That MMPI-A T scores are generally lower than those based on the MMPI adolescent norms led the developers of the MMPI-A (Butcher et al., 1992) to recommend that MMPI-A T scores of 65 or greater on the Clinical scales be considered clinically significant but that T scores between 60 and 64 also be interpreted as high scores. Greater confidence should be placed in inferences resulting from T scores that are greater than 65.

A major concern among users of the MMPI-A has been that adolescents with significant problems often do not have scores high enough to reflect those problems. For example, Hilts and Moore (2003) reported that 30% of male and 25% of female adolescents evaluated in a psychiatric inpatient setting produced valid MMPI-A protocols with no Clinical scales with T scores greater than 60. Several possible explanations for the significant number of adolescents in clinical settings having within-normal-limits (WNL) protocols have been offered. One possibility is that the absence of a K correction, such as that used with the MMPI-2, could lead to lower scores on the Clinical scales for adolescents who approached the test defensively. However, Alperin et al. (1996) demonstrated that using a K correction did not significantly reduce the number of WNL protocols among adolescent psychiatric patients. Another possibility is that adolescents in the MMPI-A normative sample answered items in the scored direction more often than adults in the MMPI-2 normative sample. Archer et al. (2001) found that a substantial number of MMPI-A items did not differentiate between adolescents in the normative sample and adolescents in clinical settings. This would lead to raw scores on MMPI-A scales having lower T-score equivalents. Consistent with this possibility is the fact that approximately 12% of the adolescents in the MMPI-A normative sample indicated that they had been referred to a therapist or counselor within 6 months of completing the MMPI-A. Hand et al. (2007) constructed revised MMPI-A norms by eliminating the adolescents in the normative sample who indicated that they had been referred to a counselor or therapist in the 6 months prior to completing the MMPI-A. Using the revised norms only slightly reduced the frequency of WNL protocols in several clinical settings. These findings suggest that perhaps some of the MMPI-A scales could be improved by eliminating the nondiscriminating items. In summary, the issue of lower scores among adolescents evaluated in clinical settings is a complex one that will require more research to try to resolve. In the meantime, clinicians using the MMPI-A should be cautious about concluding that adolescents with WNL protocols in clinical settings are not experiencing significant psychopathology.

ADMINISTRATION AND SCORING

The MMPI-A can be administered using either computer software available from the test's distributor, Pearson Assessments, or a pencil/paper version consisting of a printed booklet and a separate answer sheet. A standardized audio version of the test is also available from Pearson for test takers who have difficulties that preclude completing either the pencil/paper or computerized administrations. Although no published data are available concerning the equivalence of scores resulting from booklet, audio, or computer administration of the MMPI-A, two doctoral dissertations (Carlson, 2001; Hays, 2003) reported research indicating that pencil/paper and computer-administered versions of the MMPI-A yielded equivalent scores.

Standard English and Spanish versions of the test are available for pencil/paper, computerized, and audio formats from the test's distributor, Pearson Assessments. However, the MMPI-A has been translated into several other languages, including French, Italian, and Chinese. A full listing of approved translations of the MMPI-A and contact information for obtaining access to translated versions of the instrument are available at the University of Minnesota Press–Test Division's website (https://www.upress.umn.edu/test-division/translations-permissions/available-translations).

All of the considerations about administration of the MMPI-2, which were detailed in Chapter 2 of this book, also apply to the MMPI-A. In addition, it should be recognized that some adolescents may be too easily distracted, hyperactive, oppositional, or impulsive to complete the 478 items in a single session. When such problems are encountered, close supervision, frequent breaks, and praise and encouragement from the person administering the test may be helpful.

Once the MMPI-A has been administered, there are several scoring options available. Users should determine the scoring method to be used before administering the test because different answer sheets are needed for the various options. Hand scoring can be accomplished using templates available from the test distributor. Completed answer sheets can be mailed to Pearson Assessments for scoring. Computerized scoring can be completed using one of two software programs available from the test distributor. These software programs can produce an Extended Score Report that includes scores for all the MMPI-A scales and subscales and profiles for some of them. A computerized narrative Interpretive Report (The Minnesota Report: Adolescent Interpretive System) also is available.

MMPI-A SCALES AND THEIR PSYCHOMETRIC CHARACTERISTICS

When the MMPI-A was published in 1992, it was comprised of scales assessing response styles and substantive constructs carried over from the MMPI, as well as several new scales intended to help refine a test-user's understanding of an adolescent test taker's social, emotional, and behavioral functioning. Subsequently, additional scales were developed and added to the standard scoring. These scale sets include the Content Component scales developed by Sherwood et al. (1997) and the PSY-5 scales developed by McNulty, Harkness, et al. (1997). Forbey and Ben-Porath (1998) also developed a set of critical items for the MMPI-A.

In the next section of this chapter, descriptions of all MMPI-A scales, as well as summaries of their psychometric properties, will be provided. There are several ways in which the validity of the MMPI-A substantive scales can be assessed. To the extent that scores and configurations of scores on the MMPI-A are congruent with corresponding scores on the MMPI, interpretive information that has accumulated for the MMPI can be generalized to the MMPI-A. In addition, it is important to demonstrate that the MMPI-A scales have relevant external correlates. When possible, we will include information on both aspects of validity in our descriptions. Nonetheless, given this chapter is intended to serve as an introduction to the instrument, our descriptions will necessarily be brief. For readers interested in more information about MMPI-A scales, several excellent reference books are available (Archer, 2017; Archer & Krishnamurthy, 2002; Butcher & Williams, 2000).

MMPI-A Validity Scales

Table 14.2 provides the names and abbreviations for Validity scales scored on the MMPI-A. Non-content-based invalid responding is assessed by several scales. Cannot Say (?), originally used on the MMPI, was maintained on the MMPI-A as an index of nonresponding. Two additional Validity scales, the Variable Response Inconsistency Scale (VRIN) and the True Response Inconsistency Scale (TRIN), were developed for the MMPI-A. These scales are similar in concept to scales scored on the MMPI-2. The VRIN scale assesses inconsistent responding and is useful in identifying random protocols. The TRIN scale assesses true and false response biases. Content-based invalid

TABLE 14.2 *MMPI-A Validity Scales*

Scale	Abbreviation
Non-Content-Based Invalid Responding	
Cannot Say	?
Variable Response Inconsistency	VRIN
True Response Inconsistency	TRIN
Content Based Invalid Responding - Underreporting	
Lie	L
Defensiveness	K
Content Based Invalid Responding - Overreporting	
Infrequency	F
F1 Scale	F1
F2 Scale	F2

Note. Excerpted from *Minnesota Multiphasic Personality Inventory®-Adolescent (MMPI®-A) Manual for Administration, Scoring and Interpretation* by James N. Butcher, Carolyn L. Williams, John R. Graham, Robert P. Archer, Auke Tellegen, Yossef S. Ben-Porath, and Beverly Kaemmer. Copyright © 1992 by the Regents of the University of Minnesota. Reproduced by permission of the University of Minnesota Press. All rights reserved. "MMPI®" and "Minnesota Multiphasic Personality Inventory®" are registered trademarks of the Regents of the University of Minnesota.

responding is assessed by the L (Lie), F, and K (Defensiveness) scales, which were scored on the original MMPI and maintained in the MMPI-A. However, as described earlier, there were some significant changes made to the F scale during development of the instrument, including development of two additional scales assessing infrequent responding occurring in the first and second half of the test (i.e., F1 and F2). The F, F1, and F2 scales index overreporting. Underreporting response styles are captured by scores on L and K. Because the Validity scales of the MMPI-A are very similar to those of the MMPI-2, we would expect them to function similarly. Detailed information about adult versions of the Validity scales was provided in Chapter 3.

Non-Content-Based Invalid Responding

The VRIN scale was designed to detect random responding, one type of non-content-based invalid responding. The MMPI-A manual (Butcher et al., 1992) recommended that T scores of 75 or higher should raise concerns about random responding. Several studies have demonstrated the utility of the VRIN scale in identifying random responding (e.g., Archer & Elkins, 1999; Baer et al., 1997, 1999; Pinsoneault, 2005). However, optimal T-score cutoffs ranging from T > 51 to T > 90 have been reported. Obviously, higher cutoff scores will result in fewer false positive identifications but at the cost of more false negative identifications.

As with the MMPI-2, the TRIN scale was added to the MMPI-A during the development process and was designed to identify test takers who respond indiscriminately true or false to items without consideration of item content. The MMPI-A manual (Butcher et al., 1992) recommended that TRIN T scores equal to or higher than 75 suggest that test takers responded inconsistently to the items by answering true or false indiscriminately without consideration of item content. Archer (2017) recommended that TRIN scale T scores between 70 and 79 indicate marginal levels of response inconsistency, whereas TRIN T scores equal to or greater than 80 indicate unacceptable levels of response inconsistency. Handel et al. (2006) reported data leading them to conclude that a TRIN scale T-score cutoff of 65 was optimal in situations where the base rate of indiscriminate true or false responding is relatively low. Obviously, protocols with such high TRIN scale scores should not be interpreted.

Content-Based Invalid Responding—Overreporting

Compared with adults, relatively little research has been conducted concerning adolescents overreporting on the MMPI-A. Stein et al. (1995) published the first overreporting study with the MMPI-A. These investigators compared nonclinical adolescents who took the MMPI-A with standard instructions, nonclinical adolescents who were instructed to overreport, and adolescent psychiatric patients who took the test with standard instructions. They found that although most scales were somewhat lower than in adult overreporting studies, the pattern of scores for the adolescents who were overreporting was remarkably similar to what had previously been reported for adults who were overreporting. Although the F, Fl, and F2 scales and the F-K Index all discriminated well between adolescents who were overreporting and both nonclinical and clinical adolescents who took the test with standard instructions, the F scale was the best indicator of overreporting. An F scale raw score of 23 (T = 77 for boys and T = 89 for girls) was most effective in discriminating boys and girls who were overreporting from both boys and girls who completed the test with standard instructions in nonclinical and clinical settings.

In a study of overreporting among adolescents involved with the criminal justice system, Rogers et al. (1996) found that F, Fl, and F2 all were effective in identifying adolescents who were overreporting and that the F-K Index (> 20) yielded the best positive and negative predictive powers. These investigators also found that a separate instrument, the Structured Interview of Reported Symptoms (SIRS; Rogers, 1992) also was quite effective in identifying the adolescents who were overreporting. The combined use of the MMPI-A validity indicators and SIRS scores was more effective in identifying overreporting than either of the individual measures.

In summary, it would appear that when adolescents approach the MMPI-A with the intention of feigning serious psychopathology, they have very high F, Fl, and F2 scores and below average K scores. As with adults, these adolescents also have very high scores on most of the Clinical scales. The optimal score or index for identifying overreporting will likely differ from setting to setting and must be established according to the kinds of classification errors that one wants to minimize. However, whenever there are extremely high scores on the F scale and random and all-true or all-false responding have been ruled out by referring to the VRIN and TRIN scales, the possibility of overreporting should be considered seriously.

Content-Based Invalid Responding—Underreporting

To date, studies examining underreporting on the MMPI-A have been limited in number. Stein and Graham (1999) determined how well the MMPI-A Validity scales could detect underreporting among adolescents in a correctional/clinical inpatient setting. Adolescents who underreported tended to report fewer symptoms and problems, resulting in higher scores on scales L and K and lower scores on the Clinical scales. The underreporting pattern was similar to those reported in adult studies. The L scale seemed to work well for both boys and girls. Approximately 85% of girls from the correctional setting who were instructed to underreport and approximately 87% of girls in the comparison group who took the test with standard instructions were correctly identified by the L scale. Corresponding data for the boys were 77% and 72% in the correctional and comparison groups, respectively. However, because of the relatively small sample size in Stein and Graham's (1999) study, optimal cutoff scores for the various MMPI-A Validity scales could not be firmly established.

Baer et al. (1998) utilized community and clinical samples and instructed adolescents to complete the MMPI-A with standard instructions or with instructions to try to demonstrate excellent psychological adjustment. They also found that the L scale was the most effective way to identify underreporting.

MMPI-A Clinical Scales

The 10 standard Clinical scales of the MMPI were maintained in the MMPI-A. Although some of the scales have several fewer items than the original ones (see Table 14.1) and include some slightly rewritten items, the Clinical scales of MMPI-A are essentially the same as the corresponding scales of the MMPI and the MMPI-2. Consistent with traditional use of the MMPI with adolescents, none of the MMPI-A Clinical scales are K corrected. Chapter 4 of this book provides detailed information about the Clinical scales.

Table 14.3 reports internal-consistency and short-term, temporal-stability coefficients for the Clinical scales of the MMPI-A for boys and girls in the normative sample (Butcher et al., 1992) and longer-term temporal stability for a small group of nonclinical adolescents (Stein et al., 1998). The internal-consistency coefficients are slightly lower than the corresponding values for the MMPI-2, but most of the scales have relatively good internal consistency, especially considering that no efforts were made to ensure internal consistency when the scales were originally developed. As would be expected, the longer-term temporal stability (1 year) of the scales was somewhat lower than the shorter-term temporal stability (1 week). The temporal stability of most scales is slightly lower than for the MMPI-2. This is in keeping with generally lower stability of personality test scores for adolescents than for adults. As is the case with the MMPI-2, Scale 6 (Paranoia) has the lowest test–retest reliability coefficient of any of the Clinical scales.

The MMPI-A manual (Butcher et al., 1992) reported data concerning congruence between scores based on the MMPI-A and those based on the MMPI using the adolescent norms of Marks et al. (1974). In the MMPI-A normative sample, 95.1% of the boys and 87.8% of the girls had the same highest Clinical scale elevation. Corresponding rates for the clinical sample were 95.4% and 94.4%, respectively.

TABLE 14.3 *Internal Consistency and Temporal Stability of MMPI-A Clinical Scales*

| | Internal Consistency | | Temporal Stability | |
| | | | Short Term[a] | Long Term[b] |
Scale	Boys (n = 805)	Girls (n = 815)	Boy & Girls (n = 154)	Boy & Girls (n = 81)
1 (Hs)	0.78	0.79	0.79	0.63
2 (D)	0.65	0.66	0.78	0.66
3 (Hy)	0.63	0.55	0.70	0.50
4 (Pd)	0.63	0.68	0.80	0.68
5 (Mf)	0.43	0.40	0.82	0.59
6 (Pa)	0.57	0.59	0.65	0.51
7 (Pt)	0.84	0.86	0.83	0.69
8 (Sc)	0.88	0.89	0.83	0.54
9 (Ma)	0.61	0.61	0.70	0.54
0 (Si)	0.79	0.80	0.84	0.75

Note. Source for Internal Consistency and Short-Term Stability Data: Excerpted (Tables 13 and 14) from *Minnesota Multiphasic Personality Inventory®-Adolescent (MMPI®-A): Manual for Administration, Scoring, and Interpretation* by James N. Butcher, Carolyn L. Williams, John R. Graham, Robert P. Archer, Auke Tellegen, Yossef S. Ben-Porath, and Beverly Kaemmer. Copyright © 1992 by the Regents of the University of Minnesota. Reproduced by permission of the University of Minnesota Press. All rights reserved. "MMPI®" and "Minnesota Multiphasic Personality Inventory®" are registered trademarks of the Regents of the University of Minnesota. Source for Long-Term Stability Data: Stein, L. A. R., McClinton, B. K., Graham, J. R. (1998). Long-term stability of MMPI-A scales. *Journal of Personality Assessment, 70*, 103–108. Copyright © 1998, Lawrence Erlbaum Associates, Inc. Reproduced by permission.

[a] 1-week, test–retest interval.
[b] 1-year, test–retest interval.

However, although these data suggest the configuration of scores is quite similar across the two versions of the test, average T scores are somewhat different. For most scales, T scores on the MMPI-A are about 5 points lower than on the MMPI scored with adolescent norms. For boys, Scale 4 (Psychopathic Deviate) is about 10 T-score points lower on the MMPI-A; and for girls, Scale 9 (Hypomania) is about 10 T-score points lower on the MMPI-A. For both boys and girls, scores on Scale 0 (Social Introversion) are about the same for the two versions of the test.

There are several possible reasons for these normative differences. It may be that contemporary adolescents endorse more items in the scored direction on most scales because they are experiencing higher levels of psychopathology or are more likely to admit to experiencing psychological difficulties. However, it may also be that they are endorsing more items in the scored direction because current test instructions encourage test takers to answer all the items if they possibly can. When the earlier MMPI normative data were collected, test takers were not given as much encouragement to answer all the items, and they typically omitted more items than contemporary adolescents do. When test takers answer more items, they are likely to endorse some of them in the scored direction. Nonetheless, because of the considerable congruence between the MMPI and MMPI-A, when MMPI-A results are being interpreted, it is appropriate to use much of the information that has been reported for the MMPI with adolescents (e.g., Archer, 1992b; Archer et al., 1988; Gallucci, 1994; Hathaway & Monachesi, 1963; Marks et al., 1974; C. L. Williams & Butcher, 1989a, 1989b; Wrobel & Lachar, 1992). This information has been summarized by Archer (2017).

As mentioned earlier, it also is important to directly demonstrate the validity of the MMPI-A scales. The MMPI-A manual (Butcher et al., 1992) reports some external correlates for scores for adolescents in nonclinical and clinical settings. These data suggest there are reliable correlates of the MMPI-A scales, and the correlates are remarkably similar to those previously published for the MMPI scales. Pena et al. (1996) found that boys who had been adjudicated delinquent scored higher than boys in the MMPI-A normative sample on relevant Clinical scales. Cashel et al. (1998) identified meaningful correlates for most of the MMPI-A Clinical scales in a correctional setting. Similarly, Veltri et al. (2009) identified conceptually relevant correlates for most MMPI-A Clinical scales in samples from inpatient psychiatric and forensic settings. Handel and colleagues (2011) examined associations of the Clinical scales with broadband parent- and self-report measures of functioning in a large sample of boys and girls evaluated as part of forensic proceedings prior to the court's disposition. They demonstrated the MMPI-A Clinical scales were generally associated with the hypothesized criteria, though there were some differences in the magnitudes of correlations for girls compared to boys.

MMPI-A Clinical Scale Code Types

As when the MMPI was used with adults, scores on the Clinical scales in adolescents reflect heterogeneous constructs; and a code-type approach was adopted in an effort to provide more nuanced inferences about a test taker. Code types and their identification and interpretation were discussed in detail in Chapter 5.

The MMPI-A manual (Butcher et al., 1992) reported data concerning congruence between code types based on the MMPI-A scores and code types based on the MMPI using the adolescent norms of Marks et al. (1974). When code types are well defined (at least 5 T-score points between the lowest scale in the code type and the next highest scale), code types from the two versions of the test are quite congruent. In the normative sample, 95.2% of the boys and 81.8% of the girls had the same 2-point code type when the definition criterion of 5 T-score points was used. The corresponding rates for the clinical boys and girls were 95.0% and 91.0%, respectively. Clearly, profile configurations are quite similar for the MMPI and the MMPI-A.

Despite these similarities, the use of code-type interpretation with the MMPI-A has historically been quite controversial. This is because, although early work of Marks et al. (1974) suggested that MMPI code types of adolescents could be used to make inferences about them, later research offered only limited support for the use of code types with adolescents (Ehrenworth & Archer, 1985; C. L. Williams & Butcher, 1989a). Using a methodology similar to that of Ehrenworth and Archer, Janus et al. (1996) found that code-type descriptions based on MMPI-A norms were slightly more accurate than code-type descriptions in Ehrenworth and Archer's MMPI study.

In considering whether to adopt a code-type approach to interpretation of the MMPI-A results, it is important to also consider the question of extratest correlates of code types based on MMPI-A scales and norms. Empirical data on this question is largely lacking. However, Archer (2017) made a convincing argument that the congruence of Clinical scales of the MMPI and MMPI-A justifies using code-type descriptors based on MMPI research with adults and adolescents to generate inferences based on MMPI-A code types. Drawing on such descriptors, he provided inferences for the most frequently occurring code types among adolescents. Consideration of all these code types is beyond the scope of this chapter. Clinicians who want to use MMPI-A code types as sources of inferences should consult Archer's (2017) book. As discussed in Chapter 5 of this book, one should have more confidence on inferences based on code types that are defined and elevated.

MMPI-A Harris–Lingoes Subscales

The Harris–Lingoes subscales were discussed in some detail in Chapter 6 of this book. These scales, in slightly modified form, are available in the MMPI-A. Two of the subscales have one less item in the MMPI-A than in the MMPI-2, and some of the items have been slightly rewritten. However, these changes are so minor that the scales are comparable across the two tests.

As discussed in Chapter 6 of this book, the Harris–Lingoes subscales can be useful in understanding why test takers obtain high scores on the Clinical scales. Analysis of subscale scores can help to determine which of a variety of descriptors for elevated Clinical scales should be emphasized for a particular test taker. High scores (T ≥ 65) on the Harris–Lingoes subscales should be interpreted only when the T score on the parent Clinical scale is greater than 60.

Not much information is available concerning correlates of the Harris–Lingoes subscales for adolescents. Gallucci (1994) found that the Need for Affection (Hy2), Inhibition of Aggression (Hy5), and Naivete (Pa3) subscales functioned as inhibitory scales, whereas the Amorality (Ma1) and Psychomotor Acceleration (Ma2) subscales functioned as excitatory scales. Given the lack of research informing interpretation of these scales, we suggest a content-based approach to interpreting these scales. Interpretive inferences for the Harris–Lingoes subscales were presented in Chapter 6 of this book. As with the MMPI-2, the Harris–Lingoes subscales of the MMPI-A probably are too short and unreliable to be used as independent scales on which to base interpretation. Likewise, because little is known about the meaning of below-average scores on the Harris–Lingoes subscales, low scores should not be interpreted.

MMPI-A Scale 0 Subscales

The subscales for Scale 0 that were described in Chapter 6 of this book also are available for the MMPI-A. These subscales have the same number of items as for the MMPI-2. As with the Harris–Lingoes subscales, analysis of elevated scores (T ≥ 65) on these subscales can help clinicians understand why adolescent test takers obtained elevated scores on Scale 0. Like the Harris–Lingoes subscales, these subscales should not be used as independent scales for clinical interpretation, and low scores on the subscales should not be interpreted. High scores (T $\geq$ 65) on these subscales should be interpreted only when the T score on Scale 0 is greater than 60.

MMPI-A Supplementary Scales

Several scales that had been developed from the MMPI item pool were carried over to the MMPI-A, and several new scales were developed using the new MMPI-A item pool. These scales and their psychometric properties are described briefly below.

MacAndrew Alcoholism Scale–Revised (MAC-R)

The MacAndrew Alcoholism scale (MAC; MacAndrew, 1965) was developed using items from the original MMPI and became widely used as a screen for substance use problems. A revised version of the scale (MAC-R), with four items added to replace those deleted because of objectionable content, was included in the MMPI-2. The MMPI-A includes the revised version of the scale from the MMPI-2 minus one item, which has been replaced on the MMPI-A by another. Thus, the MAC-R scale of the MMPI-A has 49 items.

Weed et al. (1994) found that the MAC-R scale of the MMPI-A discriminated well between adolescents with substance-related difficulties and adolescents in the MMPI-A normative sample but less well between adolescents with substance-related and other mental health difficulties. However, Archer et al. (2003) found that the MAC-R scale was effective in differentiating between adolescents with comorbid substance use and other psychiatric disorders and adolescents with psychiatric disorders but not comorbid substance use disorders.

Gallucci (1997a) found that adolescents with substance use problems who scored higher on the MAC-R scale of the MMPI-A received higher therapist ratings on a scale that assessed the frequency of substance misuse behaviors. Adolescents in Gallucci's study who scored higher on the MAC-R also were rated by therapists as less likely to anticipate the consequences of their behavior and more likely to be sensation seeking and aggressive. Gallucci (1997b) reported that adolescents with substance use problems who scored higher on the MAC-R scale of the MMPI-A were more likely than those with lower scorers on this scale to be rated by treatment staff as showing behavioral undercontrol. Veltri et al. (2009) found that MAC-R scores were positively correlated with histories of substance use problems in both inpatient psychiatric and forensic samples. In a sample of adolescents undergoing predisposition forensic evaluations, Handel et al. (2011) demonstrated scores on this scale are associated with external criteria with items related to substance misuse, but less strongly than other MMPI-A indicators of substance-related difficulties such as the Alcohol/Drug Problem Acknowledgment (ACK) and Alcohol/Drug Problem Proneness (PRO) scales.

Although research concerning optimal cut scores for the MAC-R for adolescents is limited, it is our recommendation that the same cut scores recommended for adults in Chapter 8 of this book be used for adolescents. Raw scores greater than 27 suggest a strong possibility of substance use problems, and additional information about substance use should be obtained. Raw scores of 23 or lower suggest that substance use problems are not likely. Raw scores between 24 and 27 are indeterminate concerning substance use.

Alcohol/Drug Problem Acknowledgement (ACK) Scale

The ACK scale is a face-valid scale consisting primarily of items in which adolescents admit to using alcohol or other drugs and having some of the symptoms and problems associated with such use (Weed et al., 1994). Weed et al. reported that adolescents in treatment for substance-related difficulties scored higher on the ACK scale than adolescents in the MMPI-A normative sample and adolescent psychiatric patients who were not in treatment for substance use. However, this study did not report classification accuracies using the ACK scale.

Gallucci (1997a) reported that adolescents with substance-related difficulties who scored higher on the ACK scale were rated by therapists as more frequently engaging in substance use behaviors and as not anticipating the consequences of their behavior. Gallucci (1997b) found that adolescents with substance-related problems who scored higher on the ACK scale were rated by treatment staff as more likely to show behavioral undercontrol. Veltri et al. (2009) found that ACK scores were positively correlated with histories of substance use problems in both inpatient psychiatric and forensic samples. In a sample of adolescents undergoing predisposition forensic evaluations, Handel et al. (2011) demonstrated scores on this scale are associated with external criteria with items related to substance misuse.

Because of the obvious nature of the items in the ACK scale, adolescents who are denying alcohol or drug problems can easily avoid detection. However, elevated scores on the ACK scale ($T \geq 60$) indicate that adolescents are readily admitting to significant alcohol or other drug problems (Butcher et al., 1992).

Alcohol/Drug Problem Proneness (PRO) Scale

The PRO scale is an empirically derived scale developed to assess the likelihood of alcohol or other drug problems in adolescents (Weed et al., 1994). Items in the scale differentiated adolescent boys and girls in alcohol/drug treatment from adolescent boys and girls who were in treatment for psychological problems other than alcohol/drug use. The items in the scale deal with peer-group influence, sensation seeking, rule violation, negative attitudes toward achievement, problems with parents, and poor judgment (Butcher et al., 1992). Adolescents in treatment for substance use problems scored significantly higher on the PRO scale than adolescents in the MMPI-A normative sample and adolescent psychiatric patients who were not in substance use treatment programs.

Gallucci (1997a) reported that adolescents with substance-related difficulties who scored higher on the PRO scale were rated higher by therapists on a scale that assessed frequency of substance misuse behaviors. Higher scorers on the PRO scale also were rated as less likely to anticipate the consequences of their behavior and more likely to be impulsive and aggressive. Gallucci (1997b) also reported that adolescents with substance-related difficulties who scored higher on the PRO scale were rated by therapists as more likely to show behavioral undercontrol. Veltri et al. (2009) found that PRO scores were positively correlated with histories of substance-use problems in both inpatient psychiatric and forensic samples.

The MMPI-A manual (Butcher et al., 1992) suggests that T scores equal to or greater than 60 indicate a potential for developing alcohol or drug problems. However, several issues limit the confidence that we can have in the PRO scale at this time. First, no data have yet been published concerning the classification accuracy that can be achieved with this scale. Second, the label of the scale may not be appropriate. Using "proneness" in the label suggests that this scale may be assessing a vulnerability to substance-related disorders that may or may not yet have been realized. To date, all the data concerning this scale address current misuse and related difficulties, and no data have yet been published concerning potential for future substance use or related difficulties. Obviously, it should not be concluded from test data alone that an adolescent has problems with alcohol or other drugs. Third, discriminant validity of PRO scores may be limited. Handel et al. (2011) demonstrated scores on this scale are associated with scales containing items related to substance misuse, but also externalizing problems broadly, in their sample of adolescents undergoing a predisposition forensic evaluation. Given these limitations, we suggest elevated scores on this scale of the MMPI-A should be viewed as an indicator that more information should be obtained. Although preliminary data suggest that this may be a useful scale, more research is needed before we can determine whether it works as well as, or perhaps better than, the more familiar MAC-R in identifying alcohol or other drug problems in adolescents.

Immaturity (IMM) Scale

The IMM scale was developed using items in the MMPI-A item pool (Archer et al., 1992). The scale is thought to assess the degree to which adolescents report behaviors, attitudes, and perceptions of self and others that reflect immaturity in terms of interpersonal style, cognitive complexity, self-awareness, judgment, and impulse control (Butcher et al., 1992). Tentative items for the scale were identified by correlating MMPI-A items with scores from a sentence completion test of ego maturation. The items were then rated by judges concerning their relevance to the construct of ego maturation. The scale was refined by deleting items that did not add to its internal consistency and by adding other items from the MMPI-A item pool that demonstrated both a conceptual and statistical relationship to the immaturity construct.

Preliminary data indicated that higher IMM scale scores were associated with a higher incidence of academic difficulties and with disobedient, defiant, and antisocial behaviors (Butcher et al., 1992). Also, scores were inversely related to chronological age. Imhof and Archer (1997) studied the IMM scale in a relatively small sample of adolescents in residential psychiatric treatment programs. Unlike results of earlier studies, IMM scale scores were not related to chronological age but were negatively correlated with reading ability. Comparing IMM scale scores to other self-report scales, the authors concluded that higher IMM scale scorers can be expected to have a more limited capacity to think in abstract terms, to be less likely to identify with the values and beliefs of their social group, to have less capacity to perceive the world from the viewpoint of others, and to exhibit lower levels of moral development.

Zinn et al. (1999) found that IMM scale scores of college students were negatively related to level of ego development as measured by the Washington University Sentence Completion Test. Veltri et al. (2009) found very few external correlates of the IMM scale in their adolescent psychiatric and forensic samples. However, IMM scores were significantly correlated with histories of self-harm behaviors in their psychiatric sample and with histories of angry behavior in their forensic sample.

Anxiety (A) Scale

The A scale was developed to assess the most important dimension that emerged when the Validity and Clinical scales of the MMPI were factor analyzed (Welsh, 1956). The MMPI-A version of this scale has 35 of the 39 items scored on the original MMPI A scale. Archer et al. (1989) found correlate patterns for the MMPI-A version of the A scale consistent with those derived from studies of adults using the original version of the scale developed for the MMPI. Specifically, they demonstrated adolescents scoring high on the A scale were likely to be anxious, fearful, guilt-prone, and self-critical. Similar results were demonstrated for boys and girls evaluated in psychiatric and forensic contexts by Veltri et al. (2009) and in forensic contexts by Handel et al. (2011)

Repression (R) Scale

The R scale was developed to assess a second dimension that emerged when the Validity and Clinical scales of the MMPI were factor analyzed (Welsh, 1956). The MMPI-A version of this scale has 33 of the 40 items scored on the original MMPI R scale. Archer et al. (1989) reported that adolescents who scored high on the MMPI-A R scale were described as overcontrolled, inhibited, and less spontaneous than other adolescents—suggesting the adolescent version of R measures a construct similar to that of its adult counterpart.

MMPI–A Content Scales

Using procedures similar to those applied in developing the Content scales for the MMPI-2 (described in Chapter 6), C. L. Williams et al.(1992) developed a set of 15 scales to assess the basic content dimensions represented in the MMPI-A item pool. The authors rationally identified tentative items for scales, and statistical procedures were used to refine the scales. Table 14.4 lists the MMPI-A Content scales and their internal-consistency and test–retest reliability coefficients. Some of the scales are slightly modified versions of scales in the MMPI-2 (e.g., Anxiety, Depression, and Health Concerns), whereas others were developed to assess problems and concerns specific to adolescents (e.g., Conduct Problems, School Problems, and Low Aspirations).

Examination of the data in Table 14.4 indicates the internal consistencies of the MMPI-A Content scales are adequate but somewhat lower than for the corresponding MMPI-2 Content scales. As would be expected, the temporal stability over a longer time period (1 year) is somewhat lower than for a shorter time period (1 week). The temporal stability of the MMPI-A Content scales is somewhat lower than for corresponding MMPI-2 scales but comparable to that usually reported for adolescent personality scales.

In an initial effort to demonstrate the validity of the MMPI-A Content scales, C. L. Williams et al. (1992) reported extratest correlates for these scales using data from the MMPI-A normative sample and from adolescents in several different clinical settings. Sources of extratest data included adolescent self-reports, parent ratings,

TABLE 14.4 *Internal Consistency and Temporal Stability of the MMPI–A Content Scales*

| Scales | Internal Consistency | | | | Temporal Stability | |
| | Clinical Sample | | Normative Sample | | Short term[a] | Long term[b] |
	Boys (n=420)	Girls (n=293)	Boys (n=805)	Girls (n=815)	Boys & Girls (n=154)	Boys & Girls (n=81)
Anxiety (A-anx)	0.80	0.86	0.76	0.80	0.81	0.65
Obsessiveness (A-obs)	0.76	0.80	0.72	0.72	0.70	0.50
Depression (A-dep)	0.83	0.89	0.80	0.83	0.82	0.66
Health Concerns (A-hea)	0.78	0.85	0.81	0.82	0.76	0.53
Bizarre Mentation (A-biz)	0.73	0.76	0.75	0.75	0.68	0.59
Anger (A-ang)	0.75	0.79	0.69	0.66	0.72	0.45
Cynicism (A-cyn)	0.78	0.83	0.79	0.81	0.73	0.51
Alienation (A-aln)	0.72	0.75	0.69	0.75	0.62	0.53
Conduct Problems (A-con)	0.74	0.79	0.72	72	0.62	0.55
Low Self-Esteem (A-lse)	0.73	0.80	0.71	0.75	0.78	0.58
Low Aspirations (A-las)	0.63	0.63	0.55	0.59	0.66	0.61
Social Discomfort (A-sod)	0.78	0.85	0.77	0.78	0.76	0.68
Family Problems (A-fam)	0.82	0.82	0.81	0.82	0.82	0.51
School Problems (A-sch)	0.70	0.74	0.69	0.69	0.64	0.73
Negative Treatment Indicators (A-trt)	0.77	0.80	0.72	0.75	0.68	0.40

Note. Source for Internal Consistency and Short-Term Stability Data: Excerpted (Tables 21 & 22) from *Minnesota Multiphasic Personality Inventory®–Adolescent (MMPI®-A): Manual for Administration, Scoring and Interpretation* by James N. Butcher, Carolyn L. Williams, John R. Graham, Robert P. Archer, Auke Tellegen, Yossef S. Ben-Porath, and Beverly Kaemmer. Copyright © 1992 by the Regents of the University of Minnesota. Reproduced by permission of the University of Minnesota Press. All rights reserved. "MMPI®" and "Minnesota Multiphasic Personality Inventory®" are registered trademarks of the Regents of the University of Minnesota. Source for Long-Term Stability Data: Stein, L. A. R., McClinton, B. K., & Graham, J. R. (1998). Long-term stability of MMPI-A scales. Journal of Personality Assessment, 70, 103–108. Copyright © 1998, Lawrence Erlbaum Associates, Inc. Reproduced by permission.
[a] 1-week, test–retest of normative subset of normative sample, boys and girls combined.
[b] 1-year, test–retest of nonclinical sample, boys and girls combined.

clinician ratings, and information obtained from records of patients. Results supported the validity of MMPI-A Content scale scores for which construct-relevant external measures were available. However, relevant external measures for some Content scales were not available in their research. In a similar study, Veltri et al. (2009) correlated Content scale scores with information from adolescents' records in psychiatric inpatient and forensic settings. Handel et al. (2011) examined correlations between self- and parent-report measures of functioning and the Content scale scores in a sample of adolescents undergoing a predisposition forensic evaluation. Results of both studies have broadly supported the convergent and discriminant validity of most of the Content scales.

In a study conducted in an adolescent residential treatment facility, Forbey and Ben-Porath (2003) found that the Content scales added incrementally to the Clinical scales in predicting clinician ratings of psychological symptomatology. Incremental validity of the Content scales also was demonstrated in samples of psychiatric inpatients and adolescents from the community (Rinaldo & Baer, 2003). Kopper et al. (1998) found that for boys in an inpatient setting, the Alienation (A-aln) and Anxiety (A-anx) Content scales were related to scores on a self-report measure of suicide probability. For girls, the Family Problems (A-fam), Conduct Problems (A-con), and School Problems (A-sch) Content scales were related to self-reported suicide probability.

Arita and Baer (1998) reported extratest correlates for the A-anx, Depression (A-dep), Health Concerns (A-hea), A-aln, Anger (A-ang), A-con, and Social Discomfort (A-sod) Content scales for adolescents being treated at a private psychiatric hospital. They concluded the convergent and discriminant validity of scores on these scales was generally supported by the observed pattern of associations with relevant self-report measures. However, they noted scores on A-anx and A-dep did not have strong abilities for discriminating between internalizing constructs. Archer and Krishnamurthy (1994) reported that Scale 2 (Depression) and the A-dep Content scales were about equally effective in identifying adolescents with diagnoses of depression. They also reported that the A-con and Cynicism (A-cyn) Content scales and the IMM scale were related to conduct disorder diagnoses. Pena et al. (1996) reported that boys who had been adjudicated delinquent scored significantly and meaningfully higher than boys in the MMPI-A normative sample on the A-ang, A-cyn, A-con, and A-fam Content scales.

Although existing validity data concerning the MMPI-A Content scales has been encouraging, more research is needed to determine to what extent these content-based scales add to the basic Validity and Clinical scales in understanding adolescents who complete the MMPI-A. At this time, the Content scales should be used in conjunction with the basic Validity and Clinical scales. High Content scale scores often clarify the reasons for elevated scores on these other scales and help clinicians determine which of the many descriptors typically associated with these other scales should be emphasized. Scores on the Content scales should be viewed as direct communications from adolescent test takers to examiners. Because the items of the Content scales are obvious and face valid, adolescents who are trying to manage impressions of adjustment or maladjustment can do so on these scales. Therefore, the scales are most useful when the Validity scales do not indicate defensiveness or exaggeration.

MMPI-A Content Component Scales

Although the MMPI-A Content scales are more homogeneous than the Clinical scales (see Table 14.4), Sherwood et al. (1997) were able to identify meaningful clusters of items within most of the Content scales. Utilizing statistical and rational procedures similar to those used to develop the MMPI-2 Content Component scales (see Chapter 6 of this book), they developed Component scales for 13 of the 15 MMPI-A Content scales. Table 14.5 lists the MMPI-A Content Component scales.

McCarthy and Archer (1998) reported that for nine of the MMPI-A Content scales, factor analyses yielded only a single factor. For the remaining Content scales, two or three factors were identified. These results are only partially consistent with those of Sherwood et al. (1997) and suggest many Content Component scales may not be assessing distinct facets of the Content scales. More research is needed to better understand the dimensionality of the Content scales and the utility of the Content Component scales.

Information concerning internal consistency and test–retest reliability for the Content Component Scales in the MMPI-A normative sample and in an adolescent

TABLE 14.5 *MMPI-A Content Component Scales*

Depression (A–dep)

           A-dep1: Dysphoria (5 items)

           A-dep2: Self-Depreciation (5 items)

           A-dep3: Lack of Drive (7 items)

           A-dep4: Suicidal Ideation (4 items)

Health Concerns (A–hea)

           A-hea1: Gastrointestinal Complaints (4 items)

           A-hea2: Neurological Symptoms (18 items)

           A-hea3: General Health Concerns (8 items)

Alienation (A–aln)

           A-aln1: Misunderstood (5 items)

           A-aln2: Social Isolation (5 items)

           A-aln3: Interpersonal Skepticism (5 items)

Bizarre Mentation (A–biz)

           A-biz1: Psychotic Symptomatology (11 items)

           A-biz2: Paranoid Ideation (5 items)

Anger (A–ang)

           A-ang1: Explosive Behavior (8 items)

           A-ang2: Irritability (8 items)

Cynicism (A–cyn)

           A-cyn1: Misanthropic Beliefs (13 items)

           A-cyn2: Interpersonal Suspiciousness (9 items)

Conduct Problems (A-con)

>A-con1: Acting-Out Behaviors (10 items)

>A-con2: Antisocial Attitudes (8 items)

>A-con3: Negative Peer Group Influences (3 items)

Low Self-Esteem (A-lse)

>A-lse1: Self-Doubt (13 items)

>A-lse2: Interpersonal Submissiveness (5 items)

Low Aspirations (A-las)

>A-las1: Low Achievement Orientation (8 items)

>A-las2: Lack of Initiative (7 items)

Social Discomfort (A-sod)

>A-sod1: Introversion (14 items)

>A-sod2: Shyness (10 items)

Family Problems (A-fam)

>A-fam1: Familial Discord (21 items)

>A-fam2: Familial Alienation (11 items)

School Problems (A-sch)

>A-sch1: School Conduct Problems (4 items)

>A-sch2: Negative Attitudes (8 items)

Negative Treatment Indicators (A-trt)

>A-trt1: Low Motivation (11 items)

>A-trt2: Inability to Disclose (8 items)

Note. Excerpted (Table 2) from *The MMPI-A Content Component Scales: Development, Psychometric Characteristics, and Clinical Application* by Nancy E. Sherwood, Yossef S. Ben-Porath, and Carolyn L. Williams. Copyright © 1997 by the Regents of the University of Minnesota. Reproduced by permission of the University of Minnesota Press. All rights reserved. "MMPI®" and "Minnesota Multiphasic Personality Inventory®" are registered trademarks of the Regents of the University of Minnesota.

clinical sample is reported in Ben-Porath et al. (2006). The internal consistency values ranged from 0.31 to 0.81, with means of 0.56 and 0.62 for boys and girls in the normative sample, respectively. Corresponding values for the clinical sample were quite similar; 1-week, test–retest reliability of the Content Component scales ranged from 0.35 to 0.80, with a mean value of 0.65.

Given the reliability values just described, it seems clear that some of the Content Component scales are heterogeneous and unstable enough that they should not be treated as stand-alone scales. However, the Component scales can be useful in determining what kinds of items adolescents endorsed that led to their elevated scores on the Content scales. When a test taker has a T score of 60 or greater for a Content scale, the Component scales for that Content scale can be examined. If there is a difference of at least 10 T-score points between the Content Component scales, the features associated with the more elevated Content Component scale should be emphasized in interpreting the Content scale. The MMPI-A manual supplement (Ben-Porath et al., 2006) offers interpretive guidelines for the Content Component scales. Special attention should be given to the Suicidal Ideation (A-dep4) Content Component scale, as this scale reflects items with overt content regarding suicidal ideation and behavior. Even a single item endorsed in the scored direction can indicate that a suicide risk evaluation should be completed.

MMPI-A Personality Psychopathology Five (PSY-5) Scales

The development of the MMPI-2 PSY-5 scales was discussed in Chapter 7 of this book. McNulty, Harkness, et al. (1997) developed corresponding scales for the MMPI-A. In creating these scales for the MMPI-A, MMPI-2 PSY-5 items also found in the MMPI-A item pool were used as preliminary scales. Items unique to the MMPI-A were reviewed by undergraduates, and those judged to be measuring PSY-5 constructs were added to the preliminary scales. Using data from the MMPI-A normative sample and the clinical sample included in the MMPI-A manual (Butcher et al., 1992), statistical analyses were then used to refine the scales.

The labels of the MMPI-A PSY-5 scales—which are the same as the corresponding MMPI-2 scales—are reported in Table 14.6 along with internal consistency values for the MMPI-A normative and clinical samples. The values are generally similar to the values reported for the MMPI-2 PSY-5 scales (see Chapter 7 of this book). Stein et al. (1998) reported 1-year, test–retest reliability coefficients for a sample of adolescents from a public-school setting. The values ranged from 0.44 for Psychoticism (PSYC) to 0.68 for Disconstraint (DISC). Although the temporal stability of the scales is lower than for the corresponding adult scales, the values are comparable to those for other measures of adolescent personality characteristics.

Several studies have identified extratest correlates for the MMPI-A PSY-5 scales. McNulty, Harkness, et al. (1997) correlated MMPI-A PSY-5 scores with parent

TABLE 14.6 *Internal Consistency Estimates for the MMPI-A PSY-5 Scales*

PSY-5 Scale	Normative Sample		Clinical Sample	
	Boys	Girls	Boys	Girls
Aggressiveness (AGGR)	0.74	0.73	0.79	0.82
Psychoticism (PSYC)	0.76	0.74	0.74	0.78
Disconstraint (DISC)	0.74	0.72	0.72	0.75
Negative Emotionality/Neuroticism (NEGE)	0.75	0.76	0.79	0.80
Introversion/Low Positive Emotionality (INTR)	0.78	0.75	0.71	0.77

Note. Excerpted (Table 4) from the *Supplement to the MMPI®-A Manual for Administration, Scoring, and Interpretation* by Yossef S. Ben-Porath, John R. Graham, Robert P. Archer, Auke Tellegen, and Beverly Kaemmer. Copyright © 2006 by the Regents of the University of Minnesota. Reproduced by permission of the University of Minnesota Press. All rights reserved. "MMPI®" and "Minnesota Multiphasic Personality Inventory®" are registered trademarks of the Regents of the University of Minnesota.

ratings, staff ratings, and information obtained from a review of the records of boys and girls from several treatment facilities. The results supported the construct validity of the PSY-5 scales. Scores on the Aggressiveness (AGGR) scale were most strongly related to externalizing behaviors of various kinds, including aggressive behavior toward others. Scores on PSYC were associated with psychotic symptoms of various kinds. Scores on the DISC scale were associated with externalizing behaviors, including drug use, delinquency, and sexual acting out. However, DISC scale scores were not strongly related to aggressive behaviors. As expected, scores on the Negative Emotionality/Neuroticism (NEGE) scale were related most strongly to internalizing behaviors. Finally, high scorers on the Introversion/Low Positive Emotionality (INTR) scale were characterized as having internalizing characteristics.

Veltri et al. (2009) reported extratest correlates for the MMPI-A PSY-5 scales using data from large clinical and forensic samples. Their results were very similar to those of McNulty, Harkness, et al. (1997). High scorers on the AGGR scale were more likely to appear angry and to get into fights. High scorers on the PSYC scale were described as experiencing hallucinations and flashbacks. Higher scores on the DISC scale were associated with a variety of externalizing behaviors, including drug use, school behavior problems, and difficulties with the law. The strongest correlates for the NEGE and INTR scales were internalizing in nature (e.g., anxiety and depression).

Stokes and colleagues (2019) examined PSY-5 predictors of borderline personality features in a large sample of adolescents receiving treatment in an inpatient setting. They used scales from the Personality Assessment Inventory–Adolescent (PAI-A; Morey, 2007) to index borderline features. Results demonstrated scores on DISC, INTR, and NEGE were associated with these characteristics but that NEGE was the strongest individual predictor of borderline features at both the disorder and symptom level.

MMPI-A Critical Items

The use of critical items in interpreting the MMPI-2 was discussed in Chapter 6 of this book. Although previous critical item sets were developed for adults, there has been some speculation that they could also be used with adolescents. Archer and Jacobson (1993) examined endorsement frequencies of the Koss–Butcher (Koss, Butcher, & Hoffman, 1976) and Lachar–Wrobel (Lachar & Wrobel, 1979) critical items for the MMPI-2 normative sample, for the MMPI-A normative sample, and for a sample of adolescents receiving mental health services. As expected, they found that adolescents in nonclinical settings endorsed critical items much more frequently than adults in nonclinical settings and that there were not many differences in endorsement frequencies between adolescents in nonclinical and clinical settings. They interpreted these data as indicating that the Koss–Butcher and Lachar–Wrobel critical item lists would probably have little utility with adolescents and that it would be very difficult to develop a critical items list specifically for the MMPI-A.

Forbey and Ben-Porath (1998) addressed limitations of previous efforts to develop a critical item set for the MMPI-A by using a combined empirical-rational strategy. Specifically, they compared endorsement frequencies for the MMPI-A normative sample and several adolescent clinical samples and identified a set of items infrequently endorsed in the scored direction by the adolescents in the normative sample and frequently endorsed by adolescents in the clinical samples. They then examined each item in the list and retained only those whose content was judged to be of critical significance. The resulting critical item list includes 82 items that were rationally grouped into 15 categories: Aggression, Anxiety, Cognitive Problems, Conduct Problems, Depression/Suicidal Ideation, Eating Problems, Family Problems, Hallucinatory Experiences, Paranoid Ideation, School Problems, Self-Denigration, Sexual Concerns, Somatic Complaints, Substance Use/Abuse, and Unusual Thinking. Forbey and Ben-Porath (1998) concluded that their critical items "represent those developmentally appropriate adolescent concerns that, due to their critical nature, should be brought to a clinician's immediate attention."

INTERPRETING MMPI-A VALIDITY SCALE SCORES

Cannot Say Scale (?)

As with the MMPI-2, excessive item omissions lead to artificially lowered scores on the MMPI-A scales. Every effort should be made to encourage adolescents to answer as many of the items as possible. If more than 30 items are omitted, the protocol should be considered invalid, and no other scales should be interpreted (Butcher et al., 1992). If more than 10 items are omitted, the protocol should be interpreted with caution, and the omitted items should be examined to make sure that they are not concentrated on specific scales.

Variable Response Inconsistency (VRIN) Scale

The VRIN scale assesses the extent to which test takers have responded consistently to the items in the inventory. The MMPI-A manual recommends that the possibility of random responding be considered when VRIN T scores are equal to or greater than 75. As described earlier, research has suggested a wide range of scores on VRIN correctly identify both complete and partial random responding. However, these cut scores generally fall somewhere around the cutoff of $T \geq 75$ or greater recommended in the MMPI-A manual. As such, these authors recommend use of this cut score. MMPI-A protocols with such high VRIN scores should not be interpreted. It is important to note that VRIN scale scores may be less effective in detecting random responding that occurs only in the latter part of the test because relatively few VRIN item pairs occur within the last quarter of the test.

True Response Inconsistency (TRIN) Scale

The TRIN scale assesses the extent to which adolescent test takers have responded to MMPI-A items with indiscriminate true or false responding. As with the TRIN scale of the MMPI-2, T scores on the TRIN scale are always 50 or higher, with T or F added to the T score to indicate either a true or false response bias. The MMPI-A manual (Butcher et al., 1992) recommends that T scores equal to or greater than

75 indicate the possibility of a true (if in the T direction) or false (if in the F direction) response bias. MMPI-A protocols with such high TRIN scores should not be interpreted.

Infrequency (F, F1, and F2) Scales

The MMPI-A F scale is divided into two parts (F1 and F2). The F1 scale gives information about the first part of the test (items 1–236), and the F2 scale gives information about the second part of the test (items 242–470). The F scale raw score is the sum of the F1 and F2 scale raw scores. If T scores are used, scores on the F, F1, and F2 scales can be interpreted similarly.

When an adolescent obtains a T score of 70 or greater on one of the F scales, the first thing that should be done is to rule out random or careless responding. The VRIN scale (see earlier) is very useful in this regard. Next, the possibility of true response bias should be ruled out. The TRIN scale (see earlier) is helpful in evaluating this possibility. If the F scale is elevated, and scores on VRIN or TRIN suggest non-content-based invalid responding, elevations on F are likely due to this response style. In this case, as noted earlier when discussing interpretation of VRIN and TRIN, none of the MMPI-A substantive scales should be interpreted.

If neither VRIN or TRIN is elevated, scores on the F scales can be interpreted; and high scores are likely to be suggestive of either serious psychopathology or over-reporting of symptoms and problems. Scores on F1 and F2 can provide additional nuanced information. Namely, if the F1 scale is significantly elevated, substantive scales should be interpreted with great caution, if at all. If the score on F1 is within acceptable limits, and the F2 scale suggests invalid responding, the basic Validity and Clinical scales can be interpreted, but none of the other scales can. When one of the F scales' scores is elevated, interpretation of the substantive scales should be done cautiously if there is not extratest data indicating the adolescent is experiencing serious psychopathology. Generally, scores between 70T and 74T on one or more of the F scales suggest a possible problematic response pattern (Butcher et al., 1992). Scores equal to or greater than 75T indicate an even greater likelihood of problematic responding. Scores on the F scales greater than 90T are indicative of an invalidating response style in individuals without a substantiated history of severe psychopathology and suggest substantive scales should not be interpreted.

Lie (L) Scale

High scores on the L scale indicate that the adolescent test taker has approached the test in a defensive manner. They have tried to present themselves in an unrealistically favorable light, denying minor flaws and weaknesses and claiming excessive virtues (Butcher et al., 1992). Scores equal to or greater than 65T on the L scale suggest that adolescents have approached the test in such a defensive manner that the resulting scores may not reflect accurately what they really are like. If the high L score is accompanied by high scores on Clinical, Content, or other substantive scales, these scales can be interpreted; but it should be acknowledged that the scores may underrepresent symptoms and problems. If the L scale score is high, and there are no high scores on the problem-oriented scales, it is not possible to determine if the adolescent has serious problems and is covering them up or has average adjustment and is simply overstating virtues. Scores between 60T and 64T on the L scale indicate some defensiveness, which should be taken into account in interpreting the other scales.

Correction (K) Scale

Although scores on the MMPI-A Clinical scales are not K corrected, scores on the K scale can be considered a measure of defensiveness in adolescents. Scores equal to or greater than 65T suggest the possibility that the adolescent has approached the test in an invalid manner. The TRIN scale (see earlier) should be consulted to rule out the possibility of a false response bias. The MMPI-A manual (Butcher et al., 1992) recommends that a MMPI-A protocol should not be invalidated solely on the basis of the K scale. However, it should be acknowledged that when the K-scale score is high (T ≥ 65), scores on the other scales may underrepresent problems and symptoms.

INTERPRETING THE MMPI-A CLINICAL SCALES

The MMPI-A manual (Butcher et al., 1992) suggests that T scores of 65 or greater on the Clinical scales should be considered clinically significant. Scores between 60T and 64T on the Clinical scales also can be interpreted as high scores, although one should have less confidence in inferences based on scores at this lower level. Because very little is known about the meaning of low scores on the Clinical scales for adolescents, low scores should not be interpreted at this time. The interpretations of high scores on the Clinical scales are based on research with the original MMPI and with the MMPI-A. Not every interpretive statement will apply to every adolescent who has a high score on a particular scale. Inferences should be treated as hypotheses to be validated on the basis of other information available about each adolescent.

Scale 1 (Hypochondriasis)

High scores on Scale 1 generally indicate preoccupation with health, illness, and bodily functioning. Although adolescents with genuine physical disorders may obtain moderately elevated scores (T = 60–64), higher scores suggest somatic complaints that have a psychological component. High-scoring boys and girls may report fatigue and lack of energy, and high-scoring girls may report eating problems. Adolescents who score high on Scale 1 tend to have histories of poor academic performance. They are likely to be insecure and may fear failure and blame themselves for problems. They tend to be viewed by others as self-centered, demanding, and attention seeking. They also tend to be somewhat isolated from other people.

Scale 2 (Depression)

In clinical settings, high scores on Scale 2 tend to be associated with depression, low energy, guilt, pessimism, and suicidal ideation. In clinical settings, adolescents with high scores on Scale 2 often receive diagnoses of depression or dysthymia. High scorers also frequently report somatic symptoms, anxiety, fear, worry, and eating problems. They lack self-confidence, are self-critical, and perform poorly in school. They tend to be overcontrolled, submissive, shy, timid, and socially withdrawn. Because of their emotional distress, high scorers are likely to be motivated to participate in psychotherapy.

Scale 3 (Hysteria)

High scores on Scale 3 are associated with somatic symptoms, poor concentration, and sleep disturbances. In clinical samples, high scorers may report depression and suicidal ideation. High scorers tend to be immature and are viewed by others as self-centered persons who are socially involved and demanding of attention and affection. Adolescents with high scores tend to deny difficulties and lack insight into their own motives.

Scale 4 (Psychopathic Deviate)

High scores on Scale 4 are associated with a variety of acting-out and delinquent behaviors. In clinical and correctional settings, high scorers on this scale often receive conduct disorder diagnoses. High scorers resent authority and have academic and behavior problems in school and conflicts with their families. They are quite sensitive to criticism and to restrictions on their behavior. High scorers tend to be seen by others as active, assertive, and independent. They often admit to alcohol or other drug problems. High scorers often are impulsive, oppositional, and aggressive. They may show poor judgment and do not seem to learn from their experiences. They are likely to be seen by others as self-centered persons who do not accept responsibility for their own behavior. In clinical settings, high scorers may have histories of being physically abused (boys) or sexually abused (girls). High Scale 4 scorers typically are not motivated to participate in psychotherapy.

Scale 5 (Masculinity–Femininity)

As with the adult version of Scale 5, the version of Scale 5 scored on the MMPI-A has been used routinely with boys and girls and was constructed around conventional ideas about biological sex, gender, and sexual orientation. For boys, high T scores on Scale 5 suggest stereotypically feminine interest patterns; for girls, high T scores suggest stereotypically masculine interest patterns. Boys with high T scores on Scale 5 are less likely than other boys to get into trouble with the law. Girls with high T scores on Scale 5 are more likely than other girls to have academic and behavior problems in school, to have histories of learning disability, and to act out in a variety of ways. Interestingly, Hathaway and Monachesi (1963) reported that both boys and girls with higher T scores on Scale 5 were less likely to act out in delinquent ways.

Scale 6 (Paranoia)

Adolescents who score high on Scale 6 often have academic and behavior problems in school. They tend to be moody, changeable, and unpredictable. They are likely to be suspicious, guarded, evasive, and withdrawn interpersonally and are very sensitive to criticism and rejection. They tend to blame others for their own problems and difficulties. In clinical settings, self-harm behaviors and suicidal ideation are more common among high scorers than among adolescent patients in general.

Scale 7 (Psychasthenia)

High scores on Scale 7 tend to be associated with anxiety, depression, and other emotional turmoil. High scorers often have difficulty concentrating and attending, and they are indecisive. They are likely to have poor self-concepts, are self-critical and perfectionistic, and feel guilty about perceived failures. Suicidal ideation is more common among high scorers on Scale 7 than adolescent patients in general. High scorers tend to be shy and socially introverted. Clinical records of high-scoring boys may indicate histories of being sexually abused.

Scale 8 (Schizophrenia)

In clinical settings, high scorers on Scale 8 may manifest psychotic symptoms (e.g., delusions, hallucinations, or ideas of reference). They may appear to be fearful, confused, and disorganized. They are likely to be emotionally unstable and to show large shifts in mood. Somatic symptoms and drug use also may be characteristic of high scorers on this scale. High scorers tend to have academic and behavior problems in school. They are quite vulnerable to stress and may resort to excessive fantasy during times of increased stress. At times, their reality testing may be impaired. They are likely to have low self-esteem and feel inferior to others. They are described as isolated, aloof, mistrustful, and uninvolved with others. High scorers may have histories of being sexually abused. The prognosis for successful psychotherapy is not very good for high scorers on Scale 8.

Scale 9 (Hypomania)

High scorers on Scale 9 often have histories of acting-out behaviors that may include school problems and drug use. They often seem to have difficulty focusing on problems. They are likely to be resentful of authority and often behave quite impulsively. They tend to be optimistic and socially extroverted persons. They are viewed by others as being self-centered and may be grandiose in their self-appraisal. High scorers on this scale often are seen by others as deceitful and self-indulgent. They often are not very motivated to engage in psychotherapy.

Scale 0 (Social Introversion)

High scorers on Scale 0 are introverted, shy, and timid; and they are likely to have difficulty making friends. They lack self-confidence, are emotionally overcontrolled, and blame themselves for problems. They tend to have strong needs for attention, affection, and support. In clinical settings, they may report feeling depressed and suicidal. They tend not to use alcohol or drugs or to be involved in delinquent behaviors.

INTERPRETING THE MMPI-A SUPPLEMENTARY SCALES

MacAndrew Alcoholism Scale – Revised (MAC-R)

High scorers on the MAC-R scale are more likely than other adolescents to have problems related to substance use. Raw scores greater than 27 suggest a strong possibility of such problems. Raw scores between 24 and 27 are indeterminate concerning problematic substance use. Raw scores of 23 or lower suggest that substance use problems are not likely. High scorers on the MAC-R scale also are likely to display behavior undercontrol, and they are not likely to anticipate the consequences of their behavior.

Alcohol/Drug Problem Proneness (PRO) Scale

High scores on the PRO scale are associated with adolescent substance use problems. While not much information is available about PRO scale cutoff scores, the scale's authors recommended that T scores greater than 60 should raise concerns about substance use problems. It should be noted that all of the research to date deals with current substance use and not with potential for future problematic use. High scorers on this scale also tend to be impulsive, aggressive, and behaviorally undercontrolled.

Alcohol/Drug Problem Acknowledgement (ACK) Scale

High scorers on the ACK scale are likely to be directly admitting problems with alcohol and other substances. The T-score cutoff recommended by the scale's authors is 60 or greater. High scorers on the scale also tend to be impulsive and behaviorally undercontrolled.

Immaturity (IMM) Scale

High scorers on the IMM scale are likely to have a lower level of ego development than others of their chronological age. They have limited capacity to think in abstract terms and for seeing the world from the viewpoint of others. They are also less likely to identify with values and beliefs of their social group and tend to have lower levels of moral development. They are likely to have academic difficulties and to be somewhat rebellious and defiant toward authority figures.

Anxiety (A) Scale

High scorers on the A scale typically are not very well adjusted or effective. They are anxious, fearful, guilt-prone, and self-critical. They feel overwhelmed and unable to cope effectively with the demands of everyday life.

Repression (R) Scale

High scorers on the R scale tend to be overcontrolled and inhibited individuals. They are rather passive in relationships and try to avoid unpleasant confrontations and disagreeable situations.

INTERPRETING THE MMPI-A CONTENT SCALES

The MMPI-A Content scales can be very helpful in understanding patterns of scores on the basic Clinical scales. A rather wide variety of descriptors can be applied to an adolescent who has a high score on a Clinical scale. Examination of the Content scales can offer direction concerning which of these descriptors should be emphasized in interpreting the high Clinical scale score. For example, descriptors for high scores on Scale 4 for adolescents include family problems, school problems, and delinquency.

If the Content scales indicate elevation on the A-fam Content scale but not on the A-sch or A-con scales, interpretation of the Scale 4 elevation would emphasize the adolescent's problems and conflicts with family rather than school difficulties or problems with the law.

Scores on the MMPI-A Content scales also provide important information about what the adolescent wants the examiner to know about them. The item content of the scales is obvious, and adolescents are likely aware of what information they are conveying as they respond to the individual items. Adolescents who are interested in creating a particular impression of themselves can do so by carefully selecting their responses to the items that comprise these scales. Therefore, scores on the Content scales will be most informative when test takers approach the test in an honest, candid manner. The Content scales should not be interpreted when the Validity scales suggest that the adolescent has been quite defensive or has exaggerated symptoms and problems.

Scores on the MMPI-A Content scales are expressed as UT scores, as are scores on the eight basic Clinical scales. Inferences can be made about T scores equal to or greater than 60, but greatest emphasis should be placed on T scores that are equal to or greater than 65. The descriptions of high scorers on the MMPI-A Content scales that follow are based on consideration of the items in each scale and on empirically derived descriptors that have been reported for the scales (e.g., Arita & Baer, 1998; Veltri et al., 2009; C. L. Williams et al., 1992). As with the Clinical scales, not every descriptor associated with a Content scale will apply to all adolescents who have a high score on the scale. Inferences should be treated as hypotheses that are to be validated based on other information available about the adolescent.

Anxiety (A-anx)

Adolescents who score high on the A-anx scale are reporting many symptoms of anxiety, including tension, frequent worrying, and sleep disturbances. They report problems with concentration, confusion, and an inability to stay on task. They may believe that life is a strain and that their difficulties are insurmountable. They may worry about losing their minds or feel that something dreadful is about to happen to them. They seem to be aware of their problems and how they differ from others. Correlate data indicate that scores on the A-anx scale are related to general maladjustment as well as to specific symptoms such as anxiety, depression, withdrawal, and somatic complaints.

Obsessiveness (A-obs)

Adolescents who score high on the A-obs scale report worrying beyond reason, often over trivial matters. They may have ruminative thoughts about bad words or counting unimportant things. They have times when they are unable to sleep because of their worries. They report difficulty making decisions and dread changes in their lives. They report that others sometimes lose patience with them, and they often regret things they have said or done. Correlate data suggest that in clinical settings, A-obs scores are related to general maladjustment as well as dependent, anxious behaviors in boys and suicidal ideation or behaviors in girls.

Depression (A-dep)

Adolescents who score high on the A-dep scale report many symptoms of depression, including fatigue and crying spells. They are dissatisfied with their lives and feel that others are happier than they are. They may be experiencing many self-depreciative thoughts and feel that life is neither interesting nor worthwhile. They may report feeling blue and wishing they were dead, and suicidal ideation is possible. They experience social problems, report feeling lonely even when with other people, and tend to be socially withdrawn. The future seems too uncertain for them to make serious plans, and they may have periods when they are unable to "get going." They may be characterized by a sense of hopelessness and not caring. Correlate data indicate that for girls in nonclinical settings and for boys and girls in clinical settings, high scores on A-dep are indicative of depression and dysphoria. Suicidal ideation or behaviors may also be present for boys and girls in clinical settings.

Health Concerns (A-hea)

Adolescents who score high on the A-hea scale report numerous physical complaints and indicate that physical problems interfere with enjoyment of school activities and contribute to school absences. They worry about their health and may feel that their problems would disappear if only their health would improve. Correlate data offer considerable support for the A-hea scale as a measure of somatic complaints in clinical settings. For boys and girls in nonclinical settings, higher scores on this scale seem to be related to misbehavior, poor academic performance, and other school problems.

Bizarre Mentation (A-biz)

Adolescents scoring high on the A-biz scale report very strange thoughts and experiences, which may include auditory, visual, or olfactory hallucinations. They may feel that something is wrong with their minds. They may feel that they are being plotted against or that someone is trying to poison them. They may believe that others are trying to steal their thoughts, possibly through hypnosis. They may believe that evil spirits or ghosts possess or influence them. Correlate data indicate that the A-biz scale is a measure of general maladjustment in nonclinical settings, with higher scorers having problems in school and receiving low grades. For boys and girls in clinical settings, high scores on the A-biz scale are suggestive of bizarre sensory experiences and other symptoms and behaviors that may be indicative of psychosis.

Anger (A-ang)

Adolescents who score high on the A-ang scale report anger control problems. They often feel like swearing or smashing things. They may get into fights, especially when they have been drinking alcohol. They may get into trouble for breaking or destroying things. They report feeling irritable and impatient with others, and they may display their anger in order to get their way. They do not like being hurried or having people get ahead of them in line. Correlate data from clinical settings indicate that higher scorers on A-ang may have histories of assault and other acting-out behaviors. They tend to externalize blame for their problems and difficulties. Boys in these settings may also have histories of having been sexually abused.

Cynicism (A-cyn)

Adolescents scoring high on the A-cyn scale report misanthropic attitudes. They may feel that others are out to get them and will use unfair means to gain an advantage. They look for hidden motives whenever someone does something nice for them. They believe that it is safer to trust nobody because people make friends with them in order to use them. High scorers tend to assume all people secretly dislike helping others. They feel misunderstood by others and see others as jealous of them. Correlate data indicate that the A-cyn scale is not necessarily related to acting-out behavior. It may be more of an attitudinal than a behavioral measure.

Alienation (A-aln)

High scorers on the A-aln scale report considerable emotional distance from others. They believe that they are getting a raw deal from life and that no one, including their parents, cares about or understands them. They do not believe they are liked by others, nor do they get along well with their peers. They have difficulty self-disclosing and report feeling awkward when having to talk in a group. They do not appreciate hearing others give their opinions. They do not believe that others are sympathetic and feel that other people often block their attempts at success. Correlate data indicate, in both nonclinical and clinical settings, that A-aln scores are related to social problems and feelings of emotional distance from others. High scorers on this scale often report symptoms of depression and anxiety.

Conduct Problems (A-con)

Adolescents scoring high on the A-con scale report behavioral problems, which may include stealing, shoplifting, lying, breaking or destroying things, being disrespectful, swearing, and being oppositional. They say that their peers are often in trouble and frequently talk them into doing things they know they should not do. At times, they may try to make others afraid of them just for the fun of it. They are entertained by criminal behavior and do not blame people for taking advantage of others. They admit doing bad things in the past that they cannot tell anybody about. Correlate data—which were similar across nonclinical and clinical samples, genders, and criterion measures—indicate that high scorers on the A-con scale tended to have various kinds of behavior problems including delinquency, anger, aggressiveness, and problematic substance use. High scorers tend to externalize blame for their problems and difficulties.

Low Self-Esteem (A-lse)

Adolescents scoring high on the A-lse scale report very negative opinions of themselves, including being unattractive, lacking self-confidence, feeling useless, having little ability, having several faults, and not being able to do anything well. They say that they are likely to yield to others' pressure, changing their minds or giving up in arguments. They let other people take charge when problems have to be solved, and they do not feel that they are capable of planning their own future. They become uncomfortable when others say nice things about them, and at times they may become confused and forgetful. Correlate data indicate that higher scores on A-lse are related to negative views of self and poor school performance. Depression and suicidal ideation may be present among high scorers.

Low Aspirations (A-las)

High scorers on the A-las scale report low need to achieve, and they do not expect to be successful. They do not like to study and read about things, dislike science and lectures on serious topics, and prefer work that allows them to be careless. They avoid newspaper editorials and believe that the comic strips are the only interesting part of the newspaper. They report difficulty starting things and give up quickly when things go wrong. They let other people solve their problems, and they avoid facing difficulties. They believe that others block their success. They report that others tell them they are lazy. Correlate data support the A-las scale as a measure of poor achievement and limited participation in school activities. In addition, the scale is related to antisocial tendencies, such as running away, truancy, and sexual acting out in girls.

Social Discomfort (A-sod)

Adolescents with high scores on the A-sod scale report that they find it very difficult to be around others. They report being shy and prefer to be alone. They dislike having people around them and frequently avoid others. They do not like parties, crowds, dances, or other social gatherings. They tend not to speak unless spoken to, and others have told them they are hard to get to know. They have difficulty making friends and do not like to meet strangers. Correlate data suggest that the A-sod scale is a measure of social discomfort and social withdrawal. High scorers also tend to have low energy levels. Both boys and girls who score higher on this scale are likely to feel anxious and depressed. In addition, for girls, higher scores are related to eating problems and are contraindicative of aggressive and irresponsible acting-out behaviors.

Family Problems (A-fam)

Adolescents with high scores on the A-fam scale report serious problems with their parents (or primary caregivers) and other family members. Family discord, jealousy, fault-finding, anger, serious disagreements, lack of love and understanding, and limited communication characterize their families. These adolescents do not seem to feel that they can count on their families in times of trouble. They wish for the day when they are able to leave home. They feel their parents frequently punish them without cause and treat them more like children than adults. They report that their parents dislike their peer group. Correlate data indicate that high scores on the A-fam scale are related to disagreements with and between parents and to a variety of delinquent and neurotic symptoms and behaviors.

School Problems (A-sch)

High scorers on the A-sch scale report numerous difficulties in school. High scorers report poor grades, suspension, truancy, negative attitudes toward teachers, and dislike of school. The only pleasant aspect of school is being with friends. High scorers say that they do not participate in school activities, and they feel that school is a waste of time. They report frequent boredom and sleepiness at school, and they have been told that they are lazy. Some high scorers may report being afraid to go to school. Correlate data indicate that high scores on A-sch are indicative of both academic and behavioral problems at school. The scale may also be a measure of general maladjustment.

Negative Treatment Indicators (A-trt)

High scorers on the A-trt scale may report negative attitudes toward doctors and health professionals. They believe others are incapable of understanding their problems and difficulties and do not care what happens to them. They are unwilling to take charge and face their problems and difficulties, and they do not assume responsibility for the negative events in their lives. They do not feel that they can plan their own futures. They report having some faults and bad habits that they feel are insurmountable. They report great unwillingness to discuss their problems with others and indicate that there are some issues that they would never be able to share with anyone. They report feeling nervous when others ask them personal questions, and that they have secrets best kept to themselves. Treatment outcome studies with adolescents are needed to establish the external validity of the A-trt scale. Correlate data do not indicate that the scale is simply a measure of general maladjustment.

INTERPRETING CONTENT COMPONENT SCALES

Sherwood et al. (1997) developed Component scales for some of the MMPI-A Content scales. They offered some evidence that the Component scales can be helpful in understanding which Content scale correlates should be emphasized in particular cases. They suggested that the Component scales be interpreted only when the parent Content scale T score is between 60 and 75 and a Component scale T score is greater than 65. The assumption is that for Content scale T scores greater than 75, a wide array of symptoms and problems is likely to apply. Although Sherwood et al. did not specify that there should be at least a 10 T-score point difference between Component scales before interpreting them, this recommendation—which was made for the MMPI-2 Content Component scales—would seem to be appropriate for the MMPI-A scales as well.

INTERPRETING PERSONALITY PSYCHOPATHOLOGY FIVE (PSY-5) SCALES

Raw scores for each of the PSY-5 scales are converted to UT scores. T scores equal to or greater than 65 are considered to be high scores. As with other MMPI-A scale scores, interpretations can be made for T scores between 60 and 65. However, greater confidence should be placed on T scores of 65 or higher.

Aggressiveness (AGGR)

Adolescents with high scores on the AGGR scale typically engage in a variety of externalizing behaviors. They may have histories of difficulties with the law. Drug use and sexual acting out are common among high scorers. High scorers also are seen by others as angry and aggressive.

Psychoticism (PSYC)

High scores on the PSYC scale are associated with bizarre and possibly psychotic behaviors, including hallucinations. High scorers may also experience anxiety, obsessive thinking, and somatic symptoms.

Disconstraint (DISC)

High scorers on the DISC scale are characterized by a variety of externalizing behaviors. They may have problematic patterns of alcohol and other drug use, get into trouble at school and with the law, and act out in sexual ways.

Negative Emotionality/Neuroticism (NEGE)

High scores on the NEGE scale are associated with a variety of internalizing symptoms and behaviors. High scorers report feeling anxious and tense. They are self-critical and feel guilty about perceived shortcomings and failures. They also report feeling sad or blue and seem to lack energy for activities of daily life.

Introversion/Low Positive Emotionality (INTR)

High scores on the INTR scale are associated with internalizing disorders. High scorers report feeling anxious and depressed. They tend to be socially introverted and deficient in the ability to experience joy and other positive emotions.

INTERPRETING MMPI-A CRITICAL ITEMS

Forbey and Ben-Porath's (1998) critical items signal difficulties that may warrant immediate clinical attention and are organized into 15 categories: Aggression, Anxiety, Cognitive Problems, Conduct Problems, Depression/Suicidal Ideation, Eating Problems, Family Problems, Hallucinatory Experiences, Paranoid Ideation, School Problems, Self-Denigration, Sexual Concerns, Somatic Complaints, Substance Use/ Abuse, and Unusual Thinking. Critical items endorsed by a test taker are listed in the MMPI-A computerized reports available from Pearson Assessments. Inspection of an adolescent's responses to these items can provide important information about the nature and severity of problems that an adolescent has reported. However, the response to single test items should not be taken at face value as psychometrically sound indicators of psychopathology or maladjustment. Endorsed critical items can also indicate problems in need of immediate attention or further evaluation, as well as provide a starting point for discussions with the test taker about their difficulties.

MMPI-A INTERPRETIVE STRATEGY

The MMPI-2 interpretive strategy, which was presented in Chapter 11 of this book, can also be applied to the MMPI-A, although modifications that take the special life circumstances of adolescents into account are needed. In the instrument's manual,

Butcher and colleagues (1992) suggested that the following questions should be addressed in interpreting MMPI-A results:

1. Are there extratest factors that can explain the MMPI-A results?
2. What are the individual's response attitudes?
3. What are the individual's reported symptoms and behaviors? What is the likelihood of acting-out behaviors? If present, are the acting-out problems likely to be seen across settings or only in specific settings? How severe is the acting out likely to be?
4. Do problems in school play a significant role in the adolescent's clinical picture? What, if any, are they likely to be?
5. Does the adolescent admit to having a problem with alcohol or other drugs? Do they have the potential for developing such a problem?
6. What are the individual's interpersonal relationships like? Are there negative peer group influences? Are family problems significant? How do they respond to authority? Are alienation, cynicism, and isolation important factors?
7. Does the MMPI-A suggest a need for evaluation of possible physical or sexual abuse?
8. What strengths or assets are apparent in the individual?
9. What are the diagnostic implications of the MMPI-A results?
10. What treatment implications or recommendations are suggested on the basis of the MMPI-A results?

Information concerning these questions comes from examination of the individual Validity, Clinical, Supplementary, Content, Content Component, and PSY-5 scales. As suggested earlier in this chapter, for the substantive scales, T scores of 60 or greater on these scales should be considered interpretable. Greater confidence should be placed in inferences based on scales with T scores equal to or greater than 65. Because of limited information concerning the meaning of low scores on the MMPI-A, below-average scores should not be interpreted except as indicating that test takers did not admit to the problems and symptoms associated with higher scores on those scales. We cannot know if the low scorers do not have the problems and symptoms associated with high scores, are consciously denying them, or simply are not aware of them.

Sometimes the inferences based on high scores on individual scales will appear to be inconsistent, and it will be necessary to reconcile these apparent inconsistencies. The same approach recommended in Chapter 11 of this book for the MMPI-2 is appropriate for the MMPI-A. First, consider the possibility that the apparently inconsistent inferences accurately reflect different facets of the adolescent's personality and behavior. If it seems that some of the inferences are indeed inconsistent, a decision must be made concerning which inferences should be emphasized in the interpretation. In general, greater emphasis should be placed on inferences based on higher scores. Also, because the standard Validity and Clinical scales have been more thoroughly researched, greater emphasis should be placed on inferences based on these scales than on inferences based on other substantive scales. As with the MMPI-2, sometimes inferences are not based directly on scores from the MMPI-A scales. Rather, it is necessary to make higher-order inferences about adolescents based on an overall understanding of that person. Such higher-order inferences are quite acceptable, but the test interpreter should acknowledge that they do not come directly from the MMPI-A scales.

Extratest Factors

Several factors external to the MMPI-A may affect test performance and need to be taken into account in interpreting test results. Gender is an important variable; research has indicated that somewhat different descriptors are appropriate for boys and girls who have high scores on some MMPI-A scales (Butcher et al., 1992; C. L. Williams & Butcher, 1989a; Wrobel & Lachar, 1992). Reading ability is also an important factor to be considered. The MMPI-A requires approximately a seventh-grade reading ability. Having limited education, speaking English as a second language, or other factors that affect reading ability should be taken into account. When such factors are present, special attention should be given to the Validity scales. The evaluation context may also be important. An adolescent who is forced into the testing situation by parents or teachers may respond differently from one who takes the test because they are acknowledging problems and seeking help. Finally, extraordinary life circumstances that could affect test results should be considered. For example, having recently experienced a catastrophic event, such as sexual assault or the death of a parent, could lead to extreme responding on the MMPI-A, which would not reflect typical functioning of the adolescent.

Response Attitudes

Before generating inferences concerning the adolescent's symptoms, personality, and behavior, it is necessary to consider response attitudes. Are there indications that the adolescent approached the test in a manner that invalidates the results? Are there response attitudes that are not extreme enough to invalidate the results but need to be considered when interpreting the results? The standard Validity scales of the MMPI-A should be consulted in trying to answer these questions.

MMPI-A results should be considered invalid and uninterruptible if more than 30 items are omitted, if the VRIN T score is 75 or higher, or if the TRIN T score is 75 or higher (in either the true or false direction). Scores equal to or greater than 65T on the L or K scales suggest that the test taker approached the test in a defensive manner and that the scores on the other scales probably underrepresent problems and symptoms. Scores equal to or greater than 70T on the F, Fl, or F2 scales suggest the possibility of problematic responding. In such cases, the VRIN and TRIN scores should be consulted to rule out the possibility of random responding or a true or false response bias. If these possibilities are ruled out, then the elevated F scores may indicate either serious maladjustment or overreporting of symptoms and problems. Other information, especially the circumstances of the testing, should be considered in determining the most likely reasons for the high F scale scores. If it seems likely that the adolescent is overreporting, then the scores on the other scales probably overestimate problems and symptoms.

Symptoms and Behaviors

Assuming the MMPI-A results are valid and interpretable, the individual Clinical, Supplementary, Content, Content Component, and PSY-5 scale scores can be consulted to generate inferences concerning symptoms and behaviors. Although inferences can be generated from all high scores, several scales and subscales are especially important in relation to particular symptoms and problem behaviors. Inferences also can be made if a 2- or 3-point code type is present and has been described previously in the literature (see Archer, 2017).

Anxiety

Anxiety and excessive worry are suggested by high scores on Scale 7, the A-anx and A-obs Content scales, and the A Supplementary scale. High scorers on Scale 2, the A-dep Content scale, and the PSY-5 NEGE scale often report symptoms of anxiety.

Depression

High scores on Scale 2 and the A-dep Content scale are the major indicators of depression and possible suicidal ideation, particularly in clinical settings. However, high scores on Scales 3, 7, and 0; on the A-lse, A-obs, A-sod, and A-anx Content scales; and on the Sc2 (Emotional Alienation) and Sc4 (Lack of Ego Mastery, Conative) Harris–Lingoes subscales also can be suggestive of depression or suicidal ideation. Finally, high scorers on the INTR PSY-5 scale often report symptoms of depression. Because the A-dep4 Content Component Scale is made up of items dealing directly with suicidal ideas and intention, any raw score greater than zero should be taken very seriously.

Somatic Concerns

High scores on Scale 1 and on the A-hea Content scale are the clearest indicators of somatic symptoms. However, high scores on Scales 2, 3, and 8 and on the A-anx Content scale also can be indicative of somatic symptoms. Eating problems in girls have been associated with high scores on Scales 1 and 2 and the A-sod Content scale. Sleep difficulties are suggested by high scores on Scale 3, the A-obs and A-anx Content scales, and the D1 (Subjective Depression) Harris–Lingoes subscale.

Psychotic Symptoms

High scores on Scale 8, the A-biz Content scale, and the PSY-5 PSYC scale indicate the possibility of psychotic behaviors including delusions, hallucinations, ideas of reference, or disorganized thinking. High scores on the Pa1 (Persecutory Ideas), Sc3 (Lack of Ego Mastery, Cognitive), and Sc6 (Bizarre Sensory Experiences) Harris–Lingoes subscales are additional indicators of psychosis.

Poor Self-Esteem

High scores on the A-lse Content scale suggest problems with self-confidence. High scores on several Clinical scales (i.e., 1, 2, 7, 8, 0) also tend to be associated with lack of self-confidence. High scores on Scale 9 are indicative of positive self-perceptions that may at times be somewhat grandiose.

Anger

High scores on Scales 4 and 9 and the AGGR PSY-5 scale are suggestive of anger and resentment. High scores on the A-ang and A-con Content scales indicate problems with anger control.

Acting-Out Behaviors

Delinquent and acting-out behaviors are suggested by high scores on several scales and subscales. The best indicators of such behavior are high scores on Scales 4 and 9, the A-con Content scale, and the PSY-5 DISC scale. High scores on Scale 2 tend to contraindicate acting-out behavior. Some data indicate that girls who have higher T scores on Scale 5 tend to act out in various ways, whereas boys with higher T scores on Scale 5 tend not to act out. Girls with high scores on the A-sod Content scale tend not to act out. Acting out also is characteristic of adolescents who have high scores on the A-ang and A-las Content scales and on the Pd2 (Authority Problems) and Ma1 Harris–Lingoes subscales.

School Problems

The A-sch Content scale was developed specifically to assess academic and behavioral problems in school. In addition, academic problems are suggested by high scores on Scales 1, 2, 4, 5 (girls), 6, and 8 and on the A-hea, A-biz, A-lse, and A-las Content scales. Behavioral problems in school are suggested by high scores on Scales 4, 5 (girls), 6, 8, and 9, the A-hea and A-biz Content scales, and the PSY-5 DISC scale. The relationship between school problems and so many MMPI-A scales seems to indicate that adolescents develop school problems for a variety of reasons and that school problems can contribute to a variety of symptoms.

Alcohol/Drug Problems

Adolescents who have moderate (T = 60–64) or high (T ≥ 65) scores on the ACK scale are openly admitting to the use of alcohol or drugs and the problems associated with such use. However, the absence of high scores on ACK is difficult to interpret. Because of the obvious content of most items in this scale, the absence of high scores could indicate either that substance use problems are not present or that they are present and are being denied. Moderate (T = 60–64) or high (T ≥ 65) scores on the MAC-R and the PRO scale suggest problems with alcohol or drugs whether or not the adolescents are acknowledging such problems. The likelihood of problematic use is greatest if an adolescent has high scores on all three of these scales. Other indicators of possible alcohol or other drug problems include high scores on Scales 4, 8, and 9 and on the DISC PSY-5 scale. High scores on Scale 2 tend not to be associated with problematic substance use. One should not conclude from MMPI-A data that an adolescent is not experiencing substance-related difficulties. However, high scores on the scales mentioned here should alert the clinician to the possibility of substance use problems that should be evaluated more completely.

Interpersonal Relationships

Adolescents who have high scores on Scale 0, the A-sod Content scale, or the PSY-5 INTR scale are likely to be shy, introverted, and uncomfortable in social situations.

High scores on Scales 2 and 7 and on the SiI (Shyness/Self-Consciousness) subscale further support the impression of shyness and introversion. On the other hand, high scores on the Hy1 (Denial of Social Anxiety) and Pd3 (Social Imperturbability) Harris–Lingoes subscales and on Scale 9 suggest extroversion and gregariousness. Social withdrawal and isolation are suggested by high scores on Scales 1, 6, and 8; on the A-aln and A-sod Content scales; on the Pd4 (Social Alienation) and Sc1 (Social Alienation) Harris–Lingoes subscales; and on the Si2 (Social Avoidance) subscale. Adolescents who have high scores on Scale 6, on the A-cyn Content scale, or on the Pa1 Harris–Lingoes subscale are likely to be cynical, guarded, and untrusting in relationships. High scores on the A-ang Content scale are associated with irritability and lack of anger control.

High scores on Scale 4, the A-fam Content scale, and the Pd1 (Familial Discord) Harris–Lingoes subscale indicate that adolescents are describing their family circumstances very negatively. They do not see their families as loving or supportive; and they tend to be angry, resentful, and rebellious toward family members. Adolescents who have high scores on the A-con or A-lse Content scales or on the PRO scale tend to be influenced easily by peers to become involved in antisocial or delinquent acts.

Physical or Sexual Abuse

It is not possible to determine from test data whether an adolescent has been physically or sexually abused. However, some MMPI-A data suggest that adolescents with high scores on certain scales are more likely than other adolescents to have histories of having been abused. High scores on Scale 4 or the A-fam Content scale for boys suggest that the possibility of physical abuse should be considered carefully. High scores on Scales 8 (boys and girls), 4 (girls), and 7 (boys) suggest that the possibility of sexual abuse should be considered carefully. Histories of sexual abuse may be associated with high scores on the A-fam Content scale for girls and with high scores on the A-dep, A-ang, A-lse, or A-sch Content scales for boys. It should be emphasized again that high scores on these various scales should not be used to determine if abuse has occurred. Rather, high scores on these scales should alert clinicians to assess the possibility of abuse carefully if this is not already a goal of the assessment.

Strengths and Assets

Although the scales of the MMPI-A were designed to measure problems and symptoms, it is important to try to address strengths and assets when giving feedback to the adolescents, their parents, or school staff. Although the limited empirical data available for MMPI-A scales do not suggest many positive characteristics associated with high scores, research conducted on the original MMPI scales suggests some characteristics of high scorers that could be viewed as positive (Archer, 1987). High scorers on Scale 3 are described as achievement-oriented, socially involved, and friendly. High scorers on Scale 4 tend to be sociable, gregarious persons who create favorable first impressions on other people. High-scoring boys on Scale 5 are seen by others as intelligent and attaining higher levels of academic achievement. High scorers on Scale 7 can be described as conscientious. High Scale 8 scorers tend to approach problems in creative ways. High Scale 9 scorers are likely to be energetic, extroverted, and self-confident. High scorers on Scale 0 are less likely to be involved in delinquent activities.

High scores on some of the Harris–Lingoes subscales also suggest some positive characteristics. For example, high scores on Hy1 or Pd3 subscales indicate adolescents who say they are comfortable and confident in social situations. High Ma4 (Ego Inflation) scorers tend to have very favorable self-concepts (though perhaps unrealistically so at times).

Importantly, we do not recommend using low scores as being indicative of potential strengths. This is because, as stated earlier in this chapter, we cannot know if low scores on the MMPI-A scales are indicative of a lack of problems and symptoms or simply denial of them.

Diagnostic Considerations

Although there is not much research available that directly addresses the most likely diagnoses for adolescents who produce particular scores or patterns of scores on the MMPI-A, some inferences can be made on the basis of high scores on certain scales. High scores on Scale 1 or the A-hea Content scale are consistent with somatic symptom disorder diagnoses; high scores on Scale 2, the A-dep Content scale, and the INTR PSY-5 scale are consistent with depression or anxiety disorder diagnoses; high scores on Scales 4 or 9, the A-con Content scale, and the PSY-5 DISC scale often are consistent with conduct disorder diagnoses; high scores on Scale 7, the A-anx Content scale, and the NEGE PSY-5 scale are consistent with anxiety disorder diagnoses; high scores on Scale 8, the A-biz Content scale, and the PSY-5 PSYC scale are consistent with the possibility of psychotic disorders; and high scores on one or more of the alcohol/drug problem scales (i.e., MAC-R, PRO, ACK) suggest the possibility of substance-related disorders should be explored carefully.

It should be emphasized that diagnoses cannot and should not be assigned to adolescents solely on the basis of MMPI-A data. The criteria for most diagnostic categories include information that must be obtained from sources other than test data (e.g., observation, interview, history). Often the best approach is to generate a comprehensive description of the adolescent's symptoms, personality, and behavior and compare this description with the various categories described in the most current version of the diagnostic manual.

Treatment Implications

There are very limited empirical data for adolescents concerning relationships between MMPI or MMPI-A scores and treatment-related characteristics. The A-trt scale was designed to assess characteristics of adolescents that would interfere with effective psychological treatment. High scorers on this scale typically express negative attitudes toward doctors and health professionals, believe that others do not care what happens to them, accept little responsibility for their own behavior, and feel unable or unwilling to change. Obviously, characteristics such as these have very negative implications for treatment. However, it must be emphasized that there have not yet been any outcome studies conducted to evaluate the validity of A-trt scores. In addition, evidence concerning the saturation of the adult version of the A-trt scale with demoralization suggests caution is needed when interpreting high scores on the scale if the adolescent is in considerable psychological turmoil.

High scorers on Scales 2 and 7 often are experiencing enough emotional distress that they are motivated to participate in psychotherapy. By contrast, high scorers on Scales 4 and 9 often blame others for their problems, so they are not very motivated to engage in psychotherapy. The prognosis for successful psychological treatment is not very positive for high scorers on Scale 8.

Given the limited research on this topic, it is often necessary and appropriate to make higher-order inferences concerning treatment-related issues. For example, it is reasonable to infer that an adolescent who admits to a great deal of psychological turmoil (as indicated by high scores on many scales) will be more willing to cooperate in treatment than someone who does not admit to such turmoil; and that an adolescent who produces a very defensive pattern on the Validity scales of the MMPI-A would not be very open and cooperative in a therapeutic relationship. Adolescents whose MMPI-A scores (e.g., Scales 4, 9, A-ang, A-cyn, AGGR, DISC) suggest considerable anger and resentment will likely be rather uncooperative in therapy and will often test limits in relationships with therapists.

Alternative Approaches to Interpretation

There are alternative approaches to interpreting the MMPI-A. For example, Archer and Krishnamurthy (1994) developed the MMPI-A Structural Summary as a way of organizing scores using the following general factor dimensions: (a) General Maladjustment, (b) Immaturity, (c) Disinhibition/Excitatory Potential, (d) Social Discomfort, (e) Health Concerns, (f) Naivete, (g) Familial Alienation, and (h) Psychoticism. This method of summarizing MMPI-A results was based largely on a factor analysis of MMPI-A scales in the normative sample (Archer, Belevich, & Elkins, 1994). The structure that emerged in the normative sample was subsequently replicated and validated in juvenile delinquency and inpatient psychiatric samples (Archer et al., 2003; Pogge et al., 2002). For details concerning the utilization of the Structural Summary approach to MMPI-A interpretation, readers should consult Archer and Krishnamurthy's (2002) interpretive guide. Additionally, Archer, Krishnamurthy, and Jacobson (1994) and Ben-Porath and Davis (1996) have published books of case studies illustrating MMPI-A interpretation.

ILLUSTRATIVE CASE

To illustrate the interpretive strategy described in the MMPI-A manual (Butcher et al., 1992), MMPI-A scores of an adolescent boy, John, will be interpreted. The computerized Extended Score Report appended to this chapter includes John's scores and profiles. The interpretive inferences derived from his MMPI-A scores should be treated as hypotheses to be evaluated on the basis of other information available about him. The MMPI-A results should be only part of a more comprehensive evaluation. Additional cases for readers to practice interpretation with are included in the supplemental materials available for this book on the publisher's website. Please visit www.oup.com/he/graham6e to access these materials.

Background and Referral Concerns

John was a 16-year-old, White male who was referred for psychological evaluation because of problems with depression and externalizing behaviors. He was raised by his biological parents, who described John as having few problems or difficulties until he was approximately 12 years old. At that time, John began experiencing periods of depression characterized by anhedonia and amotivation, as well as extremely high levels of irritability and anger. John withdrew from previously enjoyed relationships and activities (e.g., a youth group), as well as from activities that required sustained effort (e.g., academics). His parents reported John had engaged in an escalating pattern of externalizing behaviors in the past year, such as associating with peers who were a negative influence on him and consuming alcohol and marijuana. John had also been increasingly aggressive with adult authority figures, especially his father—who was the family's disciplinarian. John was referred for evaluation and treatment after being arrested for physically assaulting his father during an argument.

Extratest Factors

John was cooperative throughout the psychological evaluation. He completed a computerized version of the MMPI-A in approximately 45 minutes, asking no questions and making no comments during the testing.

Response Attitudes

John completed the MMPI-A in a valid and interpretable manner. He omitted no items, and his VRIN scale T score of 42 and TRIN scale T score of 51 indicate that he responded to the items' contents. His T scores of 37 on the L scale and 44 on the K scale suggest that he was not defensive. In fact, these scores indicate that he was less defensive than the average adolescent. His scores on F1 (T = 52), F2 (T = 52), and F (T = 52) provided no evidence he was overreporting problems and symptoms. Rather, scores on substantive scales are likely to reflect problems and symptoms that he was experiencing. In summary, there is no reason we cannot interpret the substantive scales with confidence that they will give an accurate picture of John's psychological status.

Symptoms

John has a defined 3-point code (479), as there is at least a 5-point T score difference between his third most elevated Clinical scale score (Scale 7 and 9; both are T = 62) and the next most elevated Clinical scale (Scale 2, T = 56). The scores that comprise the code type are all greater than 60T, meaning it is interpretable. However, no descriptive information is available for this code type. John does not have a defined 2-point code because his second and third most elevated Clinical scale scores are equal (Scale 7 and 9). Thus, no code type interpretation is made, and the focus of the interpretation will be on individual scales.

Anxiety

John had a high score (i.e., T ≥ 60) on Clinical Scale 7 (T = 62), which suggests he may experience high levels of emotional turmoil. Scores on this scale can also be indicative of anxiety, but he did not achieve clinically significant elevations (i.e., T ≥ 65) on other markers of anxiety (e.g., the A-anx Content scale or PSY-5 NEGE scale) or obsessiveness (e.g., the A-obs Content scale). As such, we would emphasize the experience of emotional upset, rather than symptoms of anxiety, in our interpretation of this scale.

Depression
John achieved a clinically significant score on the A-dep Content scale (T = 79), suggesting he is likely to be feeling sad and depressed. Inspection of the Content Component Scales for A-dep indicates his elevation on this scale was driven by reports of self-depreciation (A-dep2) and low drive (A-dep3). These scores suggest he reported feeling dissatisfied with himself and the direction his life is taking, and that he struggles with motivation. Importantly, John also endorsed two items on the A-dep4 Content Component scale, which is the MMPI-A scale that contains items with obvious suicide-related content. The A-dep4 items John endorsed reflect hopelessness and suggest a suicide-risk evaluation should be undertaken.

Somatic Concerns
John is not likely to be presenting health-related concerns (T score for Scale 1 = 54; T score for A-hea = 50).

Psychotic Symptoms
John is not likely to be presenting with concerns about psychotic symptoms, as he achieved average T scores on Clinical Scale 6 and 8 (both T = 52), as well as on the A-biz Content scale and PSYC PSY-5 scale (T = 41 and 46, respectively).

Poor Self-Esteem
John's T score of 62 on the A-lse Content scale indicates he is likely to have a negative self-concept and may compare himself unfavorably to other people. Additional evidence of low self-esteem comes from elevated scores on Scales 7 and A-dep.

Anger
John has elevated scores on several primary indicators of anger (i.e., Scales 4, T = 83, and 9, T = 62; A-ang Content scale, T = 74; and AGGR PSY-5 scale, T = 65). He is likely to feel irritable and impatient with others and have problems controlling his temper. Elevations on these scales, along with the A-con Content Scale (T = 72), suggest John's anger may be expressed in direct, poorly controlled ways. He is likely to be verbally and physically aggressive toward others. Furthermore, given the elevated scores on the Pd1 Harris-Lingoes subscale (T = 80) and on the A-fam Content scale (T = 64), his anger may be directed at his family, especially his parents.

Acting-Out Behaviors
There are strong indicators of acting-out behaviors in John's MMPI-A scores. He had high or clinically significant scores on most of the primary indicators of acting out including Scales 4 (T = 83) and 9 (T = 62), the Harris-Lingoes Subscale Ma$_1$

(T = 73), the A-con Content scale (T = 72), and the PSY-5 DISC scale (T = 71). John is likely to display a variety of acting-out and delinquent behaviors. He may be prone to disagreements with authority figures, whom he is likely to resent. He is also likely to behave in oppositional, defiant, sensation-seeking, and impulsive ways.

School Problems

John achieved an average score (T = 48) on the A-sch Content scale, suggesting he did not describe himself as having difficulties in school. However, he achieved elevated scores on several other scales that could suggest problems with academic achievement and appropriate school behavior. For example, high scores on the A-dep (T = 79) and A-lse (T = 62) Content scales may indicate problems with motivation and decision making that could impact school performance. High scores on Clinical Scale 4 (T = 83) and the PSY-5 DISC (T = 71) scale are indicative of difficulties with impulsivity and boredom intolerance that could impact his ability to behave appropriately in school settings.

Alcohol/Drug Problems

Data concerning substance use problems are mixed. John's T score of 59 on the ACK scale indicates he is not admitting problematic use of substances. The T score of 59 on the MAC-R is also not consistent with substance-related difficulties. However, John endorsed several critical items related to having used alcohol and other substances, and the T score of 67 on the PRO scale raises some concern about substance use problems. It should be recognized that this scale does not include items dealing directly with substance use; and its items cover a wide array of content including family and school problems, antisocial behaviors and beliefs, and peer group influence. Regardless, given this pattern of responding, John should be further evaluated for substance-related difficulties.

Interpersonal Relationships

John is likely to be an outgoing, gregarious young man (Scale 4, T = 83; Scale 9, T = 62). However, John also reports feeling alienated from other people (Harris-Lingoes Pd4, T = 69) and sees other people as untrustworthy (A-cyn Content Scale, T = 65). His interpersonal difficulties are especially pronounced in his family relationships, as he achieved high scores on the Harris-Lingoes Pd1 (T = 80) subscale and the A-fam Content scale (T = 64). The elevated scores on these scales indicate he described his family as being characterized by a lack of love and understanding. His family is also likely to have high levels of conflict and limited positive communication.

Physical or Sexual Abuse

John achieved high scores on Clinical Scale 4 and 7, which have been associated in past research with having a history of physical and sexual abuse, respectively. There were no other indications in John's scores or item endorsements to suggest that he has been sexually or physically abused. The likelihood of these experiences should be further evaluated using data gathered from other sources of information during the assessment.

Strengths

The MMPI-A is a problem- and psychopathology-oriented instrument, and not much information is available about positive characteristics associated with its scales. However, several second-order inferences about John's strengths are possible based on his MMPI-A scores. His high scores on Scales 4 (T = 83) and 9 (T = 62) suggest John is likely to enjoy social activities and being around other people. This sociability could facilitate his engagement in meaningful, prosocial activities that would assist him in developing positive relationships, in addition to alleviating his feelings of depressed mood. One could also discuss the things that his scores suggest that he is not. For example, John is not likely to have health complaints or psychotic symptoms.

Diagnostic Considerations

John's MMPI-A scores are consistent with several diagnoses. His high scores on Clinical Scales 4 (T = 83) and 9 (T = 62), on the A-con Content scale (T = 72), and on PSY-5 AGGR (T = 65) and DISC (T = 71) scales are consistent with externalizing disorder diagnoses, such as Conduct Disorder or Oppositional Defiant Disorder. Although he is not acknowledging problems with alcohol or other substances, his clinically elevated score on the PRO scale (T = 67) suggests that substance-related diagnoses cannot be ruled out. John's high scores on Scales 7 (T = 62) and the A-dep Content scale (T = 79) are consistent with diagnoses of depression or dysthymia. Depressive disorder diagnoses also seem to be supported by his reports of having a negative view of himself (e.g., A-lse, T = 62), others (e.g., A-cyn = 65), and the future (e.g., A-dep4, T = 64). Finally, given difficulties with depressed mood in adolescence often manifest in feelings of anger and irritability, John's high scores on the A-ang Content scale (T = 74) and the PSY-5 AGGR scale (T = 65) may also support diagnoses of a depressive disorder.

Treatment Implications

John's experience of repeated difficulties with depressed mood (Scale 7, T = 62; A-dep, T = 79; A-lse = 62), his escalating pattern of angry (A-ang, T = 74), aggressive (Scale 4, T = 83; Scale 9, T = 62; A-con, T = 72; AGGR, T = 65), and impulsive (DISC, T = 71) behaviors, and deteriorating family relationships (A-fam, T = 64) indicate he could benefit from psychological treatment. Given he reported experiencing considerable emotional turmoil (e.g., Scale 7), he may be motivated for treatment. His willingness to admit to problems and difficulties while completing the MMPI-A (F1, T = 52; F2, T = 52; F, T = 52) and his lack of defensiveness (L, T = 37; K, T = 44) suggest that he may be willing to discuss problems during therapy. However, he may struggle to develop a positive relationship with his therapist given his cynical attitudes (A-cyn, T = 65) and distrust of authority figures (Scale 4, T = 83; A-con, T = 72). He may also struggle if he thinks the therapist is strongly aligned with his parents or if they are disregardful of his perspectives on the conflicts occurring in his family (A-fam = 64). His experience of hopelessness and low motivation (e.g., A-dep, T = 79) may also impact his ability to engage in therapy, and he likely feels feel incapable of dealing with his problems and unable to make positive changes in his life (A-trt, T = 81).

An initial goal for therapy should be the reduction of John's experience of psychological distress. Because he admitted to feeling hopeless and that life was not worthwhile (A-dep4, T = 64; four relevant critical items), a detailed suicide risk assessment is in order. This will be especially important given John is likely to be quite impulsive (DISC, T = 71), which can increase risk for suicidal behavior. It will also be important for the therapist to help John recognize he is capable of making meaningful changes in his life to build hope and motivation. Therapy should then address John's difficulties with depressed and angry moods (Scale 7, T = 62; A-dep, T = 79; A-ang, T = 74), which appear to have contributed to his escalating pattern of externalizing and aggressive behaviors (Scale 4, T = 83; Scale 9, T = 62; A-con, T = 72; PRO, T = 67; AGGR, T = 65). Because John's anger and aggressiveness have been primarily directed at his parents (A-fam, T = 64), careful consideration should be given to involving them in initial phases of John's individual treatment. Instead, a separate referral for family therapy or parent training and support interventions may be warranted. When working with John, the therapist should monitor the impact of John's cynical attitudes (A-cyn, T = 65), distrust of authority figures (Scale 4, T = 83; A-con, T = 72), and difficulties with motivation (A-dep, T = 79) on the therapeutic process.

Summary

John approached the MMPI-A in a valid manner, acknowledging problems and symptoms. He is experiencing emotional turmoil, including feeling depressed and angry. He has a negative view of himself, others, and the future. He may be at risk for suicidal thinking or behavior. John also experiences difficulties due to externalizing behaviors, which include angry and aggressive outbursts, as well as potential misuse of substances. He sees other people—especially his parents and other authority figures—as not being understanding or supportive. These perceptions appear to contribute to his feelings of anger, resentment, and rebelliousness.

The diagnoses most consistent with his MMPI-A scores are depressive disorder or dysthymia and adolescent-onset conduct problems. His responses to some items also endorsed by adolescents with substance-related difficulties suggest that the potential for a substance use disorder should also be further evaluated.

John's recurrent difficulties with depressed and irritable mood, escalating pattern of externalizing behaviors, and high levels of conflict with his family indicate he needs psychological intervention. He is likely to be somewhat ambivalent about treatment, feeling the need for help because of his strong distress but also believing that he will not be able to make significant positive changes. A primary goal for therapy is reduction of his psychological turmoil. Because of his high levels of hopelessness and impulsive tendencies, suicide risk monitoring should be part of treatment. The therapist and John should address his experience of depression, determining whether these difficulties are contributing to the externalizing behaviors he engages in. He could also use assistance navigating increasingly conflictual relationships with his parents.

CHAPTER APPENDIX

MMPI®-A

Minnesota Multiphasic Personality Inventory®-Adolescent

Extended Score Report

ID Number:	John
Age:	16
Gender:	Male
Date Assessed:	11/23/2015

ALWAYS LEARNING   PEARSON

MMPI-A VALIDITY AND CLINICAL SCALES PROFILE

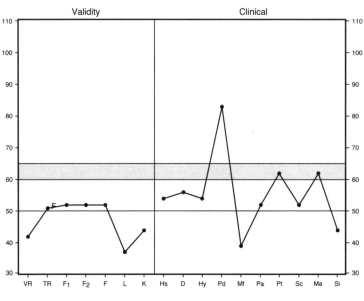

	VR	TR	F₁	F₂	F	L	K	Hs	D	Hy	Pd	Mf	Pa	Pt	Sc	Ma	Si
Raw Score:	2	9	5	6	11	0	10	10	23	23	34	17	14	27	26	27	21
T Score:	42	51	52	52	52	37	44	54	56	54	83	39	52	62	52	62	44
Response %:	100	100	100	100	100	100	100	100	100	100	100	100	100	100	100	100	100

Cannot Say (Raw):   0

Percent True: 55

Percent False: 45

Welsh Code: 4'''+79-213 68/0:5# F/K:L#

MMPI®-A Extended Score Report
11/23/2015, Page 3

John

MMPI-A CONTENT SCALES PROFILE

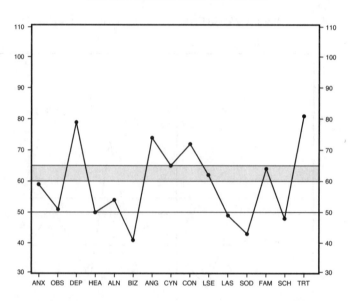

	ANX	OBS	DEP	HEA	ALN	BIZ	ANG	CYN	CON	LSE	LAS	SOD	FAM	SCH	TRT
Raw Score:	12	8	20	8	8	1	14	18	17	9	6	5	19	6	19
T Score:	59	51	79	50	54	41	74	65	72	62	49	43	64	48	81
Response %:	100	100	100	100	100	100	100	100	100	100	100	100	100	100	100

MMPI-A SUPPLEMENTARY SCALES PROFILE

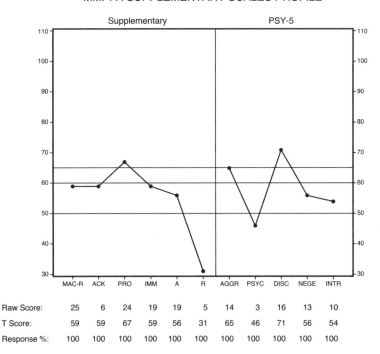

	MAC-R	ACK	PRO	IMM	A	R	AGGR	PSYC	DISC	NEGE	INTR
Raw Score:	25	6	24	19	19	5	14	3	16	13	10
T Score:	59	59	67	59	56	31	65	46	71	56	54
Response %:	100	100	100	100	100	100	100	100	100	100	100

ADDITIONAL SCALES

	Raw Score	T Score	Resp %
Harris-Lingoes Subscales			
Depression Subscales			
Subjective Depression (D_1)	17	70	100
Psychomotor Retardation (D_2)	5	51	100
Physical Malfunctioning (D_3)	5	62	100
Mental Dullness (D_4)	7	64	100
Brooding (D_5)	7	71	100
Hysteria Subscales			
Denial of Social Anxiety (Hy_1)	4	55	100
Need for Affection (Hy_2)	3	41	100
Lassitude-Malaise (Hy_3)	12	81	100
Somatic Complaints (Hy_4)	2	43	100
Inhibition of Aggression (Hy_5)	1	36	100
Psychopathic Deviate Subscales			
Familial Discord (Pd_1)	9	80	100
Authority Problems (Pd_2)	4	54	100
Social Imperturbability (Pd_3)	5	61	100
Social Alienation (Pd_4)	8	65	100
Self-Alienation (Pd_5)	9	69	100
Paranoia Subscales			
Persecutory Ideas (Pa_1)	7	60	100
Poignancy (Pa_2)	4	55	100
Naivete (Pa_3)	2	40	100
Schizophrenia Subscales			
Social Alienation (Sc_1)	10	62	100
Emotional Alienation (Sc_2)	4	59	100
Lack of Ego Mastery, Cognitive (Sc_3)	3	50	100
Lack of Ego Mastery, Conative (Sc_4)	8	65	100
Lack of Ego Mastery, Defective Inhibition (Sc_5)	2	43	100
Bizarre Sensory Experiences (Sc_6)	2	41	100
Hypomania Subscales			
Amorality (Ma_1)	6	73	100
Psychomotor Acceleration (Ma_2)	7	52	100
Imperturbability (Ma_3)	5	62	100
Ego Inflation (Ma_4)	3	42	100

	Raw Score	T Score	Resp %
Social Introversion Subscales (Ben-Porath, Hostetler, Butcher, & Graham)			
Shyness/Self-Consciousness (Si$_1$)	2	36	100
Social Avoidance (Si$_2$)	2	47	100
Alienation--Self and Others (Si$_3$)	11	60	100
Content Component Scales (Sherwood, Ben-Porath, & Williams)			
Adolescent Depression			
Dysphoria (A-dep$_1$)	2	55	100
Self-Depreciation (A-dep$_2$)	4	66	100
Lack of Drive (A-dep$_3$)	7	80	100
Suicidal Ideation (A-dep$_4$)	2	64	100
Adolescent Health Concerns			
Gastrointestinal Complaints (A-hea$_1$)	0	46	100
Neurological Symptoms (A-hea$_2$)	4	50	100
General Health Concerns (A-hea$_3$)	2	51	100
Adolescent Alienation			
Misunderstood (A-aln$_1$)	4	64	100
Social Isolation (A-aln$_2$)	0	38	100
Interpersonal Skepticism (A-aln$_3$)	2	56	100
Adolescent Bizarre Mentation			
Psychotic Symptomatology (A-biz$_1$)	0	38	100
Paranoid Ideation (A-biz$_2$)	1	53	100
Adolescent Anger			
Explosive Behavior (A-ang$_1$)	6	66	100
Irritability (A-ang$_2$)	7	64	100
Adolescent Cynicism			
Misanthropic Beliefs (A-cyn$_1$)	11	62	100
Interpersonal Suspiciousness (A-cyn$_2$)	7	61	100
Adolescent Conduct Problems			
Acting-Out Behaviors (A-con$_1$)	8	70	100
Antisocial Attitudes (A-con$_2$)	7	68	100
Negative Peer Group Influences (A-con$_3$)	0	41	100
Adolescent Low Self-Esteem			
Self-Doubt (A-lse$_1$)	8	69	100
Interpersonal Submissiveness (A-lse$_2$)	1	46	100

	Raw Score	T Score	Resp %
Adolescent Low Aspirations			
Low Achievement Orientation (A-las$_1$)	4	53	100
Lack of Initiative (A-las$_2$)	2	49	100
Adolescent Social Discomfort			
Introversion (A-sod$_1$)	3	46	100
Shyness (A-sod$_2$)	2	40	100
Adolescent Family Problems			
Familial Discord (A-fam$_1$)	13	63	100
Familial Alienation (A-fam$_2$)	5	63	100
Adolescent School Problems			
School Conduct Problems (A-sch$_1$)	0	41	100
Negative Attitudes (A-sch$_2$)	4	57	100
Adolescent Negative Treatment Indicators			
Low Motivation (A-trt$_1$)	7	67	100
Inability to Disclose (A-trt$_2$)	6	65	100

Uniform T scores are used for Hs, D, Hy, Pd, Pa, Pt, Sc, Ma, the content scales, the content component scales, and the PSY-5 scales. The remaining scales and subscales use linear T scores.

CRITICAL ITEMS (Forbey & Ben-Porath)

The MMPI-A contains a number of items whose content may indicate the presence of psychological problems when endorsed in the deviant direction. These "critical items," developed for use in clinical settings, may provide an additional source of hypotheses about the respondent. However, caution should be used in interpreting critical items since responses to single items are very unreliable and should not be treated as scores on full-length scales -- for example, an individual could easily mismark or misunderstand a single item and not intend the answer given. The content of the items and the possibility of misinterpretation make it important to keep the test results strictly confidential. Special caution should be exercised when interpreting these items in nonclinical settings.

Aggression
Item number and content omitted. (True)

Anxiety
Item number and content omitted. (True)

Conduct Problems
Item number and content omitted. (True)
Item number and content omitted. (False)
Item number and content omitted. (True)

Depression/Suicidal Ideation
Item number and content omitted. (False)
Item number and content omitted. (True)
Item number and content omitted. (True)
Item number and content omitted. (True)

Note: Item numbers and content are included in the actual reports. To protect test security, the item details do not appear in this report.

Family Problems
Item number and content omitted. (False)

Self-Denigration
Item number and content omitted. (True)
Item number and content omitted. (True)
Item number and content omitted. (True)
Item number and content omitted. (True)

Somatic Complaints
Item number and content omitted. (False)

Substance Use/Abuse
Item number and content omitted. (True)
Item number and content omitted. (False)
Item number and content omitted. (True)

End of Report

NOTE: This and previous pages of this report contain trade secrets and are not to be released in response to requests under HIPAA (or any other data disclosure law that exempts trade secret information from release). Further, release in response to litigation discovery demands should be made only in accordance with your profession's ethical guidelines and under an appropriate protective order.

ITEM RESPONSES

1: 1	2: 2	3: 2	4: 1	5: 2	6: 1	7: 1	8: 1	9: 2	10: 1
11: 2	12: 2	13: 1	14: 1	15: 1	16: 1	17: 2	18: 1	19: 1	20: 1
21: 2	22: 2	23: 1	24: 1	25: 2	26: 1	27: 2	28: 1	29: 2	30: 2
31: 1	32: 1	33: 2	34: 1	35: 1	36: 1	37: 2	38: 1	39: 2	40: 1
41: 2	42: 1	43: 1	44: 2	45: 2	46: 1	47: 2	48: 1	49: 2	50: 1
51: 1	52: 2	53: 1	54: 2	55: 1	56: 2	57: 2	58: 2	59: 2	60: 1
61: 2	62: 2	63: 2	64: 1	65: 1	66: 2	67: 2	68: 1	69: 1	70: 1
71: 2	72: 2	73: 1	74: 1	75: 1	76: 2	77: 1	78: 1	79: 2	80: 2
81: 2	82: 2	83: 2	84: 2	85: 2	86: 1	87: 2	88: 1	89: 1	90: 1
91: 2	92: 2	93: 2	94: 1	95: 2	96: 2	97: 2	98: 1	99: 1	100: 2
101: 2	102: 1	103: 1	104: 1	105: 1	106: 2	107: 1	108: 2	109: 1	110: 1
111: 1	112: 1	113: 1	114: 2	115: 1	116: 1	117: 1	118: 1	119: 2	120: 1
121: 2	122: 1	123: 1	124: 1	125: 1	126: 1	127: 1	128: 1	129: 2	130: 1
131: 2	132: 2	133: 1	134: 2	135: 2	136: 2	137: 2	138: 1	139: 2	140: 1
141: 2	142: 2	143: 2	144: 2	145: 1	146: 2	147: 1	148: 2	149: 1	150: 1
151: 2	152: 1	153: 1	154: 2	155: 2	156: 1	157: 1	158: 1	159: 2	160: 2
161: 2	162: 1	163: 2	164: 2	165: 2	166: 1	167: 1	168: 1	169: 1	170: 2
171: 1	172: 1	173: 2	174: 2	175: 2	176: 1	177: 2	178: 2	179: 1	180: 1
181: 1	182: 1	183: 1	184: 1	185: 1	186: 2	187: 2	188: 1	189: 1	190: 2
191: 1	192: 1	193: 1	194: 1	195: 1	196: 1	197: 1	198: 1	199: 2	200: 1
201: 1	202: 2	203: 1	204: 2	205: 1	206: 1	207: 2	208: 1	209: 1	210: 1
211: 2	212: 2	213: 1	214: 2	215: 2	216: 1	217: 1	218: 2	219: 1	220: 2
221: 1	222: 1	223: 1	224: 1	225: 1	226: 2	227: 2	228: 1	229: 1	230: 1
231: 2	232: 1	233: 1	234: 1	235: 2	236: 2	237: 2	238: 1	239: 1	240: 1
241: 1	242: 1	243: 1	244: 1	245: 1	246: 2	247: 1	248: 1	249: 2	250: 2
251: 2	252: 1	253: 1	254: 1	255: 1	256: 1	257: 2	258: 1	259: 1	260: 1
261: 1	262: 1	263: 1	264: 2	265: 1	266: 2	267: 1	268: 1	269: 2	270: 2
271: 1	272: 2	273: 2	274: 2	275: 2	276: 2	277: 1	278: 2	279: 1	280: 1
281: 1	282: 1	283: 2	284: 1	285: 1	286: 1	287: 2	288: 2	289: 1	290: 2
291: 2	292: 1	293: 1	294: 1	295: 1	296: 2	297: 2	298: 2	299: 2	300: 2
301: 2	302: 2	303: 2	304: 2	305: 1	306: 1	307: 2	308: 1	309: 2	310: 2
311: 1	312: 2	313: 2	314: 1	315: 2	316: 2	317: 1	318: 1	319: 2	320: 1
321: 2	322: 2	323: 1	324: 1	325: 1	326: 2	327: 2	328: 1	329: 1	330: 1
331: 1	332: 2	333: 2	334: 1	335: 1	336: 1	337: 2	338: 1	339: 1	340: 1
341: 1	342: 2	343: 2	344: 1	345: 2	346: 1	347: 1	348: 1	349: 2	350: 2
351: 1	352: 2	353: 2	354: 2	355: 2	356: 1	357: 1	358: 1	359: 2	360: 1
361: 1	362: 2	363: 2	364: 2	365: 2	366: 2	367: 2	368: 2	369: 2	370: 1
371: 1	372: 1	373: 1	374: 1	375: 1	376: 1	377: 1	378: 1	379: 1	380: 2
381: 2	382: 1	383: 2	384: 2	385: 2	386: 1	387: 1	388: 2	389: 2	390: 2
391: 1	392: 1	393: 1	394: 1	395: 2	396: 1	397: 1	398: 2	399: 1	400: 2
401: 1	402: 2	403: 1	404: 2	405: 2	406: 1	407: 2	408: 2	409: 2	410: 2
411: 2	412: 1	413: 2	414: 1	415: 1	416: 1	417: 2	418: 2	419: 1	420: 1
421: 2	422: 2	423: 2	424: 2	425: 2	426: 1	427: 1	428: 2	429: 2	430: 2

431: 2 432: 1 433: 2 434: 2 435: 1 436: 2 437: 1 438: 1 439: 2 440: 1
441: 2 442: 1 443: 2 444: 1 445: 2 446: 2 447: 1 448: 2 449: 1 450: 1
451: 2 452: 1 453: 1 454: 1 455: 1 456: 1 457: 1 458: 2 459: 2 460: 1
461: 1 462: 1 463: 2 464: 1 465: 1 466: 2 467: 1 468: 2 469: 1 470: 2
471: 2 472: 1 473: 2 474: 2 475: 2 476: 1 477: 2 478: 2

CHAPTER 15

MMPI-A-RESTRUCTURED FORM (MMPI-A-RF)

THE MMPI-A-RF IS THE most recent version of the MMPI designed for use with adolescents. Development of the MMPI-A-RF began in 2007 (Archer, 2017; Archer et al., 2016), and the process was modeled after that of the restructured, adult version of the instrument—the MMPI-2-RF (Ben-Porath & Tellegen, 2008/2011; Tellegen & Ben-Porath, 2008/2011). This approach was undertaken because the decision to retain the original Clinical scales on the MMPI-A resulted in the instrument having many of the same psychometric problems as the revised adult version of the instrument, the MMPI-2 (Butcher et al., 2001). Namely, each of the Clinical scales include heterogeneous item content and are highly inter-correlated with one another, both of which lead the scales' scores to have problems with convergent and discriminant validity (Archer et al., 2016; Tellegen et al., 2003).

As described in Chapter 7, to address psychometric problems on adult versions of the instrument, Tellegen and colleagues (2003) began by developing nine Restructured Clinical (RC) scales. These scales were intended to retain the strengths of the original Clinical scales but reflect the clinically meaningful variance of the MMPI-2 item pool in a more psychometrically optimal manner. The scale development process resulted in a measure of demoralization (i.e., RCd) and eight other scales assessing key components of the original MMPI Clinical scales (i.e., RC1–RC9). After the RC scales were complete, Tellegen and Ben-Porath (2008/2011) pursued developing additional, psychometrically efficient scales assessing other important constructs using the MMPI-2 item pool. These efforts resulted in the MMPI-2-RF (Ben-Porath & Tellegen, 2008/2011; Tellegen & Ben-Porath, 2008/2011), which is described in Chapter 12. As reviewed in that chapter, scale scores on the MMPI-2-RF have been extensively investigated and have strong evidence supporting their validity in a variety of settings (Sellbom, 2019).

Given the success of the MMPI-2-RF development process, Archer et al. (2016) elected to use a similar restructuring process when developing the MMPI-A-RF. Specifically, the primary goal was to reduce the high degree of intercorrelation between scale scores by removing the influence of a shared demoralization factor, overlapping items, and content multidimensionality. A secondary goal was to reduce the number of items on the restructured instrument due to concerns about adolescents being able to complete the 478-item MMPI-A. Further, Archer et al. (2016) sought to maintain a degree of similarity between the MMPI-A-RF and the MMPI-2-RF. With these goals in mind, the test developers began by developing MMPI-A-RF RC scales, including a measure of demoralization and scales assessing core components of each Clinical scale (with exception of Clinical Scales 5 and 0). They then developed additional new substantive scales assessing other important constructs that could be measured using the MMPI-A item pool, as well as revised versions of Validity scales assessing response styles and substantive scales assessing maladaptive personality traits.

The outcome of the development process just described was the MMPI-A-RF, a 241-item instrument intended for use with adolescents ages 14 to 18 containing six Validity scales and 42 substantive scales arranged in a hierarchical structure. Nine RC scales revised from adult versions of these scales represent the core of the MMPI-A-RF. The RC scales are augmented by five revised MMPI-A Validity scales, one new Validity scale, three new Higher-Order (H-O) scales, 25 new Specific Problems (SP) scales, and revised versions of the Personality Psychopathology Five (PSY-5) scales. Table 15.1 lists all 48 of the MMPI-A-RF scales.

TABLE 15.1 *MMPI-A-RF Scales*

Validity Scales	
VRIN-r	Variable Response Inconsistency
TRIN-r	True Response Inconsistency
CRIN	Combined Response Inconsistency
F-r	Infrequent Responses
L-r	Uncommon Virtues
K-r	Adjustment Validity
Higher-Order (H-O) Scales	
EID	Emotional/Internalizing Dysfunction
THD	Thought Dysfunction
BXD	Behavioral/Externalizing Dysfunction
Restructured Clinical (RC) Scales	
RCd	Demoralization
RC1	Somatic Complaints
RC2	Low Positive Emotions
RC3	Cynicism
RC4	Antisocial Behavior

RC6		Ideas of Persecution
RC7		Dysfunctional Negative Emotions
RC8		Aberrant Experiences
RC9		Hypomanic Activation

Specific Problems (SP) Scales

Somatic/Cognitive SP Scales

MLS	Malaise
GIC	Gastrointestinal Complaints
HPC	Head Pain Complaints
NUC	Neurological Complaints
COG	Cognitive Complaints

Internalizing SP Scales

HLP	Helplessness/Hopelessness
SFD	Self-Doubt
NFC	Inefficacy
OCS	Obsessions/Compulsions
STW	Stress/Worry
AXY	Anxiety
ANP	Anger Proneness
BRF	Behavior-Restricting Fears
SPF	Specific Fears

Externalizing SP Scales

NSA	Negative School Attitudes
ASA	Antisocial Attitudes
CNP	Conduct Problems
SUB	Substance Abuse
NPI	Negative Peer Influence
AGG	Aggression

Interpersonal SP Scales

FML	Family Problems
IPP	Interpersonal Passivity
SAV	Social Avoidance
SHY	Shyness
DSF	Disaffiliativeness

Personality Psychopathology Five (PSY-5) Scales

AGGR-r	Aggressiveness–Revised
PSYC-r	Psychoticism–Revised
DISC-r	Disconstraint–Revised
NEGE-r	Negative Emotionality/Neuroticism–Revised
INTR-r	Introversion/Low Positive Emotionality–Revised

WHO CAN TAKE THE MMPI-A-RF?

The MMPI-A-RF is intended for use with adolescents between the ages of 14 and 18 (Archer et al. 2016). Because both adult and adolescent versions of the MMPI can be used with 18-year-olds, clinicians must decide which version is most appropriate for each 18-year-old. Generally, a version of the MMPI intended for adults should be used with mature 18-year-olds who are in college or otherwise living independently. Use of an adolescent version of the MMPI is recommended for 18-year-olds who have not adopted independent lifestyles. These recommendations are based on research conducted on the MMPI-A (e.g., Shaevel & Archer, 1996), and we have no reason to believe these suggestions should be altered for the MMPI-A-RF. Determining which adolescent version of the MMPI—the MMPI-A or MMPI-A-RF—should be administered will depend on the context of the evaluation and the clinician's needs. The strengths and weaknesses of these two instruments for use in adolescent assessments will be described later in this chapter.

Norms for the MMPI-A-RF are based on those collected for the MMPI-A, which only included 14- to 18-year-olds. As such, the test is identified for use with youth who are age 14 or older. However, based on previous research with the MMPI-A (e.g., Janus et al., 1996), Archer (2017) argued the MMPI-A-RF could be administered to youth who were 12 or 13 years of age as long as they had adequate reading comprehension and life experiences sufficient to interpret the items' contents in psychologically and semantically meaningful ways. We suspect the latter of these two criteria may be seldom met by adolescents evaluated in many settings. Thus, pending additional research on this practice, we recommend the MMPI-A-RF only be administered to 12- and 13-year-old youth with great caution. Additionally, this deviation from standardized administration requirements should be noted in the interpretation of the MMPI-A-RF.

DEVELOPMENT OF THE MMPI-A-RF SCALES

Samples Used for Scale Development and Validation

The MMPI-A-RF scales were developed using archival data made available by Pearson Assessments, the distributor of the MMPI family of instruments (Archer et al., 2016). In total, the development sample was comprised of over 15,000 adolescents tested in inpatient ($n = 419$), outpatient ($n = 11,699$), correctional ($n = 1,756$), and school ($n = 1,254$) settings. There were 9,286 boys and 5,842 girls who had a mean age of 15.61 ($SD = 1.80$) in this sample. This larger sample was stratified by age so that any influence of developmental factors on scale construction could be identified.

Once scales were developed, data from several samples were used to describe the scales' psychometric properties. First, data from setting-specific subsamples within the larger development sample just described were used to calculate descriptive statistics for some scales, as well as internal consistency reliability estimates, standard error of measurement (SEM) estimates, and intercorrelations between MMPI-A and MMPI-A-RF scale scores. Similar analyses were conducted and presented using data from the MMPI-A-RF's normative sample ($N = 1,610$), which is comprised of a subset of the normative sample used for the MMPI-A. The MMPI-A-RF normative sample is described in more detail later in this chapter. A small subset of youth in the MMPI-A normative sample completed the instrument on two occasions approximately 7 days apart. Data from these youth (n = 154) were used to present test–retest reliability estimates for MMPI-A-RF scale scores. Finally, data from several samples not used for scale development were used to provide initial evidence of the scale scores' validity. These samples included a psychiatric inpatient sample (N = 302), a residential treatment facility sample (N = 372), two forensic samples (N = 521 and 199, respectively), and a medical sample (N = 165). Data in these validation samples included MMPI-A responses—from which the MMPI-A-RF can be scored—as well as a wide variety of external criteria.

Validity Scales

The MMPI-A-RF has six Validity scales. Five of these scales are revised versions of MMPI-A Validity scales; and one, Combined Response Inconsistency (CRIN), is a new scale. Several of the revised scales' names were changed during the restructuring process to describe more accurately what they assessed. For example, the MMPI-A's Lie (L) scale was renamed Uncommon Virtues (L-r) on the MMPI-A-RF to reduce the implication that high scores necessarily indicated the test taker was being dishonest. Raw scores for all Validity scales are converted to linear T scores (M = 50, SD = 10) based on responses of the MMPI-A-RF normative sample. As with the MMPI-A, the Cannot Say (CNS) scale is also used as an index of nonresponding. Scores on CNS are simply the count of unanswered items and items answered both true and false.

Variable Response Inconsistency (VRIN-r), True Response Inconsistency (TRIN-r), and Combined Response Inconsistency (CRIN) Scales

The MMPI-A-RF's VRIN-r, TRIN-r, and CRIN scales assess non-content-based invalid responding. The VRIN-r and TRIN-r scales, which assess random and fixed responding, respectively, were constructed using procedures like those used to create their adult counterparts on the MMPI-2-RF (see Chapter 12). The CRIN scale is an entirely new scale intended to provide a global index of response inconsistency.

The VRIN-r scale consists of 27 item–response pairs. When scoring this scale, a point is assigned whenever a test taker responds to two items within a pair in an inconsistent manner. For example, if a test taker indicates they wake up fresh and rested most mornings and also that their sleep is fitful and disturbed, a point would be assigned on the VRIN-r scale. The VRIN-r raw score is simply the number of inconsistencies identified in responses to the pairs of items. Raw scores are converted to linear T scores. Higher scores indicate a greater degree of inconsistent responding. Interpretive guidelines for the VRIN-r scale are presented later in this chapter.

The TRIN-r scale consists of 13 pairs of negatively correlated items for which either two true or two false answers to a pair of items indicate inconsistent responding. For example, if a test taker endorses feeling sad but also endorses being happy, a point would be assigned on the TRIN-r scale, as these responses are inconsistent. The

TRIN-r raw score is the number of true–true responses to the item pairs minus the number of false–false answers to the item pairs. To prevent scores from being negative, a constant of 5 raw score points is added to this total. A higher difference score indicates a tendency to respond in an acquiescent, content-nonresponsive manner (yea-saying), whereas a lower difference score indicates a tendency to respond in a counter-acquiescent, content-nonresponsive manner (naysaying). Difference scores are converted to linear T scores, and T scores lower than 50 are reflected. For example, a T score of 40 is reflected as a T score of 60. Thus, TRIN-r T scores cannot be lower than 50. Higher T scores indicate non-content-based, fixed responding of either an acquiescent or counter-acquiescent type, with the former being designated with the letter *T* and the latter with the letter *F* in scoring reports. Interpretive guidelines for the TRIN-r scale are presented later in this chapter.

The CRIN scale consists of the 40 item–response pairs that comprise the VRIN-r and TRIN-r scales. Because CRIN is made up of item pairs indicating both inconsistent and fixed responding, it is best described as a general index of non-content-based invalid responding. This scale was added to the MMPI-A-RF to augment VRIN-r and TRIN-r, as these latter scales are comprised of relatively fewer item pairs on the MMPI-A-RF compared to other MMPI instruments. Raw scores on CRIN are calculated by summing the number of inconsistent responses to VRIN-r item pairs, the number of true–true responses to TRIN-r item pairs, and the number of false–false responses to TRIN-r item pairs. Raw scores are converted to linear T scores. Higher scores indicate a greater degree of non-content-based invalid responding. Interpretive guidelines for the CRIN scale are presented later in this chapter.

Infrequent Responses (F-r) Scale

The F-r scale is a revised version of the MMPI-A Frequency (F) scale and is intended to assess overreporting. The scale name was changed to Infrequent Responses on the MMPI-A-RF to better describe what is assessed by the scale's scores. The F-r scale consists of 23 items that were endorsed in the keyed direction by 15% or fewer of boys and girls in the MMPI-A-RF normative sample and 20% or fewer of the adolescents in the MMPI-A-RF development sample. Some items that met these criteria were not included in the F-r scale because they appeared to the test's developers to have redundant content. Raw scores are converted to linear T scores, with higher scores indicating greater endorsement of items rarely endorsed by persons in the normative and scale development samples. Extremely high scores are indicative of an overreporting response style. Interpretive guidelines for the F-r scale are presented later in this chapter.

The Uncommon Virtues (L-r) and Adjustment Validity (K-r) Scales

The L-r and K-r scales were developed to identify underreporting on the MMPI-A-RF. These scales reflect revised versions of the MMPI-A L (Lie) and K (Correction) scales, but were renamed to reduce pejorative connotations (i.e., L) or to make the name more descriptive of the scale's purpose (i.e., K). The L-r and K-r scales were heavily based on their MMPI-2-RF counterparts, which were derived from factor analyses of MMPI-2 underreporting scales (see Chapter 12). Items scored on the MMPI-2-RF

L-r and K-r scales available in the MMIP-A item pool were used to create initial seed scales for MMPI-A-RF versions of these scales. A review of item content led to some of these preliminary items being dropped from the scales. The final MMPI-A-RF L-r scale is comprised of 11 items, while the final K-r scale is comprised of 12 items. Raw scores on the L-r and K-r scales are converted to linear T scores. Higher scores on these two scales suggest greater likelihood of underreporting. High scores on K-r reflect the disavowal of common symptoms and everyday problems, while high scores on L-r reflect reports of more virtuous behavior than the average adolescent claims. Interpretive guidelines for the L-r and K-r scales are presented later in this chapter.

Higher-Order (H-O) Scales

The H-O scales are intended to assess the major dimensions of psychological dysfunction represented by the MMPI-A-RF scales as well as provide an organizational structure for its interpretation. The H-O scales were developed by first conducting a components analysis of the MMPI-A-RF RC scales (described later in this chapter) in the psychiatric inpatient scale development subsample (n = 419). Archer et al. (2016) sought to identify three components they hypothesized would reflect internalizing, psychotic, and externalizing symptoms based on findings from studies of the MMPI-2-RF. Results suggested three relatively distinct components reflecting the hypothesized dimensions. The internalizing component was comprised of scores on RCd (Demoralization), RC1 (Somatic Complaints), RC2 (Low Positive Emotions), and RC7 (Dysfunctional Negative Emotions). The externalizing component was comprised of scores on RC4 (Antisocial Behavior) and RC9 (Hypomanic Activation). The psychosis component was comprised of scores on RC3 (Cynicism), RC6 (Ideas of Persecution), and RC8 (Aberrant Experiences), but also had a moderate cross-loading from RC4. Component scores were then derived and used to select items for the H-O scales from the MMPI-A item pool. Items that had a strong correlation with one component but not the others were selected for inclusion on an H-O scale. This process resulted in the development of three scales: Emotional/Internalizing Dysfunction (EID), Thought Dysfunction (THD), and Behavioral/Externalizing Dysfunction (BXD). Interpretive guidelines for the H-O scales are presented later in this chapter.

Restructured Clinical (RC) Scales

When developing the MMPI-A-RF, Archer et al. (2016) aimed to establish adolescent versions of the RC scales that reflected the same constructs assessed by adult versions of the RC scales. Adult versions of the RC scales were described in Chapter 7. The process of developing RC scales for the MMPI-A-RF began by developing seed scales using items scored on the MMPI-2-RF's target RC scale that were also contained in the MMPI-A item pool. These seed scales were then refined by examining the correlations of each item with other items on the seed scale (i.e., their item-to-total correlation) and via a rational review of item content.

Next, Archer et al. (2016) sought to determine if demoralization—a construct reflecting generalized distress common to many forms of psychopathology—was a distinct dimension warranting specific assessment in adolescents as had been demonstrated for adult versions of the MMPI. To accomplish this goal, each MMPI-A-RF RC seed scale's items were combined with those contained in the MMPI-A-RF seed scale for RCd and subjected to a series of exploratory factor analyses in the four setting-specific development subsamples. The developers interpreted the results of those analyses as indicating that demoralization was a source of common, substantive variance across the MMPI-A Clinical scales; and, as a consequence, was worth measuring via a MMPI-A-RF RCd scale.

Having identified seed scales for each RC scale and that the separation of variability due to generalized distress from other substantive content was warranted, the test developers proceeded to the last phase of scale development—item recruitment. In this phase, the RC seed scale scores were correlated with each of the 478 items the comprise the MMPI-A item pool. The goal was to identify items that had a pattern of strong convergent and discriminant correlations with the seed scales. In other words, the test's developers identified items that strongly correlated with one specific RC seed scale (i.e., target scale) but demonstrated either no or very small associations with all the other RC seed scales (i.e., non-target scales). Items demonstrating this pattern of association were selected for addition to the final RC scale.

The process just described resulted in the development of nine MMPI-A-RF RC scales intended to reflect demoralization and the key constructs assessed by the original Clinical scales of the MMPI (with exception of Clinical Scales 5 and 0). These scales and their abbreviations are listed in Table 15.1. Interpretive guidelines for each of these scales are presented later in this chapter. Importantly, because the MMPI-2-RF's RC scales were used as the basis for developing the MMPI-A-RF's RC scales, we expect the adolescent and adult versions of these scales have many similarities. However, the final MMPI-A-RF RC scales are not identical in composition to their adult counterparts. This is because some items scored on the MMPI-2-RF versions of these scales were removed from the MMPI-A-RF's RC seed scales. Additionally, items for MMPI-A-RF versions were recruited from the MMPI-A item pool, which contains some items not scored on the adult versions of the MMPI. Thus, we recommend the adult and adolescent versions of the RC scales should not be treated as parallel forms.

Specific Problems (SP) Scales

Archer et al. (2016) also developed a set of SP scales to measure other clinically useful constructs present in the MMPI-A item pool. As with adult versions of the instrument, the MMPI-A-RF SP scales were constructed to measure distinct Clinical scale components not represented by the RC scales, RC scale facets warranting separate assessment, and clinically significant attributes not assessed by the RC scales.

The exact procedures used to construct the MMPI-A-RF SP scales are not reported in the test's manual (Archer et al., 2016). However, the authors provide an overview of how the scales were constructed. To maintain continuity with the adult version of the instrument, the SP scales scored on the MMPI-2-RF were used as a template for the MMPI-A-RF's SP scales. However, Archer et al. (2016) indicated recognizing the importance of including scales that would assess experiences that are unique to adolescents. To ensure such experiences were identified and included on the

MMPI-A-RF, they conducted a series of factor analyses involving the 58 items scored on the MMPI-A that are not found on any adult versions of the instrument.

After identifying the key constructs for which SP scales could be developed, Archer et al. (2016) used processes like those just described for the RC scales to develop the SP scales. This included a series of factor analytic, correlational, and item-recruitment procedures that resulted in the development of 25 SP scales. As when developing the RC scales, some of these analyses were intended to minimize the contribution of demoralization to the scales (see above and Chapter 7). These scales are organized by domain, including somatic/cognitive complaints, internalizing problems, externalizing problems, and interpersonal functioning. The MMPI-A-RF SP scales are listed with their abbreviations in Table 15.1. Interpretative suggestions for these scales will be offered later in this chapter.

Notably, 19 of the MMPI-A-RF SP scales have counterparts on the MMPI-2-RF, and six are unique to the MMPI-A-RF. The adolescent SP scales with counterparts on the adult version of the instrument are likely similar to those on the MMPI-2-RF, given the MMPI-2-RF SP scales were used as a template during scale development. However, as was true for the RC scales, because items used to score the MMPI-2-RF SP scales were removed and adolescent-unique items from the MMPI-A item pool were added during the scale development process, the adolescent and adult versions of these scales are not necessarily parallel forms.

Personality Psychopathology Five (PSY–5) Scales

The PSY-5 scales of the MMPI-A-RF are revised versions of the MMPI-A PSY-5 scales, the latter of which were developed by McNulty, Harkness, and colleagues (1997). The MMPI-A-RF PSY-5 scales are intended to reflect the constructs of the PSY-5 (Harkness & McNulty, 1994), which are described in detail in Chapter 7. These scales provide a conceptual link between the MMPI-A-RF and modern models of maladaptive personality.

As reported by Archer et al. (2016), the MMPI-A-RF versions of the PSY-5 scales were created during the MMPI-A-RF test development process by two of the MMPI-A PSY-5 scales' original creators (i.e., McNulty and Harkness). Processes similar to those used to develop previous iterations of the PSY-5 scales were used (see Chapter 7) but only items retained in the MMPI-A-RF item pool after development of the other MMPI-A-RF scales was completed were considered. First, preliminary versions of the MMPI-A-RF PSY-5 scales were constructed using items from two sources. The first source was items scored on the MMPI-A PSY-5 scales that were retained in the MMPI-A-RF item pool. The second source was items identified as describing a PSY-5 construct by 100% of raters engaged in a replicated rational selection process. Next, these preliminary scales were subjected to an iterative set of analyses to derive final item assignments. This included using internal consistency analyses to examine the internal properties of the scales and examination of correlations between items and criterion measures to examine the external properties of the scale. This process resulted in the development of five MMPI-A-RF PSY-5 scales, which are comprised of 49 of the 66 items retained in the MMPI-A-RF item pool and scored on the original MMPI-A PSY-5 scales, as well as 24 items from the MMPI-A-RF item pool that were not included on the original scales. The MMPI-A-RF PSY-5 scales are listed in Table 15.1, and interpretive guidelines are presented later in this chapter.

ADMINISTRATION AND SCORING

User Qualifications
As with other MMPI instruments, the MMPI-A-RF is to be used only by persons with appropriate education and training in the use of clinical assessment instruments. The minimum qualifications for test users are determined by Pearson Assessments, the test's distributor, and details can be found on their website (pearsonassessments. com). Broadly, users must be adequately trained in the administration and interpretation of clinical assessment instruments, qualifications that can be achieved via degree programs or continuing education workshops.

Administration
As with other MMPI instruments, the MMPI-A-RF should be administered in a professional manner. General guidelines for administering the MMPI-2, which also apply to the MMPI-A-RF, were outlined in Chapter 2. Either a qualified user or someone trained by a qualified user in test administration procedures should administer the test. The test should never be administered outside a supervised setting. Additionally, despite the MMPI-A-RF having fewer items than the MMPI-A, test users need to recognize that some adolescents may still struggle to complete the test in a single session. These kinds of difficulties can arise due to fatigue, problems with inattention and distractibility, being oppositional or hyperactive, or other reasons. In these cases, close supervision, frequent breaks, and encouragement from the person administering the test can be helpful.

Before administering the MMPI-A-RF, the test-taker's ability to read and comprehend the items should be determined. The MMPI-A-RF items have a Flesch–Kincaid reading index of 4.5, suggesting slightly greater than a fourth grade reading level is needed to complete the test (Archer et al., 2016). However, as noted in Appendix D of the instrument's manual, the MMPI-A-RF contains some items that require a higher reading level. Thus, even for test takers who have the required reading skill, test users should be prepared to screen scored profiles carefully for indications of difficulties comprehending the items, which can elevate scores on scales like CNS, VRIN-r, TRIN-r, and CRIN.

The MMPI-A-RF can be administered using computer software available from the test's distributor, Pearson Assessments, or a pencil/paper version consisting of a printed booklet and a separate answer sheet. According to Pearson Assessments, completing the pencil/paper version of the test typically takes adolescents approximately 30–45 minutes, while a computerized administration typically takes 25–30 minutes. As with other versions of the MMPI, we have no reason to believe that pencil/paper and computer-administered versions of the MMPI-A-RF yield scores that are not equivalent. A standardized audio version of the test is also available from Pearson for test takers who have difficulties that preclude completing either the pencil/paper or computerized administrations. We do not recommend reading items aloud to test takers, as this practice deviates from the test's standardized administration procedures and could lead to a distortion of the test-taker's scores.

Standard English and U.S. Spanish versions of the test are available in pencil/paper, computerized, and audio formats from the test's distributor, Pearson Assessments. The MMPI-A-RF has also been translated to Korean as well as Spanish for use in Spain, South America, and Central America. The University of Minnesota Press has commissioned additional translations, and more information on approved translations is available at their website (https://www.upress.umn.edu/test-division/translations-permissions/available-translations).

Scoring

Once the adolescent has responded to the MMPI-A-RF items, scoring can be accomplished by computer or by hand. For computerized scoring, Pearson Assessment's Q-Local and Q-Global software can be used. If one of these programs was also used for test administration, then scores are quickly generated using the responses entered by the test taker. If a pencil/paper administration was completed, then users can hand enter the test-taker's responses into these programs to apply the scoring software. Completed pencil/paper response sheets can also be mailed to Pearson Assessments, where they are scored and returned to users. Finally, it is possible to hand score the MMPI-A-RF using scoring templates available from Pearson Assessments.

If digital scoring is used, test users can select a Score or Interpretive Report. The Score Report provides scores and profiles for all MMPI-A-RF scales and has the option of providing mean data for various comparison groups (e.g., mental health outpatients; psychiatric inpatients; youth in residential treatment; and youth tested in forensic, medical, or school settings). The Interpretive Report has the same information available in the Score Report but also includes a narrative interpretation along with a list of the references that were used to derive the interpretation. A sample Score Report is appended to this chapter. The case (John) was also presented in Chapter 14 of this book when the MMPI-A interpretive strategy was discussed.

PSYCHOMETRIC CHARACTERISTICS

Normative Sample

The normative sample for the MMPI-A-RF is a subset of 1,610 adolescents who comprised the MMPI-A normative sample (Archer et al., 2016). The sample was created by combining data for all 805 boys in the MMPI-A sample and data from 805 girls selected randomly from the 815 girls in the MMPI-A normative sample. Additional details concerning the MMPI-A normative sample were reported in Chapter 14 of this book. Broadly, the MMPI-A normative sample approximated the demographic breakdowns reported in the 1980 U.S. Census (Butcher et al., 1992). However, MMPI-A norms underrepresented adolescents who were Hispanic or 18 years old, and norms overrepresented youth living with both of their biological parents and those with parents who were college educated. To the extent these factors influenced application of

MMPI-A norms to adolescents with certain demographic characteristics, we expect they also influence use of the MMPI-A-RF.

To examine whether norms based on data collected in the late 1980s are still representative of today's youth, Archer et al. (2016) conducted a review of studies published between 1995 and 2012 that reported descriptive data from samples of youth who completed the MMPI-A in nonclinical settings. They argued if these descriptive data demonstrated consistent and substantive inconsistencies from mean scores in the MMPI-A normative sample, this would suggest new norms were needed for the MMPI-A-RF. They found average MMPI-A scores and their standard deviations in the reviewed studies, which represented a total of 1,899 boys and girls, were essentially identical to those produced by the MMPI-A normative sample (i.e., approximate mean T scores = 50 and standard deviations = 10). Based on this, Archer et al. (2016) concluded it was appropriate to use the MMPI-A normative sample for the MMPI-A-RF. Nonetheless, given the changing demographics of the U.S. population (e.g., Hobbs & Stoops, 2002), additional research is needed to ensure the applicability of MMPI-A-RF norms to today's youth.

Unlike the MMPI-A, which uses gendered norms, the MMPI-A-RF uses nongendered norms. The use of nongendered norms means a test-taker's standard scores on the MMPI-A-RF are based on normative data from both boys and girls. Archer et al. (2016) reported their choice to use nongendered norms for the MMPI-A-RF was based on two things. First, results of a study comparing gendered and nongendered norms for the MMPI-2 suggested few meaningful differences between the two sets of norms (Ben-Porath & Forbey, 2003). Second, gendered norms can hide important differences between groups with different gender identities (e.g., Reynolds & Kamphaus, 2002). Clinicians wanting to compare a test taker to similarly gendered individuals in the MMPI-A-RF normative sample can do this using the gendered comparison groups available in the computerized Score and Interpretative Reports available from Pearson Assessments.

Standard Scores

To standardize raw scores and facilitate interpretation, the MMPI-A-RF uses two types of T scores (i.e., standard scores with M = 50 and SD = 10). Raw scores on the substantive MMPI-A-RF scales are converted to Uniform T (UT) scores. As described in Chapter 2, use of UT scores ensures scores at a particular level have the same percentile meaning across scales. This allows for comparisons of scores across scales. However, because they have distributions that are very different than the distributions of the substantive scales, raw scores on the Validity scales are instead transformed to simple Linear T scores.

Reliability

Tables 3.2–3.6 in Archer et al. (2016) report test–retest coefficients, internal consistency coefficients (alpha), and SEM estimates in the normative sample for all the MMPI-A-RF scales. These tables also present internal consistency estimates derived in the scale development subsamples as well as SEM estimates in the combined mental health outpatient and inpatient development subsamples. Internal consistency and test–retest estimates for the Validity scales vary across scales and samples. They tend to be lower than the estimates presented for the MMPI-A-RF substantive scales, though this is expected given the limited variability of Validity scales in samples where test takers are likely to be cooperative and respond credibly. Reported SEM estimates for each Validity scale are small enough to indicate the kinds of interpretation discussed later in this chapter are justified, however.

Test–retest reliability data were based on a combined gender subset (n = 45 boys and 109 girls) of adolescents from the MMPI-A normative sample who completed the test twice, with a median test–retest interval of 7 days. Test–retest reliability coefficients ranged from 0.64 (THD) to 0.85 (EID; mdn = 0.71) for the H-O scales and from 0.56 (RC8) to 0.82 (RCd; mdn = 0.66) for the RC Scales. We expect many of the lower values observed—such as those for THD, RC6, and RC8—are a product of calculating these values in a subset of the normative sample where the base rate for this kind of serious psychopathology was very low. Test–retest coefficients for the SP scales ranged from 0.24 for Behavior-Restricting Fears (BRF) to 0.73 for Self-Doubt (SFD; mdn = 0.63). As with the H-O and RC Scales, many of the lower test–retest reliabilities for the SP scales may have been influenced by range restriction in the normative sample. The SP scales also tend to be comprised of a relatively small number of items, with some SP scales having as few as three (e.g., BRF) or four items (e.g., Substance Abuse [SUB]). This also likely impacted the stability coefficients, as scales with more items tended to be more stable than scales with fewer items. Test–retest reliability coefficients for the revised PSY-5 scales were acceptable and ranged from 0.64 for Aggressiveness–Revised (AGGR-r) and Psychoticism–Revised (PSYC-r) to 0.72 for Negative Emotionality/Neuroticism–Revised (NEGE-r; mdn = 0.70).

Internal consistency coefficients (alpha) for the H-O scales were high in the MMPI-A-RF normative sample. Alpha values ranged from 0.70 (THD) to 0.84 (EID; mdn = 0.74) and 0.70 (THD) to 0.86 (EID; mdn = 0.72) for boys and girls, respectively. As expected in samples with greater variability, these estimates were higher in the development subsamples, with typical values approximating 0.80 or higher. Internal consistency estimates for the RC scales ranged from 0.45 (RC9) to 0.80 (RCd & RC4; mdn = 0.63) and 0.52 (RC9) to 0.83 (RCd; mdn =0.66) for boys and girls in the normative sample, respectively. Lower internal consistency may be due to the shorter length of some scales as well as range restriction. These values were generally higher in the development subsamples, with typical values being greater than 0.70. Similar estimates were demonstrated by Sharf and Rogers (2020) for the RC scales in a sample of 66 youth referred for mental health services.

Archer et al. (2016) reported alpha coefficients for the SP scales in the normative sample varying from 0.36 for Interpersonal Passivity (IPP) to 0.68 for Shyness (SHY) for boys (mdn = 0.54) and 0.29 for Negative Peer Influences (NPI) to 0.73 (SHY) for girls (mdn = 0.54). These coefficients in the development subsamples were typically in the 0.60s and 0.70s. Internal consistencies of the SP scales, which have fewer items than the H-O or RC scales, tended to be lower than for the longer scales. Internal consistency coefficients (alpha) for the PSY-5 scales in the normative sample ranged from 0.57 (PSYC-r) to 0.77 for Disconstraint–Revised (DISC-r) for boys (mdn = 0.69) and 0.58 (AGGR-r) to 0.73 (DISC-r) for girls (*mdn* = 0.67). Corresponding values in development subsamples were higher, typically in the 0.70s and 0.80s.

The SEM estimates for the H-O, RC, and PSY-5 scales in both the normative and combined clinical development subsamples tended to be small, ranging from 4 to 6 points for the H-O scales, 4 to 7 points for the RC scales, and 5 to 8 points for the PSY-5 scales. Despite evidence of the SP scales having lower test–retest and internal consistency reliability, SEM estimates for the SP scales were generally similar to those reported for the H-O, RC, and PSY-5 scales. The lone exception was NPI, which comparatively had an unusually large SEM (i.e., 10 in the normative and 11 in the composite clinical samples). Overall, these data suggest observed T scores are likely to be relatively precise measures of an adolescents' true standing on the constructs assessed by these scales, though some caution may be needed when interpreting NPI scores.

In summary, the internal consistency and temporal stability of the H-O, RC, and PSY-5 scales are acceptable and comparable to those of other adolescent self-report scales. Scales with lower reliability estimates tended to be those that were relatively short in length or those assessing phenomena that occur at lower base rates among adolescents. The SP scales were particularly impacted by these issues and often had reliability estimates lower than standard conventions for acceptability. However, with the exception of NPI, the standard errors of measurement indicated T scores were relatively precise. Taken together, these findings suggest that test users should have more confidence in interpreting scores on SP scales with higher elevations as opposed to those that are only marginally elevated.

Validity

Since the MMPI-A-RF was only published in 2016, limited additional research is available to guide our understanding of its scales. There has been one broad study, however, that suggests the MMPI-A-RF's developers were successful in their efforts to improve representations of the clinically meaningful substantive content reflected in the MMPI-A item pool. Specifically, Stokes et al. (2018) examined comparability of the MMPI-A and the MMPI-A-RF in a sample of 3,516 adolescents receiving inpatient psychiatric treatment. The authors reported scores on the MMPI-A-RF RC scales were less intercorrelated than the MMPI-A Clinical scales. They also concluded RCd scores were less strongly correlated with the other MMPI-A-RF RC scales than they were with the MMPI-A Clinical scales. Overall, these two results suggest success in the test developers' efforts to reduce the influence of a shared demoralization factor and overlapping items on the psychometric properties of the MMPI-A-RF scales. Conclusions from this study also indicated many of the desirable features of the MMPI-A were carried over to the new instrument including strong assessment of response styles and inclusion of measures of personality pathology. Stokes et al. (2018) reported scores on Validity scales of the MMPI-A and MMPI-A-RF had a 92.5% rate of agreement in identifying cases as valid or invalid. They also demonstrated the revised versions of the PSY-5 on the MMPI-A-RF were strongly related to their MMPI-A counterparts and that there was not a consistent or meaningful pattern of differences in scores when derived using the MMPI-A or MMPI-A-RF versions of the scales.

While these findings suggest many similarities between the MMPI-A and MMPI-A-RF, external validity data are needed to support interpretation of the MMPI-A-RF's scales. The sections that follow summarize validity data reported in Archer et al. (2016) as well as research published in professional journals.

Validity Scales

CANNOT SAY (CNS)

CNS is the count of unscorable responses, representing both items that are unanswered and items answered both True and False. Archer et al. (2016) recommend caution when interpreting an elevated MMPI-A-RF scale with 10% or more unscorable items, as it may underestimate the test-taker's standing on the construct being assessed. Their recommendations differ from those used on previous versions of the MMPI instruments where excessive unscorable responses invalidated a profile. However, Archer et al.'s (2016) recommendations reflect a more nuanced approach to handling item omissions and are based on research conducted with the adult version of the instrument suggesting little interpretative validity is lost when up to 10% of items in scales are omitted (Dragon et al., 2012).

NON-CONTENT-BASED INVALID RESPONDING SCALES (VRIN-R, TRIN-R, CRIN)

Archer et al. (2016) indicate that when VRIN-r T scores are between 65 and 74, substantive scales should be interpreted cautiously; when VRIN-r T scores are $\geq$ 75, the test taker likely responded to items so inconsistently that scores on other scales should not be interpreted. These recommended scores appear to be based on cut scores used for the MMPI-A VRIN scale.

Archer et al. (2016) provided preliminary support for the effectiveness of VRIN-r in detecting random responding in the instrument's manual. In a computer simulation, they inserted quasi-random responses into data for half of a subsample from the MMPI-A-RF normative sample. They then calculated the correlation between MMPI-A-RF and MMPI-A Validity scales. Results indicated scores on VRIN-r were strongly associated with the MMPI-A VRIN scale (r = 0.76) as well as other scales known to be impacted by random responding (e.g., MMPI-A F scale). Additional empirical work is needed to further examine the effectiveness of VRIN-r for detecting inconsistent responding and to identify ideal cut scores.

For TRIN-r, Archer et al. (2016) recommend T scores $\geq$ 75 (T or F) suggest fixed (true or false) responding that invalidates the profile. Cautious interpretation is recommended for T Scores between 65 and 74 (T or F). As was true for VRIN-r, cut scores for TRIN-r appear to be based on recommendations for the MMPI-A TRIN scale.

Archer et al. (2016) provided preliminary support for the effectiveness of TRIN-r in detecting random responding in the instrument's manual. In a simulation study, they randomly replaced responses provided by half of a subsample from the MMPI-A-RF normative sample with "true" responses. They then calculated the correlation between MMPI-A-RF and MMPI-A Validity scales. Results indicated scores on TRIN-r were strongly associated with the MMPI TRIN scale (r = 0.93) and, to a lesser extent, other Validity scales known to be impacted by fixed true responding (e.g., the F scales). They then repeated this process instead randomly inserting "false" instead of "true" responses. The TRIN-r and TRIN scales were again highly correlated (r = 0.85). Large correlations were also observed between TRIN-r and the MMPI-A's underreporting scales (L and K). Additional research is needed to examine TRIN-r scores' effectiveness for detecting fixed responding and to establish ideal cut scores.

As noted earlier, the CRIN scale is a new Validity scale developed to assist in the detection of response inconsistency on the MMPI-A-RF. Archer et al. (2016) recommend when CRIN scores are between 65T and 74T, substantive scales should be interpreted cautiously; when CRIN T scores are ≥ 75, the test taker likely responded to items without regard to their content so frequently that scores on other scales should not be interpreted. Since this is a new scale, no published work is yet available supporting these recommendations, and additional research is needed.

In the previously described simulation studies presented in the instrument's manual (Archer et al., 2016), associations between CRIN and the MMPI-A Validity scales were also calculated. Scores on CRIN demonstrated expected patterns of association. They were most strongly associated with VRIN (r = 0.80) and the F-family scale (r = 0.73–0.79) scores in the inconsistent responses sample; VRIN (r = 0.78), TRIN (r = 0.93), and the F-family scale (r = 0.88–0.89) scores in the fixed true responses sample; and VRIN (r = 0.70) in the fixed false responses sample. These results provide initial evidence suggesting CRIN is effective in detecting non-content-based invalid responding. However, given the relative newness and limited published work on the scale, additional empirical investigation is needed. We suggest cautious interpretation of the scale's scores until such research is available.

OVERREPORTING SCALE (F–R)

As noted earlier in this chapter, the MMPI-A-RF retained a revised version of the MMPI-A F scale, F-r. Archer et al. (2016) indicate T scores between 70 and 79 on F-r indicate possible overreporting in individuals with no history or current experience of psychopathology, T scores between 80 and 89 indicate possible overreporting in individuals with no history or current experience of severe psychopathology, and T scores ≥ 90 indicate likely overreporting. The cut scores recommended by Archer et al. (2016) for F-r appear to be based on those established for the MMPI-A F scale. Additional research is needed concerning optimal cutoff scores in a variety of settings.

Archer et al. (2016) provided initial evidence supporting F-r as a measure of overreporting. They combined archival data from a sample of adolescents instructed to overreport psychopathology (n = 127; collected by Stein et al., 1998) with a randomly selected subset of youth from the MMPI-A-RF normative sample (n = 127; total N = 254). Youth were only included in the subsample if there were no indications of non-content-based invalid responding on the other MMPI-A and MMPI-A-RF Validity scales. When these two samples were combined, scores on F-r demonstrated very large correlations with the MMPI-A's F family scales (r = 0.98 for F1 & F2 to 0.99 for F). Mean scores on F-r were also elevated in the overreporting subsample

(M = 93.97, SD = 30.40). Archer et al. (2016) reported 65% of the adolescents in the overreporting sample had F-r scores above the recommended cut score of T ≥ 90, and none of the youth selected from the normative sample achieved scores above this score. Mean scores on all the RC scales except RC9 were also elevated in the overreporting sample (M = 61.37 for RC7 to 82.23 for RC4). This finding is consistent with past research indicating substantive scale scores tend to be higher for people who are overreporting symptoms and problems than for people who give credible responses (e.g., Rogers et al., 2003; see Chapter 3 for additional detail.) Overall, these data suggest the F-r scale is similar to its MMPI-A counterpart and that its scores are likely to be useful in detecting overreporting.

UNDERREPORTING SCALES (L–R, K–R)
As described earlier, the MMPI-A-RF also retained revised versions of the MMPI-A L and K scales, L-r and K-r, which are intended to measure excessive claiming of moral virtue and the denial of everyday problems and difficulties, respectively. For L-r, Archer et al. (2016) indicate T scores between 65 and 79 suggest an increasing likelihood of underreporting due to the test taker denying minor shortcomings and faults. T Scores of 80 or higher indicate the profile is likely invalid due to underreporting, as the adolescent is reporting a level of virtuousness uncommon even among adolescents raised with highly traditional or strict moral values. For K-r, Archer et al. (2016) indicate T scores between 60 and 74 suggest an increasing likelihood of underreporting due to the test taker presenting themselves as having a higher than typical level of adjustment. T Scores 80 or higher indicate the profile is likely invalid due to underreporting, as the adolescent is reporting an unusually high level of adjustment. The cut scores recommended by Archer et al. (2016) for L-r and K-r appear to be based on those established for their MMPI-A counterparts. As such, additional research is needed concerning optimal cutoff scores in a variety of settings.

Archer et al. (2016) provided initial evidence supporting L-r and K-r as measures of underreporting. Namely, using data from the forensic predisposition sample used to validate scales of the MMPI-A-RF during the development process (N = 473; collected by Handel et al. 2011), they calculated correlations between MMPI-A and MMPI-A-RF Validity scales after screening out profiles with evidence of non-content-based invalid responding on the other MMPI-A and MMPI-A-RF Validity scales. The correlation between L-r and L was 0.83 and between K-r and K was 0.80. As would be expected given both scales assess facets of a larger underreporting construct, the next largest observed correlations were between L-r and K (r = 0.44) and K-r and L (r = 0.49). Scores on K-r also had small-to-moderate, negative associations with the MMPI-A F scales (r = -0.24 for F2 to -0.33 for F1), consistent with the idea that K-r assesses the avowal of adjustment; while the F scales measure reports of maladjustment. Scores on L-r and K-r did not appear to have meaningful correlations with MMPI-A scales assessing non-content-based invalid responding (i.e., VRIN and TRIN). Overall, these data suggest L-r and K-r likely assess constructs similar to their MMPI-A counterparts, though future research should examine the effectiveness of these scales for assessing underreporting.

Substantive Scales

Most of the evidence supporting the validity of the MMPI-A-RF substantive scales comes from the instrument's manual (Archer et al., 2016). Specifically, Chapter 3 of the manual provides tables describing the correlation of MMPI-A-RF scales with the scales of the MMPI-A in the test developer's psychiatric inpatient, residential treatment, forensic predisposition, and forensic detention validation samples. Appendix G in Archer et al. (2016) presents over 17,500 correlations calculated by gender between the substantive scales of the MMPI-A-RF and external criteria in these same samples. The external criterion measures consisted of therapist ratings, intake information, record reviews, and other self-report instruments. The test authors report basing most of their interpretative recommendations on these correlational data.

HIGHER-ORDER (H-O) SCALES

In general, the correlations reported in Archer et al. (2016) support both the convergent and discriminant validity of the H-O scales. Higher scores on the EID scale are associated with many aspects of emotional distress including feeling sad, depressed, and anxious. These correlations are observed in criterion reflecting the adolescent's report as well as those from their caregivers and treatment providers. Difficulties that might be expected to occur alongside these emotional experiences are also positively associated with scores on EID, such as concerns about concentration and somatic functioning. Scores on this scale also demonstrated positive associations with reports of suicidal ideation, self-injurious behavior, and suicidal behavior fairly consistently across the validation samples. Scores on EID are unrelated, or in some settings negatively related, to measures of externalizing behaviors such as being impulsive or getting in trouble at school or with the law. In some settings, higher EID scale scores are meaningfully related to some symptoms of psychotic disorders (e.g., hallucinations). However, these types of experiences are usually more strongly associated with MMPI-A-RF scales intended to assess symptoms of psychotic disorders (e.g., THD, RC8).

Higher scores on the THD scale are associated with indicators of psychotic disorders. High scorers may report auditory or visual hallucinations and may feel persecuted by and isolated from their peers. Scores on THD are positively related to reports from the youth, their caregivers, and clinicians of feelings of depression and anxiety, though these correlations are not as strong as those demonstrated between these variables and EID. With the exception of aggressive behavior, scores on THD are not consistently associated with externalizing behaviors such as getting into trouble with the law or substance use.

Higher scores on the BXD scale are associated with a wide variety of externalizing behaviors—including oppositional and conduct-disorder-related behaviors—and having been in trouble at home, at school, and with the law. Scores on BXD are also positively associated with social conflict, verbally and physically aggressive behaviors, and associating with negative peers. Fairly consistent positive associations with reports of impulsive or poorly controlled behaviors were also demonstrated. Higher BXD scores are not related to many indicators of emotional distress, but some high scorers may report anxiety and depression. BXD scores are not strongly related to symptoms of thought dysfunction.

In sum, based on our examination of the correlates presented by Archer et al. (2016), it seems likely the three H-O scales can provide important information about the general nature of problems an adolescent is likely to be experiencing. More precise inferences about test takers are based on substantive scales assessing narrower constructs (i.e., RC, SP, and PSY-5 scales).

RESTRUCTURED CLINICAL (RC) SCALES

In the MMPI-A-RF Manual, Archer et al. (2016) presented correlations by gender for the three MMPI-A-RF scales most strongly associated with the MMPI-A scales in each of the MMPI-A-RF validation samples. These data provide some information concerning the validity of the RC scales. Scores on RCd demonstrated associations > 0.9 with Anxiety (A). They were also positively related to a large number of the Clinical and Content scales, with large to very large effect sizes. This included Clinical Scales 2, 4, 7, and 8; as well as Content Scales Depression (A-dep), Anxiety (A-anx), Alienation (A-aln), Low Self-Esteem (A-lse), Family Problems (A-fam), and Negative Treatment Indicators (A-trt). The largest and most consistent associations were with Clinical Scales 2 and 7 and Content Scales A-dep and A-anx, in line with the demoralization construct Archer et al. (2016) aimed to capture with RCd.

For the remaining RC scales, the intercorrelation data suggest the RC scales are measuring similar, if not identical, characteristics to those assessed by MMPI-A Clinical and Content scales. Scores on RC1 demonstrated associations greater than 0.9 across settings with scores on Clinical Scale 1 and the Health Concerns (A-hea) Content scale. Scores on RC1 were also positively associated, to a lesser extent, with scores on Clinical Scale 3. Intercorrelations across settings reported for other RC scales were lower, typically between 0.6 and 0.8. Scores on RC3 were consistently positively related to the Cynicism (A-cyn) Content scale. Higher scores on RC4 were associated in some settings with Clinical Scale 4, as well as with the A-fam and School Problems (A-sch) Content scales. Consistent positive associations were also demonstrated between scores on RC6 and Clinical Scale 6, RC8 and the Bizarre Mentation (A-biz) Content scale, and RC9 and Clinical Scale 9. Scores on RC7 were positively associated with the conceptually relevant Clinical Scale 7 in some settings, though Scale 7 was more consistently related to RCd. Consistent positive associations between RC7 and Obsessiveness (A-obs) were demonstrated, however, suggesting RC7 may include assessment of intrusive, distressing thoughts.

The only MMPI-A-RF RC scale that did not demonstrate large to very large associations with conceptually relevant MMPI-A Clinical and Content scales was RC2, which is intended to be a measure of low positive emotionality (Archer et al., 2016). However, across settings, scores on RC2 did demonstrate associations typically greater than 0.8 with scores on the MMPI-A Introversion/Low Positive Emotionality (INTR) PSY-5 scale. They were also moderately and positively associated with scores on the Harris–Lingoes Psychomotor Retardation (D2) subscale. This pattern of association suggests RC2 likely captures problems with experiencing positive emotionality and anhedonia, as Archer et al. (2016) intended.

While these scale intercorrelations provide some sense of what the RC scales are assessing, more useful validity information can be derived by understanding the relations between RC scale scores and external criterion measures. Generally, the correlates provided by Archer et al. (2016) support the convergent and discriminant validity of the RC scales, though there were some exceptions (e.g., RC3, RC6, RC9). These results, along with those from other empirical, published studies are described below.

In the validation samples presented by Archer et al. (2016), scores on RCd were positively and strongly related to markers of emotional distress, such as reports of being sad, depressed, and anxious, and—to a lesser extent—reports of somatic concerns. Higher scores were associated with an increased likelihood of a youth and their caregivers reporting problems in social relationships as well as difficulties with attention and concentration. Reports of suicidal ideation, as well as histories of engaging in self-injurious and suicidal behaviors, were also consistently associated with higher RCd scores. These correlations are consistent with the demoralization construct RCd is intended to assess. In terms of discriminant validity, RCd and markers of externalizing behaviors had no, or very small, associations. In some settings, higher RCd scale scores were meaningfully related to symptoms of psychotic disorders; but these types of experiences were more strongly associated with other RC scales.

Scores on RC1, which is intended to be a measure of somatic concerns, demonstrated strong, positive associations with other measures of youth- and parent-reported somatic symptoms. To a lesser extent, higher scores on RC1 were related to measures assessing depressed and anxious feelings. Scores on this scale did not generally demonstrate meaningful associations across settings with measures of externalizing or thought dysfunctions.

Scores on RC2 demonstrated positive associations with reports of depressed mood, anhedonia, low energy and fatigue, and slowed speech and movements. They were also positively related to measures of social problems, including social isolation and withdrawal. These associations are in keeping with the low positive emotionality construct this scale is intended assess. However, scores on RC2 also demonstrated small, positive associations with self-report measures of psychological distress and anxiety. Evidence of discriminant validity for scores on RC2 was strong, as they demonstrated no pattern of meaningful association with measures of externalizing or thought dysfunctions.

The RC3 scale is intended to measure a cynical worldview. The external criteria used to report correlates of MMPI-A-RF scales presented by Archer et al. (2016) did not include any explicit measures of cynical attitudes. However, scores on this scale demonstrated small associations with criteria suggesting high scorers are likely to engage in a variety of rule-breaking behaviors. These included such things as having a history of suspension or unlawful behavior, as well self-reporting engagement in behaviors that are against the rules. Additional research is needed to establish RC3 as a measure of cynicism.

Archer et al. (2016) provided strong evidence for the convergent validity of scores on RC4, which is intended to reflect disinhibited rule breaking and antisocial behaviors. Higher scores on RC4 were strongly related to youth, parent, and clinician reports of rule-breaking, oppositional, and conduct-disorder related behaviors. A variety of behaviors that had or could lead to involvement with the legal system were positively related to scores on RC4. This included both status (e.g., truancy, running away) and criminal (e.g., stealing, assault) offenses. Higher scorers on RC4 were also more likely to be described as acting in verbally and physically aggressive ways toward others and as having a history of substance use. Positive associations between markers of extraversion and negative peer associations and RC4 were also observed. Discriminant validity was strong for RC4, as no consistent association between RC4 and markers of internalizing or thought dysfunctions were observed.

Inspection of the correlates presented in Archer et al. (2016) suggests scores on RC6 were positively related to interpersonal problems reported by the youth and their caregivers, as well as observations the youth had difficulties getting along with their peers and acted in an aggressive manner. Higher scores on RC6 were also somewhat consistently related to reports of emotional distress and anxiety and problems with thinking. For boys in inpatient settings, higher scores on RC6 were related to the experience of hallucinations. Finally, small, but significant, positive associations were demonstrated between some markers of rule breaking and oppositional behavior and RC6, though these were not consistently demonstrated across settings. In sum, evidence of validity for RC6, which is intended to be a measure of persecutory thinking, was not as strong as that presented for other RC scales. This may be due to the low base rate of these types of difficulties in the validation samples or that included external criteria were not well suited for assessing persecutory ideation. Nonetheless, future research is needed to better understand what this scale may be assessing in adolescent populations.

Higher scores on RC7 were most consistently related to youth-, parent-, and clinician-reported anxiety in the correlates presented by Archer et al. (2016). Positive relations between scores on this scale and experiences likely to accompany anxiety, such as intrusive thoughts and nightmares, were also demonstrated in some of the validation samples. The negative affectivity construct intended to be assessed by scores on RC7 is theoretically distinguishable from demoralization, though the two are strongly related (Tellegen et al., 2003). Accordingly, in the validation samples, positive associations between markers of distress and depressed mood with RC7 were observed. Overall, these data support the convergent validity of RC7. However, additional work is needed to establish RC7 scores as a measure of other aspects of negative emotionality, such as excessive or impairing levels of fearfulness and anger. Scores on RC7 were not generally associated with measures of externalizing and thought dysfunctions—supporting their discriminant validity.

Scores on RC8 were positively related to markers of unusual thinking and perception across Archer et al.'s (2016) validation samples. This included higher scores on RC8 being associated with the experience of auditory or visual hallucinations, as well as clinician ratings of psychoticism. Smaller, albeit still significant, positive relations were also observed between scores on RC8 and measures of social isolation and withdrawal as well as measures of distressed, anxious, and depressed feelings. Scores on RC8 were not typically associated with more specific markers of internalizing difficulties and demonstrated little to no association with markers of externalizing behaviors.

Conceptually, RC9 reflects hypomanic activation, which includes the experience of excessive energy, racing thoughts, impulsive sensation-seeking and risk-taking behaviors (Archer et al., 2016). Correlates presented by Archer et al. (2016) provide little evidence supporting this connection, though this may be a product of the low base rate of hypomanic symptoms in the validation samples. High scores on RC9 were associated with having higher levels of energy in the validation sample of boys receiving treatment in an inpatient hospital, a sample where more extreme levels of hypomania might be expected. However, across the validation samples, scores on RC9 demonstrated moderately consistent, positive associations with markers of aggressive behavior as well as measures of having been in trouble at home, school, or with the legal system. This is congruent with correlates demonstrated for adult versions of RC9 (see summary in Sellbom, 2019). This suggests in populations where the prevalence of severe mental illness is low, scores on RC9 might be best conceptualized as assessing impulsive and excitement-seeking behaviors that are often associated with a disinhibited externalizing way of relating to the world. Future research will be needed to examine this hypothesis.

Sharf and Rogers (2020) conducted a study in 66 youth referred for mental health treatment examining the diagnostic construct validity of the MMPI-A-RF RC scales. Diagnoses were derived using symptoms counts on the Kiddie Schedule for Affective Disorders and Schizophrenia (Kaufman et al. 1997). Results of correlational analyses suggested scores on RCd, RC1, and RC7 had moderate to large positive associations with internalizing disorder diagnoses including major depressive, panic, and generalized anxiety disorders. Higher scores on RC1 were also associated with PTSD diagnoses. Higher scores on RC2 were only related to major depressive and generalized anxiety disorders. Scores on RC6 and RC8 had moderate and large positive associations, respectively, with diagnoses of schizophrenia. Higher scores on RC4 were related to externalizing conditions including having large, positive associations with oppositional, conduct, alcohol use, and drug use disorders. Scores on RC9 were not meaningfully related to any of the evaluated diagnoses. Overall, these data support the convergent and discriminant validity of the RC scales, with the exception of RC9.

SPECIFIC PROBLEMS (SP) SCALES: SOMATIC/COGNITIVE SCALES

The five Somatic/Cognitive SP scales were developed to assess general preoccupation with poor health as well as presentation of more specific somatic and cognitive difficulties. The Malaise (MLS) scale indicates the extent to which the test taker is presenting themselves as experiencing poor health that impacts their functioning. In the validation samples presented by Archer et al. (2016), scores on this scale were positively related to reported somatic concerns, fatigue, poor sleep, and problems with attention and concentration. Higher MLS scores also demonstrated associations with measures of distressed, anxious, and depressed feelings.

The content of the other four somatic/cognitive SP scales—which includes Gastrointestinal Complaints (GIC), Head Pain Complaints (HPC), Neurological Complaints (NUC), and Cognitive Complaints (COG)—focuses on circumscribed problems with physical or cognitive functioning. Because of the brevity of the scales and the homogeneity of their item content, adolescents who obtain high scores on a scale are likely to have endorsed items consistent with the label of the scale. Higher scores on COG were also consistently associated with problems with attention, concentration, and clear thinking in the validation samples presented by Archer et al. (2016). As with the MLS scale, the correlations with external criterion measures (Archer et al., 2016) indicate adolescents who score high on each of these somatic/cognitive SP scales are likely to also report having distressed, anxious, or depressed feelings.

SPECIFIC PROBLEMS (SP) SCALES: INTERNALIZING SCALES

The nine Internalizing SP scales address narrower aspects of internalizing dysfunction inherent in elevations on scales higher in the MMPI-A-RF hierarchy, including the EID, RCd, and RC7 scales. Although RC2 also reflects an internalizing construct, none of the Internalizing SP scales assess facets of this scale. The Internalizing SP scales are relatively short (3–10 items), and the content of items in each scale tends to be quite homogeneous. Thus, persons who have elevated scores on a scale likely have endorsed items consistent with the label of the scale.

For most of the Internalizing SP scales, external correlate data presented by Archer et al. (2016) suggest scores on these scales have relatively good convergent validity, but evidence of discriminant validity within the internalizing domain is limited. More specifically, most of the Internalizing SP scales are related to a conceptually relevant criteria (e.g., SFD with poor self-esteem) but are also positively associated with depression, anxiety, and other indicators of general emotional distress. Given the interrelated nature of these constructs, this pattern of associations is not entirely unexpected. The external correlates presented by Archer et al. (2016) did generally support the broader discriminant validity of these scales, as the Internalizing SP scales demonstrated no relation or negative associations with criteria assessing constructs from other domains such as markers of externalizing or thought dysfunctions.

There were a few exceptions to the general pattern of supportive validity evidence just described. Scores on the Obsessions/Compulsions (OCS), BRF, and Specific Fears (SPF) scales had limited (OCS & BRF) to no (SPF) evidence supporting the convergent validity of scores in the validation samples presented by Archer et al. (2016). This may be due to the fact that a limited number of external criteria examining aspects of obsessive–compulsive and fear-related symptoms were available in the validation samples. Nonetheless, at this time, interpretation of these scales is driven primarily by their content. Future research is needed to establish empirically based interpretative statements for these scales.

SPECIFIC PROBLEMS (SP) SCALES: EXTERNALIZING SCALES

The six SP Externalizing scales deal with acting-out behavior, and each of the scales addresses narrow manifestations of this behavior. Items in the Negative School Attitudes (NSA) scale assess beliefs about attending school, while items in the Antisocial Attitudes (ASA) scale assess attitudes that support antisocial behavior. The Conduct Problems (CNP) scale items deal with getting in trouble at school, at home, and with the law; items in the SUB scale deal with the use and misuse of alcohol or other drugs; items in the NPI scale assess the presence of peers who encourage and support inappropriate behaviors; and items in the Aggression (AGG) scale deal with anger and acting out in aggressive ways.

Many of the external correlates presented by Archer et al. (2016) are consistent with the narrow constructs reflected in these scales. For example, the NPI scale demonstrates consistent, positive associations with clinicians reporting the youth has peers who are not positive influences. However, all six Externalizing SP scales are meaningfully related to a wide variety of externalizing behaviors. In other words, each scale seems to have good convergent validity; but discriminant validity within the realm of externalizing behaviors is limited. Given the interrelated nature of these constructs, this pattern of associations is not entirely unexpected. Further, external correlates presented by Archer et al. (2016) did generally support the larger discriminant validity of these scales, as the Externalizing SP scales demonstrated no relation or negative associations with criteria assessing constructs from other domains such as markers of internalizing or thought dysfunctions.

SPECIFIC PROBLEMS (SP) SCALES: INTERPERSONAL SCALES

The five SP Interpersonal scales address adolescent test-takers' relationships with other people. The Family Problems (FML) scale assesses an adolescent's experience of conflict and low support within their families. IPP is intended to assess problems with passive, unassertive behavior, while Social Avoidance (SAV) is intended to assess social avoidance and withdrawal. The SHY scale assesses social reticence and discomfort, such as that characteristic of social anxiety. Finally, the Disaffiliativeness (DSF) scale assesses preferences for solitary activities and low levels of social closeness.

Generally, with the exception of IPP, scores on these scales were related in the expected directions to measures of the key features suggested by the scales' contents in the correlate data presented by Archer et al. (2016). Specifically, scores on FML were positively related to clinician ratings of family conflict as well as a wide range of other externalizing tendencies. Higher scores on SAV were related to being isolated and having few friends, higher scores on SHY were related to being introverted, and higher scores on DSF were related to being socially withdrawn. Additional research on IPP is needed, however, as scores on this scale only demonstrated consistent positive relations with criteria assessing distressed, depressed, and anxious feelings. These types of emotional experiences were also associated with the other Interpersonal SP scales' scores.

PERSONALITY PSYCHOPATHOLOGY FIVE SCALES-REVISED (PSY-5-R)

Examination of correlations between the original MMPI-A PSY-5 scales and the MMPI-A-RF PSY-5 scales and external criterion measures reported in Archer et al. (2016) suggests that the original and revised scales are associated with essentially the same test-taker characteristics. For most of the PSY-5 scales, evidence of convergent validity was strong. Higher scores on AGGR-r were consistently related to markers of aggression as well as other markers of antagonistic externalizing behavior. Scores on PSYC-r were strongly and positively related to markers of thought dysfunction, such as hallucinations and thought problems. A wide variety of impulsive and rule-breaking behaviors were associated with higher scores on DISC-r, congruent with the disinhibition construct intended to be assessed by this scale. Scores on Introversion/

Low Positive Emotionality–Revised (INTR-r) were positively and strongly associated with markers of anhedonia and introversion. The one exception was NEGE-r, which demonstrated a nonspecific pattern of positive associations with youth, parent, and clinician reports of distressed, depressed, and anxious moods but not narrower manifestations of negative emotionality.

Evidence of discriminant validity for the PSY-5-r also tended to be strong. One exception was that scores on PSYC-r were positively associated to a small degree with distressed, depressed, and anxious feelings, suggesting this scale may still reflect some nonspecific demoralization variability. Furthermore, AGGR-r and DISC-r appear to assess several similar behaviors (e.g., aggressive behavior). This is not unexpected considering they reflect aspects of externalizing personality traits. However, additional research that includes more targeted external criteria is likely needed to further delineate the distinctness of these scales. Further work is also likely needed examining nuanced correlates of NEGE-r and INTR-r for similar reasons. Interpretive guidelines for the PSY-5-r scales are presented later in this chapter.

MMPI-A VERSUS MMPI-A-RF

The MMPI-A-RF is intended to be an alternative, not a replacement, to the MMPI-A. There are advantages and disadvantages of each instrument. Clinicians likely need to be aware of these, as having this knowledge will be helpful in deciding which form of the test best meets the needs of a particular assessment.

There are similarities across the two instruments. First, both the MMPI-A and the MMPI-A-RF use a self-report approach in which the adolescent is asked to describe themselves and their experiences by agreeing or disagreeing with the test's items. This approach has strengths and weaknesses, which were explicated by Ben-Porath (2013). A key criticism of self-report instruments is the ability for the test taker to respond in ways that compromise the validity of their scores. Both the MMPI-A and MMPI-A-RF provide a fairly comprehensive assessment of these response styles with the Validity scales. Initial evidence suggests these scales perform similarly across the MMPI-A and MMPI-A-RF (Archer et al., 2016; Stokes et al., 2018). Second, the instruments' normative samples are comprised of a nearly identical set of adolescents intended to be representative of adolescents in the United States. As discussed in Chapter 14, there is a small body of research available for the MMPI-A norms that informs our understanding of the strengths and weaknesses of this normative sample. Because the MMPI-A-RF normative sample is nearly identical in composition, we can assume this knowledge also applies to the MMPI-A-RF. Third, the MMPI-A and MMPI-A-RF use the same process for transforming Linear T scores on the substantive scales to UT scores. This transformation assures comparability across scales (see Chapter 2 for more information about UT scores). Finally, both instruments have software available to support their administration, scoring, and interpretation. Use of these software programs can reduce the time and effort needed to include broadband measures of functioning like the MMPI-A or MMPI-A-RF in an assessment. Further, this software can reduce errors in scoring and interpretation that might impact the conclusions reached about a test taker.

Despite these many similarities, there are important differences between the MMPI-A and MMPI-A-RF that clinicians will need to consider in deciding which form to use for specific assessment purposes. Our opinion is that the MMPI-A-RF has several advantages over the MMPI-A. These include the shorter length of the test, use of nongendered norms, and a well-delineated strategy for interpretation. Although more research is needed, three additional strengths of the MMPI-A-RF may include having scales with stronger psychometric properties and strong connections to contemporary models of personality and psychopathology as well as lower recommended cut scores for interpretation of the substantive scales.

In our conversations with clinicians who regularly assess adolescents, one of their primary concerns about using the MMPI-A in their evaluations is the length of the test. At 478 items, completing the MMPI-A can be quite taxing for many adolescents, especially if they are experiencing significant psychopathology. Thus, we expect the MMPI-A-RF, which has 241 items, is likely to be viewed as an improvement. Having fewer items on the MMPI-A-RF also means less time is required for administration compared to the MMPI-A. This may be important to consider in contexts where the time allowed for an assessment is limited.

The MMPI-A uses gendered norms, while the MMPI-A-RF uses nongendered norms. We think the adoption of nongendered norms for the MMPI-A-RF is likely to represent a significant advantage. This is because, as reviewed earlier in this chapter, gendered norms can disguise, rather than illuminate, differences in personality and psychopathology observed across genders..

Another practical advantage of the MMPI-A-RF is that the interpretation strategy for the instrument is well-delineated by Archer et al. (2016) and, in our experience, is less complex than that used for MMPI-A protocols. Although in need of study, we anticipate having a straightforward interpretative strategy will decrease the time and effort required to understand and describe what a test-taker's results imply about their functioning as well as increase the reliability of interpretations. The MMPI-A-RF interpretative strategy is also likely to be easier to learn compared to those used with the MMPI-A, especially for students and others not familiar with the MMPI instruments. However, it should be noted that the same level of professional training is required for using both versions of the test.

A potential benefit of the MMPI-A-RF is having scales with psychometric properties that are similar to or better than those scores on the MMPI-A. In developing the MMPI-A-RF, Archer et al. (2016) aimed to address two recurring criticisms of the MMPI instruments—scale heterogeneity and intercorrelation. Tellegen et al. (2003) posited these problems were due to saturation of the scales with a common demoralization component. Adult versions of the RC scales, then other scales scores on the MMPI-2-RF, were developed to reduce the influence of this nonspecific distress variance (Ben-Porath & Tellegen, 2008/2011; Tellegen & Ben-Porath, 2008/2011; Tellegen et al., 2003). These efforts were successful in producing scales that demonstrated similar or stronger psychometric properties than their predecessors (see Chapters 7 and 12, but also Sellbom, 2019). Initial evidence suggests the decision to use methods like those used in developing adult versions of the RC and other MMPI-2-RF scales has resulted in similar outcomes for the MMPI-A-RF scales (Archer et al.,

2016; Stokes et al., 2018). Nonetheless, additional research is needed contrasting the psychometric performance of MMPI-A and MMPI-A-RF scale sets before we would consider this conclusion to be well supported.

Another potential benefit of the MMPI-A-RF is the stronger connections to contemporary models of personality and psychopathology. The MMPI-A-RF was created using the MMPI-2-RF as a template (Archer et al., 2016); and this latter instrument has well-established connections to models of mood and affect, maladaptive personality, and psychopathology (Lee et al., 2017; Sellbom, 2019). There is preliminary evidence these ties will also be present for the MMPI-A-RF. The empirical correlates presented by Archer et al (2016) for RCd provided strong evidence this scale measures generalized psychological distress, establishing evidence of its construct validity as a measure of the pleasantness–unpleasantness dimension of models of mood and affect (Tellegen et al., 1999a, 1999b). Principal components analyses of the MMPI-A-RF RC scales conducted by Archer et al. (2016) suggest these scales' reflect key dimensions proposed in Hierarchical Taxonomy of Psychopathology (HiTOP; Kotov et al., 2021). Stokes et al. (2018) demonstrated a high level of correspondence between MMPI-A and MMPI-A-RF versions of the PSY-5 scales. As outlined in Chapter 7, the PSY-5 scales have strong ties to models of maladaptive personality (e.g., the Alternative Model of Personality Disorders [AMPD] in the Diagnostic and Statistical Manual of Mental Disorders, 5th ed. [DSM-5]; American Psychiatric Association, 2013). Thus, while additional research will help solidify these ties, the MMPI-A-RF appears to have great potential for strong construct validity.

The last potential benefit of the MMPI-A-RF relates to its use of a lower cut score (i.e., T ≤ 60) to define a "clinically significant" substantive scale elevation than the MMPI-A (T ≤ 65). Cut scores used to identify the presence of difficulties on adult versions of the instrument have been demonstrated to have less utility when applied to adolescent versions of the instrument (Archer, 2017). This is because adolescents within the MMPI-A's normative sample endorsed a substantial number of items indicative of psychopathology, resulting in a failure of these items to differentiate between adolescents who are and are not experiencing clinical difficulties (e.g., Archer et al., 2001; Newsom et al., 2003). Findings like these have contributed to recommendations that MMPI-A substantive scale scores should be considered clinically significant at T ≤ 65, but that scores as low as T = 60 could be indicative of problems (as in Chapter 14 or Archer, 2017). This practice has been demonstrated to lower the likelihood of saying a difficulty is not present when it really is (i.e., false negatives; Fontaine et al., 2001). Thus, it seems likely the adoption of the lower cut score on the MMPI-A-RF will increase our abilities to identify problems and symptoms when they are present. The trade-off, however, is that decreasing false negative rates means false positive rates increase (i.e., saying a difficulty is present when it really is not). Research is needed to examine whether the benefits of having lower false negative rates justifies the costs of associated with having more false positives.

There also are disadvantages of using the MMPI-A-RF instead of the MMPI-A. The greatest disadvantage is that there is less research available to guide interpretation of the MMPI-A-RF scales. As noted earlier, there is a rich tradition of using some MMPI scales with adolescents, and scales on the MMPI-A have accumulated a base of research to guide interpretation (for a summary of this work, see Chapter 14 or Archer, 2017). This stands in contrast to currently available evidence supporting use of the MMPI-A-RF. While Archer et al. (2016) presented an impressive array of correlations between MMPI-A-RF scales and external criterion measures in large samples from a variety of settings, there were several scales for which appropriate external criteria for examining validity were unavailable (e.g., RC3, SPF). Their data were also inconclusive for some scales (e.g., RC9). Furthermore, these data were collected in settings where the focus is typically on clinical problems and difficulties. As such, little information about adaptive functioning and strengths an adolescent may possess are available from MMPI-A-RF data at this time. We anticipate these weaknesses will be addressed through additional empirical study. However, the pace of peer-reviewed work to supplement these data has been slow; and, as seen throughout this chapter, there are many questions about MMPI-A-RF scales in need of investigation.

Given the strengths and weaknesses of the MMPI-A and MMPI-A-RF, how might one determine which instrument to use? We think it will depend on the assessment context and the test-taker's needs. In settings where time is limited, or for youth who are likely to struggle significantly to attend and respond meaningfully to a test, the MMPI-A-RF would be preferable. It is likely to provide information about the types of difficulties a test taker is experiencing and should function effectively as a screening measure for more narrowly defined problems. In settings where more detailed descriptions are needed, the MMPI-A may be preferable given the breadth and depth of knowledge we have about its scales.

INTERPRETATION

Interpretive Guidelines

Interpretive guidelines for the Validity and substantive scales of the MMPI-A-RF are provided in the sections below. Interpretations for the Validity scales are based entirely on the guidelines offered by Archer et al. (2016). Suggested interpretations for the substantive scales are based on guidelines suggested in the MMPI-A-RF manual, our examination of the empirical correlate data presented in the MMPI-A-RF manual, and other research that has been reported since the MMPI-A-RF was published in 2016.

Notably, many of our interpretative suggestions for the substantive scales differ from those presented in the MMPI-A-RF manual (Archer et al., 2016). This may be, in part, due to our cautious approach to identifying potential inferences. Namely, inferences were generated from the MMPI-A-RF manual based on correlations between scales and criterion measures that were of at least a small effect size ($r \geq 0.20$; Cohen et al., 2002). Furthermore, current evidence suggests scales of the MMPI-A-RF likely represent similar, but not parallel, forms of scales found on adult versions of the MMPI and the MMPI-A. As such, we did not apply descriptors for MMPI-A-RF scales based on work with their counterparts from these other versions of the instrument. It is our opinion that additional research is needed to determine the accuracy of such interpretations before they are applied in practice.

As with the scales on other versions of the MMPI, inferences based on substantive scales should be treated as hypotheses that are to be compared with other information available about test takers (e.g., interview, other tests, behavioral observations). Substantive scale scores are interpreted as being clinically significant at T ≥ 60. T scores much higher than 60 suggest a greater likelihood that the listed descriptors will apply to a test taker and that listed symptoms will be more severe than those associated with less-elevated scores. Although the interpretation of low scores (i.e., T ≤ 40) on some MMPI-A-RF scales is recommended in the test's manual, no independent research is yet available to guide this interpretation. As such, the interpretive guidelines presented in this chapter for low scores are based on information and correlates presented in Archer et al. (2016).

Interpretive Guidelines for Validity Scales

Cannot Say (CNS)

When the test taker provides scorable responses to all MMPI-A-RF items, the protocol is interpretable. However, when one or more items are omitted or are unscorable, caution is indicated in the interpretation of substantive scales because the omission of items tends to lead to artificially lower scores on these scales. Thus, when one or more unscorable response is provided, the percentage of items omitted from each scale should be examined. If 10% or more of items are omitted from a scale, then elevated scores can be interpreted, but only cautiously, as they are likely to underestimate the test taker's true standing on the scale. Scales with 10% or more unscorable responses that do not reach clinically significant elevation are uninterpretable. An excessive number of unscorable responses, which Archer et al. (2016) suggest is 10 or more, may warrant exploration for potential causes. These can include such things as reading and language difficulties, severe psychopathology, obsessiveness, or lack of insight or cooperation. There may also be themes to the items that were unscorable, and this can be inspected by examining the content of the items.

Variable Response Inconsistency (VRIN-r)

HIGH SCORES (T ≥ 65)

Scores at this level indicate that the test taker responded in an inconsistent manner. T scores between 65 and 74 suggest that the protocol should be interpreted with caution. When T scores are ≥ 75, inconsistent responding is so pervasive that the protocol should not be interpreted. Scores suggesting the test taker responded inconsistently may warrant additional exploration. They can reflect intentional random responding, such as might occur if the test taker was uncooperative. Scores at this level could also reflect an unintentional inconsistency in responding that may occur if there are errors in recording their responses or cognitive, reading, or language difficulties that inhibit their understanding of the items' contents.

LOW AND AVERAGE SCORES (T = 37–64)

The test taker responded in a consistent manner, and the protocol is interpretable.

True Response Inconsistency (TRIN-r)

HIGH SCORES (T ≥ 65)

High scores on this scale indicate that the test taker responded in a fixed manner, answering True or False to items without regard to their contents. When a designation of *T* is associated with the score, the fixed responding is likely to be yea-saying (or acquiescence); whereas a designation of *F* associated with the score indicates that the fixed responding is likely to be naysaying (or nonacquiescence). Elevated scores are usually a product of an uncooperative test-taking approach. T scores between 65 and 74 indicate a tendency toward fixed responding, and the protocol should be interpreted with caution. When T scores are ≥ 75, the fixed responding is pervasive enough that the protocol should not be interpreted.

AVERAGE SCORES (T = 50–64)

Scores in this range indicate that there is no evidence of fixed responding, and the protocol is interpretable.

Combined Response Inconsistency (CRIN)

HIGH SCORES (T ≥ 65)

Scores at this level indicate the test taker responded in an inconsistent manner. T scores between 65 and 74 suggest that the protocol should be interpreted with caution. When T scores are ≥ 75, inconsistent responding is so pervasive that the protocol should not be interpreted. Scores suggesting the test taker responded inconsistently may warrant additional exploration. They can reflect intentional random responding, such as might occur if the test taker was uncooperative. Scores at this level could also reflect an unintentional inconsistency in responding such as might occur if there are errors in recording their responses or cognitive, reading, or language difficulties that inhibit their understanding of the items' contents.

LOW AND AVERAGE SCORES (T = 37–64)

The test taker responded in a consistent manner, and the protocol is interpretable.

Infrequent Responses (F-r)

T ≥ 90

Scores at this level indicate the test taker has reported a large number of symptoms that are rarely endorsed by most adolescents, even those with genuine and severe psychopathology. The VRIN-r, TRIN-r, and CRIN scales should be consulted to determine whether F-r scale scores are the product of non-content-based invalid responding. If evidence of this response style is not found, the F-r scores likely represent an attempt on the part of the test taker to appear to have much more severe psychopathology or psychological distress than is actually the case. Protocols with F-r scale scores at this level should be considered invalid and should not be interpreted.

T = 80–89
Scores at this level may indicate inconsistent responding, severe emotional distress, or overreporting. Check the VRIN-r, TRIN-r, and CRIN scales. If scores on these scales are not at acceptable levels, then the protocol should be considered invalid and should not be interpreted. If these scores are at acceptable levels, then it is important to determine whether the F-r scale scores are reflecting severe psychopathology or overreporting. For individuals for whom there is neither history nor any current indication of serious dysfunction from extratest data, scores at this level likely indicate overreporting, and the protocol should not be interpreted or only interpreted with great caution. For individuals with a history or current extratest indications of serious dysfunction, the scores at this level should be interpreted as reflecting genuine psychopathology, and the protocol can be interpreted.

T = 70–79
Scores at this level are to be interpreted similarly to T scores between 80 and 89, except the likelihood of overreporting is less than at the higher levels. The protocol can be interpreted, but with the caution that scores may to some extent overestimate the severity of symptoms and problems if there is no corroborating extratest evidence the individual has a history or is currently experiencing significant difficulties with their mental health.

T < 70
When scores are at this level, there is no evidence of significant overreporting, and the protocol can be interpreted.

Uncommon Virtues (L-r)

T ≥ 80
Since scores at this level can be a product of non-content-based invalid responding, the VRIN-r, TRIN-r, and CRIN scales should be examined. If there are no indications of this response style, then L-r scores at this level indicate the test taker has presented themselves in an overly positive and virtuous manner to such an extent that scores on substantive scales can only be interpreted with great caution. The absence of elevations on substantive scales is uninterpretable, and elevated scores on substantive scales may underestimate the problems assessed by those scales.

T = 70–79
Because L-r scores at this level may be the product of non-content-based invalid responding, check the VRIN-r, TRIN-r, and CRIN scales. If this response style is ruled out, then L-r scores at this level indicate the test taker likely presented themselves in a very positive way. The absence of elevations on substantive scales is uninterpretable, and elevated scores on substantive scales may underestimate the problems assessed by the scales. Scores at this level may also indicate someone with an upbringing that strongly stressed traditional values.

T = 65–69

Scores at this level may be the product of non-content-based invalid responding (check VRIN-r, TRIN-r, and CRIN) or an effort by test takers to present themselves in an unrealistically favorable light. Any absence of elevations on substantive scales are uninterpretable, and elevated scores may underestimate problems assessed by those scales. Scores at this level may also indicate the test taker was raised in a very traditional way.

T < 65

When scores are at this level, there is no evidence of significant underreporting, and substantive scales can be interpreted.

Adjustment Validity (K-r)

T ≥ 75

Because scores at this level can be a product of non-content-based invalid responding, check the VRIN-r, TRIN-r, and CRIN scales. If this type of invalid responding can be ruled out, then scores on K-r at this level indicate that test takers have presented themselves as remarkably well adjusted. Interpretation should proceed with considerable caution, as the scores likely represent an attempt on the part of test takers to present themselves as having much better adjustment than they really have. The absence of elevations on substantive scales is uninterpretable, and elevated scores on substantive scales likely understate the problems assessed by those scales.

T = 66–74

Because scores at this level can be a product of non-content-based invalid responding, check the VRIN-r, TRIN-r, and CRIN scales. If this type of invalid responding can be ruled out, then scores at this level on K-r may reflect either underreporting of symptoms and problems or very good psychological adjustment. For persons for whom there is no corroborating evidence of exceptional psychological adjustment, any absence of elevation on substantive scales is uninterpretable. Elevated substantive scales may underestimate the problems assessed by those scales.

T = 60–65

Non-content-based invalid responding should be ruled out by checking the VRIN-r, TRIN-r, and CRIN scales. If this response style if ruled out, then scores on K-r at this level indicate possible underreporting of symptoms and problems. For persons for whom there is corroborating evidence of poor adjustment, absence of elevations on substantive scales should be interpreted with caution. Elevated scores on substantive scales may underestimate the problems assessed by those scales.

T < 60

When scores are at this level, there is no evidence of significant underreporting, and scores on substantive scales may be interpreted.

Interpretive Guidelines for Higher–Order (H-O) Scales

The H-O Scales are broad scales assessing dysfunction in affect, thought, and behavior. High scores on the H-O scales can indicate the severity of dysfunction that an adolescent experiences, the range of symptoms a youth is experiencing within a particular domain, or both. Thus, the absence of elevation on a particular H-O scale does not necessarily mean the test taker is reporting no problems in that domain. The RC Scales and SP Scales can be used to identify more circumscribed difficulties that are being reported.

Emotional/Internalizing Dysfunction (EID)

This scale is comprised of 26 items reflecting a wide range of difficulties with emotional functioning, such as those that tend to characterize internalizing dysfunctions.

High scores (T ≥ 60) indicate adolescents who

1. report experiencing a great deal of emotional turmoil (when T score is ≥ 80, the distress is likely to be perceived as a crisis)
2. experience difficulties with sad, depressed, and anxious feelings
3. present with somatic concerns
4. have low self-esteem
5. have difficulty with attention and concentration
6. may experience suicidal ideation
7. may have histories of self-injurious or suicidal behavior
8. should be evaluated for internalizing disorders such as those characterized by depressive, anxiety, phobic, or somatic symptoms
9. may be motivated for treatment due to their high levels of emotional distress

Low scores (T ≤ 40) indicate adolescents who report a better than average level of emotional adjustment.

Thought Dysfunction (THD)

This scale is comprised of 14 items reflecting symptoms of thought dysfunction, such as unusual sensory experiences or fixed and false beliefs that may rise to the level of a delusion.

High scores (T ≥ 60) indicate adolescents who

1. report symptoms of thought dysfunction (when T score ≥ 80, the symptoms may be severe)
2. have unusual thoughts or experiences typically associated with psychosis
3. may experience auditory or visual hallucinations
4. feel distressed, depressed, and anxious
5. are isolated from others
6. have difficulties in social relationships
7. may feel persecuted by their peers
8. sometimes act aggressively toward others
9. should be evaluated for psychotic disorders (e.g., schizophrenia, delusional disorder)

10.   should be evaluated for antipsychotic medications
11.   may require treatment in a structured or secure environment

Low scores (T ≤ 40) on this scale are not interpreted.

Behavioral Externalizing Dysfunction (BXD)

This scale is comprised of 24 items reflecting difficulties due to externalizing tendencies, including impulsive, risk-taking, substance-using, and antisocial behaviors.

High scores (T ≥ 60) indicate adolescents who

1.   report engaging in a wide variety of externalizing behaviors (when ≥ 80, these behaviors are likely to have gotten them into difficulties)
2.   are oppositional and defy authority figures
3.   act in ways that are disregardful of the needs of others
4.   are seen by others as impulsive and as having poorly controlled behavior
5.   are verbally or physically aggressive in relationships
6.   have negative relationships with peers
7.   tend to associate with peers who are negative influences
8.   have histories of behavior problems in school, at home, and in their communities
9.   may have been suspended or expelled from school
10. have histories of involvement with the legal system or have engaged in behaviors that could have resulted in involvement in the legal system
11. do not typically report high levels of emotional distress but may report some symptoms of anxiety and depression
12. should be evaluated for externalizing disorders such as those characterized by impulsive, substance-use, oppositional, or antisocial behaviors
13. may lack motivation for treatment
14. are at risk for treatment non-adherence
15. may benefit from treatment targeting impulsive and disinhibited behavior

Low scores (T ≤ 40) indicate adolescents who

1.   report higher than average levels of behavioral constraint
2.   are unlikely to engage in externalizing, acting-out behaviors

Interpretive Guidelines for the Restructured Clinical (RC) Scales

The RC Scales reflect aspects of the broad domains of psychopathology captured by the H-O Scales. The RC Scales are not markers of specific disorders; rather, they assess transdiagnostic dimensions of dysfunction that can be used in identifying and describing an adolescent's difficulties, as well as during case conceptualization, treatment planning, and progress monitoring.

Demoralization (RCd)

The RCd scale is comprised of 18 items and reflects the pleasantness–unpleasantness (or happiness–unhappiness) dimension from Tellegen and colleagues' (1999a, 1999b) model of mood and affect. Scores on RCd provide an indication of the level of psychological distress and emotional discomfort an adolescent is likely to be experiencing. Conceptually, this scale corresponds with the "distress" dimension of internalizing psychopathology in the HiTOP model (Kotov et al., 2021).

High scores (T ≥ 60) indicate adolescents who

1. report feeling distressed, sad, and dissatisfied with their current life circumstances
2. report experiencing extreme psychological distress characterized by feelings of dysphoria, helplessness, and inadequacy (if T ≥ 80)
3. feel unhappy, sad, and depressed
4. feel anxious much of the time
5. struggle with attention and concentration
6. report somatic concerns
7. have poor self-concepts
8. struggle in their relationships with peers
9. may experience suicidal ideation
10. may have a history of self-injurious or suicidal behavior
11. should be evaluated for suicide risk (if suicide-related critical items are endorsed or if Helplessness/Hopelessness [HLP] ≥ 60)
12. should be evaluated for depressive and anxiety-related disorders
13. may be motivated for treatment because of emotional distress
14. may benefit from initial interventions targeting relief of emotional distress

Low scores (T ≤ 40) indicate adolescents who report higher than average levels of life satisfaction and emotional adjustment.

Somatic Complaints (RC1)

This scale is comprised of 23 items reflecting a variety of different somatic concerns. Conceptually, scores on RC1 can be linked to the somatoform factor included in dimensional models of psychopathology. This scale should be interpreted carefully in adolescents with genuine medical problems, as it can reflect these difficulties.

High scores (T ≥ 60) indicate adolescents who

1. report multiple somatic concerns, including those related to head pain or gastrointestinal or neurological symptoms
2. present with several varied somatic concerns
3. frequently have sad, depressed, and anxious feelings
4. should be evaluated for somatic symptom and related disorders if physical explanations for their reported concerns can be ruled out
5. may reject psychological explanations for their somatic concerns

Low scores (T ≤ 40) indicate adolescents who report a sense of physical well-being.

Low Positive Emotions (RC2)

This scale is comprised of 10 items reflecting the adolescent's experience of positive emotions as well as their ability and willingness to engage in relationships and activities. High scores are intended to reflect the test taker's experience of difficulties experiencing positive emotions (i.e., anhedonia), a unique component of depressive disorders. Conceptually, RC2 can be linked to the positive affect dimension of Tellegen and colleagues' (1999a, 1999b) model of mood and affect.

High scores (T ≥ 60) indicate adolescents who

1. report difficulties experiencing positive emotions and feeling socially engaged
2. have deficits in their ability to experience joy and happiness (anhedonia)
3. feel fatigued and lacking in energy
4. present with slowed speech and movements
5. tend to be isolated or withdrawn in social situations
6. feel depressed, distressed, and anxious
7. should be evaluated for depressive and other disorders characterized by anhedonia
8. should be evaluated for antidepressant medication
9. may have difficulty engaging in treatment because of low positive emotionality
10. may struggle to develop rapport with their therapist due to social withdrawal

Low scores (T ≤ 40) indicate adolescents who

1. report a high level of psychological well-being
2. report a wide range of emotionally positive experiences

Cynicism (RC3)

This scale is comprised of nine items reflecting cynical beliefs about other people's motives and behaviors. These beliefs reflect a generalized negative view of others and do not indicate the adolescent feels they are the target of uncaring or untrustworthy behavior.

High scores (T ≥ 60) indicate adolescents who

1. report cynical beliefs
2. see other people as untrustworthy, uncaring, and concerned only about themselves
3. engage in rule-breaking behaviors
4. may have difficulty forming therapeutic relationships
5. need help in developing interpersonal trust

Low scores (T ≤ 40) indicate adolescents who

1. disavow cynical beliefs
2. see others as well-intentioned and trustworthy

Antisocial Behavior (RC4)

This scale is comprised of 20 items describing a range of acting out behaviors such as substance use, rule breaking, and antisocial acts. Scores on RC4 reflect disinhibited behaviors that violate social norms or are disregardful of others. This scale conceptually aligns with the disinhibited and antagonistic externalizing spectra described in dimensional models of psychopathology.

High scores (T ≥ 60) indicate adolescents who

1. report having engaged in many risky, oppositional, and antisocial behaviors
2. engage in rule-breaking behaviors that cause problems at home, school, and in their communities
3. engage in behaviors that could result in involvement with the legal system
4. have a history of criminal charges
5. are likely to have been detained in a juvenile detention facility
6. have a history of alcohol or other drug use
7. are at increased risk for problematic substance use
8. behave in verbally and physically aggressive ways toward others
9. act in oppositional ways when interacting with authority figures
10. are extraverted and have many friends
11. tend to associate with peers who are negative influences
12. should be evaluated for disruptive behavior, impulse-control, and conduct disorders
13. should be evaluated for substance-related disorders
14. may need motivational interventions to increase participation in treatment
15. may struggle to develop a positive rapport with providers
16. may benefit from interventions targeting disinhibited, rule-breaking behavior

Low scores (T ≤ 40) indicate adolescents who

1. report higher than average levels of behavioral constraint
2. are unlikely to report histories of rule-breaking behavior, substance use, or antisocial conduct

Ideas of Persecution (RC6)

This scale consists of nine items assessing persecutory ideation ranging from the idea one is being mistreated to beliefs that one is being purposefully targeted for malicious treatment. Conceptually, this scale aligns with liabilities toward psychoticism described in dimensional models of psychopathology. It can capture beliefs that rise to the level of a delusion. However, because the items reflect a variety of ways in which an adolescent could perceive being persecuted, high scores on this scale can reflect less extreme suspicious beliefs developed because of interactions where they were singled out or mistreated (e.g., youth who experience discrimination or interpersonal trauma).

High scores (T ≥ 60) indicate adolescents who

1. report significant persecutory thinking (if ≥ 80, these may rise to the level of a paranoid delusion)
2. have difficulties in social relationships
3. have conflictual relationships with peers
4. are aggressive toward others
5. experience distressed and anxious feelings

6. may experience unusual patterns of thinking
7. need additional evaluation to clarify the presence, quality, and context of persecutory beliefs
9. should be evaluated for disorders that include psychotic symptoms (if T ≥ 80)
8. may have difficulty in forming therapeutic relationships

Low scores (T ≤ 40) on this scale are not interpreted.

Dysfunctional Negative Emotions (RC7)

This scale is made up of 11 items assessing an adolescent's experience of excessive negative emotions including anxiety, fear, irritability/anger, and apprehension. Conceptually, this scale reflects the negative affect dimension of Tellegen et al.'s (1999a, 1999b) model of mood and affect. Test takers who score high on this scale are also likely to report high levels of demoralization given the negative valence of emotions reflected in RC7's items. However, because the psychological distress reflected in demoralization tends to be present in a variety of difficulties adolescents may experience, these are distinguishable constructs.

High scores (T ≥ 60) indicate adolescents who

1. report negative emotional experiences including anxiety, fear, irritability, and apprehension
2. experience high levels of anxiety
3. experience difficulties with distressed and depressed feelings
4. may experience intrusive thoughts
5. may report having nightmares
6. should be evaluated for anxiety-related disorders
7. should be evaluated for potential need of anxiolytic medications
8. may be motivated for treatment because of emotional distress

Low scores (T ≤ 40) indicate adolescents who report below-average levels of negative emotional experiences.

Aberrant Experiences (RC8)

This scale consists of eight items inquiring about the adolescent's experience of unusual thoughts and perceptual experiences. The scale reflects positive symptoms of psychosis, such as non-paranoid delusions (e.g., ideas of reference) and sensory hallucinations. It is conceptually aligned with the thought dysfunction liability described in dimensional models of psychopathology.

High scores (T ≥ 60) indicate adolescents who

1. report unusual perceptual, cognitive, or motor experiences
2. are likely to experience visual or auditory hallucinations
3. have unusual thoughts that may rise to the level of a delusion
4. may have impaired reality testing
5. tend to be isolated or withdrawn from their peers
6. report distressed, anxious, or depressed feelings

7. should be evaluated for disorders that involve psychotic symptoms
8. should be evaluated for antipsychotic medications
9. may benefit from treatment focused on unusual patterns of thinking and perceiving

Low scores (T ≤ 40) on this scale are not interpreted.

Hypomanic Activation (RC9)

This scale consists of eight items with content reflecting experiences often associated with hypomanic activation. This includes things like excessive energy and movement, racing thoughts, and impulsive risk-taking and excitement-seeking behaviors. Conceptually, RC9 could reflect aspects of the mania subfactor in dimensional models of psychopathology, which is linked to both internalizing and though disorder spectra (Kotov et al., 2021). However, on adult versions of the instrument, items on this scale have been linked to disinhibited externalizing liability (e.g., Sellbom, 2016), likely due to their assessment of impulsive and excitement-seeking behaviors.

High scores (T ≥ 60) indicate adolescents who

1. report higher than average levels of energy and engagement with their environments
2. are aggressive
3. may have a history of behavior problems at home, school, or in the community
4. should be evaluated for mood-related disorders, including bipolar and schizoaffective disorders
5. may struggle to effectively engage in treatment due to excessive behavioral activation
6. may benefit from initial treatment focused on monitoring and stabilizing mood

Low scores (T ≤ 40) indicate adolescents who have below-average levels of activation and engagement with their environments.

Interpretive Guidelines for Specific Problems (SP) Scales

Somatic/Cognitive SP Scales

The Somatic/Cognitive SP scales assess general types of somatic and cognitive concerns that an adolescent may report. They can be helpful in discerning what kind of specific difficulties a test taker may report with their physical functioning, either when interpreting an elevated score on RC1 or when interpreting isolated SP scale elevations.

Malaise (MLS)

This scale is comprised of eight items assessing the adolescent's general perceptions of their physical health and functioning.

High scores (T ≥ 60) indicate adolescents who

1. report feelings of ill health that may interfere with their activities
2. have concerns about their physical functioning
3. feel fatigued and lacking in energy
4. experience poor sleep
5. have difficulties with attention and concentration
6. are experiencing distressed, anxious, or depressed feelings
7. should be evaluated for disorders characterized by somatic concerns including somatic-symptom disorders
8. may struggle to engage effectively in treatment because of malaise

Low scores (T ≤ 40) indicate adolescents who report a general sense of physical well-being.

Gastrointestinal Complaints (GIC)

This scale is comprised of four items with content describing gastrointestinal difficulties such as discomfort caused by nausea or vomiting.

High scores (T ≥ 60) indicate adolescents who

1. report a larger than typical number of gastrointestinal concerns
2. describe having a variety of difficulties with their physical functioning
3. are experiencing distressed, anxious, or depressed feelings
4. should be evaluated for somatic symptom disorders if physical explanations for their gastrointestinal concerns can be ruled out
5. may benefit from learning stress reduction techniques

Low scores (T ≤ 40) on this scale are not interpreted.

Head Pain Complaints (HPC)

This scale consists of four items assessing the adolescent's experience of headaches and pain.

High scores (T ≥ 60) indicate adolescents who

1. report a larger than typical number of headaches and pains
2. are experiencing distressed, anxious, or depressed feelings
3. should be considered for somatic symptom and related disorders if physical explanations for the pain can be ruled out
4. may benefit from learning stress and pain management techniques

Low scores (T ≤ 40) on this scale are not interpreted.

Neurological Complaints (NUC)

This scale is comprised of seven items reflecting problems that may be a result of neurological or psychological difficulties. This includes difficulties like unexplained numbness, dizziness, and involuntary movements.

High scores (T ≥ 60) indicate adolescents who

1. report difficulties that may have a neurological origin (e.g., problems with balance, dizziness, unexplained paralysis)

2. are experiencing distressed, anxious, or depressed feelings
3. should be evaluated for somatic symptom and related disorders if physical explanations for the reported symptoms can ruled out
4. may benefit from medical or behavioral management of symptoms if a neurological explanation for the reported symptoms is established

Low scores (T ≤ 40) on this scale are not interpreted.

Cognitive Complaints (COG)
This scale is comprised of five items assessing a range of problems with cognition and memory.

High scores (T ≥ 60) indicate adolescents who

1. report a larger than average number of cognitive difficulties
2. struggle with poor attention and concentration
3. have difficulties thinking clearly
4. are experiencing distressed, anxious, or depressed feelings
5. should be referred for neuropsychological evaluation
6. should be evaluated for neurodevelopmental disorders including ADHD

Low scores (T ≤ 40) on this scale are not interpreted.

Internalizing SP Scales
These scales are intended to assess narrow manifestations of internalizing symptoms reported by the adolescent. They represent facets of problems described by EID (all Internalizing SP scales), RCd (HLP, SFD, Inefficacy [NFC]), and RC7 (OCS, Stress/Worry [STW], Anxiety [AXY], Anger Proneness [ANP], BRF, SPF); but they can be interpreted in the absence of elevation on these higher-order scales.

Helplessness/Hopelessness (HLP)
This scale consists of 10 items asking the adolescent about their experience of hopelessness and pessimism.

High scores (T ≥ 60) indicate adolescents who

1. report feeling hopeless, helpless, and pessimistic about the future
2. are experiencing distressed, anxious, or depressed feelings
3. are likely to experience suicidal ideation
4. may have histories of self-injurious or suicidal behavior
5. may struggle with concentration and attention
6. are likely to experience academic difficulties
7. should be evaluated for depression-related disorders
8. may benefit from treatment to increase feelings of hope

Low scores (T ≤ 40) on this scale reflect the disavowal of feelings of hopelessness and helplessness.

Self-Doubt (SFD)
This scale is composed of five items reflecting low self-confidence and poor self-esteem.

High scores (T ≥ 60) indicate adolescents who

1. report a lack of self-confidence and feelings of uselessness
2. have low self-esteem
3. are experiencing distressed, anxious, or depressed feelings
4. are likely to experience suicidal ideation
5. may have histories of self-injurious or suicidal behavior
6. may struggle with concentration and attention
7. should be evaluated for depression-related disorders
8. may benefit from treatment to increase self-esteem and improve confidence

Low scores (T ≤ 40) on this scale indicate the adolescent reported high levels of self-confidence and esteem.

Inefficacy (NFC)

This scale is comprised of four items reflecting the adolescent's beliefs about their capacity to deal effectively with difficult situations.

High scores (T ≥ 60) indicate adolescents who

1. report being indecisive and ineffective in dealing with stressors
2. are passive when confronted with stressful situations
3. may tend to approach life cautiously
4. are experiencing distressed, anxious, or depressed feelings
5. are likely to experience suicidal ideation
6. may have histories of self-injurious or suicidal behavior
7. may struggle with concentration and attention
8. may benefit from treatment to decrease indecisiveness and passivity

Low scores (T ≤ 40) on this scale indicate adolescents who are decisive in stressful situations and feel efficacious.

Obsessions/Compulsions (OCS)

This scale is made up of four items reflecting obsessive thoughts and compulsive behaviors.

High scores (T ≥ 60) indicate person who

1. report an above-average level of obsessive thoughts and compulsive behaviors
2. feel anxious
3. are cautious and unlikely to take risks
4. should be evaluated for disorders involving obsessive thinking or compulsive behavior
5. may benefit from treatment intended to reduce obsessive thoughts and compulsive behavior

Low scores (T ≤ 40) on this scale indicate the adolescent reported no experience of obsessions or compulsions.

Stress/Worry (STW)

This scale is comprised of seven items describing excessive worries and resulting difficulties.

High scores (T ≥ 60) indicate person who

1. report having a large number of stressors and worries
2. are experiencing distressed, anxious, or depressed feelings
3. have problems thinking clearly
4. may struggle with concentration and attention
5. have poor self-esteem
6. are likely to experience suicidal ideation
7. may have histories of self-injurious or suicidal behavior
8. should be evaluated for stress-related disorders
9. may benefit from learning stress management techniques

Low scores (T ≤ 40) indicate adolescents who report below-average levels of stress and worry.

Anxiety (AXY)

This scale consists of four items inquiring about the adolescent's experience of anxiety and related difficulties.

High scores (T ≥ 60) indicate adolescents who

1. report feelings of anxiety, dread, and fear
2. experience high levels of anxiety
3. are likely to experience nightmares and disrupted sleep
4. may experience intrusive ideation
5. feel distressed and depressed
6. should be evaluated for anxiolytic medications

Low scores (T ≤ 40) on this scale are not interpreted.

Anger Proneness (ANP)

This scale consists of five items assessing an adolescent's experience and expression of anger.

High scores (T ≥ 60) indicate adolescents who

1. report frequently feeling irritated and angry
2. describe having experienced problems due to their angry feelings
3. are easily irritated or angered
4. act aggressively toward others
5. are likely to have been in fights or to have assaulted someone
6. have histories of rule-breaking, oppositional, and antisocial behaviors
7. should be evaluated for disruptive behavior, impulse-control, and conduct disorders

8. may benefit from treatment focused on learning and practicing anger management techniques

Low scores (T ≤ 40) on this scale indicate the adolescent reported no problems with anger.

Behavior-Restricting Fears (BRF)

This scale is comprised of three items reflecting the restriction of activities in and out of the home. These restrictions are believed to have occurred due to fearfulness such as might occur in agoraphobia (Archer et al., 2016).

High scores (T ≥ 60) indicate adolescents who

1. report having several fears that lead them to restrict their activities
2. are likely to feel distressed, anxious, and depressed
3. should be evaluated for anxiety disorders, particularly agoraphobia
4. may benefit from treatment focused on reducing the fearfulness contributing to the restriction of activities

Low scores (T ≤ 40) on this scale are not interpreted.

Specific Fears (SPF)

This scale is comprised of four items reflecting fears of specific things or environments. Empirical correlates for this scale need to be established. As such, we currently recommend only content-based interpretations.

High scores (T ≥ 60) indicate adolescents who

1. report having multiple fears, which may rise to the level of a phobia
2. may benefit from treatment aimed at reducing fearfulness

Low scores (T ≤ 40) indicate the adolescent reported a lower than average number of specific fears.

Externalizing SP Scales

These scales are intended to help identify specific manifestations of externalizing symptoms the adolescent reported. They reflect facets of BXD (all Externalizing SP scales), RC4 (NSA, ASA, CNP, SUB, and NPI), and RC9 (AGG); but they can be interpreted even in the absence of elevations on the broader scales.

Negative School Attitudes (NSA)

This scale is comprised of six items reflecting negative attitudes toward school such as beliefs that attending school is an unpleasant or unworthy activity.

High scores (T ≥ 60) indicate adolescents who

1. report a larger than typical number of negative attitudes toward school
2. experience academic problems
3. engage in a variety of rule-breaking, oppositional, and other externalizing behaviors
4. should be evaluated for problems with academic achievement and school behavior problems
5. may benefit from interventions targeting negative attitudes toward school

Low scores (T ≤ 40) on this scale indicate the youth reported fewer than typical negative attitudes toward school.

Antisocial Attitudes (ASA)

This scale consists of six items assessing attitudes that support antisocial behaviors such as believing the truth or rules should be bent if it serves one's purpose.

High scores (T ≥ 60) indicate adolescents who

1. report a variety of attitudes supportive of antisocial behavior
2. engage in a variety of rule-breaking and oppositional behaviors
3. are likely to threaten other people to get their way
4. have a history of conduct problems
5. may have engaged in a problematic pattern of substance use
6. should be evaluated for disruptive behavior, impulse-control, and conduct disorders
7. may benefit from interventions targeting antisocial attitudes

Low scores (T ≤ 40) on this scale indicate the adolescent reported a below-average number of antisocial attitudes.

Conduct Problems (CNP)

This scale is comprised of seven items assessing an adolescent's engagement in antisocial behaviors at home, at school, and in their community.

High scores (T ≥ 60) indicate adolescents who

1. report engaging in a variety of antisocial behaviors
2. are likely to engage in rule-breaking, oppositional, and antisocial behaviors
3. engage in irresponsible and impulsive behaviors
4. have a history of involvement with the legal system, such as being detained or charged
5. are likely to be aggressive toward others
6. tend to have negative relationships with their peers
7. have a history of fighting
8. are likely to have been in trouble for stealing
9. have a history of using alcohol or drugs
10. have a history of being suspended or expelled from school
11. have run away from home
12. should be evaluated for disruptive behavior, impulse-control, and conduct disorders
13. may benefit from interventions intended to reduce antisocial behaviors

Low scores (T ≤ 40) on this scale indicate the adolescent endorsed a below-average level of antisocial behavior.

Substance Abuse (SUB)

This scale consists of four items asking an adolescent about their use of alcohol or other drugs and related problems.

High scores (T ≥ 60) on this scale indicate adolescents who

1. are openly acknowledging use of alcohol, marijuana, or other substances
2. are likely to experience problems due to their use of substances
3. have histories of treatment for substance-related difficulties
4. are likely to engage in a variety of rule-breaking, oppositional, and antisocial behaviors
5. are likely to have been in trouble with the law, including being charged, detained, or placed on probation
6. have a history of running away
8. should have a detailed evaluation of their use of substances and related difficulties including assessment for potential substance-related disorders
9. may benefit from interventions targeting problematic substance use

Low scores (T ≤ 40) on this scale are not interpreted.

Negative Peer Influence (NPI)
This scale is comprised of five items describing an adolescent's involvement with peers who encourage antisocial behaviors and their caregivers' reactions to such peers.
High scores (T ≥ 60) indicate adolescents who

1. report associating with peers who encourage negative behaviors
2. are likely to have peers that encourage and support negative behaviors
3. engage in a variety of rule-breaking, oppositional, and antisocial behaviors
4. have a history of being suspended from school
5. have run away from home
6. may use alcohol or other drugs
7. may have a history of involvement with the legal system
8. should be evaluated for disruptive behavior, impulse-control, conduct, and substance-related disorders
9. may benefit from interventions intended to reduce the influence of negative peers
10. may benefit from participation in activities with positive peer influences

Low scores (T ≤ 40) on this scale are not interpreted.

Aggression (AGG)
This scale is composed of eight items reflecting the youth's engagement in aggressive behavior as well as attitudes that might support acting in an aggressive manner toward others.
High scores (T ≥ 60) indicate adolescents who

1. report acting in aggressive ways toward other people
2. engage in verbally and physically aggressive behaviors
3. are likely to make threats toward others
4. have a history of fighting
5. engage in irresponsible or impulsive behaviors
6. are likely to engage in a variety of other rule-breaking, oppositional, and antisocial behaviors

7. should be evaluated for disruptive behavior, impulse-control, and conduct disorders
8. may benefit from interventions targeting aggressive behaviors

Low scores (T < 40) indicate the adolescent reported a lower than average level of aggressive behavior.

Interpersonal SP Scales
The Interpersonal SP Scales are intended to provide information about the interpersonal functioning of the adolescent. Unlike other SP Scales, the Interpersonal Scales assess an independent domain of functioning and are not situated within the MMPI-A-RF scale hierarchy (i.e., H-O, RC, SP).

Family Problems (FML)
This scale is comprised of 11 items reflecting negative experiences the adolescent reports having within their family, such as conflict and lack of support. For adolescents whose circumstances have led them to have multiple different groups of people they perceive as family (e.g., youth who have biological and foster or adoptive families), interpreting elevations on this scale may require following up with the test taker. This is because the items do not distinguish between experiences with their family of origin versus their current family.

High scores (T ≥ 60) indicate adolescents who

1. report having negative interactions with members of their family, including conflicts and perceived lack of support
2. are likely to have families experiencing relational problems
3. act verbally or physically aggressive toward others
4. are likely to engage in a variety of rule-breaking, oppositional, and antisocial behaviors
5. experience distressed, depressed, or anxious feelings
6. should be considered for involvement in family-based treatments
7. may benefit from interventions targeting coping with family difficulties

Low scores (T ≤ 40) indicate adolescents who report past and present family environments with below-average levels of conflict.

Interpersonal Passivity (IPP)
This scale consists of four items assessing the adolescent's willingness and ability to assert themselves in social situations.

High scores (T ≥ 60) indicate adolescents who

1. report being passive and unassertive in interpersonal situations
2. describe having feelings of distress, depression, and anxiety
3. may benefit from interventions intended to increase their willingness and ability to engage in assertive behaviors

Low scores (T ≤ 40) on this scale are not interpreted.

Social Avoidance (SAV)

This scale is comprised of seven items inquiring about the adolescent's avoidance of social situations such as dances and parties.

High scores (T ≥ 60) indicate adolescents who

1. report frequently avoiding social situations and events
2. are isolated
3. have few or no friends
4. are described by others as introverted
5. describe feeling distressed, depressed, and anxious
7. may experience vegetative symptoms, such as anhedonia and slowed speech and movements (if assessed in a clinical setting)
8. should be evaluated for disorders characterized by social avoidance
9. may benefit from interventions targeting social avoidance

Low scores (T ≤ 40) indicate adolescents who report enjoying social situations and events.

Shyness (SHY)

This scale consists of nine items assessing how reticent and socially anxious the adolescent is when interacting with others.

High scores (T ≥ 60) indicate adolescents who

1. report being shy and uncomfortable around other people
2. report being easily embarrassed
3. describe themselves as having many social difficulties
4. may respond passively in social situations
5. are described by others as being introverted and isolated
6. experience feelings of distress, anxiety, and depression
7. should be evaluated for social anxiety disorder (social phobia)
8. may benefit from interventions intended to reduce social anxiety

Low scores (T ≤ 40) indicate adolescents who report little or no social anxiety.

Disaffiliativeness (DSF)

This scale is comprised of five items reflecting an adolescent's preferences for being alone and dislike of social relationships.

High scores (T ≥ 60) indicate adolescents who

1. report disliking being around other people
2. are socially withdrawn
3. describe having problems in social relationships
4. experience feelings of depression
5. may have problems with self-esteem
6. should be evaluated for disorders characterized by preferences for solitary activities
7. should be evaluated for schizoid traits (if DSF = 90)
8. may struggle to develop a positive alliance with providers

Low scores (T ≤ 40) on this scale are not interpreted.

Interpretive Guidelines for the Personality Psychopathology Five (PSY-5) Scales

As detailed in Chapter 7, the PSY-5 Scales were intended to assess adaptive and maladaptive manifestations of personality characteristics (Harkness, McNulty, & Ben-Porath, 1995). These traits are closely aligned with the AMPD presented in the DSM-5 (American Psychiatric Association, 2013) and the spectra-level dimensions outlined in the HiTOP model (Kotov et al. 2021). Versions of these scales were developed for the MMPI-A and adapted for the MMPI-A-RF due to the relative continuity of personality traits across the lifespan (McNulty, Harkness, et al., 1997).

Aggressiveness-Revised (AGGR-r)
This scale consists of 12 items with content reflecting aggressive behavior used to achieve one's goals, or instrumental aggression. The construct assessed by this scale aligns with the antagonism domain proposed in the AMPD and the antagonistic externalizing spectrum of HiTOP.

High scores (T ≥ 60) indicate adolescents who

1. report that they are interpersonally assertive and aggressive
2. tend to be verbally and physically aggressive toward others
3. have made verbal threats
4. have a history of fights
5. frequently experience anger
6. engage in a wide variety of rule-breaking, oppositional, and antisocial behaviors
7. may be impulsive, inattentive, or hyperactive
8. should be evaluated for externalizing disorders, especially conduct disorder
9. may benefit from examining costs and benefits of aggressive behavior
10. may benefit from learning anger control techniques

Low scores (T ≤ 40) indicate adolescents who report being interpersonally passive and submissive.

Psychoticism-Revised (PSYC-r)
This scale consists of 13 items describing a disconnection from consensual reality such as is reflected in symptoms of thought dysfunctions. The construct assessed by this scale aligns with the psychoticism domain proposed in the AMPD and the thought disorder spectrum of HiTOP.

High scores (T ≥ 60) indicate adolescents who

1. report unusual thought processes and perceptual experiences
2. are likely to experience psychotic symptoms
3. have unusual patterns of thinking
4. experience auditory or visual hallucinations
5. describe having nightmares
6. have distressed, anxious, or depressed feelings

7. have few positive peer relationships
8. should be evaluated for psychosis spectrum disorders and other disorders characterized by psychotic symptoms
9. may benefit from interventions targeting thought dysfunction

Low scores (T ≤ 40) on this scale are not interpreted.

Disconstraint-Revised (DISC-r)

This scale is comprised of 20 items reflecting disinhibition including poor impulse control and risk-taking. The construct assessed by this scale aligns with the disinhibition domain proposed in the AMPD and the disinhibited externalizing spectrum of HiTOP.

High scores (T ≥ 60) indicate adolescents who

1. report various manifestations of disinhibited behavior
2. engage in a variety of rule-breaking, oppositional, and antisocial behaviors
3. engage in excitement-seeking and risk-taking behaviors
4. have consumed alcohol and other drugs
5. are likely to have been suspended or expelled from school
6. are likely to have been involved in the legal system, including being charged, detained, or placed on probation
7. have histories of aggressive behavior, including fighting
8. may make impulsive decisions or show poor judgment
9. should be evaluated for disruptive behavior, impulse-control, and conduct disorders
10. may struggle in treatment due to disruptive behaviors
11. may benefit from interventions intended to reduce disinhibition and maladaptive decision making

Low scores (T ≤ 40) indicate adolescents who report low levels of behavioral disinhibition, possibly reflecting overly constrained behavior.

Negative Emotionality/Neuroticism – Revised (NEGE-r)

This scale consists of 13 items reflecting tendencies toward experiencing strong negative emotions such as anxiety, anger, and fear. The construct assessed by this scale aligns with the negative affectivity domain proposed in the AMPD and aspects of the internalizing spectrum of HiTOP.

High scores (T ≥ 60) on this scale indicate adolescents who

1. report overwhelming negative emotions
2. describe having many emotional difficulties
3. feel anxious much of the time
4. experience distressed and depressed feelings
5. have problems with attention and concentration
6. experience problems thinking clearly
7. may experience suicidal ideation

8. should be evaluated for suicide risk
9. should be evaluated for anxiety and depressive disorders
10. may be motivated for treatment because of emotional discomfort
11. may benefit from interventions targeting negative emotions

Low scores (T ≤ 40) on this scale are not interpreted.

Introversion/Low Positive Emotionality - Revised (INTR-r)

This scale is comprised of 15 items reflecting low levels of social engagement and difficulties experiencing positive emotions. The construct assessed by this scale aligns with the detachment dimensions proposed in both the AMPD and HiTOP.

High scores (T ≥ 60) on this scale indicate adolescents who

1. report fewer than average positive emotional experiences
2. feel depressed much of the time
3. experience vegetative symptoms of depression such as anhedonia and psychomotor slowing (if assessed in a clinical setting)
4. are underactive
5. experience distressed and anxious feelings
6. may be isolated and withdrawn from others
7. may struggle with trusting their peers
8. should be evaluated for depression and anxiety-related disorders
9. may benefit from interventions focused on increasing positive emotional experiences
10. may benefit from interventions intended to reduce social isolation and withdrawal

Low scores (T ≤ 40) indicate adolescents who report having many positive emotional experiences.

Interpretive Strategy

Suggestions for interpreting the MMPI-A-RF from Archer et al. (2016) are similar to those for the MMPI-2-RF (Ben-Porath & Tellegen, 2008/2011). This is appropriate given the MMPI-2-RF was used as a template for the MMPI-A-RF, leading the two instruments to be similarly structured.

When interpreting a MMPI-A-RF, the first step is to examine the Validity scales to determine whether interpretation of the substantive scales is warranted. If Validity scale scores suggest that the test taker approached the test in an invalid manner by answering items without regard their content or by overreporting, no further consideration is given to other MMPI-A-RF scores. However, sometimes Validity scale scores suggest an invalidating response style may be present but that it is not to a level that would invalidate the protocol. In these cases, substantive scales are interpreted, but only cautiously. This is because they can overestimate or underestimate the problems being reporting by the test taker. Guidelines for interpreting Validity scales are presented in Archer et al. (2016) and were summarized earlier in this chapter.

If a protocol is deemed valid and interpretable, the substantive scales are then interpreted. Archer et al. (2016) suggest MMPI-A-RF scores can be used to address five broad areas. These include (a) somatic/cognitive dysfunction, (b) emotional dysfunction, (c) thought dysfunction, (d) behavioral dysfunction, and (e) interpersonal functioning. Specific MMPI-A-RF scales are interpreted within each of these areas, and interpretation of these scales is hierarchical in nature. Inferences are made first about general areas of dysfunction (i.e., somatic/cognitive, emotional, thought, and behavioral) and then about more specific aspects of dysfunction. Inferences based on the PSY-5, which are adjacent to the larger MMPI-A-RF scale hierarchy, are then made.

The H-O, RC, SP, and revised PSY-5 (PSY-5-r) scales for each of the areas of dysfunction are listed in Table 15.2. The H-O scales allow inferences about general

TABLE 15.2 *Recommended Structure and Sources of Information for MMPI-A-RF Interpretation*

Topic	MMPI-A-RF Sources
1. Protocol Validity	
a. Content Non-Responsiveness	CNS, VRIN-r, TRIN-r, CRIN
b. Overreporting	F-r
c. Underreporting	L-r, K-r
2. Substantive Scale Interpretation	
a. Somatic/Cognitive Dysfunction	1. RC1, MLS, GIC, HPC, NUC, COG
b. Emotional Dysfunction	1. EID
	2. RCd, HLP, SFD, NFC
	3. RC2, INTR-r
	4. RC7, OCS, STW, AXY, ANP, BRF, SPF, NEGE-r
c. Thought Dysfunction	1. THD
	2. RC6
	3. RC8
	4. PSYC-r
d. Behavioral Dysfunction	1. BXD
	2. RC4, NSA, ASA, CNP, SUB, NPI
	3. RC9, AGG, AGGR-r, DISC-r
e. Interpersonal Functioning	1. FML
	2. RC3
	3. IPP
	4. SAV
	5. SHY
	6. DSF
g. Diagnostic Considerations	Most substantive scales
h. Treatment Considerations	Most substantive scales

Note. Excerpted (Table 7.1) from the *MMPI-A-RF Administration, Scoring, Interpretation, and Technical Manual* by Robert P. Archer, Richard W. Handel, Yossef S. Ben-Porath, and Auke Tellegen. Copyright © 2016 by the Regents of the University of Minnesota. Reproduced by permission of the University of Minnesota Press. All rights reserved. "MMPI-A-RF" is a registered trademark of the Regents of the University of Minnesota; "Minnesota Multiphasic Personality Inventory-Adolescent-Restructured Form" is an unregistered trademark of the Regents of the University of Minnesota.

areas of dysfunction (i.e., emotional, thought, and behavioral). There are RC scales associated with each H-O scale that allow inferences about particular facets of dysfunction suggested by elevated scores on the H-O scales. Likewise, there are SP scales associated with the RC scales that permit inferences about even more specific facets of dysfunction suggested by elevations on RC scales.

The somatic/cognitive, emotional, thought, and behavioral dysfunction area interpretations should be presented in the order of their prominence in the MMPI-A-RF protocol. This allows for interpretations to highlight the most salient problems that the test taker is likely to have. Prominence can be determined by using the RC1 scale for the somatic/cognitive area and the three H-O scales for the general emotional (EID), thought (THD), and behavioral (BXD) dysfunction areas. Start the interpretation with the area having the highest T score elevation, interpreting that scale and all the scales under it in the MMPI-A-RF hierarchy. Then, repeat this process for the remaining areas by order of elevation. Once each of these four domains has been interpreted, interpret scales in the interpersonal domain.

Within each domain, interpretation of scales should move from those that reflect the broadest dysfunction to those that reflect the narrowest dysfunction. In other words, interpretations should be ordered from the least to most specific descriptions of the test-taker's difficulties. Inferences based on the RC scales typically will be more specific than those based on the H-O scale, and SP scales will typically offer the most nuanced picture of a test-taker's difficulties. Thus, if an H-O scale is elevated, interpret this scale; then examine the RC scales associated with it (RCd, RC2, and RC7 for EID; RC6 and RC8 for THD; and RC4 and RC9 for BXD). If the T score for an RC scale is $\geq$ 60, generate inferences about the RC scale and then examine and interpret SP scales that are facets of the RC scale, making inferences about scales with T scores $\geq$ 60. Relevant PSY-5 scales should also be interpreted at this point (INTR-r for RC2, NEGE-r for RC7, PSYC-r for THD, and AGGR-r and DISC-r for BXD).

Test takers may not always produce elevated scores at all levels of the MMPI-A-RF hierarchy. In these cases, interpretation should pick up at the level of the MMPI-A-RF hierarchy where elevations (i.e., T $\geq$ 60) do occur. For example, a test taker could produce a profile with elevations on RC2, but no corresponding elevation on EID. If this were to occur, the test taker is not likely to have produced elevations on the other internalizing RC scales, RCd and RC7. This could happen if they deny problems with demoralization or negative emotions, or if they only endorse very specific facets of the dysfunction represented in these RC scales. In such a case, interpretation of the emotional dysfunction area would begin with RC2, followed by INTR-r. If the test taker had elevations on any of the SP scales reflecting facets of RCd (i.e., HLP, SFD, NFC) or RC7 (i.e., OCS, STW, AXY, ANP, BRF, SPF), or an elevation on NEGE-r, these interpretations would then be presented after the interpretation of RC2 and related scales in order of prominence.

Once scales that are elevated within all the areas have been interpreted, Archer et al. (2016) recommend looking across all the scales to provide information about diagnostic and treatment considerations so long as the assessment context warrants their inclusion. All the substantive scales (H-O, RC, SP, and PSY-5) are sources of information about diagnostic impressions and treatment implications. Archer et al.

(2016) indicated that inferences about diagnostic considerations are based in part on empirical data and are in part inferential. They also stated that inferences about treatment are not typically based on empirical data.

Archer et al. (2016) do not provide information on how to incorporate item-level interpretations into their interpretative strategy, arguing that item-level interpretation is ill-advised given problems with reliability and validity associated with responses to a single item. Instead, they recommend item-level information from critical items be used to guide follow-up interviews with test takers. We agree with this strategy.

There are two sources for obtaining important item-level information on the MMPI-A-RF. The first is from the MMPI-A-RF Score and Interpretive Reports, which provide critical responses given by test takers on the AGG, AXY, HLP, RC6, RC8, and SUB scales. These scales were identified by the test's developers as having critical item content that may require immediate attention and follow-up. Items answered in the scored direction are provided for scales for which T scores are ≥ 60.

Additional item-level information is available in the MMPI-A-RF critical items set, which was derived from the Forbey and Ben-Porath (1998) critical items developed for use with the MMPI-A. The MMPI-A-RF version includes 53 of the original 81 MMPI-A critical items. These items are arranged into 14 content categories: Aggression, Anxiety, Cognitive Problems, Conduct Problems, Depression/Suicidal Ideation, Eating Problems, Family Problems, Hallucinatory Experiences, Paranoid Ideation, School Problems, Self-Denigration, Somatic Complaints, Substance Use/Abuse, and Unusual Thinking. The Depression/Suicidal Ideation critical items category may be particularly important, as it contains all the MMPI-A-RF items that directly inquire about suicidal thinking and behavior.

Illustrative Case

In the next section, we will apply the MMPI-A-RF interpretative strategy just described to the scores for the illustrative case (John) appended to this chapter. Readers should note that this is the same case discussed in Chapter 14 in relation to the MMPI-A interpretive strategy. As with any other version of the MMPI, inferences drawn from the MMPI-A-RF should be considered only one piece of information in a more comprehensive evaluation. Additional cases for readers to practice interpretation with are included in the supplemental materials available for this book on the publisher's website. Please visit www.oup.com/he/graham6e to access these materials.

Examination of John's Validity scale scores indicates that he approached the test in an appropriate manner and that the substantive scales are interpretable, albeit cautiously. He omitted no items and his scores suggest he responded with regard to the items' contents (VRIN-r, T = 42; CRIN, T = 50), though he may have responded "true" indiscriminately at times (TRIN-r, T = 73T). This level of fixed responding does not invalidate the profile but does indicate the need to interpret the substantive scales cautiously. His scores on the content-based invalid responding indicators provide no evidence of underreporting (L-r, T = 44; K-r, T = 39) or overreporting (F-r, T = 51).

Next, we examine John's scores on the H-O and RC1 scales, which act as indicators of prominence for the four dysfunction areas in the interpretative strategy (i.e., Somatic/Cognitive, Emotional, Behavioral, and Thought Dysfunctions). Because his highest score is on the EID scale, and because that scale is T ≥ 60, we would infer that he is reporting significant signs of emotional dysfunction. We then interpret, in order of elevation, the RC scales associated with EID—RCd, RC2, and RC7—and their associated SP and PSY-5 scales. Interpretation of these scales will give a more specific picture of John's symptoms and problems.

We begin with the highest RC scale elevation, which is on the RCd scale. John's T score of 67 suggests he is reporting feeling sad, unhappy, and dissatisfied with his current life situation. He is likely to experience distressed, anxious, and depressed feelings. John achieved T scores above 60 on the HLP (T = 73), SFD (T = 62), and NFC (T = 61) scales. His scores on these scales indicate he is reporting feeling hopeless and pessimistic about the future (HLP) and likely has low self-esteem (SFD). He is also likely to approach life cautiously and passively (NFC). All of these scales suggest John may be at risk for suicidal ideation or behavior, a notion congruent with his endorsement of several critical items.

After interpreting RCd and its associated SP scales, we move to the other emotional dysfunction RC scales, RC2 and RC7. Neither is elevated, but RC2 does have an interpretable low score, so we would interpret this scale next. John's scores on RC2 (T = 37) suggests that while he is experiencing a high level of emotional distress, he also describes having a wide range of positive emotional experiences. Finally, while John does not have a significant elevation on RC7 (T = 46), his report does suggest he experiences several narrow aspects of negative emotionality. These are captured in the OCS (T = 65), STW (T = 64), and ANP (T =74) scores. The elevations on these scales suggest he is likely to frequently feel anxious (OCS, STW), worried (STW), and angry (ANP). John may be likely to experience obsessive or intrusive thoughts (OCS, STW). He is also likely to be easily irritated or angered and may act aggressively toward others when these feelings occur (ANP).

Because none of the other H-O or RC scales are elevated, we would then proceed to interpreting the SP scales within the various domains. These should be ordered by prominence. In this case, John has T scores of 73 on both MLS, a somatic/cognitive SP scale, and ASA, an externalizing SP scale. Because these two SP scales are "tied" for prominence, we must use our clinical judgment about which domain to interpret next. Given the association of somatic difficulties with internalizing difficulties, which we just discussed, we would recommend interpreting the somatic/cognitive domain next.

Within the somatic/cognitive domain, John achieved a T = 73 on MLS and T = 61 on COG. The high score on MLS suggest he is reporting having a general sense that something is wrong with his physical health and that he is likely to feel fatigued and have poor sleep. The high score on COG indicates John reports a larger than average number of cognitive difficulties. He is likely to be experiencing difficulties thinking clearly, as well problems with attention and concentration.

We would then move onto interpreting the SP scales associated with the externalizing domain, as the ASA score is the next most highly elevated (T = 73) scale in the profile. John's score on ASA suggests he is reporting attitudes supportive of antisocial behaviors. He is likely to have engaged in a wide variety of rule-breaking

534 MMPI INSTRUMENTS: ASSESSING PERSONALITY AND PSYCHOPATHOLOGY

and oppositional behaviors and may have a history of using alcohol or other substances. This latter interpretation is supported also by the elevated SUB (T = 61) and DISC-r (T = 63) scale scores. The former scale indicates John is likely to have experienced problems due to his use of substances and that he should be closely evaluated for substance-related disorders. John's last two elevations in this domain are on the PSYS-5 AGGR-r (T = 65) and DISC-r (T = 63) scales. Broadly, his scores on these scales suggest he may have personality dispositions toward antagonism (AGGR-r) and disinhibition (DISC-r). The AGGR-r score suggests John reports a wide range of instrumentally aggressive behaviors and that he is likely to be verbally and physically aggressive toward others. His score on DISC-r suggests John is likely to engage in a wide variety of behaviors characterized by poor judgment and impulsivity. This could include behaviors that get him in trouble at school or with the law, and those that reflect risk-taking.

Now that we have interpreted scales in each of the major symptom areas, we next turn to the Interpersonal Functioning scales. The only elevated interpersonal scale is FML (T = 75). Thus, none of the other interpersonal scales are interpreted. John's high score on the FML scale suggests he is reporting his family is full of conflict and that he perceives them as being unsupportive. His family is likely to be experiencing significant problems in relating to one another. John's score on this scale suggests his family may be one of the targets of his aggressive behavior as well.

We next examine all of John's scores to determine whether there is evidence to suggest that specific mental disorders should be considered. John's scores on the EID (T = 64), RCd (T = 67), Internalizing and Somatic/Cognitive SP scales MLS (T = 73), COG (T = 61), HLP (T = 73), SFD (T = 62), NFC (T = 61), OCS (T = 65), STW (T = 64), and ANP (T = 74) suggest that several internalizing diagnoses should be considered. These include depressive- and anxiety-related disorders, broadly. Narrower disorders within these larger categories, such as disorders characterized by obsessions and compulsions (OCS) or stress and worry (STW), should also be considered or further evaluated. John may also benefit from evaluation for somatic-symptoms disorders if physical origins for his malaise can be ruled out (MLS). His experience of cognitive difficulties (COG) suggests the need to consider neurodevelopmental disorders such as ADHD—a conclusion also supported by the high level of disinhibited, impulsive behavior suggested by his scores on the DISC-r (T = 63) PSY-5-r scale. John's high scores on the ANP Internalizing SP scale (T = 74)—as well as his high scores on ASA (T = 73) and SUB (T = 61) Externalizing SP scales and the AGGR-r (T = 65) and DISC-r (T = 63) PSY-5-r scales—suggest John should be evaluated for externalizing disorders other than ADHD as well. This broadly includes all the disruptive behavior, impulse-control, and conduct disorders as well as substance-related disorders. This might include considering antisocial or another Cluster B personality disorder, though given his age, we would be more likely to only describe the traits reflected in the PSY-5-r scales because they might reflect more transient manifestations of the maladaptive personality, as is common in this developmental period.

If relevant to the context, we would then examine scores on all the elevated scales to determine if there are any considerations for treatment. We usually begin by talking about engagement-related concerns. In this case, John's T score ≥ 60 on

EID, RCd, HLP, SFD, and NFC suggest he is likely to be motivated for treatment due to having a high level of emotional distress. However, he may struggle to engage effectively in treatment due to a high level of malaise (MLS) or because of disruptive behaviors (DISC-r).

We then typically discuss potential additional evaluation or outside referrals that might be needed. For John, his scores on the MMPI-A-RF suggest he needs an immediate suicide risk evaluation (RCd, HLP, SFD, NFC). This is because his scores on these scales, all of which are empirically linked to the experience of suicidal ideation and behavior (Archer et al., 2016), suggest he is experiencing a high level of emotional distress, hopelessness, and pessimism about the future. He also endorsed four of the Depression/Suicidal Ideation Critical Items, one of which has been flagged as being relevant for suicide risk assessment. We should also consider that his risk for suicide is heightened by his report of impulsive and disinhibited behavior (DISC-r). John's MMPI-A-RF profile also suggests he may benefit from additional evaluation for obsessive–compulsive and substance-related difficulties (OCS and SUB, respectively). Finally, his scores on COG suggest he may benefit from a neuropsychological evaluation to fully consider the likelihood of ADHD.

Finally, we typically turn our attention to potential treatment targets. Depending on the outcome of the suicide risk assessment described above, we might recommend interventions intended to mitigate suicide risk. More broadly, treatment targets include reducing his level of psychological distress (RCd) and indecisiveness (NFC) and increasing feelings of hope (HLP) and positive self-esteem (SFD). He may also benefit from learning anger (ANP, AGGR-r) and stress (STW) management techniques. If additional evaluation suggests significant obsessive thoughts or compulsive behaviors are present, interventions intended to address these experiences are also likely warranted (OCS). Additionally, John's MMPI-A-RF results suggest he would likely benefit from interventions broadly targeting disinhibition and poor decision making (DISC-r). Specific interventions intended to reduce attitudes supportive of antisocial (ASA) and aggressive (ANP, AGGR-r) behaviors may also be warranted. If substance-related difficulties are established, interventions targeting these behaviors may be needed (SUB). Finally, given his report of substantial family problems (FML), whether John and his family would benefit from family-based interventions should be considered.

At this point in the interpretative process, we would consider the critical responses and MMPI-A-RF critical item sets. Because John scores T ≥ 60 on HLP and SUB, items endorsed in the keyed direction are printed in his score report. He also endorsed 13/53 items in the revised Forbey and Ben-Porath (1998) critical items. These items were in the depression/suicidal ideation, family problems, self-denigration, somatic complaints, and substance use/abuse categories. Any of these items could be used to identify specific difficulties that warrant follow-up.

In summary, John appears to have approached the MMPI-2-RF in a valid manner, although some caution is needed, as he tended to answer true to items regardless of their content. John's problems are both internalizing and externalizing in nature. He is likely to be experiencing a great deal of emotional distress, feel overwhelmed by the demands of his life situation, and believe that he cannot do anything to make things better. His symptoms are likely to include feelings of ill health, stress and worry, and poor efficacy and esteem. He may be at risk for suicidal thinking or behavior. John also tends to be irritable and easily angered. He may be antagonistic and is likely to respond to provocations with verbal and physical aggression. He may use aggression instrumentally, such as to get his way. This type of aggressive behavior seems likely to be particularly salient when he is engaged in family conflicts, of which he experiences many. John tends to be disinhibited and likely makes impulsive decisions without considering their consequences. These difficulties may be exacerbated by his likely difficulties in organizing his thinking and concentration. John openly acknowledges that he uses substances and that he has attitudes supportive of antisocial behavior.

John is likely to be motivated for treatment because of the psychological and somatic distress that he is experiencing. However, there are factors that may interfere with effective treatment, such as his experience of malaise and engagement in disruptive behaviors. Several scales suggest the need for additional data gathering and external referrals. Treatment targets likely include an initial focus on decreasing his emotional turmoil, followed by interventions intended to address disinhibited, angry, and aggressive behaviors.

It can also be instructive to compare the MMPI-A-RF clinician-generated interpretation to the corresponding MMPI-A interpretation presented in Chapter 14. The MMPI-A and MMPI-A-RF reports are in agreement that John's protocols are valid and interpretable. However, the MMPI-A-RF TRIN-r score was moderately elevated, while the MMPI-A TRIN score was at an average level. This difference in elevation may be a product of the reduced number of item pairs on the MMPI-A-RF TRIN-r scale, meaning fewer items need to be answered in a similar direction to achieve an elevation. Future research should assist us in determining whether the shorter length of the MMPI-A-RF non-content-based invalid responding scales makes them more sensitive to lower levels of these types of responding.

In terms of the substantive scale interpretations, the MMPI-A and MMPI-A-RF reports agree that John is experiencing considerable psychological turmoil that may put him at risk for suicidal ideation or behavior. However, the MMPI-A suggests he has a more prominent experience of depressed mood characterized by a negative view of himself and motivational difficulties. These experiences are less salient on the MMPI-A-RF, though there were some indications of problems with self-esteem and efficacy (SFD and NFC). The MMPI-A interpretations regarding John's experience of depression came primarily from the A-dep Content scale and its component scales. While the generalized distress captured in A-dep and self-deprecation captured in A-dep2 was reflected in the SFD and NFC elevations, the Content Component scale reflecting problems with motivation that was interpreted on the MMPI-A (Low Drive; A-dep3) does not have a direct counterpart on the MMPI-A-RF. This is because no SP scales were developed for RC2 or INTR-r, the two scales most likely to capture this kind of construct. However, the interpretation of the Content Component scales on the MMPI-A is a largely content-based process. As such, it is difficult to say which of the two descriptions best describes John's true experiences.

Both the MMPI-A and MMPI-A-RF interpretations characterize John as having problems due to angry and irritable feelings and as having a high likelihood of expressing these feelings through verbally and physically aggressive behaviors. Both instruments also suggest John has antagonistic and disinhibited personality traits, which likely contribute to a pattern of risk-taking and acting-out behaviors, including substance use. However, there are fewer indications of interpersonal problems related to these tendencies on the MMPI-A-RF, with exception of both the MMPI-A and MMPI-A-RF suggesting high levels of family difficulties. Thus, the MMPI-A provides a picture of John that suggests he feels alienated from and cynical toward others, perhaps in part due to some of his behaviors, while the MMPI-A-RF does not. We think this difference may be due to the limited research on this important aspect of functioning for the MMPI-A-RF. For example, Archer et al. (2016) had few external criteria reflecting interpersonal tendencies (e.g., extraversion) and relational experiences (e.g., attachment with peers) in the external correlates they presented for MMPI-A-RF scales in the instrument's manual. For this reason, strong relations that would support interpretative recommendations were not demonstrated for many of the interpersonal scales (e.g., RC3) or were limited in breadth (e.g., SHY). Given the importance of interpersonal relationships to adolescent development, we expect, however, to see future MMPI-A-RF research on this topic.

Both the MMPI-A and MMPI-A-RF interpretations emphasize John's negative characteristics and offer limited to no information about strengths. The assessment of strengths has not historically been a key feature of the MMPI instruments, given their focus on assessing psychopathology. However, the MMPI-A scores do provide some evidence that John is extraverted, which was used to generate second-order inferences about how this could be used to improve his symptoms. Given the empirically based interpretations for the MMPI-A-RF were generated primarily from data gathered in contexts focused on describing and intervening in problems (e.g., inpatient hospital, residential center, forensic predisposition settings), the lack of external criteria focused on strengths is not surprising. Nonetheless, this is an area in which additional research is needed for the MMPI-A-RF.

The MMPI-A and MMPI-A-RF interpretations are largely in agreement about what disorders should be considered or further evaluated. Uniquely, however, the MMPI-A-RF interpretation does suggest the need for evaluation of ADHD. The two instruments also suggest similar considerations about his motivation for, and barriers to, engaging in treatment, though the MMPI-A interpretation offers additional considerations related to rapport and potential impediments to treatment progress. Scales of the MMPI-A-RF also offer little information about the likely pace and outcome of any implemented interventions. To be maximally useful to therapists, empirical work addressing how these kinds of therapeutic engagement variables are captured on the MMPI-A-RF is likely needed.

In summary, there are far more similarities than differences in the MMPI-A and MMPI-A-RF interpretations of John's protocols. As with adult versions of the instrument, the MMPI-A's richer interpretation may simply be a product of the research base informing interpretation of the MMPI-A scales. Thus, as research is conducted on the MMPI-A-RF scales, we hope to see the scales scores allow for a broader and deeper understanding of the test taker.

CLOSING COMMENTS

As mentioned at the beginning of this chapter, the MMPI-A-RF represents the most recent version of the MMPI developed for use with adolescents. The rationale underlying this alternative form and use of the widely researched MMPI-2-RF as a template suggest the MMPI-A-RF is well situated to provide information about a test taker in an efficient and psychometrically strong manner. Indeed, initial data concerning the validity of its scales' scores in a variety of settings are promising. However, additional MMPI-A-RF research is needed to adequately judge its utility in providing a nuanced view of an adolescent's social, emotional, and behavioral functioning when compared to other available instruments.

CHAPTER APPENDIX

Minnesota Multiphasic
Personality Inventory-Adolescent
Restructured Form™

Score Report

MMPI-A-RF™
Minnesota Multiphasic Personality Inventory-Adolescent-Restructured Form™
Robert P. Archer, PhD, Richard W. Handel, PhD, Yossef S. Ben-Porath, PhD, & Auke Tellegen, PhD

ID Number:	John
Age:	16
Gender:	Male
Years of Education:	Not reported
Date Assessed:	11/23/2015

ALWAYS LEARNING   **PEARSON**

MMPI-A-RF Validity Scales

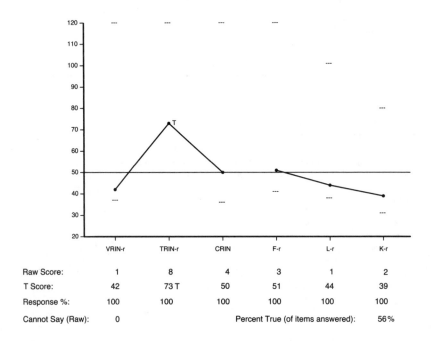

	VRIN-r	TRIN-r	CRIN	F-r	L-r	K-r
Raw Score:	1	8	4	3	1	2
T Score:	42	73 T	50	51	44	39
Response %:	100	100	100	100	100	100

Cannot Say (Raw):   0   Percent True (of items answered):   56%

The highest and lowest T scores possible on each scale are indicated by a "---"; MMPI-A-RF T scores are non-gendered.

VRIN-r	Variable Response Inconsistency	F-r	Infrequent Responses
TRIN-r	True Response Inconsistency	L-r	Uncommon Virtues
CRIN	Combined Response Inconsistency	K-r	Adjustment Validity

MMPI-A-RF Higher-Order (H-O) and Restructured Clinical (RC) Scales

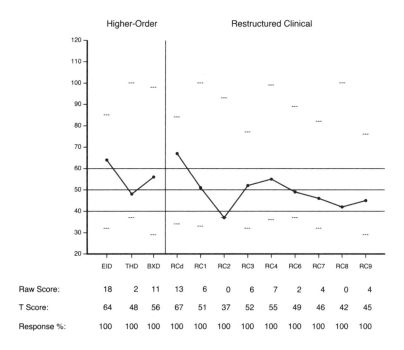

	EID	THD	BXD	RCd	RC1	RC2	RC3	RC4	RC6	RC7	RC8	RC9
Raw Score:	18	2	11	13	6	0	6	7	2	4	0	4
T Score:	64	48	56	67	51	37	52	55	49	46	42	45
Response %:	100	100	100	100	100	100	100	100	100	100	100	100

The highest and lowest T scores possible on each scale are indicated by a "---"; MMPI-A-RF T scores are non-gendered.

EID	Emotional/Internalizing Dysfunction	RCd	Demoralization	RC6	Ideas of Persecution
THD	Thought Dysfunction	RC1	Somatic Complaints	RC7	Dysfunctional Negative Emotions
BXD	Behavioral/Externalizing Dysfunction	RC2	Low Positive Emotions	RC8	Aberrant Experiences
		RC3	Cynicism	RC9	Hypomanic Activation
		RC4	Antisocial Behavior		

MMPI-A-RF Somatic/Cognitive and Internalizing Scales

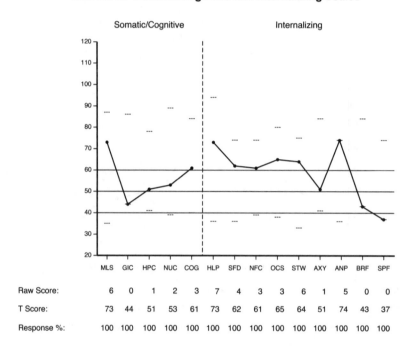

	MLS	GIC	HPC	NUC	COG	HLP	SFD	NFC	OCS	STW	AXY	ANP	BRF	SPF
Raw Score:	6	0	1	2	3	7	4	3	3	6	1	5	0	0
T Score:	73	44	51	53	61	73	62	61	65	64	51	74	43	37
Response %:	100	100	100	100	100	100	100	100	100	100	100	100	100	100

The highest and lowest T scores possible on each scale are indicated by a "---"; MMPI-A-RF T scores are non-gendered.

MLS	Malaise	HLP	Helplessness/Hopelessness	AXY	Anxiety
GIC	Gastrointestinal Complaints	SFD	Self-Doubt	ANP	Anger Proneness
HPC	Head Pain Complaints	NFC	Inefficacy	BRF	Behavior-Restricting Fears
NUC	Neurological Complaints	OCS	Obsessions/Compulsions	SPF	Specific Fears
COG	Cognitive Complaints	STW	Stress/Worry		

MMPI-A-RF Externalizing and Interpersonal Scales

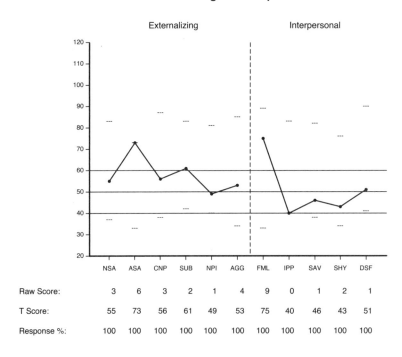

Raw Score:	3	6	3	2	1	4	9	0	1	2	1
T Score:	55	73	56	61	49	53	75	40	46	43	51
Response %:	100	100	100	100	100	100	100	100	100	100	100

The highest and lowest T scores possible on each scale are indicated by a "---"; MMPI-A-RF T scores are non-gendered.

NSA	Negative School Attitudes	FML	Family Problems
ASA	Antisocial Attitudes	IPP	Interpersonal Passivity
CNP	Conduct Problems	SAV	Social Avoidance
SUB	Substance Abuse	SHY	Shyness
NPI	Negative Peer Influence	DSF	Disaffiliativeness
AGG	Aggression		

MMPI-A-RF Personality Psychopathology Five (PSY-5) Scales

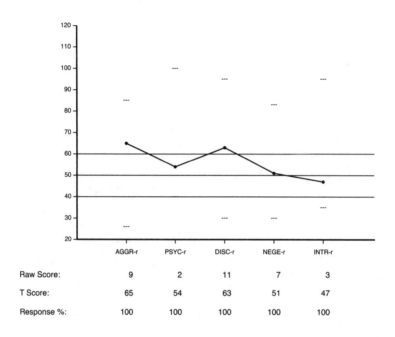

	AGGR-r	PSYC-r	DISC-r	NEGE-r	INTR-r
Raw Score:	9	2	11	7	3
T Score:	65	54	63	51	47
Response %:	100	100	100	100	100

The highest and lowest T scores possible on each scale are indicated by a "---"; MMPI-A-RF T scores are non-gendered.

AGGR-r   Aggressiveness-Revised
PSYC-r   Psychoticism-Revised
DISC-r   Disconstraint-Revised
NEGE-r   Negative Emotionality/Neuroticism-Revised
INTR-r   Introversion/Low Positive Emotionality-Revised

MMPI-A-RF T SCORES (BY DOMAIN)

PROTOCOL VALIDITY

Content Non-Responsiveness	0	42	73 T	50
	CNS	VRIN-r	TRIN-r	CRIN

Over-Reporting	51
	F-r

Under-Reporting	44	39
	L-r	K-r

SUBSTANTIVE SCALES

Somatic/Cognitive Dysfunction	51	73	44	51	53	61
	RC1	MLS	GIC	HPC	NUC	COG

Emotional Dysfunction	64	67	73	62	61
	EID	RCd	HLP	SFD	NFC

	37	47
	RC2	INTR-r

	46	65	64	51	74	43	37	51
	RC7	OCS	STW	AXY	ANP	BRF	SPF	NEGE-r

Thought Dysfunction	48	49
	THD	RC6

	42
	RC8

	54
	PSYC-r

Behavioral Dysfunction	56	55	55	73	56	61	49
	BXD	RC4	NSA	ASA	CNP	SUB	NPI

	45	53	65	63
	RC9	AGG	AGGR-r	DISC-r

Interpersonal Functioning	75	52	40	46	43	51
	FML	RC3	IPP	SAV	SHY	DSF

Note. This information is provided to facilitate interpretation following the recommended structure for MMPI-A-RF interpretation in Chapter 7 of the *MMPI-A-RF Administration, Scoring, Interpretation, and Technical Manual,* which provides details in the text and an outline in Table 7-1.

NOTE:** The final pages of this report display any items that were skipped or unscorable as well as any endorsed items that are part of a critical responses or critical items list. These sections include both the item number and content. The final page of the report includes the test taker's item level responses to every test item. These pages are not displayed in this book in order to maintain test security; however, redacted sample reports are available on the Pearson Assessments' website.

REFERENCES

Aaronson, A. L., Dent, O. B., Webb, J. T., & Kline, C. D. (1996). Graying of the critical items: Effects of aging on responding to MMPI-2 critical items. *Journal of Personality Assessment, 66*(1), 169–176. https://doi.org/10.1207/s15327752jpa6601_13

Ackerman, M. J., & Pritzl, T. B. (2011). Child custody evaluation practices: A 20-year follow-up. *Family Court Review, 49*(3), 618–628. https://doi.org/10.1111/j.1744-1617.2011.01397.x

Adkins, J. W., Weathers, F. W., McDevitt-Murphy, M., & Daniels, J. B. (2008). Psychometric properties of seven self-report measures of posttraumatic stress disorder in college students with mixed civilian trauma exposure. *Journal of Anxiety Disorders, 22*(8), 1393–1402. https://doi.org/10.1016/j.janxdis.2008.02.002

Alfano, D. P., Paniak, C. E., & Finlayson, M. A. J. (1993). The MMPI and closed head injury: A neurocorrective approach. *Neuropsychiatry, Neuropsychology, and Behavioral Neurology, 6*(2), 111–116.

Allard, G., & Faust, D. (2000). Errors in scoring objective personality tests. *Assessment, 7*(2), 119–129. https://doi.org/10.1177/107319110000700203

Allen, J. (1998). Personality assessment with American Indians and Alaska natives: Instrument considerations and service delivery style. *Journal of Personality Assessment, 70*(1), 17–42. https://doi.org/10.1207/s15327752jpa7001_2

Almagor, M., & Koren, D. (2001). The adequacy of the MMPI-2 Harris–Lingoes subscales: A cross-cultural factor analytic study of scales D, Hy, Pd, Pa, Sc, and Ma. *Psychological Assessment, 13*(2), 199–215. https://doi.org/10.1037/1040-3590.13.2.199

Alperin, J. J., Archer, R. P., & Coates, G. D. (1996) Development and effects of an MMPI-A K-correction procedure. *Journal of Personality Assessment, 67*(1), 155–168. https://doi.org/10.1207/s15327752jpa6701_12

American Educational Research Association, American Psychological Association, & National Council on Measurement in Education. (2014). *Standards for educational and psychological testing.* American Educational Research Association.

American Psychiatric Association. (1987). *Diagnostic and statistical manual of mental disorders* (3rd ed., revised).

American Psychiatric Association. (2013). *Diagnostic and statistical manual of mental disorders* (5th ed.). https://doi.org/10.1176/appi.books.9780890425596.

American Psychological Association. (1986). *Guidelines for computer-based tests and interpretations.*

American Psychological Association. (2010). Guidelines for child custody evaluations in family law proceedings. *American Psychologist, 65*(9), 863–867. https://doi.org/10.1037/a0021250

American Psychological Association. (2017). *Ethical principles of psychologists and code of conduct.*

American Psychological Association. (2020). *Publication manual of the American Psychological Association* (7th ed.). https://doi.org/10.1037/0000165-000

American Psychological Association & APA Task Force on Psychological Assessment and Evaluation Guidelines. (2020). *APA guidelines for psychological assessment and evaluation.* https://www.apa.org/about/policy/guidelines-psychological-assessment-evaluation.pdf

Anderson, J. L., & Sellbom, M. (2021). Assessing ICD-11 personality trait domain qualifiers with the MMPI-2-RF. *Journal of Clinical Psychology, 77*(4), 1090–1105. https://doi.org/10.1002/jclp.23099

Anderson, J. L., Sellbom, M., Ayearst, L., Quilty, L. C., Chmielewski, M., & Bagby, R. M. (2015). Associations between DSM-5 Section III personality traits and the Minnesota Multiphasic Personality Inventory 2–Restructured Form (MMPI-2-RF) scales in a psychiatric patient sample. *Psychological Assessment, 27*(3), 801–815. http://dx.doi.org/10.1037/pas0000096

Anderson, J. L., Sellbom, M., Bagby, R. M., Quilty, L. C., Veltri, C. O. C., Markon, K. E., & Krueger, R. F. (2013). On the convergence between PSY-5 domains and PID-5 domains and facets: Implications for assessment of DSM-5 personality traits. *Assessment, 20*(3), 286–294. https://doi.org/10.1177/1073191112471141

Anderson, J. L., Sellbom, M., Pymont, C., Smid, W., De Saeger, H., & Kamphuis, J. H. (2015). Measurement of DSM-5 section II personality disorder constructs using the MMPI-2-RF in clinical and forensic samples. *Psychological Assessment, 27*(3), 786–800. https://doi.org/10.1037/pas0000103

Anderson, J. L., Wood, M. E., Tarescavage, A. M., Burchett, D., & Glassmire, D. M. (2018). The role of dimensional personality psychopathology in a forensic inpatient psychiatric setting. *Journal of Personality Disorders, 32*(4), 447–464. https://doi.org/10.1521/pedi_2017_31_301

Anderson, W., & Bauer, B. (1985). Clients with MMPI high D-Pd: Therapy implications. *Journal of Clinical Psychology, 41*(2), 181–189. https://doi.org/10.1002/1097-4679(198503)41:2<181::AID-JCLP2270410209>3.0.CO;2-P

Anestis, J. C., Finn, J. A., Gottfried, E. D., Hames, J. L., Bodell, L. P., Hagan, C. R., Arnau, R. C., Anestis, M. D., Arbisi, P. A., & Joiner, T. E. (2018). Burdensomeness, belongingness, and capability: Assessing the interpersonal-psychological theory of suicide with MMPI-2-RF scales. *Assessment, 25*(4), 415–431. https://doi.org/10.1177/1073191116652227

Anestis, J. C., Gottfried, E. D., & Joiner, T. E. (2015). The utility of MMPI-2-RF substantive scales in prediction of negative treatment outcomes in a community mental health center. *Assessment, 22*(1), 23–35. https://doi.org/10.1177/1073191114536771

Applegate, K. L., Keefe, F. J., Siegler, I. C., Bradley, L. A., McKee, D. C., Cooper, K. S., & Riordan, P. (2005). Does personality at college entry predict number of reported pain conditions at mid-life? A longitudinal study. *The Journal of Pain, 6*(2), 92–97. https://doi.org/10.1016/j.jpain.2004.11.001

Arbisi, P. A., & Ben-Porath, Y. S. (1995). An MMPI-2 infrequent response scale for use with psychopathological populations: The Infrequency Psychopathology scale, *F(p)*. *Psychological Assessment, 7*(4), 424–431. https://doi.org/10.1037/1040-3590.7.4.424

Arbisi, P. A., & Ben-Porath, Y. S. (1998). The ability of Minnesota Multiphasic Personality Inventory-2 validity scales to detect fake-bad responses in psychiatric inpatients. *Psychological Assessment*, *10*(3), 221–228. https://doi.org/10.1037/1040-3590.10.3.221

Arbisi, P. A., & Ben-Porath, Y. S. (1999). The use of the Minnesota Multiphasic Personality Inventory-2 in the psychological assessment of persons with TBI: Correction factors and other clinical caveats and conundrums. *NeuroRehabilitation*, *13*(2), 117–125. https://doi.org/10.3233/NRE-1999-13206

Arbisi, P. A., Ben-Porath, Y. S., & McNulty, J. (2002). A comparison of MMPI-2 validity in African American and Caucasian psychiatric inpatients. *Psychological Assessment*, *14*(1), 3–15. https://doi.org/10.1037/1040-3590.14.1.3

Arbisi, P. A., Ben-Porath, Y. S., & McNulty, J. (2003a). Empirical correlates of common MMPI-2 two-point codes in male psychiatric inpatients. *Assessment*, *10*(3), 237–247. https://doi.org/10.1177/1073191103255003

Arbisi, P. A., Ben-Porath, Y. S., & McNulty, J. (2003b). Refinement of the MMPI-2 F(p) scale is not necessary: A response to Gass and Luis. *Assessment*, *10*(2), 123–128. https://doi.org/10.1177/1073191103010002002

Arbisi, P. A., Polusny, M. A., Erbes, C. R., Thuras, P., & Reddy, M. K. (2011). The Minnesota Multiphasic Personality Inventory–2 Restructured Form in National Guard soldiers screening positive for posttraumatic stress disorder and mild traumatic brain injury. *Psychological Assessment*, *23*(1), 203. https://doi.org/10.1037/a0021339

Arbisi, P. A., Rusch, L., Polusny, M. A., Thuras, P., & Erbes, C. R. (2013). Does cynicism play a role in failure to obtain needed care? Mental health service utilization among returning U.S. National Guard soldiers. *Psychological Assessment*, *25*(3), 991–996. https://doi.org/10.1037/a0032225

Arbisi, P. A., & Seime, R. J. (2006). Use of the MMPI-2 in Medical Settings. In J. N. Butcher (Ed.), *MMPI-2: A practitioner's guide* (pp. 273–299). American Psychological Association. https://doi.org/10.1037/11287-011

Arbisi, P. A., Sellbom, M., & Ben-Porath, Y. S. (2008). Empirical correlates of the MMPI-2 Restructured Clinical (RC) scales in psychiatric inpatients. *Journal of Personality Assessment*, *90*(2), 122–128. https://doi.org/10.1080/00223890701845146

Archer, R. P. (1984). Use of the MMPI with adolescents: A review of salient issues. *Clinical Psychology Review*, *41*(3), 241–251. https://doi.org/10.1016/0272-7358(84)90002-3

Archer, R. P. (1987). *Using the MMPI with adolescents*. Lawrence Erlbaum Associates.

Archer, R. P. (1992a). Minnesota Multiphasic Personality Inventory-2. In J. J. Kramer & J. C. Conoley (Eds.), *Eleventh mental measurements yearbook* (pp. 558–562). Buros Institute of Mental Measurements.

Archer, R. P. (1992b). *MMPI-A: Assessing adolescent psychopathology*. Lawrence Erlbaum Associates.

Archer, R. P. (Ed.). (2006). *Forensic uses of clinical assessment instruments*. Lawrence Erlbaum Associates.

Archer, R. P. (2017). *Assessing adolescent psychopathology: MMPI-A/MMPI-A-RF*. Routledge.

Archer, R. P., Aiduk, R., Griffin, R., & Elkins, D. E. (1996). Incremental validity of the MMPI-2 content scales in a psychiatric sample. *Assessment*, *3*(1), 79–90. https://doi.org/10.1177/107319119600300109

Archer, R. P., Belevich, J. K., & Elkins, D. E. (1994). Item-level and scale level factor structures on the MMPI-A. *Journal of Personality Assessment, 62*(2), 332–345. https://doi.org/10.1207/s15327752jpa6202_13

Archer, R. P., Bolinskey, P. K., Morton, T. L., & Farris, K. L. (2003). MMPI-A characteristics of male adolescents in juvenile justice and clinical treatment settings. *Assessment, 10*(4), 400–410. https://doi.org/10.1177/1073191103256128

Archer, R. P., Buffington-Vollum, J. K., Stredny, R. V., & Handel, R. W. (2006). A survey of psychological test use patterns among forensic psychologists. *Journal of Personality Assessment, 87*(1), 84–94. https://doi.org/10.1207/s15327752jpa8701_07

Archer, R. P., & Elkins, D. E. (1999). Identification of random responding on the MMPI-A. *Journal of Personality Assessment, 73*(3), 407–421. https://doi.org/10.1207/S15327752JPA7303_8

Archer, R. P., Elkins, D. E., Aiduk, R., & Griffin, R. (1997). The incremental validity of MMPI-2 supplementary scales. *Assessment, 4*(2), 193–205. https://doi.org/10.1177/107319119700400208

Archer, R. P., Fontaine, J., & McCrae, R. R. (1998). Effects of two MMPI-2 validity scales on basic scale relations to external criteria. *Journal of Personality Assessment, 70*(1), 87–102. https://doi.org/10.1207/s15327752jpa7001_6

Archer, R. P., & Gordon, R. A. (1994). Psychometric stability of MMPI-A modifications. *Journal of Personality Assessment, 62*(3), 416–426. https://doi.org/10.1207/s15327752jpa6203_3

Archer, R. P., Gordon, R. A., Anderson, G. L., & Giannetti, R. (1989). MMPI special scale clinical correlates for adolescent inpatients. *Journal of Personality Assessment, 53*(4), 654–664. https://doi.org/10.1207/s15327752jpa5304_2

Archer, R. P., Gordon, R. A., Giannetti, R., & Singles, J. M. (1988). MMPI scale clinical correlates for adolescent inpatients. *Journal of Personality Assessment, 52*(4), 707–721.

Archer, R. P., Griffin, R., & Aiduk, R. (1995). MMPI-2 clinical correlates for the common codes. *Journal of Personality Assessment, 65*(3), 391–407. https://doi.org/10.1207/s15327752jpa6503_1

Archer, R. P., Handel, R. W., Ben-Porath, Y. S., & Tellegen, A. (2016). *Minnesota Multiphasic Personality Inventory-Adolescent-Restructured Form (MMPI-A-RF): Manual for Administration, scoring, interpretation, and technical manual.* University of Minnesota Press.

Archer, R. P., & Jacobson, J. M. (1993). Are critical items "critical" for the MMPI-A. *Journal of Personality Assessment, 61*(3), 547–556. https://doi.org/10.1207/s15327752jpa6103_11

Archer, R. P., & Krishnamurthy, R. (1994). A structural summary approach for the MMPI-A: Development and empirical correlates. *Journal of Personality Assessment, 63*(3), 554–573. https://doi.org/10.1207/s15327752jpa6303_11

Archer, R. P., & Krishnamurthy, R. (2002). *Essentials of MMPI-A assessment.* Wiley.

Archer, R. P., Krishnamurthy, R., & Jacobson, J. M. (1994). *MMPI-A casebook.* Psychological Assessment Resources.

Archer, R. P., Maruish, M., Imhof, E. A., & Piotrowski, C. (1991). Psychological test usage with adolescent clients: 1990 survey findings. *Professional Psychology: Research and Practice, 22*(3), 247–252. https://psycnet.apa.org/doi/10.1037/0735-7028.22.3.247

Archer, R. P., & Newsom, C. R. (2000). Psychological test usage with adolescent clients: Survey update. *Assessment, 7*(3), 227–235. https://doi.org/10.1177/107319110000700303

Archer, R. P., Pancoast, D. L., & Gordon, R. A. (1992). *The development of the MMPI-A Immaturity Scale: Findings for normal and clinical samples.* Unpublished manuscript.

Archer, R. P., Stolberg, A. L., Gordon, R. A., & Goldman, W. R. (1986). Parent and child MMPI responses: Characteristics among families with adolescents in inpatient and outpatient settings. *Journal of Abnormal Child Psychology, 14*(1), 181–190. https://doi.org/10.1007/BF00917232

Archer, R. P., Handel, R. W., & Lynch, K. D. (2001). The effectiveness of the MMPI-A items in discriminating between normative and clinical samples. *Journal of Personality Assessment, 77*(3), 420–435. https://doi.org/10.1207/S15327752JPA7703_04

Arita, A. A., & Baer, R. A. (1998). Validity of selected MMPI-A content scales. *Psychological Assessment, 10*(1), 59–63. https://doi.org/10.1037/1040-3590.10.1.59

Ayearst, L. E., Sellbom, M., Trobst, K. K., & Bagby, R. M. (2013). Evaluating the interpersonal content of the MMPI-2-RF Interpersonal scales. *Journal of Personality Assessment, 95*(2), 187–196. https://doi.org/10.1080/00223891.2012.730085

Baer, R. A., Ballenger, J., Berry, D. T., & Wetter, M. W. (1997). Detection of random responding on the MMPI-A. *Journal of Personality Assessment, 68*(1), 139-151. https://doi.org/10.1207/s15327752jpa6801_11

Baer, R. A., Ballenger, J., & Kroll, L. S. (1998). Detection of underreporting on the MMPI-A in clinical and community samples. *Journal of Personality Assessment, 71*(1), 98–113. https://doi.org/10.1207/s15327752jpa7101_7

Baer, R. A., Kroll, L. S., Rinaldo, J., & Ballenger, J. (1999). Detecting and discriminating between random responding and overreporting on the MMPI-A. *Journal of Personality Assessment, 72*(2), 308–320. https://doi.org/10.1207/S15327752JP720213

Baer, R. A., & Miller, J. (2002). Underreporting of psychopathology on the MMPI-2: A meta-analytic review. *Psychological Assessment, 14*(1), 16–26. https://doi.org/10.1037/1040-3590.14.1.16

Baer, R. A., & Sekirnjak, G. (1997). Detection of underreporting on the MMPI-2 in a clinical population: Effects of information about validity scales. *Journal of Personality Assessment, 69*(3), 555–567. https://doi.org/10.1207/s15327752jpa6903_9

Baer, R. A., Wetter, M. W., & Berry, D. T. R. (1995). Effects of information about validity scales on underreporting of symptoms on the MMPI-2: An analogue investigation. *Assessment, 2,* 189–200. https://doi.org/10.1177/107319119500200209

Baer, R. A., Wetter, M. W., Nichols, D. S., Greene, R., & Berry, D. T. R. (1995). Sensitivity of MMPI-2 validity scales to underreporting of symptoms. *Psychological Assessment, 7*(4), 419–423. https://doi.org/10.1037/1040-3590.7.4.419

Bagby, R. M., Buis, T., & Nicholson, R. A. (1995). Relative effectiveness of the standard validity scales in detecting fake-bad and fake-good responding: Replication and extension. *Psychological Assessment, 7*(1), 84–92. https://doi.org/10.1037/1040-3590.7.1.84

Bagby, R. M., Marshall, M. B., Basso, M. R., Nicholson, R. A., Bacchiochi, J., & Miller, L. S. (2005). Distinguishing bipolar depression, major depression, and schizophrenia with the MMPI-2 clinical and content scales. *Journal of Personality Assessment, 84*(1), 89–95. https://doi.org/10.1207/s15327752jpa8401_15

Bagby, R. M., Nicholson, R. A., Bacchiochi, J. R., Ryder, A. G., & Bury, A. S. (2002). The predictive capacity of the MMPI-2 and PAI validity scales and indexes to detect coached and uncoached feigning. *Journal of Personality Assessment, 78*(1), 69–86. https://doi.org/10.1207/S15327752JPA7801_05

Bagby, R. M., Nicholson, R. A., Buis, T., Radovanovic, H., & Fidler, B. J. (1999). Defensive responding on the MMPI-2 in family custody and access evaluations. *Psychological Assessment, 11*(1), 24–28. https://doi.org/10.1037/1040-3590.11.1.24

Bagby, R. M., Onno, K. A., Mortezaei, A., & Sellbom, M. (2020). Examining the "traditional background hypothesis" for the MMPI-2-RF L-r scores in a Muslim faith-based sample. *Psychological Assessment, 32*(10), 991–995. https://doi.org/10.1037/pas0000941

Bagby, R. M., Rogers, R., & Buis, T. (1994). Detecting malingered and defensive responding on the MMPI-2 in a forensic inpatient sample. *Journal of Personality Assessment, 62*(2), 191–203. https://doi.org/10.1207/s15327752jpa6202_2

Bagby, R. M., Rogers, R., Buis, T., Nicholson, R. A., Cameron, S. L., Rector, N. A., Schuller, D. R., & Seeman, M. V. (1997). Detecting feigned depression and schizophrenia on the MMPI-2. *Journal of Personality Assessment, 68*(3), 650–664. https://doi.org/10.1207/s15327752jpa6803_11

Bagby, R. M., Rogers, R., Nicholson, R. A., Buis, T., Seeman, M. V., & Rector, N. A. (1997). Effectiveness of the MMPI-2 validity indicators in the detection of defensive responding in clinical and nonclinical samples. *Psychological Assessment, 9*(4), 406–413. https://doi.org/10.1037/1040-3590.9.4.406

Bagby, R. M., Ryder, A. G., Ben-Dat, D., Bacchiochi, J., & Parker, J. D. A. (2002). Validation of the dimensional factor structure of the Personality Psychopathology Five in clinical and nonclinical samples. *Journal of Personality Disorders, 16*(4), 304–316. https://doi.org/10.1521/pedi.16.4.304.24128

Bagby, R. M., Sellbom, M., Costa, P. T., Jr., & Widiger, T. A. (2008). Predicting Diagnostic and Statistical Manual of Mental Disorders-IV personality disorders with the five-factor model of personality and the Personality Psychopathology Five. *Personality and Mental Health, 2*(2), 55–69. https://doi.org/10.1002/pmh.33

Barefoot, J. C., Dahlstrom, W. G., & Williams, R. B. (1983). Hostility, CHD incidence, and total mortality: A 25-year follow-up study of 255 physicians. *Psychosomatic Medicine, 45*(1), 59–63. https://doi.org/10.1097/00006842-198303000-00008

Barefoot, J. C., Dodge, K. A., Peterson, B. L., Dahlstrom, W. G., & Williams, R. B. (1989). The Cook–Medley Hostility scale: Item content and ability to predict survival. *Psychosomatic Medicine, 51*(1), 46–57. https://doi.org/10.1097/00006842-198901000-00005

Barron, F. (1953). An ego strength scale which predicts response to psychotherapy. *Journal of Consulting Psychology, 17*(5), 327–333. https://doi.org/10.1037/h0061962

Barthlow, D. L., Graham, J. R., Ben-Porath, Y. S., & McNulty, J. L. (1999). Incremental validity of the MMPI-2 content scales in an outpatient mental health setting. *Psychological Assessment, 11*(1), 39–47. https://doi.org/10.1037/1040-3590.11.1.39

Barthlow, D. L., Graham, J. R., Ben-Porath, Y. S., & McNulty, J. L. (2004). Construct validity of the MMPI-2 College Maladjustment (Mt) scale. *Assessment, 11*(3), 251–262. https://doi.org/10.1177/1073191104268317

Barthlow, D. L., Graham, J. R., Ben-Porath, Y. S., Tellegen, A., & McNulty, J. L. (2002). The appropriateness of the MMPI-2 K correction. *Assessment, 9*(3), 219–229. https://doi.org/10.1177/1073191102009003001

Bartol, C. R. (1991). Predictive validation of the MMPI for small-town police officers who fail. *Professional Psychology: Research and Practice, 22*(2), 127–132. https://doi .org/10.1037/0735-7028.22.2.127

Bathurst, K., Gottfried, A. W., & Gottfried, A. E. (1997). Normative data for the MMPI-2 in child custody litigation. *Psychological Assessment, 9*(3), 205–211. https:// doi.org/10.1037/1040-3590.9.3.205

Baum, L. J., Archer, R. P., Forbey, J. D., & Handel, R. W. (2009). A review of the Minnesota Multiphasic Personality Inventory–Adolescent (MMPI-A) and the Millon Adolescent Clinical Inventory (MACI) with an emphasis on juvenile justice samples. *Assessment, 16*(4), 384–400. https://doi.org/10.1177/1073191109338264

Beevers, C. G., Strong, D. R., Bjorn, M., Pilkonis, P. A., & Miller, I. W. (2007). Efficiently assessing negative cognition in depression: An item response theory analysis of the Dysfunctional Attitude Scale. *Psychological Assessment, 19*(2), 199–209. https://doi .org/10.1037/1040-3590.19.2.199

Belter, R., & Piotrowski, C. (2001). Current status of doctoral-level training in psychological testing. *Journal of Clinical Psychology, 57*(6), 717–726. https://doi.org/10.1002/ jclp.1044

Ben-Porath, Y. S. (2012). *Interpreting the MMPI-2-RF.* University of Minnesota Press.

Ben-Porath, Y. S. (2013). *Self-report inventories: Assessing personality and psychopathology.* In J. R. Graham, J. A. Naglieri, & I. B. Weiner (Eds.), *Handbook of psychology: Assessment psychology* (pp. 622–644). John Wiley & Sons, Inc.

Ben-Porath, Y. S., & Butcher, J. N. (1989). Psychometric stability of rewritten MMPI items. *Journal of Personality Assessment, 53*(4), 645–653. https://doi.org/10.1207/ s15327752jpa5304_1

Ben-Porath, Y. S., Butcher, J. N., & Graham, J. R. (1991). Contribution of the MMPI-2 content scales to the differential diagnosis of schizophrenia and major depression. *Psychological Assessment, 3*(4), 634–640. https://doi.org/10.1037/1040-3590.3.4.634

Ben-Porath, Y. S., & Davis, D. L. (1996). *Case studies for interpreting the MMPI-A.* University of Minnesota Press.

Ben-Porath, Y. S., & Forbey, J. D. (2003). *Non-gendered norms for the MMPI-2.* University of Minnesota Press.

Ben-Porath, Y. S., & Forbey, J. D. (2004, May). *Detrimental effects of the K correction on clinical scale validity* [Paper presentation]. 39th Annual Symposium on Recent Developments of the MMPI-2/MMPI-A, Minneapolis, MN.

Ben-Porath, Y. S., Graham, J. R., Archer, R. P., Tellegen, A., & Kaemmer, B. (2006). *Supplement to the MMPI-A Manual for administration, scoring, and interpretation: The Content Component scales; the Personality Psychopathology Five (PSY-5) scales, and the critical items.* University of Minnesota Press.

Ben-Porath, Y. S., Graham, J. R., & Tellegen, A. (2009). *MMPI-2 Symptom Validity (FBS) Scale: Development, research findings, and interpretive recommendations.* University of Minnesota Press.

Ben-Porath, Y. S., Hostetler, K., Butcher, J. N., & Graham, J. R. (1989). New subscales for the MMPI-2 social introversion (Si) scale. *Psychological Assessment, 1*(3), 169–174. https://doi.org/10.1037/1040-3590.1.3.169

Ben-Porath, Y. S., McCully, E., & Almagor, M. (1993). Incremental validity of the MMPI-2 content scales in the assessment of personality and psychopathology by self-report. *Journal of Personality Assessment, 61*(3), 557–575. https://doi.org/10.1207/s15327752jpa6103_12

Ben-Porath, Y. S., & Sherwood, N. E. (1993). *The MMPI-2 content component scales: Development, psychometric characteristics, and clinical application.* University of Minnesota Press.

Ben-Porath, Y. S., Shondrick, D. D., & Stafford, K. P. (1995). MMPI-2 and race in a forensic diagnostic sample. *Criminal Justice and Behavior, 22*(1), 19–32. https://doi.org/10.1177/0093854895022001002

Ben-Porath, Y. S., & Stafford, K. P. (1993, August). *Empirical correlates of MMPI-2 scales in a forensic diagnostic sample: An interim report* [Paper presentation]. 101st Annual Meeting of the American Psychological Association, Toronto, Ontario.

Ben-Porath, Y. S., & Tellegen, A. (2011). *The Minnesota Multiphasic Personality Inventory-2-Restructured Form (MMPI-2-RF): Manual for administration, scoring, and interpretation.* University of Minnesota Press. Original work published in 2008.

Ben-Porath, Y. S., & Tellegen, A. (2020a). *Minnesota Multiphasic Personality Inventory-3 (MMPI-3): Manual for administration, scoring, and interpretation.* University of Minnesota Press.

Ben-Porath, Y. S., & Tellegen, A. (2020b). *Minnesota Multiphasic Personality Inventory-3 (MMPI-3): Technical manual.* University of Minnesota Press.

Ben-Porath, Y. S., & Tellegen, A. (2020c). *Minnesota Multiphasic Personality Inventory-3 (MMPI-3): User's guide for the score and clinical interpretive reports.* University of Minnesota Press.

Ben-Porath, Y. S., & Tellegen, A., & Puente, A. E. (2020). *Minnesota Multiphasic Personality Inventory-3 (MMPI-3): Manual supplement for the U.S. Spanish translation.* University of Minnesota Press.

Benton, A. L. (1949). The MMPI: A review. In O. K. Buros (Ed.), *The third mental measurements yearbook* (pp. 104–107). Rutgers University Press.

Berry, D. T., Wetter, M. W., Baer, R. A., Larsen, L., Clark, C., & Monroe, K. (1992). MMPI-2 random responding indices: Validation using a self-report methodology. *Psychological Assessment, 4*(3), 340–345. https://doi.org/10.1037/1040-3590.4.3.340

Berry, D. T. R., Adams, J. J., Clark, C. D., Thacker, S. R., Burger, T. L., Wetter, M. W., Baer, R. A., & Borden, J. W. (1996). Detection of a cry for help on the MMPI-2: An analog investigation. *Journal of Personality Assessment, 67*(1), 26–36. https://doi.org/10.1207/s15327752jpa6701_2

Berry, D. T. R., Wetter, M. W., Baer, R. A., Widiger, T. A., Sumpter, J. C., Reynolds, S. K., & Hallam, R. A. (1991). Detection of random responding on the MMPI-2: Utility of F, Back F, and VRIN scales. *Psychological Assessment, 3*(3), 418–423. https://doi.org/10.1037/1040-3590.3.3.418

Berry, D. T. R., Wetter, M. W., Baer, R. A., Youngjohn, J. R., Gass, C. S., Lamb, D. G., & Bucholz, W. D. (1995). Overreporting of closed-head injury symptoms on the MMPI 2. *Psychological Assessment, 7*(4), 517–523. https://doi.org/10.1037/1040-3590.7.4.517

Bianchini, K. J., Etherton, J. L., Greve, K. W., Heinly, M. T., &Meyers, J. E. (2008). Classification accuracy of MMPI-2 validity scales in the detection of pain-related malingering: A known-groups study. *Assessment, 15*(4), 435–449. https://doi .org/10.1177/1073191108317341

Binder, L. M., & Rohling, L. M. (1996). Money matters: Meta-analytic review of the effects of financial incentives on recovery after closed-head injury. *American Journal of Psychiatry, 153*(1), 7–10. https://doi.org/10.1176/ajp.153.1.7

Binford, A., & Liljequist, L. (2008). Behavioral correlates of selected MMPI-2 Clinical, Content, and Restructured Clinical Scales. *Journal of Personality Assessment, 90*(6), 608–614. https://doi.org/10.1080/00223890802388657

Block, A. R., Ben-Porath, Y. S., & Marek, R. J. (2013). Psychological risk factors for poor outcome of spine surgery and spinal cord stimulator implant: A review of the literature and their assessment with the MMPI-2-RF. *The Clinical Neuropsychologist, 27*(1), 81–107. https://doi.org/10.1080/13854046.2012.721007

Block, J. (1965). *The challenge of response sets: Unconfounding meaning, acquiescence, and social desirability in the MMPI.* Appleton-Century-Crofts.

Blumenthal, J. A., Barefoot, J., Burg, M. M., & Williams, R. B., Jr. (1987). Psychological correlates of hostility among patients undergoing coronary angiography. *British Journal of Medical Psychology, 60*(4), 349–355. https://doi.org/10.1111/j.2044-8341.1987. tb02754.x

Boone, D. E. (1994). Validity of the MMPI-2 Depression Content scale with psychiatric inpatients. *Psychological Reports, 74*(1), 159–162. https://doi.org/10.2466/ pr0.1994.74.1.159

Bosquet, M., & Egeland, B. (2000). Predicting parenting behaviors from Antisocial Practices Content scale scores on the MMPI-2 administered during pregnancy. *Journal of Personality Assessment, 74*(1), 146–162. https://doi.org/10.1207/s15327752jpa740110

Bow, J. N., Flens, J. R., Gould, J. W., & Greenhut, D. (2006). An analysis of administration, scoring, and interpretation of the MMPI-2 and MCMI-II/III in child custody evaluations. *Journal of Child Custody, 2*(4), 1–22. https://doi.org/10.1300/ J190v02n04_01

Bow, J. N., Gould, J. W., Flens, J. R., & Greenhut, D. (2006). Testing in child custody evaluations: Selection, usage, and Daubert admissibility. *Journal of Forensic Psychology Practice, 6*(2), 17–38. https://doi.org/10.1300/J158v06n02_02

Bowden, S. C., White, J. R., Simpson, L., & Ben-Porath, Y. S. (2014, May). Elevation discrepancies between MMPI-2 Clinical and MMPI-2-RF Restructured Clinical (RC) scales in people with seizure disorders. *Epilepsy & Behavior, 34,* 92–98. https://doi .org/10.1016/j.yebeh.2014.03.016

Bowler, R. M., Hartney, C., & Ngo, L. H. (1998). Amnestic disturbance and posttraumatic stress disorder in the aftermath of a chemical release. *Archives of Clinical Neuropsychology, 13*(5), 455–471. https://doi.org/10.1093/arclin/13.5.455

Brems, C., & Lloyd, P. (1995). Validation of the MMPI-2 Low Self-Esteem Content scale. *Journal of Personality Assessment, 65*(3), 550–556. https://doi.org/10.1207/ s15327752jpa6503_13

Bridges, S. A., & Baum, L. J. (2013). An examination of MMPI-2-RF L-r Scale in an outpatient protestant sample. *Journal of Psychology and Christianity, 32*(2), 115–123.

Brodsky, S. L. (2013). *Testifying in court: Guidelines and maxims for the expert witness* (2nd ed.). American Psychological Association.

Brodsky, S. L., & Gutheil, T. G. (2016). *The expert expert witness: More maxims and guidelines for testifying in court* (2nd ed.). American Psychological Association.

Brown, A., & Zeichner, A. (1989). Concurrent incidence of depression and physical symptoms among hostile young women. *Psychological Reports, 65*(3), 739–744. https://doi.org/10.2466/pr0.1989.65.3.739

Brown, T. A., & Sellbom, M. (2020). The utility of the MMPI-2-RF Validity scales in detecting underreporting. *Journal of Personality Assessment, 102*(1), 66–74. https://doi.org/10.1080/00223891.2018.1539003

Brown, T. G., & Fayek, A. (1993). Comparison of demographic characteristics and MMPI scores from alcohol and poly-drug alcohol and cocaine abusers. *Alcoholism Treatment Quarterly, 10*(1–2), 123–135. https://doi.org/10.1300/J020V10N01_08

Bryant, W. T., & McNulty, J. L. (2017). Which domain of the PSY-5 is most relevant to substance use? *Journal of Personality Assessment, 99*(5), 524–533. https://doi.org/10.1080/00223891.2016.1250213

Burchett, D., & Bagby, R. M. (2014). Multimethod assessment of distortion: Integrating data from interviews, collateral records, and standardized assessment tools. In C. J. Hopwood & R. F. Bornstein (Eds.), *Multimethod clinical assessment* (pp. 345–378). Guilford Press.

Burchett, D., Dragon, W. R., Smith Holbert, A. M., Tarescavage, A. M., Mattson, C. A., Handel, R. M., & Ben-Porath, Y. S. (2016). "False Feigners": Examining the impact of non-content-based invalid responding on the Minnesota Multiphasic Personality Inventory–2 Restructured Form content-based invalid responding indicators. *Psychological Assessment, 28*(5), 458–470. http://dx.doi.org/10.1037/pas0000205

Bury, A. S., & Bagby, R. (2002). The detection of feigned uncoached and coached posttraumatic stress disorder with the MMPI-2 in a sample of workplace accident victims. *Psychological Assessment, 14*(4), 472–484. https://doi.org/10.1037/1040-3590.14.4.472

Buss, A. H., & Perry, M. (1992). The Aggression Questionnaire. *Journal of Personality and Social Psychology, 63*(3), 452–459. https://doi.org/10.1037/0022-3514.63.3.452

Butcher, J. N. (1979). Use of the MMPI in personnel selection. In J. N. Butcher (Ed.), *New developments in the use of the MMPI* (pp. 165–201). University of Minnesota Press.

Butcher, J. N. (1985). Personality assessment in industry: Theoretical issues and illustrations. In H. J. Bernardin (Ed.), *Personality assessment in organizations* (pp. 277–310). Praeger.

Butcher, J. N. (1988, March). *Use of the MMPI in personnel screening* [Paper presentation]. 23rd Annual Symposium on Recent Developments in the Use of the MMPI, St. Petersburg, FL.

Butcher, J.N. (1989). *The Minnesota report: Adult clinical system.* National Computer Systems.

Butcher, J. N. (1990a). Education level and MMPI-2 measured pathology: A case of negligible influence. *MMPI-2 News and Profiles: A Newsletter of the MMPI-2 Workshops and Symposia, 1*, 3. University of Minnesota Press, Test Division.

Butcher, J. N. (1990b). *MMPI-2 in psychological treatment*. Oxford University Press.

Butcher, J. N. (1991). Screening for psychopathology: Industrial applications of the Minnesota Multiphasic Personality Inventory (MMPI-2). In J. Jones, B. D. Steffey, & D. Bray (Eds.), *Applying psychology in business: The manager's handbook* (pp. 835–850). Lexington Books.

Butcher, J. N. (1994). Psychological assessment of airline pilot applicants with the MMPI-2. *Journal of Personality Assessment, 62*(1), 31–44. https://doi.org/10.1207/s15327752jpa6201_4

Butcher, J. N. (1995). Personality patterns of personal injury litigants: The role of computer-based MMPI-2 evaluations. In Y. S. Ben-Porath, J. R. Graham, G. C. N. Hall, R. D. Hirshman, & M. S. Zaragoza (Eds.), *Forensic applications of the MMPI-2* (pp. 179–201). Sage. https://doi.org/10.4135/9781452243771.n8

Butcher, J. N., Aldwin, C. M., Levenson, M. R., Ben-Porath, Y. S., Spiro, A., & Bosse, R. (1991). Personality and aging: A study of the MMPI-2 among older men. *Psychology and Aging, 6*(3), 361–370. https://doi.org/10.1037/0882-7974.6.3.361

Butcher, J. N., Arbisi, P. A., Atlis, M. M., & McNulty, J. L. (2008). The construct validity of the Lees–Haley Fake Bad Scale: Does this measure somatic malingering and feigned emotional distress? *Archives of Clinical Neuropsychology, 23*(7–8), 855–864. https://doi.org/10.1016/j.acn.2008.10.001

Butcher, J. N., Atlis, M., & Fang, L. (2000). Effect of altered instructions on the MMIP-2 profiles of college students who are not motivated to distort their responses. *Journal of Personality Assessment, 75*(3), 492–501. https://doi.org/10.1207/S15327752JPA7503_09

Butcher, J. N., Cabiya, J., Lucio, E., & Garrido, M. (2007). *Assessing Hispanic clients using the MMPI-2 and MMPI-A*. American Psychological Association. https://doi.org/10.1037/11585-000

Butcher, J. N., Dahlstrom, W. G., Graham, J. R., Tellegen, A., & Kaemmer, B. (1989). *Minnesota Multiphasic Personality Inventory-2 (MMPI-2): Manual for administration and scoring*. University of Minnesota Press.

Butcher, J. N., Graham, J. R., & Ben-Porath, Y. S. (1995). Methodological problems and issues in MMPI, MMPI-2, and MMPI-A research. *Psychological Assessment, 7*(3), 320–329. https://doi.org/10.1037/1040-3590.7.3.320

Butcher, J. N., Graham, J. R., Ben-Porath, Y. S., Tellegen, A., Dahlstrom, W. G., & Kaemmer, B. (2001). *MMPI-2 (Minnesota Multiphasic Personality Inventory-2): Manual for administration, scoring, and interpretation* (Revised ed.). University of Minnesota Press.

Butcher, J. N., Graham, J. R., Williams, C. L., & Ben-Porath, Y. S. (1990). *Development and use of the MMPI-2 Content scales*. University of Minnesota Press.

Butcher, J. N., Hamilton, C. K., Rouse, S. V., & Cumella, E. J. (2006). The deconstruction of the Hy scale of MMPI-2: Failure of RC3 in measuring somatic symptom expression. *Journal of Personality Assessment, 87*(2), 186–192. https://doi.org/10.1207/s15327752jpa8702_08

Butcher, J. N., & Han, K. (1995). Development of an MMPI-2 scale to assess the presentation of self in a superlative manner: The S scale. In J. N. Butcher & C. D. Spielberger

(Eds.), *Advances in personality assessment, Vol. 10* (pp. 25–50). Lawrence Erlbaum Associates.

Butcher, J. N., Morfitt, R. C., Rouse, S. V., & Holden, R. R. (1997). Reducing MMPI-2 defensiveness: The effect of specialized instructions on retest validity in a job applicant sample. *Journal of Personality Assessment, 68*(2), 385–401. https://doi.org/10.1207/s15327752jpa6802_9

Butcher, J. N., & Williams, C. L. (2000). *Essentials of MMPI-2 and MMPI-A interpretation* (2nd ed.). University of Minnesota Press.

Butcher, J. N., Williams, C. L., Graham, J. R., Archer, R. P., Tellegen, A., Ben-Porath, Y. S., & Kaemmer, B. (1992). *MMPI-A: Minnesota Multiphasic Personality Inventory–Adolescent: Manual for administration, scoring, and interpretation.* University of Minnesota Press.

Butler, R. W., Foy, D. W., Snodgrass, L., Hurwicz, M., & Goldfarb, J. (1988). Combat-related posttraumatic stress disorder in a nonpsychiatric population. *Journal of Anxiety Disorders, 2*(2), 111–120. https://doi.org/10.1016/0887-6185(88)90018-7

Caillouet, B. A., Boccaccini, M. T., Varela, J. G., Davis, R. D., & Rostow, C. D. (2010). Predictive validity of the MMPI-2 PSY-5 and facets for law enforcement officer employment outcomes. *Criminal Justice and Behavior, 37*(2), 217–238. https://doi.org/10.1177/0093854809351948

Caldwell, A. B. (2006). Maximal measurement or meaningful measurement: The interpretive challenges of the MMPI-2 Restructured Clinical (RC) scales. *Journal of Personality Assessment, 87*(2), 193–201. https://doi.org/10.1207/s15327752jpa8702_09

Caldwell, A. B., Jr. (2005). The use of the MMPI-2 and the Rorschach in the child custody context: How can the MMPI-2 help child custody examiners. *Journal of Child Custody, 2*(1–2), 83–117. https://doi.org/10.1300/J190v02n01_06

Camara, W. J., Nathan, J. S., & Puente, A. E. (2000). Psychological test usage: Implications in professional psychology. *Professional Psychology: Research and Practice, 31*(2), 141–154. https://doi.org/10.1037/0735-7028.31.2.141

Canul, G. D., & Cross, J. J. (1994). The influence of acculturation and racial identity attitudes on Mexican-Americans' MMPI-2 performance. *Journal of Clinical Psychology, 50*(5), 736–745. https://doi.org/10.1002/1097-4679(199409)50:5<736::AID-JCLP2270500511>3.0.CO;2-Z

Capwell, D. F. (1945). Personality patterns of adolescent girls: II. Delinquents and non-delinquents. *Journal of Applied Psychology, 29*(4), 289–297. https://doi.org/10.1037/h0054701

Carlson, D.A. (2001). Computerized vs. written administration of the MMPI-A in clinical and non-clinical settings. *Dissertations Abstracts International: Section B: The Sciences and Engineering, 62*, 2-B.

Carmody, T. P., Crossen, J. R., & Wens, A. N. (1989). Hostility as a health risk factor: Relationships with neuroticism, Type A behavior, attentional focus, and interpersonal style. *Journal of Clinical Psychology, 45*(5), 754–762. https://doi.org/10.1002/1097-4679(198909)45:5<754::AID-JCLP2270450510>3.0.CO;2-C

Carr, J. L., & Graham, J. R. (1996). Assessing anger with the Minnesota Multiphasic Personality Inventory. In C. D. Spielberger & I. G. Sarason (Eds.), *Stress and emotion: Anxiety, anger, and curiosity* (Vol. 16, pp. 67–82). Taylor and Francis.

Carson, R. C. (1969). Interpretive manual to the MMPI. In J. N. Butcher (Ed.), *Research developments and clinical applications* (pp. 279–296). McGraw-Hill.

Carter, J. W., Nordgaard, J., & Parnas, J. (2019). Identifying non-affective psychosis in first admission patients: MMPI-2, structured diagnostic interview, and consensus lifetime best estimate. *Psychiatry Research*, *279*, 71–76. https://doi.org/10.1016/j.psychres.2019.07.010

Cashel, L., Rogers, R., Sewell, K. W., & Holliman, N. B. (1998). Preliminary validation of the MMPI-A for a male delinquent sample: An investigation of clinical correlates and discriminative validity. *Journal of Personality Assessment*, *71*(1), 49–69. https://doi.org/10.1207/s15327752jpa7101_4

Castlebury, F. K., & Durham, T. W. (1997). The MMPI-2 GM and GF scales as measures of psychological well-being. *Journal of Clinical Psychology*, *53*(8), 879–893. https://doi.org/10.1002/(SICI)1097-4679(199712)53:8<879::AID-JCLP13>3.0.CO;2-H

Castro, Y., Gordon, K. H., Brown, J. S., Anestis, J. C., & Joiner, T. E. (2008). Examination of racial differences on the MMPI-2 Clinical and Restructured Clinical scales in an outpatient sample. *Assessment*, *15*(3), 277–286. https://doi.org/10.1177/1073191107312735

Cattell, R. B., Eber, H. W., & Tatsuoka, M. M. (1970). *Handbook for the Sixteen Personality Factor Questionnaire*. Institute for Personality and Ability Testing.

Cavaiola, A. A., Strohmetz, D. B., Wolf, J. M., & Lavender, N. J. (2002). Comparison of DWI offenders with non-DWI individuals on the MMPI-2 and the Michigan Alcoholism Screening Test. *Addictive Behaviors*, *28*(5), 971–977. https://doi.org/10.1016/S0306-4603(01)00291-X

Chang, P. N., Nesbit, M. E., Youngren, N., & Robison, L. L. (1988). Personality characteristics and psychosocial adjustment of long-term survivors of childhood cancer. *Journal of Psychosocial Oncology*, *5*(4), 43–58. https://doi.org/10.1300/J077v05n04_04

Chojnacki, J. T., & Walsh, W. B. (1992). The consistency of scores and configural patterns between the MMPI and MMPI-2. *Journal of Personality Assessment*, *59*(2), 276–289. https://doi.org/10.1207/s15327752jpa5902_5

Cigrang, J. A., & Staal, M. A. (2001). Readministration of the MMPI-2 following defensive invalidity in a military job applicant sample. *Journal of Personality Assessment*, *76*(3), 472–481. https://doi.org/10.1207/S15327752JPA7603_08

Claiborn, D. D. (1995). Review of the Minnesota Multiphasic Personality Inventory–Adolescent. In J. C. Conoley & J. C. Impara (Eds.), *The twelfth mental measurements yearbook* (pp. 626–628). University of Nebraska Press.

Clark, M. E. (1994). Interpretive limitations of the MMPI-2 Anger and Cynicism Content scales. *Journal of Personality Assessment*, *63*(1), 89–96. https://doi.org/10.1207/s15327752jpa6301_7

Clark, M. E. (1996). MMPI-2 Negative Treatment Indicators Content and Content Component scales: Clinical correlates and outcome prediction for men with chronic pain. *Psychological Assessment*, *8*(1), 32–38. https://doi.org/10.1037/1040-3590.8.1.32

Cleckley, H. (1982). *The mask of sanity* (5th ed.). Mosby.

Clements, R., & Heintz, J. M. (2002). Diagnostic accuracy and factor structure of the AAS and APS scales of the MMPI-2. *Journal of Personality Assessment*, *79*(3), 564–582. https://doi.org/10.1207/S15327752JPA7903_10

Colligan, R. C., & Offord, K. P. (1988). The risky use of the MMPI Hostility scale in assessing risk for coronary heart disease. *Psychosomatics, 29*(2), 188–196. https://doi.org/10.1016/S0033-3182(88)72396-8

Cohen, J., Cohen, P., West, S. G., & Aiken, L. S. (2002). *Applied multiple regression/correlation analysis for the behavioral sciences.* Lawrence Erlbaum Associates.

Colligan, R. C., Rasmussen, N. H., Agerter, D. C., Offord, K. P., Malinchoc, M., O'Byrne, M. M., & Benson, J. T. (2008). The MMPI-2: A contemporary normative study of midwestern family medicine outpatients. *Journal of Clinical Psychology in Medical Settings, 15*(2), 98–119. https://doi.org/10.1007/s10880-008-9113-z

Comrey, A. L. (1957a). A factor analysis of items on the MMPI Depression scale. *Educational and Psychological Measurement, 17*(4), 578–585. https://doi.org/10.1177/001316445701700412

Comrey, A. L. (1957b). A factor analysis of items on the MMPI Hypochondriasis scale. *Educational and Psychological Measurement, 17*(4), 566–577. https://doi.org/10.1177/001316445701700411

Comrey, A. L. (1957c). A factor analysis of items on the MMPI Hysteria scale. *Educational and Psychological Measurement, 17*(4), 586–592. https://doi.org/10.1177/001316445701700413

Comrey, A. L. (1958a). A factor analysis of items on the MMPI Hypomania scale. *Educational and Psychological Measurement, 18*(2), 313–323. https://doi.org/10.1177/001316445801800208

Comrey, A. L. (1958b). A factor analysis of items on the MMPI Paranoia scale. *Educational and Psychological Measurement, 18*(1), 99–107. https://doi.org/10.1177/001316445801800109

Comrey, A. L. (1958c). A factor analysis of items on the MMPI Psychasthenia scale. *Educational and Psychological Measurement, 18*(2), 293–300. https://doi.org/10.1177/001316445801800206

Comrey, A. L. (1958d). A factor analysis of items on the MMPI Psychopathic Deviate scale. *Educational and Psychological Measurement, 18*(1), 91–98. https://doi.org/10.1177/001316445801800108

Comrey, A. L., & Marggraff, W. (1958). A factor analysis of items on the MMPI Schizophrenia scale. *Educational and Psychological Measurement, 18*(2), 301–311. https://doi.org/10.1177/001316445801800207

Cook, W. N., & Medley, D. M. (1954). Proposed Hostility and Pharisaic-Virtue scales for the MMPI. *Journal of Applied Psychology, 38*(6), 414–418. https://doi.org/10.1037/h0060667

Cooper-Hakim, A., & Viswesvaran, C. (2002). A meta-analytic review of the MacAndrew Alcoholism scale. *Educational and Psychological Measurement, 62*(5), 818–829. https://doi.org/10.1177/001316402236880

Corey, D. M., & Ben-Porath, Y. S. (2018). *Assessing police and other public safety personnel using the MMPI-2-RF.* University of Minnesota Press.

Corey, D. M., & Ben-Porath, Y. S. (2020). *Minnesota Multiphasic Personality Inventory-3 (MMPI-3): User's guide for the Police Candidate Interpretive Report.* University of Minnesota Press.

Corey, D. M., Sellbom, M., & Ben-Porath, Y. S. (2018). Risks associated with overcontrolled behavior in police officer recruits. *Psychological Assessment, 30*(12), 1691–1702. https://doi.org/10.1037/pas0000607

Costa, P. T., & McCrae, R. R. (1992). *NEO PI-R professional manual.* Psychological Assessment Resources.

Costello, R. M., Schneider, S. L., & Schoenfeld, L. S. (1996). Validation of a preemployment MMPI index correlated with interdisciplinary suspension days of police officers. *Psychology: Crime and Law, 2*(4), 299–306. https://doi.org/10.1080/10683169608409785

Craig, R. J. (2005). Assessing contemporary substance abusers with the MMPI MacAndrews Alcoholism scale: A review. *Substance Use & Misuse, 40,*(4), 427–450. https://doi.org/10.1081/JA-200052401

Craig, R. J., & Olson, R. E. (2004). Predicting methadone maintenance treatment outcomes using the addiction severity index and the MMPI-2 Content scales (Negative Treatment Indicators and Cynicism scales). *The American Journal of Drug and Alcohol Abuse, 30*(4), 823–839. https://doi.org/10.1081/ADA-200037548

Crighton, A. H., Marek, R. J., Dragon, W. R., & Ben-Porath, Y. S. (2017). Utility of the MMPI-2-RF Validity scales in detection of simulated underreporting: Implications of incorporating a manipulation check. *Assessment, 24*(7), 853–864. https://doi.org/10.1177/1073191115627011

Cumella, E. J., Wall, A. D., & Kerr-Almeida, N. (2000). MMPI-2 in the inpatient assessment of women with eating disorders. *Journal of Personality Assessment, 75*(3), 387–403. https://doi.org/10.1207/S15327752JPA7503_03

Dahlstrom, W. G., & Tellegen, A. K. (1993). *Socioeconomic status and the MMPI-2: The relation of MMPI-2 patterns to levels of education and occupation.* University of Minnesota Press.

Dahlstrom, W. G., & Welsh, G. S. (1960). *An MMPI handbook: A guide to use in clinical practice and research.* University of Minnesota Press.

Dahlstrom, W. G., Welsh, G. S., & Dahlstrom, L. E. (1972). *An MMPI handbook: Vol. I. Clinical interpretation.* University of Minnesota Press.

Dahlstrom, W. G., Welsh, G. S., & Dahlstrom, L. E. (1975). *An MMPI handbook: Vol. II. Research applications.* University of Minnesota Press.

Daniel, A. E., Beck, N. C., Herath, A., Schmitz, M., & Menninger, K. (1985). Factors correlated with psychiatric recommendations of incompetency and insanity. *Journal of Psychiatry & Law, 12*(4), 527–544. https://doi.org/10.1177/009318538401200406

Daubert v. Merrell Dow Pharmaceuticals, 727 F. Supp. 570 (S.D.Cal. 1989), aff'd, 951F.2d 1128 (9th Cir. 1990), vacated, 1123 S.Ct. 2786 (1993).

Davis, K. R., & Sines, J. O. (1971). An antisocial behavior pattern associated with a specific MMPI profile. *Journal of Consulting and Clinical Psychology, 36*(2), 229–234. https://doi.org/10.1037/h0030739

Dean, A. C., Boone, K. B., Kim, M. S., Curiel, A. R., Martin, D. J., Victor, T. L., Zeller, M. A., & Lang, Y. K. (2008). Examination of the impact of ethnicity on the Minnesota Multiphasic Personality Inventory-2 (MMPI-2) Fake Bad Scale. *Clinical Neuropsychologist, 22*(6), 1054–1060. https://doi.org/10.1080/13854040701750891

Dearth, C. S., Berry, D. T. R., Vickery, C. D., Vagnini, V. L., Baser, R. E., Orey, S. A., & Cragar, D. E. (2005). Detection of feigned head injury symptoms on the MMPI-2 in head injured patients and community controls. *Archives of Clinical Neuropsychology*, *20*(1), 95–110. https://doi.org/10.1016/j.acn.2004.03.004

Detrick, P., Chibnall, J. T., & Rosso, M. (2001). Minnesota Multiphasic Personality Inventory-2 in police officer selection: Normative data and relation to the Inwald Personality Inventory. *Professional Psychology: Research and Practice*, *32*(5), 484–490. https://doi.org/10.1037/0735-7028.32.5.484

Diamond, R., Barth, J. T., & Zillmer, E. A. (1988). Emotional correlates of mild closed head trauma: The role of the MMPI. *The International Journal of Clinical Neuropsychology*, *10*(1), 35–40.

Dikmen, S., Hermann, B. P., Wilensky, A. J., & Rainwater, G. (1983). Validity of the Minnesota Multiphasic Personality Inventory (MMPI) to psychopathology in patients with epilepsy. *Journal of Nervous and Mental Disease*, *171*(2), 114–122. https://doi.org/10.1097/00005053-198302000-00008

Distler, L. S., May, P. R., & Tuma, A. H. (1964). Anxiety and ego strength as predictors of response to treatment in schizophrenic patients. *Journal of Consulting Psychology*, *28*(2), 170–177. https://doi.org/10.1037/h0041457

Dodrill, C. B. (1986). Psychosocial consequences of epilepsy. In S. Filskov & T. Boll (Eds.), *Handbook of clinical neuropsychology* (Vol. 2, pp. 338–363). Wiley.

Dong, Y. T., & Church, A. T. (2003). Cross-cultural equivalence and validity of the Vietnamese MMPI-2: Assessing psychological adjustment of Vietnamese refugees. *Psychological Assessment*, *15*(3), 370–377. https://doi.org/10.1037/1040-3590.15.3.370

Dragon, W. R., Ben-Porath, Y. S., & Handel, R. W. (2012). Examining the impact of unscorable item responses on the validity and interpretability of MMPI-2/MMPI-2-RF Restructured Clinical (RC) scale scores. *Assessment*, *19*(1), 101–113. https://doi.org/10.1177/1073191111415362

Drake, L. E. (1946). A social I.E. scale for the MMPI. *Journal of Applied Psychology*, *30*(1), 51–54.

Drake, L. E., & Oetting, E. R. (1959). *An MMPI codebook for counselors*. University of Minnesota Press.

Duckworth, J., & Anderson, W. (1986). *MMPI interpretation manual for counselors and clinicians*. Accelerated Development, Inc.

Duckworth, J. C., & Duckworth, E. (1975). *MMPI interpretation manual for counselors and clinicians*. Accelerated Development, Inc.

Duckworth, M. P., & Iezzi, T. (2005). Chronic pain and posttraumatic stress symptoms in litigating motor vehicle accident victims. *The Clinical Journal of Pain*, *21*(3), 251–261. https://doi.org/10.1097/00002508-200505000-00008

Duris, M., Bjorck, J. P., & Gorsuch, R. L. (2007). Christian subcultural differences in item perceptions of the MMPI-2 Lie scale. *Journal of Psychology and Christianity*, *26*(4), 356–366.

Dush, D. M., Simons, L. E., Platt, M., Nation, P. C., & Ayres, S. Y. (1994). Psychological profiles distinguishing litigating and nonlitigating pain patients: Subtle, and not so subtle. *Journal of Personality Assessment, 62*(2), 299–313. https://doi.org/10.1207/s15327752jpa6202_10

Dusky v. United States, 362 U.S. 402 (1960).

Dwyer, S. A., Graham, J. R., & Ott, E. K. (1992). *Psychiatric symptoms associated with the MMPI-2 Content scales* [Unpublished manuscript]. Kent State University.

Edwards, A. L. (1957). *The social desirability variable in personality assessment and research.* Dryden Press.

Edwards, A. L. (1964). Social desirability and performance on the MMPI. *Psychometrika, 29*(4), 295–308. https://doi.org/10.1007/BF02289598

Edwards, E. L., Holmes, C. B., & Carvajal, H. H. (1998). Oral and booklet presentation of MMPI-2. *Journal of Clinical Psychology, 54*(5), 593–596. https://doi.org/10.1002/(SICI)1097-4679(199808)54:5<593::AID-JCLP5>3.0.CO;2-M

Egeland, B., Erickson, M. F., Butcher, J. N., & Ben-Porath, Y. S. (1991). The MMPI-2 profiles of women at risk for child abuse. *Journal of Personality Assessment, 57*(2), 254–263. https://doi.org/10.1207/s15327752jpa5702_5

Egger, J. I. M., de Mey, H. R. A., Derksen, J. J. L., & van der Staak, C. P. F. (2003). Cross-cultural replication of the five-factor model and comparison of the NEO-PI-R and MMPI-2 PSY-5 scales in a Dutch psychiatric sample. *Psychological Assessment, 15*(1), 81–88. https://doi.org/10.1037/1040-3590.15.1.81

Ehrenworth, N.V., & Archer, R.P. (1985). A comparison of clinical accuracy ratings of interpretive approaches for adolescent MMPI responses. *Journal of Personality Assessment, 49*(4) 413–421. https://doi.org/10.1207/s15327752jpa4904_9

Eichman, W. J. (1961). Replicated factors on the MMPI with female NP patients. *Journal of Consulting Psychology, 25*(1), 55–60. https://doi.org/10.1037/h0043903

Eichman, W. J. (1962). Factored scales for the MMPI: A clinical and statistical manual. *Journal of Clinical Psychology, 18*(4), 363–395. https://doi.org/10.1002/1097-4679(196210)18:4<363::AID-JCLP2270180402>3.0.CO;2-Y

Elhai, J. D., Gold, P. B., Frueh, B. C., & Gold, S. N. (2000). Cross-validation of the MMPI-2 in detecting malingered posttraumatic stress disorder. *Journal of Personality Assessment, 75*(3), 449–463. https://doi.org/10.1207/s15327752jpa7503_06

Elhai, J. D., Naifeh, J. A., Zucker, I. S., Gold, S. N., Deitsch, S. E., & Frueh, B. C. (2004). Discriminating malingered from genuine civilian posttraumatic stress disorder: A Validation of three MMPI-2 infrequency scales (F, Fp, and Fptsd). *Assessment, 11*(2), 139–144. https://doi.org/10.1177/1073191104264965

Emery, R. E., Otto, R. K., & O'Donohue, W. T. (2005). A critical assessment of child custody evaluations. *Psychological Science in the Public Interest, 6*(1), 1–29. https://doi.org/10.1111/j.1529-1006.2005.00020.x

Endicott, J., & Spitzer, R. L. (1978). A diagnostic interview: The Schedule for Affective Disorders and Schizophrenia. *Archives of General Psychiatry, 35*(7), 837–844. https://doi.org/10.1001/archpsyc.1978.01770310043002

Englert, D. R., Weed, N. C., & Watson, G. S. (2000). Convergent, discriminant, and internal properties of the Minnesota Multiphasic Personality Inventory (2nd ed.): Low Self-Esteem Content scale. *Measurement and Evaluation in Counseling and Development, 33*(1), 42–49. https://doi.org/10.1080/07481756.2000.12068995

Ezzo, F. R., Pinsoneault, T. B., & Evans, T. M. (2007). A comparison of MMPI-2 profiles between child maltreatment cases and two types of custody cases. *Journal of Forensic Psychology Practice*, *7*(2), 29–43. https://doi.org/10.1300/J158v07n02_02

Faschingbauer, T. R. (1974). A 166-item written short form of the group MMPI: The FAM. *Journal of Consulting and Clinical Psychology*, *42*(5), 645–655. https://doi .org/10.1037/h0037049

Finger, M. S., & Ones, D. A. (1999). Psychometric equivalence of the computer and booklet forms of the MMPI: A meta-analysis. *Psychological Assessment*, *11*(1), 58–66. https://doi.org/10.1037/1040-3590.11.1.58

Finn, J. A., Arbisi, P. A., Erbes, C. R., Polusny, M. A., & Thuras, P. (2014). The MMPI–2 Restructured Form Personality Psychopathology Five scales: Bridging DSM–5 Section 2 personality disorders and DSM–5 Section 3 personality trait dimensions. *Journal of Personality Assessment*, *96*(2), 173–184. https://doi.org/10.1080/00223891.2013.866569

Finn, S. E. (1996). Assessment feedback integrating MMPI-2 and Rorschach findings. *Journal of Personality Assessment*, *67*(3), 543–557. https://doi.org/10.1207/ s15327752jpa6703_10

Finn, S. E. (2007). *In our clients' shoes: Theory and techniques of therapeutic assessment.* Lawrence Erlbaum Associates.

Finn, S. E., & Tonsager, M. E. (1992). Therapeutic effects of providing MMPI-2 test feedback to college students awaiting therapy. *Psychological Assessment*, *4*(3), 278–287. https://doi.org/10.1037/1040-3590.4.3.278

First, M. B., Gibbon, M., Spitzer, R. L., Williams, J. B. W., & Benjamin, L. S. (1997). *SCID-II Personality Questionnaire.* American Psychiatric Press.

Fisher, G. (1970). Discriminating violence emanating from over-controlled vs. under-controlled aggressivity. *British Journal of Social and Clinical Psychology*, *9*(1), 54–59. https://doi.org/10.1111/j.2044-8260.1970.tb00638.x

Fontaine, J. L., Archer, R. P., Elkins, D. E., & Johansen, J. (2001). The effects of MMPI-A T-score elevation on classification accuracy for normal and clinical adolescent samples. *Journal of Personality Assessment*, *76*(2), 264–281. https://doi.org/10.1207/ S15327752JPA7602_09

Forbey, J. D., & Ben-Porath, Y. S. (1998). *A critical item set for the MMPI-A.* University of Minnesota Press.

Forbey, J. D., & Ben-Porath, Y. S. (2003). Incremental validity of the MMPI-A Content scales in a residential treatment facility. *Assessment*, *10*(2), 191–202. https://doi.org /10.1177/1073191103010002010

Forbey, J. D., & Ben-Porath, Y. S. (2008). Empirical correlates of the MMPI-2 Restructured Clinical (RC) scales in a nonclinical setting. *Journal of Personality Assessment*, *90*(2), 136–141. https://doi.org/10.1080/00223890701845161

Forbey, J. D., Ben-Porath, Y. S., & Tellegen, A. (2004, March). *Associations between and the relative contributions of the MMPI-2 Restructured Clinical (RC) and Content scales* [Paper presentation]. Society for Personality Assessment, Miami, FL.

Forbey, J. D. & Lee, T. T. C. (2011). An exploration of the impact of invalid MMPI-2 protocols on collateral measure scores. *The Journal of Personality Assessment*, *93*(6), 556–565. https://doi.org/10.1080/00223891.2011.608757

Forbey, J. D., Lee, T. T. C., & Handel, R. W. (2010). Correlates of the MMPI-2-RF in a college setting. *Psychological Assessment, 22*(4), 737–744. https://doi.org/10.1037/a0020645

Fordyce, W. E., Bigos, S. J., Batti'e, M. C., & Fisher, L. D. (1992). MMPI Scale 3 as a predictor of back injury report: What does it tell us? *Clinical Journal of Pain, 8*(3), 222–226. https://doi.org/10.1097/00002508-199209000-00006

Fraboni, M., Cooper, D., Reed, T., & Saltstone, R. (1990). Offense type and two-point MMPI code profiles: Discriminating between violent and non-violent offenders. *Journal of Clinical Psychology, 46*(6), 774–777. https://doi.org/10.1002/1097-4679(199011)46:6<774::AID-JCLP2270460612>3.0.CO;2-3

Franz, A. O., Harrop, T. M., & McCord, D. M. (2017). Examining the construct validity of the MMPI-2-RF interpersonal functioning scales using the Computerized Adaptive Test of Personality Disorder as a comparative framework. *Journal of Personality Assessment, 99*(4), 416–423. https://doi.org/10.1080/00223891.2016.1222394

Frueh, B. C., Gold, P. B., de Arellano, M. A., & Brady, K. L. (1997). A racial comparison of combat veterans evaluated for PTSD. *Journal of Personality Assessment, 68*(3), 692–702. https://doi.org/10.1207/s15327752jpa6803_14

Frueh, B. C., Smith, D. W., & Libet, J. M. (1996). Racial differences on psychological measures in combat veterans seeking treatment for PTSD. *Journal of Personality Assessment, 66*(1), 41–53. https://doi.org/10.1207/s15327752jpa6601_3

Frye v. United States, 293 F.1012 (D.C.Cir. 1923).

Fuhrman, G., & Zibbell, R. (2012). *Evaluation for child custody.* Oxford University Press.

Gallagher, R. W. (1997). *Detection of malingering at the time of intake in a correctional setting with the MMPI-2 Validity scales* [Unpublished doctoral dissertation]. Kent State University.

Gallagher, R. W., Ben-Porath, Y. S., & Briggs, S. (1997). Inmate views about the purpose and use of the MMPI-2 at the time of correctional intake. *Criminal Justice and Behavior, 24*(3), 360–369. https://doi.org/10.1177/0093854897024003003

Gallen, R. T., & Berry, D. T. R. (1996). Detection of random responding in MMPI-2 protocols. *Assessment, 3*(2), 171–178. https://doi.org/10.1177/107319119600300209

Gallucci, N. T. (1994). Criteria associated with clinical scales of Harris–Lingoes subscales of the Minnesota Multiphasic Personality Inventory with adolescent inpatients. *Psychological Assessment, 6*(3), 179–187. https://doi.org/10.1037/1040-3590.6.3.179

Gallucci, N.T. (1997a). Correlates of MMPI-A substance abuse scales. *Assessment, 4*(1), 87–94. https://doi.org/10.1177/107319119700400112

Gallucci, N. T. (1997b). On the identification of patterns of substance abuse with the MMPI-A. *Psychological Assessment, 9*(3), 224–232. https://doi.org/10.1037/1040-3590.9.3.224

Gallucci, N. T., Kay, D. C., & Thornby, J. I. (1989). The sensitivity of 11 substance abuse scales from the MMPI to change in clinical status. *Psychology of Addictive Behaviors, 3*(1), 29–33. https://doi.org/10.1037/h0080562

Gambetti, E., Zucchelli, M. M., Nori, R., & Giusberti, F. (2019). Psychological assessment in abuse and neglect cases: The utility of the MMPI-2. *Professional Psychology: Research and Practice, 50*(6), 384–394. http://dx.doi.org/10.1037/pro0000272

Gass, C. S. (1991). MMPI-2 interpretation and closed head injury: A correction factor. *Psychological Assessment, 3*(1), 27–31. https://doi.org/10.1037/1040-3590.3.1.27

Gass, C. S. (1992). MMPI-2 interpretation of patients with cerebrovascular disease: A correction factor. *Archives of Clinical Neuropsychology, 7*(1), 17–27. https://doi.org/10.1016/0887-6177(92)90015-F

Gass, C. S., & Lawhorn, L. (1991). Psychological adjustment following stroke: An MMPI study. *Psychological Assessment, 3*, 628–633. https://doi.org/10.1037/1040-3590.3.4.628

Gass, C. S., & Luis, C. A. (2001). MMPI-2 scale F(p) and symptom feigning: Scale refinement. *Assessment, 8*, 425–429. https://doi.org/10.1177/107319110100800407

Gatchel, R. J., Mayer, T. G., & Eddington, A. (2006). MMPI disability profile: The least known, most useful screen for psychopathology in chronic occupational spinal disorders. *Spine, 31*(25), 2973–2978. https://doi.org/10.1097/01.brs.0000247807.10305.5d

Gerson, A., & Fox, D. (2003). Fibromyalgia revisited: Axis II factors in MMPI and historical data in compensation claimants. *American Journal of Forensic Psychology, 21*(3), 21–25.

Gervais, R. O., Ben-Porath, Y. S., & Wygant, D. B. (2009). Empirical correlates and interpretation of the MMPI-2-RF Cognitive Complaints (COG) Scale. *The Clinical Neuropsychologist, 23*(6), 996–1015. https://doi.org/10.1080/13854040902748249

Gervais, R. O., Ben-Porath, Y. S., Wygant, D. B., & Green, P. (2007). Development and validation of a Response Bias Scale (RBS) for the MMPI-2. *Assessment, 14*(2), 196–208. https://doi.org/10.1177%2F1073191106295861

Gervais, R. O., Ben-Porath, Y. S., Wygant, D. B., & Green, P. (2008). Differential sensitivity of the Response Bias Scale (RBS) and MMPI-2 Validity scales to memory complaints. *The Clinical Neuropsychologist, 22*(6), 1061–1079. https://doi.org/10.1080/13854040701756930

Gervais, R. O., Ben-Porath, Y. S., Wygant, D. B., & Sellbom, M. (2010). Incremental validity of the MMPI-2-RF over-reporting scales and RBS in assessing the veracity of memory complaints: Erratum. *Archives of Clinical Neuropsychology, 25*(5), 473. https://doi.org/10.1093/arclin/acq052

Getter, H., & Sundland, D. M. (1962). The Barron Ego Strength scale and psychotherapy outcome. *Journal of Consulting Psychology, 26*(2), 195. https://doi.org/10.1037/h0047960

Gilberstadt, H., & Duker, J. (1965). *A handbook for clinical and actuarial MMPI interpretation.* Saunders.

Gilmore, J. D., Lash, S. J., Foster, M. A., & Blosser, S. L. (2001). Adherence to substance abuse treatment: Clinical utility of two MMPI-2 scales. *Journal of Personality Assessment, 77*(3), 524–540. https://doi.org/10.1207/S15327752JPA7703_11

Gironda, R. J. (1999). *Comparative validity of MMPI-2 scores of African Americans and Caucasians in a forensic diagnostic sample* [Unpublished doctoral dissertation]. Kent State University.

Gironda, R., & Clark, M. (2009). Psychometric properties of the MMPI-2 Restructured Form. *The Journal of Pain, 10*(4), S11. https://doi.org/10.1016/j.jpain.2009.01.048

Glassmire, D. M., Tarescavage, A. M., Burchett, D., Martinez, J., & Gomez, A. (2016). Clinical utility of the MMPI-2-RF SUI items and scale in a forensic inpatient setting: Association with interview self-report and future suicidal behaviors. *Psychological Assessment, 28*(11), 1502–1509. http://dx.doi.org/10.1037/pas0000220

Gold, P. B., & Frueh, B. C. (1999). Compensation-seeking and extreme exaggeration of psychopathology among combat veterans evaluated for posttraumatic stress disorder. *The Journal of Nervous and Mental Disease, 187*(11), 680–684. https://doi .org/10.1097/00005053-199911000-00005

Gómez, F. C., Jr., Johnson, R., Davis, Q., & Velásquez, R. J. (2000). MMPI-A performance of African and Mexican American adolescent first-time offenders. *Psychological Reports, 87*(1), 309–314. https://doi.org/10.2466/pr0.2000.87.1.309

Good, P. K., & Brantner, J. P. (1961). *The physician's guide to the MMPI.* University of Minnesota Press.

Goodwin, B. E., Sellbom, M., & Arbisi, P. A. (2013). Posttraumatic stress disorder in veterans: The utility of the MMPI–2–RF Validity scales in detecting overreported symptoms. *Psychological Assessment, 25*(3), 671–678. https://doi.org/10.1037/a0032214

Gottesman, I. I., & Prescott, C. A. (1989). Abuses of the MacAndrew MMPI alcoholism scale: A critical review. *Clinical Psychology Review, 9*(2), 223–242. https://doi .org/10.1016/0272-7358(89)90029-9

Gottfried, E. D., Anestis, J. C., Dillon, K. H., & Carbonell, J. L. (2016). The associations between the Minnesota Multiphasic Personality Inventory-2-Restructured Form and self-reported physical and sexual abuse and posttraumatic symptoms in a sample of incarcerated women. *International Journal of Forensic Mental Health, 15*(4), 323–332. http://dx.doi.org/10.1080/14999013.2016.1228088

Gottfried, E., Bodell, L., Carbonell, J., & Joiner, T. (2014). The clinical utility of the MMPI-2-RF Suicidal/Death Ideation scale. *Psychological Assessment, 26*(4), 1205–1211. http://dx.doi.org/10.1037/pas0000017

Gough, H. G. (1950). The F minus K dissimulation index for the MMPI. *Journal of Consulting Psychology, 14*(5), 408–413. https://doi.org/10.1037/h0054506

Gough, H. G., McClosky, H., & Meehl, P. E. (1951). A personality scale for dominance. *Journal of Abnormal and Social Psychology, 46*(3), 360–366. https://doi.org/10.1037/ h0062542

Gough, H.G., McClosky, H., & Meehl, P.E. (1952). A personality scale for social responsibility. *Journal of Abnormal and Social Psychology, 47*(1), 73–80. https://doi .org/10.1037/h0062924

Gould, J. W., & Martindale, D. A. (2009). *The art and science of child custody evaluations.* Guilford Press.

Graham, J. R. (1977). *The MMPI: A practical guide.* Oxford University Press.

Graham, J. R. (1978). A review of some important MMPI special scales. In P. McReynolds (Ed.), *Advances in psychological assessment* (Vol. IV, pp. 311–331). Jossey-Bass.

Graham, J. R. (1988, August). *Establishing validity of the revised form of the MMPI* [Symposium presentation]. 96th Annual Convention of the American Psychological Association, Atlanta, GA.

Graham, J.R., Barthlow, D.L., Stein, L.A.R., Ben-Porath, Y.S., & McNulty, J.L. (2002). Assessing general maladjustment with the MMPI-2. *Journal of Personality Assessment, 78*(2), 334–347. https://doi.org/10.1207/S15327752JPA7802_08

Graham, J. R., Ben-Porath, Y. S., Forbey, J. D., & Sellbom, M. (2003, June). *Relationship between T-score levels on MMPI-2 scales and symptom severity* [Paper presentation].

38th Annual Symposium on Recent Developments on the MMPI-2/MMPI-A, Minneapolis, MN.

Graham, J. R., Ben-Porath, Y. S., & McNulty, J. L. (1997). Empirical correlates of low scores on MMPI-2 scales in an outpatient mental health setting. *Psychological Assessment, 9*(4), 386–391. https://doi.org/10.1037/1040-3590.9.4.386

Graham, J. R., Ben-Porath, Y. S., & McNulty, J. L. (1999). *MMPI-2 correlates for outpatient mental health settings.* University of Minnesota Press.

Graham, J. R., & Mayo, M. A. (1985, March). *A comparison of MMPI strategies for identifying Black and White male alcoholics* [Paper presentation]. 20th Annual Symposium on Recent Developments in the Use of the MMPI, Honolulu, HI.

Graham, J. R., Schroeder, H. E., & Lilly, R. S. (1971). Factor analysis of items on the Social Introversion and Masculinity–Femininity scales of the MMPI. *Journal of Clinical Psychology, 27*(3), 367–370. https://doi.org/10.1002/1097-4679 (197107)27:3<367::AID-JCLP2270270318>3.0.CO;2-7

Graham, J. R., Smith, R. L., & Schwartz, G. F. (1986). Stability of MMPI configurations for psychiatric inpatients. *Journal of Consulting and Clinical Psychology, 54*(3), 375–380. https://doi.org/10.1037/0022-006X.54.3.375

Graham, J. R., Timbrook, R. E., Ben-Porath, Y. S., & Butcher, J. N. (1991). Code-type congruence between MMPI and MMPI-2: Separating fact from artifact. *Journal of Personality Assessment, 57*(2), 205–215. https://doi.org/10.1207/s15327752jpa5702_2

Graham, J. R., Watts, D., & Timbrook, R. E. (1991). Detecting fake-good and fake-bad MMPI-2 profiles. *Journal of Personality Assessment, 57*(2), 264–277. https://doi.org/10.1207/s15327752jpa5702_6

Greene, R. L., Robin, R. W., Albaugh, B., Caldwell, A., & Goldman, D. (2003). Use of the MMPI-2 in American Indians: II. Empirical correlates. *Psychological Assessment, 15*(3), 360–369. https://doi.org/10.1037/1040-3590.15.3.360

Greene, R. L., Weed, N. C., Butcher, J. N., Arredondo, R., & Davis, H. G. (1992). A cross-validation of MMPI-2 substance abuse scales. *Journal of Personality Assessment, 58*(2), 405–410. https://doi.org/10.1207/s15327752jpa5802_16

Greiffenstein, M. F., Baker, W. J., Gola, T., Donders, J., & Miller, L. (2002). The Fake Bad Scale in atypical and severe closed head injury litigants. *Journal of Clinical Psychology, 58*(12), 1591–1600. https://doi.org/10.1002/jclp.10077

Greiffenstein, M. F., Baker, W. J., Tsushima, W. T., Boone, K., & Fox, D. D. (2010). MMPI-2 validity scores in defense- versus plaintiff-selected examinations: A repeated measures study of examiner effects. *The Clinical Neuropsychologist, 24*(2), 305–314. https://doi.org/10.1080/13854040903456222

Grossi, L. M., Green, D., Einzig, S., & Belfi, B. (2017). Evaluation of the Response Bias Scale and Improbable Failure Scale in assessing feigned cognitive impairment. *Psychological Assessment, 29*(5), 531–541. http://dx.doi.org/10.1037/pas0000364

Gucker, D., & McNulty, J. L. (2004, May). *The MMPI-2, defensiveness and an analytic strategy* [Paper presentation]. 39th Annual Symposium on Recent Developments in the Use of the MMPI-2 and MMPI-A, Minneapolis, MN.

Gumbiner, J. (1998). MMPI-A profiles of Hispanic adolescents. *Psychological Reports, 82*(2), 659–672. https://doi.org/10.2466/pr0.1998.82.2.659

Gynther, M. D., Altman, H., & Sletten, I. W. (1973). Replicated correlates of MMPI two-point types: The Missouri Actuarial System. *Journal of Clinical Psychology, 29*(3), 263–289. https://doi.org/10.1002/1097-4679(197307)29:3<263::AID-JCLP2270290 302>3.0.CO;2-R

Haber, J. C., & Baum, L. J. (2014). Minnesota Multiphasic Personality Inventory-2 Restructured Form (MMPI-2-RF) scales as predictors of psychiatric diagnoses. *South African Journal of Psychology, 44*(4), 439–453. https://doi.org/10.1177/0081246314532788

Haggard, R. A., Stowell, A. W., Bernstein, D., & Gatchel, R. J. (2008). Relationship between the MMPI-2 and psychosocial measures in a heterogeneous pain population. *Rehabilitation Psychology, 53*(4), 471–478. https://doi.org/10.1037/a0013358

Haisch, D. C., & Meyers, L. S. (2004). MMPI-2 assessed post-traumatic stress disorder related to job stress, coping, and personality in police agencies. *Stress and Health, 20*(4), 223–229. https://doi.org/10.1002/smi.1020

Hall, G. C. N., Bansal, A. & Lopez, I. R. (1999). Ethnicity and psychopathology: A meta-analytic review of 31 years of comparative MMPI/MMPI-2 research. *Psychological Assessment, 11*(2), 186–197. https://doi.org/10.1037/1040-3590.11.2.186

Hall, G. C. N., Graham, J. R., & Shepherd, J. B. (1991). Three methods of developing MMPI taxonomies of sexual offenders. *Journal of Personality Assessment, 56*(1), 2–13. https://doi.org/10.1207/s15327752jpa5601_1

Hall, J. T., Lee, T. T. C., Ajayi, W., Friedhoff, L. A., & Graham, J. R. (2021). Associations between MMPI-2-RF internalizing RC scales and positive characteristics. *Journal of Personality Assessment, 103*(1), 1–9. https://doi.org/10.1080/00223891.2019.1677245

Hall, J. T., Lee, T. T. C., & Forbey, J. D. (2018, May). *Construct validity of the MMPI-2-RF's Demoralization (RCd) scale* [Paper presentation]. 53rd Annual MMPI Symposium, Hollywood Beach, FL.

Hall, J. T., Menton, W. H., & Ben-Porath, Y. S. (2021). Examining the psychometric equivalency of MMPI-3 scale scores derived from the MMPI-3 and the MMPI-2-RF-EX. *Assessment.* https://doi.org/10.1177/1073191121991921

Han, K., Colarelli, S. M., & Weed, N. C. (2019). Methodological and statistical advances in the consideration of cultural diversity in assessment: A critical review of group classification and measurement invariance testing. *Psychological Assessment, 31*(12), 1481–1496. https://doi.org/10.1037/pas0000731

Han, K., Weed, N. C., Calhoun, R. F., & Butcher, J. N. (1995). Psychometric characteristics of the MMPI-2 Cook-Medley Hostility scale. *Journal of Personality Assessment, 65*(3), 567–585. https://doi.org/10.1207/s15327752jpa6503_15

Hand, C. G., Archer, R. P., Handel, R. W., & Forbey, J. D. (2007). The classification accuracy of the Minnesota Multiphasic Personality Inventory–Adolescent: Effects of modifying the normative sample. *Assessment, 14*(1), 80–85. https://doi.org/10.1177/1073191106291815

Handel, R. W., & Archer, R. P. (2008). An investigation of the psychometric properties of the MMPI-2 Restructured Clinical (RC) Scales with mental health inpatients. *Journal of Personality Assessment, 90*(3), 239–249. https://doi.org/10.1080/00223890701884954

Handel, R. W., Arnau, R. C., Archer, R. P., & Dandy, K. L. (2006). An evaluation of the MMPI-2 and MMPI-A True Response Inconsistency (TRIN) scales. *Assessment, 13*(1), 98–106. https://doi.org/10.1177/1073191105284453

Handel, R. W., Archer, R. P., Elkins, D. E., Mason, J. A., & Simonds-Bisbee, E. C. (2011). Psychometric properties of the Minnesota Multiphasic Personality Inventory–Adolescent (MMPI–A) Clinical, Content, and Supplementary scales in a forensic sample. *Journal of Personality Assessment, 93*(6), 566–581. https://doi.org/10.1080/00223891.2011.608752

Handel, R. W., Ben-Porath, Y. S., Tellegen, A., & Archer, R. P. (2010). Psychometric functioning of the MMPI-2-RF VRIN-r and TRIN-r scales with varying degrees of randomness, acquiescence, and counter-acquiescence. *Psychological Assessment 22*(1), 87–95. doi: 10.1037/a0017061

Hardy, J. D., & Smith, T. W. (1988). Cynical hostility and vulnerability to disease: Social support, life stress, and physiological response to conflict. *Health Psychology, 7*(5), 447–459. https://doi.org/10.1037/0278-6133.7.5.447

Hare, R. D. (1991). *The Hare Psychopathy Checklist–Revised.* Multihealth Systems.

Hargrave, G. E., & Hiatt, D. (1987, May). *Use of the MMPI to predict aggression in law enforcement officer applicants* [Paper presentation]. 22nd Annual Symposium on Recent Developments in the Use of the MMPI, Seattle, WA.

Harkness, A. R., Finn, J. A., McNulty, J. L., & Shields, S. M. (2012). The Personality Psychopathology–Five (PSY–5): Recent constructive replication and assessment literature review. *Psychological Assessment, 24*(2), 432–443. https://doi.org/10.1037/a0025830

Harkness, A. R., & Lilienfeld, S. O. (1997). Individual differences science for treatment planning: Personality traits. *Psychological Assessment, 9*(4), 349–360. https://doi.org/10.1037/1040-3590.9.4.349

Harkness, A. R., & McNulty, J. L. (1994). The Personality Psychopathology Five (PSY-5): Issues from the pages of a diagnostic manual instead of a dictionary. In S. Strack & M. Lorr (Eds.), *Differentiating normal and abnormal personality* (pp. 291–315). Springer Publishing Company.

Harkness, A. R., & McNulty, J. L. (2006). An overview of personality: The MMPI-2 Personality Psychopathology-Five scales (PSY-5). In J. N. Butcher (Ed.), *MMPI-2: A practitioner's guide* (pp. 73–97). American Psychological Association. https://doi.org/10.1037/11287-004

Harkness, A. R., McNulty, J. L., & Ben-Porath, Y. S. (1995). The Personality Psychopathology Five (PSY-5): Constructs and MMPI-2 scales. *Psychological Assessment, 7*(1), 104–114. https://doi.org/10.1037/1040-3590.7.1.104

Harkness, A. R., McNulty, J. L., Ben-Porath, Y. S., & Graham, J. R. (2002). *MMPI-2 Personality Psychopathology Five (PSY-5) scales: Gaining an overview for case conceptualization and treatment planning.* University of Minnesota Press.

Harkness, A. R., McNulty, J. L., Finn, J. A., Reynolds, S. M., Shields, S. M., & Arbisi, P. (2014). The MMPI–2–RF Personality Psychopathology Five (PSY–5–RF) scales: Development and validity research. *Journal of Personality Assessment, 96*(2), 140–150. https://doi.org/10.1080/00223891.2013.823439

Harkness, A. R., Reynolds, S. M., & Lilienfeld, S. O. (2014). A review of systems for psychology and psychiatry: Adaptive systems, Personality Psychopathology Five (PSY–5), and the DSM–5. *Journal of Personality Assessment, 96*(2), 121–139. https://doi.org/10.1080/00223891.2013.823438

Harkness, A. R., Spiro, A., Butcher, J. N., & Ben-Porath, Y. S. (1995, August). *Personality Psychopathology Five (PSY-5) in the Boston VA Normative Aging Study* [Paper presentation]. 103rd Annual Convention of the American Psychological Association, New York, NY.

Harris, R., & Lingoes, J. (1955). *Subscales for the Minnesota Multiphasic Personality Inventory.* Mimeographed materials, The Langley Porter Clinic.

Harris, R., & Lingoes, J. (1968). *Subscales for the Minnesota Multiphasic Personality Inventory.* Mimeographed materials, The Langley Porter Clinic.

Harrison, P. L., Kaufman, A. S., Hickman, J. A., & Kaufman, N. L. (1988). A survey of tests used for adult assessment. *Journal of Psychoeducational Assessment, 6*(3), 188–198. https://doi.org/10.1177/073428298800600301

Hart, K. E. (1966). Perceived availability of different types of social support among cynically hostile women. *Journal of Clinical Psychology, 52*(4), 383–387. https://doi .org/10.1002/(SICI)1097-4679(199607)52:4<383::AID-JCLP2>3.0.CO;2-R

Hart, S. D., Cox, D. N., & Hare, R. D. (1995). *The Hare Psychopathy Checklist: Screening Version (PCL:SV).* Multi-Health Systems.

Hathaway, S. R. (1956). Scales 5 (Masculinity-Femininity), 6 (Paranoia), and 8 (Schizophrenia). In G. S. Welsh & W. G. Dahlstrom (Eds.), *Basic readings on the MMPI in psychology and medicine* (pp. 104–111). University of Minnesota Press.

Hathaway, S. R. (1965). Personality inventories. In B. B. Wolman (Ed.), *Handbook of clinical psychology* (pp. 451–476). McGraw-Hill.

Hathaway, S. R., & McKinley, J. C. (1940). A multiphasic personality schedule (Minnesota): I. Construction of the schedule. *Journal of Psychology, 10*, 249–254. https://doi.org/10.1080/00223980.1940.9917000

Hathaway, S. R., & McKinley, J. C. (1942). *The Minnesota Multiphasic Personality Schedule.* University of Minnesota Press.

Hathaway, S. R., & Monachesi, E. D. (1953). *Analyzing and predicting juvenile delinquency with the MMPI.* University of Minnesota Press.

Hathaway, S. R., & Monachesi, E. D. (1957). The personalities of predelinquent boys. *Journal of Criminal Law, Criminology, and Police Science, 48*(2), 149–163. https://doi .org/10.2307/1139488

Hathaway, S. R., & Monachesi, E. D. (1963). *Adolescent personality and behavior: MMPI patterns of normal, delinquent, dropout, and other outcomes.* University of Minnesota Press.

Hays, S. K. (2003). A computer-administered version versus paper-and-pencil-administered version of the MMPI-A. *Dissertations Abstracts International: Section B: The Sciences and Engineering, 63*, 12-B.

Hearn, M. D., Murray, D. M., & Luepker, R. V. (1989). Hostility, coronary heart disease, and total mortality: A 33-year follow-up of university students. *Journal of Behavioral Medicine, 12*(2), 105–121. https://doi.org/10.1007/BF00846545

Hedayat, M. M., & Kelly, D. B. (1991). Relationship of MMPI Dependency and Dominance scale scores to staff's ratings, diagnoses, and demographic data for day-treatment clients. *Psychological Reports, 68*(1), 259–266. https://doi.org/10.2466/pr0.1991.68.1.259

Heilbrun, A. B. (1979). Psychopathy and violent crime. *Journal of Consulting and Clinical Psychology, 47*(3), 509–516. https://doi.org/10.1037/0022-006X.47.3.509

Heilbrun, K., & Heilbrun, A. B. (1995). Risk assessment with the MMPI-2 in forensic evaluations. In Y. S. Ben-Porath, J. R. Graham, G. C. N. Hall, R. D. Hirshman, & M. S. Zaragoza (Eds.), *Forensic applications of the MMPI-2* (pp. 160–178). Sage. https://doi.org/10.4135/9781452243771.n7

Henning, J. J., Levy, R. H., & Aderman, M. (1972). Reliability of MMPI tape recorded and booklet administrations. *Journal of Clinical Psychology, 28*(53), 372–373. https://doi .org/10.1002/1097-4679(197207)28:3+<372::AID-JCLP2270280319>3.0.CO;2-Q

Hiatt, D., & Hargrave, G. E. (1988). MMPI profiles of problem peace officers. *Journal of Personality Assessment, 52*(4), 722–731. https://doi.org/10.1207/s15327752jpa5204_11

Hill, J. S., Robbins, R. R., & Pace, T. M. (2012). Cultural validity of the Minnesota Multiphasic Personality Inventory–2 empirical correlates: Is this the best we can do? *Journal of Multicultural Counseling and Development, 40*(2), 104–116. https://doi .org/10.1002/j.2161-1912.2012.00010.x

Hilts, D., & Moore, J. M., Jr. (2003). Normal range MMPI-A profiles among psychiatric inpatients. *Assessment, 10*(3), 266–272. https://doi.org/10.1177/1073191103255494

Hiscock, M., & Hiscock, C. K. (1989). Refining the forced-choice method for detection of malingering. *Journal of Clinical and Experimental Neuropsychology, 11*(6), 967–974. https://doi.org/10.1080/01688638908400949

Hjemboe, S., Almagor, M., & Butcher, J. N. (1992). Empirical assessment of marital distress: The Marital Distress Scale (MDS) for the MMPI-2. In J. N. Butcher & C. D. Spielberger (Eds.), *Advances in personality assessment: Vol. 9* (pp. 141–152). Lawrence Erlbaum Associates.

Hjemboe, S., & Butcher, J. N. (1991). Couples in marital distress: A study of personality factors as measured by the MMPI-2. *Journal of Personality Assessment, 57*(2), 216–237. https://doi.org/10.1207/s15327752jpa5702_3

Hobbs, F., & Stoops, N. (2002). *Demographic trends in the 20th Century: Census 2000 special reports*, CENSR-4. U.S. Census Bureau.

Hoelzle, J. B., & Meyer, J. (2008). The factor structure of the MMPI-2 Restructured Clinical (RC) Scales. *Journal of Personality Assessment, 90*(5), 443–455. https://doi .org/10.1080/00223890802248711

Holmes, D. S. (1967). Male-female differences in MMPI Ego Strength: An artifact. *Journal of Consulting Psychology, 31*(4), 408–410. https://doi.org/10.1037/h0024845

Houston, K. B., & Kelly, K. E. (1989). Hostility in unemployed women: Relation to work and marital experiences, social support, stress, and anger expression. *Personality and Social Psychology Bulletin, 15*(2), 175–182. https://doi.org/10.1177/0146167289152004

Houston, K. B., & Vavak, C. R. (1991). Cynical hostility: Developmental factors, psychosocial correlates, and health behaviors. *Health Psychology, 10*(1), 9–17. https://doi .org/10.1037/0278-6133.10.1.9

Hovey, H. B., & Lewis, E. G. (1967). *Semiautomatic interpretation of the MMPI*. Clinical Psychology Publishing Company.

Huber, N. A., & Danahy, S. (1975). Use of the MMPI in predicting completion and evaluating changes in a long-term alcoholism treatment program. *Journal of Studies on Alcohol, 36*(9), 1230–1237. https://doi.org/10.15288/jsa.1975.36.1230

Hunter, H. K., Bolinskey, P. K., Novi, J. H., Hudak, D. V., James, A. V., Myers, K. R., & Schuder, K. M. (2014). Using the MMPI-2-RF to discriminate psychometrically identified schizotypic college students from a matched comparison sample. *Journal of Personality Assessment, 96*(6), 596-603. https://doi.org/10.1080/00223891.2014.92 2093

Hutton, H. E., & Miner, M. H. (1995). The validation of the Megargee–Bohn Typology in African American and Caucasian forensic psychiatric patients. *Criminal Justice and Behavior, 22*(3), 233–245. https://doi.org/10.1177/0093854895022003003

Hutton, H. E., Miner, M. H., & Langfeldt, V. C. (1993). The utility of the Megargee-Bohn typology in a forensic psychiatric hospital. *Journal of Personality Assessment, 60*(3), 572–587. https://doi.org/10.1207/s15327752jpa6003_14

Hyer, L., Woods, M. G., Summers, M. N., Boudewyns, P., & Harrison, W. R. (1990). Alexithymia among Vietnam veterans with posttraumatic stress disorder. *Journal of Clinical Psychiatry, 51*(6), 243–247.

Imhof, E. A. & Archer, R. P. (1997). Correlates of the MMPI-A Immaturity (IMM) Scale in an adolescent psychiatric sample. *Assessment, 4*(2), 169–179. https://doi .org/10.1177/107319119700400206

Ingram, P. B., Golden, B. L., & Armistead-Jehle, P. J. (2020). Evaluating the Minnesota Multiphasic Personality Inventory-2-Restructured Form (MMPI-2-RF) over-reporting scales in a military neuropsychology clinic. *Journal of Clinical and Experimental Neuropsychology, 42*(3), 263–273. https://doi.org/10.1080/13803395.2019.1708271

Ingram, P. B., Kelso, K. M., & McCord, D. M. (2011). Empirical correlates and expanded interpretation of the MMPI-2-RF Restructured Clinical Scale 3 (Cynicism). *Assessment, 18*(1), 95–101. https://doi.org/10.1177/1073191110388147

Ingram, P. B., Tarescavage, A. M., Ben-Porath, Y. S., Oehlert, M. E., & Bergquist, B. K. (2021). External correlates of the MMPI-2-Restructured Form across a national sample of veterans. *Journal of Personality Assessment, 103*(1), 19–26. https://doi.org/10.1080/ 00223891.2020.1732995

Ingram, P. B., & Ternes, M. S. (2016). The detection of content-based invalid responding: A meta-analysis of the MMPI-2-Restructured Form's (MMPI-2-RF) over-reporting validity scales. *The Clinical Neuropsychologist, 30*(4), 473–496. http://dx.doi.org /10.1080/13854046.2016.1187769

Inman, T. H., Vickery, C. D., Berry, D. T. R., Lamb, D. G., Edwards, C. L., & Smith, G. T. (1998). Development and initial validation of a new procedure for evaluating adequacy of effort given during neuropsychological testing: The Letter Memory Test. *Psychological Assessment, 10*(2), 128–139. https://doi.org/10.1037/1040-3590.10.2.128

Iverson, G. L., & Barton, E. (1999). Interscorer reliability of the MMPI-2: Should TRIN and VRIN be computer scored? *Journal of Clinical Psychology, 55*(1), 65–69. https:// doi.org/10.1002/(SICI)1097-4679(199901)55:1<65::AID-JCLP6>3.0.CO;2-K

Iverson, G. L., Franzen, M. D., & Hammond, J. A. (1995). Examination of inmates' ability to malinger on the MMPI-2. *Psychological Assessment, 7*(1), 118–121. https:// doi.org/10.1037/1040-3590.7.1.118

Jackson, D. N., Fraboni, M., & Helmes, E. (1997). MMPI-2 Content scales: How much content do they measure? *Assessment, 4*(2), 111–117. https://doi .org/10.1177/107319119700400201

Jackson, D. N., & Messick, S. (1961). Acquiescence and desirability as response determinants on the MMPI. *Educational and Psychological Measurement, 21*(4), 771–790. https://doi.org/10.1177/001316446102100402

Janus, M. D., Tolbert, H., Calestro, K., & Toepfer, S. (1996). Clinical accuracy ratings of MMPI approaches for adolescents: Adding ten years and the MMPI-A. *Journal of Personality Assessment, 67*(2), 364–383. https://doi.org/10.1207/s15327752jpa6702_11

Johnson, M. E., Jones, G., & Brems, C. (1996). Concurrent validity of the MMPI-2 Feminine Gender Role (GF) and Masculine Gender Role (GM) scales. *Journal of Personality Assessment, 66*(1), 153–168. https://doi.org/10.1207/s15327752jpa6601_12

Joiner, T. E. (2005). *Why people die by suicide.* Harvard University Press.

Jones, A. (2016). Cutoff scores for MMPI-2 and MMPI-2-RF cognitive-somatic Validity scales for psychometrically defined malingering groups in a military sample. *Archives of Clinical Neuropsychology, 31*(7), 786–801. https://doi.org/10.1093/arclin/acw035

Kamphuis, J. H., Arbisi, P. A., Ben-Porath, Y. S., & McNulty, J. L. (2008). Detecting comorbid Axis-II status among inpatients using the MMPI-2 Restructured Clinical Scales. *European Journal of Psychological Assessment, 24*(3), 157–164. https://doi.org/10.1027/1015-5759.24.3.157

Kane, A. W., & Dvoskin, J. A. (2011). *Evaluation for personal injury claims.* Oxford University Press.

Kane, A. W., Nelson, E. M., Dvoskin, J. A., & Pitt, S. E. (2013). *Evaluation for personal injury claims.* In R. Roesch & P. A. Zapf (Eds.), *Best practices in forensic mental health assessment. Forensic assessments in criminal and civil law: A handbook for lawyers* (p. 148–160). Oxford University Press.

Katz, M. M., & Lyerly, S. B. (1963). Methods for measuring adjustment and social behavior in the community: I. Rationale, description, discriminative validity and scale development. *Psychological Reports, 13*(2), 503–535. https://doi.org/10.2466/pr0.1963.13.2.503

Kaufman, J., Birmaher, B., Brent, D., Rao, U., Flynn, T., Moreci, P., Williamson, D., & Ryan, N. (1997). Schedule for Affective Disorders and Schizophrenia for school-age Children-Present and Lifetime Version (K-SADS-PL): Initial reliability and validity data. *Journal of the American Academy of Child & Adolescent Psychiatry, 36*(7), 980–988. https://doi.org/10.1097/00004583-199707000-00021

Kawachi, I., Sparrow, D., Kubazansky, L. D., Spiro, A., Vokonas, P. S., & Weiss, S. T. (1998). Prospective study of a self-report Type A scale and risk of coronary heart disease: Test of the MMPI-2 Type A scale. *Circulation, 98*(5), 405–412. https://doi.org/10.1161/01.CIR.98.5.405

Keane, T. M., Malloy, P. F., & Fairbank, J. A. (1984). Empirical development of an MMPI subscale for the assessment of combat-related post-traumatic stress disorder. *Journal of Consulting and Clinical Psychology, 52*(5), 888–891. https://doi.org/10.1037/0022-006X.52.5.888

Keiller, S. W., & Graham, J. R. (1993). Interpreting low scores on the MMPI-2 clinical scales. *Journal of Personality Assessment, 61,* 211–223. https://doi.org/10.1207/s15327752jpa6102_1

Keller, L. S., & Butcher, J. N. (1991). *Assessment of chronic pain with the MMPI-2.* University of Minnesota Press.

Kelley, C. K., & King, G. D. (1979a). Behavioral correlates of the 2–7–8 MMPI profile type in students at a university mental health center. *Journal of Consulting and Clinical Psychology, 47*(4), 679–685. https://doi.org/10.1037/0022-006X.47.4.679

Kelley, C. K., & King, G. D. (1979b). Cross validation of the 2–8/8–2 MMPI code type for young adult psychiatric outpatients. *Journal of Personality Assessment, 43*(2), 143–149. https://doi.org/10.1207/s15327752jpa4302_6

Key, D. J., Fisher, R. J., & Micucci, J. A. (2020). The MMPI-2 in parenting capacity evaluations: Scale elevations and effects of underreporting. *Professional Psychology: Research and Practice, 51*(6), 630–641. https://doi.org/10.1037/pro0000320

Khazem, L. R., Anestis, J. C., Erbes, C. R., Ferrier-Auerbach, A. C., Schumacher, M. M., & Arbisi, P. A. (2021). Assessing the clinical utility of the MMPI-2-RF in detecting suicidal ideation in a high acuity, partially-hospitalized veteran sample. *Journal of Personality Assessment, 103*(1), 10–18. https://doi.org/10.1080/00223891.2020.173 9057

Kleinmuntz, B. (1961). The College Maladjustment Scale (Mt): Norms and predictive validity. *Educational and Psychological Measurement, 21*(4), 1029–1033. https://doi .org/10.1177/001316446102100432

Kleinmuntz, B. (1963). MMPI decision rules for the identification of college maladjustment: A digital computer approach. *Psychological Monographs, 77*(14), 1–22. https:// doi.org/10.1037/h0093866

Klinge, V., Lachar, D., Grisell, J., & Berman, W. (1978). Effects of scoring norms on adolescent psychiatric drug users' and nonusers' MMPI profiles. *Adolescence, 13*(49), 1–11.

Klinge, V., & Strauss, M.E. (1976). Effects of scoring norms on adolescent psychiatric patients' MMPI profiles. *Journal of Personality Assessment, 40*(1), 13–17. https://doi .org/10.1207/s15327752jpa4001_3

Knapp, R. R. (1960). A reevaluation of the validity of MMPI scales of Dominance and Social Responsibility. *Educational and Psychological Measurement, 20*(2), 381–386. https://doi.org/10.1177/001316446002000219

Knaster, C. A., & Micucci, J. A. (2013). The effect of client ethnicity on clinical interpretation of the MMPI-2. *Assessment, 20*(1), 43–47. https://doi.org/10.1177/1073191112465333

Kopper, B. A., Osman, A., & Barrios, F. X. (2001). Assessment of suicidal ideation in young men and women: The incremental validity of the MMPI-2 Content scales. *Death Studies, 25*(7), 593–607. https://doi.org/10.1080/07481180126578   .

Kopper, B. A., Osman, A., Osman, J. R., & Hoffman, J. (1998). Clinical utility of the MMPI-A Content scales and Harris–Lingoes subscales in the assessment of suicidal risk factors in psychiatric adults. *Journal of Clinical Psychology, 54*(2), 191–200. https:// doi.org/10.1002/(SICI)1097-4679(199802)54:2<191::AID-JCLP8>3.0.CO;2-V

Kornfeld, A. D. (1995). Police officer candidate MMPI-2 performance: Gender, ethnic, and normative factors. *Journal of Clinical Psychology, 51*(4), 536–540. https://doi .org/10.1002/1097-4679(199507)51:4<536::AID-JCLP2270510411>3.0.CO;2-5

Koss, M. P. (1979). MMPI item content: Recurring issues. In J. N. Butcher (Ed.), *New developments in the use of the MMPI* (pp. 3–38). University of Minnesota Press.

Koss, M. P., Butcher, J. N., & Hoffman, N. (1976). The MMPI critical items: How well do they work? *Journal of Consulting and Clinical Psychology, 44*(6), 921–928. https:// doi.org/10.1037/0022-006X.44.6.921

Kostlan, A. (1954). A method for the empirical study of psychodiagnosis. *Journal of Consulting Psychology, 18*(2), 83–88. https://doi.org/10.1037/h0054784

Kotov, R., Krueger, R. F., Watson, D., Cicero, D. C., Conway, C. C., DeYoung, C. G., Eaton, N. R., Forbes, M. K., Hallquist, M. N., Latzman, R. D., Mullins-Sweatt, S. N., Ruggero, C. J., Simms, L. J., Waldman, I. D., Waszczuk, M. A., & Wright, A. G. C. (2021). The Hierarchical Taxonomy of Psychopathology (HiTOP): A quantitative nosology based on consensus of evidence. *Annual Review of Clinical Psychology, 17*(1), 83–108. https://doi.org/10.1146/annurev-clinpsy-081219-093304

Kremyar, A. J., & Lee, T. T. C. (2021). MMPI-3 predictors of anxiety sensitivity and distress intolerance. *Assessment.* https://doi.org/10.1177/10731911211001948

Kremyar, A. J., Lee, T. T. C., Ajayi, W., Friedhoff, L. A., & Graham, J. R. (2020). Measuring positive health behaviors and outcomes with low scores on MMPI–2–RF somatic scales. *Journal of Personality Assessment, 102*(1), 36–44. https://doi.org/10.1080/00223891.2018.1514311

Krishnamurthy, R., Archer, R. P., & Huddleston, E. N. (1995). Clinical research note on psychometric limitations of two Harris–Lingoes subscales for the MMPI-2. *Assessment, 2*(3), 301–304. https://doi.org/10.1177/1073191195002003010

Krueger, R. F., Derringer, J., Markon, K. E., Watson, D., & Skodol, A. E. (2012). Initial construction of a maladaptive personality trait model and inventory for DSM-5. *Psychological Medicine, 42*(9), 1879–1890. https://doi.org/10.1017/S0033291711002674

Krueger, R. F., Markon, K. E., Patrick, C. J., Benning, S. D., & Kramer, M. D. (2007). Linking antisocial behavior, substance abuse, and personality: An integrative quantitative model of the adult externalizing spectrum. *Journal of Abnormal Psychology, 116*(4), 645–666. https://doi.org/10.1037/0021-843X.116.4.645

Kwon, P. (2002). Comment on "Effects of acculturation on the MMPI-2 scores of Asian American students." *Journal of Personality Assessment, 78*(1), 187–189. https://doi.org/10.1207/S15327752JPA7801_12

Lachar, D. (1974). *The MMPI: Clinical assessment and automated interpretation.* Western Psychological Services.

Lachar, D., Klinge, V., & Grisell, J. L. (1976). Relative accuracy of automated MMPI narratives generated from adult norm and adolescent norm profiles. *Journal of Consulting and Clinical Psychology, 44*(1), 20–24. https://psycnet.apa.org/doi/10.1037/0022-006X.44.1.20

Lachar, D., & Wrobel, T. A. (1979). Validation of clinicians' hunches: Construction of a new MMPI critical item set. *Journal of Consulting and Clinical Psychology, 47*(2), 277–284. https://doi.org/10.1037/0022-006X.47.2.277

Ladd, J. S. (1998). The F(p) Infrequency-Psychopathology scale with chemically dependent inpatients. *Journal of Clinical Psychology 54*(5), 665–671. https://doi.org/10.1002/(SICI)1097-4679(199808)54:5<665::AID-JCLP12>3.0.CO;2-B

LaDuke, C., Barr, W., Brodale, D. L., & Rabin, L. A. (2018). Toward generally accepted forensic assessment practices among clinical neuropsychologists: A survey of professional practice and common test use. *The Clinical Neuropsychologist, 32*(1), 145–164. https://doi.org/10.1080/13854046.2017.1346711

Lally, S. J. (2003). What tests are acceptable for use in forensic evaluations? A survey of experts. *Professional Psychology: Research and Practice, 34*(5), 491–498. https://doi .org/10.1037/0735-7028.34.5.491

Langwerden, R. J., van der Heijden, P. T., Egger, J. I. M., & Derksen, J. J. L. (2021). Robustness of the maladaptive personality plaster: An investigation of stability of the PSY-5-r in adults over 20 years. *Journal of Personality Assessment, 103*(1), 27–32. https://doi.org/10.1080/00223891.2020.1729772.

Lanyon, R. I. (1995). Review of the Minnesota Multiphasic Personality Inventory–Adolescent. In J. C. Conoley & J. C. Impara (Eds.), *The twelfth mental measurements yearbook* (pp. 238–239). University of Nebraska Press.

Larrabee, G. J. (2003). Detection of symptom exaggeration with the MMPI-2 in litigants with malingered neurocognitive deficit. *The Clinical Neuropsychologist, 17*(1), 54–68. https://doi.org/10.1076/clin.17.1.54.15627

Lau, L., Basso, M. R., Estevis, E., Miller, A., Whiteside, D. M., Combs, D., & Arentsen, T. J. (2017). Detecting coached neuropsychological dysfunction: A simulation experiment regarding mild traumatic brain injury. *The Clinical Neuropsychologist, 31*(8), 1412–1431. https://doi.org/10.1080/13854046.2017.1318954

Lauterbach, D., Garcia, M., & Gloster, A. (2002). Psychometric properties and predictive validity of the Mt scale of the MMPI-2. *Assessment, 9*(4), 390–400. https://doi .org/10.1177/1073191102238197

Lawrence, S. B. (1985). Clinical evaluation of competence to stand trial. In C. P. Ewing (Ed.), *Psychology, psychiatry, and the law: A clinical and forensic handbook* (pp. 41–66). Professional Resource Exchange, Inc.

Lee, T. T. C., & Forbey, J. D. (2010). MMPI-2 correlates of sexual preoccupation as measured by the Sexuality Scale in a college setting. *Sexual Addiction & Compulsivity, 17*(3), 219–235. https://doi.org/10.1080/10720162.2010.500500

Lee, T. T. C., Graham, J. R., & Arbisi, P. A. (2018). The utility of MMPI–2–RF scale scores in the differential diagnosis of Schizophrenia and Major Depressive Disorder. *Journal of Personality Assessment, 100*(3), 305–312. https://doi.org/10.1080/00223891 .2017.1300906

Lee, T. T. C., Graham, J. R., Sellbom, M., & Gervais, R. O. (2012). Examining the potential for gender bias in the prediction of symptom validity test failure by MMPI-2 symptom validity scale scores. *Psychological Assessment, 24*(3), 618–627. https://doi .org/10.1037/a0026458

Lee, T. T. C., Sellbom, M., & Hopwood, C. J. (2017). Contemporary psychopathology assessment: Mapping major personality inventories onto empirical models of psychopathology. In S. C. Bowden (Ed.), *Neuropsychological assessment in the era of evidence-based practice* (pp. 65–94). Oxford University Press.

Lee, T. T. C., Taylor, A. M., Holbert, A. M., & Graham, J. R. (2019). MMPI-2-RF predictors of interpersonal relationship characteristics in committed couples. *Psychological Assessment, 31*(9), 1118–1124. http://dx.doi.org/10.1037/pas0000735

Lees-Haley, P. R., English, L. T., & Glenn, W. J. (1991). A fake-bad scale on the MMPI-2 for personal injury claimants. *Psychological Reports, 68*(1), 203–210. https://doi .org/10.2466/pr0.1991.68.1.203

Leon, G. R., Finn, S. E., Murray, D., & Bailey, J. M. (1988). Inability to predict cardiovascular disease from hostility scores or MMPI items related to Type A behavior. *Journal of Consulting and Clinical Psychology, 56*(4), 597–600. https://doi .org/10.1037/0022-006X.56.4.597

Lessenger, L. H. (1997). Acculturation and MMPI-2 scale scores of Mexican American substance abuse patients. *Psychological Reports, 80,* 1181–1182. https://doi.org/10.2466/ pr0.1997.80.3c.1181

Lewandowski, D., & Graham, J. R. (1972). Empirical correlates of frequently occurring two-point code types: A replicated study. *Journal of Consulting and Clinical Psychology, 39*(3), 467–472. https://doi.org/10.1037/h0034018

Lilienfeld, S. O. (1996). The MMPI-2 Antisocial Practices Content scale: Construct validity and comparison with the Psychopathic Deviate scale. *Psychological Assessment, 8*(3), 281–293. https://doi.org/10.1037/1040-3590.8.3.281

Lilienfeld, S. O. (1999). The relation of the MMPI-2 Pd Harris–Lingoes subscales to psychopathy, psychopathy facets, and antisocial behavior: Implications for clinical practice. *Journal of Clinical Psychology, 55*(2), 241–255. https://doi.org/10.1002/ (SICI)1097-4679(199902)55:2<241::AID-JCLP12>3.0.CO;2-I

Lilienfeld, S. O., & Andrews, B. P. (1996). Development and preliminary validation of a self-report measure of psychopathic personality traits in noncriminal populations. *Journal of Personality Assessment, 66*(3), 488–524. https://doi.org/10.1207/ s15327752jpa6603_3

Lim, J., & Butcher, J. N. (1996). Detection of faking on the MMPI-2: Differentiation among faking-bad, denial, and claiming extreme virtue. *Journal of Personality Assessment, 67*(1), 1–25. https://doi.org/10.1207/s15327752jpa6701_1

Livingston, R. B., Jennings, E., Colotla, V. A., Reynolds, C. R., & Shercliffe, R. J. (2006). MMPI-2 code-type congruence of injured workers. *Psychological Assessment, 18*(1), 126–130. https://doi.org/10.1037/1040-3590.18.1.126

Long, K. A., & Graham, J. R. (1991). The Masculinity–Femininity scale of MMPI-2: Is it useful with normal men? *Journal of Personality Assessment, 57*(1), 46–51. https://doi .org/10.1207/s15327752jpa5701_7

Long, K. A., Graham, J. R., & Timbrook, R. E. (1994). Socioeconomic status and MMPI-2 interpretation. *Measurement and Evaluation in Counseling and Development, 27*(3), 158–177.

Lubin, B., Larsen, R. M., & Matarazzo, J. D. (1984). Patterns of psychological test usage in the United States: 1935–1982. *American Psychologist, 39*(4), 451–454. https://doi .org/10.1037/0003-066X.39.4.451

Lucio, E., Duran, C., Graham, J. R., & Ben-Porath, Y. S. (2002). Identifying faking bad on the MMPI-A with Mexican adolescents. *Assessment, 9*(1), 62–69. https://doi.org/ 10.1177/1073191102009001008

Lyons, J. A., & Scotti, J. R. (1994). Comparability of two administration formulas of the Keane Posttraumatic Stress Disorder scale. *Psychological Assessment, 6*(3), 209–211. https://doi.org/10.1037/1040-3590.6.3.209

Lyons, J. A., & Wheeler-Cox, T. (1999). MMPI, MMPI-2, and PTSD: Overview of scores, scales, and profiles. *Journal of Traumatic Stress, 12*(1), 175–183. https://doi .org/10.1023/A:1024710803042

MacAndrew, C. (1965). The differentiation of male alcoholic out-patients from nonalcoholic psychiatric patients by means of the MMPI. *Quarterly Journal of the Studies on Alcohol, 26*(2), 238–246. https://doi.org/10.15288/qjsa.1965.26.238

Marek, R. J., Anderson, J. L., Tarescavage, A. M., Martin-Fernandez, K., Haugh, S, Block, A. R., Heinberg, L. J., Jimenez, X., & Ben-Porath, Y. S. (2020). Elucidating somatization in a dimensional model of psychopathology across medical settings. *Journal of Abnormal Psychology, 129*(2), 162–176. https://doi.org/10.1037/abn0000475

Marek, R. J., & Ben-Porath, Y. S. (2017). *Using the Minnesota Multiphasic Personality Inventory-2-Restructured Form (MMPI-2-RF) in behavioral medicine settings*. In M. E. Maruish (Ed.), *Handbook of psychological assessment in primary care settings* (2nd ed., pp. 631–662). Taylor and Francis.

Marek, R. J., Ben-Porath, Y. S., Epker, J. T., Kreymer, J. K., & Block, A. R. (2020). Reliability and validity of the Minnesota Multiphasic Personality Inventory–2–Restructured Form (MMPI-2-RF) in spine surgery and spinal cord stimulator samples. *Journal of Personality Assessment, 102*(1), 22–35. https://doi.org/10.1080/002238 91.2018.1488719

Marek, R. J., Martin-Fernandez, K., Heinberg, L. J., & Ben-Porath, Y. S. (2021). An investigation of the Eating Concerns scale of the Minnesota Multiphasic Personality Inventory–3 (MMPI-3) in a postoperative bariatric surgery sample. *Obesity Surgery, 31*(12), 2335–2338. https://doi.org/10.1007/s11695-020-05113-y

Marion, B. E., Sellbom, M., & Bagby, M. R. (2011). The detection of feigned psychiatric disorders using the MMPI-2-RF overreporting Validity scales: An analog investigation. *Psychological Injury and Law, 4*(1), 1–12. https://doi.org/10.1007/s12207-011-9097-0

Marks, P. A., & Seeman, W. (1963). *Actuarial description of abnormal personality*. Williams & Wilkins.

Marks, P. A., Seeman, W., & Haller, D. L. (1974). *The actuarial use of the MMPI with adolescents and adults*. Williams & Wilkins.

Marsh, H. W., Wen, Z., Nagengast, B., & Hau, K.-T. (2012). Structural equation models of latent interaction. In R. H. Hoyle (Ed.), *Handbook of structural equation modeling* (p. 436–458). Guilford Press.

Maruta, T., Hamburgen, M. E., Jennings, C. A., Offord, K. P., Colligan, R. P., Frye, R., & Malinchoc, M. (1993). Keeping hostility in perspective: Coronary heart disease and the Hostility scale on the Minnesota Multiphasic Personality Inventory. *Mayo Clinic Proceedings, 68*(2), 109–114. https://doi.org/10.1016/S0025-6196(12)60156-6

Mattson, E. K., Nelson, N. W., Sponheim, S. R., & Disner, S. G. (2019). The impact of PTSD and mTBI on the relationship between subjective and objective cognitive deficits in combat-exposed veterans. *Neuropsychology, 33*(7), 913–921. http://dx.doi .org/10.1037/neu0000560

Mason, O., Claridge, G., & Jackson, M. (1995). New scales for the assessment of schizotypy. *Personality and Individual Differences, 18*(1), 7–13. https://doi .org/10.1016/0191-8869(94)00132-C

Mattson, C., Powers, B., Halfaker, D., Akeson, S., & Ben-Porath, Y. (2012). Predicting drug court treatment completion using the MMPI-2-RF. *Psychological Assessment, 24*(4), 937–943. https://doi.org/10.1037/a0028267

McAnulty, R. D., McAnulty, D. P., Sipp, J. E., Demakis, G. J., & Heggestad, E. D. (2014). Predictive validity of the MMPI-2 among female offenders in a residential treatment program. *Journal of Personality Assessment, 96*(6), 604–609. https://doi.org/10.1080/00223891.2014.880061

McCarthy, L., & Archer, R. P. (1998). Factor structure of the MMPI-A Content scales: Item-level and scale-level findings. *Journal of Personality Assessment, 71*(1), 84–97. https://doi.org/10.1207/s15327752jpa7101_6

McClinton, B. K., Graham, J. R., & Ben-Porath, Y. S. (1995, March). *Ethnicity and MMPI-2 substance abuse scales* [Paper presentation]. 30th Annual Symposium on Recent Developments in the Use of the MMPI-2 and MMPI-A, St. Petersburg Beach, FL.

McCord, D. M., Achee, M. C., Cannon, E. M., Harrop, T. M., & Poynter, W. D. (2017). Using the Research Domain Criteria framework to explore associations between MMPI-2-RF constructs and physiological variables assessed by eye-tracker technology. *Journal of Personality Assessment, 99*(4), 363–374. https://doi.org/10.1080/00223891.2016.1228067

McCord, D. M., & Drerup, L. C. (2011). Relative practical utility of the Minnesota Multiphasic Personality Inventory–2 Restructured Clinical Scales versus the Clinical Scales in a chronic pain patient sample. *Journal of Clinical and Experimental Neuropsychology, 33*(1), 140–146. https://doi.org/10.1080/13803395.2010.495056

McCranie, E. W., Watkins, L. O., Brandsma, J. M., & Sisson, B. D. (1986). Hostility, coronary heart disease (CHD) incidence, and total mortality: Lack of association in a 25-year follow-up study of 478 physicians. *Journal of Behavioral Medicine, 9*(2), 119–125. https://doi.org/10.1007/BF00848472

McCurdy, B. A., & Kelly, D. B. (1997). Correlations of the MMPI-2 Low Self-Esteem scale with two self-esteem measures. *Psychological Reports, 81*(3), 826. https://doi.org/10.2466/pr0.1997.81.3.826

McDermut, W., Pantoja, G., & Amrami, Y. (2019). Dysfunctional beliefs and personality traits. *Journal of Rational-Emotive & Cognitive-Behavior Therapy, 37*(4), 338–357. https://doi.org/10.1007/s10942-019-00315-5

McGrath, R. E., Sweeney, M., O'Malley, W. B., & Carlton, T. K. (1998). Identifying psychological contributions to chronic pain complaints with the MMPI-2: The role of the K scale. *Journal of Personality Assessment, 70*(3), 448–459. https://doi.org/10.1207/s15327752jpa7003_5

McKee, G. R., Shea, S. J., Mogy, R. B., & Holden, C. E. (2001). MMPI-2 profiles of filicidal, mariticidal, and homicidal women. *Journal of Clinical Psychology, 57*(3), 367–374. https://doi.org/10.1002/jclp.1018

McKinley, J. C., & Hathaway, S. R. (1940). A Multiphasic Personality Schedule (Minnesota): II. A differential study of hypochondriasis. *Journal of Psychology, 10*(2), 255–268. https://doi.org/10.1080/00223980.1940.9917001

McKinley, J. C., & Hathaway, S. R. (1944). The MMPI: V. Hysteria, hypomania and psychopathic deviate. *Journal of Applied Psychology, 28*(2), 153–174. https://doi.org/10.1037/h0059245

McKinley, J. C., Hathaway, S. R., & Meehl, P. E. (1948). The MMPI: VI. The K scale. *Journal of Consulting Psychology, 12*(1), 20–31. https://doi.org/10.1037/h0061377

McNulty, J. L., Ben-Porath, Y. S., & Graham, J. R. (1998). An empirical examination of the correlates of well-defined and not defined MMPI-2 code types. *Journal of Personality Assessment, 71*(3), 393–410. https://doi.org/10.1207/s15327752jpa7103_8

McNulty, J. L., Ben-Porath, Y. S., Graham, J. R., & Stein, L. A. R. (1997, June). *Using the Content Component scales to facilitate Content scale interpretation* [Paper presentation]. 32nd Annual Symposium on Recent Developments in the Use of the MMPI (MMPI-2 and MMPI-A), Minneapolis, MN.

McNulty, J. L., Forbey, J. D., Graham, J. R., Ben-Porath, Y. S., Black, M. S., Anderson, S. V., & Burlew, A. K. (2003). MMPI-2 Validity scale characteristics in a correctional sample. *Assessment, 10*(3), 288–298. https://doi.org/10.1177/1073191103255623

McNulty, J. L., Graham, J. R., Ben-Porath, Y. S., & Stein, L. A. R. (1997). Comparative validity of MMPI-2 scores of African American and Caucasian mental health center clients. *Psychological Assessment, 9*(4), 464–470. https://doi.org/10.1037/1040-3590.9.4.464

McNulty, J. L., Harkness, A. R., Ben-Porath, Y. S., & Williams, C. L. (1997). Assessing the Personality Psychopathology Five (PSY-5) in adolescents: New MMPI-A scales. *Psychological Assessment, 9*(3), 250–259. https://doi.org/10.1037/1040-3590.9.3.250

McNulty, J. L., & Overstreet, S. R. (2014). Viewing the MMPI-2-RF structure through the Personality Psychopathology Five (PSY-5) lens. *Journal of Personality Assessment, 96*(2), 151–157. https://doi.org/10.1080/00223891.2013.840305

Meehl, P. E. (1945). The dynamics of "structured" personality tests. *Journal of Clinical Psychology, 1*, 296–303.

Meehl, P. E. (1951). *Research results for counselors*. Minnesota State Department of Education.

Meehl, P. E. (1956). Wanted—a good cookbook. *American Psychologist, 11*(6), 263–272. https://doi.org/10.1037/h0044164

Meehl, P. E., & Dahlstrom, W. G. (1960). Objective configural rules for discriminating psychotic from neurotic MMPI profiles. *Journal of Consulting Psychology, 24*(5), 375–387. https://doi.org/10.1037/h0042233

Meehl, P. E., & Hathaway, S. R. (1946). The K factor as a suppressor variable in the Minnesota Multiphasic Personality Inventory. *Journal of Applied Psychology, 30*(5), 525–564. https://doi.org/10.1037/h0053634

Megargee, E. I. (1994). Using the Megargee MMPI-based classification system with MMPI-2s of male prison inmates. *Psychological Assessment, 6*(4), 337–344. https://doi.org/10.1037/1040-3590.6.4.337

Megargee, E. I. (2006). *Using the MMPI-2 in criminal justice and correctional settings*. University of Minnesota Press.

Megargee, E. I., Bohn, M. J., Meyer, J. E., Jr., & Sink, F. (1979). *Classifying criminal offenders: A new system based on the MMPI*. Sage.

Megargee, E. I., & Carbonell, J. L. (1995). Use of the MMPI-2 in correctional settings. In Y. S. Ben-Porath, J. R. Graham, G. C. N. Hall, R. D. Hirshman, & M. S. Zaragoza (Eds.), *Forensic applications of the MMPI-2* (pp. 127–159). Sage. https://doi.org/10.4135/9781452243771.n6

Megargee, E. I., Cook, P. E., & Mendelsohn, G. A. (1967). The development and validation of an MMPI scale of assaultiveness in overcontrolled individuals. *Journal of Abnormal Psychology, 72*(6), 519–528. https://doi.org/10.1037/h0025242

Meloy, J. R., & Gacono, C. (1995). Assessing the psychopathic personality. In J. Butcher (Ed.), *Clinical personality assessment: Practical approaches* (pp. 410–422). Oxford University Press.

Melton, G. B., Petrila, J., Poythress, N. G., Slobogin, C., Otto, R. K., Mossman, D., & Condie, L. O. (2018). *Psychological evaluations for the courts: A handbook for mental health professionals and lawyers* (4th ed.). Guilford Press.

Merritt, R. D., Balogh, D. W., & Kok, C. J. (1998). DSM-IV Cluster A personality disorder diagnosis among young adults with a 2–7–8 MMPI profile. *Assessment, 5*(3), 273–285. https://doi.org/10.1177/107319119800500307

Messick, S., & Jackson, D. N. (1961). Acquiescence and the factorial interpretation of the MMPI. *Psychological Bulletin, 58*(4), 299–304. https://doi.org/10.1037/h0043979

Michael, K. D., Furr, R. M., Masters, K. S., Collett, B. R., Spielmans, G. I., Ritter, K., Veeder, M. A., Treiber, K., & Cullum, J. L. (2009). Using the MMPI-2 to predict symptom reduction during psychotherapy in a sample of community outpatients. *Journal of Contemporary Psychotherapy, 39*(3), 157–163. https://doi.org/10.1007/s10879-008-9109-x

Mihura, J. L., Roy, M., & Graceffo, R. A. (2017). Psychological assessment training in clinical psychology doctoral programs. *Journal of Personality Assessment, 99*(2), 153–164. https://doi.org/10.1080/00223891.2016.1201978

Miller, C. S., Shields, A. L., Campfield, D., Wallace, K. A., & Weiss, R. D. (2007). Substance use scales of the Minnesota Multiphasic Personality Inventory: An exploration of score reliability via meta-analysis. *Educational and Psychological Measurement, 67*(6), 1052–1065. https://doi.org/10.1177/0013164406299130

Miller, H. A. (2004). Examining the use of the M-FAST with criminal defendants incompetent to stand trial. *International Journal of Offender Therapy and Comparative Criminology, 48*(3), 268–280. https://doi.org/10.1177/0306624X03259167

Miller, M. W., Kaloupek, D. G., Dillon, A. L., & Keane, T. M. (2004). Externalizing and internalizing subtypes of combat-related PTSD: A replication and extension using the PSY-5 Scales. *Journal of Abnormal Psychology, 113*(4), 635–645. https://doi.org/10.1037/0021-843X.113.4.636

Miller, S. N., Bozzay, M. L., Ben-Porath, Y. S., & Arbisi, P. A. (2019). Distinguishing levels of suicide risk in depressed male veterans: The role of internalizing and externalizing psychopathology as measured by the MMPI-2-RF. *Assessment, 26*(1), 85–98. https://doi.org/10.1177/1073191117743787

Monnot, M. J., Quirk, S. W., Hoerger, M., & Brewer, L. (2009). Racial bias in personality assessment: Using the MMPI-2 to predict psychiatric diagnoses of African American and Caucasian chemical dependency inpatients. *Psychological Assessment, 21*(2), 137–151. https://doi.org/10.1037/a0015316

Morey, L. C. (2007). *Personality Assessment Inventory–Adolescent (PAI-A) professional manual.* Psychological Assessment Resources.

Moultrie, J. K., & Engel, R. R. (2017). Empirical correlates for the Minnesota Multiphasic Personality Inventory-2-Restructured Form in a German inpatient sample. *Psychological Assessment, 29*(10), 1273–1289. https://dx.doi.org/10.1037/pas0000415

Muller, B. P., & Bruno, L. N. (1988, March). *The MMPI and the Inwald Personality Inventory in the psychological screening of police candidates* [Paper presentation]. 23rd

Annual Symposium on Recent Developments in the Use of the MMPI, St. Petersburg, FL.

Munley, P. H., Germain, J. M., Tovar-Murray, D., & Borgman, A. L. (2004). MMPI-2 code types and measurement error. *Journal of Personality Assessment, 82*(2), 179-188. https://doi.org/10.1207/s15327752jpa8202_6

Neal, B. (1986). The K scale (MMPI) and job performance. In J. Reese & H. Goldstein (Eds.), *Psychological services for law enforcement* (pp. 83–90). United States Government Printing Office.

Neal, L. A., Busuttil, W., Rollins, J., Herepath, R., Strike, P., & Turnbull, G. (1994). Convergent validity of measures of post-traumatic stress disorder in a mixed military and civilian population. *Journal of Traumatic Stress, 7*(3), 447–455. https://doi.org/10.1007/bf02102789

Neal, L. A., Hill, N., Hughes, J., Middleton, A., & Busuttil, W. (1995). Convergent validity of measures of PTSD in an elderly population of former prisoners of war. *International Journal of Geriatric Psychiatry, 10*(7), 617–622. https://doi.org/10.1002/gps.930100713

Neal, T. M. S., & Grisso, T. (2014). Assessment practices and expert judgment methods in forensic psychology and psychiatry: An international snapshot. *Criminal Justice and Behavior, 41*(12), 1406-1421. https://doi.org/10.1177/0093854814548449

Negy, C., Leal-Puente, L., Trainor, D. J., & Carlson, R. (1997). Mexican American adolescents' performance on the MMPI-A. *Journal of Personality Assessment, 69*(1), 205–214. https://doi.org/10.1207/s15327752jpa6901_12

Nelson, L. D., Elder, J. T., Groot, J., Tehrani, P., & Grant, A. C. (2004). Personality testing and epilepsy: Comparison of two MMPI-2 correction procedures. *Epilepsy & Behavior, 5*(6), 911–918. https://doi.org/10.1016/j.yebeh.2004.08.006

Nelson, L. D., & Marks, P. A. (1985). Empirical correlates of infrequently occurring MMPI code types. *Journal of Clinical Psychology, 41*(4), 477–482. https://doi.org/10.1002/1097-4679(198507)41:4<477::AID-JCLP2270410406>3.0.CO;2-T

Nelson, N. W., Hoelzle, J. B., Sweet, J. J., Arbisi, P. A., & Demakis, G. J. (2010). Updated meta-analysis of the MMPI-2 Symptom Validity Scale (FBS): Verified utility in forensic practice. *The Clinical Neuropsychologist, 24*(4), 701–724. https://doi.org/10.1080/13854040903482863

Nelson, N. W., Sweet, J. J., & Demakis, G. J. (2006). Meta-analysis of the MMPI-2 Fake Bad Scale: Utility in forensic practice. *The Clinical Neuropsychologist, 20*(1), 39–58. https://doi.org/10.1080/13854040500459322

Nelson, N. W., Sweet, J. J., & Heilbronner, R. L. (2007). Examination of the new MMPI-2 Response Bias Scale (Gervais): Relationship with MMPI-2 validity scales. *Journal of Clinical and Experimental Neuropsychology, 29*(1), 67–72. https://doi.org/10.1080/13803390500488546

Newman, M. L., & Greenway, P. (1997). Therapeutic effects of providing MMPI-2 test feedback to clients at a university counseling service: A collaborative approach. *Psychological Assessment, 9*(2), 122–131. https://doi.org/10.1037/1040-3590.9.2.122

Newsom, C. R., Archer, R. P., Trumbetta, S., & Gottesman, I. I. (2003). Changes in adolescent response patterns on the MMPI/MMPI-A across four decades. *Journal of Personality Assessment, 81*(1), 74–84. https://doi.org/10.1207/S15327752JPA8101_07

Nichols, D. S. (1992). Minnesota Multiphasic Personality Inventory-2. In J. J. Kramer & J. C. Conoley (Eds.), *Eleventh mental measurements yearbook* (pp. 562–565). Buros Institute of Mental Measurements.

Nichols, D. S. (2006). The trials of separating bath water from baby: A review and critique of the MMPI-2 Restructured Clinical scales. *Journal of Personality Assessment, 87*(2), 121–138. https://doi.org/10.1207/s15327752jpa8702_02

Nichols, D. S., Greene, R. L., & Schmolck, P. (1989). Criteria for assessing inconsistent patterns of item endorsement on the MMPI: Rationale, development, and empirical trials. *Journal of Clinical Psychology, 45*(2), 239–250. https://doi.org/10.1002/1097-4679(198903)45:2<239::AID-JCLP2270450210>3.0.CO;2-1

Nichols, D. S., Greene, R. L., Williams, C. L. (2009). *Gender bias in the MMPI-2 Fake Bad Scale (FBS) and FBS-r in MMPI-2-RF* [Paper presentation]. Society of Personality Assessment Chicago, Chicago, IL.

Nijdam-Jones, A., Chen, Y., & Rosenfeld, B. (2020). Detection of feigned posttraumatic stress disorder: A meta-analysis of the Minnesota Multiphasic Personality Inventory-2 (MMPI-2). *Psychological Trauma: Theory, Research, Practice, and Policy, 12*(7), 790–798. https://doi.org/10.1037/tra0000593

Noblitt, J. R. (1995). Psychometric measures of trauma among psychiatric patients reporting ritual abuse. *Psychological Reports, 77*(3), 743–747. https://doi.org/10.2466/pr0.1995.77.3.743

Nockleby, D. M., & Deaton, A. V. (1987). Denial versus distress: Coping patterns in post head trauma patients. *The International Journal of Clinical Neuropsychology, 10*(4), 145–148.

Nussbaum, D., Choudhry, R., & Martin-Doto, C. (1996). Cognitive impulsivity, verbal intelligence and locus of control in violent and nonviolent mentally disordered offenders. *American Journal of Forensic Psychology, 14*, 5–30.

O'Laughlin, S., & Schill, T. (1994). The relationship between self-monitored aggression and the MMPI-2 F, 4, 9 composite and Anger Content scale scores. *Psychological Reports, 74*(3), 733–734. https://doi.org/10.2466/pr0.1994.74.3.733

O'Reilly, B. P., Graham, J. R., Hjemboe, S. M., & Butcher, J. N. (2003, June). *The construct validity of the MMPI-2 Marital Distress Scale* [Paper presentation]. 38th Annual Symposium on Recent Developments on the MMPI-2/MMPI-A, Minneapolis, MN.

Ogloff, J. R. P. (1995). The legal basis of forensic applications of the MMPI-2. In Y. S. Ben-Porath, J. R. Graham, G. C. N. Hall, R. D. Hirschman, & M. S. Zaragoza (Eds.), *Forensic applications of the MMPI-2* (pp. 18–47). Sage. https://doi.org/10.4135/9781452243771.n2

Ogloff, J. R. P., & Douglas, K. S. (2003). Psychological assessment in forensic settings. In J. Graham & J. Naglieri (Eds.), *Handbook of psychology: Assessment psychology, Vol. 10* (pp. 345–363). John Wiley. https://doi.org/10.1002/0471264385.wei1015

Okazaki, S., & Sue, S. (1995). Cultural considerations in psychological assessment of Asian-Americans. In J. N. Butcher (Ed.), *Clinical personality assessment: Practical approaches* (pp. 107–119). Oxford University Press.

Olsen, A. M., & Veltri, C. O. C. (2019). The moderating influence of disorder on coached overreporting using the MMPI-2-RF. *Journal of Personality Assessment, 101*(3), 264–273. https://doi.org/10.1080/00223891.2018.1472099

Osberg, T. M., Haseley, E. N., & Kamas, M. M. (2008). The MMPI-2 Clinical scales and Restructured Clinical (RC) scales: Comparative psychometric properties and relative diagnostic efficiency in young adults. *Journal of Personality Assessment*, *90*(1), 81–92. https://doi.org/10.1080/00223890701693801

Osberg, T. M., & Poland, D. L. (2001). Validity of the MMPI-2 basic and Harris–Lingoes subscales in a forensic sample. *Journal of Clinical Psychology*, *57*(12), 1369–1380. https://doi.org/10.1002/jclp.1103

Osberg, T. M., & Poland, D. L. (2002). Comparative accuracy of the MMPI-2 and the MMPI-A in the diagnosis of psychopathology in 18-year-olds. *Psychological Assessment*, *14*(2), 164–169. https://doi.org/10.1037//1040-3590.14.2.164

Otto, R. K. (2002). Use of the MMPI-2 in forensic settings. *Journal of Forensic Psychology Practice*, *2*(3), 71–91. http://dx.doi.org/10.1300/J158v02n03_05

Otto, R. K., Buffington-Vollum, J. K., & Edens, J. R. (2003). Child custody evaluation. In A. M. Goldstein (Ed.), *Forensic psychology* (pp. 179–207). Wiley. https://doi.org/10.1002/0471264385.wei1111

Otto, R. K., & Collins, R. P. (1995). Use of the MMPI-2/MMPI-A in child custody evaluations. In Y. S. Ben-Porath, J. R. Graham, G. C. N. Hall, R. D. Hirshman, & M. S. Zaragoza (Eds.), *Forensic applications of the MMPI-2* (pp. 222–252). Sage. https://doi.org/10.4135/9781452243771.n10

Pace, T. M., Robbins, R. R., Choney, S. K., Hill, J. S., Lacey, K., & Blair, G. (2006). A cultural-contextual perspective on the validity of the MMPI-2 with American Indians. *Cultural Diversity and Ethnic Minority Psychology*, *12*(2), 320–333. https://doi.org/10.1037/1099-9809.12.2.320

Palav, A., Ortega, A., & McCaffrey, R. J. (2001). Incremental validity of the MMPI-2 Content scales: A preliminary study with brain-injured patients. *Journal of Head Trauma Rehabilitation*, *16*(3), 275–283. https://doi.org/10.1097/00001199-200106000-00006

Pallone, N. J. (1992). The MMPI in police officer selection: Legal constraints, case law, empirical data. *Journal of Offender Rehabilitation*, *17*(3–4), 171–188. https://doi.org/10.1300/J076v17n03_12

Pinsoneault, T. B. (2005). Detecting random, partially random, and nonrandom Minnesota Multiphasic Personality Inventory–Adolescent protocols. *Psychological Assessment*, *17*(4), 476–480. https://doi.org/10.1037/1040-3590.17.4.476

Panton, J. H. (1958). MMPI profile configurations among crime classification groups. *Journal of Clinical Psychology*, *14*(3), 305–308. https://doi.org/10.1002/1097-4679(195807)14:3<305::AID-JCLP2270140325>3.0.CO;2-9

Paolo, A. M., & Ryan, J. J. (1992). Detection of random response sets on the MMPI-2. *Psychotherapy in Private Practice*, *11*(4), 1–8.

Parker, C. A. (1961). The predictive use of the MMPI in a college counseling center. *Journal of Counseling Psychology*, *8*(2), 154–158. https://doi.org/10.1037/h0043614

Patel, K. D., & Suhr, J. A. (2020). The relationship of MMPI-2-RF scales to treatment engagement and alliance. *Journal of Personality Assessment*, *102*(5), 594–603. https://doi.org/10.1080/00223891.2019.1635488

Pena, L. M., Megargee, E. I., & Brody, E. (1996). MMPI-A patterns of male juvenile delinquents. *Psychological Assessment*, *8*(4), 388–397. https://doi.org/10.1037/1040-3590.8.4.388

Pepper, L. J., & Strong, P. N. (1958). *Judgmental subscales for the Mf scale of the MMPI.* Unpublished materials, Hawaii Department of Health, Honolulu, HI.

Persky, V. W., Kempthorne-Rawson, J., & Shekelle, R. B. (1987). Personality and risk of cancer: 20-year follow-up of the Western Electric Study. *Psychosomatic Medicine, 49*(5), 435–449. https://doi.org/10.1097/00006842-198709000-00001

Persons, R. W., & Marks, P. A. (1971). The violent 4–3 MMPI personality type. *Journal of Consulting and Clinical Psychology, 36*(2), 189–196. https://doi.org/10.1037/h0030742

Peterson, C. D., & Dahlstrom, W. G. (1992). The derivation of gender-role scales GM and GF for MMPI-2 and their relationship to scale 5 (Mf). *Journal of Personality Assessment, 59*(3), 486–499. https://doi.org/10.1207/s15327752jpa5903_5

Petroskey, L. J., Ben-Porath, Y. S., & Stafford, K. P. (2003). Correlates of the Minnesota Multiphasic Personality Inventory-2 (MMPI-2) Personality Psychopathology-Five (PSY-5) scales in a forensic assessment setting. *Assessment, 10*(4), 393–399. https://doi.org/10.1177/1073191103259006

Pinsoneault, T. B. (2007). Detecting random, partially random, and nonrandom Minnesota Multiphasic Personality Inventory-2 protocols. *Psychological Assessment, 19*(1), 159–164. https://doi.org/10.1037/1040-3590.19.1.159

Piotrowski, C. (1998). Assessment of pain: A survey of practicing clinicians. *Perceptual and Motor Skills, 86*(1), 181–182. https://doi.org/10.2466/pms.1998.86.1.181

Piotrowski, C., & Belter, R. W. (1999). Internship training in psychological assessment: Has managed care had an impact? *Assessment, 6*(4), 381–389. https://doi.org/10.1177/107319119900600408

Piotrowski, C., & Lubin, B. (1990). Assessment practices of health psychologists: Survey of APA Division 38 practitioners. *Professional Psychology: Research and Practice, 21*(2), 99–106. https://doi.org/10.1037/0735-7028.21.2.99

Pogge, D. L., Stokes, J. M., McGrath, R. E., Bilginer, L., & De Luca, V. A. (2002). MMPI-A Structural Summary variables: Prevalence and correlates in an adolescent outpatient psychiatric sample. *Assessment, 9*(4), 334–342. https://doi.org/10.1177/1073191102238152

Pope, K. S. (1992). Responsibilities in providing psychological test feedback to clients. *Psychological Assessment, 4*(3), 268–271. https://doi.org/10.1037/1040-3590.4.3.268

Pope, K. S., Butcher, J. N., & Seelen, J. (2000). *The MMPI, MMPI-2, & MMPI-A in court: A practical guide for expert witnesses and attorneys, second edition.* American Psychological Association. https://psycnet.apa.org/doi/10.1037/10331-000

Pope, K. S., Butcher, J. N., & Seelen, J. (2006). *The MMPI, MMPI-2, and MMPI-A in court: A practical guide for expert witnesses and attorneys* (3rd ed.). American Psychological Association. https://doi.org/10.1037/11437-000

Pope, M. K., Smith, T. W., & Rhodewalt, F. (1990). Cognitive, behavioral, and affective correlates of the Cook and Medley Hostility scale. *Journal of Personality Assessment, 54*(3–4), 501–514. https://doi.org/10.1080/00223891.1990.9674015

Poston, J. M., & Hanson, W. E. (2010). Meta-analysis of psychological assessment as a therapeutic intervention. *Psychological Assessment, 22*(2), 203–212. https://doi.org/10.1037/a0018679

Priest, W., & Meunier, G. F. (1993). MMPI-2 performance of elderly women. *Clinical Gerontologist, 14*(2), 3–11. https://doi.org/10.1300/J018v14n02_02

Pritchard, D. A., & Rosenblatt, A. (1980). Racial bias in the MMPI: A methodological review. *Journal of Consulting and Clinical Psychology, 48*(2), 263–267. https://doi .org/10.1037/0022-006X.48.2.263

Raley, R. K., & Bumpass, L. (2003). The topography of the divorce plateau: Levels and trends in union stability in the United States after 1980. *Demographic Research, 8,* 245–260, Article 8. https://doi.org/10.4054/DemRes.2003.8.8

Reed, M. K., Walker, B., Williams, G., McLeod, S., & Jones, S. (1996). MMPI-2 patterns in African-American females. *Journal of Clinical Psychology, 52*(4), 437–441. https:// doi.org/10.1002/(SICI)1097-4679(199607)52:4<437::AID-JCLP8>3.0.CO;2-M

Reese, P. M., Webb, J. T., & Foulks, J. D. (1968). A comparison of oral and booklet forms of the MMPI for psychiatric inpatients. *Journal of Clinical Psychology, 24*(4), 436–437. https:// doi.org/10.1002/1097-4679(196810)24:4<436::AID-JCLP2270240414>3.0.CO;2-Y

Reynolds, C. R., & Kamphaus, R. W. (2002). *The clinician's guide to the Behavior Assessment System for Children (BASC).* Guilford Press.

Rice, K. G., & Stuart, J. (2010). Differentiating adaptive and maladaptive perfectionism on the MMPI–2 and MIPS Revised. *Journal of Personality Assessment, 92*(2), 158–167. https://doi.org/10.1080/00223890903510407

Ricketts, A. J. (2003). *Validity of MMPI-2 Content scales and Content Component scales in a forensic diagnostic sample* [Unpublished doctoral dissertation]. Kent State University.

Ridenour, T. A., Miller, A. R., Joy, K. L., & Dean, R. S. (1997). "Profile" analysis of the personality characteristics of child molesters using the MMPI-2. *Journal of Clinical Psychology, 53*(6), 575–586. https://doi.org/10.1002/ (SICI)1097-4679(199710)53:6<575::AID-JCLP6>3.0.CO;2-J

Riley, J. L., III, & Robinson, M. E. (1998). Validity of MMPI-2 profiles in chronic back pain patients: Differences in path models of coping and somatization. *The Clinical Journal of Pain, 14*(4), 324–335. https://doi.org/10.1097/00002508-199812000-00010

Rinaldo, J. C. B., & Baer, R. A. (2003). Incremental validity of the MMPI-A Content scales in the prediction of self-reported symptoms. *Journal of Personality Assessment, 80*(3), 309–318. https://doi.org/10.1207/S15327752JPA8003_08

Robers, H. P. H. (1992). Ethnicity and the MMPI-2: Cultural implications and limitations for Chinese Americans. *Dissertation Abstracts International, 52,* 2311B.

Robin, R. W., Greene, R. L., Albaugh, B., Caldwell, A., & Goldman, D. (2003). Use of the MMPI-2 in American Indians: I. Comparability of the MMPI-2 between two tribes and with the MMPI-2 normative group. *Psychological Assessment, 15*(3), 351–359. https://doi.org/10.1037/1040-3590.15.3.351

Rogers, R. (1992). *Structured Interview of Reported Symptoms.* Psychological Assessment Resources. https://doi.org/10.1002/9780470479216.corpsy0957

Rogers, R., Bagby, R. M., & Chakraborty, D. (1993). Feigning schizophrenic disorders on the MMPI-2: Detection of coached simulators. *Journal of Personality Assessment, 60*(2), 215–226. https://doi.org/10.1207/s15327752jpa6002_1

Rogers, R., Gillis, J. R., McMain, S., & Dickens, S. E. (1988). Fitness evaluations: A retrospective study of clinical, criminal, and sociodemographic characteristics. *Canadian Journal of Behavioral Science, 20*(2), 192–200. https://doi.org/10.1037/h0079925

Rogers, R., Hinds, J. D., & Sewell, K. W. (1996). Feigning psychopathology among adolescent offenders: Validation of the SIRS, MMPI-A, and SIMS. *Journal of Personality Assessment, 67*(2), 244–257. https://doi.org/10.1207/s15327752jpa6702_2

Rogers, R., & McKee, G. R. (1995). Use of the MMPI-2 in the assessment of criminal responsibility. In Y. S. Ben-Porath, J. R. Graham, G. C. N. Hall, R. D. Hirshman, & M. S. Zaragoza (Eds.), *Forensic applications of the MMPI-2* (pp. 103–126). Sage.

Rogers, R., Sewell, K. W., Harrison, K. S., & Jordan, M. J. (2006). The MMPI-2 Restructured Clinical scales: A paradigmatic shift in scale development. *Journal of Personality Assessment, 87*(2), 139–147. https://doi.org/10.1207/s15327752jpa8702_03

Rogers, R., Sewell, K. W., Martin, M. A., & Vitacco, M. J. (2003). Detection of feigned mental disorders: A meta-analysis of the MMPI-2 and malingering. *Assessment, 10*(2), 160–177. https://doi.org/10.1177/1073191103010002007

Rogers, R., Sewell, K. W., & Ustad, K. L. (1995). Feigning among chronic outpatients on the MMPI-2: A systematic examination of fake-bad indicators. *Assessment, 2*(1), 81–89. https://doi.org/10.1177/1073191195002001008

Rohan, W. P. (1972). MMPI changes in hospitalized alcoholics: A second study. *Quarterly Journal of Studies on Alcohol, 33*(1), 65–76. https://doi.org/10.15288/qjsa.1972.33.065

Romero, I. E., Toorabally, N., Burchett, D., Tarescavage, A. M., & Glassmire, D. M. (2017). Mapping the MMPI-2-RF substantive scales onto internalizing, externalizing, and thought dysfunction dimensions in a forensic inpatient setting. *Journal of Personality Assessment, 99*(4), 351–362. https://doi.org/10.1080/00223891.2016.1223681

Rosch, D. S., Crowther, J. H., & Graham, J. R. (1991). MMPI derived personality description and personality subtypes in an undergraduate bulimic population. *Psychology of Addictive Behaviors, 5*(1), 15–22. https://doi.org/10.1037/h0080584

Rosen, G. M., Baldwin, S. A., & Smith, R. E. (2016). Reassessing the "traditional background hypothesis" for elevated MMPI and MMPI-2 Lie-scale scores. *Psychological Assessment, 28*(10), 1336–1343. https://doi.org/10.1037/pas0000262

Rouse, S. V., Butcher, J. N., & Miller, K. B. (1999). Assessment of substance abuse in psychotherapy clients: The effectiveness of the MMPI-2 substance abuse scales. *Psychological Assessment, 11*(1), 101–107. https://doi.org/10.1037/1040-3590.11.1.101

Ryan, J. J., Dunn, G. E., & Paolo, A. M. (1995). Temporal stability of the MMPI-2 in a substance abuse sample. *Psychotherapy in Private Practice, 14*(3), 33–41.

Sánchez, G., Ampudia, A., Jiménez, F., & Amado, B. G. (2017). Contrasting the efficacy of the MMPI-2-RF overreporting scales in the detection of malingering. *The European Journal of Psychology Applied to Legal Context, 9*(2), 51–56. http://dx.doi.org/10.1016/j.ejpal.2017.03.002

Sawrie, S. M., Kabat, M. H., Dietz, C. B., Greene, R. L., Arredondo, R., & Mann, A. W. (1996). Internal structure of the MMPI-2 Addiction Potential Scale in alcoholic and psychiatric inpatients. *Journal of Personality Assessment, 66*(1), 177–193. https://doi.org/10.1207/s15327752jpa6601_14

Schill, T., & Wang, S. (1990). Correlates of the MMPI-2 Anger Content scale. *Psychological Reports, 67,* 800–802.

Schinka, J. A., Elkins, D. E., & Archer, R. P. (1998). Effects of psychopathology and demographic characteristics on MMPI-A scale scores. *Journal of Personality Assessment, 71*(3), 295–305. https://doi.org/10.1207/s15327752jpa7103_1

Schinka, J. A., & LaLone, L. (1997). MMPI-2: Comparisons with a census-matched subsample. *Psychological Assessment, 9*(3), 307–311. https://doi.org/10.1037/1040-3590.9.3.307

Schuder, K. M., Gooding, D. C., Matts, C. W., & Bolinskey, P. K. (2016, May). Further evidence of the MMPI-2-RF's ability to discriminate psychometrically identified schizotypic college students from a matched comparison sample. *Personality and Individual Differences, 94,* 107–112. https://doi.org/10.1016/j.paid.2016.01.014

Schuldberg, D. (1992). Ego Strength revised: A comparison of the MMPI-2 and MMPI-1 versions of the Barron Ego Strength scale. *Journal of Clinical Psychology, 48*(4), 500–505. https://doi.org/10.1002/1097-4679(199207)48:4<500::AID-JCLP2270480410>3.0.CO;2-T

Schwartz, M. F., & Graham, J. R. (1979). Construct validity of the MacAndrew Alcoholism scale. *Journal of Consulting and Clinical Psychology, 47*(6), 1090–1095. https://doi.org/10.1037/0022-006X.47.6.1090

Sellbom, M. (2016). Elucidating the validity of the externalizing spectrum of psychopathology in correctional, forensic, and community samples. *Journal of Abnormal Psychology, 125*(8), 1027–1038. https://doi.org/10.1037/abn0000171

Sellbom, M. (2017). Mapping the MMPI-2-RF Specific Problems scales onto extant psychopathology structures. *Journal of Personality Assessment, 99*(4), 341–350. https://doi.org/10.1080/00223891.2016.1206909

Sellbom, M. (2019, May). The MMPI-2-Restructured Form (MMPI-2-RF): Assessment of personality and psychopathology in the twenty-first century. *Annual Review of Clinical Psychology, 15,* 149–177. https://doi.org/10.1146/annurev-clinpsy-050718-095701

Sellbom, M. (2020). Appendix B: Organization of the MMPI-3 externalizing and interpersonal scales: Assessment of disinhibited and antagonistic externalizing psychopathology. In Y. S. Ben-Porath & A. Tellegen, *Minnesota Multiphasic Personality Inventory–3 (MMPI-3): Technical manual* (pp. 111–117). University of Minnesota Press.

Sellbom, M. (2021). Examining the criterion and incremental validity of the MMPI-3 Self-Importance scale. *Psychological Assessment, 33*(4), 363–368. https://doi.org/10.1037/pas0000975

Sellbom, M., Anderson, J. L., & Bagby, R. M. (2013). Assessing DSM-5 Section III personality traits and disorders with the MMPI-2-RF. *Assessment, 20*(6), 709–722. https://doi.org/10.1177/1073191113508808

Sellbom, M., Bagby, R. M. (2008). Validity of the MMPI-2-RF (Restructured Form) L-r and K-r scales in detecting underreporting in clinical and nonclinical samples. *Psychological Assessment, 20*(4), 370–376. https://doi.apa.org/doi/10.1037/a0012952

Sellbom, M., Bagby, R. M. (2010). The detection of overreported psychopathology with the MMPI-2-RF Validity Scales. *Psychological Assessment, 22*(4), 757–767. https://doi.org/10.1037/a0020825

Sellbom, M., Bagby, R. M., Kushner, S., Quilty, L. C., & Ayearst, L. E. (2012). Diagnostic construct validity of MMPI-2 Restructured Form (MMPI-2-RF) scale scores. *Assessment, 19*(2), 176-186. https://doi.org/10.1177/1073191111428763

Sellbom, M., & Ben-Porath, Y. S. (2005). Mapping the MMPI-2 Restructured Clinical (RC) Scales onto normal personality traits: Evidence of construct validity. *Journal of Personality Assessment, 85*(2), 179–187. https://doi.org/10.1207/s15327752jpa8502_10

Sellbom, M., & Ben-Porath, Y. S. (2006). Forensic applications of the MMPI. In R. P. Archer (Ed.), *Forensic uses of clinical assessment instruments* (pp. 19–55). Lawrence Erlbaum Associates.

Sellbom, M., Ben-Porath, Y. S., & Bagby, R. M. (2008a). On the hierarchical structure of mood and anxiety disorders: Confirmatory evidence and elaboration of a model of temperament markers. *Journal of Abnormal Psychology, 117*(3), 576–590. https://doi.org/10.1037/a0012536

Sellbom, M., Ben-Porath, Y. S., & Bagby, R. M. (2008b). Personality and psychopathology: Mapping the MMPI-2 Restructured Clinical (RC) Scales onto the five factor model of personality. *Journal of Personality Disorders, 22*(3), 291-312. https://doi.org/10.1521/pedi.2008.22.3.291

Sellbom, M., Ben-Porath, Y. S., & Graham, J. R. (2006). Correlates of the MMPI-2 Restructured Clinical (RC) Scales in a college counseling setting. *Journal of Personality Assessment, 86*(1), 89–99. https://doi.org/10.1207/s15327752jpa8601_10

Sellbom, M., Ben-Porath, Y. S., Graham, J. R., Arbisi, P. A., & Bagby, R. M. (2005). Susceptibility of the MMPI-2 Clinical, Restructured Clinical (RC), and Content scales to over- and under-reporting. *Assessment, 12*, 79–85. https://doi.org/10.1177/1073191104273515

Sellbom, M., Ben-Porath, Y. S., Lilienfeld, S. O., Patrick, C. J., & Graham, J. R. (2005). Assessing psychopathic personality traits with the MMPI-2. *Journal of Personality Assessment, 85*(3), 334–343. https://doi.org/10.1207/s15327752jpa8503_10

Sellbom, M., Ben-Porath, Y. S., McNulty, J. L., Arbisi, P. A., & Graham, J. R. (2006). Elevation differences between MMPI-2 Clinical and Restructured Clinical (RC) scales: Frequency, origins, and interpretative implications. *Assessment, 13*(4), 430–441. https://doi.org/10.1177/1073191106293349

Sellbom, M., Ben-Porath, Y. S., & Stafford, K. P. (2009, March). *Examining the hierarchical structure of the MMPI-2-RF externalizing scales: Evidence of construct validity* [Paper presentation]. Society for Personality Assessment Annual Meeting, Chicago, IL.

Sellbom, M., Fischler, G. L., & Ben-Porath, Y. S. (2007). Identifying MMPI-2 predictors of police officer integrity and misconduct. *Criminal Justice and Behavior, 34*(8), 985–1004. https://doi.org/10.1177/0093854807301224

Sellbom, M., Graham, J. R., & Schenk, P. W. (2005). Symptom correlates of MMPI-2 scales and code types in a private practice setting. *Journal of Personality Assessment, 84*(2), 163–171. https://doi.org/10.1207/s15327752jpa8402_06

Sellbom, M., Graham, J. R., & Schenk, P. W. (2006). Incremental validity of the MMPI-2 Restructured Clinical (RC) scales in a private practice sample. *Journal of Personality Assessment, 86*(2), 196–205. https://doi.org/10.1207/s15327752jpa8602_09

Sellbom, M., Lee, T. T. C., Ben-Porath, Y. S., Arbisi, P. A., & Gervais, R. O. (2012). Differentiating PTSD symptomatology with the MMPI-2-RF (Restructured Form) in a forensic disability sample. *Psychiatry Research, 197*(1–2), 172–179. https://doi.org/10.1016/j.psychres.2012.02.003

Sellbom, M., & Wygant, D. B. (2018). *Forensic applications of the MMPI-2-RF: A casebook*. University of Minnesota Press.

Shaevel, B., & Archer, R. P. (1996). Effects of MMPI–2 and MMPI–A norms on T-score elevations for 18-year-olds. *Journal of Personality Assessment, 67*(1), 72–78. https://doi.org/10.1207/s15327752jpa6701_5

Sharf, A. J., & Rogers, R. (2020). Validation of the MMPI-A-RF for youth with mental health needs: A systematic examination of clinical correlates and construct validity. *Journal of Psychopathology and Behavioral Assessment, 42*(3), 527–538. https://link.springer.com/article/10.1007/s10862-019-09754-x

Sharf, A. J., Rogers, R., Williams, M. M., & Henry, S. A. (2017). The effectiveness of the MMPI-2-RF in detecting feigned mental disorders and cognitive deficits: A meta-analysis. *Journal of Psychopathology and Behavioral Assessment, 39*(3), 441–455. https://doi.org/10.1007/s10862-017-9590-1

Sharpe, J. P., & Desai, S. (2001). The revised NEO Personality Inventory and the MMPI-2 Psychopathology Five in the prediction of aggression. *Personality and Individual Differences, 31*(4), 505–518. https://doi.org/10.1016/S0191-8869(00)00155-0

Shekelle, R. B., Gale, M., Ostfeld, A. M., & Paul, O. (1983). Hostility, risk of coronary heart disease, and mortality. *Psychosomatic Medicine, 45*(2), 109–114. https://doi.org/10.1097/00006842-198305000-00003

Sherriffs, A. C., & Boomer, D. S. (1954). Who is penalized by the penalty for guessing? *Journal of Educational Psychology, 45*(2), 81–90. https://doi.org/10.1037/h0053756

Sherwood, N. E., Ben-Porath, Y. S., & Williams, C. L. (1997). *The MMPI-A Content Component scales*. University of Minnesota Press.

Shkalim, E. (2015). Psychometric Evaluation of the MMPI-2/MMPI-2-RF Restructured Clinical scales in an Israeli Sample. *Assessment, 22*(5), 607-618. https://doi.org/10.1177/1073191114555884

Shkalim, E., Almagor, M., & Ben-Porath, Y. S. (2017) Examining current conceptualizations of psychopathology with the MMPI–2/MMPI–2–RF Restructured Clinical scales: Preliminary findings from a cross-cultural study. *Journal of Personality Assessment, 99*(4), 375–383. https://doi.org/10.1080/00223891.2016.1189429

Shkalim, E., Ben-Porath, Y. S., & Almagor, M. (2016) Mapping the MMPI–2/MMPI–2–RF Restructured Clinical scales onto mood markers in an Israeli sample. *Journal of Personality Assessment, 98*(4), 430–434. https://doi.org/10.1080/00223891.2016.1146291

Shondrick, D. D., Ben-Porath, Y. S., & Stafford, K. P. (1992, May). *Forensic applications of the MMPI-2* [Paper presentation]. 27th Annual Symposium on Recent Developments in the Use of the MMPI (MMPI-2 and MMPI-A), Minneapolis, MN.

Sieber, K. O., & Meyers, L. S. (1992). Validation of the MMPI-2 Social Introversion subscales. *Psychological Assessment, 4*(2), 185–189. https://doi.org/10.1037/1040-3590.4.2.185

Siegel, J. C. (1996). Traditional MMPI-2 validity indicators and initial presentation in custody evaluations. *American Journal of Forensic Psychology, 14*(3), 55–63.

Simms, L. J., Casillas, A., Clark, L. A., Watson, D., & Doebbeling, B. N. (2005). Psychometric evaluation of the Restructured Clinical scales of the MMPI-2. *Psychological Assessment, 17*(3), 345–358. https://doi.org/10.1037/1040-3590.17.3.345

Sines, L. K. (1959). The relative contribution of four kinds of data to accuracy in personality assessment. *Journal of Consulting Psychology, 23*(6), 483–492. https://doi.org/10.1037/h0046083

Sinnett, E. R., Holen, M. C., & Albott, W. L. (1995). MMPI scores of female victims. *Psychological Reports, 76*(1), 139–144. https://doi.org/10.2466/pr0.1995.76.1.139

Sivec, H. J., Hilsenroth, M. J., & Lynn, S. J. (1995). Impact of simulating borderline personality disorder on the MMPI-2: A costs-benefits model employing base rates. *Journal of Personality Assessment, 64*(2), 295–311. https://doi.org/10.1207/s15327752jpa6402_9

Sivec, H. J., Lynn, S. J., & Garske, J. P. (1994). The effect of somatoform disorder and paranoid psychotic role-related dissimulations as a response set on the MMPI-2. *Assessment, 1*(1), 69–81. https://doi.org/10.1177/1073191194001001010

Slesinger, D., Archer, R. P., & Duane, W. (2002). MMPI-2 characteristics in a chronic pain population. *Assessment, 9*(4), 406–414. https://doi.org/10.1177/1073191102238153

Slick, D. J., Sherman, E. M. S., & Iverson, G. L. (1999). Diagnostic criteria for malingered neurocognitive dysfunction: Proposed standards for clinical practice and research. *The Clinical Neuropsychologist, 13*(4), 545-561. https://doi.org/10.1076/1385-4046(199911)13:04;1-Y;FT545

Sloan, P., Arsenault, L., Hilsenroth, M., & Harvill, L. (1996). Assessment of noncombat, war-related posttraumatic stress symptomatology: Validity of the PK, PS, and IES scales. *Psychological Assessment, 3*(1), 37–41. https://doi.org/10.1177/107319119600300104

Smith, S. R., Gorske, T. T., Wiggins, C., & Little, J. A. (2010). Personality assessment use by clinical neuropsychologists. *International Journal of Testing, 10*(1), 6–20. https://doi.org/10.1080/15305050903534787

Smith, S. R., Hilsenroth, M. J., Castlebury, F. D., & Durham, T. W. (1999). The clinical utility of the MMPI-2 Antisocial Practices Content scale. *Journal of Personality Disorders, 13*(4), 385–393. https://doi.org/10.1521/pedi.1999.13.4.385

Smith, T. W., & Frohm, K. D. (1985). What's so unhealthy about hostility? Construct validity and psychosocial correlates of the Cook and Medley Ho scale. *Health Psychology, 4*(6), 503–520. https://doi.org/10.1037//0278-6133.4.6.503

Smith, T. W., Saunders, J. D., & Alexander, J. F. (1990). What does the Cook and Medley Hostility scale measure? Affect, behavior, and attributions in the marital context. *Journal of Personality and Social Psychology, 58*(4), 699–708. https://doi.org/10.1037/0022-3514.58.4.699

Spanier, G. B. (1976). Measuring dyadic adjustment: New scales for assessing the quality of marriage and similar dyads. *Journal of Marriage and the Family, 38*(1), 15–28. https://doi.org/10.2307/350547

Spengler, P. M., Walters, N. T., Bryan, E., & Millspaugh, B. S. (2020). Attorneys' attitudes toward coaching forensic clients on the MMPI–2: Replication and extension of attorney survey by Wetter and Corrigan (1995). *Journal of Personality Assessment, 102*(1), 56-65. https://doi.org/10.1080/00223891.2018.1501568

Spiro, A., Butcher, J. N., Levenson, M. R., Aldwin, C. M., & Bose, R. (2000). Change and stability in personality: A five-year study of the MMPI-2 in older men. In J. N. Butcher (Ed.), *Basic sources on the MMPI-2* (pp. 443–462). University of Minnesota Press.

Stanley, I. H., Yancey, J. R., Patrick, C. J., & Joiner, T. E. (2018). A distinct configuration of MMPI-2-RF scales RCd and RC9/ACT is associated with suicide attempt risk among suicide ideators in a psychiatric outpatient sample. *Psychological Assessment, 30*(9), 1249–1254.

Stokes, J. M., Pogge, D. L., & Archer, R. P. (2018). Comparisons between the Minnesota Multiphasic Personality Inventory-Adolescent-Restructured Form (MMPI-A RF) and MMPI-A in adolescent psychiatric inpatients. *Psychological Assessment, 30*(3), 370–382. https://doi.org/10.1037/pas0000488

Stokes, J. M., Sapoff, M., Pogge, D. L., Zaccario, M., & Barbot, B. (2019, April). A dimensional understanding of borderline personality features in adolescence: The relationship between the MMPI-A PSY-5 scales and PAI-A borderline features. *Personality and Individual Differences, 140*, 27–32. https://doi.org/10.1016/j.paid.2018.04.025

Steffan, J. S., Morgan, R. D., Lee, J., & Sellbom, M. (2010). A comparative analysis of MMPI-2 malingering detection models among inmates. *Assessment, 17*(2), 185–196. https://doi.org/10.1177/1073191109359382

Stein, L. A. R., & Graham, J. R. (1999). Detecting fake-good MMPI-A profiles in a correctional facility. *Psychological Assessment, 11*(3), 386–395. https://doi.org/10.1037/1040-3590.11.3.386

Stein, L. A. R., Graham, J. R., Ben-Porath, Y. S., & McNulty, J. L. (1999). Using the MMPI-2 to detect substance abuse in an outpatient mental health setting. *Psychological Assessment, 11*(1), 94–100. https://doi.org/10.1037/1040-3590.11.1.94

Stein, L. A. R., Graham, J. R., & Williams, C. L. (1995). Detecting fake-bad MMPI-A profiles. *Journal of Personality Assessment, 65*(3), 415–427. https://doi.org/10.1207/s15327752jpa6503_3

Stein, L. A. R., McClinton, B. K., & Graham, J. R. (1998). Long term stability of MMPI-A scales. *Journal of Personality Assessment, 70*(1), 103–108. https://doi.org/10.1207/s15327752jpa7001_7

Stevens, M. J., Kwan, K-L., & Graybill, D. F. (1993). Comparison of MMPI-2 scores of foreign Chinese and Caucasian-American students. *Journal of Clinical Psychology, 49*(1), 23–27. https://doi.org/10.1002/1097-4679(199301)49:1<23::AID-JCLP2270490104>3.0.CO;2-O

Storm, J., & Graham, J. R. (2000). Detection of coached general malingering on the MMPI-2. *Psychological Assessment, 12*(2), 158–165. https://doi.org/10.1037/1040-3590.12.2.158

Strassberg, D. S., Clutton, S., & Korboot, P. (1991, December). A descriptive and validity study of the Minnesota Multiphasic Personality Inventory-2 (MMPI-2) in elderly Australian sample. *Journal of Psychopathology and Behavioral Assessment, 13*, 301–311. https://doi.org/10.1007/BF00960443

Strassberg, D. S., & Russell, S. W. (2000, March). MMPI-2 content scale validity within a sample of chronic pain patients. *Journal for Psychopathology and Behavioral Assessment, 22*, 47–60. https://doi.org/10.1023/A:1007524531117

Strong, D. R., Greene, R. L., Hoppe, C., Johnston, T., & Olesen, N. (1999). Taxometric analysis of impression management and self-deception on the MMPI-2 in child-custody litigants. *Journal of Personality Assessment, 73*(1), 1–18. https://doi.org/10.1207/S15327752JPA730101

Suhr, J. A. (2015). *Psychological assessment: A problem-solving approach.* Guilford Press.

Svanum, S., & Ehrmann, L. C. (1993). Screening for maladjustment in college students: An application of receiver operating characteristic curve to MMPI scales. *Journal of Personality Assessment, 60*(2), 397–410. https://doi.org/10.1207/s15327752jpa6002_15

Svanum, S., McGrew, J., & Ehrmann, L. (1994). Validity of the substance abuse scales of the MMPI-2 in a college student sample. *Journal of Personality Assessment, 62*(3), 427–439. https://doi.org/10.1207/s15327752jpa6203_4

Swan, G. E., Carmelli, D., & Rosenman, R. H. (1991). Cook and Medley Hostility and the Type A behavior pattern: Psychological correlates of two coronary-prone behaviors. In M. H. Strube (Ed.), *Type A behavior* (pp. 89–106). Sage.

Taft, R. (1957). The validity of the Barron Ego Strength scale and the Welsh Anxiety Index. *Journal of Consulting Psychology, 21*(3), 247–249. https://doi.org/10.1037/h0048538

Tanner, B. A. (1990). Composite descriptions associated with rare MMPI two-point code types: Codes that involve scale 5. *Journal of Clinical Psychology, 46*(4), 425–431. https://doi.org/10.1002/1097-4679(199007)46:4<425::AID-JCLP2270460409>3.0.CO;2-3

Tarescavage, A. M. (2015). *Predicting treatment outcomes among low back pain patients using the Minnesota Multiphasic Personality Inventory-2-Restructured Form* [Unpublished doctoral dissertation]. Kent State University.

Tarescavage, A. M., Finn, J. A., Marek, R. J., Ben-Porath, Y. S., & van Dulmen, M. H. M. (2015, March 15). Premature termination from psychotherapy and internalizing psychopathology: The role of demoralization. *Journal of Affective Disorders, 174*, 549–555. https://doi.org/10.1016/j.jad.2014.12.018

Taulbee, E. S., & Sisson, B. D. (1957). Configural analysis of MMPI profiles of psychiatric groups. *Journal of Consulting Psychology, 21*(5), 413–417. https://doi.org/10.1037/h0044567

Tellegen, A. (1982). *Brief manual for the Differential Personality Questionnaire* [Unpublished manuscript]. University of Minnesota.

Tellegen, A., & Ben-Porath, Y. S. (1992). The new uniform T scores for the MMPI-2: Rationale, derivation, and appraisal. *Psychological Assessment, 4*(2), 145–155. https://doi.org/10.1037/1040-3590.4.2.145

Tellegen, A., & Ben-Porath, Y. S. (2011). *Minnesota Multiphasic Personality Inventory-2-Restructured Form (MMPI-2-RF): Technical manual.* University of Minnesota Press. Original work published in 2008.

Tellegen, A., Ben-Porath, Y. S., McNulty, J. L., Arbisi, P. A., Graham, J. R., & Kaemmer, B. (2003). *MMPI-2 Restructured Clinical (RC) scales: Development, validation, and interpretation.* University of Minnesota Press.

Tellegen, A., Ben-Porath, Y. S., & Sellbom, M. (2009). Construct validity of the MMPI-2 Restructured Clinical (RC) scales: Reply to Rouse, Greene, Butcher, Nichols, & Williams. *Journal of Personality Assessment, 91*(3), 211–221. https://doi.org/10.1080/00223890902794192

Tellegen, A., Ben-Porath, Y. S., Sellbom, M., Arbisi, P. A., McNulty, J. L., & Graham, J. R. (2006). Further evidence on the validity of the MMPI-2 Restructured Clinical (RC) scales: Addressing questions raised by Rogers, Sewell, Harrison, and Jordan and Nichols. *Journal of Personality Assessment, 87*(2), 148–171. https://doi.org/10.1207/s15327752jpa8702_04

Tellegen, A., Watson, D., & Clark, L. A. (1999a). On the dimensional and hierarchical structure of affect. *Psychological Science, 10*(4), 297–303. https://doi.org/10.1111/1467-9280.00157

Tellegen, A., Watson, D., & Clark, L. A. (1999b). Further support for a hierarchical model of affect: Reply to Green and Salovey. *Psychological Science, 10*(4), 307–309. https://doi.org/10.1111/1467-9280.00159

Terman, L. M., & Miles, C. C. (1936). *Sex and personality: Studies in masculinity and femininity.* McGraw-Hill.

Thomas, M. L., & Locke, D. E. (2010). Psychometric properties of the MMPI-2-RF Somatic Complaints (RC1) scale. *Psychological Assessment, 22*(3), 492–503. https://doi.org/10.1037/a0019229

Thornton, V. A., Dodd, C. G., & Weed, N. C. (2020). Assessment of prescription stimulant misuse among college students using the MMPI-2-RF *Addictive Behaviors, 110.* https://doi.org/10.1016/j.addbeh.2020.106511

Timbrook, R. E., & Graham, J. R. (1992). *The meaning of low scores on the MMPI-2 clinical and content scales in a psychiatric setting* [Unpublished manuscript]. Kent State University.

Timbrook, R. E., & Graham, J. R. (1994). Ethnic differences on the MMPI-2? *Psychological Assessment, 6*(3), 212–217. https://doi.org/10.1037/1040-3590.6.3.212

Tolin, D. F., Maltby, N., Weathers, F. W., Litz, B. T., Knight, J., & Keane, T. M. (2004). The use of the MMPI-2 Infrequency-Psychopathology scale in the assessment of posttraumatic stress disorder in male veterans. *Journal of Psychopathology and Behavioral Assessment, 26*(1), 23–29. https://doi.org/10.1023/B:JOBA.0000007453.24885.39

Tombaugh, T. N. (1997). The Test of Memory Malingering (TOMM): Normative data from cognitively intact and cognitively impaired individuals. *Psychological Assessment, 9*(3), 260–268. https://doi.org/10.1037/1040-3590.9.3.260

Tran, B. N. (1996). Vietnamese translation and adaptation of the MMPI-2. In J. N. Butcher (Ed.), *International adaptations of the MMPI-2: Research and clinical applications* (pp. 175–193). University of Minnesota Press.

Trull, T. J., Useda, J. D., Costa, P. T., & McCrae, R. R. (1995). Comparison of the MMPI-2 Personality Psychopathology Five (PSY-5), the NEO-PI, and the NEO-PI-R. *Psychological Assessment, 7*(4), 508–516. https://doi.org/10.1037/1040-3590.7.4.508

Tsai, D. C., & Pike, P. L. (2000). Effects of acculturation on the MMPI-2 scores of Asian American students. *Journal of Personality Assessment, 74*(2), 216–230. https://doi.org/10.1207/S15327752JPA7402_4

Tsushima, W. T., Bridenstine, M. P., & Balfour, J. F. (2004). MMPI-2 scores in the outcome prediction of gastric bypass surgery. *Obesity Surgery, 14*(4), 528–532. https://doi.org/10.1381/096089204323013550

Tylicki, J. L., Martin-Fernandez, K. W., & Ben-Porath, Y. S. (2019). Predicting therapist ratings of treatment progress and outcomes with the MMPI-2-RF. *Journal of Clinical Psychology, 75*(9), 1673–1683. https://doi.org/10.1002/jclp.22795

Tylicki, J. L., Gervais, R. O., & Ben-Porath, Y. S. (2020). Examination of the MMPI-3 over-reporting scales in a forensic disability sample. *The Clinical Neuropsychologist.* https://doi.org/10.1080/13854046.2020.1856414

Tylicki, J. L., Phillips, T. R., Ben-Porath, Y. S., & Sellbom, M. (2020). Construct validity of the Minnesota Multiphasic Personality Inventory-2-Resructured Form scale scores in correctional settings. *Personality and Mental Health, 14*(4), 319–335. https://doi.org/10.1002/pmh.1482

Uniform Marriage and Divorce Act, 9A Uniform Laws Annotated, Sec. 316 (1979).

Urmer, A. H., Black, H. O., & Wendland, L. V. (1960). A comparison of taped and booklet forms of the Minnesota Multiphasic Personality Inventory. *Journal of Clinical Psychology, 16*(1), 33–34. https://doi.org/10.1002/1097-4679(196001)16:1<33::aid-jclp2270160114>3.0.co;2-l

van der Heijden, P. T., Egger, J. I., Rossi, G. M., & Derksen, J. J. (2012). Integrating psychopathology and personality disorders conceptualized by the MMPI–2–RF and the MCMI–III: A structural validity study. *Journal of Personality Assessment, 94*(4), 345–357. https://doi.org/10.1080/00223891.2012.656861

van der Heijden, Paul T., Egger, Jos I. M., Rossi, Gina M. P., Grundel, Gitte, & Derksen, Jan J. L. (2013). The MMPI-2-Restructured Form and the Standard MMPI-2 Clinical scales in relation to DSM-IV. *European Journal of Psychological Assessment, 29*(3), 182–188. https://psycnet.apa.org/doi/10.1027/1015-5759/a000140

Vanderploeg, R. D., Sisson, G. F. P., & Hickling, E. J. (1987). A reevaluation of the use of the MMPI in the assessment of combat-related posttraumatic stress disorder. *Journal of Personality Assessment, 51*(1), 140–150. https://doi.org/10.1207/s15327752jpa5101_13

Vaňousová, N., Brown, T. A., & Sellbom, M. (2021). Criterion and incremental validity of the MMPI-3 Eating Concerns scale in a university sample. *Journal of Clinical Psychology in Medical Settings.* https://doi.org/10.1007/s10880-021-09772-6

Velasquez, R. J. (1995). Personality assessment of Hispanic clients. In J. N. Butcher (Ed.), *Clinical personality assessment: Practical approaches* (pp. 120–139). Oxford University Press.

Velasquez, R. J., Ayala, G. X., & Mendoza, S. A. (1998). *Psychodiagnostic assessment of U.S. Latinos: MMPI, MMPI-2, and MMPI-A results.* Julian Samora Institute.

Velasquez, R. J., Gonzales, R. J., Butcher, J. N., Castillo-Canez, I., Apodaca, J. X., & Chavira, D. (1997). Use of MMPI-2 with Chicanos: Strategies for counselors. *Journal of Multicultural Counseling and Development, 25*(2), 107–120. https://doi.org/10.1002/j.2161-1912.1997.tb00321.x

Veltri, C. O., Graham, J. R., Sellbom, M., Ben-Porath, Y. S., Forbey, J. D., O'Connell, C., et al. (2009). Correlates of MMPI-A scales in acute psychiatric and forensic samples. *Journal of Personality Assessment, 91*(3), 288–300. https://doi.org/10.1080/00223890902794374

Veltri, C. O. C., & Williams, J. E. (2013). Does the disorder matter? Investigating a moderating effect on coached noncredible overreporting using the MMPI-2 and PAI. *Assessment, 20*(2), 199–209. https://doi.org/10.1177/1073191112464619

Vendrig, A. A. (1999). Prognostic factors and treatment-related changes associated with return to work in the multimodal treatment of chronic back pain. *Journal of Behavioral Medicine, 22*(3), 217–232. https://doi.org/10.1023/A:1018716406511

Vendrig, A. A., Derksen, J. J. L., & de Mey, H. R. (1999). Utility of selected MMPI-2 scales in the outcome prediction for patients with chronic back pain. *Psychological Assessment, 11*(3), 381–385. https://doi.org/10.1037/1040-3590.11.3.381

Vendrig, A. A., Derksen, J. J. L., & de Mey, H. R. (2000). MMPI-2 Personality Psychopathology Five (PSY-5) and prediction of treatment outcome for patients with chronic back pain. *Journal of Personality Assessment, 74*(3), 423–438. https://doi.org/10.1207/S15327752JPA7403_6

Verona, E., & Carbonell, J. L. (2000). Female violence and personality: Evidence of a pattern of overcontrolled hostility among one-time violent female offenders. *Criminal Justice and Behavior, 27*(2), 176–195. https://doi.org/10.1177/0093854800027002003

Viglione, D. J., Wright, D. M., Dizon, N. T., Moynihan, J. E., DuPuis, S., & Pizitz, T. D. (2001). Evading detection on the MMPI-2: Does caution produce more realistic patterns of responding? *Assessment, 8*(3), 237–250. https://doi.org/10.1177/107319110100800301

Walfish, S. (2010). Reducing MMPI-defensiveness in professionals presenting for evaluation. *Journal of Addictive Diseases, 30*(1), 75–80. https://doi.org/10.1080/10550887.2010.531666

Wallace, A., & Liljequist, L. (2005). A comparison of the correlational structures and elevation patterns of the MMPI-2 Restructured Clinical (RC) and Clinical scales. *Assessment, 12*(3), 290–294. https://doi.org/10.1177/1073191105276250

Walters, G. D. (1987). Child sex offenders and rapists in a military setting. *International Journal of Offender Therapy and Comparative Criminology, 31*(3), 261–269. https://doi.org/10.1177/0306624X8703100307

Walters, G. D., Greene, R. L., & Jeffrey, T. B. (1984). Discriminating between alcoholic and nonalcoholic Blacks and Whites on the MMPI. *Journal of Personality Assessment, 48*(5), 486–488. https://doi.org/10.1207/s15327752jpa4805_6

Walters, G. D., Greene, R. L., Jeffrey, T. B., Kruzich, D. J., & Haskin, J. J. (1983). Racial variations on the MacAndrew Alcoholism scale of the MMPI. *Journal of Consulting and Clinical Psychology, 51*(6), 947–948. https://doi.org/10.1037/0022-006X.51.6.947

Ward, L. C., & Jackson, D. B. (1990). A comparison of primary alcoholics, secondary alcoholics, and nonalcoholic psychiatric patients on the MacAndrew Alcoholism scale. *Journal of Personality Assessment, 54*(3–4), 729–735. https://doi.org/10.1080/00223891.1990.9674033

Ward, L. C., & Perry, M. S. (1998). Measures of social introversion by the MMPI-2. *Journal of Personality Assessment, 70*(1), 171–182. https://doi.org/10.1207/s15327752jpa7001_11

Wasyliw, O. E., Haywood, T. W., Grossman, L. S., & Cavanaugh, J. L. (1993). The psychometric assessment of alcoholism in forensic groups: The MacAndrew scale and response bias. *Journal of Personality Assessment, 60*(2), 252–266. https://doi.org/10.1207/s15327752jpa6002_4

Watson, C. G., Plemel, D., DeMotts, J., Howard, M. T., Tuorila, J., Moog, R., Thomas, D., & Anderson, D. (1994). A comparison of four PTSD measures' convergent

validities in Vietnam veterans. *Journal of Traumatic Stress, 7*(1), 75–82. https://doi
.org/10.1007/BF02111913

Watson, D., & Tellegen, A. (1985). Toward a consensual structure of mood. *Psychological
Bulletin, 98*(2), 219–235. https://doi.org/10.1037/0033-2909.98.2.219

Wechsler, D. (1981). *Manual for the Wechsler Adult Intelligence Scale-Revised (WAIS-R)*.
San Antonio, TX: Psychological Corporation.

Weed, N. C., Butcher, J. N., & Ben-Porath, Y. S. (1995). MMPI-2 measures of substance
abuse. In J. N. Butcher & C. D. Spielberger (Eds.), *Advances in personality assessment*
(Vol. *10*, pp. 121–145). Lawrence Erlbaum Associates.

Weed, N. C., Butcher, J. N., McKenna, T., & Ben-Porath, Y. S. (1992). New measures
for assessing alcohol and drug abuse with the MMPI-2: The APS and AAS. *Journal of
Personality Assessment, 58*(2), 389–404. https://doi.org/10.1207/s15327752jpa5802_15

Weed, N. C., Butcher, J. N., & Williams, C. (1994). Development of the MMPI-A al-
cohol/drug problems scales. *Journal of Studies on Alcohol, 55*(3), 296–302. https://doi
.org/10.15288/jsa.1994.55.296

Weed, N. C., & Han, K. (1992, May). *Is K correct?* [Paper presentation]. 27th Annual
Symposium on Recent Developments in the Use of the MMPI (MMPI-2 and MMPI-
A), Minneapolis, MN.

Weiner, I. B. (1987). Writing forensic reports. In I. B. Weiner & A. K. Hess (Eds.),
Handbook of forensic psychology (pp. 511–528). Wiley.

Weiner, I. B. (1995). How to anticipate ethical and legal challenges in personality assessments. In J. N. Butcher (Ed.), *Clinical personality assessment: Practical approaches*
(pp. 95–103). Oxford University Press. http://hdl.handle.net/10822/880190

Weisenburger, S. M., Harkness, A. R., McNulty, J. L., Graham, J. R., Ben-Porath, Y. S.
(2008). Interpreting low Personality Psychopathology-Five Aggressiveness scores on
the MMPI-2: Graphical, robust, and resistant data analysis. *Psychological Assessment,
20*(4), 403–408. https://doi.org/10.1037/a0013496

Welsh, G. S. (1956). Factor dimensions A and R. In G. S. Welsh & W. G. Dahlstrom
(Eds.), *Basic readings on the MMPI in psychology and medicine* (pp. 264–281). University
of Minnesota Press.

Welsh, G. S. (1965). MMPI profiles and factors A and R. *Journal of Clinical
Psychology, 21*(1), 43–47. https://doi.org/10.1002/1097-4679(196501)21:1<43::AID-
JCLP2270210113>3.0.CO;2-O

Wetter, M. W., Baer, R. A., Berry, D. T. R., & Reynolds, S. K. (1994). The effect of symptom information on faking on the MMPI-2. *Assessment, 1*(2), 199–207. https://doi
.org/10.1177/1073191194001002010

Wetter, M. W., Baer, R. A., Berry, D. T. R., Robison, L. H., & Sumpter, J. (1993).
MMPI-2 profiles of motivated fakers given specific symptom information: A comparison to matched patients. *Psychological Assessment, 5*, 317–323. https://doi
.org/10.1037/1040-3590.5.3.317

Wetter, M. W., Baer, R. A., Berry, D. T. R., Smith, G. T., & Larsen, L. H. (1992).
Sensitivity of MMPI-2 validity scales to random responding and malingering.
Psychological Assessment, 4(3), 369–374. https://doi.org/10.1037/1040-3590.4.3.369

Wetter, M. W., & Corrigan, S. K. (1995). Providing information to clients about psychological tests: A survey of attorneys' and law students' attitudes. *Professional Psychology: Research and Practice, 26*(5), 474–477. https://doi.org/10.1037/0735-7028.26.5.474

Wetter, M. W., & Deitsch, S. E. (1996). Faking specific disorders and temporal response consistency on the MMPI-2. *Psychological Assessment, 8*(1), 39–47. https://doi.org/10.1037/1040-3590.8.1.39

Wetter, M. W., & Tharpe, B. (1995, March). *Sensitivity of the TRIN scale on the MMPI-2* [Paper presentation], 30th Annual Symposium on Recent Developments in the Use of the MMPI-2 and MMPI-A, St. Petersburg Beach, FL.

Wetzler, S., Khadivi, A., & Moser, R. K. (1998). The use of the MMPI-2 for the assessment of depressive and psychotic disorders. *Assessment, 5*(3), 249–261. https://doi.org/10.1177/107319119800500305

Whitman, M. R., & Ben-Porath, Y. S. (2021). Distinctiveness of the MMPI-3 Self-Importance and Self-Doubt scales. *Journal of Personality Assessment, 103*(5), 613–620. https://doi.org/10.1080/00223891.2021.1883628

Whitman, M. R., Burchett, D. L., Tarescavage, A. M., Ben-Porath, Y. S., & Sellbom, M. (2020). Predictive validity of Minnesota Multiphasic Personality Inventory-2-Restructured Form scale scores in an intimate partner violence intervention program. *Criminal Justice and Behavior, 47*(8), 978–995. https://doi.org/10.1177/0093854820918003

Whitman, M. R., Kremyar, A. J., & Ben-Porath, Y. S. (2021). Using the MMPI-2-RF to assess risk of nonsuicidal self-injury among college students. *Journal of Personality Assessment, 103*(4), 455–464. https://doi.org/10.1080/00223891.2020.1801701

Whitman, M. R., Tylicki, J. L., & Ben-Porath, Y. B. (2021). Utility of the MMPI-3 validity scales for detecting overreporting and underreporting and their effects on substantive scale validity: A simulation study. *Psychological Assessment, 33*(5), 411–426. https://doi.org/10.1037/pas0000988

Whitman, M. R., Tylicki, J. L., Mascioli, R., Pickle, J., & Ben-Porath, Y. S. (2021). Psychometric properties of the Minnesota Multiphasic Personality Inventory–3 (MMPI-3) in a clinical neuropsychology setting. *Psychological Assessment, 33*(2), 142–155. http://dx.doi.org/10.1037/pas0000969

Whitney, K. A., Davis, J. J., Shepard, P. H., & Herman, S. M. (2008). Utility of the Response Bias Scale (RBS) and other MMPI-2 validity scales in predicting TOMM performance. *Archives of Clinical Neuropsychology, 23*(7–8), 777–786. https://doi.org/10.1016/j.acn.2008.09.001

Widiger, T. A. (1997). Mental disorders as discrete clinical conditions: Dimensional versus categorical classification. In S. Turner and M. Hersen (Eds.), *Adult psychopathology and diagnosis* (3rd ed., pp. 3–23). Wiley.

Wiggins, J. S. (1966). Substantive dimensions of self-report in the MMPI item pool. *Psychological Monographs: General and Applied, 80*(22), 1–42. https://doi.org/10.1037/h0093901

Wiggins, J. S. (1969). Content dimensions in the MMPI. In J. N. Butcher (Ed.), *MMPI: Research developments and clinical applications* (pp. 127–180). McGraw-Hill.

Williams, C. L. (1986). MMPI profiles from adolescents: Interpretive strategies and treatment considerations. *Journal of Child and Adolescent Psychotherapy, 3*(3), 179–193.

Williams, C. L., & Butcher, J. N. (1989a). An MMPI study of adolescents: I. Empirical validity of the standard scales. *Psychological Assessment: A Journal of Consulting and Clinical Psychology, 1*(4), 251–259. https://doi.org/10.1037/1040-3590.1.4.251

Williams, C. L., & Butcher, J. N. (1989b). An MMPI study of adolescents: II. Verification and limitations of code type classifications. *Psychological Assessment: A Journal of Consulting and Clinical Psychology, 1*(4), 260–265. https://doi.org/10.1037/1040-3590.1.4.260

Williams, C. L., Butcher, J. N., Ben Porath, Y. S., & Graham, J. R. (1992). *MMPI A content scales: Assessing psychopathology in adolescents.* University of Minnesota Press.

Williams, C. L., Ben Porath, Y. S., & Hevern, V. (1994). Item level improvements for use of the MMPI with adolescents. *Journal of Personality Assessment, 63*(2), 284–293.

Williams, R. B., Haney, T. L., Lee, K. L., Kong, Y. H., Blumenthal, J. A., & Whalen, R. E. (1980). Type A behavior, hostility, and coronary atherosclerosis. *Psychosomatic Medicine, 42*(6), 539–549. https://doi.org/10.1097/00006842-198011000-00002

Wimbish, L. G. (1984). *The importance of appropriate norms for the computerized interpretation of adolescent MMPI profiles.* Unpublished doctoral dissertation, Ohio State University, Columbus, OH.

Windle, M. (1994). Characteristics of alcoholics who attempted suicide: Co-occurring disorders and personality differences with a sample of male Vietnam era veterans. *Journal of Studies on Alcohol, 55*(5), 571–577. https://doi.org/10.15288/jsa.1994.55.571

Wolf, A. W., Schubert, D. S. P., Patterson, M., Grande, T., & Pendleton, L. (1990). The use of the MacAndrew Alcoholism scale in detecting substance abuse and antisocial personality. *Journal of Personality Assessment, 54*(3–4), 747–755. https://doi.org/10.1080/00223891.1990.9674035

Wolf, E. J., Miller, M. W., Orazem, R. J., Weierich, M. R., Castillo, D. T., Milford, J., Kaloupek, D. G., & Keane, T. M. (2008). The MMPI-2 Restructured Clinical Scales in the assessment of posttraumatic stress disorder and comorbid disorders. *Psychological Assessment, 20*(4), 327–340. https://doi.org/10.1037/a0012948

Wong, J. L., & Besett, T. M. (1999). Sex differences on the MMPI-2 substance abuse scales in psychiatric inpatients. *Psychological Reports, 84*(2), 582–584. https://doi.org/10.2466/pr0.1999.84.2.582

Woo, M., & Oei, T. P. S. (2006). The MMPI-2 Gender-Masculine and Gender-Feminine scales: Gender roles as predictors of psychological health in clinical patients. *International Journal of Psychology, 41*(5), 413–422. https://doi.org/10.1080/00207590500412185

Woo, M., & Oei, T. P. S. (2008). Empirical investigations of the MMPI-2 Gender-Masculine and Gender-Feminine scales. *Journal of Individual Differences, 29*(1), 1–10. https://doi.org/10.1027/1614-0001.29.1.1

Wright, C. V., Beattie, S. G., Galper, D. I., Church, A. S., Bufka, L. F., Brabender, V. M., & Smith, B. L. (2017). Assessment practices of professional psychologists: Results of a national survey. *Professional Psychology: Research and Practice, 48*(2), 73–78. http://dx.doi.org/10.1037/pro0000086

Wright, T. A., Quick, J. C., Hannah, S. T., & Blake Hargrove, M. (2017). Best practice recommendations for scale construction in organizational research: The development and initial validation of the Character Strength Inventory (CSI). *Journal of Organizational Behavior, 38*(5), 615–628. https://doi.org/10.1002/job.2180

Wrobel, N. H., & Lachar, D. (1992). Refining adolescent MMPI interpretations: Moderating effects of gender in prediction of descriptions from parents. *Psychological Assessment, 4*(3), 375–381. https://doi.org/10.1037/1040-3590.4.3.375

Wygant, D. B., Boutacoff, L. I., Arbisi, P. A., Ben-Porath, Y. S., Kelly, P. H., & Rupp, W. M. (2007). Examination of the MMPI-2 Restructured Clinical (RC) scales in a sample of bariatric surgery candidates. *Journal of Clinical Psychology in Medical Settings, 14*(3), 197–205. https://doi.org/10.1007/s10880-007-9073-8

Wygant, D. B., & Sellbom, M. (2012). Viewing psychopathy from the perspective of the Personality Psychopathology Five model: Implications for DSM-5. *Journal of Personality Disorders, 26*(5), 717–726. https://doi.org/10.1521/pedi.2012.26.5.717

Wygant, D. B., Sellbom, M., Gervais, R. O., Ben-Porath, Y. S., Stafford, K. P., Freeman, D. B., & Heilbronner, R. L. (2010). Further validation of the MMPI-2 and MMPI-2-RF Response Bias Scale: Findings from disability and criminal forensic settings. *Psychological Assessment, 22*(4), 745–756. https://doi.org/10.1037/a0020042

Wygant, D. B., Sellbom, M., Graham, J. R., & Schenk, P. W. (2006). Incremental Validity of the MMPI-2 PSY-5 scales in assessing self-reported personality disorder criteria. *Assessment, 13*(2), 178–186. https://doi.org/10.1177/1073191106286987

Wygant, D. B., Ben-Porath, Y. S., & Arbisi, P. A. (2004, May). *Development and initial validation of a scale to detect somatic overreporting.* Paper presented at the 39th Annual Symposium on Recent Developments in the Use of the MMPI-2 and MMPI-A. Minneapolis, MN.

Yamout, K. Z., Heinrichs, R. J., Baade, L. E., Soetaert, D. K., & Liow, K. K. (2017, March). Comparative prediction of nonepileptic events using MMPI-2 Clinical scales, Harris Lingoes subscales, and Restructured Clinical scales. *Epilepsy & Behavior, 68*, 31–34. https://doi.org/10.1016/j.yebeh.2016.12.008

Young, J. C., & Gross, A. M. (2011). Detection of response bias and noncredible performance in adult attention-deficit/hyperactivity disorder. *Archives of Clinical Neuropsychology, 26*(3), 165–175. https://doi.org/10.1093/arclin/acr013

Youngjohn, J. R., Davis, D., & Wolf, I. (1997). Head injury and the MMPI-2: Paradoxical severity effects and the influence of litigation. *Psychological Assessment, 9*(3), 177–184. https://doi.org/10.1037/1040-3590.9.3.177

Zahn, N., Sellbom, M., Pymont, C., & Schenk, P. W. (2017). Associations between MMPI-2-RF scale scores and self-reported personality disorder criteria in a private practice sample. *Journal of Psychopathology and Behavioral Assessment, 39*(4), 723–741. https://doi.org/10.1007/s10862-017-9616-8

Zinn, S., McCumber, S., & Dahlstrom, W. G. (1999). Cross-validation and extension of the MMPI-A IMM scale. *Assessment, 6*(1), 1–6. https://doi.org/10.1177/107319119900600101

AUTHOR INDEX

SUBJECT INDEX